Film:
An Anthology

compiled and

edited by

Daniel Talbot

SIMON AND SCHUSTER / NEW YORK / 1959

Acknowledgments

The editor wishes to acknowledge the following authors, representatives and publishers for their courtesy in granting permission to reprint the selections included in this anthology:

James Agee Trust for "Comedy's Greatest Era" by James Agee, © 1949 by the James Agee Trust.

George Allen & Unwin, Ltd. for "The Mechanized Muse" by Margaret Kennedy, © 1942 by George Allen & Unwin, Ltd.

Bruce Humphries, Inc., for selections from *The Art of Cineplastics* by Élie Faure, © 1923 by The Four Seas Company.

University of California Press for selections from *Film as Art* by Rudolf Arnheim, © 1957 by The Regents of the University of California.

Thomas Y. Crowell Company for "Film Reality: The Cinema and The Theatre" from *Film and Theatre* by Allardyce Nicoll, © 1936 by Allardyce Nicoll.

Estate of Robert Warshow for "The Westerner" by Robert Warshow, © 1954 by the Estate of Robert Warshow.

Manny Farber for "Underground Films," published in the November 1957 issue of *Commentary*, © 1957 by The American Jewish Committee.

Farrar, Straus and Cudahy, Inc., for "Hollywood's Surrealist Eye" from *The Hollywood Hallucination* by Parker Tyler, © 1944 by Parker Tyler.

The Free Press, Glencoe, Illinois, for selections from *Movies: A Psychological Study* by Martha Wolfenstein and Nathan Leites, © 1950 by The Free Press.

Librairie Gallimard for "How Films Are Made" from *Reflections on the Cinema* by René Clair, © 1951 by Librairie Gallimard.

Harcourt, Brace and Company, Inc., for "The Cinematographic Principle and the Ideogram" from *Film Form* by Sergei Eisenstein, translated and edited by Jay Leyda, © 1949 by Harcourt, Brace and Company, Inc.; for "The Movie Colony" from *Hollywood* by Leo C. Rosten, © 1941 by Harcourt, Brace and Company, Inc.; for "D. W. Griffith" from *The Rise of the American Film* by Lewis Jacobs, © 1939 by Lewis Jacobs; and for "Directors of the Thirties" from *Grierson on Documentary*, compiled and edited by Forsyth Hardy, © 1947 by Harcourt, Brace and Company, Inc., used by courtesy of Forsyth Hardy.

The Johns Hopkins Press for *"The Informer"* from *Novels into Films* by George Bluestone, © 1957 by George Bluestone.

Miss Pauline Kael for "Movies, the Desperate Art" from *The Berkley Book of Modern Writing No. 3*, © 1956 by The Berkley Publishing Corporation.

Alfred A. Knopf, Inc., for "The Film Age" from *The Social History of Art* by Arnold Hauser, published in 1951 by Alfred A. Knopf, Inc.

The Macmillan Company for "The Bankruptcy of Cinema as Art" by Seymour Stern, from *Movies on Trial*, edited by William J. Perlman, © 1936 by William J. Perlman.

New Directions for "The Golden Age" from *The Cosmological Eye* by Henry Miller, © 1939 by *New Directions;* reprinted by permission of *New Directions*.

W. W. Norton & Co., Inc., for "Méliès" from *The History of Motion Pictures* by Maurice Bardèche and Robert Brasillach, translated and edited by Iris Barry, © 1938 by W. W. Norton & Co., Inc.

Erwin Panofsky for "Style and Medium in the Moving Pictures," originally published in the *Bulletin of the Department of Art and Archaeology*, Princeton University, 1934.

Robert Payne for "Charlie Chaplin: Portrait of the Moralist" from *The Great God Pan*, published in 1952 by Hermitage House, © 1952 by Robert Payne.

Princeton University Press for "Caligari" from *From Hitler to Caligari* by Siegfried Kracauer, © 1947 by the Princeton University Press.

Random House, Inc., for Chapter 3 from *The Great Goldwyn* by Alva Johnston, © 1937 by Random House, Inc.

Rinehart & Company, Inc., for "Everything Has Just Gone Zoom" from *Picture* by Lillian Ross, © 1952 by Lillian Ross. The contents of the book were originally published in *The New Yorker*.

Paul Rotha for selections from *Documentary Film* by Paul Rotha, in conjunction with Sinclair Road and Richard Griffith, © 1952 by Paul Rotha. Permission granted on author's behalf by John Farquharson, Ltd., London.

Roy Publishers for selections from *Theory of the Film* by Béla Balázs, © 1952 by Roy Publishers; and for selections from *Cocteau on the Film* by Jean Cocteau, © 1954 by Roy Publishers.

Georges Sadoul for a selection from *French Film* by Georges Sadoul, © 1953 by Georges Sadoul.

Charles Scribner's Sons for "A Note on the Film" from *Feeling and Form* by Susanne Langer, © 1953 by Charles Scribner's Sons.

Simon and Schuster, Inc., for "First Night on Broadway" from *A Million and One Nights* by Terry Ramsaye, © 1926 by Simon and

Schuster, Inc., renewed 1954 by Terry Ramsaye; and for "Enter, the Movies" from *A Child of the Century* by Ben Hecht, © 1954 by Ben Hecht.

The Viking Press for "S-E-X" from *The Great Audience* by Gilbert Seldes, ©1950 by Gilbert Seldes; reprinted by permission of The Viking Press, Inc.

Vision Press, Ltd., for selections from *Film Technique and Film Acting* by V. I. Pudovkin, translated and edited by Ivor Montagu, Memorial Edition, © 1954.

Contents

Foreword

This book stems from several years of pleasurable reading in libraries and museums. Although I had always been an ardent moviegoer, I had preferred not to investigate the literature on the film or read the serious critics. I knew what I liked in a movie, I had developed my own ideas as to what constituted artistry in this medium, and I had a strong suspicion that writing on the film would tend toward press-agentry. But after watching in bug-eyed astonishment the internal movements of a major picture company in operation (I still wonder how pictures get made at all in these medieval, monolithic establishments), curiosity interposed and before long I began rummaging through hundreds of books and articles. Subsequently it struck me that here was a vital body of writing. Hence this book.

It makes no claim whatsoever to being definitive, but it does include much that is important in aesthetic and historical writing on the film. In making the following selections I was guided by an eclectic spirit. I was aware of the drawbacks of eclecticism, but I felt that it was the only way of achieving variety and diversity. In many instances there are pieces, almost side by side, which seem to flout each other. The result, I hope, is salutary.

This book comes at a time when the movies are in a funk, particularly in the United States. The movie magnates are howling and the film artists are not doing so well. (Old tunes, these, but possibly close to being over by now.) We may be witnessing the climax of the American passion play of Business vs. Art. In no other country do businessmen and artists hate each other so much as in America, and nowhere is this conflict as violent as in film making. One wishes that it were possible to trap all that energetic eidetic imagery flowing between them and to put it to good purpose. But the play will end and we know the punch lines all too well: Businessmen are swine and artists are bums.

However, without taking to euphoric optimism, I think we can point to a few encouraging signs. Hollywood the Giant has been virtually smashed. The splinters that have formed into independent production units constitute a healthy movement. Their atmosphere is partially comparable to that of the early days of film making when everybody was independent. To be sure, this has not meant— nor will it necessarily mean—that good pictures will result. The best that can be said is that it is a far better situation than we have had.

Another boost to the movies is the failure of television to keep as many people glued to their sets as it once did. The novelty was bound to wear off. Since it is doing little in the way of imaginative programming to serve its audience honorably, television's loss should become the movies' gain. Provided, of course, that the movies turn out the kind of fare that once made them lord of all the visual arts.

Finally, we can still look to the staggering amount of talent and enthusiasm for good film making in America at present. I had the opportunity, while working as the Eastern story editor for a major motion-picture company, to come upon innumerable gifted film artists. It was painful to see how tightly shut the doors were for them. The adage that all good art inevitably finds its audience is just not true of the movies. Yet the talent is there; it persists—to use an Agee-ism—with "unkillable" force. Some of it trickles into the big studios, but most of it winds up in the garage, even in our day an expedient which still produces impressive results.

   We all know what a powerful artistic and social medium the film is. It has become as meaningful an educational force in our century as the written and spoken word has been throughout the ages. In the days of my youth many of us spent entire weekends in the local movie house. I can remember my mother packing huge brown paper bags full of sandwiches, pickles, apples and pies early on Saturday mornings. I would not return home until late at night, my eyes dangerously bloodshot. It was the same story on Sundays. Having absorbed on those weekends every conceivable gesture, line, action and plot turn, my friends and I would spend the remainder of the week practicing our repertoire on street corners and in school-yards. We became masters of the hip draw, the deathfall, ferocious jaw clouting, barroom dialect, wise-guyism, cool casualness, clowning and swooning. Little did we realize then what a fantastic influence the movies were to become on our lives—on our ethics, public behavior, clothes, and even our food.

   In the same way, it is no accident that the film has attracted the attention of some of the finest minds of the past forty years—writers and thinkers who labored all their lives in various fields. Erwin Panofsky notes in his essay in this book that if suddenly all the "serious lyrical poets, composers, painters and sculptors" stopped creating, their work would scarcely be missed, whereas if films came to an abrupt halt, the result would be "catastrophic." Like painting, sculpture and the dance, the movies need not rely upon Words to charm beholders throughout the world. Unlike these three arts, the movies have in their finest works a much wider range of expression. In one sense it could be said that what painting and sculpture set out to do the movies complete: a heightened anthropomorphic vision, a continuous flowing of objects and people jammed together in moments of tenderness, spleen, melancholy, profanation and divination. A novelist often spends as much as twenty-five pages setting up an action that can take place in a second on the screen. This is the kind of breath-taking economy that is the marvel of all art.

   Unfortunately today's film maker has not profited from the older films. Today's scripts have everybody talking a blue streak, much of it nonsense. There is nothing wrong with dialogue in films, contrary to what some aestheticians think, since dialogue introduces the possibility of economy in its own way. We might say that the

*less conspicuous the speech the more effective it becomes. With-
out speech, the actor would be a pure mime. One line can avoid
several sequences of unnecessary gesture. Such films as* Citizen
Kane, A Walk in the Sun *and* Caught *come to mind readily when
I think of how artistically dialogue was used to enrich their content.
We can attribute the failure of the spoken word in films to the in-
discriminate hiring of novelists, dialogue specialists and literary men
to create scenarios. All good films must come primarily from those
who understand the workings of the eye—men like Carl Mayer, Jean
Cocteau, Max Ophuls, John Huston and René Clair.*

*If this anthology fails to present much of the important writing
on the film, it is due to the editor's shortcomings. Also there is
always the problem of space limitations, with the result that certain figures and works are bound to be neglected. The bibliography
takes up some of this slack. It should be useful to all those who are
prompted to make further investigations. If, in sum, these selections
will have been responsible for stimulating the reader into looking
at and thinking about films more meaningfully and pleasurably,
then the editor's effort has been worth while. Finally, my thanks
are due to Miss Charlotte Seitlin and Mr. Peter Schwed for their
helpful suggestions.*

DANIEL TALBOT

I

Aesthetics, Social Commentary and Analysis

This section consists of critical appreciations and evaluations of the film as an art form and a social instrument. The contributors write from such diverse backgrounds as art history and criticism, philosophy, psychology, poetry, drama criticism and film making. All of these gifted writers and thinkers are intensely aware of the socially influential and artistic potentialities of the film medium. Some of them stress form (patterns, imagery, etc.), others content (social, psychological meaning, etc.), but all share the conviction that form cannot be separated from content in any important work of art.

The

Art

of

Cineplastics

---

by Elie Faure

This selection is taken from a short book on the film entitled The Art of Cineplastics (*the Four Seas Company, Boston, 1923. The essay originally appeared as a series in English in the pages of* The Freeman, New York). *It is one of the earliest significant comments on the aesthetics of the film. Élie Faure, coming to the film as an art historian, saw in this medium its inherent plastic and architectural possibilities. Bored by the theater's static limitations, he was among the first critics to hail the film as an exciting new art form.*

Wɪᴛʜ ᴅʀᴀᴍᴀᴛɪᴄ sᴛʏʟᴇ lost, the present is just the moment for the theater to choose for its attempt to monopolize an art, or at least the instrument of an art, that is absolutely new; one that is so rich in resources that, after having transformed the spectacle, it can act on the aesthetic and social transformation of man himself with a power which I consider to exceed the most extravagant predictions made for it.[1] I see such power in the art of the moving picture that

[1] Since this essay was written, the cinegraphic production of the world does not seem to have improved. The cinema, which was severely injured by the novel of episode, has turned to the even more wretched melodrama. I still believe in it, but it is, like the other arts, a victim of the political and social chaos

I do not hesitate to regard it as the nucleus of the common spectacle
which everyone demands, as being perfectly susceptible of assuming a grave, splendid, moving character, a religious character even,
in the universal, majestic sense of the word. It can do so quite as
well as music, which began with some sort of string stretched between two sticks, struck by the finger of some poor devil, black or
yellow, blind perhaps, to an even and monotonous rhythm; it can
do so quite as well as the dance, which began with some little girl
skipping from one foot to the other, while around her other children clapped their hands; quite as well as the theater, which began
with the mimicking recital of some adventure of war or the chase
amid a circle of auditors; quite as well as architecture, which began
with the arranging of a cave, in front of which, after a fire had been
lighted, someone stretched the hide of an aurochs; quite as well as
the frescoes, the statues and the perspectives of the temple, which
began with the silhouette of a horse or a deer, dug out with a flint on
a bit of bone or ivory.

The needs and desires of man, fortunately, are stronger than his
habits. There will some day be an end of the cinema considered as
an offshoot of the theater, an end of the sentimental monkey tricks
and gesticulations of gentlemen with blue chins and rickety legs,
made up as Neapolitan boatmen or Icelandic fishermen, and ladies
really too mature for ingénue parts who, with their eyes turned
heavenward and their hands clasped, ask the benediction of heaven
and the protection of the crowd for the orphan persecuted by the
wicked rich man. It is impossible that these things should not disappear along with the theater of which they are the counterpart.
Otherwise, we must look to America and Asia, the new peoples or
those renewed by death, to bring in—with the fresh air of the oceans
and the prairies—brutality, health, youth, danger, and freedom of
action.

The cinema has nothing in common with the theater save this,
which is only a matter of appearances, and the most external and
banal appearances at that: It is, as the theater is, but also as are the

in which the whole world is floundering. Is it destined, as I would still like
to think, in a rejuvenated society, to become the art of the mass, the center
of a powerful communion in which new symphonic forms will be born in the
tumult of passion and used with aesthetic ends capable of lifting the heart?
Is it destined, if the customs of democratic society persist, to specialize like
other forms of art, to furnish sentimental insanities for the appetite of the
mob, is it destined to yield its hidden harmonies only to the initiate? I hope
not. Like the other arts it needs for its regeneration—and, in its own particular case, since it is at the beginning of its career, even to attain its first really
aesthetic phase—to be steeped completely in the needs of the people, to
be a prey to some quickening illusion.

dance, the games of the stadium and the procession, a collective spectacle having as its intermediary an actor. It is even less near to the theater than to the dance, the games or the procession, in which I see only one kind of intermediary between the author and the public. Actually the cinema presents, between the author and the public, three intermediaries: the actor—let us call him the cinemimic —the camera, and the photographer. (I do not speak of the screen, which is a material accessory, forming a part of the hall, like the setting in the theater.) This already establishes the cinema as further away from the theater than from music, in which there also exist two intermediaries between the composer and the public—i.e., the player and the instrument. Finally, and especially, there is no speaking in the cinema, which is certainly not an essential characteristic of the theater. Charlot (Charlie Chaplin), the greatest of cinemimics, never opens his mouth; and observe that the best films almost completely do without those intolerable explanations of which the screen is so prodigal.

In the cinema the whole drama unrolls in absolute silence, from which not only words, but the noise of feet, the sound of the wind and the crowds, all the murmurs, all the tones of nature are absent. The pantomime? The relationship is scarcely closer there. In the pantomime, as in the theater, the composition and the realization of the role change, more or less, every evening, which confers on both a sentimental, even impulsive, character. The composition of the film, on the other hand, is fixed once for all, and once fixed it does not change again, which gives it a character that the plastic arts are the only ones to possess. Besides, pantomime represents, by stylized gestures, the feeling and the passions brought to their essential attitudes; it is a psychological art before being a plastic art. The cinema is plastic first; it represents a sort of moving architecture which is in constant accord—in a state of equilibrium dynamically pursued—with the surroundings and the landscapes where it is erected and falls to the earth again. The feelings and the passions are hardly more than a pretext, serving to give a certain sequence, a certain probability to the action.

Let us not misunderstand the meaning of the word "plastic." Too often it evokes the motionless, colorless forms called sculptural— which lead all too quickly to the academic canon, to helmeted heroism, to allegories in sugar, zinc, papier mâché or lard. Plastics is the art of expressing form in repose or in movement by all the means that man commands: full-round, bas-relief, engraving on the wall or on copper, wood or stone, drawing in any medium, painting, fresco, the dance; and it seems to me in no wise overbold to affirm

that the rhythmic movements of a group of gymnasts or of a pro-
cessional or military column touch the spirit of plastic art far more
nearly than do the pictures of the school of David. Like painting,
moreover—and more completely than painting, since a living rhythm
and its repetition in time are what characterize cineplastics—the later
art tends and will tend more every day to approach music and the
dance as well. The interpenetration, the crossing and the association
of movements and cadences already give us the impression that even
the most mediocre films unroll in musical space.

I remember the unexpected emotions I received, seven or eight
years before the war, from certain films the scenarios of which, as it
happens, were of an incredible silliness. The revelation of what
the cinema of the future can be came to me one day; I retain an
exact memory of it, of the commotion that I experienced when I observed, in a flash, the magnificence there was in the relationship of a
piece of black clothing to the gray wall of an inn. From that moment I paid no more attention to the martyrdom of the poor woman
who was condemned, in order to save her husband from dishonor,
to give herself to the lascivious banker who had previously murdered her mother and debauched her child. I discovered, with increasing astonishment, that, thanks to the tone relations that were
transforming the film for me in a system of colors scaling from
white to black and ceaselessly commingled, moving, changing on
the surface and in the depth of the screen, I was witnessing a sudden
coming to life, a descent into that host of personages whom I had
already seen—motionless—on the canvases of El Greco, Frans Hals,
Rembrandt, Velazquez, Vermeer, Courbet, Manet.[2] I do not set
down these names at random, the last two especially. They are
those the cinema suggested to me from the first.

Later, as the medium of the screen was perfected from day to
day, as my eye became accustomed to these strange works, other
memories associated themselves with the earlier ones, till I no longer
needed to appeal to my memory and invoke familiar paintings in
order to justify the new plastic impressions that I got at the cinema.
Their elements, their complexity which varies and winds in a continuous movement, the constantly unexpected things imposed on the
work by its mobile composition, ceaselessly renewed, ceaselessly
broken and remade, fading away and reviving and breaking down,
monumental for one flashing instant, impressionistic the second fol-

[2] May I be permitted in passing to form a wish? It is that smoking be
forbidden in cinema halls, as talking is forbidden in concert halls. At the
end of an hour the atmosphere is saturated with smoke. The finest films are
clouded, lose their transparency and their quality, both in tone and in overtone.

lowing—all this constitutes a phenomenon too radically new for us even to dream of classing it with painting, or with sculpture, or with the dance, least of all with the modern theater. It is an unknown art that is beginning, one that today is as far perhaps from what it will be a century hence as the Negro orchestra, composed of a tom-tom, a bugle, a string across a calabash, and a whistle, is from a symphony composed and conducted by Beethoven.

I would point out the immense resources which, independent of the acting of the cinemimics, are beginning to be drawn from their multiple and incessantly modified relationships with the surroundings, the landscape, the calm, the fury and the caprice of the elements, from natural or artificial lighting, from the prodigiously complex and shaded play of values, from precipitate or retarded movements, such as the slow movements of those galloping horses which seem to be made of living bronze, of those running dogs whose muscular contractions recall the undulations of reptiles. I would point out, too, the profound universe of the microscopic infinite, and perhaps —tomorrow—of the telescopic infinite, the undreamed-of dance of atoms and stars, the shadows under the sea as they begin to be shot with light. I would point out the majestic unity of masses in movement that all this accentuates without insistence, as if it were playing with the grandiose problem that Masaccio, Leonardo, Rembrandt were never quite able to solve. . . . I could never come to the end of it. Shakespeare was once a formless embryo in the narrow shadows of the womb of a good dame of Stratford.

That the starting point of the art of the moving picture is in plastics seems to be beyond all doubt. To whatever form of expression, as yet scarcely suspected, it may lead us, it is by volumes, arabesques, gestures, attitudes, relationships, associations, contrasts and passages of tones—the whole animated and insensibly modified from one fraction of a second to another—that it will impress our sensibility and act on our intelligence by the intermediation of our eyes. Art, I have called it, not science. It is doubly, even trebly art, for there is conception, composition, creation, and transcription to the screen on the part of three persons, the author, the producer, the photographer, and of a group of persons, the cinemimics, as the actors may properly be called. It would be desirable, and possible, for the author to make his own film pictures, and better still if one of the cinemimics, since he cannot be his own photographer, were to be the composer and producer of the work to which he gives life and which he often transfigures by his genius. This is, of course, just what certain American cinemimics are doing, notably the admirable Charlie Chaplin. It is a moot question whether the author of the cinematographic scenario—I hesitate to create the word cineplast—should be a writer or a painter, whether the cinemimic should be a mimic or an actor. Charlie Chaplin solves all these questions; a new art presupposes a new artist.

A certain literary critic has recently deplored the sacrificing of the theater to the cinema and has bracketed Charlie Chaplin and Rigadin (an actor who was formerly known in the French theater under the name of Dranem) in the same terms of reprobation. This does not mean at all that the critic in question is unequal to his task when he sticks to the field of literature; it means simply that he does not realize the artistic significance of the cinema, nor the difference of quality that necessarily exists between the cinema and the theater and between one film and another. For, with all due respect to this critic, there is a greater distance between Charlie Chaplin and Rigadin than between William Shakespeare and Edmond Rostand. I do not write the name of Shakespeare at random. It answers perfectly to the impression of divine intoxication that Charlie Chaplin gives me, for example, in his film *An Idyll of the Fields;* it befits that marvelous art of his, with its mingling of deep melancholy and fantasy, an art that races, increases, decreases and then starts off like a flame again, carrying to each sinuous mountain ridge over which it winds the very essence of the spiritual life of the world, that mysterious light through which we half perceive that our laughter is a triumph over our pitiless insight, that our joy is the feeling of a sure eternity imposed by ourselves upon nothingness, that an elf, a goblin, a gnome dancing in a landscape of Corot, into which the privilege of reverie precipitates him who suffers, bears God himself in his heart.

We must, I think, take our stand on this. Chaplin comes from America, he is the authentic genius of a school that is looming up more and more as the first in importance in cineplastics. I have heard that the Americans greatly enjoy our French films, with their representation of French customs—a fine thing, to be sure, but without the least relation to the effects of motion which are the essential foundation of cinematographic art. The French film, as we know it, is resolutely idealistic. It stands for something like the painting of Ary Scheffer at the time when Delacroix was struggling.[3] The French film is only a bastard form of a degenerate thea-

[3] There were in France at the time these lines were written, and there have been since, interesting efforts in the direction of the true cinema. In particular, those of Monsieur Marcel L'Herbier, Monsieur H. Krauss, Monsieur Delluc.

ter and seems for that reason to be destined to poverty and death if it does not take a new turn.

The American film, on the other hand, is a new art, full of immense perspectives, full of the promise of a great future. I imagine that the taste of the Americans for the "damaged goods" that we export to them is to be explained by the well-known attraction that forms of art in a state of decomposition exercise on all primitive peoples. For the Americans are primitive and at the same time barbarous, which accounts for the strength and vitality which they infuse into the cinema. It is among them that the cinema will, I believe, assume its full significance as plastic drama in action, occupying time through its own movement and carrying with it its own space, of a kind that places it, balances it and gives it the social and psychological value it has for us. It is natural that when a new art appears in the world it should choose a new people which has had hitherto no really personal art. Especially when this new art is bound up, through the medium of human gesture, with the power, definiteness and firmness of action. Especially, too, when this new people is accustomed to introduce into every department of life an increasingly complicated mechanical system, one that more and more hastens to produce, associate and precipitate movements; and especially when this art cannot exist without the most accurate scientific apparatus of a kind that has behind it no traditions and is organized, as it were, physiologically, with the race that employs it.

Cineplastics, in fact, presents a curious characteristic which music alone, to a far less marked degree, has exhibited hitherto. In cineplastics it is far from being true, as it is in the case of the other arts, that the feeling of the artist creates the art; in cineplastics it is the art that is creating its artists. We know that the great thing we call the symphony was engendered little by little by the number and the increasing complexity of musical instruments; but before even the instrument with one string, man already sang, clapping his hands and stamping his feet; here we had a science first, and nothing but a science. There was required the grandiose imagination of man to introduce into it, at first by a timid infiltration and later by a progressive invasion breaking down all barriers, his power of organizing facts according to his own ideas, so that the scattered objects that surround him are transformed into a coherent edifice, wherein he seeks the fecund and always renewed illusion that his destiny develops in conformity with his will.

Hence come these new plastic poems which transport us in three seconds from the wooded banks of a river that elephants cross, leaving a long track of foam, to the heart of wild mountains where

distant horsemen pursue one another through the smoke of their
rifle shots, and from evil taverns where powerful shadows bend over
a deathbed in mysterious lights, to the weird half-light of submarine
waters where fish wind through grottoes of coral. Indeed—and this
comes at unexpected moments, and in comic films as well as in the
others—animals may take part in these dramas, and newborn children, too, and they participate by their play, their joys, their disappointments, their obscure dramas of instinct, all of which the theater, as it seems to me, is quite incapable of showing us. Landscapes,
too, beautiful or tragic or marvelous, enter the moving symphony in
order to add to its human meaning, or to introduce into it, after the
fashion of a stormy sky by Delacroix or a silver sea by Veronese,
the sense of the supernatural.

I have already explained why the Americans have understood, as
by instinct, the direction they should give to their visual imagination, letting themselves be guided by their love for space, movement
and action. As for the Italians, they might be reborn to the life of
conquest and lose the memory of their classic works, were they to
find in their genius for gesture and attitude and for setting (thanks
in part to the aid of their wonderful sunshine, which is like the sunshine of California) the elements of another original school, less
violent and also less sober, but presenting better qualities of composition than that of the Americans. In the cinema the Italians give us
marvelously the crowd, and the historical drama in the motionless
setting of palaces, gardens, ruins, where the ardent life that characterizes the Italian people goes on, with that quality which is theirs
of never appearing out of time or out of place. A gesticulating
drama it may be, but the gestures are true. The Italian gesture has
been called theatrical; but it is not that, for it is sincere. Giotto's
personages are not acting. If that is the impression we get from
Bolognese painting, it is because the Bolognese no longer represented the real genius of Italy. Rembrandt, up to the age of forty-
five, and Rubens are far more theatrical than all the Italian masters
down to the painters of Bologna. Italian energy alone will render
the Italian school of cineplastics capable of maintaining, in this new
art in which the Americans already excel, the plastic genius of Europe—and that by creating a form that is destined to have a great
future.[4]

In any case, the chief triumph in the American conception of
cineplastics—a triumph which the Italians approach most nearly and

[4] For the last two years the Italian film seems to be in decay. On the contrary, *Dr. Caligari* has recently revealed the powerful inventive genius of the
German film.

the French approach, alas, most remotely—seems to me to consist in this: that the subject is nothing but a pretext. The web of feeling should be nothing but the skeleton of the autonomous organism represented by the film. In time this web must be woven into the plastic drama. It is evident that this drama will be the more moving in proportion as the moral and psychological pattern that it covers is strongly, soberly and logically conducted. But that is all. The expression and the effects of that drama remain in the domain of plastics; and the web of feeling is there only to reveal and increase their value.

Shall I dare to dream of a future for the art of the moving picture, a future distant no doubt, when the actor, or, as I would prefer to call him, the cinemimic, shall disappear or at least be specialized, and when the cineplast shall dominate the drama of form that is precipitated in time? Observe, in the first place, one vital point that hitherto has not been sufficiently noted, I think, or at least the poetic consequences of which have not been made sufficiently clear. The cinema incorporates time in space. More than this, through the cinema time really becomes a dimension of space. We shall be able to see dust rising, spreading, dissipating, a thousand years after it has spurted up from the road under the hoofs of a horse; we shall be able to see for a thousand years the smoke of a cigarette condensing and then entering the ether—and this in a frame of space under our very eyes. We shall be able to understand how it may be that the inhabitants of a distant star, if they can see things on earth with powerful telescopes, are really contemporaries of Jesus, since at the moment when I write these lines they may be witnessing his crucifixion, and perhaps making a photographic or even cinematographic record of the scene, for we know that the light that illumines us takes nineteen or twenty centuries to reach them. We can even imagine, and this may modify still more our idea of the duration of time, that we may one day see this film, taken on that distant star, either through the inhabitants sending it to us in some sort of projectile or perhaps transmitting it to our screens by some system of interplanetary projection. This, which is not scientifically impossible, would actually make us the contemporaries of events which took place a hundred centuries before us, and in the very place wherein we live.

In the cinema we have indeed already made time an instrument that plays its role in the whole spatial organism, unfurling under our eyes its successive masses which are ceaselessly brought before us in dimensions that permit us to grasp their extent in surface area and in depth. Already we find in these masses pleasures of an intensity unknown hitherto. Stop the most beautiful film you know, make of it at any moment an inert photograph, and you will not obtain even a memory of the emotion that it gave you as a moving picture.

Thus in the cinema time clearly becomes necessary for us. Increasingly it forms a part of the always more dynamic idea that we are receiving about the object upon which we are gazing. We play with it at our ease. We can speed it up. We can slow it down. We can suppress it. Indeed I feel it as being formerly part of myself, as enclosed alive, with the very space which it measures and which measures it, within the walls of my brain. Homer becomes my contemporary, as my lamp upon my table before me is my contemporary, since Homer had his share in the elaboration of the image under which my lamp appears to me. Since the idea of duration enters the idea of space as a constituent element, we may easily imagine an expanded cineplastic art which shall be no more than an architecture of the idea, and from which the cinemimic will, as I have said, disappear, because only a great artist will be able to build edifices that are made and broken down and remade ceaselessly—by imperceptible passages of tone and modeling that are in themselves architecture at every moment—without our being able to seize the thousandth part of a second in which the transition takes place.

I remember witnessing something analogous to this in nature itself. At Naples, in 1906, I saw the great eruption of Vesuvius. The plume of smoke, two thousand meters high, that rose above the mouth of the volcano was spherical, outlined against the sky and sharply separated from it. Inside this cloud, enormous masses of ashes assumed form and became formless unceasingly, all sharing in the modeling of the great sphere and producing an undulation on its surface, moving and varying, but sustained, as if by an attraction at the center, in the general mass, the form and dimensions of which nothing appeared to alter. In a flash it seemed to me as I looked upon the phenomenon that I had grasped the law of the birth of planets, held by gravitation around the solar nucleus. It seemed to me that I was looking at a symbolic form of that grandiose art of which in the cinema we now perceive the germ, the development of which the future doubtless holds in store for us, namely a great moving construction ceaselessly reborn of itself under our eyes by virtue of its inner forces alone. Human, animal, vegetable and inert forms, in all their immense variety, have their share in the building of it, whether a multitude is employed on the work or whether only one man is able to realize it in its totality.

Perhaps I may explain myself further on this last point. We all know those animated drawings, very dry and thin and stiff, which are sometimes projected on the screen and are, when compared with the forms that I have been imagining, what the outlines in chalk traced on a blackboard by a child are to the frescoes of Tintoretto and the canvases of Rembrandt. Now let us suppose three or four generations devoted to the problem of giving depth to these images, not by surfaces and lines but by thickness and volumes; three or four generations devoted to modeling, by values and half tones, a series of successive movements which after a long training would gradually enter into our habits, even into our unconscious actions, till the artist was enabled to use them at will, for drama or idyll, comedy or epic, in the light or in the shadow, in the forest, the city or the desert. Suppose that an artist thus armed has the heart of a Delacroix, the power of realization of a Rubens, the passion of a Goya and the strength of a Michelangelo; he will throw on the screen a cineplastic tragedy that has come out of his whole nature, a sort of visual symphony as rich and as complex as the sonorous symphonies of the great musicians and revealing, by its precipitation in time, perspectives of infinitude and of the absolute as exalting by reason of their mystery and more moving, because of their reality for the senses, than the symphonies of the greatest of the musicians.

There is the distant future in which I believe, but of which the full realization is beyond my power of imagining. While we await the coming of the cineplast, who is as yet in the shadows of the background, there are today some admiral cinemimics and at least one cinemimic of genius, who are showing us the promise of that collective spectacle which will take the place of the religious dance that is dead, and of the philosophic tragedy that is dead, and of the mystery play that is dead—indeed of all the great dead things around which the multitude once assembled in order to commune together in the joy that had been brought to birth in the hearts of the people by the mastery over pessimism achieved by the poets and the dancers.

I am not a prophet, I cannot tell what will have become in a hundred years of the admirable creations of the imagination of a being, a cinemimic, who, alone among living things, has the privilege of knowing that though his destiny is without hope, he is yet the only being to live and think as if he had the power to take to himself eternity. Yet it seems to me that I already see what the art of that cinemimic may presume to become if, instead of permitting itself to be dragged by theatrical processes through a desolating sentimental fiction, it is able to concentrate itself on plastic processes, around a sensuous and passionate action in which we can all recognize our own personal virtues.

In every land, mankind is attempting to escape from a form of civilization which, through an excess of individualism, has become impulsive and anarchic, and we are seeking to enter a form of plastic civilization that is, undoubtedly, destined to substitute for analytic studies of states and crises of the soul, synthetic poems of masses and great ensembles in action. I imagine that architecture will be the principal expression of this civilization, an architecture whose appearance may be difficult to define; perhaps it will be the industrial construction of our means of travel—ships, trains, automobiles and airplanes—for which ports, docks, pontoons and giant cupolas will be the places of rest and relay. Cineplastics will doubtless be the spiritual ornament sought for in this period—the play that this new society will find most useful in developing in the crowd the sense of confidence, of harmony, of cohesion.

Style

and Medium

in the

Motion Pictures

by Erwin Panofsky

The following essay is one of the most important statements yet made on film aesthetics. Precisely and compactly written, it covers an enormous range of ideas and observations. In a phrase here, a suggestion there, Erwin Panofsky opens up a world of insight into the complex nature of the movie medium and its context in the history of art. What makes his approach so vital are the constant comparative references to artistic production of all kinds in epochs and civilizations gone by. The result is a remarkably clear and accurate estimate of some of the excellences and shortcomings in movies, past and present. First published in 1934, it grew out of a talk made before a Princeton audience in order to enlist its interest in the Film Library of the Museum of Modern Art, which was then being started and which, Mr. Panofsky writes, was considered "a rather queer project by most people at that time." Although the essay was revised twelve years later for Critique *magazine (Critique, Vol. 1, No. 3, January–February 1947) there was no change in the author's basic tenets, nor does he see any reason to change them today.*

F$_{\text{ILM ART}}$ is the only art the development of which men now living have witnessed from the very beginnings; and this development is all the more interesting as it took place under conditions contrary to precedent. It was not an artistic urge that gave rise to the discovery and gradual perfection of a new technique; it was a technical invention that gave rise to the discovery and gradual perfection of a new art.

From this we understand two fundamental facts. First, that the primordial basis of the enjoyment of moving pictures was not an objective interest in a specific subject matter, much less an aesthetic interest in the formal presentation of subject matter, but the sheer delight in the fact that things seemed to move, no matter what things they were. Second, that films—first exhibited in "kinetoscopes," viz., cinematographic peep shows, but projectable to a screen since as early as 1894—are, originally, a product of genuine folk art (whereas, as a rule, folk art derives from what is known as "higher art"). At the very beginning of things we find the simple recording of movements: galloping horses, railroad trains, fire engines, sporting events, street scenes. And when it had come to the making of narrative films these were produced by photographers who were anything but "producers" or "directors," performed by people who were anything but actors, and enjoyed by people who would have been much offended had anyone called them "art lovers."

The casts of these archaic films were usually collected in a "café" where unemployed supers or ordinary citizens possessed of a suitable exterior were wont to assemble at a given hour. An enterprising photographer would walk in, hire four or five convenient characters and make the picture while carefully instructing them what to do: "Now, you pretend to hit this lady over the head"; and (to the lady): "And you pretend to fall down in a heap." Productions like these were shown, together with those purely factual recordings of "movement for movement's sake," in a few small and dingy cinemas mostly frequented by the "lower classes" and a sprinkling of youngsters in quest of adventure (about 1905, I happen to remember, there was only one obscure and faintly disreputable *kino* in the whole city of Berlin, bearing, for some unfathomable reason, the English name of "The Meeting Room"). Small wonder that the "better classes," when they slowly began to venture into these early picture theaters, did so, not by way of seeking normal and possibly serious entertainment, but with that characteristic sensation of self-conscious condescension with which we may plunge, in gay company, into the folkloristic depths of Coney Island or a European kermis; even a few years ago it was the regulation attitude of the socially or intellectually prominent that one could confess to enjoying such austerely educational films as *The Sex Life of the Starfish* or films with "beautiful scenery," but never to a serious liking for narratives.

Today there is no denying that narrative films are not only "art"— not often good art, to be sure, but this applies to other media as well —but also, besides architecture, cartooning and "commercial design," the only visual art entirely alive. The "movies" have re-established that dynamic contact between art production and art consumption which, for reasons too complex to be considered here, is sorely attenuated, if not entirely interrupted, in many other fields of artistic endeavor. Whether we like it or not, it is the movies that mold, more than any other single force, the opinions, the taste, the language, the dress, the behavior, and even the physical appearance of a public comprising more than 60 per cent of the population of the earth. If all the serious lyrical poets, composers, painters and sculptors were forced by law to stop their activities, a rather small fraction of the general public would become aware of the fact and a still smaller fraction would seriously regret it. If the same thing were to happen with the movies the social consequences would be catastrophic.

In the beginning, then, there were the straight recordings of movement no matter what moved, viz., the prehistoric ancestors of our "documentaries"; and, soon after, the early narratives, viz., the prehistoric ancestors of our "feature films." The craving for a narrative element could be satisfied only by borrowing from older arts, and one should expect that the natural thing would have been to borrow from the theater, a theater play being apparently the *genus proximum* to a narrative film in that it consists of a narrative enacted by persons that move. But in reality the imitation of stage performances was a comparatively late and thoroughly frustrated development. What happened at the start was a very different thing. Instead of imitating a theatrical performance already endowed with a certain amount of motion, the earliest films added movement to works of art originally stationary, so that the dazzling technical invention might achieve a triumph of its own without intruding upon the sphere of higher culture. The living language, which is always right, has endorsed this sensible choice when it still speaks of a "moving picture" or, simply, a "picture," instead of accepting the pretentious and fundamentally erroneous "screen play."

The stationary works enlivened in the earliest movies were indeed pictures: bad nineteenth-century paintings and postcards (or waxworks à la Madame Tussaud's), supplemented by the comic strips—a most important root of cinematic art—and the subject matter of popular songs, pulp magazines and dime novels; and the films descending from this ancestry appealed directly and very intensely to a folk art mentality. They gratified—often simultaneously—first, a primitive sense of justice and decorum when virtue and industry were rewarded while vice and laziness were punished; second, plain sentimentality when "the thin trickle of a fictive love interest" took its course "through somewhat serpentine channels," or when Father, dear Father returned from the saloon to find his child dying of diphtheria; third, a primordial instinct for bloodshed and cruelty when Andreas Hofer faced the firing squad, or when (in a film of 1893–

94) the head of Mary Queen of Scots actually came off; fourth, a taste for mild pornography (I remember with great pleasure a French film of *ca.* 1900 wherein a seemingly but not really well-rounded lady as well as a seemingly but not really slender one were shown changing to bathing suits—an honest, straightforward *porcheria* much less objectionable than the now extinct Betty Boop films and, I am sorry to say, some of the more recent Walt Disney productions); and, finally, that crude sense of humor, graphically described as "slapstick," which feeds upon the sadistic and the pornographic instinct, either singly or in combination.

Not until as late as *ca.* 1905 was a film adaptation of *Faust* ventured upon (cast still "unknown," characteristically enough), and not until 1911 did Sarah Bernhardt lend her prestige to an unbelievably funny film tragedy, *Queen Elizabeth of England.* These films represent the first conscious attempt at transplanting the movies from the folk art level to that of "real art"; but they also bear witness to the fact that this commendable goal could not be reached in so simple a manner. It was soon realized that the imitation of a theater performance with a set stage, fixed entries and exits, and distinctly literary ambitions is the one thing the film must avoid.

The legitimate paths of evolution were opened, not by running away from the folk art character of the primitive film but by developing it within the limits of its own possibilities. Those primordial archetypes of film productions on the folk art level—success or retribution, sentiment, sensation, pornography, and crude humor— could blossom forth into genuine history, tragedy and romance, crime and adventure, and comedy, as soon as it was realized that they could be transfigured—not by an artificial injection of literary values but by the exploitation of the unique and specific possibilities of the new medium. Significantly, the beginnings of this legitimate development antedate the attempts at endowing the film with higher values of a foreign order (the crucial period being the years from 1902 to *ca.* 1905), and the decisive steps were taken by people who were laymen or outsiders from the viewpoint of the serious stage.

These unique and specific possibilities can be defined as *dynamization of space* and, accordingly, *spatialization of time.* This statement is self-evident to the point of triviality but it belongs to that kind of truths which, just because of their triviality, are easily forgotten or neglected.

In a theater, space is static, that is, the space represented on the stage, as well as the spatial relation of the beholder to the spectacle, is unalterably fixed. The spectator cannot leave his seat, and the setting of the stage cannot change, during one act (except for such incidentals as rising moons or gathering clouds and such illegitimate reborrowings from the film as turning wings or gliding backdrops). But, in return for this restriction, the theater has the advantage that time, the medium of emotion and thought conveyable by speech, is free and independent of anything that may happen in visible space. Hamlet may deliver his famous monologue lying on a couch in the middle distance, doing nothing and only dimly discernible to the spectator and listener, and yet by his mere words enthrall him with a feeling of intensest emotional action.

With the movies the situation is reversed. Here, too, the spectator occupies a fixed seat, but only physically, not as the subject of an aesthetic experience. Aesthetically, he is in permanent motion as his eye identifies itself with the lens of the camera, which permanently shifts in distance and direction. And as movable as the spectator is, as movable is, for the same reason, the space presented to him. Not only bodies move in space, but space itself does, approaching, receding, turning, dissolving and recrystallizing as it appears through the controlled locomotion and focusing of the camera and through the cutting and editing of the various shots—not to mention such special effects as visions, transformations, disappearances, slow-motion and fast-motion shots, reversals and trick films. This opens up a world of possibilities of which the stage can never dream. Quite apart from such photographic tricks as the participation of disembodied spirits in the action of the *Topper* series, or the more effective wonders wrought by Roland Young in *The Man Who Could Work Miracles*, there is, on the purely factual level, an untold wealth of themes as inaccessible to the "legitimate" stage as a fog or a snowstorm is to the sculptor; all sorts of violent elemental phenomena and, conversely, events too microscopic to be visible under normal conditions (such as the life-saving injection with the serum flown in at the very last moment, or the fatal bite of the yellow-fever mosquito); full-scale battle scenes; all kinds of operations, not only in the surgical sense but also in the sense of any actual construction, destruction or experimentation, as in *Louis Pasteur* or *Madame Curie*; a really grand party, moving through many rooms of a mansion or a palace. Features like these, even the mere shifting of the scene from one place to another by means of a car perilously negotiating heavy traffic or a motorboat steered through a nocturnal harbor, will not only always retain their primitive cinematic appeal but also remain enormously effective as a means of stirring the emotions and creating suspense. In addition, the movies have the power, entirely denied to the theater, to convey psychological experiences by directly projecting their content to the screen, substituting, as it were, the eye of the beholder for the consciousness of the character (as when the imaginings and hallucinations of the drunkard in the otherwise overrated *Lost Weekend* appear as stark realities instead of being described by mere words). But any attempt to convey thought and feelings exclusively, or even primarily, by speech leaves us with a feeling of embarrassment, boredom, or both.

What I mean by thoughts and feelings "conveyed exclusively, or even primarily, by speech" is simply this: Contrary to naïve expectation, the invention of the sound track in 1928 has been unable to change the basic fact that a moving picture, even when it has learned to talk, remains a picture that moves and does not convert itself into a piece of writing that is enacted. Its substance remains a series of visual sequences held together by an uninterrupted flow of movement in space (except, of course, for such checks and pauses as have the same compositional value as a rest in music), and not a sustained study in human character and destiny transmitted by effective, let alone "beautiful," diction. I cannot remember a more misleading statement about the movies than Mr. Eric Russell Bentley's in the spring number of the *Kenyon Review,* 1945: "The potentialities of the talking screen differ from those of the silent screen in adding the dimension of dialogue—which could be poetry." I would suggest: "The potentialities of the talking screen differ from those of the silent screen in integrating visible movement with dialogue which, therefore, had better not be poetry."

All of us, if we are old enough to remember the period prior to 1928, recall the old-time pianist who, with his eyes glued on the screen, would accompany the events with music adapted to their mood and rhythm; and we also recall the weird and spectral feeling overtaking us when this pianist left his post for a few minutes and the film was allowed to run by itself, the darkness haunted by the monotonous rattle of the machinery. Even the silent film, then, was never mute. The visible spectacle always required, and received, an audible accompaniment which, from the very beginning, distinguished the film from simple pantomime and rather classed it—*mutatis mutandis*—with the ballet. The advent of the talkie meant not so much an "addition" as a transformation: the transformation of musical sound into articulate speech and, therefore, of quasi pantomime into an entirely new species of spectacle which differs from the ballet, and agrees with the stage play, in that its acoustic component consists of intelligible words, but differs from the stage play and agrees with the ballet in that this acoustic component is not detachable from the visual. In a film, that which we hear remains, for good or worse, inextricably fused with that which we see; the sound, articulate or not, cannot express any more than is expressed, at the same time, by visible movement; and in a good film it does not even attempt to do so. To put it briefly, the play—or, as it is very properly called, the "script"—of a moving picture is subject to what might be termed the *principle of coexpressibility*.

Empirical proof of this principle is furnished by the fact that, wherever the dialogical or monological element gains temporary prominence, there appears, with the inevitability of a natural law, the "close-up." What does the close-up achieve? In showing us, in magnification, either the face of the speaker or the face of the listeners or both in alternation, the camera transforms the human physiognomy into a huge field of action where—given the qualification of the performers—every subtle movement of the features, almost imperceptible from a natural distance, becomes an expressive event in visible space and thereby completely integrates itself with the expressive content of the spoken word; whereas, on the stage, the spoken word makes a stronger rather than a weaker impression if we are not permitted to count the hairs in Romeo's mustache.

This does not mean that the scenario is a negligible factor in the making of a moving picture. It only means that its artistic intention differs in kind from that of a stage play, and much more from that of a novel or a piece of poetry. As the success of a Gothic jamb figure depends not only upon its quality as a piece of sculpture but also, or even more so, upon its integrability with the architecture of the portal, so does the success of a movie script—not unlike that of an opera libretto—depend, not only upon its quality as a piece of literature but also, or even more so, upon its integrability with the events on the screen.

As a result—another empirical proof of the coexpressibility principle—good movie scripts are unlikely to make good reading and have seldom been published in book form; whereas, conversely, good stage plays have to be severely altered, cut, and, on the other hand, enriched by interpolations to make good movie scripts. In Shaw's *Pygmalion*, for instance, the actual process of Eliza's phonetic education and, still more important, her final triumph at the grand party, are wisely omitted; we see—or, rather, hear—some samples of her gradual linguistic improvement and finally encounter her, upon her return from the reception, victorious and splendidly arrayed but deeply hurt for want of recognition and sympathy. In the film adaptation, precisely these two scenes are not only supplied but also strongly emphasized; we witness the fascinating activities in the laboratory with its array of

spinning disks and mirrors, organ pipes and dancing flames, and we
participate in the ambassadorial party, with many moments of impending catastrophe and a little counterintrigue thrown in for suspense. Unquestionably these two scenes, entirely absent from the
play, and indeed unachievable upon the stage, were the highlights of
the film; whereas the Shavian dialogue, however severely cut, turned
out to fall a little flat in certain moments. And wherever, as in so
many other films, a poetic emotion, a musical outburst, or a literary
conceit (even, I am grieved to say, some of the wisecracks of
Groucho Marx) entirely lose contact with visible movement, they
strike the sensitive spectator as, literally, out of place. It is certainly
terrible when a soft-boiled he-man, after the suicide of his mistress,
casts a twelve-foot glance upon her photograph and says something
less-than-coexpressible to the effect that he will never forget her. But
when he recites, instead, a piece of poetry as sublimely more-than-
coexpressible as Romeo's monologue at the bier of Juliet, it is still
worse. Reinhardt's *Midsummer Night's Dream* is probably the most
unfortunate major film ever produced; and Olivier's *Henry V* owes
its comparative success, apart from the all but providential adapta-
bility of this particular play, to so many *tours de force* that it will,
God willing, remain an exception rather than set a pattern. It com-
bines "judicious pruning" with the interpolation of pageantry, non-
verbal comedy and melodrama; it uses a device perhaps best designated as "oblique close-up" (Mr. Olivier's beautiful face inwardly
listening to but not pronouncing the great soliloquy); and, most notably, it shifts between three levels of archaeological reality: a reconstruction of Elizabethan London, a reconstruction of the events of
1415 as laid down in Shakespeare's play, and the reconstruction of a
performance of this play on Shakespeare's own stage. All this is perfectly legitimate; but, even so, the highest praise of the film will always come from those who, like the critic of the *New Yorker*, are
not quite in sympathy with either the movies *au naturel* or Shakespeare *au naturel*.

As the writings of Conan Doyle potentially contain all modern
mystery stories (except for the tough specimens of the Dashiell Ham-
mett school), so do the films produced between 1900 and 1910 pre-
establish the subject matter and methods of the moving picture as we
know it. This period produced the incunabula of the Western and the
crime film (Edwin S. Porter's amazing *Great Train Robbery* of 1903)
from which developed the modern gangster, adventure, and mystery
pictures (the latter, if well done, is still one of the most honest and
genuine forms of film entertainment, space being doubly charged

with time as the beholder asks himself not only "What is going to happen?" but also "What has happened before?"). The same period saw the emergence of the fantastically imaginative film (*Méliès*) which was to lead to the expressionist and surrealist experiments (*The Cabinet of Dr. Caligari, Sang d'un Poète*, etc.), on the one hand, and to the more superficial and spectacular fairy tales à la Arabian Nights, on the other. Comedy, later to triumph in Charlie Chaplin, the still insufficiently appreciated Buster Keaton, the Marx Brothers and the pre-Hollywood creations of René Clair, reached a respectable level in Max Linder and others. In historical and melodramatic films the foundations were laid for movie iconography and movie symbolism, and in the early work of D. W. Griffith we find, not only remarkable attempts at psychological analysis (*Edgar Allan Poe*) and social criticism (*A Corner in Wheat*) but also such basic technical innovations as the long shot, the flashback and the close-up. And modest trick films and cartoons paved the way to Felix the Cat, Popeye the Sailor, and Felix's prodigious offspring, Mickey Mouse.

Within their self-imposed limitations the earlier Disney films, and certain sequences in the later ones,[1] represent, as it were, a chemically pure distillation of cinematic possibilities. They retain the most im-

[1] I make this distinction because it was, in my opinion, a fall from grace when *Snow White* introduced the human figure and when *Fantasia* attempted to picturalize The World's Great Music. The very virtue of the animated cartoon is to animate, that is to say endow lifeless things with life, or living things with a different kind of life. It effects a metamorphosis, and such a metamorphosis is wonderfully present in Disney's animals, plants, thunderclouds and railroad trains. Whereas his dwarfs, glamourized princesses, hillbillies, baseball players, rouged centaurs and *amigos* from South America are not transformations but caricatures at best, and fakes or vulgarities at worst. Concerning music, however, it should be borne in mind that its cinematic use is no less predicated upon the principle of coexpressibility than is the cinematic use of the spoken word. There is music permitting or even requiring the accompaniment of visible action (such as dances, ballet music and any kind of operatic compositions) and music of which the opposite is true; and this is, again, not a question of quality (most of us rightly prefer a waltz by Johann Strauss to a symphony by Sibelius) but one of intention. In *Fantasia* the hippopotamus ballet was wonderful, and the Pastoral Symphony and "Ave Maria" sequences were deplorable, not because the cartooning in the first case was infinitely better than in the two others (*cf.* above), and certainly not because Beethoven and Schubert are too sacred for picturalization, but simply because Ponchielli's "Dance of the Hours" is coexpressible while the Pastoral Symphony and the "Ave Maria" are not. In cases like these even the best imaginable music and the best imaginable cartoon will impair rather than enhance each other's effectiveness. Experimental proof of all this was furnished by Disney's recent *Make Mine Music* where The World's Great Music was fortunately restricted to Prokofieff. Even among the other sequences the most successful ones were those in which the human element was either absent or reduced to a minimum; Willie the Whale, the Ballad of Johnny Fedora and Alice Blue-Bonnet, and, above all, the truly magnificent Goodman Quartet.

portant folkloristic elements—sadism, pornography, the humor engendered by both, and moral justice—almost without dilution and
often fuse these elements into a variation on the primitive and inexhaustible David-and-Goliath motif, the triumph of the seemingly
weak over the seemingly strong; and their fantastic independence of
the natural laws gives them the power to integrate space with time to
such perfection that the spatial and temporal experiences of sight and
hearing come to be almost interconvertible. A series of soap bubbles,
successively punctured, emits a series of sounds exactly corresponding
in pitch and volume to the size of the bubbles; the three uvulae of
Willie the Whale—small, large and medium—vibrate in consonance
with tenor, bass and baritone notes; and the very concept of stationary
existence is completely abolished. No object in creation, whether it
be a house, a piano, a tree or an alarm clock, lacks the faculties of organic, in fact anthropomorphic, movement, facial expression and
phonetic articulation. Incidentally, even in normal, "realistic" films
the inanimate object, provided that it is dynamizable, can play the
role of a leading character as do the ancient railroad engines in Buster
Keaton's *General* and *Niagara Falls*. How the earlier Russian films
exploited the possibility of heroizing all sorts of machinery lives in
everybody's memory; and it is perhaps more than an accident that the
two films which will go down in history as the great comical and the
great serious masterpiece of the silent period bear the names and im-
mortalize the personalities of two big ships: Keaton's *Navigator*
(1924) and Eisenstein's *Potemkin* (1925).

The evolution from the jerky beginnings to this grand climax offers
the fascinating spectacle of a new artistic medium gradually becoming
conscious of its legitimate, that is, exclusive, possibilities and limitations—a spectacle not unlike the development of the mosaic, which
started out with transposing illusionistic genre pictures into a more
durable material and culminated in the hieratic supernaturalism of
Ravenna; or the development of line engraving, which started out as
a cheap and handy substitute for book illumination and culminated in
the purely "graphic" style of Dürer.

Just so the silent movies developed a definite style of their own,
adapted to the specific conditions of the medium. A hitherto unknown language was forced upon a public not yet capable of reading
it, and the more proficient the public became the more refinement
could develop in the language. For a Saxon peasant of around 800 it
was not easy to understand the meaning of a picture showing a man
as he pours water over the head of another man, and even later many
people found it difficult to grasp the significance of two ladies stand-

ing behind the throne of an emperor. For the public of around 1910 it was no less difficult to understand the meaning of the speechless action in a moving picture, and the producers employed means of clarification similar to those we find in medieval art. One of these were printed titles or letters, striking equivalents of the medieval *tituli* and scrolls (at a still earlier date there even used to be explainers who would say, *viva voce*, "Now he thinks his wife is dead but she isn't" or "I don't wish to offend the ladies in the audience but I doubt that any of them would have done that much for her child"). Another, less obtrusive method of explanation was the introduction of a fixed iconography which from the outset informed the spectator about the basic facts and characters, much as the two ladies behind the emperor, when carrying a sword and a cross respectively, were uniquely determined as Fortitude and Faith. There arose, identifiable by standardized appearance, behavior and attributes, the well-remembered types of the Vamp and the Straight Girl (perhaps the most convincing modern equivalents of the medieval personifications of the Vices and Virtues), the Family Man, and the Villain, the latter marked by a black mustache and walking stick. Nocturnal scenes were printed on blue or green film. A checkered tablecloth meant, once for all, a "poor but honest" milieu; a happy marriage, soon to be endangered by the shadows from the past, was symbolized by the young wife's pouring the breakfast coffee for her husband; the first kiss was invariably announced by the lady's gently playing with her partner's necktie and was invariably accompanied by her kicking out with her left foot. The conduct of the characters was predetermined accordingly. The poor but honest laborer who, after leaving his little house with the checkered tablecloth, came upon an abandoned baby could not but take it to his home and bring it up as best he could; the Family Man could not but yield, however temporarily, to the temptations of the Vamp. As a result these early melodramas had a highly gratifying and soothing quality in that events took shape, without the complications of individual psychology, according to a pure Aristotelian logic so badly missed in real life.

Devices like these became gradually less necessary as the public grew accustomed to interpret the action by itself and were virtually abolished by the invention of the talking film. But even now there survive—quite legitimately, I think—the remnants of a "fixed attitude and attribute" principle and, more basic, a primitive or folkloristic concept of plot construction. Even today we take it for granted that the diphtheria of a baby tends to occur when the parents are out and, having occurred, solves all their matrimonial problems. Even today we demand of a decent mystery film that the butler, though he may

be anything from an agent of the British Secret Service to the real
father of the daughter of the house, must not turn out to be the murderer. Even today we love to see Pasteur, Zola or Ehrlich win out
against stupidity and wickedness, with their respective wives trusting
and trusting all the time. Even today we much prefer a happy finale
to a gloomy one and insist, at the very least, on the observance of the
Aristotelian rule that the story have a beginning, a middle and an
ending—a rule the abrogation of which has done so much to estrange
the general public from the more elevated spheres of modern writing.
Primitive symbolism, too, survives in such amusing details as the last
sequence of *Casablanca* where the delightfully crooked and right-
minded *préfet de police* casts an empty bottle of Vichy water into
the wastepaper basket; and in such telling symbols of the supernatural
as Sir Cedric Hardwicke's Death in the guise of a "gentleman in a
dustcoat trying" (*On Borrowed Time*) or Claude Rains's Hermes
Psychopompos in the striped trousers of an airline manager (*Here
Comes Mister Jordan*).

The most conspicuous advances were made in directing, lighting,
camera work, cutting and acting proper. But while in most of these
fields the evolution proceeded continuously—though, of course, not
without detours, breakdowns and archaic relapses—the development
of acting suffered a sudden interruption by the invention of the talking film; so that the style of acting in the silents can already be evaluated in retrospect, as a lost art not unlike the painting technique of
Jan van Eyck or, to take up our previous simile, the burin technique
of Dürer. It was soon realized that acting in a silent film neither
meant a pantomimic exaggeration of stage acting (as was generally
and erroneously assumed by professional stage actors who more and
more frequently condescended to perform in the movies), nor could
dispense with stylization altogether; a man photographed while
walking down a gangway in ordinary, everyday-life fashion looked
like anything but a man walking down a gangway when the result
appeared on the screen. If the picture was to look both natural and
meaningful the acting had to be done in a manner equally different
from the style of the stage and the reality of ordinary life; speech
had to be made dispensable by establishing an organic relation between the acting and the technical procedure of cinephotography—
much as in Dürer's prints color had been made dispensable by establishing an organic relation between the design and the technical procedure of line engraving.

This was precisely what the great actors of the silent period accomplished, and it is a significant fact that the best of them did not

come from the stage, whose crystallized tradition prevented Duse's only film, *Cenere*, from being more than a priceless record of Duse. They came instead from the circus or the variety, as was the case of Chaplin, Keaton and Will Rogers; from nothing in particular, as was the case of Theda Bara, of her greater European parallel, the Danish actress Asta Nielsen, and of Garbo; or from everything under the sun, as was the case of Douglas Fairbanks. The style of these "old masters" was indeed comparable to the style of line engraving in that it was, and had to be, exaggerated in comparison with stage acting (just as the sharply incised and vigorously curved *tailles* of the burin are exaggerated in comparison with pencil strokes or brushwork), but richer, subtler and infinitely more precise. The advent of the talkies, reducing if not abolishing this difference between screen acting and stage acting, thus confronted the actors and actresses of the silent screen with a serious problem. Buster Keaton yielded to temptation and fell. Chaplin first tried to stand his ground and to remain an exquisite archaist but finally gave in, with only moderate success (*The Great Dictator*). Only the glorious Harpo has thus far successfully refused to utter a single articulate sound; and only Greta Garbo succeeded, in a measure, in transforming her style in principle. But even in her case one cannot help feeling that her first talking picture, *Anna Christie*, where she could ensconce herself, most of the time, in mute or monosyllabic sullenness, was better than her later performances; and in the second, talking version of *Anna Karenina*, the weakest moment is certainly when she delivers a big Ibsenian speech to her husband, and the strongest when she silently moves along the platform of the railroad station while her despair takes shape in the consonance of her movement (and expression) with the movement of the nocturnal space around her, filled with the real noises of the trains and the imaginary sound of the "little men with the iron hammers" that drives her, relentlessly and almost without her realizing it, under the wheels.

Small wonder that there is sometimes felt a kind of nostalgia for the silent period and that devices have been worked out to combine the virtues of sound and speech with those of silent acting, such as the "oblique close-up" already mentioned in connection with *Henry V;* the dance behind glass doors in *Sous les Toits de Paris;* or, in the *Histoire d'un Tricheur*, Sacha Guitry's recital of the events of his youth while the events themselves are "silently" enacted on the screen. However, this nostalgic feeling is no argument against the talkies as such. Their evolution has shown that, in art, every gain entails a certain loss on the other side of the ledger; but that the gain remains a gain, provided that the basic nature of the medium is real-

ized and respected. One can imagine that, when the cavemen of
Altamira began to paint their buffaloes in natural colors instead of
merely incising the contours, the more conservative cavemen fore-
told the end of paleolithic art. But paleolithic art went on, and so will
the movies. New technical inventions always tend to dwarf the values
already attained, especially in a medium that owes its very existence
to technical experimentation. The earliest talkies were infinitely inferior to the then mature silents, and most of the present technicolor
films are still inferior to the now mature talkies in black and white.
But even if Aldous Huxley's nightmare should come true and the experiences of taste, smell and touch should be added to those of sight
and hearing, even then we may say with the Apostle, as we have said
when first confronted with the sound track and the technicolor film,
"We are troubled on every side, yet not distressed; we are perplexed,
but not in despair."

From the law of time-charged space and space-bound time, there
follows the fact that the screenplay, in contrast to the theater play,
*has no aesthetic existence independent of its performance, and that
its characters have no aesthetic existence outside the actors.*
The playwright writes in the fond hope that his work will be an
imperishable jewel in the treasure house of civilization and will be
presented in hundreds of performances that are but transient variations on a "work" that is constant. The script-writer, on the other
hand, writes for one producer, one director and one cast. Their work
achieves the same degree of permanence as does his; and should the
same or a similar scenario ever be filmed by a different director and a
different cast there will result an altogether different "play."
Othello or Nora are definite, substantial figures created by the
playwright. They can be played well or badly, and they can be "interpreted" in one way or another; but they most definitely exist, no
matter who plays them or even whether they are played at all. The
character in a film, however, lives and dies with the actor. It is not
the entity "Othello" interpreted by Robeson or the entity "Nora" interpreted by Duse; it is the entity "Greta Garbo" incarnate in a figure
called Anna Christie or the entity "Robert Montgomery" incarnate
in a murderer who, for all we know or care to know, may forever remain anonymous but will never cease to haunt our memories. Even
when the names of the characters happen to be Henry VIII or Anna
Karenina, the king who ruled England from 1509 to 1547 and the
woman created by Tolstoy, they do not exist outside the being of
Garbo and Laughton. They are but empty and incorporeal outlines
like the shadows in Homer's Hades, assuming the character of reality

only when filled with the lifeblood of an actor. Conversely, if a movie role is badly played there remains literally nothing of it, no matter how interesting the character's psychology or how elaborate the words.

What applies to the actor applies, *mutatis mutandis*, to most of the other artists, or artisans, who contribute to the making of a film: the director, the sound man, the enormously important cameraman, even the make-up man. A stage production is rehearsed until everything is ready, and then it is repeatedly performed in three consecutive hours. At each performance everybody has to be on hand and does his work; and afterward he goes home and to bed. The work of the stage actor may thus be likened to that of a musician, and that of the stage director to that of a conductor. Like these, they have a certain repertoire which they have studied and present in a number of complete but transitory performances, be it *Hamlet* today and *Ghosts* tomorrow, or *Life with Father per saecula saeculorum*. The activities of the film actor and the film director, however, are comparable, respectively, to those of the plastic artist and the architect, rather than to those of the musician and the conductor. Stage work is continuous but transitory; film work is discontinuous but permanent. Individual sequences are done piecemeal and out of order according to the most efficient use of sets and personnel. Each bit is done over and over again until it stands; and when the whole has been cut and composed everyone is through with it forever. Needless to say that this very procedure cannot but emphasize the curious consubstantiality that exists between the person of the movie actor and his role. Coming into existence piece by piece, regardless of the natural sequence of events, the "character" can grow into a unified whole only if the actor manages to be, not merely to play, Henry VIII or Anna Karenina throughout the entire wearisome period of shooting. I have it on the best of authorities that Laughton was really difficult to live with in the particular six or eight weeks during which he was doing—or rather being—Captain Bligh.

It might be said that a film, called into being by a co-operative effort in which all contributions have the same degree of permanence, is the nearest modern equivalent of a medieval cathedral; the role of the producer corresponding, more or less, to that of the bishop or archbishop; that of the director to that of the architect in chief; that of the scenario writers to that of the scholastic advisers establishing the iconographical program; and that of the actors, camermen, cutters, sound men, make-up men and the divers technicians to that of those whose work provided the physical entity of the finished product, from the sculptors, glass painters, bronze casters, carpenters and skilled masons down to the quarry men and woodsmen. And if you speak to any one of these collaborators he will tell you, with perfect *bona fides*, that his is really the most important job—which is quite true to the extent that it is indispensable.

This comparison may seem sacrilegious, not only because there are, proportionally, fewer good films than there are good cathedrals, but also because the movies are commercial. However, if commercial art be defined as all art not primarily produced in order to gratify the creative urge of its maker but primarily intended to meet the requirements of a patron or a buying public, it must be said that noncommercial art is the exception rather than the rule, and a fairly recent and not always felicitous exception at that. While it is true that commercial art is always in danger of ending up as a prostitute, it is equally true that noncommercial art is always in danger of ending up as an old maid. Noncommercial art has given us Seurat's "Grande Jatte" and Shakespeare's sonnets, but also much that is esoteric to the point of incommunicability. Conversely, commercial art has given us much that is vulgar or snobbish (two aspects of the same thing) to the point of loathsomeness, but also Dürer's prints and Shakespeare's plays. For, we must not forget that Dürer's prints were partly made on commission and partly intended to be sold in the open market; and that Shakespeare's plays—in contrast to the earlier masques and intermezzi which were produced at court by aristocratic amateurs and could afford to be so incomprehensible that even those who described them in printed monographs occasionally failed to grasp their intended significance—were meant to appeal, and did appeal, not only to the select few but also to everyone who was prepared to pay a shilling for admission.

It is this requirement of communicability that makes commercial art more vital than noncommercial, and therefore potentially much more effective for better or for worse. The commercial producer can both educate and pervert the general public, and can allow the general public—or rather his idea of the general public—both to educate and to pervert himself. As is demonstrated by a number of excellent films that proved to be great box office successes, the public does not refuse to accept good products if it gets them. That it does not get them very often is caused not so much by commercialism as such as by too little discernment and, paradoxical though it may seem, too much timidity in its application. Hollywood believes that it must produce "what the public wants" while the public would take whatever Hollywood produces. If Hollywood were to decide for itself what it wants it would get away with it—even if it should decide to "depart from evil and do good." For, to revert to whence we started, in modern life the movies are what most other forms of art have ceased to be, not an adornment but a necessity.

That this should be so is understandable, not only from a sociological but also from an art-historical point of view. The processes of all the earlier representational arts conform, in a higher or lesser degree, to an idealistic conception of the world. These arts operate from top to bottom, so to speak, and not from bottom to top; they start with an idea to be projected into shapeless matter and not with the objects that constitute the physical world. The painter works on a blank wall or canvas which he organizes into a likeness of things and persons according to his idea (however much this idea may have been nourished by reality); he does not work with the things and persons themselves even if he works "from the model." The same is true of the sculptor with his shapeless mass of clay or his untooled block of stone or wood; of the writer with his sheet of paper or his dictaphone; and even of the stage designer with his empty and sorely limited section of space. It is the movies, and only the movies, that do justice to that materialistic interpretation of the universe which, whether we like it or not, pervades contemporary civilization. Excepting the very special case of the animated cartoon, the movies organize material things and persons, not a neutral medium, into a composition that receives its style, and may even become fantastic or pretervoluntarily symbolic,[2] not so much by an interpretation in the artist's mind as by the actual manipulation of physical objects and recording machinery. The medium of the movies is physical reality as such: the physical reality of eighteenth-century Versailles—no matter whether it be the original or a Hollywood facsimile indistinguishable therefrom for all aesthetic intents and purposes—or of a suburban home in Westchester; the physical reality of the Rue de Lappe in Paris or of the Gobi Desert, of Paul Ehrlich's apartment in Frankfurt or of the streets of New York in the rain; the physical reality of engines and animals, of Edward G. Robinson and Jimmy Cagney. All these objects and persons must be organized into a work of art. They can be arranged in all sorts of ways ("arrangement" comprising, of course, such things as make-up, lighting and camera work); but there is no running away

[2] I cannot help feeling that the final sequence of the new Marx Brothers film *Night in Casablanca*—where Harpo unaccountably usurps the pilot's seat of a big airplane, causes incalculable havoc by flicking one tiny little control after another, and waxes the more insane with joy the greater the disproportion between the smallness of his effort and the magnitude of the disaster—is a magnificent and terrifying symbol of man's behavior in the atomic age. No doubt the Marx Brothers would vigorously reject this interpretation; but so would Dürer have done had anyone told him that his "Apocalypse" foreshadowed the cataclysm of the Reformation.

from them. From this point of view it becomes evident that an attempt
at subjecting the world to artistic prestylization, as in the expressionist settings of *The Cabinet of Dr. Caligari* (1919), could be no
more than an exciting experiment that could exert but little influence
upon the general course of events. To prestylize reality prior to tackling it amounts to dodging the problem. The problem is to manipulate
and shoot unstylized reality in such a way that the result has style.
This is a proposition no less legitimate and no less difficult than any
proposition in the older arts.

Film Reality:

The Cinema

and

the Theater

by Allardyce Nicoll

This selection is taken from a book called Film and Theatre (*Thomas Y. Crowell, New York, 1936), in which Mr. Nicoll investigates the differences in technique between the theater and the film. The author's main thesis is that what generally makes for dramatic credibility—and effectiveness—on the stage falls apart in the film.*

W HEN WE WITNESS a film, do we anticipate something we should not expect from a stage performance, and, if so, what effect has this upon our appreciation of film acting? At first we might be tempted to dismiss such a query or to answer it easily and glibly. There is no essential difference, we might say, save insofar as we expect greater variety and movement on the screen than we do on the stage; and for acting, that, we might reply, is obviously the same as stage acting although perhaps more stabilized in type form. Do we not see Charles Laughton, Cedric Hardwicke, Ernest Thesiger, Elisabeth Bergner now in the theater, now in the cinema? To consider further, we might say, were simply to indulge in useless and uncalled-for speculation.

Nevertheless, the question does demand just a trifle more of investigation. Some few years ago a British producing company made a film of Bernard Shaw's *Arms and the Man*. This film, after a few exciting shots depicting the dark streets of a Balkan town, the frenzied flight of the miserable fugitives and the clambering of Bluntschli onto Raina's window terrace, settled down to provide what was fundamentally a screen picture of the written drama. The dialogue was shortened, no doubt, but the shots proceeded more or less along the dramatic lines established by Shaw and nothing was introduced which he had not originally conceived in preparing his material for the stage. The result was that no more dismal film has ever been shown to the public. On the stage *Arms and the Man* is witty, provocative, incisively stimulating; its characters have a breath of genuine theatrical life; it moves, it breathes, it has vital energy. In the screen version all that life has fled, and, strangest thing of all, those characters—Bluntschli, Raina, Sergius—who are so exciting on the boards looked to the audience like a set of wooden dummies, hopelessly patterned. Performed by a third-rate amateur cast their lifeblood does not so ebb from them, yet here, interpreted by a group of distinguished professionals, they wilted and died—died, too, in such forms that we could never have credited them with ever having had a spark of reality. Was there any basic reason for this failure?

THE CAMERA'S TRUTH

The basic reason seems to be simply this—that practically all effectively drawn stage characters are types and that in the cinema we demand individualization, or else that we recognize stage figures as types and impute greater power of independent life to the figures we see on the screen. This judgment, running so absolutely counter to what would have been our first answer to the original question posited, may seem grossly distorted, but perhaps some further consideration will demonstrate its plausibility. When we go to the theater, we expect theater and nothing else. We know that the building we enter is a playhouse; that behind the lowered curtain actors are making ready, dressing themselves in strange garments and transforming their natural features; that the figures we later see on the boards are never living persons of king and bishop and clown, but merely men pretending for a brief space of time to be like these figures. Dramatic illusion is never (or so rarely as to be negligible) the illusion of reality; it is always imaginative illusion, the illusion of a period of make-believe. All the time we watch Hamlet's throes of agony we know that the character Hamlet is being impersonated by a man who

presently will walk out of the stage door in ordinary clothes
and an autograph-signing smile on his face. True, volumes have been
written on famous dramatic characters—Greek, Elizabethan English
and modern Norwegian—and these volumes might well seem to give
the lie to such assumptions. Have not Shakespeare's characters seemed
so real to a few observers that we have on our shelves books specifically concerned with the girlhood of his heroines—a girlhood the
dramas themselves denied us?

These studies, however, should not distract us from the essential
truth that the greatest playwrights have always aimed at presenting
human personality in bold theatric terms. Hamlet seizes on us, not
because he is an individual, not because in him Shakespeare has delineated a particular prince of Denmark, but because in Hamlet there
are bits of all men; he is a composite character whose lineaments are
determined by dramatic necessity, and through that he lives. Fundamentally, the truly vital theater deals in stock figures. Like a child's
box of bricks, the stage's material is limited; it is the possibilities in
arrangement that are well-nigh inexhaustible. Audiences thrill to see
new situations born of fresh sociological conditions, but the figures
set before them in significant plays are conventionally fixed and
familiar. Of Romeos there are many, and of Othellos legion. Character on the stage is restricted and stereotyped and the persons who
play upon the boards are governed not by the strangely perplexing
processes of life but by the established terms of stage practice. Bluntschli represents half a hundred similar rationalists; the idealism of
thousands is incorporated in Sergius; and Raina is an eternal stage
type of the perplexing female. The theater is populated, not by real
individuals whose boyhood or girlhood may legitimately be traced,
but by heroes and villains sprung full-bodied from Jove's brain, by
clowns and pantaloons whose youth is unknown and whose future
matters not after the curtain's fall.

In the cinema we demand something different. Probably we carry
into the picture house prejudices deeply ingrained in our beings. The
statement that "the camera cannot lie" has been disproved by millions
of flattering portraits and by dozens of spiritualistic pictures which
purport to depict fairies but which mostly turn out to be faintly disguised pictures of ballet dancers or replicas of figures in advertisements of night lights. Yet in our heart of hearts we credit the truth
of that statement. A picture, a piece of sculpture, a stage play—these
we know were created by man; we have watched the scenery being
carried in backstage and we know we shall see the actors, turned into
themselves again, bowing at the conclusion of the performance. In
every way the "falsity" of a theatrical production is borne in upon us,

so that we are prepared to demand nothing save a theatrical truth. For the films, however, our orientation is vastly different. Several periodicals, it is true, have endeavored to let us into the secrets of the moving-picture industry and a few favored spectators have been permitted to make the rounds of the studios; but for ninety per cent of the audience the actual methods employed in the preparation of a film remain far off and dimly realized. New York, we are told,

struts when it constructs a Rockefeller Center. A small town chirps when it finishes a block of fine cottages. The government gets into the newspapers for projects like Boulder Dam. It takes Hollywood approximately three days to build Rome and a morning to effect its fall, but there is very little hurrah about it. The details are guarded like Victorian virtue.

There is sound reticence on the part of a community that is usually articulate about its successes. Hollywood is in the business of building illusion, not sets. . . . The public likes to feel that the stork brought *The Birth of a Nation*. It likes to feel that a cameraman hung in the clouds—mid-Pacific—the day that Barrymore fought the whale.

That audience, accordingly, carries its prejudices with it intact. "The camera cannot lie"—and therefore, even when we are looking at Marlene Dietrich or Robert Montgomery, we unconsciously lose sight of fictional surroundings and interpret their impersonations as "real" things. Rudolph Valentino became a man who had had innumerable sheikish adventures, and into each part she took the personality of Greta Garbo was incorporated. The most impossible actions may be shown us in a film, yet Laurel and Hardy are, at their best, seen as individuals experiencing many strange adventures, not as virtuoso comedians in a vaudeville act.

How true this is was demonstrated by a film, *Once in a Blue Moon*, which has been shown in only a few theaters. The general tone of *Once in a Blue Moon* was burlesque. In it was a take-off of certain Russian films, incidental jibes at a few popular American examples, and occasional skits directed at prominent players; Jimmy Savo took the role of Gabbo the Great while one of the actresses made up to look like Katharine Hepburn. The result was dismal. In Charlie Chaplin's free fantasy there is life and interest; throughout the course of *Once in a Blue Moon* vitality was entirely lacking. Nor was the reason far to seek. We cannot appreciate burlesque in the cinema because of the fact that in serious films actor and role are indistinguishable; on the stage we appreciate it since there, in serious plays, we can never escape from separating the fictional character and its creator.

Stage burlesque is directed at an artistic method, generally the method employed by an individual player in the treatment of his parts. To caricature Irving was easy; hardly would a cinematic travesty of Arliss succeed. The presentation of this single film proved clearly the difference in approach on the part of cinema and theater public respectively. These, so generally considered identical, are seen to be controlled by quite distinct psychological elements.

Charlie Chaplin's free fantasy has been referred to above. This, associated with, say, the methods of René Clair, might well serve to demonstrate the true resources of the film; comparison with the erring tendencies of *Once in a Blue Moon* brings out clearly the genuine frontiers of the cinematic sphere. In *The Ghost Goes West* there was much of satire, but this satire was directed at life and not at art and, moreover, was kept well within "realistic" terms. Everything introduced there was possible in the sense that, although we might rationally decide that these events could not actually have taken place, we recognized that, granted the conditions which might make them achievable, they would have assumed just such forms as were cast on the screen. The ghost was thus a "realistic" one, shown now in the guise of a figure solid and opaque and now in that of a transparent wraith, capable of defying the laws of physics. In a precisely similar way is the fantasy of a Chaplin film bound up with reality. We know that the things which Charlie does and the situations in which he appears are impossible, but again, given the conditions which would make them possible, these are the shapes we know they would assume. Neither René Clair nor Charlie Chaplin steps into the field occupied by the artistic burlesque; neither is "theatrical." The former works in an independent world conceived out of the terms of the actual, and the latter, like George Arliss in a different sphere, stands forth as an individual experiencing a myriad of strange and fantastic adventures.

The individualizing process in film appreciation manifestly demands that other standards than those of the stage be applied to the screenplay. In the theater we are commonly presented with characters relatively simple in their psychological make-up. A sympathetically conceived hero or heroine is devoted in his or her love affairs to one object; at the most some Romeo will abandon a visionary Rosaline for a flesh-and-blood Juliet. For the cinema, on the other hand, greater complexity may be permitted without loss of sympathy. The heroine in *So Red the Rose* is first shown coquetting with her cousin, suggestion is provided that she has not been averse to the attentions of a young family friend, she sets her cap at a visiting Texan and grieves bitterly on receiving news of his death, and finally she discovers or rediscovers the true love she bears to the cousin. All this is done without any hint that she is a mere flirt; her affections are such as might have been those of an ordinary girl in real life and we easily accept the filmic presentation in this light. On the stage the character could not have been viewed in a similar way; there we should have demanded a much simpler and less emotionally complicated pattern if our sympathies were firmly to be held.

The strange paradox, then, results that, although the cinema introduces improbabilities and things beyond nature at which any theatrical director would blench and murmur soft nothings to the air, the filmic material is treated by the audience with far greater respect (in its relation to life) than the material of the stage. Our conceptions of life in Chicago gangsterdom and in distant China are all colored by films we have seen. What we have witnessed on the screen becomes the "real" for us. In moments of sanity, maybe, we confess that of course we do not believe this or that, but, under the spell again, we credit the truth of these pictures even as, for all our professed superiority, we credit the truth of newspaper paragraphs.

TYPE CASTING

This judgment gives argument for Pudovkin's views concerning the human material to be used in a film—but that argument essentially differs from the method of support which he utilized. His views may be briefly summarized thus: Types are more desirable in film work because of the comparative restrictions there upon make-up; the director alone knows the complete script and therefore there is little opportunity for an individual actor to build up a part intelligently and by slow gradations; an immediate, vital and powerful impression, too, is demanded on the actor's first entrance; since the essential basis of cinematic art is montage of individual shots and not the histrionic abilities of the players, logic demands the use of untrained human material, images of which are wrought into a harmony by the director.

Several of the apparent fallacies in Pudovkin's reasoning have been discussed above. There is, thus, no valid objection to the employment of trained and gifted actors, provided that these actors are not permitted to overrule other elements in the cinematic art and provided the director fully understands their essential position. That casting by type is desirable in the film seems, however, certain. Misled by theatrical ways, we may complain that George Arliss is the same in every screenplay he appears in; but that is exactly what the cinema demands. On the stage we rejoice, or should rejoice, in a performer's versatility; in the cinema unconsciously we want to feel that we are witnessing a true reproduction of real events, and consequently we are not so much interested in discerning a player's skill in diversity of character building. Arliss and Rothschild and Disraeli and Wellington are one. That the desire on the part of a producing company to make use of a particular star may easily lead to the deliberate manufacturing of a character to fit that star is true; but, after all, such a process is by no means unknown to the theater, now or in the past. Shakespeare and Molière both wrote to suit their actors, and Sheridan gave short sentimental scenes to Charles and Maria in *The School for Scandal* because, according to his own statement, "Smith can't make love—and nobody would want to make love to Priscilla Hopkins."

To exemplify the truth of these observations no more is demanded than a comparison of the stage and screen versions of *The Petrified Forest*. As a theatrical production this play was effective, moving and essentially harmonized with the conventions applying to its method of expression; lifeless and uninteresting seemed the filming of fundamentally the same material. The reasons for this were many. First was the fact that the film attempted to defy the basic law which governs the two forms; the theater rejoices in artistic limitation in space while the film demands movement and change in location. We admire Sherwood's skill in confining the whole of his action to the Black Mesa but we condemn the same confining process when we turn to see the same events enacted on the screen. Secondly, since a film can rarely bear to admit anything in the way of theatricality in its settings, those obviously painted sets of desert and mountain confused and detracted from our appreciation of the narrative. A third reason may be sought for in the dialogue given to the characters. This dialogue, following the lines provided for the stage play, showed itself as far too rich and cumbersome for cinematic purposes; not only was there too much of it, but that which sounded exactly right when delivered on the boards of the theater (because essentially in tune with theatrical conventions) seemed ridiculous, false and absurd when associated with the screen pictures. Intimately bound up with this, there has to be taken into account both the nature and the number of the dramatis personae. Sherwood's stage characters were frankly drawn as types— an old pioneer, a killer, an unsuccessful littérateur, an ambitious girl, a veteran, a businessman, a businessman's wife—each one representative of a class or of an ideal. Not for a moment did we believe that these persons were real, living human beings; they were typical figures outlining forces in present-day society. This being so, we had no difficulty in keeping them all boldly in our minds even when the whole group of them filled the stage. When transferred to the screen, however, an immediate feeling of dissatisfaction assailed us; these persons who had possessed theatrical reality could have no reality in the film; their vitality was fled; they seemed false, absurd, untrue. Still further, their number became confusing. The group of representative types which dominated the stage proved merely a jumbled mass on the screen, for the screen, although it may make use of massed effects of a kind which would be impossible in the theater, generally finds its purposes best served by concentration on a very limited number of major figures. The impression of dissatisfaction thus received was increased by the interpretation of these persons. Partly because of the words given to them, all the characters save Duke Mantee seemed to be actors and nothing else. There was exhibited a histrionic skill which might win our admiration but which at the same time was alien to the medium through which it came to us. A Leslie Howard whose stage performance was right and just became an artificial figure when, before the camera, he had to deliver the same lines he had so effectively spoken on the stage. From the lack of individualization in the characters resulted a feeling of confusion and falsity; because of the employment of conventions suited to one art and not to another vitality, strength and emotional power were lost.

PSYCHOLOGICAL PENETRATION

The full implications of such individualization of film types must be appreciated, together with the distinct approach made by a cinema audience to the persons seen by them on the screen. Because of these things, allied to its possession of several technical devices, the cinema is given the opportunity of coming into closer accord with recent tendencies in other arts than the stage. Unquestionably, that which separates the literature of today from yesterday's literature is the former's power of penetrating, psychoanalytically, into human thought and feeling. The discovery of the subconscious has opened up an entirely fresh field of investigation into human behavior, so that whereas a Walter Scott spread the action of a novel over many years and painted merely the outsides of his characters, their easily appreciated mental reactions and their most obvious passions, James Joyce has devoted an extraordinarily lengthy novel to twenty-four hours in the life of one individual. By this means the art of narrative fiction has been revolutionized and portraiture of individuals completely altered in its approach.

Already it has been shown that normally the film does not find restrictions in the scope of its material advantageous; so that the typical film approaches outwardly the extended breadth of a Scott novel. In dealing with that material, however, it is given the opportunity of delving more deeply into the human consciousness. By its subjective method it can display life from the point of view of its protagonists. Madness on the stage, in spite of Ophelia's pathetic efforts, has always appeared rather absurd, and Sheridan was perfectly within his rights when he caricatured the convention in his Tilburina and her address to all the finches of the grove. On the screen, however, madness may be made arresting, terrifying, awful. The mania of the lunatic in the German film *M* held the attention precisely because we were enabled to look within his distracted brain. Seeing for moments the world distorted in eccentric imaginings, we are moved as no objective presentation of a stage Ophelia can move us.

Regarded in this way, the cinema, a form of expression born of our own age, is seen to bear a distinct relationship to recent developments within the sphere of general artistic endeavor. While making no profession to examine this subject, one of the most recent writers on *This Modern Poetry*, Babette Deutsch, has expressed, *obiter dicta*, judgments which illustrate clearly the arguments presented above.

The symbolists [she says] had telescoped images to convey the rapid passage of sensations and emotions. The metaphysicians had played in a like fashion with ideas. Both delighted in paradox. The cinema, and ultimately the radio, made such telescopy congenial to the modern poet, as the grotesqueness of his environment made paradox inevitable for him.

And again:

The cinema studio creates a looking-glass universe where, without bottles labled "Drink me" or cakes labeled "Eat me" or keys to impossible gardens, creatures are elongated or telescoped, movements accelerated or slowed up, in a fashion suggesting that the world is made of India rubber or collapsible tin. The ghost of the future glimmers through the immediate scene, the present dissolves into the past.

Akin to these marvels is the poetry of such a man as Horace Gregory. In his *No Retreat: New York, Cassandra,* "the fluent images, the sudden close-ups, the shifting angle of vision, suggest the technique of the cinema." The method of the film is apparent in such lines as these:

Give Cerberus a nonemployment wage, the dog is hungry.
This head served in the war, Cassandra, it lost an eye;
That head spits fire, for it lost its tongue licking the paws
of lions caged in Wall Street and their claws
were merciless.

Follow, O follow him, loam-limbed Apollo, crumbling before
Tiffany's window: he must buy
himself earrings for he meets his love tonight,
(Blossoming Juliet
emptied her love into her true love's lap)
dies in his arms.

If the cinema has thus influenced the poets, we realize that inher-
ently it becomes a form of art through which may be expressed many
of the most characteristic tendencies in present-day creative endeavor.
That most of the films so far produced have not made use of the
peculiar methods inherent in the cinematic approach need not blind
us to the fact that here is an instrument capable of expressing through
combined visual and vocal means something of that analytical searching of the spirit which has formed the pursuit of modern poets and
novelists. Not, of course, that in this analytic and realistic method are
to be enclosed the entire boundaries of the cinema. The film has the
power of giving an impression of actuality and it can thrill us by its
penetrating truth to life; but it may, if we desire, call into existence
the strangest of visionary worlds and make these too seem real. The
enchanted forest of *A Midsummer Night's Dream* will always on the
stage prove a thing of lath and canvas and paint; an enchanted forest
in the film might truly seem haunted by a thousand fears and supernatural imaginings. This imaginary world, indeed, is one that our
public has cried for and demanded, and our only regret may be that
the producers, lacking vision, have compromised and in compromising
have descended to banalities. Taking their sets of characters, they
thrust these, willy-nilly, into scenes of ornate splendor, exercising
their inventiveness not to create the truly fanciful but to fashion the
exaggeratedly and hyperbolically absurd. Hotels more sumptuous
than the Waldorf-Astoria or the Ritz; liners outvying the pretentions
of the *Normandie;* speed that sets Malcolm Campbell to shame; melodies inappropriately rich—these have crowded in on us again and yet
again. Many spectators are becoming irritated and bored with scenes
of this sort, for mere exaggeration of life's luxuries is not creative
artistically.

That the cinema has ample opportunities in this direction has been
proved by Max Reinhardt's *A Midsummer Night's Dream*, which,
if unsatisfactory as a whole and if in many scenes tentative in its approach, demonstrated what may be done with imaginative forms on
the screen. Apart from the opportunity offered by Shakespeare's
theme for the presentation of the supernatural fairy world, two
things were specially to be noted in this film. The first was that cer-

tain passages which, spoken in our vast modern theaters with their sharp separation of audience and actors, become mere pieces of rhetoric devoid of true meaning and significance were invested in the film with an intimacy and directness they lacked on the stage. The power of the cinema to draw us near to an action or to a speaker served here an important function, and we could at will watch a group of players from afar or approach to overhear the secrets of soliloquy. The second feature of interest lay in the ease with which the cinema can present visual symbols to accompany language. At first, we might be prepared to condemn the film on this ground, declaring that the imaginative appeal of Shakespeare's language would thereby be lost. Again, however, second thoughts convince us that much is to be said in its defense; reference once more must be made to a subject already briefly discussed. Shakespeare's dialogue was written for an audience not only sympathetic to his particular way of thought and feeling, but gifted with certain faculties which today we have lost. Owing to the universal development of reading, certain faculties possessed by men of earlier ages have vanished from us. In the sixteenth century, men's minds were more acutely perceptive of values in words heard, partly because their language was a growing thing with constantly occurring new forms and strange applications of familiar words, but largely because they had to maintain a constant alertness to spoken speech. Newspapers did not exist then; all men's knowledge of the larger world beyond their immediate ken had to come from hearing words uttered by their companions. As a result, the significance of words was more keenly appreciated and certainly was more concrete than it is today. When Macbeth, in four lines, likened life to a brief candle, to a walking shadow and to a poor player, one may believe that the ordinary spectator in the Globe Theatre saw in his mind's eye these three objects referred to. The candle, the shadow and the player became for him mental realities.

The same speech uttered on the stage today can hardly hope for such interpretation. Many in the audience will be lulled mentally insensible to its values by the unaccustomed movement of the lines, and others will grasp its import, not by emotional imaginative understanding, but by a painful, rational process of thought. A modern audience, therefore, listening to earlier verse drama, will normally require a direct stimulus to its visual imagination—a thing entirely unnecessary in former times. Thus, for example, on the bare Elizabethan platform stage the words concerning dawn or sunlight or leafy woods were amply sufficient to conjure up an image of these things; latter-day experiments in the production of these dramas in reconstructed "Shakespearean" theaters, interesting as these may be and refreshing in their novelty, must largely fail to achieve the end so easily and with such little effort reached among sixteenth century audiences. We need, now, all the appurtenances of a decorated stage to approach, even faintly, the dramatist's purpose. This is the justification for the presentation of Shakespeare's tragedies and comedies, not in a reconstructed Globe Theatre, but according to the current standards of Broadway or of Shaftesbury Avenue.

The theater, however, can do only so much. It may visually create the setting, but it cannot create the stimulus necessary for a keener appreciation of the magic value of Shakespeare's lines. No method of stage representation could achieve that end. On the screen, on the other hand, something at least in this direction may be accomplished. In *A Midsummer Night's Dream* Oberon's appearance behind dark bespangled gauze, even although too much dwelt on and emphasized, gave force to lines commonly read or heard uncomprehendingly— "King of Shadows," he is called; but the phrase means little or nothing to us unless our minds are given such a stimulus as was here provided. Critics have complained that in the film nothing is left to the imagination, but we must remember that in the Shakespearean verse there is a quality which, because of changed conditions, we may find difficulty in appreciating. Its strangeness to us demands that an attempt be made to render it more intelligible and directly appealing. Such an attempt, through the means of expression granted to the cinema, may merely be supplying something which will bring us nearer to the conditions of the original spectators for whom Shakespeare wrote.

Normally, however, verse forms will be alien to the film. Verse in itself presupposes a certain remoteness from the terms of ordinary life, and the cinema, as we have seen, usually finds its most characteristic expression in the world that immediately surrounds us. The close connection, noted by Babette Deutsch, between cinematic expression and tendencies in present-day poetry will declare itself, not in a utilization of rhythmic speech, but in a psychological penetration rendered manifest through a realistic method.

THE WAY OF THE THEATER

If these arguments have any validity, then clearly a determined revision is necessary of our attitude toward the stage of today. That the theater ought not servilely to follow cinematic methods seems unnecessary of proof, even though we may admit that certain devices of the film may profitably be called into service by playwright and director. *She Loves Me Not* with ample justification utilized for the purpose of stage comedy a technique which manifestly was inspired by the technique strictly proper to the cinema, and various experiments in the adapting of the filmic flashback to theatrical requirements have not been without significance and value. But this way real success does not lie; the stage cannot hope to maintain its position simply by seizing on novelties exploited first in the cinema, and in general we must agree that the cinema can, because of its peculiar opportunities, wield this technique so much more effectively that its application to the stage seems thin, forced and artificial.

This, however, is not the most serious thing. Far more important is the fundamental approach which the theater during recent years has been making toward its material. When the history of the stage since the beginning of the nineteenth century comes to be written with that impartiality which only the viewpoint of distant time can provide, it will most certainly be deemed that the characteristic development of these hundred-odd years is the growth of realism and the attempted substitution of naturalistic illusion in place of a conventional and imaginative illusion. In the course of this development Ibsen stands forth as the outstanding pioneer and master. At the same time, this impartial survey may also decide that within the realistic method lie the seeds of disruption. It may be recognized that, while Ibsen was a genius of profound significance, for the drama Ibsenism proved a curse upon the stage. The whole realistic movement which strove to impose the conditions of real life upon the theater may have served a salutary purpose for a time, but its vitality was but short-lived and, after the first excitement which attended the witnessing on the stage of things no one had hitherto dreamed of putting there had waned, its force and inspiring power were dissipated. Even if we leave the cinema out of account, we must observe that the realistic theater in our own day has lost its strength. No doubt, through familiarity and tradition, plays in this style still prove popular and, popular success being the first requirement demanded of dramatic art, we must be careful to avoid wholesale condemnation; *Tobacco Road* and *Dead End* are things worthy of our esteem, definite contributions to the theater of our day. But the continued appearance and success of naturalistic plays should not confuse the main issue, which is the question whether such naturalistic plays are likely in the immediate future to maintain the stage in that position we should all wish it to occupy. Facing this question fairly, we observe immediately that plays written in these terms are less likely to hold the attention of audiences over a period of years than are others written in a different style; because bound to particular conditions in time and place, they seem inevitably destined to be forgotten, or, if not forgotten, to lose their only valuable connotations. Even the dramas of Ibsen, instinct with a greater imaginative power than many works by his contemporaries and successors, do not possess, after the brief passing of forty years, the same vital significance they held for audiences of the eighties and nineties. If we seek for and desire a theater which shall possess qualities likely to live over generations, unquestionably we must decide that the naturalistic play, made popular toward the close of the nineteenth century and still remaining in our midst, is not calculated to fulfill our highest wishes.

Of much greater importance, even, is the question of the position this naturalistic play occupies in its relations to the cinema. At the moment it still retains its popularity, but, we may ask, because of cinematic competition is it not likely to fail gradually in its immediate appeal? The film has such a hold over the world of reality, can achieve expression so vitally in terms of ordinary life, that the realistic play must surely come to seem trivial, false and inconsequential. The truth is, of course, that naturalism on the stage must always be limited and insincere. Thousands have gone to *The Children's Hour* and come away fondly believing that what they have seen is life; they have not realized that here too the familiar stock figures, the type characterizations, of the theater have been presented before them in modified forms. From this the drama cannot escape; little possibility is there of its delving deeply into the recesses of the individual spirit. That is a realm reserved for cinematic exploitation, and, as the film more and more explores this territory, does it not seem probable that theater audiences will become weary of watching shows which, although professing to be "lifelike," actually are inexorably bound by the restrictions of the stage? Pursuing this path, the theater truly seems doomed to inevitable destruction. Whether in its attempt to reproduce reality and give the illusion of actual events or whether in its pretense toward depth and subtlety in character drawing, the stage is aiming at things alien to its spirit, things which so much more easily may be accomplished in the film that their exploitation on the stage gives only an impression of vain effort.

Is, then, the theater, as some have opined, truly dying? Must it succumb to the rivalry of the cinema? The answer to that question depends on what the theater does within the next ten or twenty years. If it pursues naturalism further, unquestionably little hope will remain; but if it recognizes to the full the conditions of its own being and utilizes those qualities which it, and it alone, possesses, the very thought of rivalry may disappear. Quite clearly, the true hope of the theater lies in a rediscovery of convention, in a deliberate throwing over of all thoughts concerning naturalistic illusion and in an embracing of that universalizing power which so closely belongs to the dramatic form when rightly exercised. By doing these things, the theater has achieved greatness and distinction in the past. We admire the playhouses of Periclean Athens and Elizabethan England; in both a basis was found in frank acceptance of the stage spectacle as a thing of pretense, with no attempt made to reproduce the outer forms of everyday life. Conventionalism ruled in both, and consequently out of both could spring a vital expression, with manifestations capable of appealing not merely to the age in which they originated but to future generations also. Precisely because Aeschylus and Shakespeare did not try to copy life, because they presented their themes in highly conventional forms, their works have the quality of being independent of time and place. Their characters were more than photographic copies of known originals; their plots took no account of the terms of actuality; and their language soared on poetic wings. To this again must we come if our theater is to be a vitally arresting force. So long as the stage is bound by the fetters of realism, so long as we judge theatrical characters by reference to individuals with whom we are acquainted, there is no possibility of preparing dialogue which shall rise above the terms of common existence.

From our playwrights, therefore, we must seek a new foundation. No doubt many journeymen will continue to pen for the day and the hour alone, but of these there have always been legion; what we may desire is that the dramatists of higher effort and broader ideal do not follow the journeyman's way. Boldly must they turn from efforts to delineate in subtle and intimate manner the psychological states of individual men and women, recognizing that in the wider sphere the drama has its genuine home. The cheap and ugly simian chatter of familiar conversation must give way to the ringing tones of a poetic utterance, not removed far off from our comprehension, but bearing a manifest relationship to our current speech. To attract men's ears once more to imaginative speech we may take the method of T. S. Eliot, whose violent contrasts in *Murder in the Cathedral* are intended to awaken appreciation and interest, or else the method of Maxwell Anderson, whose *Winterset* aims at building a dramatic poetry out of common expression. What procedure is selected matters little; indeed, if an imaginative theater does take shape in our years, its strength will largely depend upon its variety of approach. That there is hope that such a theater truly may come into being is testified by the recent experiments of many poets, by the critical thought which has been devoted to its consummation and by the increasing popular acclaim which has greeted individual efforts. The poetic play may still lag behind the naturalistic or seemingly naturalistic drama in general esteem, but the attention paid in New York to Sean O'Casey's *Within the Gates* and Maxwell Anderson's *Winterset* augurs the beginning of a new appreciation, while in London T. S. Eliot's *Murder in the Cathedral* has awakened an interest of a similar kind. Nor should we forget plays not in verse but aiming at a kindred approach; Robert Sherwood's *The Petrified Forest* and S. N. Behrman's *Rain from Heaven,* familiar and apparently realistic in form, deliberately and frankly aim at doing something more than present figures of individuals; in them the universalizing power of the theater is being utilized no less than in other plays which, by the employment of verse dialogue, deliberately remove the action from the commonplaces of daily existence.

Established on these terms native to its very existence and consequently far removed from the ways of the film, the theater need have no fear that its hold over men's minds will diminish and fail. It will maintain a position essentially its own to which other arts may not aspire.

THE WAY OF THE FILM

For the film are reserved things essentially distinct. Possibility of confusion between the two has entered in only because the playhouse has not been true to itself. To the cinema is given a sphere where the subjective and objective approaches are combined, where individualization takes the place of type characterization, where reality may faithfully be imitated and where the utterly fantastic equally is granted a home, where Walt Disney's animated flowers and flames exist alongside the figures of men and women who may seem more real than the figures of the stage, where a visual imagery in moving forms may thrill and awaken an age whose ears, while still alert to listen to poetic speech based on or in tune with the common language of the day, has forgotten to be moved by the tones of an earlier dramatic verse. Within this field lies the possibility of an artistic expression equally powerful as that of the stage, though essentially distinct from that. The distinction is determined by the audience reactions to the one and to the other. In the theater the spectators are confronted by characters which, if successfully delineated, always possess a quality which renders them greater than separate individuals. When Clifford Odets declares that by the time he came to write his first play, *Awake and Sing!* he understood clearly that his interest

was not in the presentation of an individual's problems, but in those of a whole class. In other words, the task was to find a theatrical form with which to express the mass as hero . . .

he is doing no more than indicate that he has the mind and approach of a dramatist. All the well-known figures created in tragedy and comedy since the days of Aristophanes and Aeschylus have presented in this way the lineaments of universal humanity. If the theater stands thus for mankind, the cinema, because of the willingness on the part of spectators to accept as the image of truth the moving forms cast on the screen, stands for the individual. It is related to the modern novel in the same respect that the older novel was related to the stage. Impressionistic and expressionistic settings may serve for the theater —even may we occasionally fall back on plain curtains without completely losing the interest of our audiences; the cinema can take no such road, for, unless in frankly artificially created films (such as the Walt Disney cartoon), we cling to our preconceived beliefs and clamor for the three-dimensional, the exact and the authentic. In a stage play such as *Yellow Jack* we are prepared to accept a frankly formal background, because we know that the actors are actors merely; but for the treatment of similar material in *The Prisoner of Shark Island* and *The Story of Pasteur* cinematic authenticity is demanded. At first glance, we might aver that, because of this, the film had fewer opportunities for artistic expression than the stage; but further consideration will demonstrate that the restrictions are amply compensated for by an added scope. Our illusion in the picture house is certainly less "imaginative" than the illusion which attends us in the theater, but it has the advantage of giving increased appreciation of things which are outside nature. Through this the purely visionary becomes almost tangible and the impossible assumes shapes easy of comprehension and belief. The sense of reality lies as the foundation of the film, yet real time and real space are banished; the world we move in may be far removed from the world ordinarily about us; and symbols may find a place alongside common objects of little or no importance. If we apply the theory of "psychological distance" to theater and the film we realize the force of each. For any kind of aesthetic appreciation this distance is always demanded; before we can hope to feel the artistic qualities of any form we must be able to set ourselves away from it, to experience the stimulus its contemplation creates and at the same time have no call to put the reactions to that stimulus into play. This distance obviously may be of varying degrees; sometimes it is reduced, sometimes it provides a vast gulf between the observer and the art object. Furthermore the variation may be of two kinds—variation between one art and another, and variation between forms within the sphere of a single art. Music is further removed from reality than sculpture, but in music there may be an approach toward commonly heard sounds and in sculpture abstract shapes may take the place of familiar forms realistically delineated. Determination of the proper and legitimate approach will come from a consideration of the sense of distance between the observer and the object; the masterpieces in any art will necessarily be based on an adaptation to the particular requirements of their own peculiar medium of expression.

Applying this principle to theater and cinema, we will recognize that whereas there is a strong sense of reality in audience reactions to the film, always there is the fact that the pictures on the screen are two-dimensional images and hence removed a stage from actual contact with the spectators. What may happen if successful three-dimensional projection is introduced we cannot tell; at present we are concerned with a flat screen picture. This gulf between the audience and the events presented to them will permit a much greater use of realism than the stage may legitimately employ. The presence of flesh-and-blood actors in the theater means that it is comparatively easy to break the illusion proper to the theater and in doing so to shatter the mood at which any performance ought to aim. This statement may appear to run counter to others made above, but there is no essential contradiction involved. The fact remains that, when living person is set before living person—actor before spectator—a certain deliberate conventionalizing is demanded of the former if the aesthetic impression is not to be lost, whereas in the film, in which immediately a measure of distance is imposed between image and spectator, greater approaches to real forms may be permitted, even though these have to exist alongside impossibilities and fantastic symbols far removed from the world around us. This is the paradox of cinematic art.

Herein lies the true filmic realm and to these things the cinema, if it also is to be true to itself, must tend, just as toward the universalizing and toward conventionalism must tend the theater if it is to find a secure place among us. Fortunately the signs of the age are propitious; experiments in poetic drama and production of films utilizing at least a few of the significant methods basically associated with cinematic art give us authority for believing that within the next decade each will discover firmer and surer foothold and therefore more arresting control over their material. Both stage and cinema have their particular and peculiar functions; their houses may stand side by side, not in rivaling enmity, but in that friendly rivalry which is one of the compelling forces in the wider realm of artistic achievement.

A Note
on
the Film

by Susanne Langer

The following is from Susanne Langer's book on the philosophy of aesthetics, Feeling and Form *(Charles Scribner's Sons, New York, 1953). For Miss Langer the film is a new poetic art, one that appears to the beholder in what she terms "the dream mode." In the endless succession of images moving through space, past and present, the film draws upon some of the characteristics of literature, drama, poetry, painting, music and dance. This omnivorous use of many elements, Miss Langer believes, accounts for one of the film's most interesting aspects.*

HERE IS a new art. For a few decades it seemed like nothing more than a new technical device in the sphere of drama, a new way of preserving and retailing dramatic performances. But today its development has already belied this assumption. The screen is not a stage, and what is created in the conception and realization of a film is not a play. It is too early to systematize any theory of this new art, but even in its present pristine state it exhibits—quite beyond any doubt, I think—not only a new technique, but a new poetic mode. . . .

The moving camera divorced the screen from the stage. The straightforward photographing of stage action, formerly viewed as the only artistic possibility of the film, henceforth appeared as a special technique. The screen actor is not governed by the stage, nor by the conventions of the theater, he has his own realm and conventions; indeed, there may be no "actor" at all. The documentary film is a pregnant invention. The cartoon does not even involve persons merely "behaving."

The fact that the moving picture could develop to a fairly high degree as a silent art, in which speech had to be reduced and concentrated into brief, well-spaced captions, was another indication that it was not simply drama. It used pantomime, and the first aestheticians of the film considered it as essentially pantomime. But it is not pantomime; it swallowed that ancient popular art as it swallowed the photograph.

One of the most striking characteristics of this new art is that it seems to be omnivorous, able to assimilate the most diverse materials and turn them into elements of its own. With every new invention—montage, the sound track, Technicolor—its devotees have raised a cry of fear that now its "art" must be lost. Since every such novelty is, of course, promptly exploited before it is even technically perfected, and flaunted in its rawest state, as a popular sensation, in the flood of meaningless compositions that steadily supplies the show business, there is usually a tidal wave of particularly bad rubbish in association with every important advance. But the art goes on. It swallows everything: dancing, skating, drama, panorama, cartooning, music (it almost always requires music).

Therewithal it remains a poetic art. But it is not any poetic art we have known before; it makes the primary illusion—virtual history —in its own mode.

This is, essentially, *the dream mode*. I do not mean that it copies dream, or puts one into a daydream. Not at all; no more than literature invokes memory, or makes us believe that *we* are remembering. An art mode is *a mode of appearance*. Fiction is "like" memory in that is is projected to compose a finished experiential form, a "past" —not the reader's past, nor the writer's, though the latter may make a claim to it (that, as well as the use of actual memory as a model, is a literary device). Drama is "like" action in being causal, creating a total imminent experience, a personal "future" or Destiny. Cinema is "like" dream in the mode of its presentation; it creates a virtual present, an order of direct apparition. That is the mode of dream.

The most noteworthy formal characteristic of dream is that the dreamer is always at the center of it. Places shift, persons act and speak, or change or fade—facts emerge, situations grow, objects come into view with strange importance, ordinary things infinitely valuable or horrible, and they may be superseded by others that are related to them essentially by feeling, not by natural proximity. But the dreamer is always "there," his relation is, so to speak, equidistant from all events. Things may occur around him or unroll before his eyes; he may act or want to act, or suffer or contemplate; but the *immediacy* of everything in a dream is the same for him.

This aesthetic peculiarity, this relation to things perceived, characterizes the *dream mode:* it is this that the moving picture takes over, and thereby it creates a virtual present. In its relation to the images, actions, events that constitute the story, the camera is in the place of the dreamer.

But the camera *is* not a dreamer. We are usually agents in a dream. The camera (and its complement, the microphone) is not itself "in" the picture. It is the mind's eye and nothing more. Neither is the picture (if it is art) likely to be dreamlike in its structure. It is a poetic composition, coherent, organic, governed by a definitely conceived feeling, not dictated by actual emotional pressures.

The basic abstraction whereby virtual history is created in the dream mode is immediacy of experience, "givenness," or "authenticity." This is what the art of the film abstracts from actuality, from our actual dreaming.

The percipient of a moving picture sees with the camera; his standpoint moves with it, his mind is pervasively present. The camera is his eye (as the microphone is his ear—and there is no reason why a mind's eye and a mind's ear must always stay together). *He takes the place of the dreamer,* but in a perfectly objectified dream —that is, he is not in the story. The work is the appearance of a dream, a unified, continuously passing, significant *apparition.*

Conceived in this way, a good moving picture is a work of art by all the standards that apply to art as such. Sergei Eisenstein speaks of good and bad films as, respectively, "vital" and "lifeless";[1] speaks of photographic shots as "elements,"[2] which combine into "images," which are "objectively unpresentable" (I would call them poetic impressions), but are greater elements compounded of "representations," whether by montage or symbolic acting or any other means.[3] The whole is governed by the "initial general image which originally hovered before the creative artist"[4]—the matrix, the commanding form; and it is this (not, be it remarked, the artist's emotion) that is to be evoked in the mind of the spectator.

Yet Eisenstein believed that the beholder of a film was somewhat

[1] *The Film Sense,* p. 17.
[2] *Ibid.,* p. 4.
[3] *Ibid.,* p. 8.
[4] *Ibid.,* p. 31.

specially called on to use his imagination, to create his own experience of the story.[5] Here we have, I think, an indication of the powerful illusion the film makes not of things going on, but of the dimension in which they go on—a *virtual* creative imagination; for it *seems* one's own creation, direct visionary experience, a "dreamed reality." Like most artists, he took the virtual experience for the most obvious fact.[6]

The fact that a motion picture is not a plastic work but a poetic presentation accounts for its power to assimilate the most diverse materials and transform them into nonpictorial elements. Like dream, it enthralls and commingles all senses; its basic abstraction—direct apparition—is made not only by visual means, though these are paramount, but by words, which punctuate vision, and music that supports the unity of its shifting "world." It needs many, often convergent, means to create the continuity of emotion which holds it together while its visions roam through space and time.

It is noteworthy that Eisenstein draws his materials for discussion from epic rather than dramatic poetry; from Pushkin rather than Chekhov, Milton rather than Shakespeare. That brings us back to the point that the novel lends itself more readily to screen dramatization than the drama. The fact is, I think, that a story narrated does not require as much "breaking down" to become screen apparition, because it has no framework itself of fixed *space*, as the stage has; and one of the aesthetic peculiarities of dream, which the moving picture takes over, is the nature of its space. Dream events are spatial, often intensely concerned with space—intervals, endless roads, bottomless canyons, things too high, too near, too far—but they are not oriented in any total space. The same is true of the moving picture and distinguishes it—despite its visual character—from plastic art; *its space comes and goes*. It is always a secondary illusion.

The fact that the film is somehow related to dream, and is in fact in a similar mode, has been remarked by several people, sometimes for reasons artistic, sometimes nonartistic. R. E. Jones noted its freedom not only from spatial restriction, but from temporal as well.

[5] *Ibid.*, p. 33: " . . . the spectator is drawn into a creative act in which his individuality is not subordinated to the author's individuality, but is opened up throughout the process of fusion with the author's intention, just as the individuality of a great actor is fused with the individuality of a great playwright in the creation of a classic scenic image. In fact, every spectator . . . creates an image in accordance with the representational guidance, suggested by the author, leading him to understanding and experience of the author's theme. This is the same image that was planned and created by the author, but this image is at the same time created also by the spectator himself."

[6] Compare the statement in Ernest Lindgren's *The Art of the Film*, p. 92, apropos of the moving camera: "It is the spectator's own mind that moves."

Motion pictures [he said] are our thoughts made visible and audible. They flow in a swift succession of images, precisely as our thoughts do, and their speed, with their flashbacks—like sudden uprushes of memory— and their abrupt transition from one subject to another, approximates very closely the speed of our thinking. They have the rhythm of the thought-stream and the same uncanny ability to move forward or backward in space or time. . . . They project pure thought, pure dream, pure inner life."[7]

The "dreamed reality" on the screen can move forward and backward because it is really an eternal and ubiquitous virtual present. The action of drama goes inexorably forward because it creates a future, a Destiny; the dream mode is an endless Now.

[7] *The Dramatic Imagination*, pp. 17–18.

Hollywood's Surrealist Eye

by Parker Tyler

This is a chapter from The Hollywood Hallucination (*Creative Age Press, New York, 1944*), *a book on film aesthetics. The camera, as Parker Tyler suggests, is the soul of the film. With its range of mobility, its faculties of displacement and inclusion, it is finally responsible for the execution of all the imagistic power that a movie provides (or for a film's lack of such power). Here Mr. Tyler explores the camera's intricate potentialities and limitations.*

DISPLACEMENT, so familiar and democratic in surrealism and dreams, is the unofficial, veiled dictator of Hollywood. In this way, the movie city is being true to its own deep tradition. When pictures first moved, the photographer showed off their virtuosity by imitating the visual illusions of magicians—displacement of the kind practiced by sleight-of-hand artists. But the original delight-in-displacement has traveled a long road, one strewn with "corpses" of the technical advances of the cinema. Museums, such as the Museum of Modern Art Film Library in New York City, hold the documents tracing this advance, though one might say that on the surface, at least, they are placements rather than displacements; and just in the sporting sense, like an ace shot in tennis which somehow suggests a perfect "close-up," or the cinematic angle shot which displaces the normal point of vision and obtains a view unexpected of the circumstances. And there is the "swimming close-up": an eye that moves through the air with the greatest of ease, as supple as a fish in dodging the obstacles between it and the climax of its passage; one such in *Citizen Kane* goes through electric signs and past the glass of a skylight to settle its cold nose against the heroine's cheek.

As a recorder and creator of movement, the movie camera has been inevitably an instrument capable of as much displacing as placing, as much alienation as familiarizing. In moving with a more pyrotechnic virtuosity than the human eye, it has displaced *the body* of the spectator and rendered it, as carriage of perception, fluid; the eye itself has become a body capable of greater spatial elasticity than the human body, insofar as it seems a sort of detachable organ of the body. By turning one's head, one can accomplish much more in scope of perception than the movie camera, being able to see more, as they say, "at one glance." But one does not add to the clarity of that perception excepting through the limited devices of the telescope and microscope. These very instruments demonstrate that *clarity* of vision is largely a question of *attention* and thus of exclusion, narrowing. It remains for the peculiarly *alienating* faculty of the movie camera to clarify and "selectify" vision in a generally significant sense. Was it not possible to see *at one glance* the most extraordinary possibilities in such an art medium? Was the camera not a kind of monster capable of projecting marvels? Mechanical marvels, when they have appeared, have become commonplaces, but some of them manage to retain permanently the faculty of creating the wonderful.

The very soul of the cinematic medium, the camera, is the displacement of those visual conditions upon which, as a recording instrument, the camera is directly based. A wise man has said, "The camera does not lie." Why should it? Its truths are illimitable. Like all man's instruments, it is made to serve him in every potential fiber of its being. The camera first displaced color by making it implicit in pictorial values and then, in restoring it, provided a color gamut not that of either life or painting. But it displaced something more subtle than color; even more radically, it displaced that complacence which men had in subconsciously saying of a photograph, "It is very lifelike. Thank heaven it does not move!"—and the movie came as just as great a shock to those who secretly yearned to say, ". . . and look, it moves too!" Galatea moved, and answered Pygmalion's prayer; but in terms of pure movement, these having become a problem as soon as Galatea lived, Pygmalion's desire was an invitation to a greater catastrophe than perpetual and absolute inertia.

The movies alienated photography from painting by placing within it movement. This was so radical a challenge to reality that reality became a rival! After the novelty of the fantastic effects of the French pioneer Méliès wore off, it was plain that the conquest of "reality" remained. The illusion of normally clear vision and, above all, of dimension, had to be created in the artificial eye. By embracing movement, the still camera had initiated a new and different movement. The first law to be satisfied was not dimension, however, but the general articulation of the image: value and line. Méliès, of course, emphasized curiously the issue of dimension in his *Trip to the Moon*, yet at that time both still and the moving cameras had much distance to advance toward the technical perfection of the single moment of vision.

Even as late as 1925 (I am thinking specifically of *The Big Parade*), the illusion of normal pace in movement had not been created —nor, for that matter, had the distribution of values yet become easy to the eye. In order to get enough *light* into the picture, that is, in order to see the delineation of the image well enough, the pattern had to be broken up too much. Lines were too sharp in distinction to the modulation of masses—the same effect which in the still photograph of that time had provided the same virtue without the eye being overtaxed. Thus, an extra effort *to see* came into being over and above the mental and visual concentration necessary for so variegated a spectacle as the movie. It was a long time before anyone connected with the industry understood how to solve the problem of *pace*, of having the actor move so as to create an *illusion* of normal action, and by that time the camera itself was improving so much that only a subtle remodulation was necessary. Movies were then photographed—and run off—at completely arbitrary paces, creating unhappily unintentional effects.

Depth in intimate scenes—that is, of scenes in ordinary rooms— was difficult to achieve and was solved in one way by using oversized sets, there being no effort to preserve the illusion of a normal-sized room. This dual *mode de convénance* and artifice to create depth have a curious echo in the contemporary cinema musical which sometimes, in depicting a theater stage within a movie, employs effects which could not possibly exist on any stage mechanism in use in the contemporary theater. *Only the mobility of the camera makes such effects possible.* Everything connected with the moving photograph eventually had to move in its peculiar manner and assume a specific role in the whole mechanism of movie making. When sound came, it was poor since, at first, the microphone remained stationary and since reproduction was not perfected. When the microphone moved with the same ease as the camera, sound became both "natural" and adequate to the effect desired. Hence the history of cinema technique involves perpetual displacements and replacements; transparent and egregious artifices have inevitably given way to concealed or "nonchalant" ones. In one sense, while the mechanism has become more complicated, the effects have become simpler, more "natural" and direct, and, though greater in number, are complex only in proportion to the trivial content they sometimes bear. At one end of the scale is the spectacle, which is supreme today as the musical comedy; at the other is the cinema trick—the bravura offering of the keyhole type of exploitation, and by "keyhole" I mean merely the concentration on detail.

Even as actors on the stage, movie actors had to use make-up "for seeing's sake." Historically, stage make-up means character, as in masks; that is, the distance between the actor and the spectator was a definite element in determining the character mask. Primarily, the mask had meant a disguise of the real which permanently joined it to convention and symbols. Inherent, however, in the magically alienating faculty of the movies was that movie make-up implied a gradual displacement of the traditional objective of the *means* of make-up. This was because the invention of the still camera signified men's scientific desire to see more clearly—a desire to isolate reality and look at it at leisure. Thus, implying realism in culture, it implied it in artistic media. By photographing a mask, the *artifice* of the mask was expressed in distinction to the *reality of the illusion;* that is to say, the means and the end fell apart on the cinema screen to reveal a new problem in the chess of vision. The whole body of reality had in various ways to be "made up," but only in order to be more itself, to bring it closer. Therefore, in creating a purely visual intimacy between actor and audience that never before had existed, the movie displaced all the established visual conventions of dramatic expression, especially so far as the actor's person went. The point was *not* that actors should express emotions with their faces, but rather the reverse, that they should express their faces with emotions—to prove they were real, not waxworks, faces. Because of the primitive crudity of lighting, the actor's mouth, for instance, tended to become two almost undifferentiated black lines.

Moreover, the first movies were *silent*. Reality and artistic convention alike were alienated from the human portrayal. It is chiefly the absence of Bernhardt's voice which makes a somewhat grotesque marvel of her anachronistic style when seen in the movies. Visible on her face, alas, is a rapt listening to her own voice. The positive absence of sound swept away an element of reality from all living and inert images and revealed a fabulously alienated world of movements. We must not forget that normal people suddenly fixed on the moving image *the concentration of the deaf*. Not only was written dialogue and narrative in the form of captions soon deemed necessary to the photograph when it moved and told a story, but the spectator began to feel need of a further device to create the artistic illusion of unity—the "whole of reality." This was music. Why music? Obviously because it was auditory, but, more than that, because, being organized sound, music tended to contribute to the *totalized* effect of silent movement assisted by literature.

Still self-mindful, the movie camera produced clearer and more "seeable" photographs until all of a sudden—a thing which people had hardly noticed—a "surrealism" of make-up was brought to being: The black-and-white make-up, unlike the stage medium, seemed a disguise, an impediment to the reality of the effect. The presence of middle values, articulated grays, which had been relatively easy for the still camera, was suggested in cinema by the very fact that the actor's face, because it was painted, looked abnormally highlighted; it looked *too* black and white because it is in the camera's nature as an instrument of accuracy to seek effects of realism. Even after a definite middle register had been reached, expressionist values in the foreign films exploited this very abnormal, black-and-white effect. In this medium, the cinema found its photographic science displaced by the abstract dimensional devices of painting. Modern painting, with its plastic conception of movement, had invaded the field of photography from which it was previously exiled. In the most extreme example of expressionist cinema, *The Cabinet of Dr. Caligari*, fantastic in content as well as in manner, the sets were painted structural designs conveying dynamic movement and a sense of space. But this was obviously a relative, by-the-wayside device, since in the movies it is the actually mobile means which are absolute, and hence there was no contribution to the genuine cinematic marvel through such means.

In early films, however, including all those made in America, the black-and-white effects were an absolute condition of the photography and spread through the total atmosphere of the movement without demarcation between static and mobile means of conveying movement. In total relationship, paradoxically, the object in relief tended to recede, that is, to draw together because of internally unarticulated value, in relation to the arbitrary black-and-white value, which came forward purely as a result of the camera lens and the reproductive medium. This was old-fashioned movie photography. At one time Cecil B. De Mille mimicked this quality in flat *décors* and costume, so that Gloria Swanson's face was merely the stylistic climax of the entire chiaroscuro. Nothing like an expressionist or *illusory décor* was used. Instead, it was a matter of the regular or realistic interior, "stepped up" in dramatic black and white, and sometimes almost caricatured. This was by no means altogether the accident of primitive studio lighting or unassisted exteriors (the "sunlight studio"). Two classical types of the simple, tendential black-and-white motif, shy of middle values, were the bathing-girl comedy and the Keystone-cop comedy, usually combined. The female figures against the sand of the beach, the black uniforms of the cops against every light value—this was the super-real vision of the early camera; namely, the *displacement* of mobile detail in respect to a totality of the single moving image. The sportive nature of the content, embellished by the flagrant designs of bathing-suit modes, assisted in this type of "dramatization" of cinema. Unforgettable also is Charlie Chaplin's silhouette against the broad glare of the road (he still uses it), as well as that fat eel, his mustache, frantically imprisoned in the fishbowl of his face.

"Beautiful" photography in 1944 is a platitude in every first-rate studio in Hollywood—I mean specifically photography freed from every condition limiting the total representational means with clarity as an end. Yet one kind of displacement occurred in Hollywood that is altogether characteristic of its middle period of inventiveness. When the camera began to show off its realism, its ability to catch action in all its detail as well as its sweep, the spectator was brought into the aesthetic realm of physical effort and its illusory crisis of danger in a *more directly visual sense* than the stage could provide. This special effect was only gradually understood. From the beginning, Griffith, for instance, never ceased to expand the area of action (even if it meant placing a desk in the center of a large unoccupied area), desiring only to outdo the scope of the dramatic spectacle and yet to create its mobile details with some leisure. While as an artist remarkably intelligent, he failed to understand the natural possibilities of the camera, in that he assumed it was primarily extroversive, while it is equally introversive. He made many technical advances—the close-up, for example, as an accessory to the long shot, and vice versa. Working thus dialectically, this pioneering director added enormously to the dramatic vocabulary of the movies. But—dependent upon the visual psychology—there is more than one *kind* of narrative. While inferior to Griffith in ingenuity, Cecil De Mille, his successor, penetrated into the most primitive nature of the movie camera when he touched symbolically in his "bedroom dramas" upon the intimate genius of cinematic narration of images. He introduced bathroom sequences whose immodest whites exposed to the camera a secret place of light: a white mystery. In a wholly different way, Eisenstein, the Russian pioneer, realized *intimacy* with *montage*, which depends upon detail and stresses the fundamental imagery of the mind and its process of creating total thought by using objects as parts of thoughts. Thus, as a generality, the cinematic use of detail creates the subjectivity of mental states in narrative—namely, *psychology*.

Yet, of course, unless the content is dreamlike, the total effect of cinema cannot be psychological in type. Elsewhere I have stressed those forces in Hollywood working positively against that unity of effect sometimes obtained even in a second- or third-rate work of literature. Hence, when I refer to "total effects" or suggest them, I am necessarily limited to speaking of technique only. If there be no primary unity—this very rarely occurs in American pictures, much more often in foreign pictures—there is incomplete receptiveness in the spectator toward the events on the screen as they aim at a total aesthetic effect. Hence, especially if one is sensitive, he resists many aspects of the movies and automatically displaces them in the total (or "charade") scheme of cinema values. What is left then?

Always with us must be the positive accidents occurring as results of this curious struggle between forces, which we, as unusually passive spectators, reflect automatically rather than consciously. Consequently a displacement occurs *in us* corresponding to the first displacement within normal vision when the photograph appeared. I would call this an almost magical, perhaps a "surrealist," displacement of taste and accustomed finality of judgment—a ritual which begins with the sound of our change sliding down to us from the change machine at the box office. Observe that the most potent contribution of the movie camera, which is its intimate genius in recording physical action, is quite capable of isolating itself. Scenes of great and intense action, with which Hollywood movies especially have been filled, grip us most when we are involved with their intimacy, their *visual selfness*, wherein we are the miraculously protected participants through unique courtesy of the camera. This does not mean that we measure our enjoyment by equating the effect of the physical mode with that of the spiritual and emotional mode! Alas, no.

Having solved so many problems of portraying action, Hollywood technicians employ the camera's genius for sheerly pyrotechnical ends; thus, the beauty of the camera may seem most eloquent just when its material is most incongruous and trivial. In its apparently scientific function of analyzing movement (*vide* the superspeed camera and its revelations) and of bringing us into closer visual proximity with the physical world than the eye is normally capable of achieving, the Hollywood camera is capable of introducing us *into* and then *out of* an imaginative idea with the utmost arbitrariness of timing, and with a purely bravura energy. So the camera seems to possess the wildness, the compulsiveness and the interior meaning of the most instinctive life, such as that symptomatic in dreams, romantic poetry and surrealist art.

When we go over a cliff in an automobile without being in it and see a gun being fired at us without being hit by the bullet (things which we imagine by a simple transposition of spatial points), the camera's eloquence automatically is alienated from the content of the movie and becomes a more or less independent effect. Yet because the causation is evident and simple, such thrills seem as perpetually amusing as discovering how the rabbit may appear from the empty hat. The most moving effect can be derived from such an episode as one recently in *A Woman's Face*, a chase on horse sleigh through snowy mountain trails. This beautifully and dynamically photographed sequence, because its given human motives were of almost no interest, can be filled with almost any content involving human terror, and in this situation the most available content is that of dreams, half-remembered associations of our past, or subconscious or conscious literary memories. The fact that we are so physically relaxed in our theater seats corresponds to our effort to woo the visual blank of sleep, and hence our eyes are peculiarly prepared for the unexpected and the overwhelming.

Like its first imaginative efforts on the part of Méliès and others, and like the extreme literary sophistication of Cocteau's *The Blood of a Poet*, the protean personality of the movie camera is romantic and of an unpredictable and shocking entrance. It catches us like guilty or timid children in an unguarded moment. Even in certain French, German and Russian films of high artistic quality, it is evident that, in order to create the illusion of artistic unity, to keep the literary conception foremost, either fullness or depth of feeling, on the one hand, or the cinematic possibilities of narrative exploitation, on the other, have had to be slighted. The movie camera is unbelievably hospitable, delightfully hospitable—but supremely conceited. The spectator must be a suave and wary guest, one educated in a profound, naïve-sophisticated conspiracy *to see as much as he can take away with him.*

The Film Age

by Arnold Hauser

The following selection is a fragment of a chapter from Arnold Hauser's The Social History of Art *(Alfred A. Knopf, New York, 1951. Translated by Stanley Godman). This two-volume work, which was ten years in the writing, is one of the more important art histories of recent times. Proceeding from the point of view that the problems of art and literature are fundamentally sociological, Mr. Hauser examines Western art from the carvings in the caves of Altamira to the present-day film. In the last chapter of the book, from which the following is excerpted, he analyzes the similarities between the film and the prose of Proust, Joyce, Virginia Woolf and others.*

THE THEATER is in many respects the artistic medium most similar to the film; particularly in view of its combination of spatial and temporal forms, it represents the only real analogy to the film. But what happens on the stage is partly spatial, partly temporal; as a rule spatial and temporal, but never a mixture of the spatial and the temporal, as are the happenings in a film. The most fundamental difference between the film and the other arts is that, in its world-picture, the boundaries of space and time are fluid—space has a quasi-temporal time, to some extent, a spatial character. In the plastic arts, as also on the stage, space remains static, motionless, unchanging, without a goal and without a direction; we move about quite freely in it, because it is homogeneous in all its parts and because none of the parts presupposes the other temporally. The phases of the movement are not stages, not steps in a gradual development; their sequence is subject to no constraint. Time in literature—above all in the drama—on the other hand, has a definite direction, a trend of development, an objective goal, independent of the spectator's experience of time; it is no mere reservoir, but an ordered succession. Now, these dramaturgical categories of space and time have their character and functions completely altered in the film. Space loses its static quality, its serene passivity, and now becomes dynamic; it comes into being as it were before our eyes. It is fluid, unlimited, unfinished, an element with its own history, its own scheme and process of development. Homogeneous physical space here assumes the characteristics of heterogeneously composed historical time. In this medium the individual stages are no longer of the same kind, the individual parts of space no longer of equal value; it contains specially qualified positions, some with a certain priority in the development and others signifying the culmination of the spatial experience. The use of the close-up, for example, not only has spatial criteria, it also represents a phase to be reached or to be surpassed in the temporal development of the film. In a good film the close-ups are not distributed arbitrarily and capriciously. They are not cut in independently of the inner development of the scene, not at any time and anywhere, but only where their potential energy can and should make itself felt. For a close-up is not a cut-out picture with a frame; it is always merely part of a picture, like, for instance, the *repoussoir* figures in baroque painting which introduce a dynamic quality into the picture similar to that created by the close-ups in the spatial structure of a film.

But as if space and time in the film were interrelated by being interchangeable, the temporal relationships acquire an almost spatial character, just as space acquires a topical interest and takes on temporal characteristics; in other words, a certain element of freedom is introduced into the succession of their moments. In the temporal medium of a film we move in a way that is otherwise peculiar to space, completely free to choose our direction, proceeding from one phase of time into another, just as one goes from one room to another, disconnecting the individual stages in the development of events and grouping them, generally speaking, according to the principles of spatial order. In brief, time here loses, on the one hand, its uninterrupted continuity, on the other, its irreversible direction. It can be brought to a standstill: in close-ups; reversed: in flash-backs; repeated: in recollections; and skipped across: in visions of the future. Concurrent, simultaneous events can be shown successively, and temporally distinct events simultaneously—by double exposure and alternation; the earlier can appear later, the later before its time. This cinematic conception of time has a thoroughly subjective and apparently irregular character compared with the empirical and the dramatic conception of the same medium. The time of empirical reality is a uniformly progressive, uninterruptedly continuous, absolutely irreversible order, in which events follow one another as if on a conveyor belt. It is true that dramatic time is by no means identical with empirical time—the embarrassment caused by a clock showing the correct time on the stage comes from this discrepancy— and the unity of time prescribed by classicistic dramaturgy can even be interpreted as the fundamental elimination of ordinary time, and yet the temporal relationships in the drama have more points of contact with the chronological order of ordinary experience than the order of time in a film. Thus in the drama, or at least in one and the same act of a drama, the temporal continuity of empirical reality is preserved intact. Here too, as in real life, events follow each other according to the law of a progression which permits neither interruptions and jumps nor repetitions and inversions and conforms to a standard of time which is absolutely constant, that is, undergoes no acceleration, retardation or stoppage of any kind within the several sections (acts or scenes). In the film, on the other hand, not only the speed of successive events, but also the chronometric standard itself is often different from shot to shot, according as to whether slow or fast motion, short or long cutting, many or few close-ups are used.

The dramatist is prohibited by the logic of scenic arrangement from repeating moments and phases of time, an expedient that is often the source of the most intensive aesthetic effects in the film. It is true that a part of the story is often treated retrospectively in the drama, and the antecedents followed backward in time, but they are usually represented indirectly—either in the form of a coherent narrative or of one limited to scattered hints. The technique of the drama does not permit the playwright to go back to past stages in the course of a progressively developing plot and to insert them *directly* into the sequence of events, into the dramatic present —that is, it is only recently that it has begun to permit it, perhaps under the immediate influence of the film, or under the influence of the new conception of time, familiar also from the modern novel. The technical possibility of interrupting any shot without further ado suggests the possibilities of a discontinuous treatment of time from the very outset and provides the film with the means of heightening the tension of a scene either by interpolating heterogeneous incidents or assigning the individual phases of the scene to different sections of the work. In this way the film often produces the effect of someone playing on a keyboard and striking the keys ad libitum, up and down, to right and left. In a film we often see the hero first at the beginning of his career as a young man, later, going back to the past, as a child; we then see him, in the further course of the plot, as a mature man and, having followed his career for a time, we finally may see him still living after his death, in the memory of one of his relations or friends. As a result of the discontinuity of time, the retrospective development of the plot is combined with the progressive in complete freedom, with no kind of chronological tie, and through the repeated twists and turns in the time continuum, mobility, which is the very essence of the cinematic experience, is pushed to the uttermost limits. The real spatialization of time in the film does not take place, however, until the simultaneity of parallel plots is portrayed. It is the experience of the simultaneity of different, spatially separated happenings that puts the audience into that condition of suspense which moves between space and time and claims the categories of both orders for itself. It is the simultaneous nearness and remoteness of things—their nearness to one another in time and their distance from one another in space— that constitutes that spatiotemporal element, that two-dimensionality of time, which is the real medium of the film and the basic category of its world-picture.

It was discovered in a comparatively early stage in the history of the film that the representation of two simultaneous sequences of events is part of the original stock of cinematic forms. First this simultaneity was simply recorded and brought to the notice of the audience by clocks showing the same time or by similar direct indications; the artistic technique of the intermittent treatment of a double plot and the alternating montage of the single phases of such a plot developed only step by step. But later on we come across examples of this technique at every turn. And whether we stand between two rival parties, two competitors or two doubles, the structure of the film is dominated in any case by the crossing and intersecting of the two different lines, by the bilateral character of the development and the simultaneity of the opposing actions. The famous finish of the early, already classical Griffith films, in which the upshot of an exciting plot is made to depend on whether a train or a car, the intriguer or the "king's messenger on horseback," the murderer or the rescuer, reaches the goal first, using the then revolutionary technique of continuously changing pictures, flashing and vanishing like lightning, became the pattern of the denouement since followed by most films in similar situations.

The time experience of the present age consists above all in an awareness of the moment in which we find ourselves—in an awareness of the present. Everything topical, contemporary, bound together in the present moment is of special significance and value to the man of today, and, filled with this idea, the mere fact of simultaneity acquires new meaning in his eyes. His intellectual world is imbued with the atmosphere of the immediate present, just as that of the Middle Ages was characterized by an otherworldly atmosphere and that of the Enlightenment by a mood of forward-looking expectancy. He experiences the greatness of his cities, the miracles of his technics, the wealth of his ideas, the hidden depths of his psychology in the contiguity, the interconnections and dove-tailing of things and processes. The fascination of "simultaneity," the discovery that, on the one hand, the same man experiences so many different, unconnected and irreconcilable things in one and the same moment, and that, on the other, different men in different places often experience the same things, that the same things are happening at the same time in places completely isolated from each other, this universalism, of which modern technics have made contemporary man conscious, is perhaps the real source of the new conception of time and of the whole abruptness with which modern art describes life. This rhapsodic quality, which distinguishes the modern novel most sharply from the older novel, is at the same time the characteristic accountable for its most cinematic effects. The discontinuity of the plot and the scenic development, the sudden emersion of the thoughts and moods, the relativity and the inconsistency of the time standards, are what remind us in the works of Proust and Joyce, Dos Passos and Virginia Woolf of the cuttings, dissolves and interpolations of the film, and it is simply film magic when Proust brings two incidents which may lie thirty years apart as closely together as if there were only two hours between them. The way in which, in Proust, past and present, dreams and speculation join hands across the intervals of space and time, the sensibility, always on the scent of new tracks, roams about in space and time, and the boundaries of space and time vanish in this endless and boundless stream of interrelations—all this corresponds exactly to that mixture of space and time in which the film moves. Proust never mentions dates and ages; we never know exactly how old the hero of his novel is, and even the chronological relationships of the events often remain rather vague. The experiences and happenings do not cohere by reason of their proximity in time, and the attempt to demarcate and arrange them chronologically would be all the more nonsensical from his point of view as, in his opinion, every man has his typical experiences which recur periodically. The boy, the youth and the man always experience fundamentally the same things; the meaning of an incident often does not dawn on him until years after he has experienced and endured it; but he can hardly ever distinguish the deposit of the years that are past from the experience of the present hour in which he is living. Is one not in every moment of one's life the same child or the same invalid or the same lonely stranger with the same wakeful, sensitive, unappeased nerves? Is one not in every situation of life the person capable of experiencing this and that, who possesses, in the recurring features of his experience, the one protection against the passage of time? Do not all our experiences take place as it were at the same time? And is this simultaneity not really the negation of time? And this negation, is it not a struggle for the recovery of that inwardness of which physical space and time deprive us?

Joyce fights for the same inwardness, the same directness of experience, when he, like Proust, breaks up and merges well-articulated, chronologically organized time. In his work, too, it is the interchangeability of the contents of consciousness which triumphs over the chronological arrangement of the experiences, for him, too, time is a road without direction, on which man moves to and fro. But he pushes the spatialization of time even further than Proust and shows the inner happenings not only in longitudinal but also in cross sections. The images, ideas, brain waves and memories stand side by side with sudden and absolute abruptness; hardly any consideration is paid to their origins, all the emphasis is on their contiguity, their simultaneity. The spatialization of time goes so far in Joyce that one can begin the reading of *Ulysses* where one likes, with only a rough knowledge of the context—not necessarily only after a first reading, as has been said, and almost in any sequence one cares to choose. The medium in which the reader finds himself is in fact wholly spatial, for the novel not only describes the picture of a great city but also adopts its structure to some extent, the network of its streets and squares, in which people stroll about, walking in and out and stopping when and where they like. It is supremely characteristic of the cinematic quality of this technique that Joyce wrote his novel not in the final succession of the chapters, but—as is the custom in the production of films—made himself independent of the sequence of the plot and worked at several chapters at the same time.

We meet the Bergsonian conception of time, as used in the film and the modern novel—though not always so unmistakably as here

—in all the genres and trends of contemporary art. The *simultanéité des états d'âmes* is, above all, the basic experience connecting the various tendencies of modern painting, the futurism of the Italians with the expressionism of Chagall, and the cubism of Picasso with the surrealism of Giorgio de Chirico or Salvador Dali. Bergson discovered the counterpoint of spiritual processes and the musical structure of their interrelationships. Just as, when we listen properly to a piece of music, we have in our ears the mutual connection of each new note with all those that have already sounded, so we always possess in our deepest and most vital experiences everything that we have ever experienced and made our own in life. If we understand ourselves, we read our own souls as a musical score, we resolve the chaos of the entangled sounds and transform them into a polyphony of different parts. All art is a game with and a fight against chaos; it is always advancing more and more dangerously toward chaos and rescuing more and more extensive provinces of the spirit from its clutch. If there is any progress in the history of art, then it consists in the constant growth of these provinces wrested from chaos. With its analysis of time, the film stands in the direct line of this development; it has made it possible to represent visually experiences that have previously been expressed only in musical forms. The artist capable of filling this new possibility, this still empty form, with real life has not yet arrived, however.

The crisis of the film, which seems to be developing into a chronic illness, is due above all to the fact that the film is not finding its writers or, to put it more accurately, the writers are not finding their way to the film. Accustomed to doing as they like within their own four walls, they are now required to take into account producers, directors, script-writers, cameramen, art directors and technicians of all kinds, although they do not acknowledge the authority of this spirit of co-operation, or indeed the idea of artistic co-operation at all. Their feelings revolt against the idea of the production of works of art being surrendered to a collective, to a "concern," and they feel that it is a disparagement of art that an extraneous dictate, or at best a majority, should have the last word in decisions the motives of which they are often unable to account for themselves. From the point of view of the nineteenth century, the situation with which the writer is asked to come to terms is quite unusual and unnatural. The atomized and uncontrolled artistic endeavors of the present now meet for the first time with a principle opposed to their anarchy. For the mere fact of an artistic enterprise based on co-operation is evidence of an integrating tendency of which—if one disregards the theater, where it is in any case more a matter of the reproduction than the production of works of art—there had really been no perfect example since the Middle Ages, and, in particular, since the masons' lodge. How far removed film production still is, however, from the generally accepted principle of an artistic co-operative group is shown not only by the inability of most writers to establish a connection with the film, but also by such a phenomenon as Chaplin, who believes that he must do as much as possible in his films on his own: the acting of the main part, the direction, the script, the music. But even if it is only the beginning of a new method of organized art production, the—for the present—still empty framework of a new integration, nevertheless here too, as in the whole economic, social and political life of the present age, what is being striven for is the comprehensive planning without which both our cultural and material worlds threaten to go to pieces. We are confronted here with the same tension as we find throughout our social life: democracy and dictatorship, specialization and integration, rationalism and irrationalism colliding with each other. But if even in the field of economics and politics planning cannot always be solved by imposing rules of conduct, it is all the less possible in art, where all violation of spontaneity, all forcible leveling down of taste, all institutional regulation of personal initiative are involved in great though certainly not such mortal dangers as is often imagined.

But how, in an age of the most extreme specialization and the most sophisticated individualism, are harmony and an integration of individual endeavors to be brought about? How, to speak on a practical level, is the situation to be brought to an end in which the most poverty-stricken literary inventions sometimes underlie the technically most successful films? It is not a question of competent directors against incompetent writers, but of two phenomena belonging to different periods of time—the lonely, isolated writer dependent on his own resources, and the problems of the film which can only be solved collectively. The co-operative film unit anticipates a social technique to which we are not yet equal, just as the newly invented camera anticipated an artistic technique of which no one at the time really knew the range and power. The reunion of the divided functions, first of all the personal union of the director and the author, which has been suggested as a way to surmount the crisis, would be more an evasion of the problem than its solution, for it would prevent but not abolish the specialization that has to be overcome, would not bring about but merely avoid the necessity of the planning which is needed. Incidentally, the monistic-individual principle in the discharge of the various functions, in place of a collectively organized division of labor, not merely corresponds externally and technically to an amateurish method of working, but it also involves a lack of inner tension which is reminiscent of the simplicity of the amateur film. Or may the whole effort to achieve a production of art based on planning have been only a temporary disturbance, a mere episode, which is now being swept away again by the torrent of individualism? May the film be perhaps not the beginning of a new artistic era, but merely the somewhat hesitant continuation of the old individualistic culture, still full of vitality, to which we owe the whole of postmedieval art? Only if this were so would it be possible to solve the film crisis by the personal union of certain functions—that is, by partly surrendering the principle of collective labor.

The film crisis is, however, also connected with a crisis in the public itself. The millions and millions who fill the many thousands of cinemas all over the world from Hollywood to Shanghai and from Stockholm to Cape Town daily and hourly, this unique world-embracing league of mankind, have a very confused social structure. The only link between these people is that they all stream into the cinemas, and stream out of them again as amorphously as they are pumped in; they remain a heterogeneous, inarticulate, shapeless mass with the only common feature of belonging to no uniform class or culture. This mass of cinema-goers can hardly be called a "public" proper, for only a more or less constant group of patrons can be described as such, one which is able to some extent to guarantee the continuity of production in a certain field of art. Public-like agglomerations are based on mutual understanding; even if opinions are divided, they diverge on one and the same plane. But with the masses who sit together in the cinemas and who have undergone no previous common intellectual formation of any kind, it would be futile to look for such a platform of mutual understanding. If they dislike a film there is such a small chance of agreement among them as to the reasons for their rejection of the film that one must assume that even general approval is based on a misunderstanding.

The homogeneous and constant public units which, as mediators between the art producers and the social strata with no real interest in art, had always discharged a fundamentally conserving function were, as we know, dissolved with the advancing democratization of the enjoyment of art. The bourgeois subscription audiences of the state and municipal theaters of the last century still formed a more or less uniform, organically developed body, but with the end of the repertory theater even the last remains of this public were scattered and since then an integrated audience has come into being only in particular circumstances, though in some cases the size of such audiences has been bigger than ever before. It was on the whole identical with the casual cinema-going public which has to be caught by new and original attractions every time and over and over again. The repertory theater, the serial-performance theater and the cinema mark the successive stages in the democratization of art and the gradual loss of the festive character that was formerly more or less the property of every form of theater. The cinema takes the final step on this road of profanation, for even to attend the modern metropolitan theater showing some popular play or other still demands a certain internal and external preparation—in most cases seats have to be booked in advance, one has to keep to a fixed time and to prepare for an occupation that will fill the whole evening—whereas one attends the cinema *en passant*, in one's everyday clothes and at any time during the continuous performance. The everyday point of view of the film is in perfect accordance with the improvisation and unpretentiousness of cinema-going.

The film signifies the first attempt since the beginning of our modern individualistic civilization to produce art for a mass public. As is known, the changes in the structure of the theater and reading public, connected at the beginning of the last century with the rise of the boulevard play and the *feuilleton* novel, formed the real beginning of the democratization of art which reaches its culmination in mass attendance of cinemas. The transition from the private theater of the princes' courts to the bourgeois state and municipal theater and then to the theater trusts, or from the opera to the operetta and then to the revue, marked the separate phases of a development characterized by the effort to capture ever wider circles of consumers, in order to cover the costs of the growing investments. The outfit for an operetta could still be sustained by a medium-sized theater, that of a revue or a large ballet had already to travel from one big city to the next; in order to amortize the invested capital, the cinema-goers of the whole world have to contribute to the financing of a big film. But it is this fact that determines the influence of the masses on the production of art. By their mere presence at theatrical performances in Athens or the Middle Ages they were never able to influence the ways of art directly; only since they have come on the scene as consumers and paid the full price for their enjoyment have the terms on which they hand over their shillings become a decisive factor in the history of art.

There has always been an element of tension between the quality and the popularity of art, which is not by any means to say that the broad masses of the people have at any time taken a stand against qualitatively good art in favor of inferior art on principle. Naturally, the appreciation of a more complicated art presents them with greater difficulties than the more simple and less developed, but the lack of adequate understanding does not necessarily prevent them from accepting this art—albeit not exactly on account of its aesthetic quality. Success with them is completely divorced from qualitative criteria. They do not react to what is artistically good or bad, but to impressions by which they feel themselves reassured or alarmed in their own sphere of existence. They take an interest in the artistically valuable, provided it is presented so as to suit their mentality—that is, provided the subject matter is attractive. The chances of success of a good film are from this point of view better from the very outset than those of a good painting or poem. For, apart from the film, progressive art is almost a closed book today for the uninitiated; it is intrinsically unpopular, because its means of communication have become transformed in the course of a long and self-contained development into a kind of secret code, whereas to learn the newly developing idiom of the film was child's play for even the most primitive cinema public. From this happy constellation one would be inclined to draw far-reaching optimistic conclusions for the future of the film, if one did not know that that kind of intellectual concord is nothing more than the state of a paradisian childhood and is probably repeated as often as new arts arise. Perhaps all the cinematic means of expression will no longer be intelligible even to the next generation, and certainly the cleft will sooner or later arise that even in this field separates the layman from the connoisseur. Only a young art can be popular, for as soon as it grows older it is necessary, in order to understand it, to be acquainted with the earlier stages in its development. To understand an art means to realize the necessary connection between its formal and material elements; as long as an art is young, there is a natural, unproblematical relation between its content and its means of expression—that is to say, there is a direct path leading from its subject matter to its forms. In the course of time these forms become independent of the thematic material, they become autonomous, poorer in meaning and harder to interpret, until they become accessible only to a quite small stratum of the public. In the film this process has hardly begun, and a great many cinema-goers still belong to the generation which saw the birth of the film and witnessed the full significance of its forms. But the process of estrangement already makes itself felt in the present-day director's forgoing of most of the so-called "cinematic" means of expression. The once so popular effects produced by different camera angles and maneuverings, changing distances and speeds, by the tricks of montage and printing, the close-ups and the panoramas, the cut-ins and the flashbacks, the fade-ins, fade-outs and dissolves, seem affected and unnatural today, because the directors and cameramen are concentrating their attention, under the pressure of a second, already less film-minded generation, on the clear, smooth and exciting narration of a story and believe they can learn more from the masters of the *pièce bien faite* than from the masters of the silent film.

The

Bankruptcy

of

Cinema

as Art

by Seymour Stern

Written in 1936, the following is an interesting example of how polemical film criticism can get. In it the author reveals a crusader's concern for the unlimited potentialities of the film as art, and an enraged frustration at the poor quality of the movies made at that time. Some of the films which Mr. Stern regarded as "half-baked" have since become, through a distorted sense of values, screen "classics." This piece appeared originally in an anthology entitled The Movies on Trial, *compiled and edited by William J. Perlman, and published by The Macmillan Company, New York, 1936. Most of the selections, including the Seymour Stern piece, were written originally for that book.*

THE MOVIE PRODUCERS, being men of low intelligence and even lower courage, refused to experiment."—GILBERT SELDES, *The Movies and the Talkies.*

"The American film industry has above all lacked originality, courage and resource. It has left such things to the despised Scandinavians, Germans, and Russians."—JOHN GOULD FLETCHER, *The Crisis of the Film.*

"When the Future of Hell is written in this series, a large number of pages will have to be reserved for the Americans who make films."—ERNEST BETTS, *Heraclitus, or the Future of Films.*

TWENTY YEARS AFTER *The Birth of a Nation,* nineteen years after *Intolerance,* and ten after *Potemkin,* the cinema as a fine art, in every country of the world, presents a picture of absolute bankruptcy. In those countries, notably Germany and the Soviet Union, where within the last decade the most promising and fruitful creative developments were witnessed, today there exists absolutely nothing which can be considered as evidence of a noble use of the film as an instrument of creative expression. The initial promise of the German cinema, projected during the early '20s in a number of films of a high order of excellence—*The Last Laugh, Variety, Siegfried, Kriemhild's Revenge, Dr. Mabuse, The Golem, Secrets of the Soul, The Street, Vanina,* Lubitsch's *The Loves of Pharaoh* and *Sumurun, Caligari,* Buchowetzki's *Danton,* etc.—was forced to remain unfulfilled; the German cinema, the first important one to develop on the European continent, had already fallen into a condition of premature decay at least five years before Hitler came into power. By 1933 little was left of it to be destroyed by the Nazis, and it is said that their use of the film for purposes of war propaganda has proved singularly dull, ineffective and beneath the standards of the lowest American commercialism.

In the U.S.S.R.—the only country that can boast a film university—the picture is almost as dismal. In 1925 Eisenstein's *Potemkin* marked the beginning of the golden age of the Soviet cinema. This epochal film was to Soviet film art what Griffith's *The Birth of a Nation* was to the cinema in general: the first major creative achievement. In the subsequent five years there emerged in the Workers' and Peasants' Republic at least three directors of extraordinary creative ability—Sergei Eisenstein, Vsevolod Pudovkin and Alexander Dovzhenko—and there appeared, both by them and by their students and followers, at least a dozen other films—*Ten Days That Shook the World, Old and New, The End of St. Petersburg, Mother, Storm over Asia, Arsenal, Earth, A Fragment of an Empire, The New Babylon, Old Siberia, China Express, Turk-Sib,* and others—which collectively represent the greatest advance in the field of cinematic art since the masterpieces of David Wark Griffith. Sometime around 1930, this torrential Russian outburst of creativity began to slacken. Today, a mere decade after the production of *Potemkin,* it is a matter of common observation that Eisenstein, Pudovkin and Dovzhenko, though alive and in excellent health, have practically stopped producing films in the land of the Soviets. Not a single other Russian director has arisen who even remotely approaches any one of these three in originality and power, and the best that contemporary Soviet production can offer may be seen in such meager tripe as *The Youth of Maxim* and in such meretricious or hopelessly ordinary films as *Three Songs about Lenin, Petersburg Nights* and the much vaunted *Chapayev.* Whatever the reasons, the fact remains that film art in any large and ample sense of the term is now a thing of the past, perhaps also of the future, in the Soviet Republic. But it is *not* a thing of the present there.

Casting a swift eye across the rest of Europe, we see nothing in the form of significant creative film work that deserves even passing notice. The commercial cinemas of England and the Continent continue to grind out their heavy-handed imitations of the standardized Hollywood program product. Up to a few years ago, this dreary spectacle was relieved on occasion by isolated French productions (not to mention the German art cinema at the height of its glory) of a definite creative caliber—*Finis Terrae, The Fall of the House of Usher, David Golder, The Little Match Girl, Faces of Children, Tragedy of the Street, Poil de Carotte*, etc.—and by the enthusiastic constructive activity of the English film societies and film magazines. But today, no alternatives to the market junk of the big commercial European film companies gladden the eye. The French experimental cinema has been dead for at least three years; no single picture equal in aesthetic merit or in sincerity of conception to *The Passion of Joan of Arc*, or to the earlier *Crainquebille*, has been put forth in France or elsewhere on the Continent; no spectacle of a dignity and significance remotely comparable to that of the early *Monna Vanna*, the greatest of all European mass films, has even been attempted within the past five years; René Clair, who at best is absurdly overrated, has long degenerated into a formula; and the film-art movement of England, which barely managed to summon up enough energy two years ago to register a feeble and belated protest against Upton Sinclair's destruction of Eisenstein's Mexican film,[1] today is all but a pleasant memory of yesteryear. In a word, while the European film industries continue uninterruptedly with their programs of popular drivel and their desperate duplications of Hollywood, the European cinema as a creative force in Western civilization is utterly and hopelessly dead.

If we turn to the United States, we may possibly expect to find a

[1] For the benefit of readers not familiar with the details of Eisenstein's Mexican film: The film epic of Mexico originally known as *"Que Viva Mexico!"* was privately financed by Mr. and Mrs. Upton Sinclair and a few of their friends during the Russian director's sojourn in America in 1931–32. After the production was completed, Sinclair had the entire negative of 232,000 feet edited, under his own supervision, by an independent commercial producer. Eisenstein's original intention was ignored, the original conception of *"Que Viva Mexico!"* hopelessly distorted, and the negative indiscriminately mutilated. Sinclair's handiwork was released as *Thunder over Mexico*. The outrage was vigorously protested by radicals, intellectuals and art lovers everywhere; in Mexico, Sinclair's market version was banned after threat of a general strike by Mexican labor. The original negative, however, has not yet been saved. This catastrophe definitely marks the end of a long period of splendidly creative film work throughout the world.

very different state of affairs here. America, after all, is the birthplace of the motion picture; it was America that produced Griffith, the first creative force in this medium. But we are slated to receive a great disappointment if we entertain any notions that the American cinema, creatively considered, is in a better condition than the current European or Soviet cinema. Griffith has ceased to be the "dominant mind" (as Gilbert Seldes once called him), i.e., the single major creative influence, of the American screen, after twenty years of unchallenged ascendancy; Stroheim, for all his titanic labors on *Greed*, today struggles for dictatorship; and the original crowd of cloak-and-suit manufacturers who gained possession of the industry in its pioneer days—before it had half a chance to realize a fraction of the creative aims and functions envisioned for it by its early enthusiasts—are more solidly in the saddle of power than ever before. It is worse today because now they have the big bankers behind them, who lend financial and strategic support to their position. Their regimentation of Hollywood, of those working on their payrolls, has been complete; they have successfully suppressed any single creative mind that might get out of hand and attempt to use the cinema according to some other, possibly more civilized, conception than their own. It is *their* tradition of film making, *their* interpretation of what the public wants, *their* tastes and standards that have triumphed. Except for a handful of intelligent but futile subproducers, they have peopled their studios, from executive office to prop department, with their own kind.

As the special concern of this essay is with the American rather than with the world cinema, it will be worth while to examine more closely the present condition of the medium in this country and to make a sweeping survey of the causes which have led to its debasement.

Even a superficial inspection of contemporary American cinema reveals certain inescapable features. First of all, no conceivable mental gymnastics can lead one to imagine that a film *art* worthy of the name exists here today. Every consistent student of the motion picture knows that the present period of American cinema represents a distinct degeneration from the period dominated by Griffith. Between *The Birth of a Nation* (1915) and *Isn't Life Wonderful?* (Griffith's last important picture, released in 1925), there appeared a number of works of major value—*Intolerance, Broken Blossoms, America*, Stroheim's *Greed*—to which there are not even near-counterparts today. These remain unrivaled save by the grand masterpieces of the silent Soviet cinema—possibly also, with reservations, by a few isolated independent productions such as Murnau's *Tabu*. Already five years before the advent of the talk film, a rank misconception of the nature of film montage[2] had gained ascendancy over the formal creative experimentations of Griffith, and when *Isn't Life Wonderful?* appeared—I consider it the last serious creative film work to have been done in the United States—it failed at the box office; though it contained superficially popular elements, its subtly formalized treatment of the material could not compete with the smooth, brilliant and highly polished surface finish of such uncinematic bits of persiflage as Lubitsch's sex comedies (how inferior, by the way, to his fine film work in Germany), or with such pseudoartistic concoctions as Murnau's *Sunrise* and King Vidor's *The Crowd.*

After 1925 Griffith's decline was rapid and complete. His elemental, but exciting and dramatically adequate, formal methods were superseded, first by the dubious camera tricks which marred even the best of the German films and which inevitably captured the fancy of the Hollywood people, who used the new "foreign" devices to spice up their stereotyped product; and a short time later by the great Russian silent films, where his methods of photography and cutting were realized to the nth degree and developed, at least in some instances, into entirely new forms. Since Griffith's decline as the foremost American director, it is a simple matter to trace the progressive artistic degradation of the American film. Unfortunately, space does not permit of such details as would make a review of this process dramatically exciting to the film student. Six months ago Seldes informed the readers of Scribner's magazine that in the past five years, i.e., since the inception of the talk film, not a single picture of the highest order of importance had been produced in the United States. If to this statement be added the fact that Griffith's style form (the first in the history of the cinema) has not been supplanted here by any other equally potent formal development, but has merely been followed by a strictly utilitarian, cut-and-dried technique, of doubtful aesthetic value and which for the most part does not belong to the medium, the creative bankruptcy of the latter can be duly estimated.

However, this condition is neither freakish nor ephemeral, as may be the case at present in Russia, nor is it a mere temporary setback to a normally abundant artistic growth. Its roots, I believe, are fixed fast in the subsoil of the American screen world—in the caliber of

---

[2] Montage: For the benefit of readers to whom this term is new, it will suffice to define it here as the formative creation, through the agency of film cutting, of the movements and rhythms of the photographed film and their organization into a continuity pattern. The creative act, or process, of film montage is the very essence of cinematic art. In Hollywood the term has been characteristically distorted to mean something to which it has absolutely no relation—i.e., a short transitional or connective sequence consisting of a rapid jumble of trick shots photographed from unusual angles.

personality that prevails among the film makers themselves, and ultimately, of course, in the mentality of American audiences. Simply stated, the fundamental cause amounts to the failure of the American film people to apprehend the real powers, capacities and resources of the cinema, beyond those necessary to a standardized, straightforward narrative technique. Their failure may be partially explained in that the majority of them, particularly the directors, cameramen and executives, are not, and have never been, essentially of the cinema. Essentially they are vaudevillians, stage people, circus people, manufacturing people, shrewd merchants, but not, except in a small number of instances, people who were "born to the element." It is certainly significant that they refer to themselves as "showmen," and to the cinema as the "show business." For while they have managed the mechanical apparatus with professional skill, the technical and artistic culture of the film, its revolutionary traditions, its untouched creative capacities, its inherent potentialities as a thing freed from theater, from painting and from literature—these have all escaped them, the very issues implicit in these phases of cinema remaining as foreign to their experience as a book of Chinese verse. Thus, it is no wonder that every new Russian or German or French film of creative significance takes them by surprise, sweeps them off their feet, dazzles, frightens them; they had never suspected these new forms, these fresh, yet easily conceivable ways of picturizing content, these new patterns of photographic style and filmic continuity. A *Potemkin*, a *Ten Days That Shook the World*, a *Passion of Joan of Arc*, a *Cabinet of Dr. Caligari*, Tisse's photographic work on *"Que Viva Mexico!"*—such products of creative ingenuity and experimental daring shock and bewilder the Hollywood practitioners who, with, or perhaps despite, their wealth of resources and studio machinery, have not managed to conceive a single new form of montage relationships in all the years that have passed since *Intolerance*. The industry's one experiment along these lines was the Fox film *The Power and the Glory* (1933). In spite of the solemnity of certain critics who praised it, this picture was a sadly half-baked attempt to dramatize the retrospect of a man's life by projecting its salient episodes in *non*chronological order—a departure from the simple, straight-line structure of traditional American continuity, which amounted to nothing more than Fejos' *The Last Moment* in a new framework, with two or three sequences placed "out of order"' (as the Fox people explained it) to lend "novelty" to the retrospect. In itself this device was merely one of half a dozen radical measures of the same category which Griffith invented as far back as 1916 when he designed *Intolerance* on four parallel lines of sectional flashbacks and united the separate climaxes in a single gigantic filmic rhythm. The industry's film, made by professional experts, failed. The juggling around of the retrospect episodes was not dramatically sagacious or psychologically imperative; on the screen it merely demonstrated what had been in the minds of its creators from the first—a pointless, and somewhat vulgar, novelty. But *Intolerance,* a work achieved independently of the American film industry, was no mere showman's novelty. Conceived and executed as a creative experiment, it projected a system of image relationships—rhythm and counterpoint, present action and retrospect, detail and totality, close-up and perspective—in a grand architectonic design which became, under Griffith's direction, a cinematic fugue. Yet this monumental work, the supreme masterpiece of the American screen, dates back practically twenty years—when the movies were "in their infancy." How can it be maintained, as it is today by a few misguided critics and intellectuals, that the American film has advanced as an art form when in the interim it has not dared one-tenth as much as this? The point is, of course, that it has not only not advanced, it has definitely retrogressed. For in the beginning there was Griffith; but today what is there? Standardized routine continuity; standardized photography; standardized laboratory process; mock realism; artificial landscapes; a submergence per formula of all pictorial elements inherent in any given story; and, as a crowning feature of Hollywood professionalism, the trick transitional or connective sequence, with standardized "montage" by Vorkapich—a sample of the "influence" of Soviet film technique on American film production!

It is an unalterable principle of aesthetic criticism that no art actually progresses except as it learns to express itself in its own native terms. On this basis, the American screen, creatively viewed, is hardly entitled to the grandiose claims of "progress" which its publicity departments and its deluded magnates are continually making for it. "No new form of art," writes Fletcher, "has ever been brought into the world under such favorable circumstances as has the film; and no new form of art has so little justified its claim to be ranked as an art at all. That is the extraordinary paradox that lies at the root of all discussion of cinema art." At any rate, no art has ever been so heavily financed; but to what advantage even at its experimental best? *David Copperfield?* This embarrassingly overrated film was neither fish nor fowl; (1) it was only middling Dickens, and (2) it was decidedly poor cinema. The hopeless state of film criticism in this country is beautifully demonstrated by the acclaim with which this picture was received in the more unsophisticated intellectual circles. *Crime without Passion?* Can this piece—so far superior to the Hollywood prod-

uct, yet so far beneath even the minor achievements of world cinema
—possibly be admitted as a "contribution"?[3] *Our Daily Bread?* Was it
not a shame to waste this excellent title? In brief, the best "bold," "audacious," "different," "experimental" attempts that Hollywood dares
to offer are easily put to shame by a Soviet documentary film, a German legend picture, a French *surréaliste* work. It cannot be otherwise. For to their ignorance on a multitude of intellectual and artistic
matters the Hollywood film people add ignorance of the powers and
capacities of their own medium; to a superficial knowledge of elementary film technique even the best of them fail to apply a willingness
to experiment. A few camera tricks, some very good photography
and lighting in their own native style, a vague notion that montage
means "trick transitions" or "a lot of quick cuts"—this is the full extent both of the knowledge and of the practice, by Hollywood, of
cinema as art.

All this leads to the conclusion that in at least one respect the Hollywood people have scored a major victory. One traditional intention,
heroically sustained since the earliest days of the film industry, has
been realized at last—with a literalness and a consistency that are
positively breathtaking. This is the age-old dream of the Hollywood
movie crowd, executives and directors alike, to make the screen the
living duplicate of the stage. Stupendous triumph! No longer need
they wrestle with the stringent dynamic exigencies of the silent,
black-and-white film! Today the talk film, color film, depth film
make feasible a literal, a devastatingly absolute transplantation of the
stage onto the screen, and—think of it!—Broadway can be brought to
Middletown! This was the dream, the one serious longing of the
movie magnates (apart from money), that animated all their efforts
in the earliest days, that later caused them to hire renowned stage
directors in the face of Griffith's repeated demonstrations of the future of the motion picture along native lines of development. But
Griffith's films, which should have taught them everything, taught
them nothing beyond elementary lessons in the technique of climax
construction—the best things in his films were too subtle and delicate;
they were not adaptable to story treatment of a cheaper fiber. True,
the movie people stood in awe of *The Birth of a Nation* (they have
maintained a decent respect for it down the years principally because

---

[3] *The Informer?* Much was heard through the industry in praise of this film;
the experts had forgotten, or probably had never known, Grüne's *The Street*,
the San Francisco sequences of *Greed*. Though unquestionably the most distinguished American picture of the current year, it was nevertheless not in any
degree the masterpiece that critics, "experts" and newcomers to the screen imagined it, and after several viewings one wondered whether the director's accidental moment of filmic consciousness could be repeated.

of the eighteen million dollars' profit which it brought in), but from Griffith's other important pictures, especially those (*Intolerance* and *Broken Blossoms*) from which they should have taken a cue as to the further development of film technique, they learned exactly nothing. Even the more obvious mechanical innovations which came in abundance from Griffith in the earlier days were slow in penetrating. Thus, they saw *Intolerance*, with its myriad moving-camera shots, yet they did not see it; five years later, when the German films took them by storm, they became aware of the moving camera, which they promptly hailed as a German invention![4] This slowness in utilizing new cinematic devices has not been a characteristic of American film activity during the past five years. A multitude of effective innovations are in use today. But their use is appallingly superficial; they are surface ornaments of the film. No revolutionary organic change has come into the humdrum technique of film production in America.

Of course, underlying this barbarous indifference to the evolution of the motion picture along its only legitimate path has always been Hollywood's notorious obsession with the idea of turning the screen into a living replica of the stage. Already in 1921, only five years after the release of *Intolerance*, the Hollywood crowd was consciously striving to break away from any and all forms of film montage that tended to shorten the individual shot and extend the dynamics of the shot into complex forms of shot relationship. Griffith's use of overtone in *Broken Blossoms* (anticipating Eisenstein and Pudovkin by nearly ten years) meant as little to them as if it had never existed. This was not the sort of evolution the movie magnates had in mind when they screamed to the public about the "progress" of the industry. The kind of progress they meant was precisely the progressive approximation of film technique to the technique of the speaking stage. Thus, though Griffith had created thousands of separate shots in *The Birth of a Nation* and *Intolerance* (despite the immense number of subtitles, both these pictures are impeccable models of continuity pattern and filmic rhythm), the movie crowd of the '20s, as if ani-

---

[4] Readers not familiar with the history of the American film industry may find it difficult to appreciate this delicious bit of irony. The joke consists in Griffith's introduction of advanced styles of moving-camera shots in the Babylonian and modern episodes of *Intolerance*, produced in 1916. Hollywood, with the wealth of a kingdom behind it, ignored this new device by the leading American director and waited for five years until the Germans, with practically no production money to speak of, copied the device *ad nauseam* and sent it back under the banner of German studio craftsmanship! The American producers thereupon reproached their directors for not having thought of it first themselves! This is only one of a thousand examples of that phenomenal opaqueness which has characterized the "picture minds" of the professional Hollywood experts from the first days of the industry to the present.

mated by a perverse instinct, argued that this basis of film construction was wrong. Why mount the separate elements of a movement in a
series of related images when you can show the movement in its entirety in one or two general shots? Rhythm? Rhythm? That's really
Art, isn't it? Then why bother with it? Their reasoning, such as it was,
ran very much along this line. The result was—the lengthening of the
individual shot on the screen *nearly a decade before the actual invention of the talk film.* Almost any American production during the period of the 1920s, if examined today, will testify to this progressive
degeneration in continuity form (since the time of Griffith's major
film work), with its corresponding loss in dramatic vitality. The
Hollywood people went blithely ahead, holding the shot on the
screen immeasurably longer than Griffith's incorruptible cinematic
instinct had ever allowed him to hold it even in his bad pictures, and
through this practice, utterly devastating in its effect on the formal
principles established by Griffith, other idiocies set in. The most
glaring of these was the reduction to a minimum of the number of
detail shots; attention to significant detail, which is a characteristic of
all true creative expression, is to this day consistently avoided in
Hollywood pictures. Second: the elimination of practically all *close-
ups* except those featuring the star; it ought to be plain to everyone
that a voluptuous concentration on the superficial glamour of the
featured players of a film is hardly provocative of an intelligent response. Third: an extensive, and frequently wholesale, substitution
of the *lap dissolve* for the direct cut in almost every American film
from 1925 down to the present. No technical knowledge is required
to realize that when an endless number of shots "melt" (dissolve) into
each other in slow "mixes," without regard to the tempo of the action
in each shot, the rhythm of the continuity is bound to suffer. But
rhythm, which is the moving spirit of Art, is a minus quantity in
Hollywood. Its existence has hardly been suspected by the experts.
Fourth: increased use of the *trick shot* for its own sake to compensate
(at intervals) for the slowing down of the cutting pace of the picture.
In contrast, note the work of two stylists, Griffith and Stroheim. Note
the extremely sparing, and then very cunning, use of any kind of
trick shot in Griffith's films; the practically complete absence of trick
shots in *Greed.* Montage, which merely means the system of relationship between the shots, is practically canceled out of existence when
the continuity is dominated by trick shots.—In short, what happened
may be summed up as a general *alteration* of the technique of picture
making to meet the requirements of the "make-the-screen-like-the-
stage" idea, which demanded smoothness in place of dynamics, surface finish in place of significant emphasis, clever transitional "effects"

in place of organic structural development of the whole continuity.

By 1930, the mechanical realization of the talk film invention relieved the Hollywood people of the burdensome necessity of creating
silent talk films through subtitles and sustained shots, as they had been
doing for years during the "silent era." Arrival of the apparatus—
they had been waiting for it eagerly since the beginning—was merely
a signal to adjust themselves from what had been talk films in effect
to films that talked in actuality: the "revolution," as the publicity departments termed it, was a quite bloodless and easy affair—because
in reality it was no revolution at all! In one of the early talkies, *The
Letter*, single shots of characters speaking run on the screen for four
and five minutes at a time. This was a great step "ahead"; in the silent
days it would have been necessary to intercut these same shots with
at least two or three subtitles, and none of the shots would have
lasted on the screen for more than about one minute (a long time as
screen action goes). Now, thanks to *actual* speech, it was possible to
reduce both camera and cutting to their minimum functions—the
nearest step yet made toward their complete eradication. Today, five
years after the appearance of the invention, the length of the average
shot in the average Hollywood picture has been slightly shortened
again—cutting is slightly more frequent. But by no stretch of the
imagination can it be held that, in making a picture under Hollywood
studio restrictions (other limitations aside), it is either feasible or permissible for a director to mount a film with emphasis on the cutting
pace or with subordination of dialogue to continuity pattern and
filmic rhythm. On the eve of the final victory (i.e., perfection of the
three-dimensional film) of the "make-the-screen-like-the-stage" idea,
these lines by Gilbert Seldes, written many years ago, have a re-
sounding pertinence:

It ought to have been clear to everyone that the alliance between the
stage and the screen was a mistake. It had actually failed. But its effect
persisted. This muddle-headed idea that because the screen *could* use
the material and the people of the stage, it was at its best when doing so,
is responsible for the retarded development of the movie in America,
giving it, at the age of twenty-five, the mentality of a child of six. . . .
Like a child brought up in a dark room, it shrank from the light, like a
cripple it preferred not to move. And light and movement are its life.[5]

The Hollywood people have never been impressed by such strictures. They cannot conceive of taking Film seriously, that is, as Art,
and there is something faintly ironical in the fact that the volumes

[5] *The Movies and the Talkies*, p. 54.

of analytical material which have been written on the motion picture during the past twenty years have completely escaped them. Today, with the three-dimensional film practically ready for use, they await its arrival with something akin to the excitement of a child who expects a new toy. This statement by Gregg Toland, one of the leading cameramen of Hollywood, may be taken as representative of the attitude of the entire industry:

It will mean that we will not need so many close-ups in our movies as we use today [sic]. Now we must bring the camera close to the face of the actor to show the important emotions. But with the actors standing out clearly and roundly, as in our three-dimensional experiments, we can keep our camera back and follow them, like on a stage, and each motion will be clearly recorded.[6]

The statement would be complete had he added that their enthusiasm for the three-dimensional film has nothing whatever to do with the possibilities of its amplifying the resources of film montage, but is due solely to the realization that this invention will literally fulfill the American producers' dream of making the screen resemble the stage to the nth degree of similitude.

After the foregoing rather wholesale condemnation of the American cinema, it would seem only fair and an evidence of plain common sense to add a word of appraisal of the Hollywood entertainment film as such—i.e., not as serious art; in other words, to give the devil his due. If it is true that Hollywood as an institution is the enemy of real art, of culture per se, it is also true that, purely as a popular entertainment catering to an inevitably shallow vein of sentiment, the Hollywood product during the past five or six years has undergone a great improvement. (Incidentally, this improvement has come about wholly within the industry itself and in spite of the repressive influence of those perennial pests, the Church and the censor boards, which continue to have a deplorable effect on film making in this country.) Taken for what it is, the American entertainment film stands today as the best of its kind in the world. Compare the average Hollywood picture with the average European program product; the superiority of the former is overwhelming and beyond dispute. Of course, this may be merely another way of saying that one brand of poison is better than other brands of the same poison; but, however you choose to look at it, the fact remains that the Hollywood movie is immeasurably superior to its many imitations throughout the world. True, the pretentious vacuities

[6] New York *Times*, January 20, 1935. Italics mine.

of Josef "von" Sternberg and the lumbering theatrics of Cecil B.
De Mille are still here; but over and against these, the more modern
type of picture represents a new set of values that is greatly in advance of the formulas of the older showmen.

The brilliant advances in surface finish and in swiftness, economy,
and ingenuity of plot that have been made since the advent of the
talkie are a matter of striking observation. These are the qualities
thanks to which the American entertainment film justly outshines
its rivals on the world market. It possesses most of the good points
of any fine manufactured product, such as a car, a refrigerator or
an aluminum utensil. It is efficiently contrived and put together;
it fits its purpose as a popular emotional excitant, just as these articles fulfill a universal utility, and, like these, it possesses immense,
if superficial, physical attractiveness.[7] A beautiful example of a common program picture that hits the high-water mark of this type of
mechanical excellence was *The Mystery Woman*, produced by
Fox Films early in 1935. The story of this film was the usual slick
affair devised out of a most plausible improbability and lubricated
throughout by a perfectly ubiquitous cleverness. Hundreds of such
products are turned out of the Hollywood factories. At best these
pictures manifest a vigilant attention to dramatic efficacy, which,
however, more often than not degenerates into the mere opportun-
ism of melodrama but which at least has the minimum virtue of
keeping audiences awake. Like all popular art, much vitality, much
spontaneous dash and animation, together with much that is meretricious and hackneyed, goes into the content of these films; like all
popular art, they belong to "the people." As such they are naturally
full of a primitive optimism; not infrequently, as in films of the type
of *Seventh Heaven* and *Life Begins*, they seem almost grotesque in
their amiable acceptance of the bitterest tragedies. Such attitudes,
however, are quite in keeping with the dominant quality of the
Hollywood product, surface finish—i.e., the sensuous lushness with
which each scene is pictorially realized. The seductive glamour of
physical objects in these films—clothes, furniture, automobiles, drawing rooms, not to mention the complexion and figures of the screen

[7] The strictly utilitarian function of the Hollywood "entertainment" film
cannot be sufficiently emphasized. Consider, for example, the increasing output
of propaganda pictures for war and fascism. These pictures, glorifying the
Army, the Navy, the gangster-police, the right of the individual to acquire
wealth through the exploitation of others, etc., may be so much rubbish, cul-
turally speaking, but they are supremely effective in sustaining the prestige of
the ruling class at times when the American system speeds to ruin. Like the
Church, Hollywood serves its prescribed utilitarian mission—in the interests of
wealth, war and the psychological enslavement of the populace.

stars—is considered the supreme triumph of Hollywood photographers and laboratories. Like refrigerators, automobiles and kitchen utensils, their product must "sell."

In this regard arises the question of whether or not the superficial progress of the Hollywood film warrants a shift in critical attitude. It is the fashion nowadays, especially among the young intellectuals who write for the liberal magazines, to temporize agreeably with current film production, and they have even managed to discover a number of self-styled "classics" in the course of their new rapport with the industry. Thus, we find them acclaiming a picture like *It Happened One Night* as a "classic of the American screen." *It Happened One Night* was, in effect, a delightfully spontaneous and charming picture, not without its priceless moments of humor. However, it is absolutely certain that it will not be remembered five years hence; as comedy, neither the film nor the mind behind it transcended the framework of strictly popular values. This fact alone, as every developed critic knows, is sufficient to damn any effort that becomes a candidate for the title of a work of art. But the acclaim which this and similar pictures receive from the intellectuals is painful evidence of the laxness and vague-mindedness of American film criticism. Even the most picture-wise of the New York newspaper critics (usually excepting André Sennwald), who ordinarily may be expected to know better, take a cue from the bright boys of the liberal press; it is not uncommon to find them writing solemnly about the "style" of such directors as Milestone, Sternberg, Capra, Boleslavsky, Le Roy, Cukor, King Vidor, etc., as if there were any fundamental distinctions to personalize the single standardized style common to all of them, or about some good routine program film as if it were a fresh, new, singular contribution to Film Art, flouting the formulas and conventions of popular entertainment. This practice is tantamount to writing profound critical essays about the "style" of Mary Roberts Rinehart, Elinor Glyn, Rex Beach and Harold Bell Wright; yet it does not seem to disturb the film critics. Despite Vachel Lindsay and Gilbert Seldes, motion picture criticism has never succeeded in becoming a vital branch of American letters; but it seems to me on a lower level today than it was ten or even fifteen years ago.

In the last analysis, the whole issue comes down to this: Putting aside the individual achievements of Griffith and the single masterpiece of Stroheim, the American cinema of the past two decades has made no fundamental progress. None of its advances, except along strictly mechanical lines, has been of real significance; none of the basic viewpoints of its practitioners toward the making of motion pictures has changed or progressed in any real sense. Twenty years after the capital American achievements in the realm of cinematic art—*Intolerance* and *The Birth of a Nation*—the Hollywood film industry remains, as in the far-gone days of the nickelodeons, the foe of real art, the retarder of real cinematic progress—in short, the greatest single retroactive, anticultural influence in the world today. Projected in the light of a noble conception of Film Art, the best Hollywood products of our time are poor and contemptible things; in them there are no horizons, no imaginative heights, no passion, no ecstasy. Even in their "serious" moments, they are essentially trivial, ordinary, banal—like the businessmen who produce, direct and photograph them, and like the masses who, hypnotized by Hollywood surface finish, give the businessmen ample reason to continue production along the same lines. In preparing a subject for the screen, every idea, every situation, has to be "adapted," i.e., translated into the visual and dynamic terms of Film. But in Hollywood, this process of screen adaptation means something else besides: It means the reduction of every story to the lowest level of human intelligence, the assimilation of every idea to the spirit and grain of the universal Average Man. This is merely another way of saying that Hollywood film production automatically implies the suppression of creative imagination, the elimination of any and all possible moments of poetry in any given subject, and an enforced standardization of the style of the individual director, an obliteration of his temperament, to meet the requirements of popular taste. The outcome of this factory process, through which every subject is put, may be, and frequently is, more charming, more "entertaining," than description of the process itself would indicate. But even at its best, the Hollywood product invariably emerges from the factory a negative quantity. A major agency of expression, it has neither enriched human life nor added one jot to the development of human consciousness. It has not presented a single fresh perspective of the world, nor projected a single significant vision of man and his destiny (the one American effort in this direction, *Intolerance*, dates back two decades). In brief, except in the case of Griffith, the American screen has not contributed to the general enlightenment of the human race in any degree commensurate with its powers to do so. In place of this culture, it has offered what the movie merchants call "sensational show values"—the half-truths, the superstitions, the vapid and sensual daydreams of the crowd.

It goes without saying that these severe strictures are, and have been, repeated *ad nauseam*, that they are sadly and brutally obvious. Certain alarming symptoms of contemporary film criticism, together with the increasing indifference to higher values of the more intelligent sections of the film-going public, necessitate a reiteration of the facts. The real danger is that the intelligent minority audiences, for want of better filmic nourishment, will come to reject anything better than the current movie fare of tinsel and candied pseudo art. Then the prostitution of taste will be complete.

One question remains: What, if anything, can be done to regenerate this wayward behemoth, the American cinema? Any and all suggestions are apt to be feeble in view of the really formidable obstacles that beset the problem. In spite of the best possible remedies, the fact must not be lost sight of that control of the film industry proper is still vested in the present crowd and that the vacuous entertainment film will continue to be produced in immense quantities for a long time to come. Nevertheless, one or two radical innovations should be obvious:

1. Above everything else, a university of the cinema, patterned after the one in Moscow but with emphasis on the formal and aesthetic problems of the motion picture, should definitely be established here. It is a trifle absurd to consider that the Soviet Union, a new nation confronted with a thousand and one crucial problems involving its very survival as a society, should be the only country in the world today that can boast of an institution of film culture, while in the United States, where the cinema as art received its original impetus, nothing exists except a few courses of doubtful value in "cinematography" in universities of Southern California and a highly commercialized course in "scenario writing" in a New York university. An American film university should be subsidized by the government in the interests of America's foremost art. The courses should be completely divorced from the exigencies of commercial film production, and under no circumstances, save at the peril of the university's future, should a single magnate, executive, supervisor or producer from the Hollywood film industry be permitted to be a member of the board of trustees or perform any function whatever unless it be that of a voluntary benefactor. As a symbol of the university's educational direction and of its attitude toward Film as a cultural medium, a statue of Griffith should dominate the main foyer.

2. A Theater of the Cinema should be established in at least every large city of the United States. Here the great films of all countries and of all periods should be projected in constant revivals. Each theater should have a library of the cinema, consisting of well-preserved prints of old films and also of literature on the motion picture. To obviate the danger of control by ignorant distributors

and petty racketeers, as happened with several of the film-arts guild organizations five or six years ago, all the theaters throughout the country should be controlled by a central theater in New York City, in the same manner as the branches of a great metropolitan library. A nationwide system of exhibition centers of this nature would solve the distribution problem for minority audiences who are fed up with the standard entertainment product.

3. Entirely apart from the Theater of the Cinema, the film-art movement itself should be revived. There should be a resurrection of film societies for purposes of discussion of the nature and destiny of the cinema, just as there are music clubs, Dickens societies, etc. The chief purpose of these clubs, however, will be to heighten interest in the exhibition of classics and experimental films at the theaters of the cinema. Through these organizations, thousands of new individuals will be attracted to Film Art. All the organizations together should issue a magazine, along the lines of *Experimental Cinema*, for the twofold purpose of making propaganda for the film-art movement and publishing critical and technical articles of value.

4. Independent creative film production should be subsidized by the government as the logical fruition of its support of the film university. The tragic exclusion from the industry of thousands of talented young men and women all over the country in favor of distinctly inferior and even degenerate talent should give the government pause. The money for these projects can be obtained by levying a culture tax on all members of the Hollywood film industry receiving salaries of $100 a week and over.

5. A nationwide campaign should be organized, using the screen itself as the principal instrument of propaganda, against censorship of the motion picture by the Church and the censor boards. The American film will never become a mature art form until its champions succeed in freeing it from these ancient pests. Until this is done, it will be useless further to discuss the question of "what is wrong with the movies."

A concluding word: I am fully aware that this program for the regeneration of the American screen is hopelessly ideal and that it has not one chance in a million of being realized here for at least a century to come. I offer it, nevertheless, because only in this light can we see what is wrong with and about our greatest art. The practical solutions of practical men have all inevitably failed; they have been concerned with immediate stopgaps and surface reforms, not with fundamental changes that really change. As with society itself, so with the motion picture, the "practical" minds are the impractical ones; the shortest, easiest solution is the longest, hardest solution. One Griffith is worth the whole tribe of movie magnates; one *Intolerance* is worth all the "good" films Hollywood has ever made. This is merely another way of saying that the only final remedy for whatever ails any medium of human expression is a *creative* remedy, not a moral or a social or a political remedy. When this idea is fully understood by those who wish to "revolutionize" the movie in this country, a real revolution will be possible; then, and not before then, will the cinema become the glory, instead of the pointless joke, of American civilization.

The

Mechanized

Muse

----

by

Margaret Kennedy

In this witty essay (published as a P.E.N. Book by George Allen & Unwin, Ltd., London, 1942) Margaret Kennedy examines the atmosphere in which scenarios are created and the plight of the screenwriter who is given books, plays, biographies to adapt. It is particularly frustrating, Miss Kennedy notes, for the screenwriter with aspirations of becoming a "screen Keats." What emerges on the screen is usually a far cry from his original intention—a situation that could be remedied, she suggests, by allowing the writer to edit the film.

I

ONCE UPON a time, about fifteen years ago, the manufacturers and salesmen of a particular patent collar stud met for their annual luncheon at a famous London hotel. It was a genial gathering, for they had brought their wives with them, and champagne cocktails were served freely. The percentage of old acquaintance was high. Conversation was animated, for Travelers know how to talk. Backs were slapped and good stories were told in corners. Little wives simpered shyly; big wives were graciously patronizing.

These people looked happy and they had sound reasons for being so. They knew what they were doing. They knew what they wanted. The Collar Stud, from which all blessings flowed, brooded over them like a tribal totem. None of them was troubled by any doubts as to the nature and purpose of a collar stud. They made it and they sold it. It provided them with a job and a future, it paid rent, rates and school bills, it put new three-pieces onto the backs of the little wives and pearls round the necks of the big ones. All collar studs are good and useful objects, and their own was the best on the market.

In the general hubbub the arrival of several queer-looking strangers was at first overlooked. Later on everybody began to wonder who they could be. For they seemed ill at ease and friendless. They drank but did not talk, and stood eying their neighbors with a kind of suspicious curiosity. Beside the dapper, eupeptic Collar Studs they looked shabby and bilious. And they had a peevish expression which no retailer would have found persuasive—the air of people who dislike what they are doing and are far from sure of what they want.

After an interval they began to drift together into a little group. They seemed to have met before, though they took little visible pleasure in recognizing one another. Finding themselves thus stranded in an alien kraal, they were forced into a kind of Stanley-Livingstone cordiality and exchanged a few moody salutations. They marveled to see themselves, and each other, where they were. No suspicion had as yet crossed their minds that they must have got into the wrong party. On the contrary, the entrance of a famous actress strengthened their conviction that they had got into the right one.

Everybody stared at her, and nobody felt inclined to tell her that she ought not to be there. For the Collar Studs, who had worshiped her for years, were delighted to meet her and to have the privilege of bringing her a cocktail. Besides, she gave nobody a chance to get in a word edgewise . She picked out, at a glance, their Big Chief and told him that his idea was simply marvelous. She was crazy about it. But did he really think that the films, now that they had begun to talk, would kill the stage?

"I'm afraid," he stammered, "that I can't . . . ."

"You can't say *what's* going to happen? Oh, I know. Nobody can. That's why this party is such a wonderful idea, with the *entire* film world turned upside down and everything. Because the sooner we all get together . . . I mean, what *is* a talking film? A sort of photographed play? Because, in that case . . . ."

At this point a well-known stage director appeared and took her away, explaining that this was the wrong party. She went, with a show of reluctance which delighted the Collar Studs.

"Why do I have to go? This is a lovely party. I'm sure it's nicer than your party. *They* don't belong here either—" pointing to the Stanley-Livingstone group, "and you don't make them come."

The director looked them over and recognized one or two faces. He said, without much enthusiasm, "They don't. I must. They're authors. . . ."

He shepherded his morose flock upstairs and downstairs and along corridors and round corners until they reached the right party, which was indeed not nearly so nice. An act of hospitality was being committed, but nobody was quite sure by whom, or for what purpose. Its totem was the Sound Film, which had recently burst upon the world and placarded London with invitations to the public to SEE AND HEAR their favorite stars. Most of the guests were strangers to one another. Members of the upside-down film world were there, hoping to be turned right way up by closer contact with the stage, with authors, with anyone who might tell them what to do next. The stage was there in the hope that this new portent might signify translation rather than death. Authors were there because their agents had told them to go.

As a totem, the Sound Film was neither so familiar nor so kindly as the Collar Stud. It might be big with benefits but it was also a menace and threatened ruin to numberless people. There was money in it; everybody was sure of that, but they were sure of nothing else. Even those who hoped to make it and sell it had no clear idea as to its nature and purpose. They could scarcely have come to any agreement as to what it ought to be.

It is wonderful that so many people should still be able to share the optimism of Mr. Lambkin, in his prize poem:

> When Science has discovered something more,
> We shall be happier than we were before.

For Science is always showering down upon us these disconcerting benefits, these miraculous implements, which we neither desire nor deserve. And our attempts to make use of them, though sometimes comic, are often grim.

On this occasion comedy prevailed. Science was offering a wonderful baby, a Midas, an infant Hercules, to anyone who could improvise a cradle large enough to hold it. None of the Arts felt inclined to accept responsibility. The showmen, the purveyors of entertainment, were ready enough to accept paternity and pay for its keep, but they could not cradle it. Nor could they purvey something which did not as yet exist. The tools, only, existed. Nobody knew how it should be cherished, nurtured and fed.

Nothing quite like this has ever happened before in the whole history of Art. It is to be hoped that nothing like it will ever happen again; but Science has grown so fond of presenting us with these unspecified tools, means without an end, that further surprises of this kind are more than likely. Development, in the past, has always followed a reverse order. The inspiration, the idea, the desire to make a pattern, has preceded the technical apparatus. The painter has devised new methods, has experimented with new colors and surfaces, the better to execute designs which are already in his head. Stages have been enlarged and improved for the better performance of a drama already in existence.

But in this case technical apparatus outran inspiration. Here was a new medium of expression, a way of telling stories, of creating suspense, exciting emotion, arousing both the intellect and the imagination; here was spectacle assisted by sound, music interpreted visually, and drama set free from the limitations of the stage. But nobody felt any impulse to make use of it. Cave men, scratching bison and deer upon the rock, would have found little in a modern studio that they could use. Shepherds, piping on their oaten reeds, would have made sad work of most of the instruments in a Wagnerian orchestra. Peasant mummers, bellowing *St. George* in a farmhouse kitchen, felt no need of a curtain and a revolving stage. Yet—cave man, shepherd and peasant—each had his own rough, primitive idea of what a satisfactory drawing, or tune, or play, should be. As much can scarcely be said of the first fabricators of sound films. They had no notion of what they wanted to make. Nor had the public much notion of what it wanted to see and hear. The artist and his audience were equally at a loss.

The unlimited possibilities of this new medium were in themselves drawbacks which mitigated its value to Art. For all the arts grow up from the soil, as it were, of their own limitations. In every medium there must always be some things which the artist cannot do, and some which are not worth doing. He works within these bounds. And the sense of being unable to do certain things drives him ever more deeply into the study of what is possible. It is a challenge, and his response is to make a pattern. He invents a form, a shape, a character, a design, which defeats the impossible by making it irrelevant. Where nothing seems to be impossible it is difficult for form to emerge.

Form, in Art, is constantly changing, as the tools improve and the field widens. But it is always there, and always must be there, for it is the very essence of the whole business. The fewer, the more primitive, the tools, the more rigid the form; the more limited the medium, the greater the compensation sought in pattern.

For twenty years the silent film, developing inside its inherent
limitations, had been making progress toward its own kind of form
and shape. Sound was denied to it; therefore its tendency was to
make sound irrelevant. Obliged to rely upon the eye alone, it was
exploring the field of visual experience and learning how to reject all
material which could not be treated visually. Captions were disappearing. The picture was less and less liable to be interrupted by
printed placards telling the audience what was happening and what
the characters were saying to one another. A technique had been
evolved which could largely dispense with them. Actors emerged
who felt no need of speech. Charlie Chaplin, for instance, felt the
need of it so little that, when the sound film was invented, he
refused the new tool and continued, for many years, to act silently.
For him, as for all great artists, the limitation had become the
inspiration; the impossible was also the superfluous. Truth, for him,
was not to be found in speech.

A comparison of pictures made in 1906 with those made in 1926 will
immediately demonstrate how fast human beings were catching up
with the machine; how intelligence and imagination were getting to
work with a new tool. It is true that the mechanics also improves. The
pictures of 1926 do not wink and blink and jerk, as do those of 1906.
Better cameras, projectors, lighting and apparatus of all sorts had been
introduced. But the progress in the mechanical element is small
compared with the progress in the human element, in treatment and
cutting, in the ground covered by actors and directors. The actors
in the earliest pictures were ridiculous, not because they were badly
photographed, but because they did not understand the first principles of screen acting. They were stage actors playing at dumb
crambo; at every turn they were hampered because they could not
speak. And they tried, by a violent multiplicity of gesture, to make
up for the dialogue which had been denied to them.

One of the earliest screen dramas, shown now as a museum piece,
contains a scene between a Roman Patrician and a Christian Maiden
who is awaiting martyrdom in the amphitheater. He wishes to persuade her to recant and marry him. Both parts were played by
skilled actors, artists on the three-dimensional stage. But their performance would have disgraced a charade in the nursery.

He flings his hands out persuasively, a great many times.
She shakes her head vehemently and points upward.
He shrugs his shoulders.
She makes the Sign of the Cross.
He joins his hands in earnest entreaty.

Again she shakes her head and points upward.

He takes to looking upward too.

He falls on his knees and begins to pat his own head, in order to indicate that he desires immediate baptism.

She smiles and nods repeatedly.

The lions, to whom this tongue-tied pair were eventually thrown, were far better screen actors because they felt no wish to talk. Human beings were reduced to the level of Robinson Crusoe and Man Friday, conversing by signs and pointing down their own throats to show that they were hungry.

Yet we have often known that Charlie was hungry, though he did not point down his own throat and no caption informed us of the fact. Our fellow creatures tell us an infinite number of things about themselves, without words and without Man Friday gestures, had we but eyes to see. Hungry men do not invariably announce that they starve, yet they can be recognized. So can lovers, any day of the week. Direct verbal statements are crude and often misleading. Very few people reveal themselves in what they say. They are not capable of defining their thoughts and feelings with any degree of accuracy. Or, if they are, they generally prefer to keep their mouths shut. A frightened man may speak bravely; it is only by small involuntary gestures that he betrays himself. He yawns, not because he is sleepy, but in a reflex action from nervous tension. Little boys, going in to bat in a house match, yawn as they stroll nonchalantly out across the pitch. The company assembled in a dentist's waiting room may rustle the illustrated weeklies with outward calm, but the silence is punctuated by enormous yawns. Privates John Bates, Alexander Court and Michael Williams, grumbling, joking and arguing in undertones as they waited for day to break over the field of Agincourt, may have had a great deal to say for themselves, but nothing more eloquent than the yawns which probably filled up the pauses.

In fact, all the *brouhaha* of the spoken word often obscures truth instead of revealing it. And deaf people, who must rely upon their eyes, are sometimes abnormally sensitive to the emotional atmosphere around them.

These were truths which the silent film had begun to explore in the years between 1906 and 1926. It treated speech as something superfluous. It concentrated upon all those other ways in which humanity reveals itself. It asked the public to use its eyes, to develop some of the extra visual sensibility of the deaf, and the public was beginning to respond.

Captions and clumsy symbolism were discarded as film acting drew nearer to truth. In 1912 an innocent young girl was always obliged to go about hugging an armful of lilies, at any rate in the earlier sequences of the picture, in order that the audience might know just exactly what sort of girl she was. If, on first catching sight of the villain, she dropped these lilies, and if he was subsequently seen to trample on them, the public again knew what to expect; nobody was surprised to see her, after a suitable time lapse, wandering in the snow with a little shawled bundle in her arms. By 1926 these devices were out of date. They were no longer necessary, because the acting was nearer to truth and audiences were quicker in the uptake. Screen actresses had learned how to look, approximately, like inexperienced girls; the public was more ready to recognize an unsophisticated girl when it saw one. Both had come to realize that such a girl, even if she can speak, does not go about the world loudly proclaiming her own inexperience. Far from it. She is probably consumed by the ambition to be thought extremely sophisticated, and it would be a great mistake to listen to the little dear. Her conversation is intended to convince the world that she is the Scarlet Woman. But her eyes, her mouth, her hands, her feet, the majestic poise with which she conceals her inner uncertainties, the little hops and skips into which she lapses when she is off her guard—these proclaim her for what she is.

After twenty years the art of the silent film was still only in its infancy. It was still crude. But it was developing, and the response, the awareness, of the public was developing too. Things easily perceived and understood by the average film fan in 1926 would have passed right over his head in 1912. Moreover this art had already become, in some degree, esoteric. The average film fan could take points which were imperceptible to people who seldom visted the cinema.

In the early days, the dumb-crambo days, many intelligent, cultivated, sensitive people rushed to the conclusion that art could never emerge from moving pictures. Moved by curiosity, they visited the cinema once or twice, admitted its marvelous ingenuity and then decided that they had no more time to waste on it. They could not believe that it would ever become a vehicle of truth or beauty. What they had seen was crude, childish and ridiculous. Even as a joke it palled.

For many years they never went near a picture house and derided those who did. They continued to cultivate their imaginations, intellects and sensibilities in other ways. But, in the nineteen-twenties, they began to drift back to the cinema, lured by the genius of Chaplin and other great comedians, and prepared to scoff at anything which was not farce. They still found much at which to scoff. The thing was still crude, childish and ridiculous. But it was something else. It had developed, in the interval, a kind of subtlety which was new to them and which they could not always follow, for all their superiority of taste.

"They ask so much of the imagination," complained one old gentleman, who would never have grumbled at the imaginative demands made by any other form of art. "I suppose if you see the things often enough you get a sort of knack. I must say I could follow it better when they used to throw words on the screen to tell us what had happened."

The ground covered in twenty years had been considerable. How the silent film would have developed, and what it would have been today, is now merely a matter for speculation. For, in the late nineteen-twenties, Science discovered something more. Sound was added to sight. The machine once more took charge of the artist, and a discarded element had to be reintroduced into the pattern.

II

Of all the guests assembled at that luncheon party, the authors had most to hope for and least to fear. Their own profession was not seriously threatened. Nobody had gone so far as to suggest that Talking Films might kill the circulating library.

Authors' film rights had been a valuable subsidiary source of income for several years, and there seemed to be no likelihood that the demand for stories would diminish. But hitherto the author had been chiefly concerned with the sale of his material and had had little to do with the retelling of his story in the new medium. He might be invited to collaborate in alterations to the story line, or to edit the captions, but he could not have much say in a business where the technique so essentially differed from his own. Many authors deliberately abstained from ever seeing the film versions of their books, taking it for granted that little or nothing of their original conception would survive. Words were their medium. Their art lay in the manipulation of words, both in dialogue and in narrative. They could not avoid a certain distrust for a form of storytelling which had dispensed with words.

Now, however, the case was altered. Words were going to be needed again. Screen characters were going to talk. It seemed likely

that word experts would be called in. Authors began to hope that
their special technical experience might be hired out very profitably.

Hired out it was, on a scale so lavish as to astonish even their
agents. Hollywood briefed them recklessly; it was no rare thing to
find three or four distinguished novelists and playwrights at work
upon one story. They were hired on the strength of their success in
their own craft, and not because they had had any previous interest
in, or experience of, picture making. For a certain number of days,
weeks or months they worked on the script. Frequently they dis-
liked one another, and sometimes they never even met. As the shooting date drew nearer, and the script became more chaotic, more
authors were called in. Nor did this period of activity come to an
end because the script was ready, or because anybody concerned
was satisfied with it. Only when the picture had to go on the floor
did it stop. During the last available twenty-four hours some *Émi-
nence Grise*, who lurks unseen in every studio, produces a shooting
script.

The shooting script is a kind of lucky dip. It resembles no previous
script but has traces of half a dozen earlier versions scattered over
it. Screen credit for the authors is assured to them under their contracts, but most of them are secretly determined to disown it in the
Last Day.

It may seem surprising that distinguished novelists and playwrights should have submitted to such treatment. The very high
pay is not the only explanation. Screen work was a new and amusing
experience to many of them, and some became genuinely interested
and anxious to explore the possibilities of this new medium. The
more conscientious suffered severe twinges, for they had really
made some effort to understand what it was that they were required
to do, and nobody could tell them, for nobody knew. They did
not like to take money and credit when not a line of their dialogue,
not one of their suggestions, had survived in the shooting script.
Nor could they ever be quite sure whether their material was
rejected because it was unsuitable or simply because "these silly
people don't even know their own silly business."

Others became excessively knowing and acquired a technical
vocabulary which should have impressed the cameraman, if any
cameraman ever read a script. They knew all about panning and
tracking and were careful to distinguish between a dissolve and a
fade-out. But in the final lucky dip they seldom fared better than
their colleagues.

"I think I could do it all very well," said an elderly novelist who had been engaged to work on her first screen adaptation, "if it wasn't for this Continuation they keep talking about. But I am to have a Continuation Expert to help me."

By this she meant Continuity, a bugbear which haunted all authors at that time. We hear less of it nowadays; in fact it is growing so old-fashioned that our younger screenwriters will soon be asking what it was. But ten years ago it was regarded as something so mysterious, so highly technical, that nobody outside the Industry could possibly be expected to understand it. When first authors were hired to write scripts they usually found themselves yoked with Continuity Experts, bred in the studios, who also wrote scripts but who did not seem to rate as authors.

Continuity merely means the bridging of gaps in time and space. It is the art of informing the audience that the scene has leaped from London to Paris, or that an hour, a week, a month have elapsed in the twinkling of an eye. In the very early days it was thought sufficient to display a caption which said:

PARIS!

And a time lapse was marked by another caption saying:

ONE WEEK LATER.

Subsequently it was felt that these bald little notices broke the illusion. An attempt was made to elaborate them and to infuse them with some emotional significance. They said:

CAME THE DAWN. . . .

Or:

THE PLAYGROUND OF EUROPE—ST. MORITZ.

In the next stage they were eliminated altogether. It was incompatible with the growing artistry of the silent film that the audience should be continually switching from pictures to letter print, from looking to reading. Information of this kind must be conveyed pictorially. When the story moved to Paris, a shot of the Eiffel Tower was inserted. If a week had to elapse, a calendar was shown with a hand coming up and tearing off the leaves.

But then it was felt that these Eiffel Towers and calendars, popping irrelevantly into the picture, were scarcely an improvement on captions. Continuity devices became more elaborate. Efforts were made to weave them into the fabric of the story itself.

In 1932 an author received a story outline with the direction, "Emily proceeds to Venice by a suitable continuity device." In a mood of ill-judged merriment she asked if the train would be considered a suitable continuity device. She learned that it would not. For if all the people in screen dramas were to be seen getting into trains every time they go somewhere else, then there would be too many pictures of people getting into trains. But, it was added, this was not a matter which need worry her. A continuity expert would attend to it. And the continuity expert took Emily for a ride in a punt at Henley and then dissolved the punt, with Emily in it, into a gondola, and that was a continuity device. But the story had to be knocked about considerably in order to lure Emily into the punt.

All this, in its turn, became old-fashioned a year or two later. Script Managers discovered that elaborate continuity devices were unnecessary. Something much more abrupt and natural would suffice, after all. Why, anyway, did Emily go to Venice? Not to ride in a gondola but to see her dying mother. The audience is interested in Emily, not geography. It will be quite sufficient to cut from a picture of Emily snatching up a suitcase to a picture of a table covered with medicine bottles.

Somebody ill! says the audience. *This must be Mother in that foreign place. Yes! There she is . . . lying in bed. Coo! Doesn't she look bad? Emily will be properly upset to find her like this. Who's this? A nun? Ah, they have nuns to nurse them in foreign places. This must be this place Venice and soon we shall see Emily coming. . . .*

These developments sprang from a growing sensitiveness to the reactions of the audience, a more accurate power to forecast what the audience will think and feel. With the power to forecast came the artist's desire, and the artist's skill, to control these reactions, to rivet attention on the essential and significant. If Emily is the theme, then the purpose of every object shown to the audience must be to excite more and more interest in Emily. In the earliest pictures it would have been quite possible to see Emily's face registering terror, with open mouth and staring eyeballs, at some perfectly unexplained cause. The effect of this was to make us want to leave off looking at Emily. It filled us with curiosity to know what had frightened her so much and we wanted to see it too. The picture would then shift to a herd of maddened buffaloes charging down the gorge. After this interruption it would go back, with somewhat diminished impetus, to Emily. In a modern picture these shots would almost certainly be reversed. We would see Emily strolling all unconscious down the gorge. We would then see the buffaloes, realize her danger, and immediately feel a strong desire to see Emily again and watch her as she realizes it too. The sight of her terrified face has then a double effect, as it fulfills a wish already in our minds.

We may believe that we wish to see Emily because she is our favorite star. We do not realize how much this wish has been stimulated by a transposition of shots. Her acting and personality would have been handicapped in the earlier sequence. The later sequence enhances them.

The Industry, having taken thirty-five years to make all these discoveries, was naturally inclined to regard them as technical mysteries, very difficult for a newcomer to understand. At least another thirty-five years must elapse before authors could be trusted to grasp them. Even today an author is only reluctantly permitted to undertake entire responsibility for a script. He may have had ten years' experience, he may have a dozen scripts to his credit, but he is still offered the services of some stripling who will explain to him the dangers of a time lapse and make sure that he gets Emily and the buffaloes in the right order.

Authors are called in by the Industry to do three things: (1) To adapt novels, plays, biography and other material for the screen. (2) To supply dialogue. (3) To write original stories. They are sometimes asked for an adaptation without dialogue and are frequently asked for dialogue alone. They might also be asked for an original story without dialogue. Jane Austen, had she lived today, might have been asked to supply the "story" of *Pride and Prejudice* without any of the characterization, any of the idiomatic touches, which lie in her dialogue. "Mr. Collins proposes to Elizabeth" would have been thought sufficient. No more from her, as an artist, would have been required. And the actual proposal of Mr. Collins might then have been written by Mr. Ernest Hemingway. Nor is this all. She might well be asked to supply the story with dialogue, and, in the shooting script, half of her original dialogue might be retained and the other half might have been rewritten by Mr. P. G. Wodehouse, Mr. Charles Morgan and Miss Stevie Smith, if her employers could secure their services.

To playwrights and novelists this may seem fantastic. But it is very natural that dialogue should not be rated highly among people who have spent twenty years learning how to do without it, and who never asked to have it put back into the pattern. Back it is, but its relative importance is still undetermined. For emphasis, in the talking picture, is still visual rather than aural. It is not a duet of sight and sound. Disney, in some of his later cartoons, especially *Fantasia*, has made experiments in this direction. He has tried to create such a duet by dint of the extreme simplification of cartoon drawing, which makes a comparatively small demand upon the eye. But, even so, many people found that the simultaneous demands upon eye and ear were too much for them—that if they looked they could not listen and if they listened they could not look.

It may be that the public will catch up with Disney; the human race may, in a year or two, develop new faculties of co-ordinated attention. Or perhaps Disney may experiment upon lines of still greater simplification until he has discovered how much the average human being can see and hear simultaneously. But all these experiments will only carry the art of the moving cartoon still further away from the art of the moving photograph, which frankly subordinates the ear to the eye.

ADAPTATIONS

In the case of a novel this means cutting out a great deal of material and turning comment into action. Where the novelist explains, the film must exhibit. The screen writer must find a dramatic visual substitute for a passage like this:

Thus we see her in a strange state of isolation. To have lost the God-like conceit that we may do what we will, and not to have acquired a homely zest for doing what we can, shows a grandeur of temper which . . . forswears compromise. But, if congenial to philosophy, it is apt to be dangerous to the Commonwealth. (EUSTACIA VYE in *The Return of the Native*.)

This is not as difficult as might at first appear. Such a character is not uncommon. Many people in the audience may have met such a woman, and summed her up, though not quite in the same words. *She cries for the moon*, they might say, *and nothing else will satisfy her. It's impossible to argue with such people and they make a lot of trouble.* They will recognize the type, when they meet it on the screen, if something about the woman reminds them of old Aunt Isobel, who eventually grew so impossible that she had to be shut up. Aunt Isobel would march straight through ponds and rivers, straight past notices which told her to keep off the grass or beware of the bull, and, when she came to a nine-foot brick wall which she *could* not climb, she just sat down and screamed. If Eustacia is seen doing something of the sort, on her first appearance in the picture, she will be recognized as an incipient Isobel.

The author must devise these slight, natural, easily recognized indications of type. And, in any case, he must try to explain to his employers the meaning of such a passage. For he is working with people who seldom read, who have a profound and intelligible mistrust of the written word. That is one of the reasons why he has been called in. He is accustomed to take the written word quite seriously, and he will tell them what is in the book.

"I don't get this girl, this Eustacia Vye," they will say. "Why did she act that way? What sort of girl was she? How do you see her, Mr. Scribble?"

"Like your Aunt Isobel," says Scribble, if he knows his job.

As soon as this is clear they may possibly show more ingenuity than he does in devising signposts which shall direct the memory of the audience to its own Aunt Isobel. But they do not easily recognize a written description of a character. They do not deal in words. They scarcely think in words. Scribble, whose profession it is to manipulate words, who is never satisfied until he has found the *mot juste*, may jump to the conclusion that there is no such thing as wordless cerebration, and that the Industry does not, cannot, think. He is completely wrong. But the thought processes of the Industry must always be a profound mystery to him.

Here is a true story. An actor once held up all activity on the floor for half an hour while he complained that one of his lines was out of character. He was playing an impoverished aristocrat showing the heroine round his house and apologizing for its disorder. The line was "You see, there has been no lady in the house since my mother died." He maintained that "lady" was quite wrong; "no woman in the house" would be more natural. What? said the Industry. Call his mother a woman? Surely not? The man was an aristocrat!

The argument grew heated. Scribble, who was present, supported the actor. He said bitterly that "woman" had been the word in his script, but that some so-and-so had altered it to "lady" in the shooting script. But he merely embittered the contest by flourishing the Old School Tie and asserting that all Etonians call their mothers women. Whereupon those present who did not happen to have been educated at Eton came out strongly on the side of "lady." At last the actor solved the problem by demanding a Bible.

After a good deal of agitation and telephoning, just as a lorry was about to set out for London with orders to bring back a gross of Bibles, news went round that there was one, actually in the studio.

It belonged to somebody's dresser. It was brought to the actor and he looked up a text.

"'Woman, what have I to do with thee?' There! You see? Our Lord called His mother a woman. And what was good enough for Our Lord ought to be good enough for anybody."

This carried immediate conviction and "woman" was adopted, to the profound astonishment of Scribble. As an argument, it grows more telling the more one considers it. Here was a controversy on a matter of taste. How are such things ever to be settled? Woman or lady, napkin or serviette—who is to be the arbiter? Can any authority be cited? Was there ever any person whose taste is likely to be accepted as infallible by all sorts and conditions of men? Only one. But Scribble would never have thought of it, in spite of his preoccupation with the *mot juste*.

Generally speaking, literary merit in the material to be adapted greatly hampers the screenwriter. The finer the novel or play, the more formidable the difficulties of adaptation. In a great work of art nothing is irrelevant. To cut any part of it is to damage the whole. In a great work of art the medium is so wedded to the subject that it becomes impossible to think of them apart. To take the *writing* out of a great novel is to run a risk of emptying out the baby with the bath. And, if any story has been perfectly told in one medium, what motive can there be for retelling it in another?

Most screenwriters prefer to work on an ill-written, second-rate book, toward which they have no conscience, but which has some situation or character which has caught at their imagination. This serves as a *Jew of Malta* to their *Merchant of Venice*. A bald literal translation of some inferior Continental novel is ideal material, provided that the book has some tinder in it which will kindle the tow of the storyteller's imagination.

Not infrequently authors are required to retell some foreign novel or play, Anglicizing the characters and giving the story an English setting. This is a very tricky business. The characters can speak in a perfectly colloquial idiom, wear English clothes, play cricket and drink tea. But they remain obstinately foreign. Their actions are never quite comprehensible to an English audience.

Very small slips can do a great deal of damage. When the French picture *Prison sans Barreaux* was retold in an English version, the scene was laid in France but most of the Gallic flavor was removed, with unhappy results. This was most apparent in a sequence where a cow gave birth to a calf in a byre attached to a sort of female Borstal. By a series of misunderstandings, the prison doctor was called in and remained closeted in the byre for most of the night, with one

of the inmates of the prison, a young girl of seventeen; and this tête-
à-tête was too much for his discretion. In the French version this
girl wore a long black dress and clutched round her thin shoulders
a little white shawl, the kind of shawl that Frenchwomen are fond
of wearing in emergencies, because emergencies are often so drafty.
Its "foreignness" carried off the unlikelihood of such an incident.
They do so many queer things on the Continent. In a French reformatory, one thought, it is perhaps possible that the *pensionnaires* are
allowed to spend their nights in byres, alone with attractive young
men. But in the English version she wore a businesslike white linen
coat, and the whole incident became incredible. The authorities
who provided that coat would never have allowed such a thing to
happen.

The great difficulty, in such adaptations, is the translation of sentiment. The material is rarely first-rate and its popularity in its own
country has therefore been largely sentimental. And, just as the
sentiment of one generation becomes the laughingstock of the next,
so does the sentiment of one nation leave another cold. Characters
created on a purely sentimental formula have often no appeal save
for a local and temporary public. And sometimes they will take the
grand tour; outmoded in their country, they will find a new public
elsewhere. Our grandfathers wept over Little Nell. We mock at
her. But she is said to have had a tremendous vogue in Russia in the
nineteen-twenties.

Some years ago an English author was discussing with a Central
European director the plot of a Hungarian novel which he wished
her to transpose into English suburban life. She complained that there
was not one passably decent character in the book. They all acted
solely from motives of greed, appetite, cowardice or self-interest,
they showed the most complete callousness in their attitude to one
another and seemed to be entirely devoid of any sense of responsibility or moral obligation. She feared that they might be thought
unsympathetic and asked if the story might not be altered a little.
Could they not behave rather less badly? Might not extenuating
circumstances be introduced? Might it not at least be possible for
some of them to show signs of distress, scruple, or inner conflict?

The director said coldly, "That is your British hypocrisy. In my
country an audience interests himself in a girl who has stealed five
pounds because she is wanting a new hat. In your country she must
have stealed for bread for her old grandmother."

"Perhaps," said Miss Scribble, somewhat nettled. "But I really do
think I had better turn some of these cads into hypocrites."

"*Was heisst* cads?"

"Cads? Oh, well . . . all the people in this book are cads."

"So? Then everybody is cad."

"That is a very sentimental thing to say."

"If you will excuse, it is you that I find sentimental. If you wish, I am cynic."

Miss Scribble heatedly asserted that there is not a pin to choose between cynicism and sentimentality. Both are ways of dodging truth. Both spring from timidity and conceit.

"Both have the lie in the soul," said she, "and if one stinks of moral cant, the other stinks of intellectual cant."

This tirade achieved an unexpected and undeserved success. The director's English was scanty but he did recognize one word which he had often heard in Hollywood. His integrity as a cynic wavered.

"It will stink?" he said anxiously. "Why aren't you telling me this before? If it will stink the story must be altered so."

British sentiment and, if we are to judge by the pictures which come to us from the United States, American sentiment is of the kind which appeals to extroverts. We like a conflict, hearts of gold, and a happy ending. We like to see men challenging fate and battling with circumstances. We like to see good triumph over evil. We overstress, perhaps, the importance of action, and we like to believe that some kindly Providence will always intervene to make sure that "the Boy gets the Girl and the dough." We do not want to see the real world but a world "remolded nearer to the heart's desire."

European sentiment, in many countries during the past twenty years, has often been defeatist and fatalist. It dwells on the futility of action and shows men as the helpless pawns of circumstance. This has found frequent expression in the Little Victim theme, in stories of cruelty to children, such as *Mädchen in Uniform, Poil de Carotte, Maternité,* and in numerous stories of prisons and convicts. These spectacles of unbridled injustice, oppression and sadism, of children mishandled, of confidence and innocence betrayed, have generally been somewhat misunderstood by English audiences. They have been received as stern human documents, scarcely to be rated as entertainment, and their realism has been commended by people who imagine that sentimentality always wears rose-colored spectacles. But these subjects can evoke a purely sentimental response—luxurious tears and a cozy sense that we are all poor things and all bound to get a raw deal. People who regard themselves as victims like pictures about victimization. They can feel with the victim and, at the same time, somewhat perversely revel in the power of the oppressor. They do not

want to see good triumph over evil. That has not been their own experience and they are unwilling to believe that anyone, anywhere, is
getting a better deal. They too do not want to see the real world.
They would rather see something a little worse than the truth. But this
brand of sentimentality, though nearly all the Little Victim pictures
were intended to purvey it, completely misses fire with an English
audience. Extroverts invariably begin to ask why somebody did not
interfere. In most of these stories there are one or two kindly characters, nurses, warders, teachers, doctors or priests, who see and deplore
what is going on, but who never seem to have heard of the National
Society for the Prevention of Cruelty to Children. An English audience sits waiting impatiently for somebody to do something and goes
away feeling that they cannot have got any N.S.P.C.C. in these
foreign places.

This fact is so well known that such films are generally modified
before they are sent to London. The final sequences are reshot.
Somebody does interfere, at the last moment, and a perfunctory
happy ending is tacked on as a concession to "British sentimentality."
The version of *Mädchen in Uniform* shown everywhere on the
Continent ended with a tortured child leaping from the top of a
building to lie, mangled and dead, at the feet of the fiendish head
mistress. But a special version was made for England, in which her
schoolmates pulled her back into safety and the sympathetic junior
mistress, on whom our hopes had been vainly fixed throughout the
picture, and who had been a passive spectator of the scene, observed
smugly, "A great tragedy has been averted."

The adaptation of a stage play presents a new series of problems.
To indicate character is a comparatively simple matter, for the dramatist has already done a good deal of the work. Unlike the novelist,
he has been obliged to forgo the advantage of telling the audience
about his characters and has maneuvered them into revealing themselves. Also there is less material to be cut. Expansion rather than
compression is the problem; the task is to break up a form which
hampers screen narrative. Scenes which, in the play, all took place
in one room now more naturally occur in different parts of the
house. The characters can be sent out of the house to play cricket,
as in *Quiet Wedding*. Incidents which the dramatist has been obliged
to indicate as happening "off" must be brought back into the story,
since very few things can be allowed to happen "off" on the screen.

The whole buildup of the scenes and acts must be broken until
no trace of it remains. For the film, like life, has neither curtains nor

intervals. It goes right on. Each act, in a play, is built up so as to
lead to a climax and a curtain, upon which the audience is content
to pause and to be told nothing more for ten minutes. The intervals
have their place in the rhythm of a play. But in a film this climax
must be so treated that the audience is prepared to go on without a
pause. Each scene, in a play, is shaped as a steppingstone to the climax, therefore each scene must be reshaped. In a film there are no
exits and entrances. An actor does not make an exit from the picture;
the picture moves away from him. And stage dialogue, though it has
some superficial resemblance to screen dialogue, can seldom be transposed without great alteration in emphasis.

DIALOGUE

Since they are wordmongers, authors are perhaps entitled to regard themselves as dialogue specialists. And it is true that good dialogue can add greatly to the value of a film, just as a good libretto
is of value in an opera. But, where there is so much to engage the
eye, the audience does not listen very attentively; dialogue should
not demand too much concentration. It should be natural and convincing, but it should be used to illustrate and amplify points which
are made in many other ways.

Screen dialogue is much more natural than stage dialogue, for
stage actors are obliged to reveal themselves almost entirely by
speech. It is true that they support speech by timing, gesture and expression, but these do not play so large a part as they can in a film,
where the faces of the actors can be equally well seen by everybody
in the audience and where emphasis can be increased by close-ups or
changes of shot. A film can show a man talking in a high moral tone,
and then call attention to his foot pressing the foot of his neighbor's
wife under the table. That man is revealed as a hypocrite without a
word of dialogue, by a gesture and a change of shot which makes sure
that everyone sees it. Because of this peculiar capacity for emphasizing
small but significant things it can afford to be more lifelike than the
stage; it can dispense with the overemphasis upon which stage actors
often have to depend in order to get a point across.

It makes a perfectly different use of setting and background.
When the curtain goes up on a scene in a theater the audience immediately takes in the setting, receives the intended impression of
luxury, squalor, respectability or Bohemianism, and then takes it
for granted through the rest of the scene. In a film the setting can
be brought forward at any time to reinforce the action. On the stage

a woman mourning the death of her child has to be given words to convey the terrible emptiness of her life and heart, in order that the audience may understand why it is that she tries to steal somebody else's child. On the screen a shot of the empty, tidy nursery, with the toys all put away on their shelves, will tell part of this story without any words from her.

Rhetoric is very difficult to manage on the screen, and so are any long, intricately built-up speeches. This is partly because of the frequent changes of shot and angle, necessitated by the inherent flatness of the screen. The audience is kept from being irritated by this flatness because the camera goes round the subject giving frequent, but slight, variations of distance and angle, so that an illusion of roundness is produced. These shots are so skillfully strung together that the audience is hardly aware of them; but they interrupt the rhythm of long speeches. It would be impossible, for instance, to hold the same shot during the whole of one of Hamlet's soliloquies, and very difficult to synchronize it with a variety of shots. It can be done; but a screenwriter should not ask too much of the boys in the cutting room. If he finds that more than half of "To be or not to be" is gone, he must not jump to the conclusion that this is because they do not appreciate poetry. They may appreciate it so well that they shrink from the task of breaking it up into shots.

Television, which is far more stereoscopic, is a more suitable medium for poetry or rhetoric. If Science should discover something more, in the shape of a stereoscopic screen projector, one shot could be held much longer before an audience would grow tired of it. But, in that case, screen technique would have to be scrapped entirely and we should all have to start all over again. The eye would become quite dizzy, whirled from one scene to another, if it saw all those scenes in the round. The whole of screen technique is based on the fact that a number of objects can be shown to people in rapid succession.

Important or informative screen dialogue should be carried on in short speeches and short sentences. There is no place for the outburst, the torrent of words running up to a climax and a dramatic announcement, which so often heralds a curtain on the stage. These outbursts nearly always have to be "written down" in a screen adaptation. They are not natural. In real life, people do not say, "Oh this is the last straw! I won't bear it. I've kept silent for years, but now . . . wallah . . . wallah . . . wallah . . . because *he is my son!*" (Curtain.) They do not shout for five minutes before coming to the matter nearest their hearts. They begin with it. They say, "He's my son! Yes he is! I've kept quiet about it for years, but now this is the

last straw . . . wallah . . . wallah . . . wallah. . . ." And they go
on and on, repeating themselves and letting fall further items of
startling information, until somebody brings them an aspirin.

On the other hand, long discursive monologues, of the kind favored by Miss Bates, can be very effective on the screen. They can
run on like a kind of obbligato accompaniment. There is, in *Femme
du Boulanger*, an immensely long drunken monologue by Raimu.
It accompanies him from place to place, to church, through the
streets, to the presbytery, back to his own bakery; it ranges over
a multitude of topics and it is addressed to many different people;
it contains no information necessary to the story and there is no
one sentence in it which could not quite well be cut. The whole
is a most poignant, most convincing utterance of a heartbroken man.
To hear it is to be grateful that sound has been brought back into the
pattern.

ORIGINAL STORIES

An author is seldom invited to write an original screen story unless a vehicle is wanted for a particular star. And that task is tolerable
only if he happens to have an overwhelming admiration for the star's
personality. Unless he himself desires to see nothing save that one
face, to hear nothing save that one voice, he will find it hard to write
dialogue which is to be treated, for the most part, unilaterally, so
that anything said by actors other than the star will be said by faceless ghosts, while the attention of the audience is concentrated on
the star's face listening. In fact he must be convinced that nothing
he writes can have any value unless it is interpreted, directly or indirectly, by that one individual.

But any author can, if he is enough of an enthusiast, write an original script, all out of his own head, and try to persuade some company to accept it. Should he succeed in doing this he will be pretty
certain to break his heart. For it is only then that he will fully realize
how anomalous his position is, and how small the chance that any
fraction of his idea will ever find its way to the screen. So long as
his task has been merely to adapt other people's material he may
manage to accept this fate philosophically. But, where his own creation is concerned, he cannot feel the same detachment. It will come
as a bitter blow to him if he finds that some other author has been
summoned to alter his story line or touch up his dialogue.

The practice of hiring several authors to work, often quite independently, on the same story is comprehensible only when it is re-

membered that the Industry is composed of self-contained groups of experts. Each group knows its own job but makes no pretense of knowing much about the jobs of the others. Authors are not regarded as creators. They are merely called upon to supply an ingredient in the pudding. The chef is a director whom they may possibly have never met. They are specialists and should stick to their lasts. A Bessarabian novel, by an unknown Mr. Protopopov, has been purchased because it contains material congenial to a Lithuanian star. It is a story about the love of a sophisticated society woman for a plowboy. Mr. Michael Arlen is a specialist in sophisticated society women. Miss Sheila Kaye-Smith knows all about plowboys. Therefore it would seem very natural to the Industry to invite them to collaborate on the script, or to ask Miss Kaye-Smith to make a treatment and then send it to Mr. Arlen so that he might put in some sophistication. No insult would be intended to either. But these possibilities are intolerable to the author of an original script.

It is true that a few, a very few, authors command sufficient prestige to secure a clause in their contracts stipulating that nothing in their scripts shall be changed. This means that a script written by them, and them alone, lies about on chairs in the studio while the picture is being shot. But that is very often all it means. In the present conditions of picture making there is no Guardian Angel to watch over the story on its perilous journey from script to screen. No clause in any contract can ensure that the author's true conception will survive.

Much has been said of the changes which can overtake a play during production. A group gets to work on it and each person in that group has a slightly different idea of what it ought to be. The author continually finds that the emphasis is altered, that serious scenes are being played for comedy, that comic scenes are being treated very solemnly, and that the wrong character is walking away with the play. But this is negligible in comparison with what can happen to a screen story by the time directors, art directors, actors, cameramen, sound technicians and cutters have done with it.

Even if all these gentry were willing and anxious to carry out the author's ideas (and many of them are) he has no established means of communicating with them or of explaining what he wants. He has some sort of position in the theater. Everybody knows who and what he is. But he has none in the studio. There is his script, lying about on chairs. But no script, however persuasive, can convey his ideas to a community which never reads. So long as the poor fellow confines himself to setting down his ideas on paper, he may as well stick

to dialogue assignments, or to adapting Bessarabian novels for Lithuanian stars.

III

And why, it may here be asked, should any author ever want to
write an original script? It is true that the art of the screen is daily
becoming more beautiful, more subtle and more significant; that
pictures are being made which challenge the most critical standards.
But what does the screen offer to the storyteller which the novel
and the play do not offer? As a medium, has it any unique advantages?

It has, in the first place, an arbitrary power over the attention
of its audience which no other storytelling medium can exert. It can
completely exclude the irrelevant and decide absolutely what is to be
seen and heard.

It has an unlimited range of emphasis—an emphasis which can be
intolerably crude but which can also be infinitely subtle. It can call
attention at any moment to any object, indicate a contrast, or build
up an association of ideas. Its power to suggest, rather than to state,
is limited of course by the degree of suggestibility in the public,
but that is a limitation which applies to every medium. At present
the common denominator of suggestibility may be low, because the
art is still in its infancy and has to create its own public as it develops.
But the unexplored regions in this field are vast and fascinating.

The screen is more natural and lifelike than the stage, and it has
a greater freedom of movement in time and space. It is more dramatic
than the novel. It can suggest, in a few seconds, things which the
novelist must take many pages to describe. It has the apparatus for
saying what cannot be said *in words*. What the novelist is forced
to make explicit the film can merely imply.

It can, for instance, show how the same person, the same scene,
can appear quite differently to different people. It can show the
world as seen by two lovers, dining together in a popular restaurant—
a noble hall, vast, commodious and beautifully decorated, faultless
service, exquisite music, and themselves, superbly handsome in each
other's eyes, the center of the scene. The picture carries us from
their minds to the mind of a jaundiced old gentleman sitting at the
next table. The camera becomes his eye instead of theirs. And simply
by dint of ingenious photography, by a change in angles, shots and
lighting, by emphasis on other details, the same scene appears quite
differently. A shabby, awkward boy and his fat sweetheart are

munching a bad dinner in a tawdry, overcrowded room, where the waiters have dirty hands and the band plays out of tune.

It can show how the same scene appears quite differently to one person on different occasions: It can carry us from the mind of childhood to the mind of middle age and show how the vast lake, the mysterious forest, and the lofty mountain can shrink, in later years, to a small duckpond, a copse and a hillock.

It can indicate those variations of pace, those deviations in our sense of time, of which we are hardly conscious, but which are implicit in all our emotions. For it is a fact that we seldom live at the same pace for two consecutive hours. Whatever our watches may tell us, we know that an hour spent with a bore is ten times longer than an hour spent with our heart's choice. The pace quickens as we grow older. The days of childhood are endless. In middle age the weeks rattle past like telegraph posts beside a train. When we say, of a recent event, "How long ago that seems!" we mean that intervening emotional experiences have set a wide gulf between then and now. When we say, of a long-past event, "Why! It seems only yesterday!" we mean that the emotional gap, in this respect, is small. To many people nowadays the year 1937 must seem as remote as the Flood. But a happy couple, celebrating their golden wedding, may still feel that they have only just got back from their honeymoon because their love, during fifty years, has remained unchanged.

The more violent the emotion, the more erratic does our time sense become. Anyone who has been through a car or railway accident will testify to this. Between the moment when a crash is seen to be inevitable and the moment when it actually occurs there may be a time lapse of a few seconds. To the people concerned it may seem like a hundred years. Very slowly the two cars creep toward each other. There appears to be ample opportunity for everyone to get out, walk home, eat a good supper and go to bed. "It was like a slow-motion picture," they say when describing the experience afterward. Or they may have had the reverse impression. "Everything seemed to happen at once," they say, meaning that a number of things happened consecutively but that their own emotional state was such that they were unaware of any time lapse at all.

Most people would declare that these are illusions; that the rational conception of time, as something measured out to us by the Greenwich Observatory, is the true conception. But many, having said this, will go to church and sing, with perfect conviction, "A thousand ages in Thy sight Are like an evening gone." This statement ignores

Greenwich completely and suggests that our emotional illusions about time do really bring us nearer to ultimate truth than do our rational faculties.

This see-saw in our dual conception of time is one of

> . . . those obstinate questionings
> Of sense and outward things,
> Fallings from us, vanishings;
> Blank misgivings of a creature
> Moving about in worlds not realized . . .
> Which, be they what they may,
> Are yet the fountain light of all our day,
> Are yet a master light of all our seeing;
> Uphold us, cherish, and have power to make
> Our noisy years seem moments in the being
> Of the eternal silence: truths that wake,
> To perish never. . . .

There can be no higher function for Art than to concern itself with those truths which perish never, and to stress those obstinate questionings. No human activity can properly be described as an art unless it can do this. For, surely, it is those very questionings which have driven men, in all ages, to break out into art—to seek for a harmony, a design, a rhythm, which they desire and which they do not find in sense and outward things.

In the matter of our double time sense, the film can suggest far more than a play or a novel simply by turning a handle at a varying pace, by making things happen more quickly or more slowly, so that we are aware of that rhythm in our lives which defies both reason and the clock. This is a field which has been as yet scarcely explored, but it surely will be. Experiments were made, even in the days of the silent film, in such pictures as *Warning Shadows*. And a very effective use of varying pace was made in the opening sequence of *Carnet de Bal*, where a woman is recollecting her youth and her first ball. Everything is a little slower than normal life; in a fairylike ballroom, with snowy pillars and regal chandeliers, a long row of white-clad girls stands waiting . . . the long row of beautiful young men advances step by step . . . each couple, moving as if half in a dream, begins to waltz. The effect is one of timeless ecstasy, with all life, all the years, still to come, still to be enjoyed.

Toward the end of the picture she returns to the same town and the same hall and dances there, for old time's sake, with one of her former beaux, now a prosperous barber and the father of a large family. The hall is a tawdry, dingy place, only half its remembered size. Sulky girls sit waiting for partners. The dancers trot round and round perfunctorily. But among them, for a moment, she catches a glimpse of a ghost, a young girl in a white dress, and across the screen waltz those other feet, moving in a slower rhythm.

But the greatest advantage of the screen medium is a power which it shares with poetry to fuse humanity with its setting, to charge even inanimate objects with emotional significance.

It can show the entrance to a hospital, with one of those wooden bars which swing to and fro as the people go in and out, full of their own cares and fears. A woman appears—a woman whose story we know. Someone she loves has just died in the hospital. She walks straight down the steps, pushes through the barrier and passes swiftly out of the picture. The camera holds the wooden bar which swings, after she has passed, backward and forward, until it comes to rest. Like rings spreading out on water when a stone is thrown into a pool, this movement can amplify the significance of the sorrow which has passed by, can remind us that she is not the first, nor will she be the last, to set that bar swinging.

This is poetry. Only a poet can do this with a piece of wood. In this way does a poet achieve that touch of universality which is essential if pathos is to be raised to tragedy. In any story of individual suffering there must be a point at which we feel that it touches some greater theme—not so much that this is the common lot as that this is part of something greater than any one person's lot, that it has echoes of "the still, sad music of humanity." If we cannot be made to feel this, if we are not lifted on the wings of poetry, a spectacle of suffering becomes simply painful and constricting. It does not elevate our minds or expand our hearts.

Poetry has this power to enlarge the individual by catching up, into his emotional orbit, so much that we usually think of as outside ourselves, as inanimate and insensible. When Wordsworth's Lucy died, the whole vast, turning earth had for him but one significance. It was a grave for Lucy.

> No motion has she now, no force,
> She neither hears nor sees:
> Rolled round in earth's diurnal course
> With rocks and stones and trees.

Very little screen poetry has been made as yet. Fifty years of experiment have not lifted this new art much above the level of prose. But it is possible to hope that, at the end of another fifty years, poets may have taken to making pictures. And when they do, then at last full use will be made of the medium, with its suggestive subtlety, its rhythm, its deliberate variation of pace, its complete exclusion of anything outside the pattern.

Poets have already written some very good scripts. Here is one which could be shot as it stands. It is a sequence showing the escape of two lovers from a castle full of enemies; they are living in terms of obstacles and dangers, so that every lamp is a menace, every fluttering curtain a threat.

> Down the wide stairs a darkling way they found.
> In all the house was heard no human sound.
>
> A chain dropped lamp was flickering by each door.
>
> The arras, rich with horseman, hawk and hound,
> Fluttered in the besieging wind's uproar;
>
> And the long carpets rose along the gusty floor.
>
> They glide, like phantoms, into the wide hall;
> Like phantoms to the iron porch they glide;
>
> There lay the porter in uneasy sprawl,
>
> With a huge empty flagon by his side.
>
> The wakeful bloodhound rose and shook his hide.
> But his sagacious eye an inmate owns:
>
> By one, and one, the bolts full easy slide
> The chains lie silent on the footworn stones.
>
> The key turns,
>   and the door upon its hinges groans.
>
> And they are gone. . . .

IV

But there is really no such thing as screen *writing*. A script is not meant to be read, as novels, poems and plays are read. It is no more a work of literature than is the recipe for a pudding. So long as the meaning is grasped, and the recipe followed, it would serve its purpose if it were written in pidgin English. The trouble is that the recipe is never followed; the orchestra never plays the notes which the composer has set down.

But the screen can tell a story. And storytellers have, for some hundreds of years, made use of the written word; so that there is still a tendency to call all storytellers writers.

The wholesale buying up of novels and plays must be only a phase in the development of screen storytelling. Why should the Industry send out for its material in this manner? Simply because it has, as yet, so few screen composers of its own. Most storytellers still prefer to say what they have to say in some other medium, in spite of the possibilities offered to them by the screen.

And why is this?

It is because the conditions of screen storytelling are, at present, so discouraging to any genuine artist. The screen composer has no place in the scheme of things, no means of carrying his vision of life and truth safely through this dogfight of technicians. Nor has he any position in the cutting room, where the emphasis, which is the true soul of his story, will be determined.

A picture must be a group production, just as operas, symphonies and plays are group productions. But no group production can ever be classed as a great work of art unless it has the stamp of one predominating, creative mind. This single signature, in screen art, is at present the signature of the director. And while this is the case no screen Keats is ever likely to supply scripts.

It may be asked why directors do not take to writing their own stories. They are fine artists. Why should they be content with such unsatisfactory material? Surely they could themselves turn out something better than the mangled remains of a Bessarabian novel, chewed over by half a dozen Scribbles? Why should not one of them turn poet and write his own script?

The answer is probably that they would if they could but they can't. As well might it be suggested that Toscanini and Beecham, since they are fine artists, ought to be able to compose their own symphonies. The art of direction, of ruling groups of people and inducing them to supply certain effects, does not often coexist with that contemplative faculty which is essential to a poet. For poets are seldom at their best when bellowing through a megaphone. They do not like crowds; they have no special talent for leadership or organization. They like to lead quiet lives in the country, or in small university towns. They need regular meals and a good deal of sleep. But a director lives in the arena. He often has to do without sleep for weeks on end and subsists on ham sandwiches, gulped down between spells at the megaphone.

If screen poetry should ever reach the heights destined for it, perhaps the supremacy of directorship may turn out to have been a

passing phase. It may be that in time screen composers will have
fought their way into such a position that they can insist on their
own signature. That is to say, they will write their score, their recipe,
turn it over to a director to be shot, and supervise the cutting personally, so as to secure that particular design, rhythm and emphasis
upon which their poetry depends. They would have to learn how to
be cutters as an essential part of their training. The director's role
would more nearly approximate that of the conductor of an
orchestra.

Such a development seems, at the moment, to be impossible. The
immense cost of picture making stands in its way and hampers
experiment. Screen art is obliged to serve a very large public and
must seek a common denominator in taste, and in emotional and
intellectual appeal. But many things may operate, as time goes on,
to reduce the cost of picture making.

The popularity of the cinecamera, among amateurs, was growing
rapidly before the war. In its wake came the home projector. This
at present is silent. But a sound projector in every home is not a
more fantastic idea than the promise of wireless telegraphy in every
home would have seemed thirty years ago. And, when a great many
homes have their own projectors, their owners will not be content
merely to see the films they have made of themselves surf-bathing
last summer. The buying and hiring of films may grow up, just as
the sale of gramophone records has grown up. A vast new field
would be opened to picture makers. They would be able to deal with
the public more directly; they would not have to be governed by the
policy or prejudice of distributors. Films of all lengths and kinds, on
all subjects, would be demanded: stories, documentaries, nature
and travel films. If this new market grows up, the Industry will have
to branch out in many ways to supply it.

Films intended for a small audience, a family, possibly only one
person, in a dwelling room, would have to be different from those
intended for a crowd in a hall. Anyone who has seen a popular film
run through in a small room, for one or two spectators, must have
noticed how wrong the pitch seems to be. It is directed at something
in him which he should share with several hundred people who are
not there. But if films for the home are ever produced there will not
be this need to seek, and satisfy, a great common denominator. There
will not be one film public but dozens—as many publics as there are
for novels or gramophone records. And among these publics the
screen Keats may get his chance.

If the signature of a great poet is ever to be put on a film, some
corner in the studio must be found for him and his ivory tower; he

must have a face and a name and the Industry must recognize him for what he is. But it is difficult at present to guess in which department the materials for that ivory tower are being collected.

The practice of hiring "authors" to write for the screen is already on the wane. There is growing up, in the Industry, an increasing supply of screenwriters who are not interested in any other form of storytelling, who can do all that novelists and playwrights used to do, and who understand much better what is wanted. What original scripts they may keep locked away in their desks is best known to themselves; they are generally kept busy on the works of Mr. Protopopov. Their signature is not known to the public, though their names appear in credit titles. But perhaps they may one day produce a screen Keats.

The notion of an author-cutter, with sufficient authority to sit on a director, is so revolutionary that most screenwriters would reject it. They talk hopefully of their ambition someday to make their *own pictures*. But at present the only man who makes pictures is a director. And if they ever become directors they will inevitably find that they are making other people's pictures. Nor is it probable that those of them who might succeed in directorship have got the most interesting screen poetry locked away in their desk drawers. So that it is not certain that our screen Keats will emerge from the script department.

Perhaps, one day, some cutter will grow tired of making patterns out of other people's material, and the mutiny may start at that end of the studio.

Or perhaps some director may desert the arena for the ivory tower. He may decide that his art is creative rather then executive. Retaining all his prestige and decisive authority, he may toss his megaphone to some trusted subordinate and quit the hurly-burly of the floor. In his office he will build a sanctuary where he can be vacant and pensive, and cultivate that "inward eye" which turns the thing seen into the imagined thing; where he can woo this foundling, this Tenth Muse, this *dea ex machina*, of whom we know, at present, so little.

Directors

of the

Thirties

by John Grierson

John Grierson was largely responsible for the wide use of documentary films by the British Government Service public-information program in the 1920s. He was the first to use the word "documentary" in describing Robert Flaherty's Moana. *In writing about feature "story" films he inevitably based his criticisms on their social and political content. The following selection is taken from* Grierson on Documentary *(Harcourt, Brace, New York, 1947), edited by Forsyth Hardy. It gives a kaleidoscopic view of the work of some of the well-known directors of the 1930s.*

JOE STERNBERG is one of the few directors whose every work one sees as a matter of course. He stepped rather suddenly into the film world in 1925 with a film called *The Salvation Hunters,* which he had financed with his last five thousand dollars. He has been interesting ever since. *The Salvation Hunters* was a young man's gamble. His stars were taken from the ranks of Poverty Row extras; his story was right outside the Hollywood tradition. It was a sad romantic affair of how a young man tried to escape from the dreary existence of a dredger. The dredger with its slime was, of course, symbolic. The ending, with its two young lovers moving off into the rising sun, was equally symbolic. Sternberg began with a great hankering for good things.

The simple, rather naïve and sentimental idealism of that first effort should be remembered when *Shanghai Express* is considered. Dietrich stars. Like that exotic and meaningless lady herself, the film is a masterpiece of the toilette. That only. Its photography is astonishing; its sets are expensive and detailed to an ingenious and extravagant degree; its technique in dissolve and continuity is unique. The film might be seen for its good looks alone. But it is cold-bloodedly lacking in every virtue which made Sternberg a lad of promise.

A great deal must have happened over the years to turn the simple romanticist into this sophisticated purveyor of the meretricious Dietrich. I wish I knew what it was. I knew Sternberg just after his *Salvation Hunters* and liked him immensely. He had made a fine picture for Metro called *The Exquisite Sinner* and had been heaved off the payroll for adding some genuine local color to a Breton scene.

It struck me that sensibility of his peculiarly intensive and introspective sort was not a very healthy equipment for a hard world, and, in face of his strange progress, I am sure I was right. There is, as you can imagine, no place for the introspectionist in a commercial film world which is as objective in its conceptions as in its accounts. A director of this instinct is bound to have a solitary and (as commerce goes) an unsuccessful life of it. Sternberg, I think, was weak. Hating the notion of this commercial unsuccess, he has thrown his sensibility to the winds and accepted the hokum of his masters. His aesthetic conscience is now devoted to making the hokum as good-looking as possible. It is, indeed, almost pathologically good-looking, as by one whose conscience is stricken.

I detail this Sternberg saga because it tells more clearly than any personal story I know how even great spirits may fail in film. The temptation of commercial success is a rather damnable one. There are dollars past dreaming and power and publicity to satisfy every vanity for anyone who will mesmerize the hicks of the world.

I watched Sternberg make still another picture, *The Woman of the Sea*, for Chaplin. The story was Chaplin's, and humanist to a degree: with fishermen that toiled, and sweated, and lived and loved as proletarians do. Introspective as before, Sternberg could not see it like Chaplin. Instead, he played with the symbolism of the sea till the fishermen and the fish were forgotten. It would have meant something just as fine in its different way as Chaplin's version, but he went on to doubt himself. He wanted to be a success, and here plainly and pessimistically was the one way to be unsuccessful. The film as a result was neither Chaplin's version nor Sternberg's. It was a strangely beautiful and empty affair—possibly the most beautiful I have ever seen—of net patterns, sea patterns and hair in the wind. When a director dies, he becomes a photographer.

With *Shanghai Express* Joe Sternberg has become the great Josef von Sternberg, having given up the struggle for good: a director so successful that even Adolf Zukor is pleased to hold his hand for a brief condescending moment. He has made films with Jannings and George Bancroft: *Paying the Penalty, Docks of New York,* others of equally exquisite hokum; and Paramount has blessed his name for the money they made. Once from the top of the tree he made a last desperate gesture to his past in *The Case of Lena Smith,* a fine film which failed; but that is now forgotten and there will never be a repetition. He has found Dietrich and is safe for more dollars, more power, more success than ever. What irresolute director would not launch a thousand cameras for Dietrich, giving up hope of salvation hereafter? Sternberg has. He has the "Von" and the little warm thankful hand of Adolf Zukor for his pains.[1]

Shanghai Express follows the progress of a train from Peking to Shanghai, finding its story among the passengers as *The Blue Express* did. Dietrich is Shanghai Lily, a lady of no reputation. Clive Brook is an old lover meeting her again, hating her past, but still very much in love with her. They fall into the hands of Chinese revolutionaries and Dietrich saves Clive, and Clive saves Dietrich; and in that last mutual service the dust is shaken out of the Lily's petals and the doubter damns himself for having doubted. This high argument is staged with stupendous care, stupendous skill, and with an air of most stupendous importance.

I remember one shot of the Shanghai express pulling into a way-side station in the early evening. It is one of the half-dozen greatest shots ever taken, and I would see the film for that alone. It is, however, the only noble moment in the film. The scenes of Chinese life are massive, painstaking to the point of genius in their sense of detail and presented very pleasantly in dissolve; the minor acting is fine; but the rest is Dietrich. She is shown in seven thousand and one poses, each of them photographed magnificently. For me, seven thousand poses of Dietrich (or seventy) are Dietrich *ad nauseam.* Her pose of mystery I find too studied, her make-up too artificial, her every

---

[1] Among later films in which Sternberg directed Marlene Dietrich were *The Devil Is a Woman* and *The Scarlet Empress.* In 1938 Sternberg visited Britain and announced his intention to make a film version of Zola's *Germinal.* During the war Sternberg directed a short documentary, *The Town,* for the U.S.O.-W.I.—F.H.

gesture and word too deliberate for any issue in drama save the very gravest. Sternberg perhaps is still after that ancient intensity. When themes are thin it is a hankering that can bring one very close to the ridiculous.

Erich von Stroheim is the crazy man of the film world. He cut *Greed* to sixty reels and defied Hollywood to make it less, at which they sacked him and hired an infidel to bring it down to a humble ten. They are always sacking Von Stroheim. The infidel cut and cut and gave up at twenty-five, and, when he too was fired, explained that Stroheim's sixty was a masterpiece, anyway.

Of course, Hollywood respected Von Stroheim for his stand at sixty. Anyone who will threaten to entertain you for twelve hours on end is plainly in the grand manner. They gave him yet another and yet another film to do. Each time the story has been the same. Stroheim has gone whoopee and shot to the moon, and found himself unemployed before the picture hit the headlines.

He paid himself into the *première* of his own *Merry Widow*, though *The Merry Widow* went on to make a fortune. *The Wedding March*, which followed, became one of those traditional productions, like *Ben Hur*, which company after company fail on. It soared into the millions. I saw great slices of it shot and great hunks of financiers' hair torn from the roots in the process. But not a frame of what I saw appeared in the final version. When Paramount bought and finished the film, Stroheim was on the outside as before.

Yet for most of us Von Stroheim is the director of all directors, and I think largely because of this superlative disregard for the financiers who back him. If he feels like shooting, he shoots, and damns the pennies. If he wants one last detail on a set, he will hold up the world at a thousand dollars per tick to get it. If the gesture of a single tenth-rate extra is to be perfected, he will rehearse it for a couple of hours and hold every star in the cast waiting till it is done. The public issue of the film means nothing to him in comparison with its issue in craftsmanship.

The principals in the desert scene of *Greed* he put into hospital by actually shooting the scene in Death Valley and sweating them under the Californian sun till they achieved the realism he wanted. That sort of thing does not, I know, prove him a great artist, but it does demonstrate a virtue which is necessary in some measure to every director. Surrounded by a thousand technicians and a thousand interests which conflict with his job of pure creation, a director has to have something of Lenin in him to come through. Strangely enough, there is not an artist who ever appeared under him who will

hear a word against Von Stroheim. In a world of commercial flip-flap
he does stand so surely for the larger intensities of art.[2]

The Lost Squadron uses him as an actor only, in yet another of
those sinister Teutonic roles he made famous. The interesting point
is that he is cast as the crazy film director he is supposed to be: with
such a passion for realism that he pours acid on control wires and
sacrifices the lives of his stunt airmen for a movie effect.

This sort of thing, of course, is not quite the measure of Von
Stroheim the director; for if he did smash things to pieces to get his
stuff, be sure he took the biggest wallop himself.

Just for a minute, however, you do get something like a genuine
picture of the man: when, standing dreadfully erect before the set,
he screams, "Cameras!" I have seen him do that with very similar
passion, and I have seen him go off the hoop as he does subsequently,
and be very much the bloodcurdling creature of temperament he
demonstrates. It is worth seeing. He is the villain of the piece in this
case, but you may believe with me that a single gesture of such
villainy is worth a great deal of more flat-footed orthodoxy. "What
are a few deaths to the art of Benvenuto?"

The case of William Wyler is a rather curious one. He is an odd
member of the Laemmle tribe: origin Swiss; and, like every other
member of the tribe across the world, he has answered the tocsin
of Uncle Carl and joined the family at Universal City. But there
must be something in the Laemmle blood, because Wyler has taken
a line of his own. He is very nearly the most serious of Hollywood's
directors, and almost certainly the best poet. I have a notion he will
become the director we once expected Vidor to be. Like Vidor he
wanders in strange country but, unlike Vidor, he has the courage
of it.

Hell's Heroes, a film of the early thirties, told the queer story of
three bad hombres who sacrificed their lives to deliver a child to a
frontier town, and Wyler directed it magnificently. With its perverse parallel to the tale of the Three Wise Men, the delivery of the
child on Christmas Day, and the last man falling dead as the local
choir broke into the carol of "Holy Night," the story itself missed
hokum by a hairbreadth. Only a director of unusual ability could
have steered it past into genuine emotion.

In *A House Divided*, Wyler lives dangerously again. Here the

<hr/>

[2] Although he has made regular appearances as an actor in American and
French films, Von Stroheim has not directed any further films. He wrote a
novel of Hungarian gypsy life, *Paprika*, in 1935 and a story for M-G-M which
was filmed as *Between Two Women* (1937).—F.H.

story concerns the father-and-son theme which Eugene O'Neill made great in *Desire under the Elms* and Douglas in *The House with the Green Shutters*. In this case the son is weak and the father is strong, the father takes a new wife, and wife and son fall in love with each other. The story is set against a background of sea. Walter Huston plays the father.

I saw Huston play the father role in the New York Theatre Guild's production of *Desire under the Elms*. He played it for the great and intense thing it is, and caught the Calvinist passion of the role with a certainty that seemed a trifle bewildering in the atmosphere of metropolitan America. When Calvinism has disappeared from its own country, dare one expect to find it honored among the Philistines? But if that was strange, it is stranger still to find the outlook and the issue reappearing in a Hollywood film.

I am all for this William Wyler; he has a taste for the greater gestures and is still steering them past the hokum they so easily invoke. It is difficult to stage a tough old warrior of the Calvinist school, and achieve sympathy for him. If there is kindness in him, he would not show it; and ninety per cent of the slovenly little humanities which people expect will wither under his discipline. But Wyler and Huston put him over. It is not often that the ancient virtue of pity and terror creeps into a film. Here it does.

Cecil B. De Mille is out of fashion among the critics. But, as is my custom, I have seen *The Sign of the Cross* twice over and am still an unrepentant admirer. There is no director to touch him in command of the medium: certainly none who strikes such awe into my professional mind. I have only to see his crowds and continuities, yes, and images too, to think of the Milestones and Pudovkins as so many amateurs. How good and fine an artist he is may possibly be another matter. Too many judges announce contempt for his bathtubs and debauches for me to disrespect their finding. Personally I like both his bathtubs and his debauches, for the sufficient (I hope technical) reason that they are the biggest and the best in cinema. No man short of a Napoleon of movie would dare them, and De Mille is almost casual in their making.

There is another measure of De Mille. He is the only Jewish[3] director who is not afraid of being his Jewish self; and the thin and squeamish Western mind may not therefore be fit judge of his Oriental opulence. He is our only Oriental director. Not a picture of his but comes slap out of the Old Testament. They are the hotcha

[3] This is an error. Cecil B. De Mille was an Episcopalian.—D.T.

bits the Old Testament only mentions: the fiestas in Gomorrah, the celebrations before the calf of gold, the amami nights in the palace of Solomon; the living, pulsing, luxuriating aspect of the Hebrew life, which the parsons, Hebrew and otherwise, have suppressed.

The Sign of the Cross by a curious irony is the best of them all, better even than *The Ten Commandments*. It takes a Jew possibly to appreciate the Christian story, and for a number of reasons. It is at heart a Jewish story; it is a story of a humility which no other race knows anything about; and the oppression which is the other half of it can properly be understood only by a people who, back of everything they say, do or pretend, have the most vivid sense and knowledge of oppression in the world. On both sides, Basil Wright told me that the Negroes in Jamaica went crazy over *The Sign of the Cross:* for the same reason, I suggest, that De Mille went whoopee in the making of it. The luxury of Poppæa's bath of asses' milk and of the Lesbian dance in the house of Marcus is out-luxuried by the massacre of the Christians before Nero. It is gloriously horrifying, as by one who understands both the delight of Nero and the delight of the Christians. Only a Jew, I believe, could understand both points of view.

G. W. Pabst, in *Kameradschaft*, tells how French miners and German miners help each other in a mining disaster and break through the frontier to help each other. The frontier is the enemy, with every foolish enmity and every foolish memory of war and international misunderstanding symbolized in it. The conquering spirit of the future is the realization of common feelings and common ends on both sides of it.

Pabst has a fierce international idealism tucked away in his Teutonic interior. It blazes up in this film and adds both power and importance to everything he describes. The miners, the villages, the scrambling crowds, the desperate sorties in the exploding mine might be the ordinary material of melodrama. The larger theme invests them with the quality of epic. These people achieve something beyond themselves.

I think the mixture of French and German in which the dialogue is carried on is no deterrent in taking the points of the story. The whole affair swings ahead in unmistakable fashion, from the German side to the French, from family to family, and from the mine disaster itself to the ethical issue of the film.

Pabst's construction is the one I like best in cinema. He builds his little individual stories only slightly into the march of events. They punctuate it and give it point, and whatever the emphasis on lost sons and brothers and lovers, the march of events never ceases to be the principal concern. The mining exteriors are superb: the crowd scenes are handled with a skill which I doubt if many other directors in cinema can match. The staging (and particularly the finishing) of single episodes is brief and strong and—for the most part—natural. The disaster itself is all the more impressive because it does not tumble over itself to be sensational. The explosion comes with a low half-suppressed roar, which is sinister by the very suppression. There are a hundred other such details of fine direction: of tappings which go frantic at the realization of relief, of men that laugh when they find their relatives are alive, of others so distraught that they can only see back through rescuing gas masks to the gas masks of war. There are effects in the film which tear one to shreds.

My only complaint against Pabst is an old one. He means the best things in the world, but he means them sometimes too obviously. He cannot let well alone, but must keep on underlining things already emphasized. He is the Galsworthy of the screen: similar in the quality of his mind though a trifle superior in the field of his sympathies. The frontier theme, for example, is played to the point of symbolic handclasps and international embraces. The excellence of the previous demonstration makes both of them feeble and unnecessary. Pabst wags a finger at you and insults your imagination like any parson.

On a swift generalization it is remarkable how Fritz Lang's instinct runs to bigger ideas than any other director; but it is just as remarkable how little he ever makes of them. *M* is in the grandiose manner Lang established in such films as *Metropolis*. Its theme is taken from the Düsseldorf murders. Its hero is a sex pervert who murders little girls.

By its subject matter the film is unusual in all conscience, but I doubt if, on examination, it proves to be anything more than a plain thriller. Lang's photography is always excellent, of course, and his description of a mood or situation can often be brilliantly brief. In this example the murder of one child is followed in the adventures of a toy balloon; and the approaching growing and finally commanding mania of the murder is translated in the simple whistling of a motif from Grieg. But, if we look behind to the theme itself, we find that Lang's inspiration is only second-rate.

Metropolis, for all its pretension of setting and high-flying issue between capital and labor, concluded sillily and sentimentally that "it was love that made the world go round." As H. G. Wells pointed out at the time, it was an infant conception, without knowledge of society or science. Lang, I think, only ever peeps into the great problems. Looking into the hinterlands of space and time and the mind itself—in *The Girl in the Moon*, in *Metropolis*, in *Mabuse*, and in *M*—he is satisfied in the end with the honors of melodrama.[4]

The concluding scene of *M* is in the basement of an old battered distillery. The murderer has been run down, not by the police but by the thieves of the town, who find that the now desperate activities of the law are spoiling their business. To effect his running down, the thieves have organized the city beggars to watch every quarter, every street and every section of a street. But with the murderer crushed and cringing before the underworld, the whole drama is climaxed in a trial scene in which thief and pervert argue the relative merits of their case. It is a fantastic way of bringing so derelict a spirit as the Düsseldorf murderer into the realms of sympathy, but obviously not a tragic way.

It may possibly be asked if the whole idea of the film is not a little perverse: if anything is to be gained by creating sympathy for such a character. The test is always in the telling. Whatever the derelict— a creature of jealousy like Othello, or ambition like Macbeth, or of madness like this man from Düsseldorf—it makes no odds in theory to the writer of tragedy. As a human figure, both possible in fact and relatable in fact to the warring issues of existence, he can be brought to sympathy and made an instrument of great appreciation and great art. The sociological argument is beside the point. If he must be kicked from the social midst—hanged, imprisoned, or shut in a padded cell—the sociologist may be done with him. The artist is not. By that very fate he becomes for the tragedian the broken, incomplete figure of man who gives him his occasion and his opportunity.

When Peter Lorre, who plays the murderer, screams out "I couldn't help it!" you will probably be moved. That is the center of the piece, the theme itself; terrifying and, in the usual curious way, uplifting. But in that poignant moment one appreciates all the more the opportunity that has been lost. If this was the story, if this possession by devils and most foul destruction by devils was the story, the film's theatrical excursions into underworld organization, housebreaking and the like are irrelevant. Lang has, as usual, peeped into his big subject and been satisfied with a glimpse. The best that

[4] Fritz Lang left Germany in 1933 after he had made *Das Testament von Dr. Mabuse*, described as "the first anti-Nazi film." In Hollywood he has made, among other films, *Fury* and *You Only Live Once* on themes with a strong sociological basis. *Man Hunt* and *Hangmen Also Die* were wartime anti-Nazi films. His current films, *Woman in the Window* and *Scarlet Street*, are psychological thrillers.—F.H.

can be said for the film is that no other director one knows would have thought of the Düsseldorf murderer for his hero. In this Lang shares honors with Dostoevsky and the best of them. But Lang has only thought of his subject; he has not felt it. *M*, like *Frankenstein*, is a full-blown tragedy that has been diminished in the creation to a mere "sensational."

Ernst Lubitsch is one of the master craftsmen of the cinema. Consider, for example, *The Man I Killed*, the tragic antiwar story of the French youth who, conscience-stricken for his killing of a German youth, goes to make peace with the German's people. You may consider the story sentimental in its substance—for, war or no war, we do a lot of killing in our day—but you will have no doubt at all about Lubitsch. I cannot remember a film so beautifully made, so completely fine in its execution.

Perhaps I can indicate its quality better by describing a simpler illustration. Before Flaherty went off to the Aran Islands to make his *Man of Aran*, I had him up in the Black Country doing work for the E.M.B. He passed from pottery to glass, and from glass to steel, making short studies of English workmen. I saw the material a hundred times, and by all the laws of repetition should have been bored with it. But there is this same quality of great craftsmanship in it which makes one see it always with a certain new surprise. A man is making a pot, say. Your ordinary director will describe it; your good director will describe it well. He may even, if good enough, pick out those details of expression and of hands which bring character to the man and beauty to the work. But what will you say if the director beats the potter to his own movements, anticipating each puckering of the brows, each extended gesture of the hands in contemplation, and moves his camera about as though it were the mind and spirit of the man himself? I cannot tell you how it is done, nor could Flaherty. As always in art, to feeling which is fine enough and craft which is practiced enough, these strange other-world abilities are added.

Lubitsch does not often depart from comedy to make serious films. His last one was *The Patriot* in the late days of the Silents, with Emil Jannings as the mad Czar Paul. It was a huge performance with great acting, intense action, and some amazing camera movements in the corridors of the palace.

The Man I Killed is a simpler film, lower in key, with none of the mad happenings of *The Patriot* to build on. The youth, praised by the priest, goes on his journey. The German family, living on the

memory of their dead son, receive him as a friend of the son, and he
finds it impossible to make the confession he intended. There are
scenes of the old citizens of the German town at their beer; there are
some homely interiors; and the only happenings are that the old
father comes to like this foreign youth and turns from his hatred of
the French, and the German youth's girl falls in love with the man he
was killed by. Little enough, if you like, to make movement of, or
make climactic intensities of. But Lubitsch's camera glides magically
in and out of these ordinary scenes, taking the details of expression
and character and essential story on its way. Watch it particularly
in the last scene, as it goes from the youth playing his violin to the
girl, to the old couple, and watch how there is expectation, and
expectation surprised, in every foot of the gyro's passage. The actors
are Lionel Barrymore, Phillips Holmes and Nancy Carroll. As always
happens under Lubitsch direction, they were never so modulated or
so good.

Lubitsch sketches his character with a single pose, or a single
gesture, taken in the camera's stride. He does his work so easily that
you hardly know it is being done.

Only half a dozen directors make a personal contribution to their
work which is recognizable and unique. René Clair is one. He may
not be as solid a performer as Pudovkin nor as slick a one as Lubitsch,
but for his power to do something new and fine and entirely his own
he stands as high as any of them. He has power of fantasy and fairy
tale; he can jumble sound and sight together to make a crazy quilt of
good sense; and he is, above all, French.

For sheer brilliance of direction I begin to think that there are only
two directors worth recording: Clair himself and Lubitsch. Lubitsch
perhaps has an advantage on the big sets, but when it comes to the
intimacies, none can pull a face out of a crowd or build up a sequence
of tenement detail like Clair. And, in liking his neighbors as he does,
he has the unique distinction of liking them all equally, whether
they are artists or apaches or policemen or thieves or doctors or duns,
or moral or not.

Le Million is a bright and brilliant film, full of wit and fun, and
very, very ably directed. The story is a delightful trifle about an
artist who wins a million francs in a lottery but whose winning ticket
is stolen with his coat and passed from hand to hand over the length
and breadth of Paris. The pursuit of the coat is a slapstick affair with
Clair squeezing each sequence of studio and underworld and police
station and opera house for its every detail of fun. In lesser hands

Le Million would have been a comedy. In Clair's it has become a fairy tale. There is magic in it.[5]

A new Hitchcock film is something of an event in the English year. Hitchcock has a personal style of his own in direction, which can be recognized. He has a long record of good work, with large slices here and there of supremely intelligent work. He is known to have a freer hand than most in direction and to have odd thoughts of greatness. It is no wonder, therefore, if in criticism we exalt him a trifle. With a national cinema growing up under our eyes, we need strong and individual directors more than anything else. Financiers and impresarios you can buy two a penny. Directors who have something to say and the power to say it, you can only close your fingers and wish for.

Rich and Strange is the story of a young couple who cross the earthball on a holiday, and drift, in shipboard fashion, to new loyalties. An adventuress so-called disrupts the male and a colonial planter disrupts the female. In the main it is a meandering tale built up on the slim behaviorism of two or three characters and the minutiae of their relationships. The end of the story is that the couple are shipwrecked and saved by a Chinese junk. In that oddest of all spots in the world they discover the great mercy of having a baby.

The most important thing about the film is not so much the story. It is the sudden emphasis it lays on weaknesses in Hitchcock's make-up. I have guessed before that these existed, but have never seen so clearly what new opportunities of direction must be given him if he is to build up his talent to the very grand affair we expect it to be.

In trying new material Hitchcock has found himself outside both his experience and his imagination. He has already proved himself as a director of London types and Londonesque melodrama. This new and greater canvas of seven seas and half a world has caught him short. Think of the theme for a moment. You have in the background the journey across the earthball, and Marseilles and Suez, and Colombo and Singapore to play with. That must surely mean something to the story. You may think of it simply as a cosmic journey on which something happened to happen. You may think of it more deeply as a demonstration of the fact that even the world and its

---

[5] Clair made *A Nous la Liberté*, *Le Quatorze Juillet*, and *Le Dernier Milliardaire* in France before coming to Britain to direct *The Ghost Goes West* for Korda. His Hollywood films have included *It Happened Tomorrow*, a futuristic fantasy, and *Ten Little Indians*, adapted from the story by Agatha Christie. He returned to France shortly after the end of the war.—F.H.

wonders can only teach people to be themselves. Whatever you
think, you cannot avoid the background. It is the material of your
drama and your cinema both.

The success of the film as a study of people and as a slice of cinema
depended, therefore, on Hitchcock's ability to make that journey
live. He fails, and entirely because his mind does not quite appreciate
the wonders of the world he is trying to use. He is in this sense the
supreme provincial your true-born Londoner tends to be. He knows
people, but not things, situations and episodes, but not events. His
sense of space, time and the other elements of barbarian religion is
almost nil.

The shipwreck is like the ship itself, a fake and a frost, composed
of half a dozen studio effects. The scenes abroad have nothing that
influence the story even by a trifle. They cannot be rich and strange
because not one of them is newly observed. It would have been good
to have added to the film some sense of strange trafficking and curious
merchandise, but, if anything, the greater weakness is the weakness
of the ship. By its very nature a ship is a living thing, worth the grace
of cinema, and in missing it Hitchcock has very literally missed the
boat. It is not as Hitchcock makes it, just a collection of rails to look
over, and evening skies to go moony about. It moves; it passes with
not a little triumph through an entire ocean, with all sorts of things
stowed away in its mysterious belly.

But let me indicate the charm of Hitchcock's direction of his
separate episodes. You will have heard before now of "the Hitchcock
touch." This consists in his great ability to give a novel twist to his
sketch of an episode. The man and woman are quarreling desperately
in some Oriental room: Hitchcock punctuates that episode with the
apologetic entry of a Chinese who wants to sweep the floor. The
man, again, has just clinched his appointment for a first essay in infidelity: he walks idiotically into a ventilator. The film is full of details of the kind, sometimes amusing, always clever, sometimes merely
clever.

I would suggest that Hitchcock's concentration on such details
is at least a part of his worry in the world. Reaching for the smart
touch, as often as not he irresponsibly destroys the characters he has
been building up and throws away his sequence. In Chaplin you do
not mind the beaded story of moments and episodes. In a dramatic
director like Hitchcock you must. A film is not like the celebrated
Rosary, an affair of moments to be counted over, every one apart.
It is a procession of people and events that march along: preferably,
of course, going somewhere.

I believe the highbrows, in their praise of him, have sent Hitch-

cock off in the wrong direction, as they have sent many another:
Chaplin, for example. They have picked out his clever little pieces,
stressed them and analyzed them till they are almost everything in
his directorial make-up. We have waited patiently for the swing of
event (preferably of great event) to come into his films, something
that would associate him more profoundly with the dramatic wants
of common people. Something serious, I am afraid, will have to happen to Hitchcock before we get it.[6]

I have seldom seen an English film that gave me so much pleasure
as *Dance Pretty Lady*. If you would see how movement should be put
together and most ordinary exits and entrances turned into a poetry
of movement, you will find a whole curriculum in this film. And
more. One of Anthony Asquith's great talents is his power of giving
conversational point to action and character. He slips in details of
observation which are, on their own account, a running commentary
on both. Plastered hair, a stiff collar, or a room's decorations become
in his hands a character sketch; the window of a hansom cab under-
lines a period. There is no other director can do it so well; there is
no other director can even do it.

Always, too, looking at Asquith's films, you realize how well he
knows his painters. I suppose the little references to one or another,
the consciousness in this case that Dégas should not be shamed in his
own subject, can mean little to some audiences. Asquith can at least
defend himself on the Kantian maxim, that one may only appreciate
as one would wish the whole world to appreciate. It is a maxim
never, never in evidence in the film world, but heaven knows cinema
could do with a little of it.

Dance Pretty Lady is a delight to the eye: be assured of that. I
cannot, however, say so much for its appeal to the imagination. It
represents filigree work, most delicate, on a story that could not
possibly make a big film. A little ballet dancer (much too young to
be allowed to fall in love with anybody) falls in love with a sculptor.
She will not let him have her "because she would feel a sneak." The
sculptor goes off in a tantrum. The girl, annoyed by the tantrum,
lets another man, "a dirty rotter," have her instead. The sculptor
comes back for a quick and sudden and quite banal happy ending.

That is the tiding of great joy which Asquith (of Balliol and I

[6] *Rich and Strange* (1931) followed *Blackmail* and preceded Hitchcock's
crime thrillers which were to become part of the British film tradition. His
later British films included *The Man Who Knew Too Much, The Thirty-Nine
Steps, The Lady Vanishes,* and *Jamaica Inn* (with Charles Laughton). American
productions have included *Rebecca, Foreign Correspondent, Suspicion, Shadow
of a Doubt,* and the controversial *Lifeboat.*—F.H.

know not what other traditions of English leadership) has spent a year in fetching us. A more cynical and shameful waste of time I cannot imagine. I may tend to overemphasize our need for leadership and the film's great capacity for giving it, but was there ever another film director trained so specifically and deliberately and cold-bloodedly for the job as Asquith? This is it, bless you. Claptrap about a virginity. Why, the entire sentiment that makes a plot like that possible went into discard with the good prosperous complacent old Victoria. It was, relatively, an important matter then. But it is mere infant fodder now when you consider the new problems we carry in our bellies, and think of the new emphases we must in mercy to ourselves create out of our different world.

Flaherty was sitting with me at *Dance Pretty Lady*, and he is a good judge. He was as fascinated as I was myself. But his summing up was this: "If that boy ever gets a story you will see the film of your life." It is a trouble to know whether Asquith is denied the big story by his masters, or is by his own nature powerless to find it.[7]

I think, myself, that like many other brilliant young men of his training and generation, he is a damned sight too remote from ordinary things to discover it easily. It is not enough to recognize bigness by its classical reference (for this Asquith can do on his head); it must be recognized, without reference at all, out of one's own most private sense of importance, if there is to be power of revelation. I cannot tell you what the secret is, but it should be plain on the face of it that there are more powerful spirits to be called from the deep than you are likely to get from stories of this sort.

Michael Powell is a young director who promises to stand up presently in the publicity line with Asquith and Hitchcock. I threw him a bouquet for his film *Rynox*, and in *Star Reporter* he again demonstrates the same solid ability and (more important still) the same solid certainty of himself. The story is by Philip MacDonald, the detective writer, and by Ralph Smart, who made the film on Port Sunlight. Powell not only makes a slick businesslike job of it, but gets a very considerable size into his presentation of one or two of the sequences. This is going some for a film produced at speed.

The passage showing the arrival of the *Berengaria* demonstrates a unique power of observation which promises much. His angles are strong, his continuity, shot by shot, direct and definite. Powell can

[7] Asquith's most successful film in the pre-war period was *Pygmalion*, made with Leslie Howard. His war films included *Freedom Radio*, *We Dive at Dawn*, a story of the submarine service, and *The Way to the Stars* (in America *Johnny in the Clouds*) a notably fine story-documentary of Anglo-American co-operation in the air.—F.H.

certainly see things. One only waits now for evidence of his powers to recognize ideas. *Rynox* was the story of an insurance swindle; *Star Reporter* is the story of a stolen diamond with a Fleet Street reporter marrying into Mayfair. This sort of thing may be all right to practice on but it obviously cannot be taken seriously. Powell must step presently into something more sensible.[8]

It is a waste of time to consider what Eisenstein would have done with *Thunder Over Mexico*, if he had been allowed to cut it. The fact is that he was not allowed, and alibis that the cutting was done "in exact accord" with Eisenstein's script are merely silly. One might as well talk of writing a George Moore novel from George Moore's notes; for with Eisenstein, as with Moore, the style is nearly everything. He is not a poet like Pudovkin, whose conceptions are themselves emotional and uplifting, nor a finely descriptive director like Flaherty, whose observations are of themselves intimate. His raw material is common documentary, and sometimes very common. It is his power of juxtaposition that counts, his amazing capacity for exploding two or three details into an idea. It is not how his actors act, nor yet how the camera looks at them, that is important in Eisenstein, for his acting is often bad and his camera work meretricious: it is the odd reference he adds to his actors' presence that gives meaning and tempo to their lives. Say this for brief, that Eisenstein is detailed and cold in his shooting, and that he only warms his stuff to life when he starts putting it together. It is his method of approach; and there could be no genuine Eisenstein film without it.

Thunder Over Mexico might have been a good film with Eisenstein, or it might not; without him it is pretty dull stuff, without style, without idea, and without construction. What I hear was intended to be a vast description of the Mexican spirit turns out to be a niggardly slow-told tale of how a peasant girl was raped by a feudal lord and how her peasant lover rebelled and was executed.

There is a symbolic sequence at the beginning which is meant to describe the age-long suffering of the Mexican people. It is full of dissolves, superimpositions and wipes, in a manner never before associated with Eisenstein; and I cannot understand its presence. If Eisenstein intended it, he has certainly deviated from his own stalwart doctrine. He was always an enemy of such vague methods of mental

[8] It was not long before this invitation was accepted. Powell made *The Edge of the World* (1935–37) on Foula in the Shetlands and, during the war, films of such quality as *49th Parallel* (*The Invaders* in America), *The Life and Death of Colonel Blimp*, *One of Our Aircraft is Missing*, *A Canterbury Tale*, and *I Know Where I'm Going.*—F.H.

association as are represented by the draping of symbolic figures across the landscape; and I remember how he raged at the symbolic example of *Joan of Arc* when I once put it to him. This sequence, if it is anything, is just bad *Joan of Arc*. The tale of rape follows, in a setting of heavily filtered clouds and foreground cactus. The clouds and the cactus will pass for great photography among the hicks, but they are, of course, easy meat for anyone with a decent set of filters. The lovely molding of form, the brilliance of near and intimate observation, which you get in *Moana*, say, are a mile away and beyond. These are superficial qualities only. But, as I suggest, one never looked to Eisenstein for great photography or intimate observation, and one's only disappointment is that Hollywood has fallen for these clouds and things and let the film go to the devil for the sake of its glycerined scenic effects. The types on the other hand are superb, for no one holds a candle to Eisenstein when it comes to picking face. The acting, too, is much better than we have associated with Eisenstein in the past, though never as fine in its nuances of reaction as we get in Pudovkin.

But there you are and what of it? The significance that Eisenstein might have added to the tale is not there; and types, acting and glycerined clouds cannot turn a simple tale of village rape into the passion of a people. There were other things up Eisenstein's sleeve, or he is not the dialectician I have always taken him for.

Pudovkin's *A Simple Case* was a dreadful little film with an ingenious use of slow motion, a host of lovely images, and no point. *Deserter* is Pudovkin on the rebound: more complex in his effects, surer in his technical hand, and even stronger in his theme than he was in *The End of St. Petersburg*. If you remember your Dostoevsky or your Joyce or your Melville you will know how leisurely the masterpieces may sometimes proceed: how, damning the audience, they may sometimes fly suddenly off the earth, or, by perversity, from off the earth back to terra firma again, without a by your leave: taking good pains to bore the lesser minds with inconsequent pondering on the guts of whales and the exact clinical nature of disease and disaster. *Deserter* has something of this curious strength. If, in its hobbling from one odd chapter to another, as it freely does, the film extends your patience, you will respect it, as like as not, for the size it brings. Only the little fellows care what twiddling echoes go round your pipes and, sycophantically, measure the music to suit you. The big fellows call their own tune. You will certainly have time to consider this matter, for the film runs nearly a couple of hours, in innumerable acts and subdivisions of acts, shifting from scene to scene in titles, and sometimes plain blackouts, as I cannot remember anything doing so variously since *Antony and Cleopatra*.

When you come to consider the continuing theme of the film you will be wise to look for none, but content yourself with the vast description it gives of the world today: of high-powered industry, of unemployment, of poverty, of the accumulating fire of public effort, of the stresses and storms between men and men which economic disaster has brought in its train. The net effect is of great tragedy, in which the beauties of blue sky and morning, ships and machinery, young faces and hopeful faces, are strangely stifled in the common disaster. For long passages there is argument: as of dictatorship, leadership, solution; and you will not need to know Russian to know every turn of the dialectic. But you will regard even this as part of a necessary effort.

For my part, I shall only record that no film or novel or poem or drama has sketched so largely the essential story and the essential unhappiness of our time, or brought them so deeply to the mind.

I have met some of the great men of cinema, but can think of none more impressive in his mind and presence than the American-born, Canadian-trained explorer, Robert Flaherty. Since 1921 when he brought *Nanook* out of the arctic and abandoned his discovering of Belcher Islands and mapping of Northern Labrador for cinema, he has stood uncompromisingly for everything that is fine in film. The story of his long fight with Hollywood is perhaps the best of all Hollywood stories, because it is the single one in which personal advantage has been sacrificed at every turn for a decent result.

Nanook was the simple story of an Eskimo family and its fight for food, but its approach to the whole question of film-making was something entirely novel at the time it was made. It was a record of everyday life so selective in its detail and sequence, so intimate in its shots, and so appreciative of the nuances of common feeling, that it was a drama in many ways more telling than anything that had come out of the manufactured sets of Hollywood. In *Moana* Flaherty adopted the same method with the Samoans. Without actors, almost without acting, he built up in his camera what he considered the essential story of their lives. The second film stated the difference of his approach even better than *Nanook*. Because of the great financial success of the first film Flaherty found himself commissioned by the film people to "make another *Nanook*." It is their way to repeat themselves. Hollywood could only think of other food agonies, the different climate and circumstance of Samoa notwithstanding. In the issue it was disappointed, as it was bound to be. Flaherty's film was the story of how the Samoans, blessedly freed from the more primitive pains of life, had still to invent pain to demonstrate their manhood. He made the story of the Tattoo. Hollywood, asking for battles with sharks, got the loveliness of a ceremonial prayer to the gods. And asking for dark-skinned bathing belles, they got a quiet, dignified young heroine with a flower in her ear, who danced superbly but could not possibly be confused with whoopee. In desperation they issued the film as "The Love Life of a South Sea Siren," and gave it a prologue of jangling guitars and shimmying chorus girls.

After even more desperate battles in the making and abandoning of *White Shadows of the South Seas* (the bathing belles this time included), and a film on the Red Indian rain dance, which crashed because of a Hollywood insistence on love story, Flaherty made his expedition to the Aran Islands and was given a decent independence.

When I spoke with him on the Arans he was full of the possibilities of the British documentary cinema. If on these islands—only so many hours from London—there was this story of romantic life ready to the camera, how many more must there be! He mentioned the Hebrides and the Highlands, and sketched out a film of Indian village life. He spoke of the tales of fine craftsmanship which must be tucked away in the Black Country. But first, he emphasized, there must be the process of discovery and freedom in discovery: to live with the people long enough to know them. He talked with a certain rising fury of the mental attitude of the studio-bred producer who hangs a slicked-out story of triangles against a background of countryside or industry. Rather must the approach be, to take the story from out the location, finding it essentially there: with patience and intimacy of knowledge as the first virtues always in a director. He referred to a quotation I once wrote for him in New York, when his seemingly tardy method of production was first an issue in the studios. It was Plato's description of his metaphysic where he says that no fire can leap up or light kindle till there is "long intercourse with the thing itself, and it has been lived with." No doubt the studios, with their slick ten or fifteen-day productions of nothing in particular, still disagree with Flaherty and Plato profoundly. His idea of production is to reconnoiter for months without turning a foot, and then, in months more perhaps, slowly to shape the film on the screen: using his camera first to sketch his material and find his people, then using his screen, as Chaplin uses it, to tell him at every turn where the path of drama lies.

No director has the same respect as Flaherty for the camera; indeed very few of them even trouble to look through the camera while it is shooting their scenes. Flaherty, in contrast, is always his own "first cameraman." He spoke almost mystically of the camera's capacity for seeing beyond mortal eye to the inner qualities of things. With Fairbanks he agrees that children and animals are the finest of all movie actors, because they are spontaneous, but talks also of the movements in peasants and craftsmen and hunters and priests as having a special magic on the screen because time or tradition has worn them smooth. He might also add—though he would not—that his own capacity for moving the camera in appreciation of these movements is an essential part of the magic. No man of cameras, to my knowledge, can plan so curiously, or so bewilderingly anticipate a fine gesture or expression.

Flaherty's ideal in the new medium is a selective documentation of sound similar at all points to his selective documentation of movement and expression in the silent film. He would use the microphone, like the camera, as an intimate attendant on the action: recording the accompanying sounds and whispers and cries most expressive of it. He says the language does not matter at all, not even the words, if the spirit of the thing is plain. In this point as in others, Flaherty's cinema is as far removed from the theatrical tradition as it can possibly be. His screen is not a stage to which the action of a story is brought, but rather a magical opening in the theater wall, through which one may look out to the wide world: overseeing and overhearing the intimate things of common life which only the camera and microphone of the film artist can reveal.

Comedy's

Greatest

Era

by James Agee

Although James Agee wrote this article in 1949 (it was published in the September 5, 1949, issue of Life), nothing has happened to American film comedy in the interim to out-date it. In fact, if he were writing this piece as of today, his conviction that the works of Charlie Chaplin, Harry Langdon, Mack Sennett and Harold Lloyd stand out as cinematic monuments would be stronger than ever. Possibly the comic potentialities of Ernie Kovacs would be worth mentioning, but he is still new to films. One can only hope that Kovacs will be given a chance to display his endless bag of tricks. This would seem unlikely, however, for the sad fact remains that the difference between today's and yesterday's comedians is that the former are at the mercy of the complexities and difficulties of large-scale production, while the latter had total control over their material.

IN THE LANGUAGE of screen comedians four of the main grades of laugh are the titter, the yowl, the belly laugh and the boffo. The titter is just a titter. The yowl is a runaway titter. Anyone who has ever had the pleasure knows all about a belly laugh. The boffo is the laugh that kills. An ideally good gag, perfectly constructed and played, would bring the victim up this ladder of laughs by cruelly controlled degrees to the top rung, and would then proceed to wobble, shake, wave and brandish the ladder until he groaned for mercy. Then, after the shortest possible time out for recuperation, he would feel the first wicked tickling of the comedian's whip once more and start up a new ladder.

The reader can get a fair enough idea of the current state of screen comedy by asking himself how long it has been since he has had that treatment. The best of comedies these days hand out plenty of titters and once in a while it is possible to achieve a yowl without overstraining. Even those who have never seen anything better must occasionally have the feeling, as they watch the current run or, rather, trickle of screen comedy, that they are having to make a little cause for laughter go an awfully long way. And anyone who has watched screen comedy over the past ten or fifteen years is bound to realize that it has quietly but steadily deteriorated. As for those happy atavists who remember silent comedy in its heyday and the belly laughs and boffos that went with it, they have something close to an absolute standard by which to measure the deterioration.

When a modern comedian gets hit on the head, for example, the most he is apt to do is look sleepy. When a silent comedian got hit on the head he seldom let it go so flatly. He realized a broad license, and a ruthless discipline within that license. It was his business to be as funny as possible physically, without the help or hindrance of words. So he gave us a figure of speech, or rather of vision, for loss of consciousness. In other words he gave us a poem, a kind of poem, moreover, that everybody understands. The least he might do was to straighten up stiff as a plank and fall over backward with such skill that his whole length seemed to slap the floor at the same instant. Or he might make a cadenza of it—look vague, smile like an angel, roll up his eyes, lace his fingers, thrust his hands palms downward as far as they would go, hunch his shoulders, rise on tiptoe, prance ecstatically in narrowing circles until, with tallow knees, he sank down the vortex of his dizziness to the floor and there signified nirvana by kicking his heels twice, like a swimming frog.

Startled by a cop, this same comedian might grab his hatbrim with both hands and yank it down over his ears, jump high in the air, come to earth in a split violent enough to telescope his spine, spring thence into a coattail-flattening sprint and dwindle at rocket speed to the size of a gnat along the grand, forlorn perspective of some lazy back boulevard.

Those are fine clichés from the language of silent comedy in its infancy. The man who could handle them properly combined several of the more difficult accomplishments of the acrobat, the dancer, the clown and the mime. Some very gifted comedians, unforgettably Ben Turpin, had an immense vocabulary of these clichés and were in part so lovable because they were deep conservative classicists and never tried to break away from them. The still more gifted men, of course, simplified and invented, finding out new and

much deeper uses for the idiom. They learned to show emotion
through it, and comic psychology, more eloquently than most language has ever managed to, and they discovered beauties of comic
motion which are hopelessly beyond reach of words.

It is hard to find a theater these days where a comedy is playing;
in the days of the silents it was equally hard to find a theater which
was not showing one. The laughs today are pitifully few, far between, shallow, quiet and short. They almost never build, as they
used to, into something combining the jabbering frequency of a
machine gun with the delirious momentum of a roller coaster. Saddest of all, there are few comedians now below middle age and there
are none who seem to learn much from picture to picture, or to try
anything new.

To put it unkindly, the only thing wrong with screen comedy
today is that it takes place on a screen which talks. Because it talks,
the only comedians who ever mastered the screen cannot work, for
they cannot combine their comic style with talk. Because there is a
screen, talking comedians are trapped into a continual exhibition of
their inadequacy as screen comedians on a surface as big as the side
of a barn.

At the moment, as for many years past, the chances to see silent
comedy are rare. There is a smattering of it on television—too often
treated as something quaintly archaic, to be laughed at, not with.
Some two hundred comedies—long and short—can be rented for
home projection. And a lucky minority has access to the comedies
in the collection of New York's Museum of Modern Art, which is
still incomplete but which is probably the best in the world. In the
near future, however, something of this lost art will return to regular
theaters. A thick straw in the wind is the big business now being done
by a series of revivals of W. C. Fields's memorable movies, a kind
of comedy more akin to the old silent variety than anything which
is being made today. Mack Sennett now is preparing a sort of pot-
pourri variety show called *Down Memory Lane* made up out of his
old movies, featuring people like Fields and Bing Crosby when they
were movie beginners, but including also interludes from silents.
Harold Lloyd has re-released *Movie Crazy*, a talkie, and plans to
revive four of his best silent comedies, *Grandma's Boy*, *Safety Last*,
Speedy and *The Freshman*. Buster Keaton hopes to remake at feature
length, with a minimum of dialogue, two of the funniest short comedies ever made, one about a porous homemade boat and one about a
prefabricated house.

Awaiting these happy events, we will discuss here what has gone
wrong with screen comedy and what, if anything, can be done about

it. But mainly we will try to suggest what it was like in its glory in the years from 1912 to 1930, as practiced by the employees of Mack Sennett, the father of American screen comedy, and by the four most eminent masters: Charlie Chaplin, Harold Lloyd, the late Harry Langdon and Buster Keaton.

Mack Sennett made two kinds of comedy: parody laced with slapstick, and plain slapstick. The parodies were the unceremonious burial of a century of hamming, including the new hamming in serious movies, and nobody who has missed Ben Turpin in *A Small Town Idol*, or kidding Erich von Stroheim in *Three Foolish Weeks* or as *The Shriek of Araby*, can imagine how rough parody can get and still remain subtle and roaringly funny. The plain slapstick, at its best, was even better: a profusion of hearty young women in disconcerting bathing suits, frisking around with a gaggle of insanely incompetent policemen and of equally certifiable male civilians sporting museum-piece mustaches. All these people zipped and caromed about the pristine world of the screen as jazzily as a convention of water bugs. Words can hardly suggest how energetically they collided and bounced apart, meeting in full gallop around the corner of a house; how hard and how often they fell on their backsides; or with what fantastically adroit clumsiness they got themselves fouled up in folding ladders, garden hoses, tethered animals and each other's headlong cross-purposes. The gestures were ferociously emphatic; not a line or motion of the body was wasted or inarticulate. The reader may remember how splendidly upright wandlike old Ben Turpin could stand for a Renunciation Scene, with his lampshade mustache twittering and his sparrowy chest stuck out and his head flung back like Paderewski assaulting a climax and the long babyish back hair trying to look lionlike, while his Adam's apple, an orange in a Christmas stocking, pumped with noble emotion. Or huge Mack Swain, who looked like a hairy mushroom, rolling his eyes in a manner patented by French romantics and gasping in some dubious ecstasy. Or Louise Fazenda, the perennial farmer's daughter and the perfect low-comedy housemaid, primping her spit curl; and how her hair tightened a good-looking face into the incarnation of rampant gullibility. Or snouty James Finlayson, gleefully foreclosing a mortgage, with his look of eternally tasting a spoiled pickle. Or Chester Conklin, a myopic and inebriated little walrus stumbling around in outsize pants. Or Fatty Arbuckle, with his cold eye and his loose, serene smile, his silky manipulation of his bulk and his satanic marksmanship with pies (he was ambidextrous and could simultaneously blind two people in opposite directions).

The intimate tastes and secret hopes of these poor ineligible dunces were ruthlessly exposed whenever a hot stove, an electric fan or a bulldog took a dislike to their outer garments: agonizingly elaborate drawers, worked up on some lonely evening out of some Godforsaken lace curtain; or men's underpants with big round black spots on them. The Sennett sets—delirious wallpaper, megalomaniacally scrolled iron beds, Grand Rapids *in extremis*—outdid even the underwear. It was their business, after all, to kid the squalid braggadocio which infested the domestic interiors of the period, and that was almost beyond parody. These comedies told their stories to the unaided eye, and by every means possible they screamed to it. That is one reason for the India ink silhouettes of the cops, and for convicts and prison bars and their shadows in hard sunlight, and for barefooted husbands, in tigerish pajamas, reacting like dervishes to stepped-on tacks.

The early silent comedians never strove for or consciously thought of anything which could be called artistic "form," but they achieved it. For Sennett's rival, Hal Roach, Leo McCarey once devoted almost the whole of a Laurel and Hardy two-reeler to pie throwing. The first pies were thrown thoughtfully, almost philosophically. Then innocent bystanders began to get caught into the vortex. At full pitch it was Armageddon. But everything was calculated so nicely that until late in the picture, when havoc took over, every pie made its special kind of point and piled on its special kind of laugh.

Sennett's comedies were just a shade faster and fizzier than life. According to legend (and according to Sennett) he discovered the tempo proper to screen comedy when a green cameraman, trying to save money, cranked too slow.[1] Realizing the tremendous drumlike power of mere motion to exhilarate, he gave inanimate objects a mischievous life of their own, broke every law of nature the tricked camera would serve him for and made the screen dance like a witches' Sabbath. The thing one is surest of all to remember is how toward the end of nearly every Sennett comedy, a chase (usually called the "rally") built up such a majestic trajectory of pure anarchic motion that bathing girls, cops, comics, dogs, cats, babies, automoblies, locomotives, innocent bystanders, sometimes what seemed like a whole city, an entire civilization, were hauled along head over heels in the wake of that energy like dry leaves following an express train.

[1] Silent comedy was shot at twelve to sixteen frames per second and was speeded up by being shown at sixteen frames per second, the usual rate of theater projectors at that time. Theater projectors today run at twenty-four, which makes modern film taken at the same speed seem smooth and natural. But it makes silent movies fast and jerky.

"Nice" people, who shunned all movies in the early days, condemned the Sennett comedies as vulgar and naïve. But millions of less pretentious people loved their sincerity and sweetness, their wild-animal innocence and glorious vitality. They could not put these feelings into words, but they flocked to the silents. The reader who gets back deep enough into that world will probably even remember the theater: the barefaced honky-tonk and the waltzes by Waldteufel, slammed out on a mechanical piano; the searing redolence of peanuts and demirep perfumery, tobacco and feet and sweat; the laughter of unrespectable people having a hell of a fine time, laughter as violent and steady and deafening as standing under a waterfall.

Sennett wheedled his first financing out of a couple of ex-bookies to whom he was already in debt. He took his comics out of music halls, burlesque, vaudeville, circuses and limbo, and through them he tapped in on that great pipeline of horsing and miming which runs back unbroken through the fairs of the Middle Ages at least to ancient Greece. He added all that he himself had learned about the large and spurious gesture, the late decadence of the Grand Manner, as a stage-struck boy in East Berlin, Connecticut, and as a frustrated opera singer and actor. The only thing he claims to have invented is the pie in the face, and he insists, "Anyone who tells you he has discovered something new is a fool or a liar or both."

The silent-comedy studio was about the best training school the movies have ever known, and the Sennett studio was about as free and easy and as fecund of talent as they came. All the major comedians we will mention worked there, at least briefly. So did some of the major stars of the '20s and since—notably Gloria Swanson, Phyllis Haver, Wallace Beery, Marie Dressler and Carole Lombard. Directors Frank Capra, Leo McCarey and George Stevens also got their start in silent comedy; much that remains most flexible, spontaneous and visually alive in sound movies can be traced, through them and others, to this silent apprenticeship. Everybody did pretty much as he pleased on the Sennett lot, and everybody's ideas were welcome. Sennett posted no rules, and the only thing he strictly forbade was liquor. A Sennett story conference was a most informal affair. During the early years, at least, only the most important scenario might be jotted on the back of an envelope. Mainly Sennett's men thrashed out a few primary ideas and carried them in their heads, sure that better stuff would turn up while they were shooting, in the heat of physical action. This put quite a load on the prop man; he had to have the most improbable apparatus on hand—bombs, trick telephones, what not—to implement whatever idea might suddenly turn up. All kinds of things did—and were recklessly used. Once a low-comedy auto got out of control and killed the cameraman, but he was not visible in the shot, which was thrilling and undamaged; the audience never knew the difference.

Sennett used to hire a "wild man" to sit in on his gag conferences, whose whole job was to think up "wildies." Usually he was an all but brainless, speechless man, scarcely able to communicate his idea; but he had a totally uninhibited imagination. He might say nothing for an hour; then he'd mutter, "You take . . ." and all the relatively rational others would shut up and wait. "You take this cloud . . ." he would get out, sketching vague shapes in the air. Often he could get no further; but thanks to some kind of thought transference, saner men would take this cloud and make something of it. The wild man seems in fact to have functioned as the group's subconscious mind, the source of all creative energy. His ideas were so weird and amorphous that Sennett can no longer remember a one of them, or even how it turned out after rational processing. But a fair equivalent might be one of the best comic sequences in a Laurel and Hardy picture. It is simple enough—simple and real, in fact, as a nightmare. Laurel and Hardy are trying to move a piano across a narrow suspension bridge. The bridge is slung over a sickening chasm, between a couple of Alps. Midway they meet a gorilla.

Had he done nothing else, Sennett would be remembered for giving a start to three of the four comedians who now began to apply their sharp individual talents to this newborn language. The one whom he did not train (he was on the lot briefly but Sennett barely remembers seeing him around) wore glasses, smiled a great deal and looked like the sort of eager young man who might have quit divinity school to hustle brushes. That was Harold Lloyd. The others were grotesque and poetic in their screen characters in degrees which appear to be impossible when the magic of silence is broken. One, who never smiled, carried a face as still and sad as a daguerreotype through some of the most preposterously ingenious and visually satisfying physical comedy ever invented. That was Buster Keaton. One looked like an elderly baby and, at times, a baby dope fiend; he could do more with less than any other comedian. That was Harry Langdon. One looked like Charlie Chaplin, and he was the first man to give the silent language a soul.

When Charlie Chaplin started to work for Sennett he had chiefly to reckon with Ford Sterling, the reigning comedian. Their first picture together amounted to a duel before the assembled professionals. Sterling, by no means untalented, was a big man with a florid Teutonic style which, under this special pressure, he turned on full blast.

Chaplin defeated him within a few minutes with a wink of the mustache, a hitch of the trousers, a quirk of the little finger.

With *Tillie's Punctured Romance*, in 1914, he became a major star. Soon after, he left Sennett when Sennett refused to start a landslide among the other comedians by meeting the raise Chaplin demanded. Sennett is understandably wry about it in retrospect, but he still says, "I was right at the time." Of Chaplin he says simply, "Oh well, he's just the greatest artist that ever lived." None of Chaplin's former rivals rates him much lower than that; they speak of him no more jealously than they might of God. We will try here only to suggest the essence of his supremacy. Of all comedians he worked most deeply and most shrewdly within a realization of what a human being is, and is up against. The Tramp is as centrally representative of humanity, as many-sided and as mysterious, as Hamlet, and it seems unlikely that any dancer or actor can ever have excelled him in eloquence, variety or poignancy of motion. As for pure motion, even if he had never gone on to make his magnificent feature-length comedies, Chaplin would have made his period in movies a great one singlehanded even if he had made nothing except *The Cure*, or *One A.M.* In the latter, barring one immobile taxi driver, Chaplin plays alone, as a drunk trying to get upstairs and into bed. It is a sort of inspired elaboration on a soft-shoe dance, involving an angry stuffed wildcat, small rugs on slippery floors, a Lazy Susan table, exquisite footwork on a flight of stairs, a contretemps with a huge, ferocious pendulum and the funniest and most perverse Murphy bed in movie history—and, always made physically lucid, the delicately weird mental processes of a man ethereally sozzled.

Before Chaplin came to pictures people were content with a couple of gags per comedy; he got some kind of laugh every second. The minute he began to work he set standards—and continually forced them higher. Anyone who saw Chaplin eating a boiled shoe like brook trout in *The Gold Rush*, or embarrassed by a swallowed whistle in *City Lights*, has seen perfection. Most of the time, however, Chaplin got his laughter less from the gags, or from milking them in any ordinary sense, than through his genius for what may be called *inflection* —the perfect, changeful shading of his physical and emotional attitudes toward the gag. Funny as his bout with the Murphy bed is, the glances of awe, expostulation and helpless, almost whimpering desire for vengeance which he darts at this infernal machine are even better.

A painful and frequent error among tyros is breaking the comic line with a too-big laugh, then a letdown; or with a laugh which is out of key or irrelevant. The masters could ornament the main line beautifully; they never addled it. In *A Night Out* Chaplin, passed out, is hauled along the sidewalk by the scruff of his coat by staggering Ben Turpin. His toes trail; he is as supine as a sled. Turpin himself is so drunk he can hardly drag him. Chaplin comes quietly to, realizes how well he is being served by his struggling pal, and with a royally delicate gesture plucks and savors a flower.

The finest pantomime, the deepest emotion, the richest and most poignant poetry were in Chaplin's work. He could probably panto-mime Bryce's *The American Commonwealth* without ever blurring a syllable and make it paralyzingly funny into the bargain. At the end of *City Lights* the blind girl who has regained her sight, thanks to the Tramp, sees him for the first time. She has imagined and anticipated him as princely, to say the least; and it has never seriously occurred to him that he is inadequate. She recognizes who he must be by his shy, confident, shining joy as he comes silently toward her. And he recognizes himself, for the first time, through the terrible changes in her face. The camera just exchanges a few quiet close-ups of the emotions which shift and intensify in each face. It is enough to shrivel the heart to see, and it is the greatest piece of acting and the highest moment in movies.

Harold Lloyd worked only a little while with Sennett. During most of his career he acted for another major comedy producer, Hal Roach. He tried at first to offset Chaplin's influence and establish his own in-dividuality by playing Chaplin's exact opposite, a character named Lonesome Luke who wore clothes much too small for him and whose gestures were likewise as un-Chaplinesque as possible. But he soon realized that an opposite in itself was a kind of slavishness. He dis-covered his own comic identity when he saw a movie about a fight-ing parson: a hero who wore glasses. He began to think about those glasses day and night. He decided on horn rims because they were youthful, ultravisible on the screen and on the verge of becoming fashionable (he was to make them so). Around these large lensless horn rims he began to develop a new character, nothing grotesque or eccentric, but a fresh, believable young man who could fit into a wide variety of stories.

Lloyd depended more on story and situation than any of the other major comedians (he kept the best stable of gagmen in Hollywood, at one time hiring six); but unlike most "story" comedians he was also a very funny man from inside. He had, as he has written, "an unusually large comic vocabulary." More particularly he had an expertly ex-pressive body and even more expressive teeth, and out of his the-saurus of smiles he could at a moment's notice blend prissiness, breezi-ness and asininity, and still remain tremendously likable. His movies

were more extroverted and closer to ordinary life than any others of
the best comedies: the vicissitudes of a New York taxi driver; the
unaccepted college boy who, by desperate courage and inspired in-
eptitude, wins the Big Game. He was especially good at putting a
very timid, spoiled or brassy young fellow through devastating
embarrassments. He went through one of his most uproarious
Gethsemanes as a shy country youth courting the nicest girl in town
in *Grandma's Boy*. He arrived dressed "strictly up to date for the
Spring of 1862," as a subtitle observed, and found that the ancient
colored butler wore a similar flowered waistcoat and moldering cut-
away. He got one wandering, nervous forefinger dreadfully stuck
in a fancy little vase. The girl began cheerfully to try to identify
that queer smell which dilated from him; Grandpa's best suit was
rife with mothballs. A tenacious litter of kittens feasted off the
goose grease on his home-shined shoes.

Lloyd was even better at the comedy of thrills. In *Safety Last*,
as a rank amateur, he is forced to substitute for a human fly and to
climb a medium-sized skyscraper. Dozens of awful things happen to
him. He gets fouled up in a tennis net. Popcorn falls on him from a
window above, and the local pigeons treat him like a cross between
a lunch wagon and St. Francis of Assisi. A mouse runs up his britches
leg, and the crowd below salutes his desperate dance on the window
ledge with wild applause of the daredevil. A good deal of this full-
length picture hangs thus by its eyelashes along the face of a building.
Each new floor is like a new stanza in a poem; and the higher and
more horrifying it gets, the funnier it gets.

In this movie Lloyd demonstrates beautifully his ability to do more
than merely milk a gag, but to top it. (In an old, simple example of
topping, an incredible number of tall men get, one by one, out of
a small closed auto. After as many have clambered out as the joke
will bear, one more steps out: a midget. That tops the gag. Then the
auto collapses. That tops the topper.) In *Safety Last* Lloyd is driven
out to the dirty end of a flagpole by a furious dog; the pole breaks
and he falls, just managing to grab the minute hand of a huge clock.
His weight promptly pulls the hand down from IX to VI. That would
be more than enough for any ordinary comedian, but there is further
logic in the situation. Now, hideously, the whole clockface pulls
loose and slants from its trembling springs above the street. Getting
out of difficulty with the clock, he makes still further use of the instrument by getting one foot caught in one of these obstinate
springs.

A proper delaying of the ultrapredictable can of course be just as
funny as a properly timed explosion of the unexpected. As Lloyd

approaches the end of his horrible hegira up the side of the building in *Safety Last,* it becomes clear to the audience, but not to him, that if he raises his head another couple of inches he is going to get murderously conked by one of the four arms of a revolving wind gauge. He delays the evil moment almost interminably, with one distraction and another, and every delay is a suspense-tightening laugh; he also gets his foot nicely entangled in a rope, so that when he does get hit, the payoff of one gag sends him careening head downward through the abyss into another. Lloyd was outstanding even among the master craftsmen at setting up a gag clearly, culminating and getting out of it deftly, and linking it smoothly to the next. Harsh experience also taught him a deep and fundamental rule: Never try to get "above" the audience.

Lloyd tried it in *The Freshman.* He was to wear an unfinished, basted-together tuxedo to a college party, which would gradually, fall apart as he danced. Lloyd decided to skip the pants, a low-comedy cliché, and lose just the coat. His gag men warned him. A preview proved how right they were. Lloyd had to reshoot the whole expensive sequence, build it around defective pants and climax it with the inevitable. It was one of the funniest things he ever did.

When Lloyd was still a very young man he lost about half his right hand (and nearly lost his sight) when a comedy bomb exploded prematurely. But in spite of his artificially built-out hand he continued to do his own dirty work, like all of the best comedians. The side of the building he climbed in *Safety Last* did not overhang the street, as it appears to. But the nearest landing place was a roof three floors below him, as he approached the top, and he did everything, of course, the hard way, i.e., the comic way, keeping his bottom stuck well out, his shoulders hunched, his hands and feet skidding over perdition.

If great comedy must involve something beyond laughter, Lloyd was not a great comedian. If plain laughter is any criterion—and it is a healthy counterbalance to the other—few people have equaled him, and nobody has ever beaten him.

Chaplin and Keaton and Lloyd were all more like each other, in one important way, than Harry Langdon was like any of them. Whatever else the others might be doing, they all used more or less elaborate physical comedy; Langdon showed how little of that one might use and still be a great silent-screen comedian. In his screen character he symbolized something as deeply and centrally human, though by no means as rangily so, as the Tramp. There was, of course, an immense difference in inventiveness and range of virtuosity. It seemed as if Chaplin could do literally anything, on any instrument in the orchestra. Langdon had one queerly toned, unique little reed. But out of it he could get incredible melodies.

Like Chaplin, Langdon wore a coat which buttoned on his wishbone and swung out wide below, but the effect was very different: he seemed like an outsized baby who had begun to outgrow his clothes. The crown of his hat was rounded and the brim was turned up all around, like a little boy's hat, and he looked as if he wore diapers under his pants. His walk was that of a child which has just got sure on its feet, and his body and hands fitted that age. His face was kept pale to show off, with the simplicity of a nursery school drawing, the bright, ignorant, gentle eyes and the little twirling mouth. He had big moon cheeks, with dimples, and a Napoleonic forelock of mousy hair; the round, docile head seemed large in ratio to the cream-puff body. Twitchings of his face were signals of tiny discomforts too slowly registered by a tinier brain; quick, squirty little smiles showed his almost prehuman pleasures, his incurably premature trustfulness. He was a virtuoso of hesitations and of delicately indecisive motions, and he was particularly fine in a high wind, rounding a corner with a kind of skittering toddle, both hands nursing his hatbrim.

He was as remarkable a master as Chaplin of subtle emotional and mental process and operated much more at leisure. He once got a good three hundred feet of continuously bigger laughs out of rubbing his chest, in a crowded vehicle, with Limburger cheese, under the misapprehension that it was a cold salve. In another long scene, watching a brazen show girl change her clothes, he sat motionless, back to the camera, and registered the whole lexicon of lost innocence, shock, disapproval and disgust, with the back of his neck. His scenes with women were nearly always something special. Once a lady spy did everything in her power (under the Hays Office) to seduce him. Harry was polite, willing, even flirtatious in his little way. The only trouble was that he couldn't imagine what in the world she was leering and pawing at him for, and that he was terribly ticklish. The Mata Hari wound up foaming at the mouth.

There was also a sinister flicker of depravity about the Langdon character, all the more disturbing because babies are premoral. He had an instinct for bringing his actual adulthood and figurative babyishness into frictions as crawly as a fingernail on a slate blackboard, and he wandered into areas of strangeness which were beyond the other comedians. In a nightmare in one movie he was forced to fight a large, muscular young man; the girl Harry loved was the prize. The young man was a good boxer; Harry could scarcely lift his gloves. The contest took place in a fiercely lighted prize ring, in a prodigious pitch-dark arena. The only spectator was the girl, and she was rooting against Harry. As the fight went on, her eyes glittered ever more brightly with blood lust and, with glittering teeth, she tore her big straw hat to shreds.

Langdon came to Sennett from a vaudeville act in which he had fought a losing battle with a recalcitrant automobile. The minute Frank Capra saw him he begged Sennett to let him work with him. Langdon was almost as childlike as the character he played. He had only a vague idea of his story or even of each scene as he played it; each time he went before the camera Capra would brief him on the general situation and then, as this finest of intuitive improvisers once tried to explain his work, "I'd go into my routine." The whole tragedy of the coming of dialogue as far as these comedians were concerned —and one reason for the increasing rigidity of comedy ever since— can be epitomized in the mere thought of Harry Langdon confronted with a script.

Langdon's magic was in his innocence, and Capra took beautiful care not to meddle with it. The key to the proper use of Langdon, Capra always knew, was "the principle of the brick." "If there was a rule for writing Langdon material," he explains, "it was this: His only ally was God. Langdon might be saved by the brick falling on the cop, but it was *verboten* that he in any way motivate the brick's fall." Langdon became quickly and fantastically popular with three pictures, *Tramp, Tramp, Tramp, The Strong Man* and *Long Pants;* from then on he went downhill even faster. "The trouble was," Capra says, "that high-brow critics came around to explain his art to him. Also he developed an interest in dames. It was a pretty high life for such a little fellow." Langdon made two more pictures with high-brow writers, one of which (*Three's a Crowd*) had some wonderful passages in it, including the prize-ring nightmare; then First National canceled his contract. He was reduced to mediocre roles and two-reelers which were more rehashes of his old gags; this time around they no longer seemed funny. "He never did really understand what hit him," says Capra. "He died broke [in 1944]. And he died of a broken heart. He was the most tragic figure I ever came across in show business."

Buster Keaton started work at the age of three and a half with his parents in one of the roughest acts in vaudeville ("The Three Keatons"); Harry Houdini gave the child the name Buster in admiration for a fall he took down a flight of stairs. In his first movies Keaton teamed with Fatty Arbuckle under Sennett. He went on to become one of Metro's biggest stars and earners; a Keaton feature cost about

$200,000 to make and reliably grossed $2 million. Very early in his movie career friends asked him why he never smiled on the screen. He didn't realize he didn't. He had got the deadpan habit in variety; on the screen he had merely been so hard at work it had never occurred to him there was anything to smile about. Now he tried it just once and never again. He was by his whole style and nature so much the most deeply "silent" of the silent comedians that even a smile was as deafeningly out of key as a yell. In a way his pictures are like a transcendent juggling act in which it seems that the whole universe is in exquisite flying motion and the one point of repose is the juggler's effortless, uninterested face.

Keaton's face ranked almost with Lincoln's as an early American archetype; it was haunting, handsome, almost beautiful, yet it was irreducibly funny; he improved matters by topping it off with a deadly horizontal hat, as flat and thin as a phonograph record. One can never forget Keaton wearing it, standing erect at the prow as his little boat is being launched. The boat goes grandly down the skids and, just as grandly, straight on to the bottom. Keaton never budges. The last you see of him, the water lifts the hat off the stoic head and it floats away.

No other comedian could do as much with the deadpan. He used this great, sad, motionless face to suggest various related things: a one-track mind near the track's end of pure insanity; mulish imperturbability under the wildest of circumstances; how dead a human being can get and still be alive; an awe-inspiring sort of patience and power to endure, proper to granite but uncanny in flesh and blood. Everything that he was and did bore out this rigid face and played laughs against it. When he moved his eyes, it was like seeing them move in a statue. His short-legged body was all sudden, machinelike angles, governed by a daft aplomb. When he swept a semaphorelike arm to point, you could almost hear the electrical impulse in the signal block. When he ran from a cop his transitions from accelerating walk to easy jog trot to brisk canter to headlong gallop to flogged-piston sprint—always floating, above this frenzy, the untroubled, untouchable face—were as distinct and as soberly in order as an automatic gearshift.

Keaton was a wonderfully resourceful inventor of mechanistic gags (he still spends much of his time fooling with Erector sets); as he ran afoul of locomotives, steamships, prefabricated and overelectrified houses, he put himself through some of the hardest and cleverest punishment ever designed for laughs. In *Sherlock Jr.*, boiling along on the handlebars of a motorcycle quite unaware that he has lost his driver, Keaton whips through city traffic, breaks up a tug-of-war, gets a shovelful of dirt in the face from each of a long line of Rockette-timed ditchdiggers, approaches at high speed a log which is hinged open by dynamite precisely soon enough to let him through and, hitting an obstruction, leaves the handlebars like an arrow leaving a bow, whams through the window of a shack in which the heroine is about to be violated, and hits the heavy feet first, knocking him through the opposite wall. The whole sequence is as clean in motion as the trajectory of a bullet.

Much of the charm and edge of Keaton's comedy, however, lay in the subtle leverages of expression he could work against his nominal deadpan. Trapped in the side wheel of a ferryboat, saving himself from drowning only by walking, then desperately running, inside the accelerating wheel like a squirrel in a cage, his only real concern was, obviously, to keep his hat on. Confronted by Love, he was not as deadpan as he was cracked up to be, either; there was an odd, abrupt motion of his head which suggested a horse nipping after a sugar lump.

Keaton worked strictly for laughs, but his work came from so far inside a curious and original spirit that he achieved a great deal besides, especially in his feature-length comedies. (For plain hard laughter his nineteen short comedies—the negatives of which have been lost—were even better.) He was the only major comedian who kept sentiment almost entirely out of his work, and he brought pure physical comedy to its greatest heights. Beneath his lack of emotion he was also uninsistently sardonic; deep below that, giving a disturbing tension and grandeur to the foolishness, for those who sensed it, there was in his comedy a freezing whisper not of pathos but of melancholia. With the humor, the craftsmanship and the action there was often, besides, a fine, still and sometimes dreamlike beauty. Much of his Civil War picture *The General* is within hailing distance of Mathew Brady. And there is a ghostly, unforgettable moment in *The Navigator* when, on a deserted, softly rolling ship, all the pale doors along a deck swing open as one behind Keaton and, as one, slam shut, in a hair-raising illusion of noise.

Perhaps because "dry" comedy is so much more rare and odd than "dry" wit, there are people who never much cared for Keaton. Those who do cannot care mildly.

As soon as the screen began to talk, silent comedy was pretty well finished. The hardy and prolific Mack Sennett made the transfer; he was the first man to put Bing Crosby and W. C. Fields on the screen. But he was essentially a silent-picture man, and by the time the Academy awarded him a special Oscar for his "lasting contribution to the comedy technique of the screen" (in 1938), he was no longer active. As for the comedians we have spoken of in particular, they were as badly off as fine dancers suddenly required to appear in plays.

Harold Lloyd, whose work was most nearly realistic, naturally coped least unhappily with the added realism of speech; he made several talking comedies. But good as the best were, they were not so good as his silent work, and by the late '30s he quit acting. A few years ago he returned to play the lead (and play it beautifully) in Preston Sturges' *The Sin of Harold Diddlebock*, but this exceptional picture—which opened, brilliantly, with the closing reel of Lloyd's *The Freshman*—has not yet been generally released.

Like Chaplin, Lloyd was careful of his money; he is still rich and active. Last June, in the presence of President Truman, he became Imperial Potentate of the A.A.O.N.M.S. (Shriners). Harry Langdon, as we have said, was a broken man when sound came in.

Up to the middle '30s Buster Keaton made several feature-length pictures (with such players as Jimmy Durante, Wallace Beery and Robert Montgomery); he also made a couple of dozen talking shorts. Now and again he managed to get loose into motion, without having to talk, and for a moment or so the screen would start singing again. But his dark, dead voice, though it was in keeping with the visual character, tore his intensely silent style to bits and destroyed the illusion within which he worked. He gallantly and correctly refuses to regard himself as "retired." Besides occasional bits, spots and minor roles in Hollywood pictures, he has worked on summer stages, made talking comedies in France and Mexico and clowned in a French circus. This summer he has played the straw hats in *Three Men on a Horse*. He is planning a television program. He also has a working agreement with Metro. One of his jobs there is to construct comedy sequences for Red Skelton.

The only man who really survived the flood was Chaplin, the only one who was rich, proud and popular enough to afford to stay silent. He brought out two of his greatest nontalking comedies, *City Lights* and *Modern Times*, in the middle of an avalanche of talk, spoke gibberish and, in the closing moments, plain English in *The Great Dictator*, and at last made an all-talking picture, *Monsieur Verdoux*, creating for that purpose an entirely new character who might properly talk a blue streak. *Verdoux* is the greatest of talking comedies though so cold and savage that it had to find its public in grimly experienced Europe.

Good comedy, and some that was better than good, outlived silence, but there has been less and less of it. The talkies brought one great comedian, the late, majestically lethargic W. C. Fields, who could not possibly have worked as well in silence; he was the toughest and the most warmly human of all screen comedians, and *It's a Gift* and *The Bank Dick*, fiendishly funny and incisive white-collar comedies, rank high among the best comedies (and best movies) ever made. Laurel and Hardy, the only comedians who managed to preserve much of the large, low style of silence and who began to explore the comedy of sound, have made nothing since 1945. Walt Disney, at his best an inspired comic inventor and teller of fairy stories, lost his stride during the war and has since regained it only at moments. Preston Sturges has made brilliant, satirical comedies, but his pictures are smart, nervous comedy-dramas merely italicized with slapstick. The Marx Brothers were sidesplitters but they made their best comedies years ago. Jimmy Durante is mainly a night-club genius; Abbott and Costello are semiskilled laborers, at best; Bob Hope is a good radio comedian with a pleasing presence, but not much more, on the screen.

There is no hope that screen comedy will get much better than it is without new, gifted young comedians who really belong in movies, and without freedom for their experiments. For everyone who may appear we have one last, invidious comparison to offer as a guidepost.

One of the most popular recent comedies is Bob Hope's *The Paleface*. We take no pleasure in blackening *The Paleface;* we single it out, rather, because it is as good as we've got. Anything that is said of it here could be said, with interest, of other comedies of our time. Most of the laughs in *The Paleface* are verbal. Bob Hope is very adroit with his lines and now and then, when the words don't get in the way, he makes a good beginning as a visual comedian. But only the beginning, never the middle or the end. He is funny, for instance, reacting to a shot of violent whisky. But he does not know how to get still funnier (i.e., how to build and milk) or how to be funniest last (i.e., how to top or cap his gag). The camera has to fade out on the same old face he started with.

One sequence is promisingly set up for visual comedy. In it, Hope and a lethal local boy stalk each other all over a cow town through streets which have been emptied in fear of their duel. The gag here is that through accident and stupidity they keep just failing to find each other. Some of it is quite funny. But the fun slackens between laughs like a weak clothesline, and by all the logic of humor (which is ruthlessly logical) the biggest laugh should come at the moment, and through the way, they finally spot each other. The sequence is so weakly thought out that at that crucial moment the camera can't afford to watch them; it switches to Jane Russell.

Now we turn to a masterpiece. In *The Navigator* Buster Keaton

works with practically the same gag as Hope's duel. Adrift on a ship
which he believes is otherwise empty, he drops a lighted cigarette. A
girl finds it. She calls out and he hears her; each then tries to find the
other. First each walks purposefully down the long, vacant starboard
deck, the girl, then Keaton, turning the corner just in time not to see
each other. Next time around each of them is trotting briskly, very
much in earnest; going at the same pace, they miss each other just
the same. Next time around each of them is going like a bat out of
hell. Again they miss. Then the camera withdraws to a point of van-
tage at the stern, leans its chin in its hand and just watches the whole
intricate superstructure of the ship as the protagonists stroll, steal
and scuttle from level to level, up, down and sidewise, always managing to miss each other by hairbreadths, in an enchantingly neat
and elaborate piece of timing. There are no subsidiary gags to get
laughs in this sequence and there is little loud laughter; merely a quiet
and steadily increasing kind of delight. When Keaton has got all he
can out of this fine modification of the movie chase he invents a fine
device to bring the two together: the girl, thoroughly winded, sits
down for a breather, indoors, on a plank which workmen have left
across sawhorses. Keaton pauses on an upper deck, equally winded
and puzzled. What follows happens in a couple of seconds at most:
Air suction whips his silk topper backward down a ventilator; grab-
bing frantically for it, he backs against the lip of the ventilator,
jackknifes and falls in backward. Instantly the camera cuts back to
the girl. A topper falls through the ceiling and lands tidily, right
side up, on the plank beside her. Before she can look more than
startled, its owner follows, head between his knees, crushes the
topper, breaks the plank with the point of his spine and proceeds to
the floor. The breaking of the plank smacks Boy and Girl together.

It is only fair to remember that the silent comedians would have as
hard a time playing a talking scene as Hope has playing his visual ones,
and that writing and directing are as accountable for the failure as
Hope himself. But not even the humblest journeymen of the silent
years would have let themselves off so easily. Like the masters, they
knew, and sweated to obey, the laws of their craft.

The

Westerner

---

by Robert Warshow

Because of its obvious symbolism, scenic possibilities and message-proneness, the Western movie has always been a favorite among film makers. Unfortunately a lot of nonsense has been written about the alleged hidden meanings in Westerns. Robert Warshow's analysis of several well-known Westerns is a distinct exception (published in Partisan Review, *March 1954). It is one of the very few statements that fully explores the significance of style and content in this genre.*

They that have power to hurt and will do none,
That do not do the thing they most do show,
Who, moving others, are themselves as stone,
Unmoved, cold, and to temptation slow;
They rightly do inherit heaven's graces,
And husband nature's riches from expense;
They are the lords and owners of their faces,
Others but stewards of their excellence.

The two most successful creations of American movies are the gangster and the Westerner: men with guns. Guns as physical objects, and the postures associated with their use, form the visual and emotional center of both types of films. I suppose this reflects the importance of guns in the fantasy life of Americans; but that is a less illuminating point than it appears to be.

The gangster movie, which no longer exists in its "classical" form, is a story of enterprise and success ending in precipitate failure. Success is conceived as an increasing power to work injury, it belongs to the city, and it is of course a form of evil (though the gangster's death, presented usually as "punishment," is perceived simply as defeat). The peculiarity of the gangster is his unceasing, nervous activity. The exact nature of his enterprises may remain vague, but his commitment to enterprise is always clear, and all the more clear because he operates outside the field of utility. He is without culture, without manners, without leisure, or at any rate his leisure is likely to be spent in debauchery so compulsively aggressive as to seem only another aspect of his "work." But he is graceful, moving like a dancer among the crowded dangers of the city.

Like other tycoons, the gangster is crude in conceiving his ends but by no means inarticulate; on the contrary, he is usually expansive and noisy (the introspective gangster is a fairly recent development), and can state definitely what he wants: to take over the North Side, to own a hundred suits, to be Number One. But new "frontiers" will present themselves infinitely, and by a rigid convention it is understood that as soon as he wishes to rest on his gains, he is on the way to destruction.

The gangster is lonely and melancholy, and can give the impression of a profound worldly wisdom. He appeals most to adolescents with their impatience and their feeling of being outsiders, but more generally he appeals to that side of all of us which refuses to believe in the "normal" possibilities of happiness and achievement; the gangster is the "no" to that great American "yes" which is stamped so big over our official culture and yet has so little to do with the way we really feel about our lives. But the gangster's loneliness and melancholy are not "authentic"; like everything else that belongs to him, they are not honestly come by: he is lonely and melancholy not because life ultimately demands such feelings but because he has put himself in a position where everybody wants to kill him and eventually somebody will. He is wide open and defenseless, incomplete because unable to accept any limits or come to terms with his own nature, fearful, loveless. And the story of his career is a nightmare inversion of the values of ambition and opportunity. From the window of Scarface's bulletproof apartment can be seen an electric sign proclaiming, "The World Is Yours," and, if I remember, this sign is the last thing we see after Scarface lies dead in the street. In the end it is the gangster's weakness as much as his power and freedom that appeals to us; the world is not ours, but it is not his either, and in his death he "pays" for our fantasies, releasing us momentarily both from the concept of success, which he denies by caricaturing it, and from the need to succeed, which he shows to be dangerous.[1]

The Western hero, by contrast, is a figure of repose. He resembles the gangster in being lonely and to some degree melancholy. But his melancholy comes from the "simple" recognition that life is unavoidably serious, not from the disproportions of his own temperament. And his loneliness is organic, not imposed on him by his situation but belonging to him intimately and testifying to his completeness. The gangster must reject others violently or draw them violently to him. The Westerner is not thus compelled to seek love; he is prepared to accept it, perhaps, but he never asks of it more than it can give, and we see him constantly in situations where love is at best an irrelevance. If there is a woman he loves, she is usually unable to understand his motives; she is against killing and being killed, and he finds it impossible to explain to her that there is no point in being "against" these things: they belong to his world.

Very often this woman is from the East and her failure to understand represents a clash of cultures. In the American mind, refinement, virtue, civilization, Christianity itself, are seen as feminine, and therefore women are often portrayed as possessing some kind of deeper wisdom, while the men, for all their apparent self-assurance, are fundamentally childish. But the West, lacking the graces of civilization, is the place "where men are men"; in Western movies, men have the deeper wisdom and the women are children. Those women in the Western movies who share the hero's understanding of life are prostitutes (or, as they are usually presented, barroom entertainers)—women, that is, who have come to understand in the most practical way how love can be an irrelevance, and therefore "fallen" women. The gangster, too, associates with prostitutes, but for him the important things about a prostitute are her passive availability and her costliness; she is part of his winnings. In Western movies, the important thing about a prostitute is her quasi-masculine independence: nobody owns her, nothing has to be explained to her, and she is not, like a virtuous woman, a "value" that demands to be protected. When the Westerner leaves the prostitute for a virtuous woman—for love—he is in fact forsaking a way of life,

---

[1] I discussed gangster movies at greater length in an article called "The Gangster as Tragic Hero" (*PR*, February 1948).

though the point of the choice is often obscured by having the prostitute killed by getting into the line of fire.

The Westerner is par excellence a man of leisure. Even when he wears the badge of a marshal or, more rarely, owns a ranch, he appears to be unemployed. We see him standing at a bar, or playing poker—a game which expresses perfectly his talent for remaining relaxed in the midst of tension—or perhaps camping out on the plains on some extraordinary errand. If he does own a ranch, it is in the background; we are not actually aware that he owns anything except his horse, his guns, and the one worn suit of clothing which is likely to remain unchanged all through the movie. It comes as a surprise to see him take money from his pocket or an extra shirt from his saddlebags. As a rule we do not even know where he sleeps at night and don't think of asking. Yet it never occurs to us that he is a poor man. There is no poverty in Western movies, and really no wealth either; those great cattle domains and shipments of gold which figure so largely in the plots are moral and not material quantities, not the objects of contention but only its occasion. Possessions too are irrelevant.

Employment of some kind—usually unproductive—is always open to the Westerner, but when he accepts it, it is not because he needs to make a living, much less from any idea of "getting ahead." Where could he want to "get ahead" to? By the time we see him, he is already "there"; he can ride a horse faultlessly, keep his countenance in the face of death, and draw his gun a little faster and shoot it a little straighter than anyone he is likely to meet. These are sharply defined acquirements, giving to the figure of the Westerner an apparent moral clarity which corresponds to the clarity of his physical image against his bare landscape; initially, at any rate, the Western movie presents itself as being without mystery, its whole universe comprehended in what we see on the screen.

Much of this apparent simplicity arises directly from those "cinematic" elements which have long been understood to give the Western theme its special appropriateness for the movies: the wide expanses of land, the free movement of men on horses. As guns constitute the visible moral center of the Western movie, suggesting continually the possibility of violence, so land and horses represent the movie's material basis, its sphere of action. But the land and the horses have also a moral significance; the physical freedom they represent belongs to the moral "openness" of the West—corresponding to the fact that guns are carried where they can be seen. (And, as we shall see, the character of land and horses changes as the Western film becomes more complex.)

The gangster's world is less open, and his arts not so easily identifiable as the Westerner's. Perhaps he too can keep his countenance, but the mask he wears is really no mask; its purpose is precisely to make evident the fact that he desperately wants to "get ahead" and will stop at nothing. Where the Westerner imposes himself by the appearance of unshakable control, the gangster's pre-eminence lies in the suggestion that he may at any moment lose control; his strength is not in being able to shoot faster or straighter than others, but in being more willing to shoot. "Do it first," says Scarface, expounding his mode of operation, "and keep on doing it!" With the Westerner, it is a crucial point of honor *not* to "do it first"; his gun remains in its holster until the moment of combat.

There is no suggestion, however, that he draws the gun reluctantly. The Westerner could not fulfill himself if the moment did not finally come when he can shoot his enemy down. But because that moment is so thoroughly the expression of his being, it must be kept pure. He will not violate the accepted forms of combat though by doing so he could save a city. And he can wait. "When you call me that—smile!"—the villain smiles weakly, soon he is laughing with horrible joviality, and the crisis is past. But it is allowed to pass because it must come again; sooner or later Trampas will "make his play," and the Virginian will be ready for him.

What does the Westerner fight for? We know he is on the side of justice and order, and of course it can be said he fights for these things. But such broad aims never correspond exactly to his real motives; they only offer him his opportunity. The Westerner himself, when an explanation is asked of him (usually by a woman), is likely to say that he does what he "has to do." If justice and order did not continually demand his protection, he would be without a calling. Indeed, we come upon him often in just that situation, as the reign of law settles over the West and he is forced to see that his day is over; those are the pictures which end with his death or with his departure for some more remote frontier. What he defends, at bottom, is the purity of his own image—in fact his honor. This is what makes him invulnerable. When the gangster is killed, his whole life is shown to have been a mistake, but the image the Westerner seeks to maintain can be presented as clearly in defeat as in victory: he fights not for advantage and not for the right, but to state what he is, and he must live in a world which permits that statement. The Westerner is the last gentleman, and the movies which over and over again tell his story are probably the last art form in which the concept of honor retains its strength.

Of course I do not mean to say that ideas of virtue and justice and courage have gone out of culture. Honor is more than these things; it is a style, concerned with harmonious appearances as much as with desirable consequences, and tending therefore toward the denial of life in favor of art. "Who hath it? he that died o' Wednesday." On the whole, a world that leans to Falstaff's view is a more civilized and even, finally, a more graceful world. It is just the march of civilization that forces the Westerner to move on; and if we actually had to confront the question it might turn out that the woman who refuses to understand him is right as often as she is wrong. But we do not confront the question. Where the Westerner lives it is always about 1870—not the real 1870, either, or the real West—and he is killed or goes away when his position becomes problematical. The fact that he continues to hold our attention is evidence enough that, in his proper frame, he presents an image of personal nobility that is still real for us.

Clearly, this image easily becomes ridiculous; we need only look at William S. Hart or Tom Mix, who in the wooden absoluteness of their virtue represented little that an adult could take seriously; and doubtless such figures as Gene Autry or Roy Rogers are no better, though I confess I have seen none of their movies. Some film enthusiasts claim to find in the early, unsophisticated Westerns a "cinematic purity" that has since been lost; this idea is as valid, and finally as misleading, as T. S. Eliot's statement that *Everyman* is the only play in English that stays within the limitations of art. The truth is that the Westerner comes into the field of serious art only when his moral code, without ceasing to be compelling, is seen also to be imperfect. The Westerner at his best exhibits a moral ambiguity which darkens his image and saves him from absurdity; this ambiguity arises from the fact that, whatever his justifications, he is a killer of men.

In *The Virginian*, which is an archetypal Western movie as *Scarface* or *Little Caesar* are archetypal gangster movies, there is a lynching in which the hero (Gary Cooper), as leader of a posse, must supervise the hanging of his best friend for stealing cattle. With the growth of American "social consciousness," it is no longer possible to present a lynching in the movies unless the point is the illegality and injustice of the lynching itself; *The Ox-Bow Incident*, made in 1943, explicitly puts forward the newer point of view and can be regarded as a kind of "anti-Western." But in 1929, when *The Virginian* was made, the present inhibition about lynching was not yet in force; the justice, and therefore the necessity, of the hanging is never questioned—except by the schoolteacher from the East, whose refusal to understand serves as usual to set forth more

sharply the deeper seriousness of the West. The Virginian is thus
in a tragic dilemma where one moral absolute conflicts with another
and the choice of either must leave a moral stain. If he had chosen
to save his friend, he would have violated the image of himself that
he had made essential to his existence, and the movie would have
had to end with his death, for only by his death could the image
have been restored. Having chosen instead to sacrifice his friend to
the higher demands of the "code"—the only choice worthy of him,
as even the friend understands—he is none the less stained by the
killing, but what is needed now to set accounts straight is not his
death but the death of the villain Trampas, the leader of the cattle
thieves, who had escaped the posse and abandoned the Virginian's
friend to his fate. Again the woman intervenes: Why must there be
more killing? If the hero really loved her, he would leave town, refusing Trampas' challenge. What good will it be if Trampas should
kill him? But the Virginian does once more what he "has to do"
and in avenging his friend's death wipes out the stain on his own
honor. Yet his victory cannot be complete: no death can be paid for
and no stain truly wiped out; the movie is still a tragedy, for though
the hero escapes with his life, he has been forced to confront the
ultimate limits of his moral ideas.

This mature sense of limitation and unavoidable guilt is what
gives the Westerner a "right" to his melancholy. It is true that the
gangster's story is also a tragedy—in certain formal ways more
clearly a tragedy than the Westerner's—but it is a romantic tragedy,
based on a hero whose defeat springs with almost mechanical inevitability from the outrageous presumption of his demands: the gangster is *bound* to go on until he is killed. The Westerner is a more
classical figure, self-contained and limited to begin with, seeking
not to extend his dominion but only to assert his personal value, and
his tragedy lies in the fact that even this circumscribed demand
cannot be fully realized. Since the Westerner is not a murderer but
(most of the time) a man of virtue, and since he is always prepared
for defeat, he retains his inner invulnerability and his story need
not end with his death (and usually does not); but what we finally
respond to is not his victory but his defeat.

Up to a point, it is plain that the deeper seriousness of the good
Western films comes from the introduction of a realism, both physi-
cal and psychological, that was missing with Tom Mix and William
S. Hart. As lines of age have come into Gary Cooper's face since
The Virginian, so the outlines of the Western movie in general have
become less smooth, its background more drab. The sun still beats

upon the town, but the camera is likely now to take advantage of this illumination to seek out more closely the shabbiness of buildings and furniture, the loose, worn hang of clothing, the wrinkles and dirt of the faces. Once it has been discovered that the true theme of the Western movie is not the freedom and expansiveness of frontier life, but its limitations, its material bareness, the pressures of obligation, then even the landscape itself ceases to be quite the arena of free movement it once was, but becomes instead a great empty waste, cutting down more often than it exaggerates the stature of the horseman who rides across it. We are more likely now to see the Westerner struggling against the obstacles of the physical world (as in the wonderful scenes on the desert and among the rocks in *The Last Posse*) than carelessly surmounting them. Even the horses, no longer the "friends" of man or the inspired chargers of knight-errantry, have lost much of the moral significance that once seemed to belong to them in their careering across the screen. It seems to me the horses grow tired and stumble more often than they did, and that we see them less frequently at the gallop.

In *The Gunfighter*, a remarkable film of a couple of years ago, the landscape has virtually disappeared. Most of the action takes place indoors, in a cheerless saloon where a tired "bad man" (Gregory Peck) contemplates the waste of his life, to be senselessly killed at the end by a vicious youngster setting off on the same futile path. The movie is done in cold, quiet tones of gray, and every object in it—faces, clothing, a table, the hero's heavy mustache—is given an air of uncompromising authenticity, suggesting those dim photographs of the nineteenth-century West in which Wyatt Earp, say, turns out to be a blank untidy figure posing awkwardly before some uninteresting building. This "authenticity," to be sure, is only aesthetic; the chief fact about nineteenth-century photographs, to my eyes at any rate, is how stonily they refuse to yield up the truth. But that limitation is just what is needed: by preserving some hint of the rigidity of archaic photography (only in tone and *décor*, never in composition), *The Gunfighter* can permit us to feel that we are looking at a more "real" West than the one the movies have accustomed us to—harder, duller, less "romantic"—and yet without forcing us outside the boundaries which give the Western movie its validity.

We come upon the hero of *The Gunfighter* at the end of a career in which he has never upheld justice and order, and has been at times, apparently, an actual criminal; in this case, it is clear that the hero has been wrong and the woman who has rejected his way of life has been right. He is thus without any of the larger justifications and

knows himself a ruined man. There can be no question of his "re-
deeming" himself in any socially constructive way. He is too much
the victim of his own reputation to turn marshal as one of his old
friends has done, and he is not offered the sentimental solution of a
chance to give up his life for some good end; the whole point is that
he exists outside the field of social value. Indeed, if we were once allowed to see him in the days of his "success," he might become a
figure like the gangster, for his career has been aggressively "antisocial" and the practical problem he faces is the gangster's problem:
there will always be somebody trying to kill him. Yet it is obviously
absurd to speak of him as "antisocial," not only because we do not
see him acting as a criminal, but more fundamentally because we do
not see his milieu as a society. Of course it has its "social problems"
and a kind of static history: civilization is always just at the point of
driving out the old freedom; there are women and children to represent the possibility of a settled life; and there is the marshal, a bad man
turned good, determined to keep at least his area of jurisdiction at
peace. But these elements are not, in fact, a part of the film's "realism," even though they come out of the real history of the West; they
belong to the conventions of the form, to that accepted framework
which makes the film possible in the first place, and they exist not to
provide a standard by which the gunfighter can be judged, but only
to set him off. The true "civilization" of the Western movie is always
embodied in an individual, good or bad is more a matter of personal
bearing than of social consequences, and the conflict of good and bad
is a duel between two men. Deeply troubled and obviously doomed,
the gunfighter is the Western hero still, perhaps all the more because
his value must express itself entirely in his own being—in his presence,
the way he holds our eyes—and in contradiction to the facts. No
matter what he has done, he *looks* right, and he remains invulnerable
because, without acknowledging anyone else's right to judge him,
he has judged his own failure and has already assimilated it, understanding—as no one else understands except the marshal and the barroom girl—that he can do nothing but play out the drama of the gun
fight again and again until the time comes when it will be he who
gets killed. What "redeems" him is that he no longer believes in this
drama and nevertheless will continue to play his role perfectly; the
pattern is all.

  The proper function of realism in the Western movie can only be
to deepen the lines of that pattern. It is an art form for connoisseurs,
where the spectator derives his pleasure from the appreciation of
minor variations within the working out of a pre-established order.
One does not want too much novelty; it comes as a shock, for instance,

when the hero is made to operate without a gun, as has been done in several pictures (e.g., *Destry Rides Again*), and our uneasiness is allayed only when he is finally compelled to put his "pacifism" aside. If the hero can be shown to be troubled, complex, fallible, even eccentric, or the villain given some psychological taint or, better, some evocative physical mannerism, to shade the colors of his villainy, that is all to the good. Indeed, that kind of variation is absolutely necessary to keep the type from becoming sterile; we do not want to see the same movie over and over again, only the same form. But when the impulse toward realism is extended into a "reinterpretation" of the West as a developed society, drawing our eyes away from the hero if only to the extent of showing him as the one dominant figure in a complex social order, then the pattern is broken and the West itself begins to be uninteresting. If the "social problems" of the frontier are to be the movie's chief concern, there is no longer any point in re-examining these problems twenty times a year; they have been solved, and the people for whom they once were real are dead. Moreover, the hero himself, still the film's central figure, now tends to become its one unassimilable element, since he is the most "unreal."

The Ox-Bow Incident, by denying the convention of the lynching, presents us with a modern "social drama" and evokes a corresponding response, but in doing so it almost makes the Western setting irrelevant, a mere backdrop of beautiful scenery. (It is significant that *The Ox-Bow Incident* has no hero; a hero would have to stop the lynching or be killed in trying to stop it, and then the "problem" of lynching would no longer be central.) Even in *The Gunfighter* the women and children are a little too much in evidence, threatening constantly to become a real focus of concern instead of simply part of the given framework, and the young tough who kills the hero has too much the air of juvenile criminality; the hero himself could never have been like that, and the idea of a cycle being repeated therefore loses its sharpness. But the most striking example of the confusion created by a too conscientious "social" realism is in the celebrated *High Noon.*

In *High Noon* we find Gary Cooper still the upholder of order that he was in *The Virginian,* but twenty-four years older, stooped, slower moving, awkward, his face lined, the flesh sagging, a less beautiful and weaker figure, but with the suggestion of greater depth that belongs almost automatically to age. Like the hero of *The Gunfighter,* he no longer has to assert his character and is no longer interested in the drama of combat; it is hard to imagine that he might once have been so youthful as to say, "When you call me that—smile!" In fact, when we come upon him he is hanging up his guns and his marshal's

badge in order to begin a new, peaceful life with his bride, who is a
Quaker. But then the news comes that a man he sent to prison has
been pardoned and will get to town on the noon train; three friends of
this man have come to wait for him at the station, and when the freed
convict arrives the four of them will come to kill the marshal. He is
thus trapped; the bride will object, the hero himself will waver much
more than he would have done twenty-four years ago, but in the end
he will play out the drama because it is what he "has to do." All this
belongs to the established form (there is even the "fallen woman"
who understands the marshal's position as his wife does not). Leaving
aside the crudity of building up suspense by means of the clock, the
actual Western drama of *High Noon* is well handled and forms a
good companion piece to *The Virginian*, showing in both conception
and technique the ways in which the Western movie has naturally
developed.

But there is a second drama along with the first. As the marshal
sets out to find deputies to help him deal with the four gunmen, we
are taken through the various social strata of the town, each group
in turn refusing its assistance out of cowardice, malice, irresponsibility, or venality. With this we are in the field of "social drama"—of
a very low order, incidentally, altogether unconvincing and displaying a vulgar antipopulism that has marred some other movies of
Stanley Kramer's. But the falsity of the "social drama" is less important than the fact that it does not belong in the movie to begin with.
The technical problem was to make it necessary for the marshal to
face his enemies alone; to explain *why* the other townspeople are not
at his side is to raise a question which does not exist in the proper
frame of the Western movie, where the hero is "naturally" alone and
it is only necessary to contrive the physical absence of those who
might be his allies, if any contrivance is needed at all. In addition,
though the hero of *High Noon* proves himself a better man than all
around him, the actual effect of this contrast is to lessen his stature:
he becomes only a rejected man of virtue. In our final glimpse of him,
as he rides away through the town where he has spent most of his
life without really imposing himself on it, he is a pathetic rather than
a tragic figure. And his departure has another meaning as well; the
"social drama" has no place for him.

But there is also a different way of violating the Western form.
This is to yield entirely to its static quality as legend and to the
"cinematic" temptations of its landscape, the horses, the quiet men.
John Ford's famous *Stagecoach* (1938) had much of this unhappy
preoccupation with style, and the same director's *My Darling Clementine* (1946), a soft and beautiful movie about Wyatt Earp, goes

further along the same path, offering indeed a superficial accuracy
of historical reconstruction, but so loving in execution as to destroy
the outlines of the Western legend, assimilating it to the more sentimental legend of rural America and making the hero a more dangerous
Mr. Deeds. (*Powder River*, a recent "routine" Western shamelessly
copied from *My Darling Clementine*, is in most ways a better film;
lacking the benefit of a serious director, it is necessarily more concerned with drama than with style.)

The highest expression of this aestheticizing tendency is in George
Stevens' *Shane*, where the legend of the West is virtually reduced
to its essentials and then fixed in the dreamy clarity of a fairy tale.
There never was so broad and bare and lovely a landscape as Stevens
puts before us, or so unimaginably comfortless a "town" as the little
group of buildings on the prairie to which the settlers must come for
their supplies and to buy a drink. The mere physical progress of the
film, following the style of *A Place in the Sun*, is so deliberately
graceful that everything seems to be happening at the bottom of a
clear lake. The hero (Alan Ladd) is hardly a man at all, but something
like the Spirit of the West, beautiful in fringed buckskins. He emerges
mysteriously from the plains, breathing sweetness and a melancholy
which is no longer simply the Westerner's natural response to
experience but has taken on spirituality; and when he has accomplished his mission, meeting and destroying in the black figure of Jack
Palance a Spirit of Evil just as metaphysical as his own embodiment
of virtue, he fades away again into the more distant West, a man
whose "day is over," leaving behind the wondering little boy who
might have imagined the whole story. The choice of Alan Ladd to
play the leading role is alone an indication of this film's tendency.
Actors like Gary Cooper or Gregory Peck are in themselves, as
material objects, "realistic," seeming to bear in their bodies and their
faces mortality, imitation, the knowledge of good and evil. Ladd is
a more "aesthetic" object, with some of the "universality" of a piece
of sculpture; his special quality is in his physical smoothness and
serenity, unworldly and yet not innocent, but suggesting that no
experience can really touch him. Stevens has tried to freeze the
Western myth once and for all in the immobility of Alan Ladd's
countenance. If *Shane* were "right," and fully successful, it might
be possible to say there was no point in making any more Western
movies; once the hero is apotheosized, variation and development
are closed off.

Shane is not "right," but it is still true that the possibilities of
fruitful variation in the Western movie are limited. The form can

keep its freshness through endless repetitions only because of the special character of the film medium, where the physical difference between one object and another—above all, between one actor and another—is of such enormous importance, serving the function that is served by the variety of language in the perpetuation of literary types. In this sense, the "vocabulary" of films is much larger than that of literature and falls more readily into pleasing and significant arrangements. (That may explain why the middle levels of excellence are more easily reached in the movies than in literary forms, and perhaps also why the status of the movies as art is constantly being called into question.) But the advantage of this almost automatic particularity belongs to all films alike. Why does the Western movie especially have such a hold on our imagination?

Chiefly, I think, because it offers a serious orientation to the problem of violence such as can be found almost nowhere else in our culture. One of the well-known peculiarities of modern civilized opinion is its refusal to acknowledge the value of violence. This refusal is a virtue, but like many virtues it involves a certain willful blindness and it encourages hypocrisy. We train ourselves to be shocked or bored by cultural images of violence, and our very concept of heroism tends to be a passive one: we are less drawn to the brave young men who kill large numbers of our enemies than to the heroic prisoners who endure torture without capitulating. In art, though we may still be able to understand and participate in the values of the *Iliad*, a modern writer like Ernest Hemingway we find somewhat embarrassing: there is no doubt that he stirs us, but we cannot help recognizing also that he is a little childish. And in the criticism of popular culture, where the educated observer is usually under the illusion that he has nothing at stake, the presence of images of violence is often assumed to be in itself a sufficient ground for condemnation.

These attitudes, however, have not reduced the element of violence in our culture but, if anything, have helped to free it from moral control by letting it take on the aura of "emancipation." The celebration of acts of violence is left more and more to the irresponsible—on the higher cultural levels to writers like Céline, and lower down to Mickey Spillane or Horace McCoy, or to the comic books, television, and the movies. The gangster movie, with its numerous variations, belongs to this cultural "underground" which sets forth the attractions of violence in the face of all our higher social attitudes. It is a more "modern" genre than the Western, perhaps even more profound, because it confronts industrial society on its own ground— the city—and because, like much of our advanced art, it gains its effects by a gross insistence on its own narrow logic. But it is anti-

social, resting on fantasies of irresponsible freedom. If we are brought
finally to acquiesce in the denial of these fantasies, it is only because
they have been shown to be dangerous, not because they have given
way to a better vision of behavior.[2]

In war movies, to be sure, it is possible to present the uses of violence
within a framework of responsibility. But there is the disadvantage
that modern war is a co-operative enterprise; its violence is largely
impersonal, and heroism belongs to the group more than to the
individual. The hero of a war movie is most often simply a leader,
and his superiority is likely to be expressed in a denial of the heroic:
you are not supposed to be brave, you are supposed to get the job
done and stay alive (this too, of course, is a kind of heroic posture,
but a new—and "practical"—one). At its best, the war movie may
represent a more civilized point of view than the Western, and if it
were not continually marred by ideological sentimentality we might
hope to find it developing into a higher form of drama. But it cannot
supply the values we seek in the Western.

Those values are in the image of a single man who wears a gun on
his thigh. The gun tells us that he lives in a world of violence, and even
that he "believes in violence." But the drama is one of self-restraint:
the moment of violence must come in its own time and according to
its special laws, or else it is valueless. There is little cruelty in Western
movies, and little sentimentality; our eyes are not focused on the
sufferings of the defeated but on the deportment of the hero. Really,
it is not violence at all which is the "point" of the Western movie,
but a certain image of man, a style, which expresses itself most clearly
in violence. Watch a child with his toy guns and you will see: what
most interests him is not (as we so much fear) the fantasy of hurting
others, but to work out how a man might look when he shoots or is
shot. A hero is one who looks like a hero.

Whatever the limitations of such an idea in experience, it has always
been valid in art and has a special validity in an art where appearances
are everything. The Western hero is necessarily an archaic figure;
we do not really believe in him and would not have him step out of
his rigidly conventionalized background. But his archaicism does not
take away from his power; on the contrary, it adds to it by keeping
him just a little beyond the reach both of common sense and of

[2] I am not concerned here with the actual social consequences of gangster
movies, though I suspect they could not have been so pernicious as they were
thought to be. Some of the compromises introduced to avoid the supposed bad
effects of the old gangster movies may be, if anything, more dangerous, for the
sadistic violence that once belonged only to the gangster is now commonly
enlisted on the side of the law and thus goes undefeated, allowing us (if we wish)
to find in the movies a sort of "confirmation" of our fantasies.

absolutized emotion, the two usual impulses of our art. And he has, after all, his own kind of relevance. He is there to remind us of the possibility of style in an age which has put on itself the burden of pretending that style has no meaning, and, in the midst of our anxieties over the problem of violence, to suggest that even in killing or being killed we are not freed from the necessity of establishing satisfactory modes of behavior. Above all, the movies in which the Westerner plays out his role preserve for us the pleasures of a complete and self-contained drama—and one which still effortlessly crosses the boundaries which divide our culture—in a time when other, more consciously serious art forms are increasingly complex, uncertain, and ill-defined.

Underground

Films

---

by Manny Farber

Films such as those noted in the following essay (Commentary, Nov. 1957)—modest, unpretentious films with a hard core of what Mr. Farber calls "masculine" truth—are rarely produced these days. The more risky and BIG film production becomes, the less likelihood there is for the making of tight, flawlessly executed melodramas, a genre which achieved distinction during the past twenty-five years. There is room for debate about the ultimate artistic value of these films, but there can be no question about their expert craftsmanship or their sharp observation of the details of human behavior.

THE SADDEST THING in current films is watching the long-neglected action directors fade away as the less-talented De Sicas and Zinnemanns continue to fascinate the critics. Because they played an anti-art role in Hollywood, the true masters of the male action film—such soldier-cowboy-gangster directors as Raoul Walsh, Howard Hawks, William Wellman, William Kieghley, the early, pre-*Stagecoach* John Ford, Anthony Mann—have turned out a huge amount of unprized second-gear celluloid. Their neglect becomes more painful to behold now that the action directors are in decline, many of them having abandoned the dry, economic, life-worn movie style that made their observations of the American he-man so rewarding. Americans seem to have a special aptitude for allowing History to bury the toughest, most authentic native talents. The same tide that has swept away Otis Ferguson, Walker Evans, Val Lewton, Clarence Williams, and J. R. Williams into near oblivion is now in the process of burying a group that kept an endless flow of interesting roughneck film passing through the theaters from the depression onward. The tragedy of these film-makers lies in their having been consigned to a Sargasso Sea of unmentioned talent by film reviewers whose sole concern is not continuous flow of quality but the momentary novelties of the particular film they are reviewing.

Howard Hawks is the key figure in the male action film because he shows a maximum speed, inner life, and view, with the least amount of flat foot. His best films, which have the swallowed-up intricacy of a good soft-shoe dance, are *Ceiling Zero, Only Angels Have Wings, The Big Sleep*, and *The Thing*. Raoul Walsh's films are melancholy masterpieces of flexibility and detailing inside a lower-middle-class locale. Walsh's victories, which make use of tense broken-field journeys and nostalgic background detail, include *They Drive By Night, White Heat*, and *Roaring Twenties*. In any Bill Wellman operation, there are at least four directors—a sentimentalist, deep thinker, hooey vaudevillian, and an expedient short-cut artist whose special love is for mulish toughs expressing themselves in drop-kicking heads and somber standing around. Wellman is at his best in stiff, vulgar, low-pulp material. In that set-up, he has a low-budget ingenuity which creates flashes of ferocious brassiness, an authentic practical-joke violence (as in the frenzied inadequacy of Ben Blue in *Roxie Hart*) and a brainless hell-raising. Anthony Mann's inhumanity to man, in which cold mortal intentness is the trademark effect, can be studied best in *The Tall Target, Winchester 77, Border Incident*, and *Railroaded*. The films of this tin-can De Sade have a Germanic rigor, caterpillar intimacy, and an original dictionary of ways in which to punish the human body. Mann has done interesting work with scissors, a cigarette lighter, and steam, but his most bizarre effect takes place in a taxidermist's shop. By intricate manipulation of athletes' bodies, Mann tries to ram the eyes of his combatants on the horns of a stuffed deer stuck on the wall.

The film directors mentioned above did their best work over a decade ago when it was possible to be a factory of unpretentious picture-making without frightening the front office. During the same period and later, less prolific directors also appear in the uncompromising action film. Of these, the most important is John Farrow, an urbane vaudevillian whose forte, in films like *The Big Clock* and *His Kind of Woman*, is putting a fine motoring system beneath the veering slapstick of his eccentric characterizations. Though he has tangled with such heavyweights as Book-of-the-Month and Hemingway, Zoltan Korda is an authentic hard-grain cheapster telling his stories through unscrubbed action, masculine characterization, and violent explorations inside a fascinating locale. Korda's best films—*Sahara, Counterattack, Cry the Beloved Country*—are strangely active films in which terrain, jogs, and people get curiously interwoven in a ravening tactility. William Kieghley, in *G Men* and *Each Dawn I Die*, is the least sentimental director of gangster careers. After the bloated philosophical safecrackers in Huston's *Asphalt Jungle*, the smallish cops and robbers in Kieghley's work seem life-size. Kieghley's handling is so right in emphasis, timing, and shrewdness that there is no feeling of the director breathing, gasping, snoring over the film.

The tight-lipped creators whose films are mentioned above comprise the most interesting group to appear in American culture since the various groupings that made the 1920s an explosive era in jazz, literature, silent films. Hawks and his group are perfect examples of the anonymous artist, who is seemingly afraid of the polishing, hypocrisy, bragging, fake educating that goes on in serious art. To go at his most expedient gait, the Hawks type must take a withdrawn, almost hidden stance in the industry. Thus, his films seem to come from the most neutral, humdrum, monotonous corner of the movie lot. The fascinating thing about these veiled operators is that they are able to spring the leanest, shrewdest, sprightliest notes from material that looks like junk, and from a creative position that on the surface seems totally uncommitted and disinterested. With striking photography, a good ear for natural dialogue, an eye for realistic detail, a skilled inside-action approach to composition, and the most politic hand in the movie field, the action directors have done a forbidding stenography on the hard-boiled American handyman as he progresses through the years.

It is not too remarkable that the underground films, with their twelve-year-old's adventure-story plot and endless palpitating movement, have lost out in the film system. Their dismissal has been caused by the construction of solid confidence built by daily and weekly reviewers. Operating with this wall, the critic can pick and discard without the slightest worry about looking silly. His choice of best salami is a picture backed by studio build-up, agreement amongst his colleagues, a layout in *Life* Magazine (which makes it officially reasonable for an American award), and a list of ingredients that anyone's unsophisticated aunt in Oakland can spot as a distinguished film. This prize picture, which has philosophical undertones, pan-fried domestic sights, risqué crevices, sporty actors and actresses, circuslike gym-

nastics, a bit of tragedy like the main fall at Niagara, has every reason
to be successful. It has been made for that purpose. Thus, the year's
winner is a perfect film made up solely of holes and evasions, covered
up by all types of padding and plush. The cavity filling varies from
one prize work to another, from *High Noon* (cross-eyed artistic
views of a clock, silhouettes against a vaulting sky, legend-toned
walking, a big song), through *From Here to Eternity* (Sinatra's
private scene-chewing, pretty trumpeting, tense shots in the dark and
at twilight, necking near the water, a threatening hand with a broken
bottle), to next year's winner which will probably be a huge ball of
cotton candy containing either Audrey Hepburn's cavernous grin
and stiff behind or more of Zinnemann's glacéed picture-making. In
terms of imaginative photography, honest acting, and insight into
American life there is no comparison between an average underground triumph (*The Tall Target*) and the trivia that causes a critical
salaam across the land. The trouble is that no one asks the critics'
alliance to look straight backward at its "choices," i.e. a horse-drawn
truckload of liberal schmaltz called *The Best Years of Our Lives*.
These ridiculously maltreated films sustain their place in the halls of
fame simply because they bear the label of art in every inch of their
reelage. Praising these solemn goiters has produced a climate in which
the underground picture-maker, with his modest entry and soft-shoe
approach, can barely survive.

However, any day now, Americans may realize that scrambling
after the obvious in art is a losing game. The sharpest work of the
last thirty years is to be found by studying the most unlikely, self-
destroying, uncompromising, roundabout artists. When the day
comes for praising infamous men of art, some great talent will be
shown in true light: people like Weldon Kees, the early Robert
DeNiro, James Agee, Isaac Rosenfeld, Otis Ferguson, Val Lewton, a
dozen comic-strip geniuses like the creator of "Harold Teen," and
finally a half dozen directors, such as the master of the ambulance-
speedboat, flying-saucer movie: Howard Hawks.

The films of the Hawks-Wellman group are *underground* for more
reasons than the fact that the director hides out in the subsurface
reaches of his work. The hard-bitten action film finds its natural
home in caves; the murky, congested theaters, looking like glorified
tattoo parlors on the outside and located near bus terminals in big
cities. These theaters roll action films in what, at first, seems like a
nightmarish atmosphere of guzzling, snoring, clicking flashlights,
ice-cream vending, and amazing restlessness. After a while, the clatter
and congested tinniness is swallowed by the atmosphere of shabby
transience, prints that seem overgrown with jungle moss, sound tracks

infected with hiccups. The spectator watches two or three action films go by, and leaves feeling as though he were a pirate discharged from a giant sponge.

The cut-throat atmosphere in the itch house is reproduced in the movies shown there. Hawks's *The Big Sleep* not only has a slightly gaseous, sub-surface, Baghdad-ish background, but its gangster action is engineered with a suave, cutting efficacy. Walsh's *Roaring Twenties* is a jangling barrelhouse film which starts with a top gun bouncing downhill, and, at the end, he is seen slowly pushing his way through a lot of Campbell's Scotch broth. Wellman's favorite scene is a group of hard-visaged ball bearings standing around—for no damned reason and with no indication of how long or for what reason they have been standing. His worst pictures are made up simply of this moody, wooden standing around. All that saves the films are the little flurries of bulletlike acting that give the men an inner look of credible orneriness and somewhat stupid mulishness. Mann likes to stretch his victims in crucifix poses against the wall or ground, and then peer intently at their demise with an icy surgeon's eye. Just as the harrowing machine is about to run over the wetback on a moonlit night, the camera catches him sprawled out in a harrowing image. At heart, the best action films are slicing journeys into the lower depths of American life: dregs, cast-outs, lonely hard wanderers caught in a buzz saw of niggardly intricate devious movement.

The projects of the underground directors are neither experimental, liberal, slick, spectacular, low-budget, epical, improving, or flagrantly commercial like Sam Katzman two-bitters. They are faceless movies taken from a type of half-polished trash writing that seems like a mixture of Burt L. Standish, Max Brand, and Raymond Chandler. Tight, cliché-ridden melodramas about stock musclemen. A stool pigeon gurgling with a scissors in his back; a fat, nasal-voiced gang leader, escaped convicts, power-mad ranch owners with vengeful siblings, a mean gun with an Oedipus complex and migraine headaches, a crooked gambler trading guns to the redskins, exhausted GIs, an incompetent kid hoodlum hiding out in an East Side building, a sickly-elegant Italian barber in a plot to kill Lincoln, an underpaid shamus signing up to stop the blackmailing of a tough millionaire's depraved thumb-sucking daughter.

The action directors accept the role of hack so that they can involve themselves with expedience and tough-guy insight in all types of action: barnstorming, driving, bulldogging. The important thing is not so much the banal-seeming journeys to nowhere that make up the stories, but the tunneling that goes on inside the classic Western-gangster incidents and stock hoodlum-dogface-cowboy types. For instance, Wellman's lean elliptical talents for creating brassy cheapsters and making gloved references to death, patriotism, masturbation, suggest that he uses private runways to the truth, while more famous directors take a slow, embalming surface route.

The virtues of action films expand as the pictures take on the outer appearance of junk jewelry. The underground's greatest mishaps have occurred in art-infected projects where there is unlimited cash, studio freedom, an expansive story, message, heart, and a lot of prestige to be gained. Their flattest, most sentimental works are incidentally the only ones that have attained the almond-paste-flavored eminence of the Museum of Modern Art's film library, i.e. *Gl Joe*, *Public Enemy*, and *Scarface*. Both Hawks and Wellman, who made these overweighted mistakes, are like basketball's corner man: their best shooting is done from the deepest, worst angle. With material that is hopelessly worn out and childish (*Only Angels Have Wings*), the underground director becomes beautifully graphic and modestly human in his flexible detailing. When the material is like drab concrete, these directors become great on-the-spot inventors, using their curiously niggling, reaming style for adding background detail (Walsh), suave grace (Hawks), crawling mechanized tension (Mann), veiled gravity (Wellman), svelte semicaricature (John Farrow), modern Gothic vehemence (Phil Karlson), and dark, modish vaudeville (Robert Aldrich).

In the films of these hard-edged directors can be found the unheralded ripple of physical experience, the tiny morbidly life-word detail which the visitor to a strange city finds springing out at every step. The Hawks film is as good on the mellifluous grace of the impudent American hard rock as can be found in any art work; the Mann films use American objects and terrain—guns, cliffs, boulders, an 1865 locomotive, telephone wires—with more cruel intimacy than any other film-maker; the Wellman film is the only clear shot at the mean, brassy, clawlike soul of the lone American wolf that has been taken in films. In other words, these actioneers—Mann and Hawks and Kieghley and, in recent times, Aldrich and Karlson—go completely underground before proving themselves more honest and subtle than the water buffaloes of film art: George Stevens, Billy Wilder, Vittorio De Sica, Georges Clouzot. (Clouzot's most successful work, *Wages of Fear*, is a wholesale steal of the mean physicality and acrid highway inventions in such Walsh-Wellman films as *They Drive by Night*. Also, the latter film is a more flexible, adroitly ad-libbed, worked-in creation than Clouzot's eclectic money-maker.)

Unfortunately, the action directors suffer from presentation problems. Their work is now seen repeatedly on the blurred, chopped,

worn, darkened, commercial-ridden movie programs on TV. Even
in the impossible conditions of the "Late Show," where the lighting
is four shades too dark and the porthole-shaped screen defeats the
movie's action, the deep skill of Hawks and his tribe shows itself.
Time has dated and thinned out the story excitement, but the ability
to capture the exact homely-manly character of forgotten locales
and misanthropic figures is still in the pictures, along with pictorial
compositions (Ford's *Last of the Mohicans*) that occasionally seem
as lovely as anything that came out of the camera box of Billy Bitzer
and Mathew Brady. The conditions in the outcast theaters—the
Lyric on Times Square, the Liberty on Market Street, the Victory
on Chestnut—are not as bad as TV, but bad enough. The screen
image is often out of plumb, the house lights are half left on during
the picture, the broken seats are only a minor annoyance in the unpredictable terrain. Yet, these action-film homes are the places to
study Hawks, Wellman, Mann, as well as their near and distant
cousins.

The underground directors have been saving the American male
on the screen for three decades without receiving the slightest credit
from critics and prize committees. The hard, exact defining of male
action, completely lacking in acting fat, is a common item *only* in
underground films. The cream on the top of a *Framed* or *Appointment with Danger* (directed by two first cousins of the Hawks-
Walsh strain) is the eye-flicking action that shows the American
body—arms, elbow, legs, mouths, the tension profile line—being used
expediently, with grace and the suggestion of jolting hardness.
Otherwise, the Hollywood talkie seems to have been invented to
give an embarrassingly phony impression of the virile action man.
The performance is always fattened either by coyness (early Robert
Taylor), unction (Anthony Quinn), histrionic conceit (Gene
Kelly), liberal knowingness (Brando), angelic stylishness (Mel Ferrer), oily hamming (José Ferrer), Mother's Boy passivity (Rock
Hudson), or languor (Montgomery Clift). Unless the actor lands
in the hands of an underground director, he causes a candy-coated
effect that is misery for any spectator who likes a bit of male truth
in films.

After a steady diet of undergrounders, the spectator realizes that
these are the only films that show the tension of an individual intelligence posing itself against the possibilities of monotony, bathos, or
sheer cliché. Though the action film is filled with heroism or its absence, the real hero is the small detail which has arisen from a stormy
competition between lively color and credibility. The hardness of
these films arises from the aesthetic give-and-go with banality. Thus,

the philosophical idea in underground films seems to be that nothing is easy in life or the making of films. Jobs are difficult. Even the
act of watching a humdrum bookstore scene from across the street
has to be done with care and modesty to evade the type of butter-
slicing glibness that rots the Zinnemann films. In the Walsh film, a
gangster walks through a saloon with so much tightroped ad-libbing
and muscularity that he seems to be walking backward through the
situation. Hawks's achievement of moderate toughness in *Red River*,
using Clift's delicate languor and Wayne's claylike acting, is remarkable. As usual, he steers Clift through a series of cornball fetishes
(like the Barney Google Ozark hat and the trick handling of same)
and graceful, semi-collegiate business: stances and kneelings and
snake-quick gunmanship. The beauty of the job is the way the cliché
business is needled, strained against without breaking the naturalistic
surface. One feels that his is the first and last hard, clamped-down,
imaginative job Clift does in Hollywood—his one non-mush performance. Afterward, he goes to work for Zinnemann, Stevens,
Hitchcock.

The small buried attempt to pierce the banal pulp of underground
stories with fanciful grace notes is one of the important feats of the
underground director. Usually, the piercing consists in renovating a
cheap rusty trick that has been slumbering in the "thriller" director's handbook—pushing a "color" effect against the most resistant
type of unshowy, hard-bitten direction. A mean butterball flicks a
gunman's ear with a cigarette lighter. A night-frozen cowboy shud-
ders over a swig of whisky. A gorilla gang leader makes a cannon-
aded exit from a barber chair. All these bits of congestion are like
the lines of a hand to a good gun movie; they are the tracings of
difficulty that make the films seem uniquely hard and formful. In
each case, the director is taking a great chance with clichés and forcing them into a hard natural shape.

People don't notice the absence of this hard combat with low,
commonplace ideas in the Zinnemann and Huston epics, wherein the
action is a game in which the stars take part with confidence and
glee as though nothing can stop them. They roll in parts of drug
addicts, tortured sheriffs, success depending on how much sentimental bloop and artistic japery can be packed in without encoun-
tering the demands of a natural act or character. Looking back on
a Sinatra film, one has the feeling of a private whirligig performance
in the center of a frame rather than a picture. On the other hand,
a Cagney performance under the hands of a Kieghley is ingrained
in a tight, malignant story. One remembers it as a sinewy, life-marred

exactness that is as quietly laid down as the smaller jobs played by the Barton MacLanes and Frankie Darros.

A constant attendance at the Lyric-Pix-Victory theaters soon impresses the spectator with the coverage of locales in action films. The average gun film travels like a shamus who knows his city and likes his private knowledges. Instead of the picture-postcard sights, the underground film finds the most idiosyncratic spot of a city and then locates the niceties within the large nicety. The California Street hill in San Francisco (*Woman in Hiding*) with its old-style mansions played in perfect night photography against a deadened domestic bitching. A YMCA scene that emphasizes the wonderful fat-waisted-middle-aged-physicality of people putting on tennis shoes and playing handball (*Appointment with Danger*). The terrorizing of a dowdy middle-aged, frog-faced woman (*Born to Kill*) that starts in a decrepit hotel and ends in a bumbling, screeching, crawling murder at midnight on the shore. For his big shock effect, director Robert Wise (a sometime member of the underground) uses the angle going down to the water to create a middle-class mediocrity that out-horrors anything Graham Greene attempted in his early books on small-time gunsels.

Another fine thing about the coverage is its topographic grimness, the fact that the terrain looks worked over. From Walsh's *What Price Glory* to Mann's *Men at War*, the terrain is special in that it is used, kicked, grappled, worried, sweated up, burrowed into, stomped on. The land is marched across in dark threading lines at twilight, or the effect is reversed with foot soldiers in white parkas (*Fixed Bayonets*) curving along a snowed-in battleground as they watch troops moving back—in either case the cliché effect is worked credibly inward until it creates a haunting note like the army diagonals in *Birth of a Nation*. Rooms are boxed, crossed, opened up as they are in few other films. The spectator gets to know these rooms as well as his own hand. Years after seeing the film, he remembers the way a dulled waitress sat on the edge of a hotel bed, the weird elongated adobe in which ranch hands congregate before a Chisholm Trail drive. The rooms in big-shot directors' films look curiously bulbous, as though inflated with hot air and turned toward the audience, like the high-school operetta of the 1920s.

Of all these poet-builders, Wellman is the most interesting, particularly with Hopper-type scenery. It is a matter of drawing store fronts, heavy bedroom boudoirs, the heisting of a lonely service station, with light furious strokes. Also, in mixing jolting vulgarity (Mae Clarke's face being smashed with a grapefruit) with a space composition dance in which the scene seems to be constructed before your eyes. It may be a minor achievement but when Wellman finishes with a service station or the wooden stairs in front of an ancient saloon, there is no reason for any movie realist to handle the subject again. The scene is kept light, textural, and as though it is being built from the outside in. There is no sentiment of the type that spreads lugubrious shadows (Kazan), builds tensions of perspective (Huston), or inflates with golden sunlight and finicky hot air (Stevens).

Easily the best part of underground films are the excavations of exciting-familiar scenery. The opening up of a scene is more concerted in these films than in other Hollywood efforts, but the most important thing is that the opening is done by road-mapped strategies that play movement against space in a cunning way, building the environment and event before your eyes. In every underground film, these vigorous ramifications within a sharply seen terrain are the big attraction, the main tent. No one does this anatomization of action and scene better than Hawks, who probably invented it—at least, the smooth version—in such 1930s gunblasts as *The Crowd Roars*. The control of Hawks's strategies is so ingenious that when a person kneels or walks down the hallway, the movement seems to click into a predetermined slot. It is an uncanny accomplishment that carries the spectator across the very ground of a giant ranch, into rooms and out again, over to the wall to look at some faded fight pictures on a hotel wall—as though he were in the grip of a spectacular, mobile "eye." When Hawks landscapes action—the cutting between light tower and storm-caught plane in *Ceiling Zero*, the vegetalizing in *The Thing*, the shamus sweating in a greenhouse in *The Big Sleep*—the feeling is of a clever human tunneling just under the surface of terrain. It is as though the film has a life of its own that goes on beneath the story action.

However, there have been many great examples of such veining by human interactions over a wide plane. One of the special shockers, in *Each Dawn I Die*, has to do with the scissoring of a stooly during the movie shown at the penitentiary. This Kieghley-Cagney effort is a wonder of excitement as it moves in great leaps from screen to the rear of a crowded auditorium: crossing contrasts of movement in three points of the hall, all of it done in a sinking cavernous gloom. One of the more ironic criss-crossings has to do with the coughings of the stuck victim played against the screen image of zooming airplanes over the Pacific.

In the great virtuoso films, there is something vaguely resembling this underground maneuvering, only it goes on above the story.

Egocentric padding that builds a great bonfire of pyrotechnics over a gapingly empty film. The perfect example is a pumped-up fist fight that almost closes the three-hour *Giant* film. This ballroom shuffle between a reforming rancher and a Mexican-hating luncheonette owner is an entertaining creation in spectacular tumbling, swinging, back-arching, bending. However, the endless masturbatory "building" of excitement—beautiful haymakers, room-covering falls, thunderous sounds—is more than slightly silly. Even if the room were valid, which it isn't (a studio-built chromium horror plopped too close to the edge of a lonely highway), the room goes unexplored because of the jumbled timing. The excess that is so noticeable in Stevens' brawl is absent in the least serious undergrounder, which attains most of its crisp, angular character from the modesty of a director working skillfully far within the earthworks of the story.

Underground films have almost ceased to be a part of the movie scene. The founders of the action film have gone into awkward, big-scaled productions involving pyramid-building, a passenger plane in trouble over the Pacific, and postcard Westerns with Jimmy Stewart and his harassed Adam's-apple approach to gutty acting. The last drainings of the underground film show a tendency toward moving from the plain guttural approach of *G Men* to a Germanically splashed type of film. Of these newcomers, Robert Aldrich is certainly the most exciting—a lurid psychiatric stormer who gets an overflow of vitality and sheer love for movie-making into the film. This enthusiasm is the rarest item in a dried, decayed-lemon type of movie period. Aldrich makes viciously anti-Something movies—*Attack* stomps on Southern rascalism and the officer sect in war, *The Big Knife* impales the Zanuck-Goldwyn big shot in Hollywood. The Aldrich films are filled with exciting characterizations—by Lee Marvin, Rod Steiger, Jack Palance—of highly psyched-up, marred, and bothered men. Phil Karlson has done some surprising modern Gothic treatments of the Brink's hold-up (*Kansas City Confidential*) and the vice-ridden Southern town (*The Phenix City Story*). His movies are remarkable for their endless outlay of scary cheapness in detailing the modern underworld. Also, Karlson's work has a chilling documentary exactness and an exciting shot-scattering belligerence.

There is no longer a literate audience for the masculine picture-making that Hawks and Wellman exploited, as there was in the 1930s. In those exciting movie years, a smart audience waited around each week for the next Hawks, Preston Sturges, or Ford film—shoe-stringers that were far to the side of the expensive Hollywood film.

That underground audience, with its expert voice in Ferguson and its ability to choose between perceptive trash and the Thalberg pepsin-flavored sloshing with Tracy and Gable, has now oozed away. It seems ridiculous, but the Fergusonite went into fast decline during the mid-1940s when the movie market was flooded with fake underground films—plushy thrillers with neo-Chandler scripts and a romantic style that seemed to pour the gore, histrionics, décor out of a giant catsup bottle. The nadir of these films: an item called *Singapore* with Fred MacMurray and Ava Gardner.

The straw that finally breaks the back of the underground film tradition is the dilettante behavior of intellectuals on the subject of oaters. Aesthetes and upper bohemians now favor horse operas almost as wildly as they like the cute, little-guy worshipings of De Sica and the pedantic, interpretive reading of Alec Guinness. This fad for Western films shows itself in the inevitable little magazine review which finds an affinity between the subject matter of cowboy films and the inner aesthetics of Cinemah. The Hawks-Wellman tradition, which is basically a subterranean delight that looks like a cheap penny candy on the outside, hasn't a chance of reviving when intellectuals enthuse in equal amounts over Westerns by Ford, Nunnally Johnson, J. Sturges, Stevens, Delmar Daves. In Ferguson's day, the intellectual could differentiate between a stolid genre painter (Ford), a long-winded cuteness expert with a rotogravure movie sense (Johnson), a scene painted with a notions-counter eye and a primly naïve manner with sun-hardened bruisers (John Sturges), and a *Boys' Life* nature lover who intelligently half prettifies adolescents and backwoods primitives (Daves). Today, the audience for Westerns and gangster careers is a sickeningly frivolous one that does little more than play the garbage collector or make a night court of films. With this highbrow audience, which loves banality and pomp more than the tourists at Radio City Music Hall, there is little reason to expect any stray director to try for a hidden, meager-looking work that is directly against the serious-art grain.

Movies, the Desperate Art

by Pauline Kael

In the following essay, which has been revised slightly for this book, Miss Kael expresses justifiable despair over the inadequacy of much film criticism as well as the downright staleness of Hollywood and also of many avant-garde film makers. In suggesting that today's audience has been conditioned by suave-looking films that probably would have been passed up by the more adult and more discriminating audiences of the twenties and thirties, she has hit upon a useful approach for judging movies. (This essay was published originally in The Berkley Book of Modern Writing No. 3, edited by William Phillips and Philip Rahv, the Berkley Publishing Corp., New York, 1956.)

THE FILM CRITIC in the United States is in a curious position: the greater his interest in the film medium, the more enraged and negative he is likely to sound. He can assert his disgust, and he can find ample material to document it, but then what? He can haunt film societies and re-experience and reassess the classics, but the result is an increased burden of disgust; the directions indicated in those classics are not the directions Hollywood took. A few writers, and not Americans only, have taken a rather fancy way out: they turn films into Rorschach tests and find the most elaborate meanings in them (bad acting becomes somnambulism, stereotyped situations become myths, and so forth). The deficiency of this technique is that the writers reveal a great deal about themselves but very little about films.

SIZE

Hollywood films have attempted to meet the "challenge" of television by the astonishingly simple expedient of expanding in size; in the course of this expansion the worst filmic tendencies of the past thirty years have reached what we may provisionally call their culmination. Like a public building designed to satisfy the widest public's concept of grandeur, the big production loses the flair, the spontaneity, the rhythm of an artist working to satisfy his own conception. The more expensive the picture, the bigger the audience it must draw, and the fewer risks it can take. The big film is the disenchanted film: from the outset, every element in a multi-million-dollar production is charged with risk and anxiety, the fear of calamitous failure—the loss of "big" money. The picture becomes less imaginative in inverse ratio to its cost. But the idiot solution has worked: size *has* been selling, and Hollywood has learned to inflate everything, even romance (*Three Coins in the Fountain*) or murder mystery (*Black Widow*)—the various genres become indistinguishable. A "small" picture would probably seem retrogressive to Hollywood—as if the industry were not utilizing its full resources, and, indeed, when the CinemaScope screen contracts for an "old-fashioned"-size picture, the psychological effect is of a going *back*. Films must be big to draw the mass audience, but the heroes and heroines, conceived to flatter the "ordinary," "little" persons who presumably make up the audience, must be inanities who will offend no one.

The magic that films advertise is the magic of bloated production methods—it is no longer the pyramid the company photographed at Gizeh which is the selling point (that has become too easy) but the pyramid they have *built*. It is the "magic" of American industry—the feats of production presumed to be possible nowhere else (musical extravaganzas like *Easy to Wed* or *Latin Lovers* are incarnations of American speed and efficiency, vigor and abundance, held together by the conviction that all this is the good life). Abroad, especially, the glamour of American movies emanates from the wastefulness of Hollywood methods as much as from the land of plenty revealed in film stories.

Those who see the era of the wide screen and the traveling camera crew as encouraging evidence that movies will once again become magical and exciting recall their childhood when the wonder of film lay in the extraordinary scope of the camera. But the panoramic views of a CinemaScope or VistaVision production are about as magical as a Fitzpatrick travelogue, and the actors are not unlike the girls that travelogue makers love to place at the entrance to each glorious temple—commonplace, anachronistic and reassuring. In a film like *Soldier of Fortune* the story material and the exotic backgrounds do not support each other (as they do in Carol Reed's *The Outcast of the Islands*); the company goes to Hong Kong to tell a story that could just as easily be told in Southern California—the location shots are used to make the familiar seem unusual.

The split between background and foreground in pictures with foreign settings develops into schizophrenia in historical and Biblical spectacles. A reconstruction of Egypt (usually filtered through Maxfield Parrish) means authenticity; the audience is supposed to feel that the film is "real" and important because the background material has been thoroughly researched (the sets are real sets). But the heroes and heroines are not really intended to look of the period at all; the audience might lose its bearings if Susan Hayward or Alan Ladd did not hold them in the familiar present. Would *20,000 Leagues under the Sea* have been such a commercial success if Kirk Douglas had not been there to destroy the illusion of the nineteenth century? The emotions and actions recorded by novelists and historians might insult American tastes and mores; audiences rest easier when characters do only those things modern young men and women are supposed to do (Salome can dance, but she can't get the head). Accuracy (or what passes for accuracy) in background details becomes enormously important—it gives the shoddy, sexy films the sanction of educational and religious values. (The fantastic emphasis on accurate sets and costumes may indicate also a last desperate stand by the artists and technicians who have failed to grapple with the most restrictive censorship—the tastes of the national audience—but who still cling to some kind of pride in their work.) There is a crude appeal in Hollywood's "realism." Arliss made up to look like Disraeli was a living display of ingeniousness for the same public that appreciates a painted horse that looks real enough to ride. There is an instinct for what the public respects that works beneath film methods: the backgrounds of *Seven Brides for Seven Brothers* are painted to fool the audience into seeing real snow on real mountains. In proving that it can make things look real (reality rates higher with the mass audience than style and illusion) Hollywood comes full circle—back to before the beginnings of art.

Hollywood follows the mass audience and the mass audience follows Hollywood; there is no leader. The worst of the past is preserved with new dust. How many films that we once groaned at do we now hear referred to nostalgically? When the bad is followed by the worse, even the bad seems good. (Film addicts talk about *Grand Hotel* or Busby Berkeley's choreography, as if *those* were the days.) The hostility toward art and high-browism that infects much of our culture helps to explain the popularity of so many untrained and untalented screen performers. Richard Burton and Daniel O'Herlihy do not stimulate the fans; Tony Curtis, Tab Hunter, Janet Leigh, Jane Powell do. Fans like untrained actors; perhaps they like even the embarrassment of untrained actors (why should they tolerate the implied criticism of speech or gesture that derives from a higher culture?). The office girl says, "No, I don't want to go see Howard Keel—he was a professional singer, you know." The tastes of the mass audience belong to sociology, not aesthetics. Those who make big films do not consider primarily the nature of the medium and what they want to do with it, they try to keep ahead of the mass audience.

As the mass media developed, the fine points of democratic theory were discarded, and a parody of democracy became public dogma. The film critic no longer considers that his function is the formation and reformation of public taste (that would be an undemocratic presumption); the old independent critic who would trumpet the good, blast the bad, and tell his readers they were boobs if they wasted their money on garbage, gives way to the amiable fellow who feels responsible not to his subject matter but to the tastes of his stratum of the public. Newspaper critics are, in many cases, not free to attack big films (too much is at stake), but they are usually free to praise what they wish; yet they seem too unsure of themselves, too fearful of causing a breach with their readers, to praise what may be unpopular. It is astonishing how often they attack the finest European productions and the most imaginative American ones—safe targets. Attitudes become more important than judgments. The critic need not make any definite adverse comments; his descriptive tone is enough to warn his readers off. Praise which includes such terms as "subtle," "low-keyed" or "somber" is damnation; the critic saves his face but helps kill the movie.

There are people, lots of them, who take big pictures seriously. What is one to say to the neo-Aristotelianism of the salesgirl who reports, "I saw *The Student Prince* last night—it was so wonderful and so sad. I cried and cried, and when it was over, why, I just felt all cleaned out." Only snobs howl at *Duel in the Sun* ($11.3 million gross), and if you crawled out on *Quo Vadis* ($10.5 million gross) you not only showed your disrespect for heavy labor, you implied contempt for those who were awed by it. Hollywood productions are official parts of American life, proofs of technological progress; derision is subversive. You will be reproved with "What right have you to say *Samson and Delilah* is no good when millions of people liked it?" and you will be subjected to the final devastation of "It's all a matter of taste and one person's taste is as good as another's." One does not make friends by replying that although it *is* all a matter of taste (and education and intelligence and sensibility) one person's taste is *not* as good as another's.

Three or four years ago, films by Huston and Zinnemann and, at times, Mankiewicz, Kazan and a few others, stood out from the thick buttered-up products and showed the working of individual creative responsibility. The wide screen and the rediscovery of Christianity have restored films to their second childhood. In the thirties we thought Cecil B. De Mille passé; the American film of 1955 represents his full triumph. In the infancy of films there was promise and fervor; the absurdities were forgivable—we could find them amusing and primitive because we thought we saw the beginnings of a prodigy and we knew there were real obstacles ahead. But this synthetic infancy is monstrous—a retracing of the steps, not to discover the lost paths of development, but to simulate the charms of infancy—and, for all we know, there may be a return to each previous (and doomed) period of film. Something must be done to keep a huge film in motion—in desperation everything gets thrown in. *Grand Hotel* itself becomes a model: put in enough characters and stories and perhaps the huge screen will fuse what it encompasses (Mankiewicz' *The Barefoot Contessa*, Kazan's *East of Eden*, as well as *Violent Saturday, Soldier of Fortune, The Cobweb*). The biggest productions often look like a compendium of the worst filmic crimes of the past, achieving a really massive staleness. Some directors, feeling possibly that spectacles are a joke, attempt elaborate spoofs like *Athena* or *Jupiter's Darling*. But films have got so close to no conviction and no believability that there is very little difference when they cross the line into satire of themselves. If an audience can accept *Mambo* as a serious film, how is it to know, the next week, that *Many Rivers to Cross* is supposed to be funny? When the spectacular production scale is used for comedy, audiences may be too stunned by size and expense to see the humor.

One reason recent spectacles are so much worse than the earliest ones is the addition of sound; it was bad enough to look at the

Saviour on the cross, now we must hear his gasps. And the wide screen, which theoretically expands filmic possibilities in certain areas of material, in general limits what can be done—while the areas in which it offers possibilities will probably never be explored. A master could use the vast medium; he could even find themes and dialogue adequate to it (*The Dynasts* or *Peer Gynt* perhaps—or *Road to Damascus*), but what master would be entrusted with the cost of such a venture? It was Michael Todd who enlisted the Yugoslav Army for *War and Peace* ("We're going to make this movie accurate down to the last bit of hairdress and harness") while David Selznick, the Civil War behind him, commands another *War and Peace* (even the legions and larders of Hollywood may be exhausted building the steppes of Russia). Selznick and his peers continue the worst heritage of Griffith, not the visual inventiveness which is his glory but the spread of his conceptions and the spliced sentiments and ideas which substituted for structure. Erich von Stroheim's synopses of *Walking down Broadway* and *Queen Kelly* (recently published in *Film Culture*) are extraordinary documents (as high-school themes they would be hilarious); is it possible that early film makers did not realize that they were heirs to *any* traditions, that because the film medium was new they thought it should be approached with an empty mind? The egotism of the self-taught, which is a practical, though often paranoid, defense against commercial pressure, has had considerable effect on film development. The megalomaniacs who make films can think of no bigger subject than *War and Peace* (Italians, Finns and Russians all race to complete their versions); what can they do next—recreate the creation of the world? All these companies but one will probably lose their shirts; if *all* lose their shirts, perhaps producers will heed the Tolstoyan lesson and learn to approach film making with the economy of a peasant.

ACTION

The best films of recent years have not been spectacles and they have not been geared to a large audience; they have made more and more demands on concentrated attention. The trained eye of an adult may find magic in the sustained epiphanies of *Day of Wrath*, the intricate cutting and accumulating frenzy of *La Règle du Jeu*, the visual chamber drama of *Les Parents Terribles*. American attempts in these directions have met with resistance not only from the public but from American film critics as well. The critics' admiration for "action" and "the chase" leads them to praise sleazy suspense films but to fret over whether *A Streetcar Named Desire* or *The Member of the Wedding* is really "cinematic."

For the gullible, advertising provides a rationale for spectacles (the duplication of big historical events is edifying, and the films themselves are triumphs comparable in status to the original events); a more sophisticated audience finds its own rationale for suspense films: crime and punishment suggest some connection with the anxieties and terrors of modern man. The police pursuing a mad killer in the most routine chase seems more "realistic" than a spectacle, and have not some film theorists decided that the chase is "pure cinema"? Suspense films may reflect modern anxieties but they don't deal with them; the genre offers the spring of tension, the audience recoils. For critics, the suspense film has been a safety valve: they could praise it and know themselves to be in accord both with high "technical" standards and a good-size audience.

But critics have been quick to object to a film with a difficult theme, a small camera range, or a markedly verbal content (they object even when the words are worth listening to). Because action *can* be extended over a wide area on the screen, they think it must be—or what they're seeing isn't really a movie at all. The camera is supposed to get outside, even when it has no place to go. According to *Time*, *The Member of the Wedding* "comes most vibrantly alive when it forsakes the one-set stage original and untrammeled by high-flown talk, roves through the neighborhood, e.g., Frankie's journey through blaring, glaring honky-tonk town." The drama, however, was in the "high-flown talk," and the excursion into town was the least dramatically interesting sequence in the film (and, as a matter of fact, the camera moved more fluidly within the room than it did outside). *Miss Julie* was a beautifully executed "cinematic" treatment of a play with the action extended over acres and generations. Yet when it was over one wanted to see the play itself —that confined, harrowing drama which had been dissipated in additional material and lyrical compositions from nature. The closed framework employed in *Les Parents Terribles* could have brought us *Miss Julie* as we could never see it on the stage, with the camera intensifying our consciousness of the human face and body, picking up details, and directing the eye toward the subtleties of performance. The film *Miss Julie* treats the play as if stage and screen were opposed media and the play had to be subjected to a chemical change. (What is chemically changed in the process is the material and meaning of the play.) But, of course, it was dramatists like Strindberg and Ibsen who reformed stage movement and acting technique and created the modern style—the style to which virtually all film directors are indebted. They are the dramatists who taught film how to behave.

Concerned to distinguish between the "proper" functions of stage and screen, critics tend to overlook that most important dramatic function which they share: the revelation of human character. Instead of asking, "Does the film mean anything?" they ask, "Does the film move?" It is not surprising that there should be many in the mass audience who can see action only in a cavalry charge, but it is surprising how many film critics have the same basic notion of action. (The idea that filmic action must be red-blooded turns up in surprising places. Why did Olivier as Hamlet feel it necessary to throw Ophelia down as if to break every bone in her body?) Most of the elements they condemn as "stagy" were taken over from films anyway—the theatrical devices of Tennessee Williams, for example. Kazan's transition from stage director to film director was so smooth because he had already been adapting film techniques to the stage. The most widely applauded "advanced" staging derives from films: revolving stages (*Lady in the Dark*) simulate rapid cutting, scrim sets (*Death of a Salesman*) conjure variable perspectives, unit sets (*Tea and Sympathy*) attempt a controlled panorama, light-plot sets (*The Trial*) imitate the whole process of the dissolve and montage. And to confound the issue, Griffith and the other film pioneers who developed these techniques extracted them in large part from Max Reinhardt—who was bursting the bounds of the stage frame. Few, if any, of the devices of film originated exclusively with film.

The giveaway in the critics' demand for action is that fine films in which the camera is brilliantly active over considerable terrain often disturb and displease them; they found *Miracle in Milan* too fantastic and imaginative, *Los Olvidados* too grim, *The Beggar's Opera* too contrived, *The Earrings of Madame De* too chic and decadent. When they asked for action they didn't mean action with intellectual content (they want the chase to be pure). One of the strongest critical terms of condemnation is that a film is *slow*. This is understood to mean dull, but what it may really indicate is complexity or subtlety. Renoir's lovely comedy *The Golden Coach* was described as "slow" (and died at the box office), though after sitting through it twice I still had not had time to catch up with everything in it. Those who are used to films which underscore and overscore every point for them are bewildered when they are required to use their own eyes and ears—nothing seems to be going on. Perhaps the effects of a few decades of radio have been underestimated: film audiences don't want images to carry the dramatic idea; they don't know what's happening unless there are words to tell them. And they want the same kind of words they are used to on the radio. When the simplest kind of visual image is added to the verbal plane of soap opera or radio humor, you have the style of Hollywood films. One of the reasons for their extraordinary popularity all over the world is that once the audience gets used to this visual-verbal redundancy (which is remarkably easy to understand) it dislikes the effort of adjusting to more complex types of film. The patrons of "action" houses, steady customers for the heroics of Jeff Chandler or Rory Calhoun, are displeased only when there is some content that slows up the "action." The speed of Hollywood films is a necessity; there is nothing for the eye to linger on and nothing verbal that requires thought.

So many film pedants have insisted that one portion "belongs" to the camera and one portion "belongs" to the stage that it has become a mark of culture to discuss movies in terms of their cinematic properties and their theatrical deviations. In place of this tug of war (which would split both film and stage down the middle) may one propose simple basic terms for the evaluation of film: does the frame of meaning support the body of photographic, directorial, and acting styles; and conversely, do these styles define the frame of meaning? Examples of this integrity are Keaton's *The Navigator* or *The General*, Guitry's *Les Perles de la Couronne, On Approval, The Fallen Idol, Rashomon.* There are other examples, where the meaning may vitiate our interest in the film, but where the film is obviously of a piece—*The Maltese Falcon* or *Sunset Boulevard.* The integration of meaning and style is almost always the result of the director's imaginative grasp of the story material and control over the production. A great film is one in which the range of meaning is so imaginatively new, compelling, or exciting that we experience a new vision of human experience (*Grand Illusion*). One might also call a film great because it triumphantly achieves a style (René Clair's *Le Million*) or because it represents a new method and approach (*Potemkin*). Only rarely does an American film, as a whole, sustain an interesting range of meanings, but frequently there are meaningful sections and efforts in a film. For example, the theme of *On the Waterfront* is inflated and the directorial style is overscaled, but certain sections of the film are more dramatically meaningful than anything else in recent American movies. When the latent meanings in the material are disintegrated in the photography, direction and acting, we have fiascoes like *The Caine Mutiny* and *The Bridges of Toko-Ri.* When the meanings are too obvious and

too absurd to support the body, we have the typical bloated film
(*The Prodigal, Garden of Evil, Daddy Long Legs*, or that Cinema-
Scope edition of *The Reader's Digest, A Man Called Peter*).

ACADEMIC "CRAFTSMANSHIP"

The serious, literate audiences share with the larger American audience the fear of being duped. Even the small audiences at cinema
guilds and art houses are suspicious of new artists, who might be
charlatans pulling tricks and willfully obscuring things. Americans
are susceptible to the widespread democratic propaganda that the
really great artists of history were simple and lucid; they don't
want to be *had*. Music lovers who listen to nothing later than Mo-
zart are saved from errors in taste; they are certain to consider
themselves discriminating. The film audience dedicated to Pudovkin
or von Stroheim or the early René Clair are playing it just as safe.

While it is not easy to recognize or understand new art, meticulous, ponderous craftsmanship—the emulation of already recognized
art—can be appreciated at once. George Stevens used to direct some
pictures with good moments (*Alice Adams, The More the Merrier*);
now that he makes heavy, expensive pictures full of obese nuances
(*I Remember Mama, A Place in the Sun, Shane*) he is highly regarded. Literate carefulness is the much advertised "quality" of
Samuel Goldwyn productions (assemble "distinguished" writers, a
costly story property, director and actors and technicians with artistic reputations, and you have a "prestige" picture—though the results may suggest the old Community Chest slogan "Suppose nobody cared . . ."). The production values of a Goldwyn picture
(*The North Star, The Best Years of Our Lives, Hans Christian Andersen*) are not as banal and vulgar as those of *A Woman's World*,
but crudity has often been the only sign of life in American movies;
the prestige picture sacrifices even this feeble vitality for an impressive façade.

The look of solid, serious construction seems to be very important
to the educated audience; they are fearful of approving the films
of Cocteau—perhaps, like Gulley Jimson, he may be painting for
pleasure on walls that are collapsing. Readers who put down *The
Horse's Mouth* and ask anxiously if Gulley Jimson is really supposed to be a great painter are, no doubt, part of the same audience
that feels reassured when George Stevens says, "I don't make films
for pleasure." Work without joy is respectable; it doesn't raise
doubts that it may not be serious. Cocteau, with his enigmas and

ambiguities, is he not perhaps trying to put something over? His high style is suspicious; members of the serious audience don't want to go out on a limb for something that may turn out to be merely chic and fashionable. Though they are educated beyond the fat production values of routine pictures, they still want the fat of visible artistic effort. And there is something they want even more, something they value even higher than "artistic values"—the fat of "important ideas" and paraphrasable content (in the thirties, Warner Brothers was the chief purveyor; in the late forties, Stanley Kramer took over). While the less educated mass audience may be in awe of the man-hours and banker's dollars that go into a colossal production, the educated audience, uncertain and self-sacrificial, respects the good a movie will do for others.

PRESSURES

Our films are stuffed with good intentions. A *Life* editorial pointed out that "in 1951 Americans bought more tickets to symphony concerts than they did to baseball games. . . . The hunger of our citizenry for culture and self-improvement has always been grossly underestimated." Is it hunger or is it a nutritional deficiency? These educated people of conscience don't feel they should waste their time; they reserve their interest for films with praiseworthy aims. The themes favored by the serious audience in the thirties and forties—race relations and mob violence—are perfectly good themes, but treatment of them in conformity with the moral and social aims of conscientious people bleached the interest out. The morally awakened audience banished the early subhuman racial stereotypes from the screen; they developed their own stereotypes—which they must know to be lies and yet feel are *necessary* lies. Could Melville's *Benito Cereno* be filmed, a century after it was written, without a barrage of protests from the educated audience—an audience that cannot admit to the dread and terror of Melville's white man held captive by Negroes?

It is the enlightened message, e.g., *Gentleman's Agreement*, that people must be educated into tolerance; prejudice is wrong. Any motives indicated for the prejudice must be superficial or wrongheaded, so that the prejudiced character can be exposed, if not to himself, at least to the audience. At the lowest level in *It's a Big Country* (a bottom-grade big picture) the Jewish soldier was the usual Hollywood boy next door, and the woman's hostility toward him was the product of sheer ignorance; we left her enlightened by the recognition that he was exactly like the boy next door, only better, and she was about to correspond with his mother. At a more complex level in *Crossfire* the Jew-hater was a fanatic who never learned; but what the audience saw was once again the liberal stereotype: the murdered Jew was a decorated war hero. (Suppose the murdered man was a draft dodger, or a conscientious objector, would the audience then feel no sting, would the fanatic have been justified in killing him?) In John Sturges' *Bad Day at Black Rock* (one of the few reasonably good films to come out of Hollywood this year) the pattern is the same: the period is 1945 and the victim of the townspeople is a murdered Japanese farmer—this time it is the victim's son (killed in action) who is the decorated war hero. By a quota system, war films admitted carefully selected minority representatives, clean-cut Jewish and Negro soldiers whose participation in the national defense apparently gave them a special claim to equality over and above mere membership in the human species. Can it be that even in liberal thinking there is a stigma which can be rubbed off only if minority characters behave heroically?

The fantasy structure is familiar: We have had countless movie heroines who sin (i.e., express sexual passion) and repent by way of almost automatic illegitimate births and various forms of social condemnation. Eventually they "work off" the sin by self-sacrifice, commonly the sacrifice of mother for child. This pleasure-pain bookkeeping (for which the production code, and hence the pressure groups, are partly responsible) tells you that you pay for pleasure by the sacrifice of all future pleasures. Can it be that for the middle classes, Jews and Negroes also need to work off something? Pinky gave up the white doctor and dedicated her life to her people; in what sense they were her people at all it was hard to say, but as a partly Negro heroine she was expected to behave sacrificially—like the escaped convict she had to return to prison to pay her debt to society.

How effective, one wonders, are the "necessary" lies of well-meaning people when the mass audience lives in a world full of the very people that the movies tell us are figments of prejudiced thinking—the Negroes of Harlem or the Fillmore, the Jews of Broadway and Central Park West, and the Hollywood producers of the Hillcrest Country Club, with its own gentleman's agreement (no Gentiles accepted). Films may "expose" anti-Semitism or anti-Negroism but they dare not deal with Semitism or Negroism (the existence of which they deny). Behind the pressures that destroy the thematic possibilities in race relations (and similar pressures obtain in sex relations) is the fear that some portions of the public are not intelligent enough to understand that if one Jew is pictured as aggressive, this does not mean that all are aggressive; or if one Negro pulls a knife in a fight, all will; or, for that matter, if one dentist over-charges, all do. This fear has been played upon by the leaders of minorities and pressure groups: Negroes or Jews are made to feel that because others might associate them with the actions of Jose-phine Baker or Walter Winchell, they are somehow responsible for those actions. Any Italian or doctor or psychiatrist on the screen is considered as a *representative* of the group, who might, by his action, discredit the whole group. In order to protect themselves, minorities act upon the premise which they ascribe to the ignorant public.

The situation is not simple. Art derives from human experience, and the artist associates certain actions and motivations with certain cultural and vocational groups because that is how he has observed and experienced them. Would Jews be so fearful of the depiction of Jewish characters as ostentatious and vulgar, aggressive and secre-tive, if they did not recognize that these elements often converge in "Jewishness"? Would Negroes be so sensitive to the images of sullen bestiality and economic irresponsibility if they did not feel the im-pact? It is the germ of observed truth that pressure groups fear a germ which infects only the individual but which the group treats as epidemic. The whole group becomes defensive under the guid-ance of pressuring leaders who inoculate them with false responsi-bilities. All these inoculations have produced a real democratic disease: a mass culture made up of stereotypes, models, whitewashes, smiles and lies. To allow the artist to treat his experience freely may be dangerous, but it is a step toward the restoration of individual responsibility. And how else can American indifference and cyni-cism be cured?

Truth is feared most of all in the visualization of sex relations. The presumption is that romantic models of happiness are less dangerous than truth, that if youngsters saw in films the same kind of problems they experience and see all about them, they would be "misled" into believing that human relations are often difficult, painful and un-satisfactory, that society is unwilling to consider the problems of adolescents, and that the impetus for divorce is not an absurd, un-motivated quarrel which will be patched up in the last reel (*Phfft!*) but a miserable impasse. These lies are certainly more dangerous than truth; the split between the romantic glorifications of love, marriage and family life and our actual mores adds to the perplexity and guilt of those whom the films seek to protect.

Films do not suffer from the pressure to do something; they turn into drivel because of the pressures not to do almost everything. One may suspect that there is something fundamentally corrupt in a concept of democracy which places safety, harmony and conformity above truth. The educated audience deplores the films offered to the less educated audience, but, in order to protect the ignorant, and in the cause of democracy, they effectively prevent an exploration of the living world. Art, perhaps unfortunately, is not the sphere of good intentions.

IS ANYTHING LEFT?

If there are almost no films (except the suspense variety) set in contemporary America, the reason is clear: there are almost no modern themes acceptable to the mass audience. The treatment of historical subjects generally reduces them to nothing (*Desirée*), but it is easier to dress up nothing in a foreign or period setting. The hollowness of the big productions is a direct result of the effort to please the public while doing nothing that might displease countless sections within the public. (A competent movie like *Blackboard Jungle* has to fight its way against pressure groups and legal action.) To a marked degree, the effort is self-defeating: when nothing is left to hang the *décor* on, audiences get bored. They were amazed and delighted when *On the Waterfront* and, before that, *From Here to Eternity* made contact with some areas in their experience; it's as if they had forgotten that movies could mean anything at all. It may be that such box-office successes as *The Robe* and *Quo Vadis* are among the last belches of the giant. Spectacles will cease to be events, and audiences can be more comfortably bored at home. Tony Curtis and Janet Leigh can easily transfer to television, which has inherited not only the worst of radio and vaudeville but the content of B movies as well (the dreary humors of family life). Americans do have some sort of taste: they will accept mediocrity, but they don't like to *pay* for it. Vaudeville died because people refused to support it in its decrepitude, but they were perfectly willing to listen to its ghost on the radio. They will suffer, on television, chopped-up, incoherent prints of bad movies—the very worst specimens of what destroyed their enthusiasm for going out to a theater. (David Riesman's suggestion that people over thirty may be staying away from theaters because "films are too mature, move too fast, for older people to catch on to and catch up with" is altogether remarkable. No doubt, Americans as they age do tend to lose the youngsters' lively interest in the world, but American movies show the same middle-aged spread. To a sociologist, movies can be a constant source of material on up-to-date habits and manners. But one interested in film as an art form finds these surface shifts about as significant as a sculptor finds the cosmetic lore of Forest Lawn. Riesman offers us possibilities of "mature" comedy. Documentary camera in hand, one would like to follow the proposed team of "humanists and social scientists" as they "come together to see what each set of skills might contribute to heighten the awareness of Americans of all ages for the imaginative qualities of their best films." The man who described for us the outlines of the American mousetrap now calls for mice to walk in. Skilled teamwork, having already destroyed movies, will now take over movie criticism.)

Americans don't have to go to the movies at all. They spend as much money on equipment for fishing as they do at movie box offices; they spend as much on hunting and bowling. Sports not only invite participation, they provide suspense about the outcome (something which our movies have failed to do for a long time); sports are geared to leisure interests, travel, photography and a whole range of consumer goods—casual clothes, equipage. And sports comprise the proper interests for getting along and getting ahead in a sociable way.

Drama, on the other hand, posits intense interest in the character and destiny of the individual, and American culture is indifferent, and even hostile, to strong individuality. The American film is no longer concerned with characters of real dramatic stature; it gives the actor few chances for any interesting or full characterizations and often constricts acting possibilities to the barest minimum. Films do not center as much as they used to on one or two heroic individuals who were often engaged in a grand passion, or a drive toward money or power, or even in some struggle against society and conventions. The new heroes and heroines of film and television are dismaying—not because they're not attractive and presentable (often they're competently played), but because they represent the death of drama as we have known it. They are not protagonists in any meaningful sense; they represent the voice of adjustment, the caution against individuality, independence, emotionality, art, ambition, personal vision. They represent the antidrama of American life. Biblical spectacles convey magnitude of character by magnitude of close-up. Film versions of the lives of the "great" turn out to be success stories drawn from the mass media—Knute Rockne, Marty Mahrer, Glenn Miller, Eva Tanguay, Ruth Etting, Jackie Robinson, Houdini, Cole Porter, Rodgers and Hart, Sigmund Romberg, Jane Froman, "Crazy-Legs" Hirsch, Lou Gehrig, Joe Louis, etc. And with Valentino, Al Jolson, Eddie Cantor, and the projected Jean Harlow and Theda Bara, Hollywood feeds upon itself—a confection only for jaded palates. The heroism of Hollywood is the gift of itself to the world: *A Star Is Born* is the epic of Hollywood's self-sacrifice. The new path for success is to enact the success of someone else in the same field; when you have reached the summits, you re-enact your own success.

Other arts show an internal logic in their development, the constant solving of aesthetic challenges; films have changed simply by following the logic of the market. When one cycle was exhausted, a new personality (embodying some recognizable form of human experience and a new kind of sexual excitement) in a new type of picture usually set off another. Joan Crawford doing the Charleston on the table in *Our Dancing Daughters* incarnated a new youthful abandon for her period, just as Valentino had brought dark, exotic sensuality to his, and Fairbanks joy of life to his. Bette Davis introduced a more complicated sexual character—driving, neurotic. When the public interest in gangsters and the socially downtrodden was exhausted, and the war over, Hollywood lacked a social orientation. Kirk Douglas injected something new into melodrama: he represented a new type—the guy who's got the stuff, but who is really a wrong guy, the ambitious heel in a disoriented society. Now Marlon Brando breathes some life into films: he projects the tensions of displaced, alienated American youth—characters who reject the hypocritical society that denies their instincts. Refresher personalities don't, of course, stay fresh; their roles become stale; the public becomes satiated. Idolatry turns to mockery and boredom, and new idols appear. When his magic was gone, it didn't matter that Charles Boyer was an excellent actor. Sometimes the public gets the full spectacle of the fall: John Barrymore became a buffoon. And the public was more than willing to turn Garbo into a national butt of humor.

Though even the biggest stars have not remained at the zenith, we are now witnessing a desperately contrived effort to keep them there: waning stars provide the "big" names for the big productions. Clark Gable or Gary Cooper, Robert Taylor or James Stewart add size and importance, but do they have any vital star quality left? Advertising announces "the *new* Greer Garson" or "Lana as you've never seen her before"—obviously the public wasn't buying the old Greer or Lana. Can Hollywood manufacture the artificial asteroid? (Joan Crawford has come to represent the tenacity of a woman determined to remain a star: her survival power is the only drawing power she has left. She shows us her legs to prove that they are *still* good.) From time to time newspapers or the radio play upon the popular nostalgia about old favorites, but the public stopped buying a Norma Shearer or a Janet Gaynor long before they faded. The camera itself uses up an Esther Williams rapidly; her expressive resources are so limited that close-ups are like billboard ads—the image is constant, only the backgrounds vary. Can a new refresher find so much as a toe hold in the blubber of big films? The old big name or the actor who can impersonate a model American is safer than a challenging new personality; the studios are rather resentful of Brando's drawing power: what big pictures does he really fit into? He will, of course, be remade to fit.

When the remains of Christianity are returned to their caskets, Hollywood may delve into Buddhism or Mohammedanism (all gods are pretty much alike and resemblance to the Christian god will, no doubt, lend the others a certain respectability). This step is foreshadowed in *The Egyptian.* A clash of cymbals announces the name of Darryl F. Zanuck, but, with all modesty, the letters of fire are reserved for the postscript: "All these things happened thirteen centuries before the birth of Christ." (Obviously the producers would like to get precedence on *The Robe*—an estimated $19 million gross.) Why should Americans be offended by other religions when they can all be depicted as anticipations of the true faith? Hollywood will probably also "adjust" itself. *Rogue Cop* is a somewhat longer and bigger version of the typical glossy MGM melodrama of the thirties and forties. It is what might be called the "academic commercial" film—competently done, considering that it's not worth doing. Can films like this, over a period of time, draw people away from television and into theaters? It's more than doubtful—the material of television drama *is* old movie melodrama; when films recapitulate their past, they're in a deadlock with television. And the film becomes increasingly subject to pressure. That *Rogue Cop* has been banned in some states, at the insistence of police departments who argue that the crooked cop of the film might give some juvenile delinquents the wrong idea about policemen, suggests that there is almost no subject matter left for the mass-audience film. When everybody knows that there is widespread police corruption, the movies are not supposed to show even one cop who isn't a model (the police have good reason to be so sensitive). Obviously if one made a film about an incompetent teacher's effect upon a child, or dramatized the results of a doctor's mistaken diagnosis, one would be in trouble. (Artists, on the other hand, may be pictured as pathological cowards, cheats and murderers—they're not organized.) Every group wants glorification, but even glorification carries risks (audiences can be derisive about the discrepancies between film and fact), so perhaps it is safer to leave all subjects untouched. This feat is virtually accomplished in films like *White Christmas* and *The Long Gray Line*. Fear of offending someone—anyone—may help to account for the death of American film comedy. Films like *Roxie Hart, His Girl Friday, A Letter to Three Wives,* and the Preston Sturges comedies didn't seem so important when we had them; in retrospect, after a *Sabrina*, they acquire new luster. While serious drama is smothered by moral restrictions and the preordained ending (characters must get their "just deserts"), the verve and zest of comedy dribble away when you're half afraid to make a joke of anything.

WHO CARES ABOUT MOVIES?

It may be that in a few years the film situation will be comparable to the present stage situation. The few dozen Broadway plays a year are supplemented by thousands of little theaters and college groups. It would not be unlikely that a few hundred big houses showing big Hollywood productions would be surrounded by a swarm of small "art" houses, catering to a fairly limited audience and showing foreign films, revivals and new American films—experimental or, at least, inexpensive ones. The art houses might even be forced to help finance small new films. Good American films like *The Treasure of Sierra Madre* have often failed financially—possibly because they attempted to succeed in the wrong places; if Hollywood could make good pictures on a low-budget basis, book them into art houses, and give them months and even years to return the investment, they might show a modest profit.

Small houses cannot grow to a swarm on foreign films alone. After the initial enthusiasm for French, Italian and English films, Americans begin to lose interest. The acceptance of life in European films, the acceptance of joys and defeats, does not make vital contact with American experience. We do not live in those terms, and *our* terms are apparently somewhat incomprehensible to Europeans. Representations of Americans in foreign films always feel wrong to an American audience. It is true we are shallow, but we are not carefree and irresponsible, we are shallowly *serious*. Even the worst American films have often had more energy than the imports. English comedies, with their high level of craftsmanship, their quiet charm and their tiny scope, become almost as wearisome to us as the shoddy tasteless products of Hollywood. Success within such small limits is ultimately not very interesting, especially to Americans. *Genevieve* is delightful, but have you missed anything if you didn't see it? And just how many *Genevieves* do you want to see? The economy of the enterprise is so straitened; you can't accuse the English of not fulfilling large intentions because they don't aim very high. Where is the insolence that gives bite to comedy? The English have their own way of playing it safe. Not every moving picture can be great or even good, and there can be no objection to honest failure or modest success. But every work of art has a core of risk and it is around this core that the work takes form.

Our commercialized culture never integrates all the individuals with energy and talent. They constitute a reserve of independence and dissidence, and idiosyncrasy. And in this reserve there is, perhaps, a more vital hope for the American film.

There are people who can sit around for hours discussing early films, giving detailed accounts of dialogue, action, gesture, even costume, exchanging remembered reactions to Colin Clive, or what Nils Asther was like in *The Bitter Tea of General Yen*, or Bette Davis in *Cabin in the Cotton*. Sentiment and romance may be attached to the memories, but, more important, these people remember movies because they were alert to them. They were fascinated by what went on in the films—the personalities, the talents, the inadvertences, the reactions of the audience, the mélange of techniques, the actress working against hopeless material, the director injecting a clever bit of business, the glaring close-ups as in a strip tease revealing the human material. The people who love movies are a knowing audience; the early period of going to movies has not deadened their taste, it has cultivated it. They are capable of judging in advance just about what a given production will be like, though they may want to taste for themselves the precise flavor even of horseradish. Films are at the mercy of this knowing audience: it goes to see everything it can in a film, and often comes out with much more than it was intended to see. In a sense, every movie is a documentary: the actor is as exposed as the tenant farmer, the sets as exposed as the Aran Islands. In one way or another, everyone who goes to the movies knows this; when the film fails to hold the attention of the audience and when the theater situation permits, the disgruntled patrons comment on what is exposed to them.

Just as there are people alive to poetry but blind to painting, there are literate people who don't care for movies. The quality of most Hollywood films has made it easy for them to say they are not interested, without even that nod at acknowledging a failing that usually accompanies the statement that one draws a blank on opera or poetry. They tend, in fact, to view lack of interest in films as evidence of superiority and to be contemptuous of the "low tastes" of those who go to films frequently (many of them *do* go to movies—in guilty secrecy). One is inclined to suspect that these people who dismiss movies as a lost cause and a circus for the masses never could tell a good picture from a poor one.

With all the waste and disappointment, growing up at the films was, for our generation, an extraordinary education of the senses. We were in almost at the beginning, when something new was added to human experience. In high school and college we formed friendships as much on the basis of film tastes as of literature or politics. When the commercialized Hollywood films could no longer satisfy our developing tastes, *Le Jour se Lève* and *La Grande Illusion* restored us. After more than fifteen years one still recalls the rage one felt toward the college boy who was so busy pointing out the biographical falsifications in *Beethoven* that he had no eyes for Harry Bauer. Arguments about films were formative, and, by the logic of developing taste, those who cared enough to argue found that film-going resulted in disgust. It took a couple of decades for Hollywood films to wear us out; we wearied more quickly of the imports. While in the mass audience older people abandoned movies to the kids, we could not abandon film-going any more than we could give up other vital appetites.

Cocteau, after revivals of *Blood of a Poet*, emerged as the most important film maker, not necessarily because one especially liked the film, but because Cocteau suggested to us the shattering possibilities of an artist using the medium for his own ends, not just to make movies, but to say what he wanted to say in movies. Because of him, we began to look at films in a new way: we were no longer merely audience, we were potential film makers. And we discovered new ancestors. Searching through early film experiments, looking for the excitement that our senses told us the medium could produce, we found the early experimenters who had discovered the film medium for themselves. When we arrived at the infant beginnings of film art, we realized that we had grown up in a period of steady decline, scarcely aware of what films had started out to be.

From the beginning, American film makers have been crippled by business financing and the ideology it imposed: they were told that they had an obligation to entertain the general public, that this was a democratic function and a higher obligation than to give their best to a few hundred or a few million people. This "obligation" forced even the early innovators to lard their work with sentimentality. And this "obligation" has contributed to fear of the medium itself—they began to use titles and music to explain and add to what they were already doing with images; when sound became possible, they were fearful of imaginative or difficult speech and music. It is clear now that there is more than one audience, and that artists must judge their own obligations. The film artist knows what happened to the innovators; he knows he can't expect the banks and studios to finance him. Fortunately his experience at expensive movies should have surfeited him—his tastes need not be so extravagant. If he wants to make movies he must cadge and borrow and save and fill out fellowship forms and beg from foundations—like other American artists. And if he produces a squiggly little mess of abstract patterns or a symbolic drama full of knives, keys and figures receding in the night, at least the responsibility is where it should be.

The responsibility is on the artist, even when he tries to evade responsibility. If, so far, American experimental and "little" films haven't received much support, most of them haven't deserved it, either. All too frequently, after an evening of avant-garde cinema, one wants to go see a movie (at least a little fresh air comes in through the holes in Hollywood plots). Though avant-garde film makers don't always know what they're doing when they make a film, they demonstrate a marvelous talent for the post-factum scenario; often their greatest effort at composition is in explaining away the lack of it in their films. They become so adept at escaping consideration of their failures and limitations that they rarely develop at all; what they fail to put in they deride you for not seeing there. You're supposed to find a whole world of meaning in that three-minute cinepoem. The times are out of joint: the poisonous atmosphere of Hollywood premieres is distilled to pure pretension at avant-garde premieres. Object to the Hollywood film and you're an intellectual snob, object to the avant-garde films and you're a Philistine. But, while in Hollywood, one must often be a snob; in avant-garde circles one must often be a Philistine.

This is from Gilbert Seldes' The Great Audience (*The Viking Press, New York, 1950*), *a book which examines various aspects of radio, television and the movies. Here Mr. Seldes rakes the Production Code over the coals. Since its formulation in the twenties, it has been a pox on directors and writers, causing them to smuggle in, wherever they can, "illicit" goods. Unhappily this has resulted in falsification, evasion and the inevitable portrayal of love and sex as a dirty business.*

S-e-x

by Gilbert Seldes

THE CODE itself is flanked by "Reasons Supporting the Preamble of the Code," "Reasons Underlying the General Principles," and "Reasons Underlying Particular Applications"; all contain important items, of which the following are the most significant.

From the Code:

SEX

The sanctity of the institution of marriage and the home shall be upheld. Pictures shall not infer that low forms of sex relationship are the accepted or common thing.

1. *Adultery and Illicit Sex*, sometimes necessary plot material, must not be explicitly treated, or justified, or presented attractively.

2. *Scenes of Passion*
   a. These should not be introduced except where they are definitely essential to the plot.
   b. Excessive and lustful kissing, lustful embraces, suggestive postures and gestures are not to be shown.
   c. In general, passion should be treated in such manner as not to stimulate the lower and baser emotions.

3. *Seduction or Rape*
   a. These should never be more than suggested, and then only when essential for the plot. They must never be shown by explicit method.
   b. They are never the proper subject for comedy.

The fourth item forbids "any inference of sex perversion," the fifth bans the subject of white slavery, and the sixth bars "sex relationship between the white and black races." The seventh declares that sex hygiene and venereal diseases are not subjects for theatrical motion pictures, the eighth opposes showing scenes of "*actual child birth,* in fact or in silhouette," and the ninth says simply that "children's sex organs are never to be exposed."

That is the total of the Code's specifications under the heading of "Sex." Under "Profanity" a few illuminating notes are to be found. Among the words and phrases not to be used are "bat" and "broad" if applied to a woman—also "tart" and "whore"; nor "madam" (relating to prostitution); and "traveling salesman and farmer's daughter jokes" are out. The adjective "hot" is not to be applied to women, and "fairy" (in a vulgar sense) and "pansy" (not so qualified) are forbidden. Under "Repellent Subjects" (after brutality and possible gruesomeness, branding of people or animals) the code notes that "the sale of women or a woman selling her virtue" must be treated "within the careful limits of good taste."

"The Reasons Underlying Particular Applications" begin with the statement that "*sin and evil* enter into the story of human beings and hence in themselves are valid dramatic material." (All italics are in the original.)

Under "Sex": "Out of regard for the sanctity of marriage and the home, the *triangle,* that is, the love of a third party for one already married, needs careful handling. The treatment should not throw sympathy against marriage as an institution."

The language of the Code and its appendices is often obscure and in discussing sex is generally offensive. But the quotation above is a masterpiece of "careful handling" in itself; by this definition the "triangle" is one-sided; it does not involve the love of "one already married" for "a third party," only the reverse. The fixed rule that actuality must be distorted could not be better illustrated. Within this definition of the triangle, romance and sentimentality are possible, as the long devotion of a lover to a married woman who either does not return his love or is merely waiting for her husband to die before yielding. Comedy is possible, since a hopeless love can be made ridiculous. But neither adultery nor divorce is possible. The basic section of the Code, as quoted above, concedes the existence of adultery and allows its use if it is not made attractive; the "Reasons" blandly assume that adultery does not exist. However—

Scenes of passion must be treated with an honest acknowledgment of human nature and its normal reactions. Many scenes cannot be presented without arousing dangerous emotions on the part of the immature, the young, or the criminal classes.

Even within the limits of *pure love*, certain facts have been universally regarded by lawmakers as outside the limits of safe presentation.

In practice, what the Code calls "pure love" is pure because it is passionless; in day-to-day operations, the Code authority eliminates scenes of passion, and human nature and its normal reactions are not honestly acknowledged. Perhaps the most degrading effect of the Code is the mean and mawkish concept of marriage it has forced upon the movies.

The next explanation concerns the love "which society has always regarded as wrong." This is a wild exaggeration; certain sections of society, at certain times, have held adultery in esteem and considered marital fidelity an evidence of low moral standards, lack of enterprise, or sheer bad luck. The semantics of the Code need study. The additional phrase about love "which has been banned by divine law" refers, presumably, to the Seventh Commandment. This "impure love" must not

be presented as *attractive and beautiful;*
be the subject of comedy or farce or treated as material for laughter;
be presented in such a way as to *arouse passion* on the part of the audience;
be made to seem *right and permissible;*
be detailed in method and manner.

The other sections of the Code, the "Reasons Supporting the Preamble" and the "Reasons Underlying the General Principles," supply the moral and philosophical groundwork for the specific commandments on sex. They compose a self-justification of the Code, and in one respect they are cogent and clear. The motion picture "has special MORAL OBLIGATIONS" because it affects audiences in special ways. Neither the aesthetes who saluted the movies nor those who despised them were particularly interested in effects and obligations; the churchmen who worked out the Code have the advantage. They saw that

this art appeals at once to *every class;*
this art *reaches places* unpenetrated by other forms of art;
the exhibitors' theaters are built for the masses, for the mature and immature. . . . Films . . . can with difficulty be confined to certain groups;
a book describes; a film vividly presents . . . by apparently living people;
a book reaches the mind through the words merely; a film reaches the eyes and ears through the reproduction of actual events.

I refrain from adding italics to those of the Code; if the last words above had been emphasized, they would require much thought; presumably they mean the reproduction of events on the sound stages, as suggested above by "apparently living people." The Code is aware of the remarkable illusion of reality produced by the movies, as witness:

the reaction to a film depends on the vividness of presentation;
the film [unlike newspapers which are "after the fact"] gives the events in the process of enactment and with the apparent reality of life;

and even of the moral effect of the star system:

. . . the audience is . . . ready to confuse actor and actress and characters they portray, and it is most receptive of the emotions and ideals presented by their favorite stars.

Finally, the Code delivers its own fundamental concept of the motion picture. In contrast with entertainment "which tends to degrade human beings or to lower their standards of life and living," the movies are primarily to be regarded as "ENTERTAINMENT which tends to improve the race, or at least to re-create and rebuild human beings exhausted with the realities of life." Reference is made to "the healthy reactions to healthful sports, like baseball, golf," and to the "unhealthy reactions to sports like cock-fighting, bull-fighting, bear-baiting, etc." The gladiatorial combats and "the obscene plays

of Roman times" are mentioned to demonstrate the effect they had
on ancient nations; wrong entertainment "lowers the whole living
conditions and moral ideas of a race."

The vexing question of the relation between Art and Morals is
discussed, not lucidly, but with conviction:

Art can be *morally good.* . . . Art can be *morally evil.* . . . It has often
been argued that art in itself is unmoral, neither good nor bad. This is
perhaps true of the THING which is music, painting, poetry, etc. But the
thing is the PRODUCT of some person's mind and the intention of that mind
was either good or bad morally when it produced the thing. Besides the
thing it has its EFFECT upon those who come into contact with it; . . . as
a product of a mind and the cause of definite effects, it has a deep moral
significance and an unmistakable moral quality.
. . . The motion pictures . . . have their moral quality from the intention of the minds which produce them and from their effects on the moral
lives and reactions of their audiences. This gives them a most important
morality.
1. They reproduce the morality of the men who use the pictures as a
medium for the expression of their ideas and ideals.
2. They affect the moral standards of those who, through the screen, take
in these ideas and ideals.

The first of these numbered statements is either meaningless or
is a gross libel on writers, producers, directors and actors. The morality of the movies is imposed upon them. If "the men who use the
pictures as a medium" refers to the owners of the studios and the
distributors of the pictures, it is possible to say that their morality is
"reproduced," but not that their ideas and ideals are expressed. The
second statement, if it is true, puts upon the entertainment film
(which is fundamentally considered to be the same as the amusement
film) an intolerable moral burden. Again the Code sidesteps actuality.

Following the Code from its specific thou-shalt-nots to its philosophy produces a strange effect of sympathy; the Code so patently
does not say what it wants most to say, that all life must be carefully
falsified to conform to an ethical ideal; it acknowledges *"sin and evil*
. . . [as] . . . *valid dramatic material"* and promptly becomes
entangled in details of good taste; an amateur semanticist, a logician,
an untutored shrewd Yankee of the time of Thoreau, a modern
adolescent, could tear the argument to shreds. It is a self-defeating
document because if its premises are true, if the movies are responsible for moral standards, if they re-create and rebuild human beings, if
like other works of art they are "the presentation of human thought,

emotion, and experience, in terms of an appeal to the soul through the senses," then they cannot possibly function under an imposed Code; only movies made purely for distraction, appealing to the mass minority, can be made in this way. The positive demands of distributors dovetail nicely with the negative commandments of the Code; both demand an art from which, as far as possible, all "human thought, emotion, and experience" have been eliminated, and at times the distributors and the backers of the Code have expressed great satisfaction with their success.

I believe that the Production Code, as it operates today, does actual, demonstrable harm to the community; although I do not exaggerate the influence of the movies (or any other art) I think that the Code, its frivolous applications, and the evasions it encourages have become a dangerous and destructive element in American life. I have not cited the passages, more numerous and explicit, on the handling of crime, since it is well known that Code approval has been given to pictures of the astounding and totally meaningless brutality which has become the distinguishing mark of the American film and has penetrated to comedy and psychological drama; while the forces of law and order have become as violent as the criminal whom the Code forbids the movies to glorify. Here the Code has been either powerless or indifferent; the rules governing all the aspects of sex are the ones upon which the Code insists, and on the consequences of these rules the Code must stand.

The prime effect of the Code is to create a sexual morality which no moralist, no great religious leader, no church has ever tolerated. It is as mythical as the social and economic contrivances of the movies are. "Driven out and compelled to be chaste," the creative artists in the movies have fabricated a world of fantasy. Like all imaginary worlds it has its own rules:

Pure love, as the Code calls it, is not sexual; it may have what the physiologists call "secondary sexual characteristics," but it's not physical.

If love is sensual, it is immoral and occurs only between a "wicked" character and a weak one.

Consequently, good women are fundamentally sexless (compare any good wife and mother with any old-fashioned "vamp" or contemporary "good-bad" woman).

A further consequence—the sexual relation, the actuality of passion between man and woman, exists outside the marriage re-

lationship exclusively; within the sacrament of marriage, passion
is outlawed.

Essential to all of these laws of behavior is the idea that while men
may at times derive pleasure from sexual love, women never do. This
concept was familiar long before the Code was established, and from
Clara Bow to Greta Garbo the movies presented a series of women
who looked with innocence or surprise or distaste, but never with
pleasure, upon the advances of the lustful male; at the same time the
movies presented endless variations of the vampire, the siren who
lured men to their destruction, following some obscure purpose of
her own, revenge, perhaps, or ambition, or desire for power, but
not for the ecstasy of passion or the simple pleasure of getting into
bed with a man.

The word commonly used in describing movies and movie actresses is "sexy"; the word commonly used to describe living people
of strong sexual enterprise is "passionate." Since the movies are forbidden to display sensuality, "sexy" is a proper adjective; it implies
an as-if state, not an actual one. Just as the word "manly" is never
used about a man, as "womanly" is used only for secondary attributes of women, "sexy" refers to the superficial and the immature
aspects of the relation between men and women, to the apparatus of
seduction and not to the pains or pleasures if seduction succeeds, to
provocation, not to satisfaction.

Winthrop Sargeant (whom *Life* designated "the most philosophical of our editors") discussed Rita Hayworth and concluded: "It
has remained for Americans of the hard-boiled twentieth century to
enthrone Aphrodite as the supreme deity of their popular religion,
to portray her rather dubious machinations as the most exalting and
satisfying of human experiences, and to subscribe with unquestion-
ing faith to her incessant litany that sex is the most important thing
in the world." Commenting on these words and the movies' "obsessive cult of love" in general, Lloyd Morris, in *Not So Long Ago*,
wrote: "And this . . . seemed to be all that the movies had found
to say . . . on the subject of love." Mr. Morris' section on the movies in his book is generally well balanced, bringing in the athleti-
cism of a Douglas Fairbanks against the It Girl and modifying Mr.
Sargeant's excesses by noting other, more scholarly investigations
which conclude that Hollywood's presentation of love has "very
little psychological validity." The point still needs making that the
Greeks had no goddess of the non-act of sex. The silver-limbed implacable Aphrodite was caught in bed with Ares, held by the net of
chains her husband had forged, and "a roar of unquenchable laugh-

ter rose from the blessed gods" at the sight; the girdles she fastened around the thighs of her votaries were unloosed by men as promptly as possible, "and they took their joy of love together." There might be something farcical in love or something tragic; the appetite for love made the gods treacherous and led men and women to heroic sacrifice or to the murder of those who stood in their way. It was not the only desire of humankind, but it was recognized for what it was and faithfully rendered in myth and epic and drama. It was not romanticized and it was not falsified.

It is a possible argument that nothing true or significant about sex can be said in so universal a medium as the movies. It is also possible to take the word of those European novelists who tell us that Americans know nothing of love, because that would at least explain our acceptance of the movie substitute for the real thing. Both of these arguments have the merit of candor; they acknowledge the false image of love presented on the screen. I do not think either has general application, and the simplest explanation of all is, I believe, the soundest: the movies are made primarily for an audience of children and adolescents. The audience begins to go to the movies at the age when myths are sufficient; it continues to go during the romantic phase of adolescence. The presentation of mature passions might bewilder such an audience. Adults who remain fervent patrons have perhaps not reached the phase of reality or have retreated from it. They may find consolation in the bright lies that the movies tell about love, as they may find it in the low-pitched and agonized falsifications of the daytime serial.

The movie substitute for love serves for a time, for some people. The majority of those who know anything about the real thing find that substitute unacceptable. Since the movies have an impressive atmosphere of reality and their version of non-love is presented to adolescents at the formative period of their lives, they may themselves be contributing to the unhappiness in marriage of the American people. Certainly half a century of upholding the sanctity of the marriage bond has not diminished the number of divorces on the grounds of adultery, and if we are approaching a single standard for men and women it is the standard of accepted promiscuity. Perhaps this is the inevitable result of presenting love as trivial, marriage as sexless, and cohabitation as an act to be delayed as long as possible.

There is no question about the sexiness of the movies, their tendency to reduce all other human relations to familiar terms in a sexual equation. In European movies set against the background of postwar rubble and desolation, the actuality of sexual passion plays a part; the most intelligent of the American pictures in that setting,

A Foreign Affair, is more realistic than most in rendering the atmosphere of a broken civilization, but the picture turns into a charade in which Jean Arthur and Marlene Dietrich represent the familiar figures of the good (cold) woman and the bad one (who is not cold). Cecil De Mille thrives on the sexiness he injects into his Biblical extravaganzas; and other specialists use history or science or the lives of composers to the same ends. To the superficial moralist, this preoccupation with sex is in itself dubious; to our European critics it is ridiculous because the preoccupation is real, the sex is not.

In the depths of the depression Paramount signed Mae West, despite her sensational career as a merchant of provocative sexual tidbits, and, ignoring the threats of censorship, proceeded to make several pictures with her. These constitute the exception; the character portrayed by Miss West always expressed the liveliest anticipations of pleasure from the embraces of men, and romantic love was brushed aside with a knowing wink. The character was promiscuous and friendly, impure love was essentially used for comic effect, and the pictures were as refreshing as if the Wife of Bath had suddenly appeared on the screen. The Code was in existence when Paramount, driven by economic pressure, dared to flout it; a few years later the administration of the Code was fully organized, and Miss West's work, while never reduced to the mincing politeness of the usual screen character, suffered.

The exceptional, almost unique quality of the early Mae West pictures was that by implication she was portraying a "bad woman" who was thoroughly enjoying life. The vamps of the silent pictures were intense and tortured; Miss West's characters were good company. Just as the vamps were followed by Clara Bow, the It Girl, who suggested that the ideal mate for the American man was the captain of the girls' basketball team in the local high school, the cheerful courtesan of Mae West was followed by the character usually described as the "good-bad" girl. This is not the conventional dramatic figure of the harlot with a heart of gold; appearances are against the girl, but she herself is no wanton, she gets no pleasure out of it; and her goodness lies in the passionless wish to be united in respectable marriage to the hero: In *Movies, a Psychological Study*, Dr. Martha Wolfenstein and Dr. Nathan Leites suggest that the forbidden wishes of the audience are realized in the "false appearances" of the movies, "since we can enjoy the suggested wish fulfillments without emphatic guilt." I cannot quarrel with this analysis, but I am left wondering what the ultimate effect of all these "false appearances" may be.

A note should be made of one of the rare instances of the appearance of common reality in the movies. At the request of Woody Van Dyke, who directed *The Thin Man*, the writing team of Frances Goodrich and Albert Hackett provided several scenes between William Powell and Myrna Loy which were in the bantering tone that later became standard practice. These scenes managed to suggest, and the director underlined, the important fact that a man and his own wife were in love with each other, took pleasure in each other's company, and (by the single deft motion with which Powell removed the dog Asta from Miss Loy's berth) intended to sleep together.

These exceptions are remembered precisely because they managed to violate the prevailing customs of the films. Or, it might be said, because they correspond to the customs of the country.

One of the customs of the country is divorce, and nothing in the Code specifically instructs the producers on the handling of this subject. In practice the movies have created a mythology of divorce, the essence of which is that divorced couples always remarry. This usually takes place after the husband has escaped from sex, represented by a wicked woman, or the wife has seen through a plausible cad with whom she has been tempted to enjoy impure love.

The minor myths create the proper atmosphere:

Divorce occurs for trivial reasons only; it is the consequence of hasty tempers or misunderstandings or a desire to rise in the world of society or finance.

Divorce does not occur because of sexual incompatibility or incompetence.

Divorce does not occur because of adultery.
The way to prevent divorce is for the wronged partner to pretend to be in love with someone else.

Alternatively, if the wronged partner is the wife, she can take off her horn-rimmed glasses.

Husbands and wives are much together during divorce proceedings; if they are not, and a divorcee marries again, all the forces of nature combine to prevent the consummation of the second marriage, giving time for the first husband to reappear and win the wife back.

The motion-picture equivalent of the old shivaree should provide material for a sociologist. The Production Code says: "The treatment of bedrooms must be governed by good taste and delicacy"; and the "Reasons Underlying" offer this explanation: "Certain places are so closely and thoroughly associated with sexual life or with sexual sin that their use must be carefully limited." In the mythology of marriage this has come to mean that the bridal night is a long series of accidents through which young lovers are kept from entering or staying in the same room after nightfall. It is, in effect, a long strip tease, a source of merriment innocent only in the technical sense. The ingenuity of picture makers in creating new obstacles to the consummation of marriage is admirable, unless perhaps it is pathological to set up They Shall Not Cohabit as the great commandment for the legally married.

The devices for keeping lovers apart before they are married fall into a conventional pattern; they are a courteous bow to established morality and can produce delightful moments like the "Walls of Jericho" sequence in *It Happened One Night*. The plotting to prevent man and wife from going to bed has to be more elaborate; the moral system represented is not one accepted by the audience; the play is for laughs that cover a sniggering lewdness. Perhaps as good an example as any is *I Was a Male War Bride*, which had the added attraction of dressing Cary Grant in women's clothes and reduced the whole unhappiness of our postwar armies of occupation to a series of obstacles to cohabitation.

The current interpretation of the Code has drained away from the marriage sacrament all its seriousness; if, in fact, the sacrament hallows and makes acceptable to God and man a passion otherwise brutish, it is only a mockery if the passion does not exist; the small and silly emotions rendered in the movies hardly require sanctification.

That is the suicidal consequence of the Code: it sets out to uphold the sanctity of the institution of marriage and ends by undermining the moral foundation upon which marriage stands. Marriage is—or can be—a profoundly satisfying way to live, full of tensions, hardships, pleasures, excitements; constantly threatened, sometimes triumphant; it persists because it fulfills certain requirements, because in marriage men and women, satisfying their natural impulses, become creators, not only of their children, but of themselves. But this is not marriage à la Code. With its fundamentally irreligious concept of marriage, the Code has succeeded in bringing to the screen a relation between men and women which is more ignoble than the meanest marriages of common experience. The economic pressures, the sudden drunken impulses, the vanities and fears and lusts that sometimes drive people to marry are powerful and urgent. Out of them can come hatred or love or degradation; but in any case, life. Out of marriage in the movies nothing can come.

The

Informer

by George Bluestone

The following selection is a chapter from a book entitled Novels into Film (*the Johns Hopkins Press, Baltimore, Maryland, 1957*). *This is a subject that causes anxiety and pain among those who favor "faithful" adaptations of novels into films, and annoyance for the screenwriter who feels no such obligation. The fact is that, generally speaking, serious "literary" novels rarely lend themselves to good screen adaptations. Most outstanding film makers prefer a banal novel with obvious visual ingredients, for the simple reason that the problem of translating them from word to screen presents no complications.*

The Informer, by Liam O'Flaherty, appeared in 1925 to a reception of mixed reviews. O'Flaherty was recognized as a "subjective naturalist,"[1] a peripheral voice in the Irish Renaissance who possessed a passionate, even compelling style, and as a kind of psychological realist who understood the violent tendencies beneath the calm exterior of human behavior. If his work was uneven, or inconclusive, or poorly plotted, it was, nevertheless, deeply felt. Earlier that year, a kind of allegorical composite of O'Flaherty's main themes—the Irish peasant, his struggles, his explosive passions, his rebellious

[1] See John M. Manley and Edith Rickert, *Contemporary British Literature,* 3rd edition (New York, 1935), p. 45.

221

nationalism—had appeared in his novel *Black Souls*. The main character, Fergus O'Connor, a wanderer who alights in the quiet peasant community of Rooruck on the shores of Inverara and sets off a violent erruption because of his passion for the wife of a native villager, looks ahead to the explosive style of *The Informer*.

Around 1930, John Ford, who had already been directing Hollywood films for sixteen years, became interested in the story and began, without success at first, to get his studio to approve it. In 1935, encouraged by the success of *The Lost Patrol*, a low-budgeted production the year before, Ford and his writer, Dudley Nichols, all but sneaked the film into production on their own.

Known as a "sleeper" in trade jargon, *The Informer* is said to have cost $243,000, a small sum by present-day standards. The picture was shot in three weeks and "Ford declared it was the easiest he ever made."[2] The executives had reason to be astounded when Victor McLaglen's acting (in the role of Gypo Nolan), John Ford's direction, and Dudley Nichols' script all won Academy Awards, and the New York film critics judged *The Informer* the best film of 1935. For certainly *The Informer* defied most of Hollywood's conventions. It had no happy ending. The hero, though physically powerful, did not repel whole armies of Indians or Arabs with a single carbine. The hero's woman was unmistakably a prostitute. The hero's romantic dreams remained unfulfilled. The setting and circumstances of the drama were, as we shall see, more controversial than Ford had imagined. Why, then, did it make such a lasting impression on critics and audiences alike?

The bare story, as portrayed in the film, is simple enough. On "a certain night in strife-torn Dublin—1922" during the height of the Sinn Fein rebellion against the British, Gypo Nolan, a brutish hulk of a man, betrays his friend Frankie McPhillip for twenty pounds by revealing his whereabouts to enemy soldiers. As a result, Frankie is shot down while trying to escape from his own home. In order to protect himself, Gypo accuses another man, the tailor Rat Mulligan, then tries to drown his sin in a long night of drink and revelry. Taken before a rebel court of inquiry, which is supervised by Commandant Dan Gallagher, head of the revolutionary organization, he finally breaks down and confesses. Mulligan has an airtight alibi; and Mary McPhillip, the dead man's sister, proves Gypo's testimony false. Awaiting execution, Gypo manages to escape and hide away in the room of the streetwalker for whom he had wanted the money in the first place. While he sleeps, Katie Madden, the girl, goes to Commandant Gallagher to plead for Gypo's life and unwittingly

2 Lewis Jacobs, *The Rise of the American Film* (New York, 1939), p. 480.

gives him away. Gypo, pursued by the revolutionaries, is mortally wounded by pistol fire. Finally he drags himself into a church where the dead man's mother kneels at her morning prayers. Gypo confesses and begs forgiveness, which Mrs. McPhillip grants. Exultant in the mother's mercy, Gypo collapses into death.

In outline, these events roughly follow the movement of the book. The film's major characters are generally derived from the novel, and whole selections of dialogue remain more or less intact. For example, when O'Flaherty's Katie first finds Gypo in a pub, after he has received the reward money, she asks him if he has robbed a church. When he sees that the notion is repugnant to her, he says, "It wasn't a church. It was a sailor off an American ship," and he warns her that he will get into trouble if she says anything about it.[3]

"Who? Me?" Katie laughs aloud, "What d'ye take me for? An informer or what?" At the sound of the word, Gypo bounds up, as if struck, and cries, "What are ye talkin' about informin' for?"

These lines, with slight pruning, appear intact in the film. And the novel's closing scene reads almost exactly like the film scenario.

But to trace the literal carry-over from book to film is to say very little about the artistic mutation. It tells us nothing of how a linguistic medium is changed to a visual medium. It sheds little light on how the director arranges his scenes, or composes his shots, or uses his lighting, or edits his sound track, or prunes his dialogue, or what governs the director's deletions, additions, and alterations. Yet in tracing the history of any adaptation, a consideration of deletion, addition, and alteration presses itself upon one very quickly. For almost invariably these are more striking, if not numerically greater, than the carry-over. The very confrontation of a different medium imposes a different mode of thinking. Dudley Nichols, the screenwriter who worked with Ford on the film, even goes so far as to suggest that deviations from the original had become his central problem. "I am prompted," he writes, "to explain the method by which I *translated* Mr. O'Flaherty's novel into the language of the film; some new method had to be found by which to make the psychological action photographic"[4] (italics mine). It is almost as if the film maker must destroy the old medium in order to catch its essence in the new.

Daniel Taradash, who did the adaptation of *From Here to Eternity*, makes a similar statement about this duality of retention and

[3] Liam O'Flaherty, *The Informer* (Harrisburg, Pa., 1945), p. 30. Originally published by Harcourt, Brace, New York, in 1925. The text is from the 1945 edition.

[4] Dudley Nichols, *Twenty Best Film Plays*, ed. with John Gassner (New York, 1943), p. xxxvi.

deletion. He writes: "The matter of responsibility in adapting a fine novel is, I guess, mostly a matter of respect for the material. . . . You have to be bold in breaking away from the book when it becomes necessary. But there are certain key scenes and definite aspects of character, which have to be retained."[5]

If we can fix upon those elements in the film version that are carried over from their source, and those which depart from it, we ought, in the process, to illuminate the essential limits and possibilities of film and novel both.

Lester Asheim, in his content analysis of twenty-four film adaptations of novels, breaks down his deviations into the general areas of dialogue, character, action, setting, and narrative summary. For the purposes of *The Informer*, these distinctions are not quite so clear. As one reviewer pointed out, ". . . rarely has an American picture achieved such a consistent unity of emotional tone" because "outer and inner world are interfused."[6] We may, then, examine character and action together, because alterations in the first so closely influence alterations in the second. In an urban setting charged with political tension, and especially under Ford's direction, where setting and space severely highlight Gypo's inner moods, the elements are inextricable.

The inextricable relationship is not accidental. Nichols himself says, "I transferred the action of the drama from its original, rather special setting to a larger and more dramatic conflict which had national connotations."[7] John Howard Lawson seems to agree that this mutation is an improvement: "Nichols recognized the importance of establishing a social framework that was not defined in O'Flaherty's novel."[8] And earlier, "*The Informer* reflected the changing temper of the American people in 1935, the impact of social forces breaking through the barriers that monopoly had erected around the industry."[9] In the transference we ought to expect, then, that the particular circumstances of the Irish Revolution will be generalized for American consumption. What we may perhaps be unprepared for (granting that Lawson and Nichols have evaluated the process correctly) is the way in which such mutations parallel changes in the characters and reinterpret O'Flaherty's original intention.

[5] Jerry Wald, "Screen Adaptation," *Films in Review*, V (February 1954), p. 64.
[6] William Troy, "Judas in Dublin," *The Nation*, CXL (May 22, 1935), p. 610.
[7] Nichols, p. xxxvii.
[8] John Howard Lawson, *Theory and Technique of Playwrighting and Screenwriting* (New York, 1949), p. 437.
[9] *Ibid.*, p. 350.

Let us look first at some of the characters who are dropped completely. Frankie McPhillip's father, in the novel, is a chairman of the bricklayers' trade-union, "a thoroughly respectable, conservative Socialist" who is "utterly fanatical in his hatred of the status of the workingman." He prides himself on having put Frankie into a good job as an insurance agent and resents his failure to live up to his respectable position. When Gypo appears at the wake and Mrs. McPhillip identifies him as a friend, Mr. McPhillip bursts out:

What kind of friend d'ye call that waster that never did a day's work in his life? That ex-policeman! . . . It's the likes o' him that's brought Frankie to his death an' destruction. Them an' their revolutions. It's in Russia they should be where they could act the cannibal as much as they like, instead of leadin' good Irishmen astray. Why don't they get out of here and go back to England where they came from.

In the film, for all practical purposes, Frankie has no father, and the absence is never questioned, let alone explained.

Gypo's girl in the book, Katie Fox (who becomes Katie Madden in the film), has a rival named Connemara Maggie, who works at Aunt Betty's, a high-class brothel. It is Connemara Maggie rather than Katie who favors Gypo toward the end of his nocturnal revelry. Katie is furious not only because Gypo abandons her when he finds himself solvent but also because Katie is associated with Biddy Burke's, a much seedier, lower-class brothel.

Katie, too, has a roommate, named Louisa Cummins, an old bedridden hypochondriac with whom Gypo must contend when he takes refuge from his pursuers. Her presence does little but add grotesqueness to the room, which, as we shall see, is alien to the mood which the film tries to evoke. On Louisa Cummins' bedpost hangs a statue of Saint Joseph,

suspended from a thick nail by a rough, knotted cord. The cord was hung around the statue's neck, in a noose. That statue was not suspended there out of crude respect, as might be supposed. It was hung there as a blasphemous protest against the incompetence of the saint. Four years before she had made a Novena to Saint Joseph, requesting a cure for muscular rheumatism, and because her request was not granted she hung up the statue by the neck.

Neither Connemara Maggie nor Louisa Cummins appears in the movie.

One more deletion among these peripheral characters ought to
shed additional light on the nature of the film's omissions. One of
the figures whom Gypo encounters in the course of his drunken
binge is a character named Crank Shanahan. Shanahan shows up
drunk at the fish-and-chips shop where Gypo is treating his friends
to food. Described as a crank who is in the habit of attending every
political meeting in the city, Crank Shanahan takes up his usual
occupation of "agitating and preaching in a loud shrill voice his own
peculiar philosophy of social life. That philosophy was revolt against
every existing institution, habit or belief. He was called an anarchist,
but he was not an anarchist. He was just a fanatic who was dissatisfied
with life." Shanahan takes part in the general tumult which passes
for political discussion, but his reputation as a neurotic who is given
"to fearfully morbid thoughts," to locking himself up at night and
putting cotton wool in his ears "lest he might hear a sound," pre-
cludes anyone's taking him seriously. With a single roar from Gypo,
he and everyone else fall silent. The voice of strength makes political
discussion seem querulous and weak. Thus the deleted characters,
who are capable of slipping into the anonymity of a crowd, are
grotesque, vehement about political convictions (and usually absurd
ones), or given to pointing up class distinctions. All these, apparently, were irrelevant to the film makers' intention.

The addition of characters in the film, on the other hand, is much
more sparse. Aside from a few Black and Tan officers who appear
in a scene that was written into the film, there are only two major
additions—a blind man who functions more as a symbol than a character, and a little crony named Terry whom Gypo picks up early in
his night of carousing. Terry is a sharp-tongued and totally oppor-
tunistic little Irishman who tags along with Gypo, inflating his ego
and pacifying him, but only as long as Gypo has money in his
pocket. He becomes a kind of nimble mind governing the actions of
Gypo's strong but more slow-witted body. Terry's motive is unmistakable. At one point, when he thinks Gypo has run out of cash,
he tauntingly deserts him. But when Gypo pulls out another roll of
bills, Terry quickly ingratiates himself again. Gypo has gone in
search of Katie Madden, but through a kind of glib repartee which
Gypo cannot match, Terry leads him to Aunt Betty's—"the finest
shebeen in town"—continually flattering the big man by calling him
"King Gypo," or bragging to the brothel's middle-class patrons that
his friend is "rich as Craysus." When the emissaries come to take
Gypo to the court of inquiry, Terry is stuck with the last round of
drinks. Aunt Betty calls the bouncer, for whom Terry is clearly
no match without Gypo. Now he is helpless. But his wit does not

fail him. These are the last words we hear him say: "I have a queer feeling there's going to be a strange face in heaven in the morning." Like the porter's soliloquy in Macbeth, Terry's comic words have a deeper meaning. For it is Gypo's face, not his, which will be seen in heaven by morning. In the novel Gypo goes to his fate alone. In the film, he has a kind of clever fool to goad him there.

If additions and deletions are striking, alterations in the surviving characters are perhaps more significant. For in almost every carry-over we find a marked change. In the case of Dan Gallagher, the change is nothing less than startling. As portrayed by Preston Foster in the film, Gallagher is a clean-cut, pipe-smoking, trench-coated revolutionary leader who inspires respect and confidence. Rational in his decisions, Gallagher is fair-minded in Gypo's case without failing to be decisive. He constantly reiterates the motif that the informer must be found because the entire organization is in danger. "One traitor can destroy an army," he tells his confederates after his first meeting with Gypo. And when Dan tells Katie, who comes to plead for Gypo's life, that the organization gave Gypo the benefit of every doubt, that he, Dan, is powerless to grant her request because "I didn't pass sentence on him. The court did," he has no other choice because Gypo has endangered "the lives of hundreds of other men who are fighting for what they believe in," and we have no reason to doubt his sincerity. If anything, the neatness of the characterization tends to make Dan Gallagher dull.

In his relations with Mary McPhillip, Frankie's sister, Dan is wholly honorable. They profess love for each other on several occasions, and, though it is never overtly stated, the implication is that only the conditions of war prevent their being married.

The novel's Dan Gallagher bears little correspondence to Preston Foster's portrayal. O'Flaherty presents him as a complex public figure. His position is indicated by three contrasting reports which have appeared in three diverse sources. The leading organ of "the English aristocracy" prints a story which reads in part:

This flower of Irish manhood grew on an obscure dunghill, in the daily practice of all these virtues, which are indigenous to the Irish soil, if one is to believe the flowery utterances of the politicians on St. Patrick's Day. His father was a small peasant farmer in Kilkenny. Having assisted very probably in the gentle assassination of a few of his landlord's agents in the past, he reverently decided to devote the activities of his promising son to the service of God. He succeeded in making himself famous in the ecclesiastical seminary in which he was being prepared for the priesthood, by smashing the skull of one of the Roman priests during a dispute on the playground.

An extract from an article in the leading organ of the American Revolutionary Organization reads in part:

> When the glorious history of the struggle for proletarian liberation in Ireland comes to be written, the name of Comrade Dan Gallagher will stampede from cover to cover in one uninterrupted blaze of glory. . . . No other living man has given nobler service to the world revolution than this sturdy fighter, who rules the workers of Dublin with greater power than is wielded by the Irish bourgeoisie, who are still nominally in the saddle.

And finally, a secret report sent back to the "International Executive of the Revolutionary Organization," which had sent an agent over from the Continent for a three-month tour of Ireland, reads in part:

> For the moment it would be a tactical blunder to expel Comrade Gallagher from the International. At the same time there can be no doubt that the Irish section has deviated entirely from the principles of revolutionary Communism as laid down in the laws of the International. Comrade Gallagher rules the national Organization pure and simply as a dictator.

Ironically, the film's Dan Gallagher corresponds to the portrait suggested by the American Revolutionary Organization, while the novel's Dan corresponds to a cross between the character in the English journal and the report to the Continental International. In the novel, he is clearly ruthless, sadistic, loveless, terrified at losing power, a kind of incarnation of the naked intelligence.

A contrast between corresponding scenes in the film and book will sufficiently dramatize the alteration. In both media, Dan asks Mary to testify at the court of inquiry. In the film, after establishing the loophole in Gypo's alibi, Dan gently asks Mary to appear as a witness. "I will if you need me," she says. She expresses fear for Dan's safety and longs deeply for an end to the fugitive life. Now that Frankie is dead, she couldn't bear having something happen to Dan, too. The dialogue is conventional, almost stilted, and the scene begins and ends with a show of affection.

The novel's Dan likewise expresses fear, but the fear is only for himself. Before visiting Mary, he vows to stamp out the informer because "The least little rift . . . Then it's all up with *me*." Shortly after, at the McPhillip house, he asks Mary to come with him to the court of inquiry. Instead of complying, she is terrified and Gallagher has to persuade her. Mary is less moved by his plea than by his physical magnetism. "She wanted to rush away and to shout, but the fascination of his voice was upon her." They enter into a discussion of their relationship, and Gallagher persists in asking her to "join him." Finally, she asks hesitantly, "Do you mean . . . to . . . to . . . marry you?" This is part of his answer:

"Oh rot . . . These ridiculous conventions. Not only have I no respect for them, but they don't enter my consciousness. . . . Marriage . . . is truly a capitalist word meaning an arrangement for the protection of property so that legitimate sons could inherit it. So I don't have to argue with it in my own mind in order to rid myself of a belief in it. . . . I am a hundred years before my time."

"Tell me, Dan," Mary asks, "do you believe in anything?" In the kind of near-ranting we have already observed in two deleted characters, Mr. McPhillip and Crank Shanahan, Gallagher goes on:

"No . . . I believe in nothing fundamentally. And I don't feel pity. Nothing fundamental that has consciousness capable of being understood by a human being exists, so I don't believe in anything, since an intelligent person can only believe in something that is fundamental. . . ."

Small wonder that occasionally Dan will pull himself up short and say, "But wait a minute. I haven't worked that out fully yet."

If Gallagher's capacity for theorizing is inconclusive and ambiguous, his sadism and cruelty are not. At the court of inquiry, the novel's Gallagher reveals none of Gallagher's patient reasonableness in the film. He indulges in sheer mental torture to break Gypo down and relishes the big man's agony. He becomes "demented, drunk with the fury of hatred." Even when the ordinarily hardened revolutionaries are reviled by Gypo's humiliation, by "the sight of a human soul stripped naked of the covering of civilization," Gallagher still revels in the spectacle. The combination of Gallagher's barely audible voice, gone suddenly "soft and sweet like a girl's," and Gypo's trying to kiss Gallagher's boots in a final plea for mercy is so grotesque as to be virtually impossible to render in cinematic terms. Later, when Gypo escapes, Gallagher vows, in the throes of his own terror, to catch the informer at all costs. "That hulking swine can do his best," he tells Mary, "I will drain his blood before dawn." Where the Dan of the film sends his confederates to get

Gypo, and mercifully draws the shade to shield Katie from the sight, the Dan of the novel is eagerly in at the kill. He fires the mortal shot and stands there in front of Gypo "smiling dreamily now, with distant, melancholy eyes."

Let it be said, in Mary's defense, that even though her fictional characterization is more complicated than the placid colleen we see on the screen, O'Flaherty's Mary is at once more recognizable and more intense. When we first see her in the novel, she is truly grieved over Frankie's death, but we are told that ever since "she got a position two years before as clerk in the offices of Gogarty and Hogan," she had hated Frankie's revolutionary activities. Once a sympathizer without organizational affiliation, she has allowed her white-collar job to turn her against the "whole theory of revolution." She has also turned religious and has got the notion that she would like to convert Dan Gallagher. Drawn to him by his cold but magnetic power, she turns against him at the end when it is clear he is beyond redemption. After the court of inquiry, she asks, exactly like the Mary of the film, "Why can't we have peace? Why must we be killing one another?" And when Dan sets out in his final pursuit of Gypo, Mary assails him bitterly. "Murderer, murderer," she cries after him "until they stuffed her mouth."

Like Dan and Mary, Gypo's girl Katie undergoes a metamorphosis from the book to the film. In the film, she is still a prostitute but has good reason to be one. Gypo doesn't support her, and when he disposes of a dandy who is trying to pick her up she gets angry and tells him to keep his fine principles because she "can't afford them." She is willing to offer him companionship even when he has no money and agrees to hide him when he escapes from Gallagher's men. She has scruples about informing, and when Gypo tells her what he has done, she replies sadly, "You don't know what you've done to me. . . . I'd lay down my life for you, ye poor blind old boy." While Gypo sleeps, she goes to Gallagher to plead for Gypo's life and tries to take part of his guilt upon herself. She is sorry for the words spoken to him in anger, "Shamin' him for his poverty and blamin' him for mine and puttin' the idea into his head." Only unwittingly does she reveal where Gypo is hiding.

O'Flaherty's conception of Katie is quite different. The novel's Katie has been expelled from the Revolutionary Organization on a charge of public prostitution. But her fall is not forced by poverty; it is gratuitous. She is known even among her colleagues as "a drug fiend, a slattern, an irresponsible creature." She is physically less attractive, more degenerate than John Ford's Katie. Though she also loves Gypo "in her own amazing way," she neither motivates his

informing nor shares his guilt. Moreover, she does not try to inter-
cede for him with the revolutionaries. On the contrary, for reasons
which are not entirely clear in the book, she decides, while Gypo
sleeps, to turn him over to Gallagher. The last we hear of her, before she willfully betrays Gypo, she has been intercepted running
down a road, "mad with dope."

Finally, Frankie McPhillip himself, the betrayed man, undergoes a
marked change from book to film. In the hands of John Ford, he is
a fugitive from the Black and Tans, who want him for murder.
Although we never learn whom he has murdered, or under what
circumstances, it does not seem to matter. We are left to infer that
Frankie killed his victim in the line of patriotic duty, that the Tans
are after him for political reasons. Clean-cut and likable, he has
slipped into the city with the fog to see his family. When he talks
to Gypo to ask if the Tans have set a guard around his house, he
reminds the big man of the old days when they used to pull off
"jobs" together. A great pair they were, with Gypo's muscles and
Frankie's brain. Before he leaves, Frankie signals encouragingly and
says, "Up the rebels." When Gypo informs, we feel that Frankie has
been utterly and unjustly betrayed.

O'Flaherty's Frankie is not quite so engaging. We learn that he
has murdered "the secretary of the local branch of the Farmers'
Union during the farm laborers' strike at M———." Later we learn
that the farm secretary was killed not during a political skirmish
but during a drunken binge. Carousing with Gypo and two women,
Frankie runs across his victim quite by accident and shoots him
without provocation. He and Gypo bolt without making any attempt to cover their tracks and come into Dublin with a flimsy tale
which endangers the entire organization. Moreover, Frankie has
come into the city at this point not only to see his mother before he
dies but also to communicate with the executive committee as well.
Frankie is afraid he's dying of consumption and has come to ask for
money. The phrase "Up the rebels" never appears. O'Flaherty's
characterization does not by any means justify Gypo's betrayal. But
because the novel's Frankie is much less worth saving, Gypo's act
seems less monstrous.

What do these deletions, additions, and alterations amount to? In
general, they endow the film characters with a nobility, honesty,
and reasonableness which the originals do not possess. The grossest
physical characteristics are played down. The contrasts between
Gypo's brutishness and the placid goodness of Mary and Mrs. Mc-
Phillip, on the one hand, and the verbal dexterity of Frankie and
Terry on the other, are sharply delineated. In the case of Dan Gal-

lagher, the quantitative change is so great that a qualitative change results. Like the harsh naturalistic details, the political issues are toned down or relegated to the background. At least part of the change in accent is understandable for nonaesthetic reasons. Aside from the general problem of translating an Irish tale for American audiences, we know that Liam O'Flaherty was deeply concerned with the intricacies of Irish nationalism, whereas John Ford was more centrally concerned with constructing a film story. In 1941, an interviewer for the *Christian Science Monitor* raised the question of whether Ford, after *The Informer* and *The Grapes of Wrath*, had committed himself to doing movies with social significance. Pointing out that he had done a great variety of films, including Westerns, comedies, and films with tragic endings, Ford answered, ". . . when I make a picture, I try to find people I like in situations that I think are dramatic,"[10] and Ford, as always, seemed content to leave it at that. Add Ford's primary interest in dramatic stories to the exigencies of the Production Code and the necessity of working for an American audience, and the shifted emphasis becomes more comprehensible.

At any rate, Ford should not have been surprised that his careful pruning of grotesqueries and politics would still not satisfy local interests. An enlightening exchange on the content of *The Informer*, which appeared in the pages of *Commonweal*, in 1936, serves to shed light on the impossibility of ever dissociating entirely a controversial setting from its dramatic story. In the issue of March 6, Rev. E. Oliver Boyle writes a communication to the magazine, protesting the recent award by the New York film critics to *The Informer* as the best production of the year.[11] Father Boyle argues that the film distorts facts: (1) In 1922—after Dail Eireann, in the wake of such Black and Tan barbarism as the destruction of the city of Cork in December 1920, had officially declared the Republic—the word "informer" had become a term of opprobrium and horror to all good Irishmen, but O'Flaherty and Ford lead us to believe that informing was not an uncommon occurrence. (2) The sign, "10 pounds to America," which leads Gypo to inform is misleading; Father Boyle argues that even if an Irishman had twenty pounds, he would have found it impossible either to get a passport or to buy passage for the money. (3) At a time when every grammar school child was singing "The Soldier's Song," it was unthinkable that a patriotic Irishman would *want* to go to America. (4) Father Boyle disap-

---

[10] Frank Daugherty, "John Ford Wants It Real," *Christian Science Monitor* (June 21, 1941), p. 5.
[11] Rev. E. Oliver Boyle, *Commonweal*, XXIII (March 6, 1936), 525.

proves of the way the Gaelic chant is mumbled at Frankie McPhillip's wake. (5) The scene in the brothel and the characterization of Katie Madden is degrading to Irish womanhood.

In the issue of April 3, an answer to Father Boyle appears by Rev. Edward S. Schwegler.[12] Father Schwegler states quite strongly that he doubts whether the film can be criticized either on "historical" or "decency" grounds. He is amazed at the class-C rating which was conferred on the film by the Legion of Decency, and he argues that, on the contrary, it is the precise point of the picture that Gypo's betrayal *was* exceptional, that we are shown quite clearly, after all, the tragic effect of such perfidy. He demonstrates that with the twenty pounds commonly offered for information leading to the whereabouts of Irish Republican Army leaders, one *could* get a passport *and* afford a ticket. He says that the Gaelic chant *is* sometimes mumbled at wakes and that an old Irish lady had remarked to him on how realistic had seemed to her this sequence in the film. And what, Father Schwegler wants to know, has the mumbling of the Gaelic chant got to do with the decency of a film anyway? Furthermore, the only suggestion of prostitution in the film occurs when the dandy tries to pick up Katie, but Gypo gallantly cuts it short by tossing him into the street. Besides, the character of Katie is not at all typical of Celtic womanhood, which, according to Father Boyle, had been severely maligned. Much more typical of Irish womanhood is Frankie's sister, Mary. Surely one could scarcely find a sweeter and more wholesome colleen. Finally, it is not quite accurate, says Father Schwegler, to say that the Legion of Decency had condemned the film. Catholics were clearly split on the issue, and the Legion of Decency decision had merely represented Catholic opinion in Chicago. The International Federation of Catholic Alumnae, on the other hand, had recommended the film highly as adult entertainment. The proof of the pudding is that now, according to Father Schwegler, the International Federation is doing the reviewing for the Legion of Decency, while the Chicago faction is out in the cold. We may concur in Father Schwegler's observation that the weakness in the position of the Chicago school, and of Father Boyle himself, results inevitably from the dual fallacy of overlooking the positive aspects of a film, and of generalizing from particulars which falsify the whole.

If Ford and Nichols intended to avoid such controversy by widening the specific Dublin setting, they were not wholly successful. And if they intended to tone down the horror, it is hard to account for the impression of William Troy, who reviewed the film for

[12] Rev. Edward S. Schwegler, *Commonweal*, XXIII (April 3, 1936), 637-38.

The Nation. The film, Mr. Troy contends, gives an even more terrifying impression than the novel of the events of 1922.[13] The changes, apparently, were not going to protect the film or the studio either from controversy or from sheer misunderstanding. If the mutations we have already noted are to be justified, they must be justified on other grounds.

Perhaps a more direct and closer examination of the central figure, Gypo Nolan, will help uncover some of these grounds. The first thing we notice is that in the novel much of the special flavor of Gypo's character, the manner of his involvement with others, is achieved through peculiarly linguistic devices. More particularly, O'Flaherty relies heavily on internal monologue, metaphor, and especially on recurrent animal imagery. The idea of informing on Frankie appears to Gypo as an "uncouth ogre that was prowling around in his brain." At another point, "His jaws set like the teeth of a bear trap that has been sprung fruitlessly." There is repeated reference to his tufted eyebrows, "twitching ominously like snouts." Without his hat, Gypo's head appears "naked, hummocked . . . like a badly shorn sheep." At the fish-and-chips shop, he towers above the crowd "like some primeval monster." Later the street, "with its dirt and its squalor, was a savage sauce to whet his appetite for the riotous feast. . . ." When a woman in the brothel resists him and calls him a "pig," his face contorts, his head going from right to left "like a ram that is going to charge an enemy." In his terror at the court of inquiry, he lets go a "muffled scream like a dumb animal in mortal agony," and when he tries to escape with five men hanging on to him, he appears "like Laocoön entwined with snakes." At other points in the narrative, Gypo or his compatriots are likened to insects, heifers, snails, vipers, oxen, swine, bulls, and cats. The savage, primeval, and demonic run like motifs through O'Flaherty's prose.

Aside from bestial analogies, similes frequently appear to reinforce a physical action: "He raised Mulholland's body from the ground . . . like a book which he wanted to read"; he hits a man who goes down "like a bag of nails dropped on an iron deck"; Gypo walks away, his trousers "brushing with the sound of hay being cut with a scythe."

Internal monologue and literary figures of speech are all but impossible to translate to celluloid. The film, which must render its meanings in moving images, resists both these devices. And yet the texture of the narrative prose, which is so largely supported by both monologue and metaphor, must be rendered in cinematic equiva-

13 Troy, p. 610.

lents. Ford and Nichols have solved this problem by devising an
elaborate set of symbols which function on both literal and ana-
logical levels. These symbols are in turn supported by a careful
arrangement of visual and aural renditions of Gypo's subjective
conflicts.

Some of these symbols, like the all-pervasive fog, relieved only
occasionally by the flare of light from a doorway or the bloom of
a fireplace in a room, are direct carry-overs from the novel. In the
book, Gypo's hat is used explicitly as a symbol of security. At one
point, he loses it, and hence becomes irrational: "terror again invaded his mind. If they discovered the hat they might be able to
discover the identity of that ponderous fellow who had gone into
the police-station. . . ." But the moment he retrieves the hat, his
confidence returns. In the film, the cap is also used as a symbolic
prop. When Gypo is cocky and sure of himself, the cap sits on his
head at a jaunty angle. When he is nervous and unsure, as in the
Tan headquarters, or at the court of inquiry, he twists it nervously
in his hand, or uses it to wipe the perspiration from his face. Toward
the end, from the time of his imprisonment to his death, Gypo goes
bareheaded.

Similarly, in both book and film, the twenty pounds is used literally for cash transactions, and analogically as a symbol of Gypo's
undoing. He spends the money in two ways—either as an act of
desperate self-gratification, to forget his deed, or as an act of
impulsive generosity, to share what he has. In both versions, he
treats his fair-weather friends to food and drink, gives a despised
woman in the brothel enough money to get her home, and delivers
the remains to Katie. But in the film, the meaning of the money is
reinforced. An epigraph is added at the beginning: "Then the Judas
repented himself—and cast down the thirty pieces of silver—and
departed," which makes explicit the implied theme of the novel,
and helps round out the religious framework. But in the long run,
whether Gypo spends the money selfishly or generously, the reward is cursed. Bartley Mulholland, Gallagher's cat-eyed man, trails
Gypo relentlessly, adding up the pounds which Gypo spends, each
pound becoming another tally in Gypo's final accounting.

A series of visual symbols which do not appear in the novel,
however, are boldly added to the film, and it is here, more than
anywhere else perhaps, that we find the greatest evidence of the Ford-
Nichols signature. Working from mere clues in O'Flaherty's narrative, Ford and Nichols construct a series of full-blown cinematic
details which become suffused with subjective ideas. For example,
O'Flaherty shows the betrayal growing in Gypo exclusively through

interior monologue. As Gypo talks to Frankie at the Dunboy House, a "monstrous idea" prowls into his head "like an uncouth beast straying from a wilderness into a civilized place where little children are alone." Later, the "ghoulish thing" comes back like a specter into his mind until finally, "There were two facts in his brain. First, the fact of his meeting with McPhillip. Second, the fact of his having no money for the night."

Dudley Nichols tells us precisely how this growing awareness appears in the film: "A poster offering a reward for information concerning Gypo's friend became the symbol of the evil idea of betrayal, and it blows along the street, following Gypo; it will not leave him alone. It catches on his leg and he kicks it off. But still it follows him and he sees it like a phantom in the air when he unexpectedly comes upon his fugitive friend."[14] Still later, during Gypo's first interview with Dan, a copy of the poster burns slowly in the fireplace, the flames distorting and consuming Frankie's features. No such poster appears in the novel, but its adoption enables the film makers to render O'Flaherty's meaning in purely visual terms.

Again, when Gypo leaves Tan headquarters in the novel, with the money still fresh in his pocket, he hears a menacing footstep. It turns out to be only a ragged old woman. She mutters something unintelligible. "Then she bared her ragged teeth. Was it an omen?" The woman does not appear again. In the film, the old woman becomes a blind man, who is not dropped but appears at intervals throughout the film. When Gypo encounters him outside Tan headquarters, he grips the blind man's throat in sudden guilt. The blind man, Nichols tells us,

is a symbol of the brute conscience, and Gypo releases him when he discovers the man cannot see. But as Gypo goes on to drown his conscience in drink, the tapping of the blind man's stick follows him; we hear it without seeing the blind man as Gypo hears his guilt pursuing him in his own soul. Later, when he comes face to face with his conscience, for a terrifying moment he tries to buy it off—by giving the blind man a couple of pounds, a lordly sum.[15]

Nichols might have added that the blind man appears for the last time at the court of inquiry where his sheer presence is even more electrifying than his brief testimony as a witness.

14 Nichols, p. xxxvi.
15 *Ibid.*, p. xxxvii. Arthur Mizener acknowledges the structural effectiveness of this and other symbolic devices in "The Elizabethan Art of Our Movies," *Kenyon Review,* IV (Spring, 1942), p. 189 ff.

Even more striking is what Ford and Nichols do to O'Flaherty's Chapter 2. In its entirety, the chapter reads:

At thirty-five minutes past seven Francis Joseph McPhillip shot himself dead while trying to escape from No. 44 Titt Street, his father's house. The house had been surrounded by Detective-Sergeant McCartney and ten men. Hanging by his left hand from the sill of the back-bedroom window on the second floor, McPhillip put two bullets into McCartney's left shoulder. While he was trying to fire again, his left hand slipped and lost its hold. The pistol muzzle struck the edge of the sill. The bullet shot upward and entered McPhillip's brain through the right temple.

When they picked him out of the orange box in the back garden where he fell, he was quite dead.

In the film, we see, as at the end of the novel's Chapter 1, Gypo making his nervous claim for the reward money. But we cut instantly to a shot of the soldiers loading onto lorries. We hear the motors revving up. Back in the office, Gypo sits in the foreground, his head bare and bowed, the major and his officer at the window in the background, watching the preparations outside. Gypo looks up at a clock, whose ticking we hear quite clearly. The flashing light of the pendulum, underscoring the headlights of the lorries, casts an hypnotic gleam in Gypo's eyes. The clock reads five minutes past six. In Lewis Jacobs' phrase, "we have a prescience of relentless evil."[16] The ticking continues into the next scene, where we see Frankie entering his house to surprise his mother and sister. There, another clock, reading sixteen minutes after six, "welds the transition structurally." The soldiers surprise Frankie at his meal. In the confusion, he climbs out on the windowsill, but the Tans rush in to block the alleyway. Frankie fires, hitting one of the men, but another soldier shoots him mortally with a submachine gun. The violent noise stops as suddenly as it began. We see only Frankie's hand now, slipping slowly from the window, hear only the sound of his nails dragging across the sill. Stunned with horror, Frankie's mother sinks to the floor.

Back at headquarters, Gypo is still sitting in the same position. The ringing of a phone breaks the silence, sharply replacing the ticking of the clock. A sentry answers and informs the major that Frankie McPhillip was killed trying to escape. In cold silence, the major throws some bills upon the table, and an officer contemptu-

[16] Jacobs, p. 482.

ously pushes the money toward Gypo with his cane. "Show him out the back way," the officer says.

The last important innovation is that very model of a ship, representing the dream of passage to America, which so disturbed Father Boyle. At the moment that Gypo is seized in the novel with the impulse to report Frankie, he is not looking at a ship model (with a sign above it reading "10 pounds to America: Information Within"). He is looking into the window of a saddler's shop, but all he sees are a pair of spurs. Later, he daydreams not about himself and Katie sailing to America in formal wedding attire, but of his lost romantic youth: ". . . a mad longing seized him for the protection of the environment of his youth, the countryside of a Tipperary village, the little farm, the big red-faced kindhearted mother, who hoped he would become a priest." To American audiences the injected dreams of marriage and ocean voyage are likely to seem more familiar than the longing for a Tipperary village, but the film has the added advantage of giving the symbol greater continuity. Gypo passes the window once with Katie; then again with Terry; and he ends with the superimposed fantasy. These appearances are joined, both visually and dramatically, in a way which the bright spurs and boyhood reminiscences of the novel never achieve. (Both Father Boyle and Father Schwegler, incidentally, seem unaware that the ship image never appears in the book, or that Liam O'Flaherty had little to do with the film adaptation.)

Curiously, it is at precisely these points of deviation from the novel that the film seems to have won its greatest critical support. William Troy considered Frankie's death scene one of the finest in cinema literature. And even Otis Ferguson, the reviewer for *The New Republic*, who raised one of the very few dissenting voices against the film, admitted the power of the early sequences, where most of these innovations appear.[17]

As suggested earlier, the symbols which conform to the film's realistic demands are reinforced by still other cinematic devices. A carefully worked out musical score is used to parallel rather than counterpoint the action. Some of the musical accents arise from the scene itself. In the first sequence, for example, Gypo stops to listen to a street tenor sing the romantic ballad, "Rose of Tralee."

> The pale moon was rising above the green mountain,
> The sun was declining beneath the blue sea
> When I strayed with my love to the pure crystal fountain . . .

[17] Otis Ferguson, "The Informer," *The New Republic*, LXXXIII (May 29, 1935), p. 76.

As he sings, a patrol of Tan soldiers come by and frisk him for weapons, then toss him a coin. Although the tenor sings on without interruption, the oppressed atmosphere of the city has been strikingly suggested. Moreover, Gypo has been vaguely moved by the song, and a moment later he is looking at the ship model in the tourist window, dreaming.

The street singer appears again outside Frankie's house, where the wake is being held. Once more, his ballad is appropriate to the occasion:

> The minstrel boy to the war has gone,
> In the ranks of death you'll find him.

With Terry, Gypo goes carousing through the streets singing "The Wearing o' the Green," which is picked up at later intervals by the sound track. At Aunt Betty's, to bolster another kind of mood, Gypo calls for a rendition of "All Those Endearing Young Charms."

The sound track score is carefully cued to emphasize the emotional tones of particular scenes. The themes of the blind man and the minstrel boy, the money, the informer, and "The Wearing o' the Green" are woven together in a loose kind of medley which sounds at appropriate tempos. For example, at the court of inquiry, while Dan is adding up the money that Gypo has spent, the music builds to a crescendo and quickly breaks at the moment when Gypo, trapped by the evidence, drops all pretenses and breaks down.

More revealing than the musical accompaniment, however, is the way in which Ford finds visual and aural substitutes for Gypo's interior monologues. For example, when Gypo first sees the poster, we see superimposed upon the screen an image of Gypo and Frankie in a bar singing a soldier's song. When Gypo is met by the real Frankie at the Dunboy House, we see a different image superimposed. This time it is the poster which Gypo had seen a little while before. We know that his temptation has begun. Again, during Gypo's last escape toward Katie's room, the superimposed poster appears once more, like a misty dream, this time dark and glowering, full of accusation. At the brothel, the despised woman, to whom Gypo later gives the money, dissolves for a moment, and Gypo thinks he is seeing Katie. Finally, after the betrayal, Gypo sits in a pub trying to formulate a plan. He seems to hear Frankie's mocking voice, "Ah, Gypo, I'm your brain. You're lost . . . You're lost. . . ."

Considering all these devices, it is surprising to find the *Christian*

Science Monitor reporter explaining that Ford "rarely uses trick shots, but frames every take carefully from the straight-on angle." What Ford has really done here is to employ neither the trick shot nor the straight-on angle—it is hardly a question of that—but to use every resource of the camera to render the tortured consciousness of Gypo Nolan.

After a careful tracing out of the mutations which take place in John Ford's film, we are left with one remaining problem. How, in searching out these visual equivalents, does Ford evoke the kind of pity and terror for Gypo which the novel apparently failed to do? As we indicated earlier, the novel met with nothing like the unanimity of approval accorded the film. *The New Statesman*, appreciating the book as a study in the "psychology of revolution," seemed uneasy because "the terrors of fact mow and gibber through these pages."[18] *The Saturday Review of Literature* said, "One contemplates Gypo with a purely objective emotion, as one might look upon a figure by Rodin, equally brutish, equally strong, equally impotent."[19] *The New Republic* was even more severe. It complained that a "harsh, unrhythmic play of words occasionally rises to a flash of power, but more often becomes monotonous. The Dublin underworld is here—backstreets, brothels, and bestiality—but nothing of significance emerges from background or theme."[20] *The Spectator*, on the assumption that "It is good sometimes that the Beelzebub in humanity should be made manifest," was one of the few which broke through the hard bindings of a modifying clause to say something positive: "Gypo, though a brute, cunning and malevolent as any hungry tiger, is truly a man and dies like a man, strong in his soul."[21]

At first glance one would think that John Ford's Gypo would be even harder to center on sympathetically. The softening of supporting characters—the diminution of their harshness—ought to make his sin less venial, for the offense is greater. In the novel, Gypo is less sharply distinguished from the other characters. They all seem more or less covered with the gray mire of sin. In O'Flaherty's world, Gypo has much less to sin against, as we have already noted in the case of Frankie McPhillip. In Ford's world, Frankie is more innocent, Gallagher more benevolent, Katie more noble, and each is hurt as well as offended by Gypo's act. But in a curious way, this sharper differentiation throws Gypo's character into the kind of dramatic

18 *The New Statesman*, xxv (October 10, 1925), p. 727.
19 *The Saturday Review of Literature*, ii (October 17, 1925), p. 227.
20 *The New Republic*, xlv (December 9, 1925), p. 93.
21 *The Spectator*, cxxxv (October 3, 1925), p. 560.

relief which is hard to find in the book. Because his sin in the film appears to be greater, his suffering and redemption take on more tragic overtones. In the book, Katie's jealousy and Dan's hatred are unequivocal. But in the film, Gypo succeeds in dividing his characters against themselves. He induces emotional conflict in Katie and Dan and even in Mrs. McPhillip. Their affection for Gypo begins to war against their sense of justice, and the affection derives from the added dimension of goodness in themselves. Of the four major supporting roles, only Mary, and Katie for no more than an instant, exhibit this conflict in O'Flaherty's original. Having little or no affection for Gypo to begin with, the novel's characters respond more simply than they do in the film. Since the beast imagery is so insistent in O'Flaherty, we can feel little more than horror at Gypo's final degradation. In the film, the depths and the heights are both more clearly defined and more clearly contrasted. If O'Flaherty has the worst of the terror, then Ford has the best of the pity.

Again, looking at clues in the novel, we can see how Ford visually builds up our sympathy for Gypo. In the novel, Gypo is put upon by intelligent men. What frightens him most about the Revolutionary Organization is its likeness to an all-pervasive mind. Gypo suffers the loss of Frankie's intelligence, and the severe, almost malignant oppression of Dan's. In the film, Terry is introduced to enforce the continuity between them. "King Gypo," he keeps calling him, and we remember, dramatically, how unlike a king he is.

In the novel, Gypo undergoes a kind of psychological division of identity. At moments, he actually forgets that it was he who had gone into the police station. When he runs into Bartley Mulholland at the fish-and-chips place, he asks, "Hear anythin' about what I was tellin' ye? I mean about the fellah that informed on Frankie McPhillip?" Moments of that forgetfulness are carried over into the film. Outside the pub, a man sees Gypo and asks, "Usen't he be pals with Frankie McPhillip who was shot by the Black and Tans tonight?" With Terry's help, Gypo forces the man to say, "May the Lord have mercy on his soul," as if he were genuinely, if drunkenly, concerned about treating a friend's name with respect. He really *has* forgotten. At the court of inquiry, he sees Rat Mulligan and, forgetting the circumstances of the meeting, greets the sick man with friendly concern. He consistently meets Bartley's coldness with warmth and openness. And when he blurts out at the wake, "I'm sorry for yer trouble, Mrs. McPhillip," we feel that his grief is genuine. By the time he breaks down and tells Dan, "I didn't know what I was doing, I didn't know what I was doing," we are prepared to believe him. It is as if he were trying to suppress a monstrous

part of himself. That he recognizes it as monstrous endows his re-
pentance with a kind of tragic awareness.

In the film, Gypo carries even further the acts of instinctive
generosity which occur in the book. Not only does he share his
money with friends and cronies and the girl in the brothel, but he
presses money on the blind man, remains faithful to Katie throughout, and submits to the betrayal as much for her sake as for the
price of a meal and a bed.

Finally, we are made to feel grudging admiration for his strength.
Forced to drop the bestial tropes of O'Flaherty's prose, Ford substitutes a series of visual movements which amply demonstrate
Gypo Nolan's enormous strength. In every instance, there is a sense
in which the exhibition is either innocent or partially justified. First
we see him picking up the dandy who tries to accost Katie, and
tossing him into the street. The man outside the pub whom Gypo
challenges for staring at him strikes Gypo first before Gypo lays
him out. The policeman who ends up in the street beside this man,
"sweet and peaceful as the babes in the woods," as Terry says, also
initiates the assault on Gypo. Later, Gypo picks up Katie as if she
were weightless, and at Aunt Betty's and the fish-and-chips shop,
he is continually hoisting women upon his shoulder with hardly any
effort at all. The little man who challenges him at the shebeen is
brushed off like a fly. Gypo's exhibitions of strength, then, are
never cruel, or at least there is nothing in them to compare with
the sadism of O'Flaherty's Dan Gallagher. Yet we have been prepared for his breaking out of the cell where he sits awaiting death.
During his escape, he turns a guard's jaw into "jelly," but this time
he is fighting for his life. Even after he has been shot several times,
he summons enough strength to reach the church. His sheer vitality
reinforces all the other carefully constructed traits which are used
to enlist our sympathy. At the end, Gypo is more a victim than a
victimizer.

Granted, then, the medial, formal, and thematic changes which
are dictated almost as much by a shift in audience, taboos, and conventions as by the artistic sensibility of the film makers, shall we say
that the film is a violation of the original? I think not. What the film
loses in savagery, brutality, violence, pessimism and terror, it gains
in consistency of tone, sharper delineation of character, tighter
integration of theme, and greater enlistment of pity. Margaret Kennedy makes a relevant observation on the general problem in *The
Mechanized Muse:* "In a great work of art," she writes, "the
medium is so wedded to the subject that it becomes impossible to
think of them apart. To take the *writing* out of a great novel is to

run the risk of emptying out the baby with the bath . . . if any story has been perfectly told in one medium, what motive can there be for retelling it in another?"[22] That is why, she continues, "Most screenwriters prefer to work on an ill-written, second-rate book, toward which they have no conscience, but which has some situation or character which has caught the imagination."

In the particular instance of *The Informer*, though Ford retains the kind of respect toward his original which Daniel Taradash calls for, the cumulative changes are so great that the result is a new species. A quantitative concern with additions, deletions, and alterations ends up as a qualitative problem. There is a sense, as we have seen, in which a careful film adaptation goes to the original not as a finished work (though this tends to be less true of the classics), but as a kind of raw material, much as the novelist approached *his* experiences. Like D. W. Griffith, such a director scarcely needs the writer at his side. Dudley Nichols tells us that Griffith, like Shakespeare, "took his stories where he found them—*Broken Blossoms* from Thomas Burke, *The Birth of a Nation* from a second-rate historical novelist. . . . Collaborating in a sense with such writers, he was able by his own genius to create masterpieces, just as Shakespeare found the seed for *Hamlet* in Saxo Grammaticus. . . ."[23]

That is why, if one is asked, "How do you like the Greek *Electra?*" one must reply, "By whom? Sophocles or Euripides?" And if one is asked, "How do you like *The Informer?*" one must reply, "By whom? O'Flaherty or Ford?"

[22] Margaret Kennedy, *The Mechanized Muse* (London, 1942), p. 29.
[23] Nichols, p. xxii.

Movies:

A

Psychological

Study

by

Martha Wolfenstein

and Nathan Leites

The following selection consists of sections of a book bearing the same title (The Free Press, Glencoe, Illinois, 1950). In this work the authors, using the methods of cultural anthropology, undertake an investigation of American movies (also some British and French) from the latter part of 1945 to 1949. Their aim is to isolate certain aspects of contemporary morality in these countries and indicate how they are reflected in the themes and styles of their movies. The authors are primarily interested in examining the real-life fantasies centering around work, sex, play and family that consistently show up in the films of these countries.

WILL IT EVER TAKE THE PLACE OF BASEBALL?

IN *Love Affair*, a film of the '30s, a Continental lady-killer is on an ocean liner bound for the United States. A telegram which he has just received from an enamored lady blows out of his hand. The American heroine picks it up, reads it with an ironical smile, and hands it back to him with the question, "Will it ever take the place of baseball?"

This query (which recalls "Is sex necessary?") suggests a way of achieving detachment. Most of the time, under the pressure of fun morality, we maintain the image of ourselves as being in a state of perpetual readiness to rise to any amorous occasion. But there are moments when, under the guise of comedy or humor, it is a relief to disparage the whole affair. In a similar way, businessmen may find relief from incessant and strenuous activity by calling it all a racket. For a moment the tension relaxes, and it becomes possible to ask, "Is it really worth all the bother?" This momentary, joking renunciation of impulse is perhaps the American version of Buddhist retirement from the world. In the movies the comic hero may express this freedom from impulse, or may dare to prefer child-like pleasures to more difficult adult ones. Bob Hope reclines in a harem, surrounded by beautiful girls, and sucks a lollipop (*The Road to Morocco*). At first glance, he appears ludicrous for not taking advantage of his opportunities. But under the comic façade, another pleasure is provided, that of emancipation from the demand for impulse achievement. The comic hero demonstrates a certain wisdom.

American film comedies repeatedly present unused sexual opportunities as occasions for amusement. Their pleasant tone derives partly from a belief that there will be plenty of other chances, partly from the fiction that impulses will always be ready to seize on the next opportunity. But at bottom the missed opportunity seems to be a relief, like being provided with a good excuse for getting out of an examination. Frequently the situation is arranged so that one or both members of the couple have no wish to take advantage of the opportunity, which they have not sought to begin with. In most cases the value of the lost opportunity is diminished by introducing various anaphrodisiac devices: discomforts, distractions, a temporary ludicrousness in the appearance of one or both partners. In *Guest Wife*, the heroine and her husband's best friend are posing as husband and wife. They are not really interested in each other at all. It is just an elaborate hoax that the friend feels forced to play on his boss, who believes him to be married. As guests of the boss, the bogus couple are forced to share a bedroom. The wife, to teach the friend a lesson, pretends that she has fallen in love with him. Her advances throw him into a panic. Clad in pajamas which he has clumsily pulled on over his clothes, he takes refuge on a porch where he gets drenched by a shower.

The Sailor Takes a Wife is a comedy about a wedding night that repeatedly fails to materialize. The young couple, who have married after a few hours' acquaintance, set up housekeeping in a hastily acquired apartment. The difficulties of initiating marital relations are symbolized by the malfunctioning of material appurtenances. The elevator does not work except capriciously and unexpectedly. The windows are stuck shut. The young husband is almost swallowed up by a folding couch which he is struggling to open into a bed. The girl, who had hitherto seemed very attractive, now appears in a pair of heavy, long-sleeved pajamas, and with her hair done up in little-girlish pigtails. When the young man laughs at this costume, she runs to the bedroom and locks the door.

The fairly frequent discrepancy between movie advertisements and movie content may have a similar impact to that of the missed opportunity. The advertisements may suggest a greater prominence of love-making than appears in the film. In an extreme case, *The Bells of St. Mary's*, where the two stars played a Catholic priest and a nun, the advertisements showed their profiles juxtaposed, with clerical collar and headdress eliminated. Presumably audiences do not manifest too much disappointment when a film reveals less amorous content than the advertisements would lead them to expect. They may think of themselves as wanting sex and feel relieved to be exempted from it.

Missed opportunities rarely constitute a permanent loss. There are always plenty of other chances. The couples who spend the night together without anything happening frequently marry in the end. The classic case was *It Happened One Night*, the well-known film of the '30s, in which the hero and heroine reproduced for their wedding night the circumstances of the earlier night together when they had divided the room between them. The last scene showed the falling of the blanket curtain which had served as a barrier. Similarly in *Lady on a Train* and *Runaround* a harmless night spent together is a prelude to marriage. In *The Sailor Takes a Wife*, the three-times-postponed wedding night is finally consummated.

In French films, missed opportunities are more apt to be occasions for endless regret. The lost occasion is not recapturable. There tends to be a fatal discrepancy in the timing of desire and opportunity. (Failure in various kinds of timing pervades the plots of French films.) When the chance is provided, the wish to take advantage of it has not yet matured; when the desire is there, the opportunity is denied. Fate behaves in a niggardly and mocking way. In the old René Clair film *Sous les Toits de Paris*, the hero brings home to his room a girl of rather easy virtue who has no place to go for the night. He gives up his bed to her while he sleeps in a chair. Later he falls in love with her. She is going to come to live with him, and he happily prepares his shabby little room, putting flowers on the table, a loaf of bread and a bottle of wine. An unfortunate chance intervenes and the hero is taken to jail. When he gets out, he finds his girl already with another man. In his room the mice are gnawing the bread which was to have been his wedding cake.

In *Les Enfants du Paradis*, the hero brings to his room the beautiful woman with whom he has fallen in love. She begins to undress but he feels there should be more preliminary soul-searching and mutual avowals, and he leaves her. She immediately becomes the mistress of his best friend, whose room is next door. Numerous other difficulties intervene, the hero and the heroine both marry. It is not till years later that they return to the same room. They repeat the words they said on the first occasion and try to deceive themselves that they can have their chance again. They spend one night together. Then his wife comes to plead and weep, and the heroine leaves, presumably never to return. Besides expressing the rarity of opportunities, this film presents a further contrast to the American pattern. In American films, the ever renewed opportunity is always the same; time effects no changes. The unused chance reappears as bright and shiny as ever. In *Les Enfants du Paradis*, the attempt of the hero and heroine to make the later meeting a repetition of the first points up the hopeless transformation of their circumstances.

The British *Brief Encounter* also presents a lost opportunity as irretrievable. The difficulty here is in raising the intensity of impulse sufficiently to overcome serious scruples. The middle-aged man and woman, both married, who have fallen in love with each other, are ready at one moment to forget everything but their love. They go to an apartment which the hero has borrowed for the occasion, but they are interrupted. The heroine is overwhelmed with shame, all her reluctance is rearoused; the hero, struggling with his own bad conscience, lacks sufficient force to persuade her a second time. Shortly afterward they separate. Similarly in *Sleeping Car to Trieste*, a married man and a young woman are starting out somewhat apprehensively for an interlude of illicit love on the Continent. On the train they become accidentally involved in a criminal investigation and their intended relation is exposed. When they reach their destination they part without going through with their plan. Here, as often happens in British films, accidents have the effect of activating guilt instead of providing exemption. In contrast to *Les Enfants du Paradis*, where the hero and heroine long for a second chance, in these British films internal obstacles prevent them from seeking it. American films usually express the confident expectation that impulses will be sufficiently resolute in the end to bring the couple together, the more so as they are free from guilt; the missed opportunity is a proof of their virtue. American films express an equal confidence in an inexhaustible series of opportunities. This double confidence, combined with a less manifest relief in exemption from love-making, makes the lost opportunity a situation of comedy rather than pathos.

LOVE WITHOUT TEARS

It is probably a characteristic American conviction that suffering is pointless and unnecessary. In keeping with this, love in American films rarely involves suffering. The numerous possibilities of tragic love, familiar in Western literature, find new counterparts here. Lovers do not show the unreasoning obstinate attachment which might involve hopeless longing for someone unattainable, or rage and despair at the loss of the loved one. There is little feeling that it is sweet to be tortured by the loved one; such treatment does not bind the victim to the tormentor, as sometimes happens in British films (*The Seventh Veil, They Were Sisters*). There is a tendency for feelings to become quickly detached from a loved one who has proved disappointing by not loving in return, or by dying, or by turning out to be a criminal. The lover may then decide that this was not love or was not the right person. There is thus little danger of being dragged down by love for an unworthy person; love is awarded to the person who deserves it. Complementing and rewarding this flexibility of feeling is the wealth of opportunity. Replacements, temporary or permanent, are readily available in case of a temporary or permanent defection of the loved one.

This plenitude of possibilities consoles the rejected suitor. In *Two Guys from Milwaukee*, the man who has just been turned down by his girl boards an airplane and is dazzled by the discovery that his favorite movie actress, Lauren Bacall, is sitting beside him. Although Humphrey Bogart comes up a moment later to claim his seat, the impact of the revelation is not lost: there is another dream girl just around the corner. In *The Well-Groomed Bride*, the heroine, whose bridegroom is diverted at the last moment by an old sweetheart, quickly switches to an even more attractive man who is conveniently at hand. Her disillusionment with the bridegroom and her falling in love with the new man have progressed concurrently, thus eliminating the danger of an even momentary emotional void. In *Wonderman*, when the bride is kept waiting at the church and it seems clear that the bridegroom is not going to show up (he has in fact been murdered, and his place has been taken by his twin brother, who is in love with another girl), the bride accepts the offer of the best man to take the bridegroom's place. In *Mildred Pierce*, when the heroine's divorced husband is thrown over by his lady friend, he at once calls up his ex-wife and asks her out to dinner. During the break in her marriage, the heroine has consoled herself with another highly attractive man. However, she now shifts back to her husband. In *The Sailor Takes a Wife*, the rejected suitor of the heroine and the vamp who had made a play for the hero end up by consoling each other. In these rapid changes no one is for long without a partner. The feelings of shame and guilt which Americans seem to associate with being alone are as far as possible avoided.

Emotional entanglements which suggest ironic possibilities are satisfactorily resolved by an appropriate adjustment of feelings. In *The Fallen Angel*, the impecunious hero falls in love with a beautiful mercenary woman. In order to win her he schemes to get the fortune of a small-town heiress, a sweet, colorless girl, whom he rushes into a hasty marriage. Immediately afterward the mercenary one is murdered. Instead of suffering bitter regrets for her loss or for his loveless marriage which has now become pointless, he achieves a quick transformation of feelings which enables him to find satisfaction in the changed circumstances. The day after the murder, he finds that the dead woman has already become unreal for him; at the same time he discovers an unexpected attractiveness in his wife, and he is soon genuinely in love with her.

The possibility of lovers suffering prolonged uncertainty about each other is avoided. In *Pride of the Marines*, the young man and the girl have been going together for some time, but when he enters the service there have been no definite commitments. In saying goodbye, the young man says that they've had a lot of good times together and, considering the uncertainty of things, they had better leave it at that. We then see him pacing the platform of the railroad station alone—he has asked her not to come to see him off—and he looks very lonely. Suddenly the girl appears and throws herself into his arms. It turns out that he has an engagement ring in his pocket, and he has just time to slip it on her finger before the train pulls out.

Lovers who are temporarily deprived of a loved one are apt to be provided with someone to love them in the meantime. They are thus not left in the unpleasant position of being unwanted and lonely. Also, they have a chance to turn the tables by refusing the love of the newcomer. The American remake of the British *Stolen Life* illustrates this. The heroine has just become friends with the

hero when her bad twin sister takes him away from her. It is only
after a considerable time and several tragic upsets that the heroine,
who continues to love the hero throughout, finally gets him. In the
British version, she has no consolation in the interim; she mainly
goes sailing by herself. The American version supplies her with an
attractive suitor whom she in turn repulses. She does not find a new
love—after all, she is going to get the hero in the end. But instead
of waiting for him in solitude, she is occupied with warding off
the not too distasteful advances of another man. *This Love of Ours*
has a similar pattern. The heroine has been driven from her home
by her husband, who mistakenly suspects her of infidelity. In the
long interval before their reunion, she acquires an attractive, understanding, and devoted suitor, whom she in turn rejects.

Where love disappointment is not compensated by the appearance
of a temporary or permanent substitute for the lost loved one, other
consolations may be provided. The two girl singers in *Night and Day*
remain in love with the song-writer hero, who reciprocates only
with a comradely affection. One of the singers becomes a top
musical-comedy star; the other accepts the patronage of a series of
millionaires. The ex-Marine in *Till the End of Time*, temporarily
disappointed by his girl, immediately reverts to the comradeship of
his war buddies. They get drunk together and plan to buy a ranch
where they will all go off to live.

Where continued attachment to a loved one would involve serious trouble, feelings become detached. This may happen where the
hero has fallen in love with a woman who later turns out to be a
criminal (*Framed, Dead Reckoning*).This pattern contrasts with one
which is frequent in French films. The lover may be thrown into
self-destructive despair on learning that the previously idealized
loved one is criminal (*La Passionnelle*) or be provoked to murder
by her infidelity (*Quai des Orfèvres*). But love once committed to
this woman cannot be detached. Women may similarly persist in
loving a man who leads them into a life of crime (*Panique*), or
who repulses their love (*Falbalas, Torrents*). This feeling of being
hopelessly bound is alien to American films. Love tends to be reasonable and righteous. The hero who withdraws his love from the
woman who turns out to be bad is exercising the principle of conditional love which he learned from his mother: you have to be
good if you want to be loved.

Where a disappointed lover is not provided with a new partner,
there is nevertheless little indulgence in grief, rage, or envy, but
rather a quick shift to nonpainful feelings. In *Adventure*, the heroine's girl friend, who had at first made a big play for the hero, greets

the news of their marriage with an effusive "I love you both!" and immediately assumes the role of friend of the family. The necessity of mourning beyond a minimum for a dead loved one is also denied. A long painful process of detachment of feelings is not recognized. In *My Reputation*, the widowed heroine denies that there is anything painful about the memories evoked by the old house. In *Young Widow*, when the heroine returns to her job after an interlude of being haunted by memories of her dead husband, she expresses regret that she did not go back to work sooner: she has been wasting her time.

The rare characters who submit to suffering from loss of love are apt to appear as comic or weak. The hero of *Hold That Blonde* develops comical symptoms after having been rejected by his fiancée. He becomes a kleptomaniac and his ears wiggle every time he sees a pretty girl. He has to be told by a psychiatrist to get himself another sweetheart. In *The Strange Love of Martha Ivers*, the man who continues to love a woman who despises him is a consistently weak character. He has allowed his father to arrange his marriage, permitted himself to be used to cover up his wife's crimes and to advance her ambitions. All he can do about it is get drunk. In the end he commits suicide.

With the many expedients for avoiding suffering in love, it is not surprising that few love relations turn out unhappily. If we consider the central love story, and define unhappiness by death or defection, only one sixth of American films have love ending unhappily. French films show love turning out unhappily half of the time. The proportion of unhappy love in British films seems to fall between these two.

The hazards of love are further reduced by the fact that scarcely anyone tries to force anything on a loved one. The lover does not imperiously demand conformity to his wishes, nor does he practice any serious deception to get what he wants. In *My Reputation*, where the domestically inclined heroine falls in love with the playboy, there is little danger that she will be ruined or that he will be trapped. Neither has the inclination to take advantage of the other. The situation is easily resolved by a transformation of his feelings, so that his wishes coincide with hers. In *The Fallen Angel*, the original exploitative intentions of the hero fail to materialize. Almost immediately after he has married the heroine for her money, he confesses this to her, then makes good by falling in love with her. Even the exceptionally demanding and possessive wife in *Leave Her to Heaven* does not feel that she can force on her husband her requirement that they live in complete mutually absorbed isolation. Instead she kills anyone who threatens to invade their solitude. In an exceptional case, *The Killers*, the bad woman uses the hero as a fall guy for her crimes and the enamored hero allows himself to be used.

Aside from a few exceptions, however, men and women are not made vulnerable by emotional susceptibility. Dangers in American films tend to take the form of external violence, not of inner conflict. The threat of falling hopelessly in love with someone bad or exploitative or unloving, and so having one's life destroyed, seems unreal. The shot in the dark, the beating in the lonely shack in the woods, or the false crime accusation—these are the images of danger. In American films, men and women may, and often do shoot each other. They do not break each other's hearts.

THE HERO AS FATHER

It is, as Margaret Mead has pointed out, characteristic of American family life that parents tend to bring up their children differently from the way in which they themselves were brought up. This has been partly related to immigrant backgrounds, partly to the more general expectation that children should surpass their parents. Correspondingly, movie heroes and heroines tend to have relations with their children which are different from those their parents have with them. The hero's father, we have seen, is usually well disposed and inconsequential. The hero as father tends to exercise more influence on his son's life. Where the hero's relation to his father has been prosaic, the hero's relation to his son tends to be dramatic, a matter of life and death. In *Adventure*, the hero, who has been away at sea for months, returns home to find to his surprise that his wife (who had been estranged from him when he went away) has just given birth to a son. The child, however, seems to be stillborn; the doctor is working over it without noticeable results. The hero, elated at the appearance of the son, confident that the son will live, takes the baby from the doctor's hands and breathes life into him. In *Too Young to Know*, the hero returns from the war to find that his estranged wife has borne a son and given him away for adoption. The hero is anxious to get his son back and succeeds in retrieving him. In *Tomorrow Is Forever* the hero's wife bears him a son after he has been presumed to be lost in the First World War. The hero, who has been badly maimed and has allowed himself to be considered dead, turns up in disguise many years later as a visitor in the house of his wife, who has since married again. He is elated when he discovers he has a son and assumes an influential role in relation to a major decision in the son's life. It is early in the Second World War, before America's entry, and the boy is eager to enlist in the RCAF. The hero recognizes in his son the same idealistic motives which had led him to volunteer in the First World War, and strengthens his resolve. The mother, fearful for her son's safety, resents the influence of this stranger, as she takes him to be, and nearly throws him out of the house. In the end, the hero succeeds in communicating to the mother his enthusiasm for the son's enterprise, and the son goes off with the mother's blessing.

The hero's son is his immortality. This is explicitly stated by the child's mother where the hero is, or is presumed to be dead (*To Each His Own, Tomorrow Is Forever*). It is not easy to picture the hero as being in the same way a perpetuation of his insignificant father; in any case, this idea is never expressed. The continuity of generations extends forward, not back.

The hero tends to receive more love from his daughter than the older-generation father. As we have seen, the daughter frequently has the older-generation father to herself but does not derive intense gratification from this monopoly. In contrast to this, the younger-generation father inspires intense love in his daughter, who strives unsuccessfully to get exclusive possession of him. In *This Love of Ours*, the hero for a time lives alone with his daughter. When the girl was very young, he took her away from her mother, whom he suspected of infidelity. He has told her that her mother is dead, and she maintains a shrine to her mother's memory in the garden. This situation, agreeable to the daughter, is disrupted by the reappearance of the mother. The father has known for a long time that his suspicions of her were ungrounded. He finally succeeds in finding her, and persuades her to come home for the daughter's sake. The daughter, who is told that this is her father's new wife, bitterly resents her intrusion. She prefers the old dead mother with the shrine in the garden to the new live one who usurps her place in the house. She tells her father that things were nicer when there were just the two of them, and tries to turn him against the mother by communicating her discovery that the mother was a night-club entertainer. She almost succeeds in driving the mother away. But after getting hints from an old friend of the family, she recognizes her as her real mother and stops her just as she is going out the front door, suitcase in hand.

A stepfather may allow a fuller expression of the daughter's longings. In *The Secret Heart*, a daughter's devotion to her father reappears as love for her stepmother's suitor. In the beginning the girl's father appears as a querulent drunkard who devotes himself mainly to playing soulful music on the piano. The daughter idealizes him, feels she is the only one who understands him, and intensely resents her stepmother, who sometimes manifests impatience with the father. In an alcoholic depression the father walks off a moonlit cliff. The daughter becomes moody, withdrawn, hypochondriacal, and spends her time playing her father's favorite pieces. She revives when an attractive, long-term suitor of her stepmother reappears. The girl misinterprets his friendly interest in her, believes that he reciprocates her love, and gets a shock when she overhears an affectionate passage between him and the stepmother. She rushes out into the night and contemplates stepping off the same fatal cliff, but is stopped in time. Eventually she is led to see that her father was not as wonderful, nor her stepmother as bad as she had thought; that her prospective stepfather is not for her; and that the nice boy of her own age who has been hanging around is acceptable.

In *Mildred Pierce*, the daughter of the heroine despises her mother and loves first her father, then her stepfather. She has an affair with the stepfather and kills him when he tells her that she is silly and her mother admirable. In *Sentimental Journey*, a less mature adopted daughter is left alone with the father after the mother's death. The girl tries to carry out the wish of the mother, whom she loved devotedly, to take the mother's place and take care of the father. The father resists this substitution. After protractedly rejecting the little girl, however, he becomes reconciled to her out of obedience to his dead wife's wishes.

These younger-generation fathers of daughters tend to be colorless and intensely loved figures, whose fate is incidental to a central mother-daughter drama. Their stiff emptiness is perhaps related to the fact that they always make the conventionally correct choice, preferring the older to the younger of the two women, regardless of whether the younger one is a possible love object. This tendency to avoid any disturbingly intense love of the hero for his daughter or stepdaughter recalls the tendency to make his mother emotionally unimportant for him. Thus there is, on the manifest level, a tendency for familial women to evoke no serious feelings.

An exception occurs in *The Red House*, in which an adoptive father intensely loves his adopted daughter. In contrast to the previously mentioned fathers who are bland, handsome, youngish and docile, this father is aging, ugly, crippled, dominant, terrible in his rage, dangerous, and, as it eventually appears, mad and a murderer. He lives alone with his old sister and a beautiful young adopted daughter, on a lonely farm next to an allegedly haunted wood. The wood is in fact guarded by a brutal young man hired by him. The secret of the wood, unveiled in the end, is that the father years before murdered the mother of the adopted daughter, whom he loved, together with her husband, and buried their bodies in a house in the wood. The adopted daughter, toward whom he is possessive, falls in love with a young man. They explore the forbidden wood, pursued by sudden blows on the head and rounds of shotgun fire. The father becomes patently mad, confuses the adopted daughter with her mother and almost re-enacts the earlier murder with the girl as victim. Her young man comes to the rescue at the last moment and the old man commits suicide.

In French and British films a father or father-surrogate may intensely love a daughter without assuming the stigmata of the father figure in *The Red House*. In French films, the father figure is apt to be the hero who suffers out of love for a familial woman, typically a daughter figure instead of a mother figure. This love of an aging man for a daughter figure is likely to be a second edition of a love for a forbidden woman, which reaches from one generation to another but now with the age relations reversed. The father figure is portrayed sympathetically, as a man overcome by inappropriate feelings which cause suffering to himself as much as to others. He is not violent. In the end he may prevent others from getting what they want, but without fulfilling his own wishes. In *Symphonie Pastorale*, a pastor falls in love with his adopted daughter, a beautiful blind girl whom he has rescued and educated. An intense rivalry develops between him and his son for the girl's affections. After an operation which restores her sight, she falls in love with the younger man. But the possessive father drives him away, and in the end the girl drowns herself. In *Le Silence Est d'Or*, a comic variant of the same theme, the father figure, who loves the girl and could prevent the happiness of the young couple, becomes resigned and brings them together.

In British films, a father figure may have an intense possessive love for a daughter or daughter-surrogate in a way which differs from both the American and French versions. While remaining partially sympathetic, this English father figure tends to be somber and cruel, and at the same time fascinating, binding the daughter to him in spite of her mixed feelings. In *The Seventh Veil*, the heroine's guardian maintains an aloof and domineering attitude toward her. When he discovers her musical talent, he becomes a severe taskmaster, keeping her at her work and promoting her successful career. When she falls in love, he enforces his authority as her guardian, reminds her that she may not even leave the house without his permission, and takes her away on a concert tour where he and she are constantly together. Eventually, in spite of his watchfulness, she falls in love again and, being of age now, threatens to leave him. He falls into a rage, demanding that she stay with him, and, when she refuses, beats her with his cane. She runs away with her new young man, is hurt in an auto accident, becomes disoriented, attempts suicide, and is treated by a psychiatrist. Finally, presented with the two still devoted suitors and her guardian to choose from, she goes to her guardian. This English father figure is domineering but weak; he rages out of fear of being deserted. Before his ward comes to live with him, he lives alone in an austere mansion where the portrait of his haughty and beautiful mother (who ran off with a foreign musician when her son was a child) occupies a prominent place. His moroseness and cruelty, and especially his rage at the threat of being deserted, are related to his past disappointment and loneliness.

This terrifying but weak English father figure may easily pass over the boundary between sympathetic and unsympathetic. The father in *They Were Sisters* brutally exploits the mother and selfishly monopolizes the daughter. The mother devotes herself with timid servility to his needs and is rewarded by contempt and mockery. She is so afraid of him that she hardly dares to stay away for a day on a holiday with her sisters. On rare occasions she feels that she cannot bear any more of his oppression and resolves to leave him. He then produces a simulated heart attack, becomes helplessly dependent, and implies that he would die without her. This father (in contrast to the typical father figures in American films discussed above) prefers his daughter to his wife. The daughter, whom he presses into service as a secretary, is his indispensable companion and confidante, and he treats her with respect. He is possessive toward her and destroys without a qualm the letters addressed to her by a young man in whom she has become interested. The wife, after a particularly devastating quarrel, runs out of the house and, blinded by tears, collides with an oncoming automobile and is killed. In the subsequent legal investigation of the accident, a question is raised about the state of mind of the dead woman immediately preceding the fatal event. The husband, preoccupied with his good repute, tells about the serene happiness of their family life. The sister of the dead wife denies this with asperity. It becomes an urgent issue for him whether his daughter will support him or not. At this point the daughter again meets the young man she loves, learns that he has been writing to her and infers that her father has suppressed the letters. In a final encounter between father and daughter, he appeals for her support and she refuses it. We see him last in the hall of the law courts, alone.

THE HEROINE AS MOTHER

American movie heroines tend to find motherhood full of anxieties and frustrations. Where the heroine has a son, the child's father is usually dead or absent (*Adventure, My Reputation, Tomorrow Is Forever, Too Young to Know, To Each His Own*). In the heroine's relation to her son, quarrels, separations, fears of separation, and disappointment about his insufficient love are prominent.

In *Too Young to Know*, the heroine gives birth to a son after her husband has quarreled with her and left her. She allows her child to be adopted by a childless couple. In *To Each His Own*, the heroine gives birth to a son after her lover, a World War I ace, has been killed. It is when the father of the child is already dead that a heroine is apt to show an intense wish to have the child. One rarely finds a heroine manifesting comparable eagerness to bear a child to a man who is still alive. The heroine in *To Each His Own* risks her life to give birth to her son after her doctor has advised an abortion for medical reasons. She then devises a scheme to make the baby appear to be a foundling so that she can adopt him without arousing suspicion. The scheme miscarries, and the child is adopted by another woman. A series of humiliations and disappointments develops as the heroine tries to get her son back and win his love. She applies for the job of nursemaid in the house of the adoptive mother, but is refused. Later, she virtually blackmails the adoptive mother into giving the boy back to her. But he suffers from loneliness for the adoptive mother and the heroine sends him back. Many years later she meets the son, now a Second World War aviator, introduces herself as an old friend of the family, and offers to put him up at her apartment while he is on leave. He goes to stay with her, but again she suffers rebuffs and disappointments. The son wants to spend all his time with his fiancée and rudely brushes aside this spinsterish, inexplicably sentimental old friend of the family. It is only at the last moment that he learns her identity and calls her Mother.

In *Tomorrow Is Forever*, the heroine gives birth to a son after her husband is supposed to have been killed. Later, when the son is grown up, the mother suffers from the typical anxiety about losing him. While she is untroubled at the prospect of his loving someone else and behaves graciously toward his fiancée, she is panicky about his wish to enlist in the RCAF. Her opposition to her son's plans, rationalized by her political isolationism, precipitates family quarrels. The reappearance of her first husband helps to resolve the conflict; the heroine's anxiety about her son becomes less acute, and she is able to let him go.

In *Claudia and David*, a more temporary absence of the father creates the typical situation in which the mother is left alone with the son and suffers anxiety about losing him. The young couple go off to a party, leaving their little son at home. The husband becomes absorbed in a business deal and cannot be disturbed. The wife is overwhelmed by an apprehension that the child has become ill during their absence and asks another man at the party to drive her home. They find the little boy having convulsions, and he is barely saved by the combined efforts of the party guest and the old housekeeper. When the husband returns, the wife is furious with him for having been absent in this emergency. Here the presumable rage of the heroines of the other films against the absent fathers of their children, rendered inexpressible because of the real or supposed death of these fathers, finds its outlet. Later in this film, the other component of the constellation, the death or near-death of the father, occurs: the husband is almost killed in an automobile accident.

In *My Reputation*, the heroine, whose husband has just died, is left with two preadolescent sons. They are about to leave for boarding school, and the mother plans a picnic celebration on the eve of their departure. Just as they get into the station wagon, a bunch of the boys' friends drive up and invite them to a party. The mother urges them to accept; they leave her with alacrity, and she is left holding the picnic bag. Some time later the mother, after an interlude of intense loneliness, falls in love with a new man. This relationship arouses gossip, and the boys, when they return for the Christmas holidays, are snubbed by their friends because of it. They become enraged with their mother and run away to their grandmother's house. The mother comes after them and with tearful explanations succeeds in reconciling them. The major role of the sons in the life of this heroine is deprivational.

Johnny Belinda presents perhaps most fully the legend of the heroine and her son. The father is not only absent, but the heroine does not even remember her single sexual contact with him. She is a deaf-mute whose native cleverness and prettiness have been brought out by the kindly interest of a young doctor. A neighborhood rowdy, impressed by her transformation, rapes her. (This is a backwoods variant on the theme of the plain girl getting prettied up and getting her man. Evoking lingering puritanical misgivings about sexual attractiveness, this story relates: a plain girl gets prettied up, gets raped.) The heroine, rescued from lifelong loneliness by the appearance of her son, adores him. However, like other young mothers in films, she is in danger of losing him. The father of the child, who alone knows of his relationship, turns up and is moved by paternal feelings for the handsome infant. He tries to take the baby away and the mother shoots him. Here the death of the father recurs, and the hostility of the mother toward him, suggested by other films, is manifest. The heroine, on trial for murder, is separated from her son, suffers intensely from his absence, but finally has him restored to her.

A recurrent theme in these films of the heroine and her son is the absence of the father, who may descend from heaven in an airplane to beget the child and then fly off never to be seen again (*To Each His Own*). We may recognize in this the American film version of the widely recurring myth of the birth of the hero. In its rudiments the myth (told of Buddha, Jesus, Romulus and Remus, etc.) reduces the relation of the mother and father to a transient contact; the father, a supernatural being, descends briefly to beget the son and then disappears, so that the mother remains virtually a virgin, with the son as the only man in her life. This fantasy, as analyzed by Otto Rank, gratifies the son's longing to exclude the father and have the mother to himself. If we try to see what is distinctive in the American treatment of this myth, it seems to be partly the emphasis on the independence and competence of the mother left to herself (notably the brilliant career woman of *To Each His Own*), partly the stress on her hostility to the father (which is clearest where she kills him in *Johnny Belinda*). The emphasis in the American treatment falls even more on the threat to the mother that she will lose the son, that she will be disappointed in her love for him. This theme is underscored in the melodramas which we shall analyze presently where the hero is frequently bent on disappointing the disguised mother figure who seeks his love, who seems to have been involved with another man but really loves only the hero. This disappointment of the mother by the son is a major trend in the movie plots reflecting mother-son relations and suggests as a possible source a specially intense love disappointment of the son in relation to the mother, a disappointment for which compensation is sought in these fantasied reversals of the situation.

The myth of the birth of the hero also recalls *The Miracle of Morgan's Creek*. There the heroine has become pregnant from an overnight marriage with a soldier who has disappeared and whom she has forgotten completely due to a blow on the head which she

suffered on the same night. Her position is that of an unwed mother-
to-be. She is shown at Christmas time with her old father, who is
trying to cheer her up. The father, alluding to her imminent maternity, reminds her of the birth of Christ, who was also born in
humble circumstances, and, as he might have added, of a virgin
mother. The allusion may have seemed out of key in the comic
context, but is justified as comparative mythology. The heroine's
father in the film goes on to prophesy that her child may become
president of the United States. The heroine does in fact achieve
great fame from her maternity, as she gives birth to sextuplets. Needless to say, they are all boys. The relation of these films to the myth
of the hero's birth is confirmed by the circumstance that it is a son
(or sons), not a daughter, who is born to the mother alone. Another recurrent feature of these films is that the heroine finds an
obliging, unaggressive, devoted man who unprotestingly assumes the
paternity of her fatherless son or sons. In *The Miracle of Morgan's
Creek*, he is a particularly pronounced sucker type, who, incapable
of having got a girl in trouble, gets himself into all kinds of scrapes
in his efforts to protect her. In the end he is dazzled and disoriented
by being given credit for the sextuplets.

The heroine's relation to her son contrasts with her relation to
her father. As we have seen, the relation with the father is un-
disturbed by the intense and painful feelings which appear in relation to the son. The heroine suffers disappointment for unrequited
love, fears of separation, separation, and fears of death in connection
with her son. None of these feelings is apt to appear in connection
with her father. This again illustrates the tendency of American
films to direct intense familial feelings toward the present and future, and away from the past generation.

The heroine is frequently apt to assume a maternal role toward
her father or a father substitute. In this relation she is likely to be
more sure and better appreciated than in her relation to her son. Her
maternal relation to an old man may be symbolized by her pulling
him out of the water, saving his life. Thereafter she feels responsible
for taking care of him, nicknames him Pop and takes him to live
with her (*Stork Club*). She may support her old father, and when
he misbehaves, threaten to withdraw his allowance (*She Wouldn't
Say Yes*). The exchange of the father figure who remains so devoted and easy to mother for the son who is so hard to hold on to
occurs in *Apartment for Peggy*. The heroine twice saves the life of
the old professor with whom she lives (who reminds her of her
grandfather and whom she calls Pop). She loses her son, who dies
at birth. (This episode is associated, as usual, with the absence of

the child's father.) The old professor, consoling the heroine for the loss of the child, tells her that she has restored him to life.

The frustrations of the heroine in relation to her son contrast with the picture of the hero in relation to his daughter. As we have seen, the hero as father is greatly loved by his daughter, who is usually disappointed in not being able to win sufficient love from him in return. In the total balance sheet of love and disappointment, the hero tends to be more loved than loving in relation to mother, daughter, or mother substitute. The most stressed theme is the disappointment of the familial woman.

The heroine also tends to be unhappy in relation to her daughter, whom she loves intensely and who does not love her in return. As with the son there is suffering through separation, but there is not the same anxiety about the possible death of the daughter. Instead there is the threat of the daughter's hostility. The mother-daughter conflict, which is expressed only weakly and incidentally in the older generation, is here fully developed. In *Mildred Pierce* the heroine loves her daughter more than anything else. The girl remains hostile and competitive toward the mother throughout. The heroine is extremely ambitious for her daughter, and impatient with her rather ineffectual husband, who fails to provide the family with the means for a life of sufficiently high status. The husband finds a less exacting woman to comfort him for his unhappiness at home, and the heroine goes to work, at first as a waitress. When the daughter discovers this, despite her mother's efforts at concealment, she taunts her mother with being a low-class woman and says it is not surprising that the well-bred father should have left her. The daughter maintains this attitude even when the competent mother has easily and rapidly risen to being the owner of a large chain of restaurants. The girl takes advantage of the wealth now at her disposal to lead a fast life, mainly running around with an upper-class playboy who has previously had an affair with her mother. When the mother reproaches her, she replies that the mother naturally cannot understand or share their mode of life. The mother slaps her face, and the girl runs away from home to become a singer in a low-grade night club. The heroine, after an interlude of distress, decides to marry the playboy, who is impecunious and attracted equally by her charms and her business. She wants to offer the playboy's family mansion as a home of such high status that the daughter will come back. The ruse succeeds and there is a brief happy reunion of mother and daughter. However, the daughter pursues her affair with her new stepfather. After a short time he becomes bored with her; she reproaches him for his withdrawal and he retorts by telling her how much less interesting she is than her mother. Piqued by this, she kills him. The mother, discovering his body, infers what has happened. First she tries to make another suitor of hers the fall guy for the crime. When this fails, she confesses to it herself. The daughter, brought face to face with the mother in the police station, attacks the mother for having, as she supposes, betrayed her, and thus gives herself away. The movie ends with the daughter being led away to jail, while the mother leaves the courthouse at dawn, accompanied by her first husband—he has come back to stand by her, and they become reunited.

The daughter tends to express mixed feelings about the mother's ambitions for her. As we have seen in *Mildred Pierce*, she uses the fulfillment of her mother's ambitions as a weapon against the mother: having acquired, in response to the mother's demands, standards appropriate to a higher status, she turns them against the mother and despises her as less well-bred than herself. Alternatively she spites the mother by threatening to move downward in the status scale, when she becomes a singer in a low-class café.

In *Desert Fury*, the mother, a bootlegger's widow, runs a successful gambling house in a small Western town, where she is snubbed by the women of good society. Ambitious for her daughter, she keeps sending her away to upper-class boarding schools. But the girl always tells her schoolmates about her mother's business, precipitates snubs from them, and then leaves school in a rage, driving home in her flashing station-wagon-style roadster. She insists to her mother that she wants to come to work in the gambling place. There is a long-drawn-out conflict between mother and daughter over the mother's demand that the girl rise higher and the girl's wish to imitate her mother. This conflict becomes acute when the girl falls in love with a gambler-gangster with whom the mother was connected in the past, and whom the mother knows to be a thoroughly bad lot. Against her mother's strenuous opposition, the girl runs off with this man, becomes disillusioned with him just in time to escape being murdered by him. The mother is so relieved to see the girl safely returned that she is ready to yield on the point of the girl's working in the gambling place. However, by now the girl has sufficiently satisfied her rebellious low-life strivings and is ready to settle down with a nice young man. His accepted place in the community will make it possible for her to become dissociated from her origins.

This Love of Ours is another film whose central theme is a mother's great love for her daughter, her suffering about being separated from the daughter, and the daughter's hostility and contempt toward her. It is frequent in Western culture for the daughter to feel more or less consciously that the mother (who has sexual relations with the father) is a low woman, while she (whose communion with the father is spiritual) can satisfy the higher side of the father's nature which the mother fails to understand. The American pattern of family life, in which each generation is supposed to surpass the preceding, and where the mother particularly is the bearer of this ambition for the children, gives a special emphasis to this common theme. The daughter's sour-grapes attitude toward the mother as a love rival may easily assume the form of social snobbery.

The characteristic demand for achievement which American mothers make on their children presumably works considerable emotional hardship on them: they feel they must fulfill the mother's ambitions in order to be loved. By their provocative behavior the daughters in *Mildred Pierce* and *Desert Fury* rebel against the mother's achievement demands. The daughter turns the fulfillment of the mother's demands into a weapon against the mother. She retaliates for her mother's making love conditional by refusing to love the mother. Alternatively, she tries to test whether the mother will love her anyhow, flouting the mother's achievement demands by plunging into low life or obstinately adhering to the level of her origin. Presumably this expresses a longing for the mother's unconditional love, and a wish to be like her instead of having to become alienated from her by superior achievement.

Sentimental Journey is a wish-fulfillment fantasy which provides for the joint gratification of the mother's wish to elevate the daughter and the daughter's wish to identify with the mother. It is a "family romance" in which a fine lady adopts a poor orphan girl. The child is spiritually the true daughter of the mother, enjoying a delicate fantasy life similar to that which the mother recalls from her childhood. Thus the external elevation of the daughter simply makes it possible for her to express her soul and brings her into communion with the mother instead of forcing her away. The mother, knowing she is soon to die, has adopted the girl to take her place with her supposedly childlike husband. The girl is inducted into such routines as bringing her adoptive father breakfast in bed, and instructed in the practices of overprotection. When the mother dies, this is the last thing the girl would wish, since the mother is the one person she loves, and she has not yet achieved a good relation with the father. Following the mother's instructions, frequently reinforced by spirit communications, the girl tries to take the mother's place with the father. However, he has never liked the girl, resenting the close tie between her and the mother which seemed to exclude him. It was, in fact, as the result of a quarrel, in which the father demanded that the girl be sent away, that the mother suffered a fatal heart attack. The girl was thus unwittingly guilty of setting the dilemma, either Mother goes or I go. After the mother's death, the father hesitates to go through with his plan to send the child away. However, the girl is eventually so impressed with his distaste for her that she runs away to the seashore where she first met the mother. The father is prompted by the voice of the mother, in the form of a phonograph recording (the more ethereal child receives posthumous messages from the mother without material mediation), to realize how much it means to the dead wife that he should love the child in her place. He rushes out to the nocturnal shore in time to snatch the distracted child from the waves.

In this film the daughter concentrates all her love on the mother. It is probably significant for the American situation that this variant occurs where the conflict between mother and daughter over the mother's ambitions for the daughter is obviated.

II

Theory

and

Technique

This group of selections is of a more technical nature than those in the previous section. Although Balázs, Arnheim and Cocteau go into aesthetic considerations, their pieces are theoretical—in the sense that they are all trying to formulate a set of propositions (implied or stated) about the film medium. Pudovkin, Eisenstein and Clair, all master film makers, are more concerned with the technical side of film composition. The case of Rotha is somewhat special in that he presents a theory on the necessity of using a sociological and political approach for both the documentary and the conventional dramatic film.

Film

Technique

_____

by V. I. Pudovkin

The following selection consists of two sections from Pudovkin's Film Technique *(Vision Press, Ltd., England, 1954. This edition also includes Pudovkin's* Film Acting, *first published in Russia in 1933. Translated by Ivor Montagu). First published in Russia in 1929, the book still holds up as a remarkably perceptive and practical statement on film theory and technique. Simply and lucidly written, it anatomizes every aspect of film creation.*

METHODS OF TREATMENT OF THE MATERIAL

(Structural Editing)

A CINEMATOGRAPH film, and consequently also a scenario, is always divided into a great number of separate pieces (more correctly, it is built out of these pieces). The sum of the shooting script is divided into sequences, each sequence into scenes, and, finally, the scenes themselves are constructed from a whole series of pieces (script scenes) shot from various angles. An actual scenario, ready for use in shooting, must take into account this basic property of

267

the film. The scenarist must be able to write his material on paper exactly as it will appear upon the screen, thus giving exactly the content of each shot as well as its position in sequence. The construction of a scene from pieces, a sequence from scenes, and reel from sequences, and so forth, is called *editing*. Editing is one of the most significant instruments of effect possessed by the film technician and, therefore, by the scenarist also. Let us now become acquainted with its methods one by one.

EDITING OF THE SCENE

Everyone familiar with a film is familiar with the expression "close-up." The alternating representation of the faces of the characters during a dialogue; the representation of hands, or feet, filling the whole screen—all this is familiar to everyone. But in order to know how properly to use the close-up, one must understand its significance, which is as follows: The close-up directs the attention of the spectator to that detail which is, at the moment, important to the course of the action. For instance, three persons are taking part in a scene. Suppose the significance of this scene consists in the *general* course of the action (if, for example, all three are lifting some heavy object); then they are taken simultaneously in a *general* view, the so-called long shot. But suppose any one of them changes to an independent action having significance in the scenario (for example, separating himself from the others, he draws a revolver cautiously from his pocket); then the camera is directed on him alone. His action is recorded separately.

What is said above applies not only to persons, but also to separate parts of a person, and objects. Let us suppose a man is to be taken apparently listening calmly to the conversation of someone else, but actually restraining his anger with difficulty. The man crushes the cigarette he holds in his hand, a gesture unnoticed by the other. This hand will always be shown on the screen separately, in close-up, otherwise the spectator will not notice it and a characteristic detail will be missed. The view formerly obtained (and is still held by some) that the close-up is an "interruption" of the long shot. This idea is entirely false. It is no sort of interruption. It represents a proper form of construction.

In order to make clear to oneself the nature of the process of editing a scene, one may draw the following analogy. Imagine yourself observing a scene unfolded in front of you, thus: A man stands near the wall of a house and turns his head to the left; there appears another man slinking cautiously through the gate. The two are fairly widely distant from one another—they stop. The first takes some object and shows it to the other, mocking him. The latter clenches his fists in a rage and throws himself at the former. At this moment a woman looks out of a window on the third floor and calls, "Police!" The antagonists run off in opposite directions. Now, how would this have been observed?

1. The observer looks at the first man. He turns his head.

2. What is he looking at? The observer turns his glance in the same direction and sees the man entering the gate. The latter stops.

3. How does the first react to the appearance on the scene of the second? A new turn by the observer; the first takes out an object and mocks the second.

4. How does the second react? Another turn; he clenches his fists and throws himself on his opponent.

5. The observer draws aside to watch how both opponents roll about fighting.

6. A shout from above. The observer raises his head and sees the woman at the window shouting.

7. The observer lowers his head and sees the result of the warning—the antagonists running off in opposite directions.

The observer happened to be standing near and saw every detail, saw it clearly, but to do so he had to turn his head, first left, then right, then upward, whithersoever his attention was attracted by the interest of observation and the sequence of the developing scene. Suppose he had been standing farther away from the action, taking in the two persons and the window on the third floor simultaneously, he would have received only a general impression, without being able to look separately at the first, the second, or the woman. Here we have approached closely the basic significance of editing. Its object is the showing of the development of the scene in relief, as it were, by guiding the attention of the spectator now to one, now to the other separate element. The lens of the camera replaces the eye of the observer, and the changes of angle of the camera—directed now on one person, now on another, now on one detail, now on another —must be subject to the same conditions as those of the eyes of the observer. The film technician, in order to secure the greatest clarity, emphasis, and vividness, shoots the scene in separate pieces and, joining them and showing them, directs the attention of the spectator to the separate elements, compelling him to see as the attentive observer saw. From the above the manner in which editing can even work upon the emotions is clear. Imagine to yourself the excited observer of some rapidly developing scene. His agitated glance is thrown rapidly from one spot to another. If we imitate this glance with the camera we get a series of pictures, rapidly alternating pieces, creating a *stirring scenario editing construction*. The reverse would be long pieces changing by mixes, conditioning a calm and slow editing construction (as one may shoot, for example, a herd of cattle wandering along a road, taken from the viewpoint of a pedestrian on the same road).

We have established, by these instances, the basic significance of the constructive editing of scenes. It builds the scenes from separate pieces, of which each concentrates the attention of the spectator only on that element important to the action. The sequence of these pieces must not be uncontrolled, but must correspond to the natural transference of attention of an imaginary observer (who, in the end, is represented by the spectator). In this sequence must be expressed a special logic that will be apparent only if each shot contains an impulse toward transference of the attention to the next. For example, (1) a man turns his head and looks; (2) what he looks at is shown.

EDITING OF THE SEQUENCE

The guidance of the attention of the spectator to different elements of the developing action in succession is, in general, characteristic of the film. It is its basic method. We have seen that the separate scene, and often even the movement of one man, is built up upon the screen from separate pieces. Now, the film is not simply a collection of different scenes. Just as the pieces are built up into scenes endowed, as it were, with a connected action, so the separate scenes are assembled into groups forming whole sequences. The sequence is constructed (edited) from scenes. Let us suppose ourselves faced with the task of constructing the following sequence: Two spies are creeping forward to blow up a powder magazine; on the way one of them loses a letter with instructions. Someone else finds the letter and warns the guard, who appears in time to arrest the spies and save the magazine. Here the scenarist has to deal with simultaneity of various actions in several different places. While the spies are crawling toward the magazine, someone else finds the letter and hastens to warn the guard. The spies have nearly reached their objective; the guards are warned and rushing toward the magazine. The spies have completed their preparations; the guard arrives in time. If we pursue the previous analogy between the camera and an observer, we now not only have to turn it from side to side, but also to move it from place to place. The observer (the camera) is now on the road shadowing the spies, now in the guardroom recording the confusion, now back at the magazine showing the spies at work, and so forth. But, in combination of the separate scenes (editing), the former law of sequence succession remains in force. A consecutive sequence will appear upon the screen only if the attention of the spectator be transferred correctly from scene to scene. And this correctness is conditioned as follows: The spectator sees the creeping spies, the loss of the letter, and finally the person who finds the letter. The person with the letter rushes for help. The spectator is seized with inevitable excitement—Will the man who found the letter be able to forestall the explosion? The scenarist immediately answers by showing the spies nearing the magazine—his answer has the effect of a warning, "Time is short." The excitement of the spectator—Will they be in time?—continues; the scenarist shows the guard turning out. Time is very short—the spies are shown beginning their work. Thus, transferring attention now to the rescuers, now to the spies, the scenarist answers with actual impulses to increase the spectator's interest, and the construction (editing) of the sequence is correctly achieved.

There is a law in psychology that says if an emotion gives birth to a certain movement, by imitation of this movement the corresponding emotion can be called forth. If the scenarist can effect in even rhythm the transference of interest of the intent spectator, if he can so construct the elements of increasing interest that the question, "What is happening at the other place?" arises and at the same moment the spectator is transferred whither he wishes to go, then the editing thus created can really excite the spectator. One must learn to understand that editing is in actual fact a compulsory and deliberate guidance of the thoughts and associations of the spectator. If the editing be merely an uncontrolled combination of the various pieces, the spectator will understand (apprehend) nothing from it; but if it be co-ordinated according to a definitely selected course of events or conceptual line, either agitated or calm, it will either excite or soothe the spectator.

EDITING OF THE SCENARIO

The film is divided into reels. The reels are usually equal in length, on an average from 900 to 1,200 feet long. The combination of the reels forms the picture. The usual length of a picture should not be more than from 6,500 to 7,500 feet. This length, as yet, involves no unnecessary exhaustion of the spectator. The film is usually divided into from six to eight reels. It should be noted here, as a practical hint, that the average length of a piece (remember the editing of scenes) is from 6 to 10 feet, and consequently from 100 to 150 pieces go to a reel. By orientating himself on these figures, the scenarist can visualize how much material can be fitted into the scenario. The scenario is composed of a series of sequences. In discussing the construction (editing) of the scenario from sequences, we introduce a new element into the scenarist's work—the element of so-called dramatic continuity of action that was discussed at the beginning of this sketch. The continuity of the separate sequences when joined together depends not merely upon the simple transference of attention from one place to another, but is conditioned by the development of the action forming the foundation of the scenario. It is important, however, to remind the scenarist of the following point: A scenario has always in its development a moment of greatest tension, found nearly always at the end of the film. To prepare the spectator, or, more correctly, preserve him, for this final tension, it is especially important to see that he is not affected by unnecessary exhaustion during the course of the film. A method, already discussed, that the scenarist can employ to this end is the careful distribution of the titles (which always distract the spectator), securing compression of the greater quantity of them into the first reels, and leaving the last one for uninterrupted action.

Thus, first the action of the scenario is worked out, the action is then worked out into sequences, the sequences into scenes, and these constructed by editing from the pieces, each corresponding to a camera angle.

EDITING AS AN INSTRUMENT OF IMPRESSION

(Relational Editing)

We have already mentioned, in the section on editing of sequences, that editing is not merely a method of the junction of separate scenes or pieces, but is a method that controls the "psychological guidance" of the spectator. We should now acquaint ourselves with the main special editing methods having as their aim the impression of the spectator.

Contrast.—Suppose it be our task to tell of the miserable situation of a starving man; the story will impress more vividly if associated with mention of the senseless gluttony of a well-to-do man.

On just such a simple contrast relation is based the corresponding editing method. On the screen the impression of this contrast is yet increased, for it is possible not only to relate the starving sequence to the gluttony sequence, but also to relate separate scenes and even separate shots of the scenes to one another, thus, as it were, forcing the spectator to compare the two actions all the time, one strengthening the other. The editing of contrast is one of the most effective, but also one of the commonest and most standardized, of methods, and so care should be taken not to overdo it.

Parallelism.—This method resembles contrast but is considerably wider. Its substance can be explained more clearly by an example. In a scenario as yet unproduced a section occurs as follows: A workingman, one of the leaders of a strike, is condemned to death; the execution is fixed for 5 A.M. The sequence is edited thus: A factory owner, employer of the condemned man, is leaving a restaurant drunk; he looks at his wrist watch: four o'clock. The accused is shown—he is being made ready to be led out. Again the manufacturer; he rings a doorbell to ask the time: four-thirty. The prison wagon drives along the street under heavy guard. The maid who opens the door—the wife of the condemned—is subjected to a sudden senseless assault. The drunken factory owner snores on a bed, his leg with trouser end upturned, his hand hanging down with wrist watch visible; the hands of the watch crawl slowly to five o'clock. The workman is being hanged. In this instance two thematically unconnected incidents develop in parallel by means of the watch that tells of the approaching execution. The watch on the wrist of the callous brute, as it were, connects him with the chief protagonist of the approaching tragic denouement, thus ever present in the consciousness of the spectator. This is undoubtedly an interesting method, capable of considerable development.

Symbolism.—In the final scenes of the film *Strike*, the shooting of workmen is punctuated by shots of the slaughter of a bull in a stockyard. The scenarist, as it were, desires to say: Just as a butcher fells a bull with the swing of a pole-axe, so, cruelly and in cold blood, were the workers shot down. This method is especially interesting because, by means of editing, it introduces an abstract concept into the consciousness of the spectator without use of a title.

Simultaneity.—In American films the final section is constructed from the simultaneous rapid development of two actions, in which the outcome of one depends on the outcome of the other. The end of the present-day section of *Intolerance* . . . is thus constructed. The whole aim of this method is to create in the spectator a maximum tension of excitement by the constant forcing of a question, such as, in this case, Will they be in time? Will they be in time?

The method is a purely emotional one, and nowadays overdone almost to the point of boredom, but it cannot be denied that of all the methods of constructing the end hitherto devised it is the most effective.

Leitmotiv (*reiteration of theme*).—Often it is interesting for the scenarist especially to emphasize the basic theme of the scenario. For this purpose the method of reiteration exists. Its nature can easily be demonstrated by an example. In an antireligious scenario that aimed at exposing the cruelty and hypocrisy of the Church in the employ of the Tsarist régime the same shot was several times repeated: a church bell slowly ringing and, superimposed on it, the title, "The sound of bells sends into the world a message of patience and love." This piece appeared whenever the scenarist desired to emphasize the stupidity of patience, or the hypocrisy of the love thus preached.

The little that has been said above of relational editing naturally by no means exhausts the whole abundance of its methods. It has merely been important to show that constructional editing, a method specifically and peculiarly filmic, is, in the hands of the scenarist, an important instrument of impression. Careful study of its use in pictures, combined with talent, will undoubtedly lead to the discovery of new possibilities and, in conjunction with them, to the creation of new forms.

THE ENVIRONMENT OF THE FILM

All the action of any scenario is immersed in some environment that provides, as it were, the general color of the film. This environment may, for example, be a special mode of life. By more detailed examination, one may even regard as the environment some separate peculiarity, some special essential trait of the given mode of life selected. This environment, this color, cannot, and must not, be rendered by one explanatory scene or a title; it must constantly pervade the whole film, or its appropriate part, from beginning to end. As I have said, the action must be immersed in this background. A whole series of the best films of recent times has shown that this emphasis by means of an environment in which the action is immersed is quite easily effected in cinematography. The film *Tol'able David* shows us this vividly. It is also interesting that the effecting of the unity of this color of a film is based upon the scarcely communicable ability to saturate the film with numerous fine and correctly observed details. Naturally it is not possible to require of the scenarist that he shall discover all these details and fix them in writing. The best that he can do is find their necessary abstract formulation, and it is the affair of the director to absorb this formulation and give it the necessary plastic shape. Remarks by the scenarist such as, perhaps, "There was an insufferable smell in the room," or "Many factory sirens vibrated and sang through the heavy, oil-permeated atmosphere," are not in any sense forbidden. They indicate correctly the relation between the ideas of the scenarist and the future plastic shaping by the director. It may already now be said with a fair degree of certainty that the most immediate task next awaiting the director is that very solution by filmic methods of the descriptive problems mentioned. The first experiments were carried out by the Americans in showing a landscape of symbolic character at the beginning of a film. *Tol'able David* began with the picture of a village taken through a cherry tree in flower. The foaming, tempestuous sea symbolized the leitmotiv of the film *The Remnants of a Wreck.*

A wonderful example, affording unquestionably an achievement of this kind, are the pictures of the misty dawn rising over the corpse of the murdered sailor in *The Battleship Potemkin.* The solution of these problems—the depiction of the environment—is an undoubted and important part of the work on the scenario. And this work naturally cannot be carried out without direct participation by the director. Even a simple landscape—a piece of nature so often encountered in films—must, by some inner guiding line, be bound up with the developing action.

I repeat that the film is exceptionally economical and precise in its work. There is, and must be, in it no superfluous element. There is no such thing as a neutral background, and every factor must be collected and directed upon the single aim of solving the given problems. For every action, insofar as it takes place in the real world, is always involved in general conditions—that is, the nature of the environment.

The action of the scenes may take place by day or by night. Film directors have long been familiar with this point, and the effort to render night effects is to this day an interesting problem for film directors. One can go further. The American, Griffith, succeeded in the film *America* in obtaining, with marvelous tenderness and justness, gradations of twilight and morning. The director has a mass of material at his disposal for this kind of work. The film is interesting, as said before, not only in that it is able to concentrate on details, but also in its ability to weld to a unity numerous materials, deriving from widely embraced sources.

As example, this same morning light: To gain this effect, the director can use not only the growing light of sunrise, but also numerous correctly selected, characteristic processes that infallibly relate themselves with approaching dawn in the apprehension of the spectator. The light of lampposts growing paler against the lightening sky, the silhouettes of scarcely visible buildings, the tops of trees tenderly touched with the light of the not yet ascended sun, awakening birds, crowing cocks, the early morning mist, the dew— all this can be employed by the director, shot, and in editing built to a harmonious whole.

In one film an interesting method was used of representing the filmic image of a dawn. In order to embrace in the editing construction the feeling of growing and ever wider expanding light, the separate shots follow one another in such wise that at the beginning, when it is still dark, only details can be seen upon the screen. The camera took only close-ups, as if, like the eye of man in the surrounding dark, it saw only what was near to it. With the increase of the light the camera became ever more and more distant from the object shot. Simultaneously with the broadening of the light, broader and broader became the view field embraced by the lens. From the close-ups in darkness the director changed to ever more distant long shots, as if he sought directly to render the increasing light, pervading everything widely and more widely. It is notable that here is employed a pure technical possibility, peculiar only to the film, of communicating a very subtle feeling.

It is clear that work on the solution of problems of this kind is bound up so closely with the knowledge of film technique, so organically with the pure directorial work of analysis, selection of the material, and its unification in creative editing, that such problems cannot, independently of the director, be resolved for him by the scenarist alone. At the same time, it is, as already mentioned, absolutely essential to give the expression of this environment in which the action of every film is immersed, and accordingly, in the creation of the scenario, it is indispensable for the director to collaborate in the work.

THE CHARACTERS IN THE ENVIRONMENT

I should like to note that in the work of one of the strongest directors of the present day, David Griffith, in almost every one of his films, and indeed especially in those in which he has reached the maximum expression and power, it is almost invariably the case that the action of the scenario develops among characters blended directly with that which takes place in the surrounding world.

The stormy finale of the Griffith film is so constructed as to strengthen for the spectator the conflict and the struggle of the heroes to an unimagined degree, thanks to the fact that the director introduces into the action gale, storm, breaking ice, rivers in spate, a gigantic roaring waterfall. When Lillian Gish, in *Way Down East*, runs broken from the house, her happiness in ruins, and the faithful Barthelmess rushes after her to bring her back to life, the whole pursuit of love behind despair, developing in the furious tempo of the action, takes place in a fearful snowstorm; and at the final climax, Griffith forces the spectator himself to feel despair, when a rotating block of ice, on it cowering the figure of a woman, approaches the precipice of a gigantic waterfall, itself conveying the impression of inescapable and hopeless ruin.

First the snowstorm, then the foaming, swirling river in thaw, packed with ice blocks that rage yet wilder than the storm, and finally the mighty waterfall, conveying the impression of death itself. In this sequence of events is repeated, on a large scale, as it were, the same line of that increasing despair—despair striving to make an end, for death, that has irresistibly gripped the chief character. This harmony—the storm in the human heart and the storm in the frenzy of nature—is one of the most powerful achievements of the American genius. This example shows particularly clearly how far-reaching and deep must be that connection, between the content of the scenario and the director's general treatment, that adds strength and unity to his work. The director not only transfers the separate scenes suggested by the scenarist each into movement and form, he has also to absorb the scenario in its entirety, from the theme to the final form of the action, and perceive and feel each scene as an irremovable, component part of the unified structure. And this can be the case only if he be organically involved in the work on the scenario from beginning to end.

When the work on the general construction has been finished, the theme molded to a subject, the separate scenes in which the action is realized laid down, then only do we come to the period of the hardest work on the treatment of the scenario, that stage of work when, already concrete and perceptible, that filmic form of the picture that will result can be foreseen; do we come to the period of the planning out of the editing scheme for the shots, of the discovery of those component parts from which the separate images will later be assembled.

To bring a waterfall into the action does not necessarily mean to create it on the screen. Let us remember what we said regarding the creation of a filmic image that becomes vivid and effective only when the necessary details are correctly found. We come to the stage of utilizing the pieces of real space and real time for the future creation of filmic space and filmic time. If it may be said at the beginning of the process that the scenarist guides the work—and that the director has only to pay attention so as properly to apprehend it organically, and so as, not only to keep contact with it at every given moment, but to be constantly welded to it—now comes a change. The guide of the work is now the director, equipped with that knowledge of technique and that specific talent that enables him to find the correct and vivid images expressing the quintessential element of each given idea. The director organizes each separate incident, analyzing it, disintegrating it into elements, and simultaneously thinking of the connection of these elements in editing. It is here of special interest to note that the scenarist at this later stage, just as the director in the early stages, must not be divorced from the work. His task it is to supervise the resolution to editable shape of every separate problem, thinking at every instant of the basic theme—sometimes completely abstract, yet current in every separate problem.

Only by means of a close collaboration can a correct and valuable result be attained. Naturally one might postulate as the ideal arrangement the incarnation of scenarist and director in one person. But I have already spoken of the unusual scope and complexity of film creation that prevents any possibility of its mastery by one person. Collectivism is indispensable in the film, but the collaborators must be blended with one another to an exceptionally close degree.

Theory

of the

Film

by Béla Balázs

*The following fragments are se-
lected from* Theory of the Film:
Character and Growth of a New
Art *by Béla Balázs (Roy Publishers, New York, 1953. Translated
from the Hungarian by Edith
Bone). Balázs ranks as one of the
most important thinkers on film
art. He had extremely interesting
things to say about every imaginable aspect of the film—sound,
lighting, dialogue, film societies, sociology of the film, and many
others.*

I
IN PRAISE OF THEORY

DANGERS OF IGNORANCE

WE ALL KNOW and admit that film art has a greater influence on
the minds of the general public than any other art. The official
guardians of culture note the fact with a certain amount of regret
and uneasiness. But too few of us are sufficiently alive to the dangers that are an inevitable consequence of this fact. Nor do we
realize clearly enough that we must be better connoisseurs of the
film if we are not to be as much at the mercy of perhaps the greatest

intellectual and spiritual influence of our age as to some blind and irresistible elemental force. And unless we study its laws and possibilities very carefully, we shall not be able to control and direct this potentially greatest instrument of mass influence ever devised in the whole course of human cultural history. One might think that the theory of this art would naturally be regarded as the most important field for present-day art theory. No one would deny today that the art of the motion picture is *the* popular art of our century —unfortunately not in the sense that it is the product of the popular spirit but the other way round, in the sense that the mentality of the people, and particularly of the urban population, is to a great extent the product of this art, an art that is at the same time a vast industry. Thus the question of educating the public to a better, more critical appreciation of the films is a question of the mental health of the nations. Nevertheless, too few of us have yet realized how dangerously and irresponsibly we have failed to promote such a better understanding of film art.

WHY ARE PEOPLE NOT TAUGHT
TO APPRECIATE FILMS?

Nowadays social considerations are taken into account in the cultural sphere no less than in others. Nevertheless, the aesthetics of the film are nowhere included in the official teaching of art appreciation. Our academies have sections for literature and every established art, but none for the new art of our day—the film. It was not until 1947 that the first film maker was elected to the French *Académie*. At our universities there are chairs for literature and all arts except that of the film. The first art academy which included the theory of film art in its curriculum was opened in Prague in 1947. The textbooks used in our secondary schools discuss the other arts but say nothing of the film. Millions hear about the aesthetics of literature and painting who will never make use of such knowledge because they read no books and look at no pictures. But the millions who frequent the movies are left without guidance—no one teaches them to appreciate film art.

NEED FOR GENERAL CULTURE

There are numerous film schools in the world and no one denies that there may be need of a theory of the film—for specialists. In

Paris, in London, and elsewhere, film institutes and scientific film societies have been formed to study the "science" of the film. But what is needed is not specialized knowledge; it is a general level of culture. No one who had not the faintest conception of literature or music would be considered well educated. A man who had never heard of Beethoven or Michelangelo would be out of place among people of culture. But if he has not the faintest idea of the rudiments of film art and had never heard of Asta Nielsen or David Wark Griffith, he might still pass for a well-educated, cultured person, even on the highest level. The most important art of our time is that about which one need know nothing whatever. And yet it is an urgent need that we should cultivate enough discrimination to influence the art which shapes the popular taste in the highest degree. Until there is a chapter on film art in every textbook on the history of art and on aesthetics; until the art of the film has a chair in our universities and a place in the curriculum of our secondary schools, we shall not have firmly established in the consciousness of our generation this most important artistic development of our century.

II
DER SICHTBARE MENSCH

This chapter, which deals with the visual culture developed through the silent film, is taken from my book *Der Sichtbare Mensch*. In it I hailed the silent film as a turning point in our cultural history, not suspecting that the sound film would soon come to oust it. The truth which stated a then existing reality has remained true, but the reality it dealt with has bolted like a runaway horse and has made new observations and interpretations necessary. Nevertheless, this chapter may be of interest not merely as a chapter in the history of film theory. Nor does it perhaps retain its interest only because the picture still remains the essence of the film and its visual content. Lines of development are never rigidly set. They often proceed in a roundabout way, throwing the light of old knowledge onto new paths through dialectical interaction. Because I believe that we have now come to such a doubling back in the development of the film, when the already once accomplished and then again lost achievements of the silent film are about to be revalued and restored, I want to quote here what I wrote in 1923 about the silent film:

The invention of printing gradually rendered illegible the faces of men. So much could be read from paper that the method of conveying meaning by facial expression fell into desuetude.

Victor Hugo wrote once that the printed book took over the part played by the cathedral in the Middle Ages and became the carrier of the spirit of the people. But the thousands of books tore the *one* spirit, embodied in the cathedral, into thousands of opinions. The word broke the stone into a thousand fragments, tore the church into a thousand books.

The visual spirit was thus turned into a legible spirit and visual culture into a culture of concepts. This of course had its social and economic causes, which changed the general face of life. But we paid little attention to the fact that, in conformity with this, the faces of individual men, their foreheads, their eyes, their mouths, had also of necessity and quite concretely to suffer a change.

At present a new discovery, a new machine is at work to turn the attention of men back to a visual culture and give them new faces. This machine is the cinematographic camera. Like the printing press, it is a technical device for the multiplication and distribution of products of the human spirit; its effect on human culture will not be less than that of the printing press.

For not to speak does not mean that one has nothing to say. Those who do not speak may be brimming over with emotions which can be expressed only in forms and pictures, in gesture and play of feature. The man of visual culture uses these not as substitutes for words, as a deaf-mute uses his fingers. He does not think in words, the syllables of which he sketches in the air like the dots and dashes of the Morse code. The gestures of visual man are not intended to convey concepts which can be expressed in words, but such inner experiences, such nonrational emotions as would still remain unexpressed when everything that can be told has been told. Such emotions lie in the deepest levels of the soul and cannot be approached by words that are mere reflections of concepts; just as our musical experiences cannot be expressed in rationalized concepts. What appears on the face and in facial expression is a spiritual experience which is rendered immediately visible without the intermediary of words.

In the golden age of the old visual arts, the painter and sculptor did not merely fill empty space with abstract shapes and forms, and man was not merely a formal problem for the artist. Painters could paint the spirit and the soul without becoming "literary," for the soul and the spirit had not yet been confined in concepts capable of expression only by means of words; they could be incarnated without residue. That was the happy time when paintings could still have a "theme" and an "idea," for the idea had not yet been tied to the concept and to the word that named the concept. The artist could present in its primary form of manifestation the soul's bodily incarnation in gesture or feature. But since then the printing press has grown to be the main bridge over which the more remote interhuman spiritual exchanges take place and the soul has been concentrated and crystallized chiefly in the word. There was no longer any need for the subtler means of expression provided by the body. For this reason our bodies grew soulless and empty—what is not in use deteriorates.

The expressive surface of our body was thus reduced to the face alone and this not merely because the rest of the body was hidden by clothes. For the poor remnants of bodily expression that remained to us the little surface of the face sufficed, sticking up like a clumsy semaphore of the soul and signaling as best it could. Sometimes a gesture of the hand was added, recalling the melancholy of a mutilated torso. In the epoch of word culture the soul learned to speak but had grown almost invisible. Such was the effect of the printing press.

Now the film is about to inaugurate a new direction in our culture. Many million people sit in the picture houses every evening and purely through vision, experience happenings, characters, emotions, moods, even thoughts, without the need for many words. For words do not touch the spiritual content of the pictures and are merely passing instruments of as yet undeveloped forms of art. Humanity is already learning the rich and colorful language of gesture, movement and facial expression. This is not a language of signs as a substitute for words, like the sign language of the deaf-and-dumb—it is the visual means of communication, without intermediary, of souls clothed in flesh. Man has again become visible.

Linguistic research has found that the origins of language lie in expressive movement—that is, that man when he began to speak moved his tongue and lips to no greater extent than the other muscles of his face and body—just as an infant does today. Originally the purpose was not the making of sounds. The movement of tongue and lips was at first the same spontaneous gesturing as every other expressive movement of the body. That the former produced sounds was a secondary, adventitious phenomenon, which was only later used for practical purposes. The immediately visible message was thus turned into an immediately audible message. In the course of this process, as in every translation, a great deal was lost. It is the expressive movement, the gesture, that is the aboriginal mother-tongue of the human race.

Now we are beginning to remember and relearn this tongue. It is still clumsy and primitive and very far removed as yet from the refinements of word art. But already it is beginning to be able sometimes to express things which escape the artists of the word. How much of human thought would remain unexpressed if we had no music! The now developing art of facial expression and gesture will bring just as many submerged contents to the surface. Although these human experiences are not rational, conceptual contents, they are nevertheless neither vague nor blurred, but as clear and unequivocal as is music. Thus the inner man, too, will become visible.

But the old visible man no longer exists today and the new visible man is not yet in existence. As I have said before, it is the law of nature that unused organs degenerate and disappear, leaving only rudiments behind. The animals that do not chew lose their teeth. In the epoch of word culture we made little use of the expressive powers of our body and have therefore partly lost that power. The gesturing of primitive peoples is frequently more varied and expressive than that of the educated European whose vocabulary is infinitely richer. A few more years of film art and our scholars will discover that cinematography enables them to compile encyclopedias of facial expression, movement and gesture, such as have long existed for words in the shape of dictionaries. The public, however, need not wait for the gesture encyclopedia and grammars of future academies; it can go to the pictures and learn it there.

We had, however, when we neglected the body as a means of expression, lost more than mere corporal power of expression. That which was to have been expressed was also narrowed down by this neglect. For it is not the same spirit, not the same soul that is expressed once in words and once in gestures. Music does not express the same thing as poetry in a different way—it expresses something quite different. When we dip the bucket of words in the depths, we bring up other things than when we do the same with gestures. But let no one think that I want to bring back the culture of movement and gesture in place of the culture of words, for neither can be a substitute for the other. Without a rational, conceptual culture and the scientific development that goes with it there can be no social and hence no human progress. The connecting tissue of modern society is the word spoken and written, without which all organization and planning would be impossible. On the other hand fascism has shown us where the tendency to reduce human culture to subconscious emotions in place of clear concepts would lead humanity.

What I am talking about is only art and even here there is no question of displacing the more rational art of the word. There is no reason why we should renounce one sort of human achievement in favor of another. Even the most highly developed musical culture need not crowd out some more rational aspect of culture.

But to return to the simile of the bucket: we know that the wells that dry up are the wells from which no water is dipped. Psychology and philology have shown that our thoughts and feelings are determined a priori by the possibility of expressing them. Philology is also aware that it is not only concepts and feelings that create words, but that it is also the other way round: words give rise to concepts and feelings. This is a form of economy practiced by our mental constitution which desires to produce unusable things just as little as does our physical organism. Psychological and logical analysis has shown that words are not merely images expressing our thoughts and feelings but in most cases their a priori limiting forms. This is at the root of the danger of stereotyped banality which so often threatens the educated. Here again the evolution of the human spirit is a dialectical process. Its development increases its means of expression and the increase of means of expression in its turn facilitates and accelerates its development. Thus if then the film increases the possibilities of expression, it will also widen the spirit it can express.

Will this newly developing language of facial expression and expressive gesture bring human beings closer to each other or the contrary? Despite the tower of Babel there were concepts common to all behind the different words and one could also learn the languages of others. Concepts on the other hand, have, in civilized communities, a content determined by convention. A universally valid grammar was an even more potent unifying principle holding together the individuals who in bourgeois society were prone to become estranged and isolated from each other. Even the literature of extreme subjectivism used the common vocabulary and was thus preserved from the loneliness of final misunderstanding.

But the language of the gestures is far more individual and personal than the language of words, although facial expression, too, has its habitual forms and conventionally accepted interpretations, to such an extent that one might—and should—write a comparative "gesturology" on the model of comparative linguistics. Nevertheless this language of facial expression and gesture, although it has a certain generally accepted tradition, lacks the severe rules that govern grammar and by the grace of our academies are compulsory for us all. No school prescribes that you must express your cheerfulness by this sort of smile and your bad humor with that sort of wrinkled brow. There are no punishable errors in this or that facial expression, although children doubtless do observe and imitate such conventional grimaces and gestures. On the other hand, these are more immediately induced by inner impulses than are words. Yet it will probably be the art of the film after all which may bring together the peoples and nations, make them accustomed to each other, and lead them to mutual understanding. The silent film is free of the isolating walls of language differences. If we look at and understand each other's faces and gestures, we not only understand, we also learn to feel each other's emotions. The gesture is not only the outward projection of emotion, it is also its initiator.

The universality of the film is primarily due to economic causes —which are always the most compelling causes. The making of a film is so expensive that only very few nations have a home market sufficient to make film production pay. But one of the preconditions of the international popularity of any film is the universal comprehensibility of facial expression and gesture. Specific national characteristics will in time be permissible only as exotic curiosities and a certain leveling of "gesturology" will be inevitable. The laws of the film market permit only universally comprehensible facial expressions and gestures, every nuance of which is understood by princess and working girl alike from San Francisco to Smyrna. We now already have a situation in which the film speaks the only universal, common world language understood by all. Ethnic peculiarities, national specialties sometimes can lend style and color to a film, but can never become factors in causing the story to move on, because the gestures which convey the meaning and decide the course of the action must be uniformly comprehensible to every audience everywhere, otherwise the producer will lose money on the film.

The silent film helped people to become physically accustomed to each other and was about to create an international human type. When once a common cause will have united men within the limits of their own race and nation, then the film which makes visible man equally visible to everyone will greatly aid in leveling physical differences between the various races and nations and will thus be one of the most useful pioneers in the development toward an international universal humanity.

III
THE CLOSE-UP

As we have already said, the basis of the new form-language is the moving cinematographic camera with its constantly changing viewpoint. The distance from the object and with it the size and number of objects in the frame, the angle and the perspective all change incessantly. This movement breaks up the object before the camera into *sectional pictures*, or "shots," irrespective of whether that object is moving or motionless. Sectional pictures are not details of a whole film. For what is being done is not to break up into its constituent parts a picture already taken or already envisaged. The result of this would be detail; in this case one would have to show every group and every individual in a crowd scene from the same angle as the one from which they are seen in the total picture; none of the people or things could move—if they did, they would no longer be details of the same total. What is done is not to break up into detail an already existent, already formed total picture, but to show a living, moving scene or landscape as a synthesis of sectional pictures, which merge in our consciousness into a total *scene* although they are not the parts of an existent immutable mosaic and could never be made into a total single *picture*.

WHAT HOLDS THE SECTIONAL PICTURE TOGETHER?

The answer to this question is: the montage or cutting, the mobile composition of the film, an architecture in time, not space, of which much more is to be said later. For the time being we are interested in the psychological question of why a scene broken up into sectional pictures does not fall apart but remains a coherent whole, remains in the consciousness of the spectator a consistent unity in both space and time. How do we know that things are happening simultaneously and in the same place, even though the pictures pass before our eyes in temporal sequence and show a real passing of time?

This unity and the simultaneity of pictures proceeding in time is not produced automatically. The spectator must contribute an association of ideas, a synthesis of consciousness and imagination to which the film-going public had first to be educated. This is that visual culture of which we have spoken in previous chapters.

But the sectional picture (or "shot") must be correctly ordered and composed. There may be shots which slip out of the whole and in respect of which we no longer feel that we are in the same place and see the same scene as in the preceding shots. This is a matter for the director, who can, if he chooses, make the spectator feel the continuity of the scene, its unity in time and space even if he has never once shown him a total picture of the whole scene for his orientation.

This is done by including in every shot a movement, a gesture, a form, a something which refers the eye to the preceding and following shots, something that protrudes into the next shot like the branch of a tree or a fence, like a ball that rolls from one frame to the other, a bird that flies across, cigar smoke that curls in both, a look or gesture to which there is an answer in the next shot. But the director must be on his guard not to change the angle together with the direction of movement—if he does, the change in the picture is so great as to break its unity. The sound film has simplified this job of remaining in step. For sound can always be heard in the whole space, in each shot. If a scene is enacted, say, in a night club, and we hear the same music we will know that we are in the same night club even if in the shot itself we see nothing but a hand holding a flower or something of the sort. But if we suddenly hear different sounds in this same shot of a hand we will assume, even if we don't see it, that the hand holding the flower is now in a quite different place. For instance, to continue the picture of the hand holding the rose—if instead of dance music we now hear the twittering of birds, we will not be surprised if, when the picture widens into a long shot, we see a garden and the owner of the hand picking roses. This sort of change-over offers opportunities for good effects.

SOUND IS INDIVISIBLE

This totally different nature of sound has a considerable influence on the composition, montage and dramaturgy of the sound film. The sound camera cannot break up sound into sections or shots as the cinematographic camera can break up objects. In space, sound is always heard indivisibly and homogeneously; that is, it has the same character in one part of space as in any other; it can only be louder or softer, closer or more distant and mixed with other sounds in differing ways. In the night club, for instance, we may first hear only dance music and then the loud talking and laughter of a noisy company at one of the tables may almost drown it.

SOUND IN SPACE

All sound has an identifiable place in space. By its timbre we can tell whether it is in a room, or a cellar, in a large hall or in the open air. This possibility of placing sound also helps to hold together shots the action of which takes place in the same space. The sound film has educated our ear—or might and should have educated it—to recognize the timbre of sound. But we have made less progress in our aural than in our visual education. In any case, the sound film which could use sound as its artistic material in a similar way as the silent film had used the visual impression was soon superseded by the talkie, which was in a sense a step backward toward the photographed theater.

THE FACE OF THINGS

The first new world discovered by the film camera in the days of the silent film was the world of very small things visible only from very short distances, the hidden life of little things. By this the camera showed us not only hitherto unknown objects and events: the adventures of beetles in a wilderness of blades of grass, the tragedies of day-old chicks in a corner of the poultry-run, the erotic battles of flowers and the poetry of miniature landscapes. It brought us not only new themes. By means of the close-up the camera in the days of the silent film revealed also the hidden mainsprings of a life which we had thought we already knew so well. Blurred outlines are mostly the result of our insensitive shortsightedness and superficiality. We skim over the teeming substance of life. The camera has uncovered that cell-life of the vital issues in which all great events are ultimately conceived; for the greatest landslide is only the aggregate of the movements of single particles. A multitude of close-ups can show us the very instant in which the general is transformed into the particular. The close-up has not only widened our vision of life, it has also deepened it. In the days of the silent film it not only revealed new things, but showed us the meaning of the old.

VISUAL LIFE

The close-up can show us a quality in a gesture of the hand we never noticed before when we saw that hand stroke or strike something, a quality which is often more expressive than any play of the features. The close-up shows your shadow on the wall with which you have lived all your life and which you scarcely knew; it shows the speechless face and fate of the dumb objects that live with you in your room and whose fate is bound up with your own. Before

this you looked at your life as a concertgoer ignorant of music listens to an orchestra playing a symphony. All he hears is the leading melody; all the rest is blurred into a general murmur. Only
those can really understand and enjoy the music who can hear the
contrapuntal architecture of each part in the score. This is how we
see life: only its leading melody meets the eye. But a good film with
its close-ups reveals the most hidden parts in our polyphonous life,
and teaches us to see the intricate visual details of life as one reads
an orchestral score.

LYRICAL CHARM OF THE CLOSE-UP

The close-up may sometimes give the impression of a mere naturalist preoccupation with detail. But good close-ups radiate a tender
human attitude in the contemplation of hidden things, a delicate so-
licitude, a gentle bending over the intimacies of life-in-the-minia-
ture, a warm sensibility. Good close-ups are lyrical; it is the heart,
not the eye, that has perceived them.

Close-ups are often dramatic revelations of what is really happening under the surface of appearances. You may see a medium
shot of someone sitting and conducting a conversation with icy
calm. The close-up will show trembling fingers nervously fumbling
a small object—sign of an internal storm. Among pictures of a comfortable house breathing a sunny security, we suddenly see the evil
grin of a vicious head on the carved mantelpiece or the menacing
grimace of a door opening into darkness. Like the leitmotiv of impending fate in an opera, the shadow of some impending disaster
falls across the cheerful scene.

Close-ups are the pictures expressing the poetic sensibility of the
director. They show the faces of things and those expressions on
them which are significant because they are reflected expressions of
our own subconscious feeling. Herein lies the art of the true cameraman.

In a very old American film I saw this dramatic scene: the bride
at the altar suddenly runs away from the bridegroom whom she
detests, who is rich and who has been forced on her. As she rushes
away she must pass through a large room full of wedding presents.
Beautiful things, good things, useful things, things radiating plenty
and security smile at her and lean toward her with expressive faces.
And there are the presents given by the bridegroom: faces of things
radiating touching attention, consideration, tenderness, love—and
they all seem to be looking at the fleeing bride, because she looks

at them; all seem to stretch out hands toward her, because she feels they do so. There are ever more of them—they crowd the room and block her path—her flight slows down more and more, then she stops and finally turns back.

IV
THE FACE OF MAN

The basis and possibility of an art of the film is that everyone and everything looks what it is

Every art always deals with human beings; it is a human manifestation and presents human beings. To paraphrase Marx: "The root of all art is man." When the film close-up strips the veil of our imperceptiveness and insensitivity from the hidden little things and shows us the face of objects, it still shows us man, for what makes objects expressive are the human expressions projected onto them. The objects only reflect our own selves, and this is what distinguishes art from scientific knowledge (although even the latter is to a great extent subjectively determined). When we see the face of things, we do what the ancients did in creating *gods* in man's image and breathing a human soul into them. The close-ups of the film are the creative instruments of this mighty visual anthropomorphism.

What was more important, however, than the discovery of the physiognomy of things was the discovery of the human face. Facial expression is the most subjective manifestation of man, more subjective even than speech, for vocabulary and grammar are subject to more or less universally valid rules and conventions, while the play of features, as has already been said, is a manifestation not governed by objective canons, even though it is largely a matter of imitation. This most subjective and individual of human manifestations is rendered objective in the close-up.

A NEW DIMENSION

If the close-up lifts some object or some part of an object out of its surroundings, we nevertheless perceive it as existing in space; we do not for an instant forget that the hand, say, which is shown by the close-up belongs to some human being. It is precisely this connection which lends meaning to its every movement. But when Griffith's genius and daring first projected gigantic "severed heads"

onto the cinema screen, he not only brought the human face closer
to us in space, he also transposed it from space into another dimension. We do not mean, of course, the cinema screen and the patches
of light and shadow moving across it, which, being visible things,
can be conceived only in space; we mean the expression on the face
as revealed by the close-up. We have said that the isolated hand
would lose its meaning, its expression, if we did not know and
imagine its connection with some human being. The facial expression on a face is complete and comprehensible in itself and therefore we need not think of it as existing in space and time. Even if
we had just seen the same face in the middle of a crowd and the
close-up merely separated it from the others, we would still feel
that we have suddenly been left alone with this one face to the exclusion of the rest of the world. Even if we have just seen the owner
of the face in a long shot, when we look into the eyes in a close-up,
we no longer think of that wide space, because the expression and
significance of the face has no relation to space and no connection
with it. Facing an isolated face takes us out of space, our consciousness of space is cut out and we find ourselves in another dimension:
that of physiognomy. The fact that the features of the face can be
seen side by side, i.e., in space—that the eyes are at the top, the ears
at the sides and the mouth lower down—loses all reference to space
when we see, not a figure of flesh and bone, but an expression or
in other words when we see emotions, moods, intentions and
thoughts, things which although our eyes can see them, are not in
space. For feelings, emotions, moods, intentions, thoughts are not
themselves things pertaining to space, even if they are rendered
visible by means which are.

MELODY AND PHYSIOGNOMY

We will be helped in understanding this peculiar dimension by
Henri Bergson's analysis of time and duration. A melody, said Bergson, is composed of single notes which follow each other in sequence—i.e., in time. Nevertheless a melody has no dimension in
time, because the first note is made an element of the melody only
because it refers to the next note and because it stands in a definite
relation to all other notes down to the last. Hence the last note,
which may not be played for some time, is yet already present in
the first note as a melody-creating element. And the last note com-
pletes the melody only because we hear the first note along with it.
The notes sound one after the other in a time sequence, hence they

have a real duration, but the coherent line of melody has no dimension in time; the relation of the notes to each other is not a phenomenon occurring in time. The melody is not born gradually in the course of time but is already in existence as a complete entity as soon as the first note is played. How else would we know that a melody is begun? The single notes have duration in time, but their relation to each other, which gives meaning to the individual sounds, is outside time. A logical deduction also has its sequence, but premise and conclusion do not follow one another in time. The process of thinking as a psychological process may have duration; but the logical forms, like melodies, do not belong to the dimension of time.

Now facial expression, physiognomy, has a relation to space similar to the relation of melody to time. The single features, of course, appear in space; but the significance of their relation to one another is not a phenomenon pertaining to space, no more than are the emotions, thoughts and ideas which are manifested in the facial expressions we see. They are picturelike and yet they seem outside space; such is the psychological effect of facial expression.

How is the countryside turned into landscape? Not every bit of nature is a landscape in itself. The countryside has only a topography, which is a thing that can be exactly reproduced on a military map. But the landscape expresses a mood, which is not merely objectively given; it needs the co-operation of subjective factors before it can come into existence. The phrase is "the mood of the landscape" but there is no mood save that of some human being and those who look at the countryside with the greatest objectivity—a farmer, for instance—would be least likely to see any sort of "mood" in it. "Mood" is the feeling of the painter, the artist, not of the plowman, the shepherd or the woodcutter, whose business with nature is not of the soul but of the body, a practical, not artistic, activity.

The landscape is the physiognomy of some countryside, as seen by the painter who can put it on his canvas, but also by the cameraman who can shoot it with an appropriate setup. It is as though the countryside were suddenly lifting its veil and showing its face, and on the face an expression which we recognize though we could not give it a name. There have already been several landscape artists of genius in the film, artists of that moving landscape which has not only a physiognomy, but mimicry and gesture too. On these landscapes the clouds gather, the mist drives, the reeds tremble and shiver in the wind, the branches of the trees nod and toss and the shadows play hide-and-seek—these are film landscapes which wake at daybreak and darken to tragedy at the setting of the sun. There is no painter born whose motionless pictures could match this experience.

The following two essays and a section of a third are from Film as Art *(University of California Press, 1957. This book is an adaptation of* Film, *Faber and Faber, London, 1933. It was originally published in Germany under the title* Film als Kunst). *It is one of the most outstanding books on film theory and aesthetics—a work that belongs on the same shelf with the writings of Balázs, Pudovkin and Eisenstein. In this book Mr. Arnheim examines the kinesthetic possibilities of the film, more particularly what it is in the dynamics of motion picture composition that is capable of producing such visual magic. The author sets out to show, very convincingly, how each new technical advance—sound, color, 3-D—has worked against the artistic potentialities of the film medium.*

Film

as Art

---

by Rudolph Arnheim

FILM AND REALITY

Film RESEMBLES painting, music, literature, and the dance in this respect—it is a medium that may, but need not, be used to produce artistic results. Colored picture post cards, for instance, are not art and are not intended to be. Neither are a military march, a true-confessions story, or a strip tease. And the movies are not necessarily film art.

There are still many educated people who stoutly deny the possibility that film might be art. They say, in effect, "Film cannot be art, for it does nothing but reproduce reality mechanically." Those who defend this point of view are reasoning from the analogy of painting. In painting, the way from reality to the picture lies via the artist's eye and nervous system, his hand and, finally, the brush that puts strokes on canvas. The process is not mechanical like that of photography, in which the light rays reflected from the object are collected by a system of lenses and are then directed onto a sensitive plate where they produce chemical changes. Does this state of affairs justify our denying photography and film a place in the temple of the Muses?

It is worth while to refute thoroughly and systematically the charge that photography and film are only mechanical reproductions and that they therefore have no connection with art—for this is an excellent method of getting to understand the nature of film art.

With this end in view, the basic elements of the film medium will be examined separately and compared with the corresponding characteristics of what we perceive "in reality." It will be seen how fundamentally different the two kinds of image are, and that it is just these differences that provide film with its artistic resources. We shall thus come at the same time to understand the working principles of film art.

THE PROJECTION OF SOLIDS UPON A PLANE SURFACE

Let us consider the visual reality of some definite object such as a cube. If this cube is standing on a table in front of me, its position determines whether I can realize its shape properly. If I see, for example, merely the four sides of a square, I have no means of knowing that a cube is before me, I see only a square surface. The human eye, and equally the photographic lens, acts from a particular position and from there can take in only such portions of the field of vision as are not hidden by things in front. As the cube is now placed, five of its faces are screened by the sixth, and therefore this last only is visible. But since this face might equally well conceal something quite different—since it might be the base of a pyramid or one side of a sheet of paper, for instance—our view of the cube has not been selected characteristically.

We have, therefore, already established one important principle: If I wish to photograph a cube, it is not enough for me to bring the object within range of my camera. It is rather a question of my position relative to the object, or of where I place it. The aspect chosen above gives very little information as to the shape of the cube. One, however, that reveals three surfaces of the cube and their relation to one another shows enough to make it fairly unmistakable what the object is supposed to be. Since our field of vision is full of solid objects, but our eye (like the camera) sees this field from only one station point at any given moment, and since the eye can perceive the rays of light that are reflected from the object only by projecting them onto a plane surface—the retina—the reproduction of even a perfectly simple object is not a mechanical process but can be set about well or badly.

The second aspect gives a much truer picture of the cube than the first. The reason for this is that the second shows more than the first—three faces instead of only one. As a rule, however, truth does not depend on quantity. If it were merely a matter of finding which aspect shows the greatest amount of surface, the best point of view could be arrived at by purely mechanical calculation. There is no formula to help one choose the most characteristic aspect; it is a question of feeling. Whether a particular person is "more himself" in profile than full face, whether the palm or the outside of the hand is more expressive, whether a particular mountain is better taken from the north or the west cannot be ascertained mathematically—they are matters of delicate sensibility.

Thus, as a preliminary, people who contemptuously refer to the camera as an automatic recording machine must be made to realize that even in the simplest photographic reproduction of a perfectly simple object, a feeling for its nature is required which is quite beyond any mechanical operation. We shall see later, by the way, that in artistic photography and film, those aspects that best show the characteristics of a particular object are not by any means always chosen; others are often selected deliberately for the sake of achieving specific effects.

REDUCTION OF DEPTH

How do our eyes succeed in giving us three-dimensional impressions even though the flat retinas can receive only two-dimensional images? Depth perception relies mainly on the distance between the two eyes, which makes for two slightly different images. The fusion of these two pictures into one image gives the three-dimensional impression. As is well known, the same principle is used in the stereoscope, for which two photographs are taken at once, about the same distance apart as the human eyes. This process cannot be used for film without recourse to awkward devices, such as colored spectacles, when more than one person is to watch the projection. For a single spectator it would be easy to make a stereoscopic film. It would only mean taking two simultaneous shots of the same incident a couple of inches apart and then showing one of them to each eye. For display to a larger number of spectators, however, the problem of stereoscopic film has not yet been solved satisfactorily—hence the sense of depth in film pictures is extraordinarily small. The movement of people or objects from front to back makes a certain depth evident—but it is necessary only to glance into a stereoscope, which makes everything stand out most realistically, to recognize how flat the film picture is. This is another example of the fundamental difference between visual reality and film.

The effect of film is neither absolutely two-dimensional nor absolutely three-dimensional, but something between. Film pictures are at once plane and solid. In Ruttmann's film *Berlin* there is a scene of two subway trains passing each other in opposite directions. The shot is taken looking down from above onto the two trains. Anyone watching this scene realizes, first of all, that one train is coming toward him and the other going away from him (three-dimensional image). He will then also see that one is moving from the lower margin of the screen toward the upper and the other from the upper toward the lower (plane image). This second impression results from the projection of the three-dimensional movement onto the screen surface, which, of course, gives different directions of motion.

The obliteration of the three-dimensional impression has as a second result a stronger accentuation of perspective overlapping. In real life or in a stereoscope, overlapping is accepted as due merely to the accidental arrangement of objects, but very marked cuts result from superimpositions in a plane image. If a man is holding up a newspaper so that one corner comes across his face, this corner seems almost to have been cut out of his face, so sharp are the edges. Moreover, when the three-dimensional impression is lost, other phenomena, known to psychologists as the constancies of size and shape, disappear. Physically, the image thrown onto the retina of the eye by any object in the field of vision diminishes in proportion to the square of the distance. If an object a yard distant is moved away another yard, the area of the image on the retina is diminished to one quarter of that of the first image. Every photographic plate reacts similarly. Hence in a photograph of someone sitting with his feet stretched out far in front of him the subject comes out with enormous feet and much too small a head. Curiously enough, however, we do not in real life get impressions to accord with the images on the retina. If a man is standing three feet away and another equally tall six feet away, the area of the image of the second does not appear to be only a quarter of that of the first. Nor if a man stretches out his hand toward one does it look disproportionately large. One sees the two men as equal in size and the hand as normal. This phenomenon is known as the constancy of size. It is impossible for most people, excepting those accustomed to drawing and painting—that is, artificially trained—to see according to the image on the retina. This fact, incidentally, is one of the reasons the average person has trouble copying things "correctly." Now an essential for the functioning of the constancy of size is a clear three-dimensional impression; it works excellently in a stereoscope with an ordinary photograph, but hardly at all in a film picture. Thus, in a film picture, if one man is twice as far from the camera as another, the one in front looks very considerably the taller and broader.

It is the same with the constancy of shape. The retinal image of a table top is like the photograph of it; the front edge, being nearer to the spectator, appears much wider than the back; the rectangular surface becomes a trapezoid in the image. As far as the average person is concerned, however, this again does not hold good in practice; he *sees* the surface as rectangular and draws it that way too. Thus the perspective changes taking place in any object that extends in depth are not observed but are compensated unconsciously. That is what is meant by the constancy of form. In a film picture it is hardly operative at all—a table top, especially if it is near the camera, looks very wide in front and very narrow at the back.

These phenomena, as a matter of fact, are due not only to the reduction of three-dimensionality but also to the unreality of the film picture altogether—an unreality due just as much to the absence of color, the delimitation of the screen, and so forth. The result of all this is that sizes and shapes do not appear on the screen in their true proportions but distorted in perspective.

LIGHTING AND THE ABSENCE OF COLOR

It is particularly remarkable that the absence of colors, which one would suppose to be a fundamental divergence from nature, should have been noticed so little before the color film called attention to it. The reduction of all colors to black and white, which does not leave even their brightness values untouched (the reds, for instance, may come too dark or too light, depending on the emulsion), very considerably modifies the picture of the actual world. Yet everyone who goes to see a film accepts the screen world as being true to nature. This is due to the phenomenon of "partial illusion." The spectator experiences no shock at finding a world in which the sky is the same color as a human face; he accepts shades of gray as the red, white and blue of the flag; black lips as red; white hair as blond. The leaves on a tree are as dark as a woman's mouth. In other words, not only has a multicolored world been transmuted into a black-and-white world, but in the process all color values have changed their relations to one another; similarities present themselves which do not exist in the natural world; things have the same color which in reality stand either in no direct color connection at all with each other or in quite a different one.

The film picture resembles reality insofar as lighting plays a very important role. Lighting, for instance, helps greatly in making the shape of an object clearly recognizable. (The craters on the surface of the moon are practically invisible at full moon because the sun is perpendicular and no shadows are thrown. The sunlight must come from one side for the outlines of the mountains and the valleys to become visible.) Moreover, the background must be of a brightness value that allows the object to stand out from it sufficiently; it must not be patterned by the light in such a way that it prevents a clear survey of the object by making it appear as though certain portions of the background were part of the object or vice versa.

These rules apply, for example, to the difficult art of photographing works of sculpture. Even when nothing but a "mechanical" reproduction is required, difficulties arise which often puzzle both the sculptor and the photographer. From which side is the statue to be taken? From what distance? Shall it be lighted from the front, from behind, from the right or left side? How these problems are solved determines whether the photograph or film shot turns out anything like the real object or whether it looks like something totally different.

DELIMITATION OF THE IMAGE AND DISTANCE
FROM THE OBJECT

Our visual field is limited. Sight is strongest at the center of the retina, clearness of vision decreases toward the edges, and, finally, there is a definite boundary to the range of vision due to the struc-

ture of the organ. Thus, if the eyes are fixed upon a particular
point, we survey a limited expanse. This fact is, however, of little
practical importance. Most people are quite unconscious of it, for
the reason that our eyes and heads are mobile and we continually
exercise this power, so that the limitation of our range of vision
never obtrudes itself. For this reason, if for no other, it is utterly
false for certain theorists, and some practitioners, of the motion
picture to assert that the circumscribed picture on the screen is an
image of our circumscribed view in real life. That is poor psychology. The limitations of a film picture and the limitations of
sight cannot be compared because in the actual range of human
vision the limitation simply does not exist. The field of vision is in
practice unlimited and infinite. A whole room may be taken as a
continuous field of vision, although our eyes cannot survey this
room from a single position, for while we are looking at anything
our gaze is not fixed but moving. Because our head and eyes move
we visualize the entire room as an unbroken whole.

It is otherwise with the film or photograph. For the purpose of
this argument we are considering a single shot taken with a fixed
camera. We shall discuss traveling and panorama shots later. (Even
these aids in no sense replace the natural range of vision nor are they
intended to do so.) The limitations of the picture are felt immediately. The pictured space is visible to a certain extent, but then
comes the edge which cuts off what lies beyond. It is a mistake to
deplore this restriction as a drawback. I shall show later that on the
contrary it is just such restrictions which give film its right to be
called an art.

This restriction (though also the lack of any sense of the force of
gravity) explains why it is often very difficult to reproduce intel-
ligibly in a photograph the spatial orientation of the scene depicted.
If, for example, the slope of a mountain is photographed from below, or a flight of steps from above, the finished picture surprisingly
will often give no impression of height or depth. To represent an
ascent or descent by purely visual means is difficult unless the level
ground can somehow be shown as a frame of reference. Similarly
there must be standards of comparison to show the size of anything.
To show the height of trees or of a building, for instance, human
figures may be introduced beside them. A man in real life looks all
round him when he is walking; and even supposing he is going up
a mountain path with his eyes fixed on the ground at his feet, he
still has a sense of the general lie of the surrounding country in his
mind. This perception comes to him chiefly because his muscles
and his sense of balance tell him at every instant exactly in what

relation his body stands to the horizontal. Hence he can continually assess correctly the visual impression of the slanting surface. In contrast to such a man is one who is looking at a photograph or screen picture. He must depend upon what his eyes tell him without any assistance from the rest of his body. Moreover, he has only that part of the visual situation which is included within the confines of the picture to help him get his bearings.

The range of the picture is related to the distance of the camera from the object. The smaller the section of real life to be brought into the picture, the nearer the camera must be to the object, and the larger the object in question comes out in the picture—and vice versa. If a whole group of people is to be photographed, the camera must be placed several yards away. If only a single hand is to be shown, the camera must be very close, otherwise other objects besides the hand will appear in the picture. By this means the hand comes out enormously large and extends over the whole screen. Thus the camera, like a man who can move freely, is able to look at an object from close to or from a distance—a self-evident truth that must be mentioned inasmuch as from it is derived an important artistic device. (Variations of range and size can also be obtained by lenses of different focal lengths. The effects are similar but involve no change of the distance from the object and, therefore, no change of perspective.)

How large an object appears on the screen depends partly on the distance at which the camera was placed from it, but partly also on how much the picture is enlarged when the finished film is projected. The degree of enlargement depends on the lens of the projection machine and on the size of the theater. A film may be shown in whatever size is preferred—as small as the pictures in a child's magic lantern or gigantic as in a movie palace. There is, however, an optimum relationship between the size of the picture and its distance from the spectators. In a motion picture theater the spectator sits relatively far away from the screen. Hence the projection must be large. But those watching pictures in a living room are quite close to the screen and therefore the projection may be much smaller. Nevertheless, the range of sizes used in practice is wider than is altogether desirable. In large theaters the projection is larger than in small ones. The spectators in the front rows naturally see a much larger picture than those in the back rows. It is, however, by no means a matter of indifference how large the picture appears to the spectator. The photography is designed for projection of a particular relative size. Thus in a large projection,

or when the spectator is near the picture, movements appear more
rapid than in a small one, since in the former case a larger area has
to be covered than in the latter. A movement which seems hurried
and confused in a large picture may be perfectly right and normal
in a smaller one. The relative size of the projection, moreover,
determines how clearly the details in the picture are visible to the
spectator; and there is obviously a great difference between seeing
a man so clearly that one can count the dots on his tie, and being
able to recognize him only vaguely—more especially since, as has
been pointed out, the size in which the object is to appear is used
by the film director to obtain a definite artistic effect. Thus by the
spectator's sitting too near or too far away a most disagreeable and
obvious misrepresentation of what the artist intended may arise.
Up to the present it is impossible to show a film to a large audience
so that each member of it sees the picture in its right dimensions.
After all, spectators must, as far as possible, be placed one behind
the other, because when the rows of seats extend too far sideways
those sitting at the ends will see the picture distorted—and that is
even worse.

ABSENCE OF THE SPACE-TIME CONTINUUM

In real life every experience or chain of experiences is enacted for
every observer in an uninterrupted spatial and temporal sequence.
I may, for example, see two people talking together in a room. I am
standing fifteen feet away from them. I can alter the distance between us; but this alteration is not made abruptly. I cannot suddenly
be only five feet away; I must move through the intervening space.
I can leave the room; but I cannot suddenly be in the street. In
order to reach the street I must go out of the room, through the
door, down the stairs. And similarly with time. I cannot suddenly
see what these two people will be doing ten minutes later. These
ten minutes must first pass in their entirety. There are no jerks in
time or space in real life. Time and space are continuous.

Not so in film. The period of time that is being photographed
may be interrupted at any point. One scene may be immediately
followed by another that takes place at a totally different time. And
the continuity of space may be broken in the same manner. A
moment ago I may have been standing a hundred yards away from
a house. Suddenly I am close in front of it. I may have been in
Sydney a few moments ago. Immediately afterward I can be in
Boston. I have only to join the two strips together. To be sure, in

practice this freedom is usually restricted in that the subject of the film is an account of some action, and a certain logical unity of time and space must be observed into which the various scenes are fitted. For time especially there are definite rules which must be obeyed.

Within any one film sequence, scenes follow each other in their order of time—unless some digression is introduced as, for example, in recounting earlier adventures, dreams or memories. Within such a flashback, again, time passes naturally, but the action occurs outside the framework of the main story and need not even stand in any precise time relationship ("before" or "after") to it. Within individual scenes the succession of separate events implies a corresponding sequence of time. If, for example, a long shot of a man raising a revolver and firing it is shown, the raising and firing cannot be shown again afterward as a close-up. To do so would be to make a sequence of events that were in fact simultaneous.

That things are happening simultaneously is of course most simply indicated by showing the events in one and the same picture. If I see someone writing at a table in the foreground and someone else in the back playing the piano, the situation is self-explanatory as far as time is concerned. This method is, nevertheless, often avoided for artistic reasons and the situation composed of separate shots.

If two sequences of the action are to be understood as occurring at the same time they may simply be shown one after the other, in which case, however, it must be obvious from the content that simultaneity is intended. The most primitive way of giving this information in a silent film is by printed titles. ("While Elise was hovering between life and death, Edward was boarding the liner at San Francisco.") Or something of this sort: A horse race has been announced to begin at 3:40. The scene is a room full of people who are interested in the race. Someone pulls out a watch and shows the hands pointing to 3:40. Next scene—the racecourse with the horses starting. Events occurring simultaneously may also be shown by cutting up the various scenes and alternating the sections so that the progress of the different events is shown by turns.

Within the individual scenes the time continuum must never be disturbed. Not only must things that occur simultaneously not be shown one after the other, but no time must be omitted. If a man is going from the door to the window, the action must be shown in its entirety; the middle part, for example, must not be suppressed and the spectator left to see the man starting from the door and then with a jerk arriving at the window. This gives the feeling of a violent break in the action, unless something else is inserted so that the intervening time is otherwise occupied. Time may be dropped in the course of a scene only to produce a deliberately comic effect—as, for instance, when Charlie Chaplin enters a pawnbroker's shop and emerges instantly without his overcoat. Since to show complete incidents would frequently be dull and inartistic, because superfluous, the course of the action is sometimes interrupted by parts of scenes taking place simultaneously somewhere else. In this way it can be arranged to show only those moments of each event which are necessary for the action without patching together things that are incoherent in time. Apart from this, each scene in a good film must be so well planned in the scenario that everything necessary, and only what is necessary, takes place within the shortest space of time.

Although the time continuum within any individual scene must remain uninterrupted, the time relationship between scenes that occur at different places is undefined in principle so that it may be impossible to tell whether the second scene takes place before, during, or after the first. This is very clearly shown in many educational films where there is no connection in time but only in subject. As, for example: ". . . not only rabbits but also lions may be tamed." First picture—performing rabbits. Within this scene the continuity of time must be observed. Second picture—lion taming. Here too the continuity of time must not be broken. These two scenes, however, have no sort of time connection. The lion taming may go on before, during or after the performance with the rabbits. In other words, the time connection is of no consequence and therefore does not exist. Similar situations arise occasionally in narrative films.

If sequences are meant to follow each other in time, the content of the film must make this relationship clear, precisely as in the case of simultaneity, because the fact that two sequences follow each other on the screen does not indicate in itself that they should be understood as following each other in time.

Film can take far greater liberties with space and time, however, than the theater can. To be sure, in the theater it is also permissible to have one scene occur at quite a different time and place from the preceding scene. But scenes with a realistic continuity of place and time are very long-drawn-out and allow of no break. Any change is indicated by a definite interruption—the curtain is lowered or the stage darkened. It might, nevertheless, be imagined that an audience would find it disturbing to see so many disconnected events on one and the same stage. That this is not so is due to a very curious fact:

the illusion given by a play (or film) is only partial. Within any particular scene value is laid on naturalism. The characters must talk as people do in real life, a servant like a servant, a duke like a duke. (But even here we have this restriction: the servant and the duke are to talk clearly and sufficiently loudly—that is, really, too clearly and loudly.) An ancient Roman lamp must not be placed to light a modern drawing room nor a telephone by Desdemona's bed. Yet the room has only three walls—the fourth, the one that should intervene between the stage and the audience, is missing. Any audience would laugh if a piece of scenery fell down and revealed the wall of the room to be nothing but painted canvas, or if the crack of a shot were heard some seconds before the revolver was fired. But every audience takes it for granted that on the stage a room has only three walls. This deviation from reality is accepted because the technique of the stage demands it. That is to say, the illusion is only partial.

The stage is, so to speak, in two different but intersecting realms. It reproduces nature, but only a part of nature—separate in time and space from the actual time and space of the "house," where the audience is located. At the same time, the stage is a showcase, an exhibit, the scene of action. Hence it comes into the domain of the fictitious. The component of illusion is relatively strong in theater because an actual space (the stage) and an actual passage of time are given. The component of illusion is very slight when we are looking at a picture—for example, a photograph lying on the table in front of us. The photograph, like the stage, represents a particular place and a particular time (a moment of time), but it does not do this as is done in the theater with the aid of an actual space and an actual passage of time. The surface of the picture *signifies* a pictured space; and that is so much of an abstraction that the picture surface in no way gives us the illusion of actual space.

Film—the animated image—comes midway between the theater and the still picture. It presents space, and it does it not as on the stage with the help of real space, but, as in an ordinary photograph, with a flat surface. In spite of this, the impression of space is for various reasons not so weak as in a still photograph. A certain illusion of depth holds the spectator. Again, in contrast with the photograph, time passes during the showing of a film as it does on the stage. This passage of time can be utilized to portray an actual event but is, nevertheless, not so rigid that it cannot be interrupted by breaks in time without the spectator feeling that these breaks do violence to it. The truth is that the film retains something of the nature of a flat, two-dimensional picture. Pictures may be displayed

for as long or short a time as one pleases, and they can be shown
next to one another even if they depict totally different periods
in time.

Thus film, like the theater, provides a partial illusion. Up to a
certain degree it gives the impression of real life. This component
is all the stronger since in contrast to the theater the film can actually portray real—that is, not simulated—life in real surroundings.
On the other hand, it partakes strongly of the nature of a picture in
a way that the stage never can. By the absence of colors, of three-
dimensional depth, by being sharply limited by the margins on the
screen, and so forth, film is most satisfactorily denuded of its realism. It is always at one and the same time a flat picture post card
and the scene of a living action.

From this arises the artistic justification for what is called montage. It was pointed out above that film, which records real situations on strips of celluloid that may be joined together, has the
power of placing in juxtaposition things that have no connection at
all in real time and space. This power was, however, primarily a
purely mechanical one. One might expect the spectator to be overcome by a physical discomfort akin to seasickness when watching
a film that had been composed of different shots. For example: In
Scene 1 a man is discovered ringing the front doorbell of a house.
Immediately following appears a totally different view—the interior
of the house with a maid coming to answer the door. Thus the
spectator has been jerked violently through the closed door. The
maid opens the door and sees the visitor. Suddenly the viewpoint
changes again and we are looking at the maid through the visitor's
eyes—another breakneck change within the fraction of a second.
Then a woman appears in the background of the foyer and in the
next moment we have bridged the distance separating us from her,
and we are close beside her.

It might be supposed that this lightning juggling with space would
be most unpleasing. Yet everyone who goes to the movies knows
that actually there is no sense of discomfort, but that a scene such
as the one just described can be watched with perfect ease. How
can this be explained? We have been talking as though the sequence
had actually taken place. But it is not real and—which is of the
greatest importance—the spectators have not the (complete) illusion
of its reality. For, as has already been said, the illusion is only partial
and film gives simultaneously the effect of an actual happening and
of a picture.

A result of the "pictureness" of film is, then, that a sequence of
scenes that are diverse in time and space is not felt as arbitrary. One

looks at them as calmly as one would at a collection of picture post cards. Just as it does not disturb us in the least to find different places and different moments in time registered in such pictures, so it does not seem awkward in a film. If at one moment we see a long shot of a woman at the back of a room, and the next we see a close-up of her face, we simply feel that we have "turned over a page" and are looking at a fresh picture. If film photographs gave a very strong spatial impression, montage probably would be impossible. It is the partial unreality of the film picture that makes it possible.

Whereas the theater stage differs from real life only in that the fourth wall is missing, the setting of the action changes, and the people talk in theatrical language, the film deviates much more profoundly. The position of the spectator is continually changing, since we must consider him located at the station point of the camera. A spectator in the theater is always at the same distance from the stage. At the movies the spectator seems to be jumping about from one place to another; he watches from a distance, from close to, from above, through a window, from the right side, from the left; but actually this description, as has been said, is altogether misleading, because it treats the situation as physically real. Instead, pictures taken from the most various angles follow one another, and although the camera position had to be changed continually when they were taken, the spectator is not obliged to duplicate all this commotion.

Many people who are accustomed to clear thinking will feel that this theory of "partial illusion" is vague and equivocal. Is not the very essence of illusion that it should be complete? Is it possible, when one is surrounded by one's own friends and sitting in a chair at home in New York, to imagine oneself in Paris? Can one believe that one is looking at a room when a moment ago a street was there? Yes; one can. According to an outdated psychology that is still deeply rooted in popular thought, an illusion can be strong only if it is complete in every detail. But everyone knows that a clumsy childish scribble of a human face consisting of two dots, a comma, and a dash may be full of expression and depict anger, amusement or fear. The impression is strong, though the representation is anything but complete. The reason it suffices is that in real life we by no means grasp every detail. If we observe the expression on somebody's face, we are far from being able to say whether he had blue eyes or brown, whether he was wearing a hat or not, and so on. That is to say, in real life we are satisfied to take in essentials; they give us all that we need to know. Hence if these essentials are reproduced we are content and obtain a complete impression that is all the more artistic for being so strongly concentrated. Similarly, in film or theater, so long as the essentials of any event are shown, the illusion takes place. So long as the people on the screen behave like human beings and have human experiences, it is not necessary for us to have them before us as substantial living beings nor to see them occupy actual space—they are real enough as they are. Thus we can perceive objects and events as living and at the same time imaginary, as real objects and as simple patterns of light on the projection screen; and it is this fact that makes film art possible.

ABSENCE OF THE NONVISUAL WORLD
OF THE SENSES

Our eyes are not a mechanism functioning independently of the rest of the body. They work in constant co-operation with the other sense organs. Hence surprising phenomena result if the eyes are asked to convey ideas unaided by the other senses. Thus, for example, it is well known that a feeling of giddiness is produced by watching a film that has been taken with the camera traveling very rapidly. This giddiness is caused by the eyes participating in a different world from that indicated by the kinesthetic reactions of the body, which is at rest. The eyes act as if the body as a whole were moving; whereas the other senses, including that of equilibrium, report that it is at rest.

Our sense of equilibrium when we are watching a film is dependent on what the eyes report and does not as in real life receive kinesthetic stimulation. Hence certain parallels which are sometimes drawn between the functioning of the human eye and the camera—for instance, the comparison between the mobility of the eyes and that of the camera—are false. If I turn my eyes or my head, the field of vision is altered. Perhaps a moment ago I was looking at the door; now I am looking at the bookcase; then at the dining-room table, then at the window. This panorama, however, does not pass before my eyes and give the impression that the various objects are moving. Instead I realize that the room is stationary as usual, but that the direction of my gaze is changing, and that that is why I see other parts of the motionless room. This is not the case in film. If the camera was rotated while the picture was being shot, the bookcase, table, window and door will proceed across the screen when the picture is projected; it is they which are moving. For since the camera is not a part of the spectator's body like his head and his eyes, he cannot tell that it has been turned. He can see the objects on the screen being displaced and at first is led to assume that they are in motion. In Jacques Feyder's *Les Nouveaux Messieurs*, for example, there is a scene in which the camera passes rapidly along a long wall covered with posters. The result is that the wall seems to move past the camera. If the scene that has been photographed is very simple to understand, if it is easy to get one's bearings in it, the spectator corrects this impression more or less rapidly. If, for instance, the camera is first directed toward a man's legs and if it then pans slowly up toward his head, the spectator knows very well that the man did not float feet first past a stationary camera. Film directors, however, often turn or shift the camera for taking pictures that are not so easy to grasp, and then a sensation of drifting supervenes which may be unintentional and may easily make the audience feel dizzy. This difference between the movements of the eyes and those of the camera is increased because the film picture has, as was said above, a fixed limit, whereas the field of vision of our eyes is practically unbounded. Fresh objects are continually appearing within the frame of the picture and then disappearing again, but for the eyes there is an unbroken space continuum through which the gaze wanders at will.

Thus there is relativity of movement in film. Since there are no bodily sensations to indicate whether the camera was at rest or in motion, and if in motion at what speed or in what direction, the camera's position is, for want of other evidence, presumed to be fixed. Hence if something moves in the picture this motion is at first seen as a movement of the thing itself and not as the result of a movement of the camera gliding past a stationary object. In the extreme case this leads to the direction of motion being reversed. If, for example, a moving car is filmed from a second one which is overtaking the first, the finished picture will show a car apparently traveling backward. It is, however, possible to make clear which movement is relative and which absolute by the nature and behavior of the objects shown in the picture. If it is obvious from the picture that the camera was standing on a moving car, that is, if parts of this car are seen in the picture, and, contrary to the landscape, they stay in the same place in the picture, the car will be perceived as moving and the surrounding landscape as stationary.

There is also a relativization of spatial co-ordinates—above, below, and so forth. To this are partly due the phenomena we described above in the section on the "Delimitation of the Image." A photograph of a slanting surface may not give an appearance of slope because there is no sensation of gravity to help the spectator realize "up and down." It is impossible to feel whether the camera was standing straight or was placed at an angle. Therefore, as long as there is nothing to indicate the contrary, the projection plane is perceived as vertical. If the camera is held over a bed to show from above the head of a man lying in it, the impression may easily be given that the man is sitting upright and that the pillow is perpendicular. The screen is vertical, although since the camera was turned downward it actually represents a horizontal surface. This effect can be avoided only by showing enough of the surroundings in the picture to give the spectator his bearings.

As regards the other senses: No one who went unprejudiced to watch a silent film missed the noises which would have been heard if the same events had been taking place in real life. No one missed the sound of walking feet, nor the rustling of leaves, nor the ticking of a clock. The lack of such sounds (speech, of course, is also one of them) was hardly ever apparent, although they would have been missed with a desperate shock in real life. People took the silence of the movies for granted because they never quite lost the feeling that what they saw was after all only pictures. This feeling alone, however, would not be sufficient to prevent the lack of sound being felt as an unpleasant violation of the illusion. That this did not happen is again connected with what was explained above: that in order to get a full impression it is not necessary for it to be complete in the naturalistic sense. All kinds of things may be left out which would be present in real life, so long as what is shown contains the essentials. Only after one has known talkies is the lack of sound conspicuous in a silent film. But that proves nothing and is not an argument against the potentialities of silent film, even since the introduction of sound.

It is much the same with the sense of smell. There may be people who if they see a Roman Catholic service on the screen imagine that they can smell incense; but no one will miss the stimulus. Sensations of smell, equilibrium or touch are, of course, never conveyed in a film through direct stimuli, but are suggested indirectly through sight. Thence arises the important rule that it is improper to make films of occurrences whose central features cannot be expressed visually. Of course a revolver shot might occur as the central point of a silent film; a clever director could afford to dispense with the actual noise of the shot. It is enough for the spectator to see the revolver being fired and possibly to see the wounded man fall. In Josef von Sternberg's *The Docks of New York* a shot is very cleverly made visible by the sudden rising of a flock of scared birds.

ARTISTIC USE OF THE DELIMITATION OF THE
PICTURE AND OF THE DISTANCE FROM THE OBJECT[1]

Since our eyes can move freely in every direction, our field of vision is practically unlimited. A film image, on the other hand, is definitely bounded by its margins. Only what appears within these margins is visible, and therefore the film artist is forced—has the opportunity—to make a selection from the infinity of real life. In other words, he can choose his "motif." The delimitation of the image is as much a formative tool as perspective, for it allows of some particular detail being brought out and given special significance; and, conversely, of unimportant things being omitted, surprises being suddenly introduced into the shot, reflections of things that are happening "off" being brought in.

Moreover, a frame is an absolute essential if the decorative qualities of a picture are to be displayed; one can consider the filling of the canvas, the allotment of space, and so forth, only if there are definite limits to act as framework for the pictorial design. The frame of the image consists of two vertical and two horizontal lines. Every vertical and horizontal line occurring in the shot, therefore, will be supported by these axes. Slanting lines appear as slanting because the margins of the picture are straight, that is, vertical and horizontal, for every deviation requires some visible standard of comparison to show from what it deviates.

In a good film image, all lines and other directions stand in well-balanced relation to one another and to the margins. They support one another as parallels or are in contrast; they form a quiet or a restless pattern, a complicated or a simple one; and similarly with the distribution of dark and light masses. If the screen were infinitely large, there could be no question of a good organization of the surface, for, in order to achieve it, there must be a limited space to organize. There is no balance in the infinite, except perhaps in wallpaper designs where there is a serial uniformity, which, of course, is hardly applicable to the film.

The question of the size and proportion of the image is quite topical at present. Abel Gance in his Napoleon film took certain scenes for a triptych screen. At the performance three projectors operated simultaneously, so that a sort of panoramic strip resulted, which could be surveyed at a single glance only from a considerable dis-

[1] This is a section from the second essay in *Film as Art*, entitled "The Making of a Film."

tance. In America, too, various experiments have been made with enlarged screens. Nevertheless, the greater the surface of projection, the more difficult it is to organize the picture meaningfully. The temptation to increase the size of the screen goes with the desire for colored, stereoscopic and sound film. It is the wish of people who do not know that artistic effect is bound up with the limitations of the medium and who want quantity rather than quality. They want to keep on getting nearer to nature and do not realize that they thereby make it increasingly difficult for film to be art.

The experiments with various-sized screens have once again raised the question as to how far the internationally standardized rectangular shape is artistically satisfactory. Statistical inquiries have been made to discover what shapes were preferred by the great masters. The Russian director Eisenstein during his stay in Hollywood gave a lecture advocating the square screen, within which horizontal and vertical rectangles of any proportion could be formed by using different-shaped masks. "Neither the vertical nor the horizontal shape alone is ideal," he said. "How may the vertical and horizontal tendencies of the film image be satisfied simultaneously? The battlefield for such a conflict is easily found—it is the square. The square is the only shape which is capable of producing all possible rectangles, if portions at the sides or top and bottom are masked. It may also be used as a whole, in order to impress upon the spectator the cosmic finality of its squareness—particularly in a dynamic sequence of different dimensions, from a tiny square in the middle up to the all-embracing square that includes the whole screen."

In the beginnings of photography, and thus also of film art, only all-inclusive images were taken—that is, pictures that contained the whole of the event or object to be represented. Close-ups—a pair of hands, or half a face—could have been taken then as now, but they were not. Things that are technically possible are utilized only after the idea has penetrated that by their means useful and valuable results can be achieved, and not merely forbidden or unsound ones. If one wanted to take a shot of a man, his complete figure, or at least the whole upper part of his body, had to be in the picture. The margins of the screen were considered only in a negative sense—they must not cut parts of anything off. Interest was concentrated entirely on what was to be photographed, and not at all on the manner in which this was to be done. That sections and isolated details could be used creatively was a revolution, the same revolution that had to take place for all the other features of the film medium before it could become art. Just as Cecil B. De Mille's customers objected to having pictures in which faces were only partially illuminated, so it seemed absurd intentionally to cut up a natural object by the margins of the picture. Nowadays, after only a few years have passed, it has become fashionable even for quite mediocre directors to let the range finder go wild from time to time.

In the film *The Cameraman*, Buster Keaton is in love with a girl who works at a press photograph agency. The following scene takes place: It is early morning. The office is being opened up, the employees arrive. The reception room with the counter at which customers are received is shown. This is where the girl works. She enters, takes her coat off and settles down. Suddenly the camera is shifted a little, and now a hitherto invisible corner of the waiting room comes into the picture, and there sits Buster Keaton, staring stupidly in front of him. He has been sitting there all night waiting to see the girl. This shows that even a long shot may actually be, in a sense, nothing but a detail shot. "Long shot" is of course a relative and inexact term, which cannot be defined, unless by saying, "A long shot includes the whole of everything that is relevant to the particular total situation." In practice it would be called a long shot if (as in this case) a whole office were shown. But that crucial corner occupied by Buster Keaton does not come into the picture and the whole effect of the shot depends on this. The same event might have been shown in this way: The girl comes up the stairs, opens the door into the office and sees Buster Keaton sitting in the corner. But the whole absurd and extravagant effect arises from the fact that the spectator believes himself to be seeing all there is to see—an ordinary office with ordinary people working in it—and suddenly, as if he had fallen from the skies, the ridiculous, infatuated boy is discovered, as though waiting from time immemorial in the midst of this business-like office, in which nothing out of the ordinary is expected. The psychological shock which is given to the spectator might be described theoretically as follows: A complete whole is shown, and the spectator has been lulled to a false security; suddenly the total structure of this whole is altered by an insignificant twist which seems incongruous with what has gone before. Something of the same effect is achieved when Charlie Chaplin is seen in *Smart People* marvelously turned out in a top hat and tails; but only the upper part of his body is shown, and suddenly it is discovered that he has no trousers on and is standing there in his underpants. Here again the part that is shown (the upper part of the body) suggests a complete picture (smartly dressed man) and the disclosure shows in quite a different light what has already been seen and turns it into a caricature.

Now for an example of an entirely different kind. Sternberg's *The Docks of New York* has a scene in which a suicide jumps off a boat.

Nothing is shown in the shot except the quivering surface of the water in which is seen the reflection of the boat with the woman standing up and then jumping overboard. The woman is shown indirectly by her reflection in the water. The next moment, however, the woman herself is seen falling into the water, at the very spot where her reflection has been. This unexpected sequence of the direct upon the indirect view is most impressive. The effect is achieved by a careful choice of what is to be photographed. The camera is so placed that the most important part of the shot, namely, the boat with the woman on board, does not come in at all—a position which is quite absurd from the standpoint of ordinary representation of an object. The important part of the event, the only reason for which the shot has been taken, only throws its reflection into the picture. But the spectator, who perhaps might have watched a direct shot of the event with merely passing interest, is caught and thrilled by the unusualness of the presentation.

Similar artistic "tricks" are used frequently. They have almost become conventions—such as the shadow of the creeping villain appearing dark against a light wall. Indeed a shadow often acts as the announcer; it appears before the person throwing it comes on the scene, and by this means directs the audience's interest and attention to whatever is approaching.

The true virtue of the delimited image appears from the "close-up." The smaller the detail to be photographed, the larger it comes out in the picture. The close-up not only helps the artist give an enlargement of something which would not be obvious as a mere detail of a long shot—for example, that someone's eyes are filled with tears or that a mouse is sitting in a corner of a room—but it also takes some characteristic feature out of the whole. Very often the film artist will introduce his audience to a new situation by means of some such detail. The pendulum of a clock may be shown, then the whole clock, then the camera travels farther back, and people appear sitting in a room and looking anxiously at the clock. The clock is the vital point of the scene and is therefore shown first. In Pabst's *The Diary of a Lost Girl* the reformatory is introduced in the following manner: The hard, ill-natured face of the teacher with hair strained back from her forehead is shown first; then that she is rhythmically beating a gong; then the camera is moved back, and it is seen that she is standing at the head of a table at which the girls are having dinner and are putting the spoons to their mouths in time to the strokes on the gong. Here again the central point, which is at the same time a detail illustrative of the situation, is picked out so as to direct the spectators' attention along the right lines, and also to provide a certain element of surprise; for a gradual revelation starting from the detail is much more exciting, seizes the spectators' interest much more than if the whole scene were given at once.

A sequence of scenes leading like this from the detail to the total picture can be given in various ways. Either the whole and the detail can be taken separately and joined together in the finished strip, in which case the shots go from one to the next with a jerk; or else the camera is moved backward, the shot being continuously turned, so that what appears on the screen becomes at the same time smaller and more comprehensive—that is, the detail which was at first large becomes gradually small and slips into its place in the whole scene. Or, thirdly, the camera may be left in position, while the operator works with mobile masks, so that at first the greater part of the picture remains dark and some detail of the scene—say a head—is seen in a small (round) setting, as if through a hole in a curtain. Starting from this hole, then, the whole shot "fades in."

There are still other ways of using close-ups, and these are much less easy to fit into any definite scheme. In *The Docks of New York* there is a love scene between a sailor and a prostitute. They are sitting drinking, and there is not much sign of love. Then a close-up is cut in, an uncannily lewd detail: she lustfully strokes his naked arm with indecent tattoo marks all over it, as he ripples the muscles on it for her amusement. The same scene taken as a long shot would not be nearly as effective. Instead of the whole man, only his arm appears, a sturdy, naked, lewdly decorated thing—a clever application of the principle of *pars pro toto:* this woman sees nothing of the man but power, nudity, muscle.

Similar examples can be found in any film: the feet of a man going upstairs, so as to indicate visually the sound of the steps; the legs of a couple of lovers. Feyder's *Les Nouveaux Messieurs* has a scene depicting the ceremonial opening of a number of new buildings in a workmen's colony. The Minister is in a hurry and makes his inspection more and more rapidly, until the whole procession is positively running. Then comes a close-up: a fat man in the procession, no one in particular, mopping his brow. This man has been picked out as the type of all his fellow sufferers. In Pudovkin's *Mother* the scenes taking place in the law courts are ushered in by rapidly successive close-ups of the cold gray ashlars of the building, and in one case a huge shot of the boot of one of the soldiers on guard, a dark uncanny apparition, which is an excellent introduction to the mood of the following scenes. The Russians, indeed, have created an entirely new technique of close-ups.

The possibility of varying the range of the image and the distance from the object thus provides the film artist with the means of splitting up the whole of any scene easily without interfering with reality. Parts may represent the whole, suspense may be created by leaving what is important or remarkable out of the picture. Certain portions may be emphasized so as to induce the spectator to seek symbolic meaning in their appearance. Particular attention may be focused on essential details.

The close-up, however, has one serious drawback. It easily leaves the spectator in the dark as to the surroundings of the object or part of the object. This is especially true in a film where there are too many close-ups, where hardly any long shots are given, as for instance in Dreyer's *The Passion of Joan of Arc*, or in a number of Russian films. The close-up shows a human head, but one cannot tell where the man is to whom the head belongs, whether he is indoors or outdoors, and how he is placed in regard to other people—whether close or distant, turning toward them or away from them, in the same room with them or somewhere else. A superabundance of close-ups very easily leads to the spectators' having a tiresome sense of uncertainty and dislocation. Thus a film artist will generally find himself obliged not to use close-ups alone but only in conjunction with long shots that will give the necessary information as to the situation in general.

On the other hand, however, the film artist has a valuable means of expression, which is denied to the stage, in the power of choosing his distance from his subject. In a theater the spectator always remains at the same distance from the scene of action, and hence events and objects can only be shown within certain limits of size. The subtleties of facial expression, for instance, are lost for the majority of the spectators, who are not seated close to the stage. Indeed, unless gifted with very sharp eyes or by making use of the unsatisfactory, because falsifying, assistance of opera glasses, the audience even in the first balcony will be able to catch only a fraction of what is shown on the stage.

It is, however, not only technical matters of visual acuity that are under discussion. The constant distance of the spectator from the stage makes for an unchangeable evaluation of properties and actions on the stage "according to size," which is most important aesthetically. From a visual standpoint the movements of the actors, their costumes, the sets, are only effective up to a fairly low degree of differentiation. Film can enlarge this range of validity and, which is more important, it can shift it. The spectator may have been looking at a whole room but the next minute the camera can provide quite a different scene on the same spot, in which quite different things form the center of interest, quite different objects come out large and important, and possibly everything that was important in the long shot a moment ago has been omitted. Of a room containing two people only a tiny half-yard-square patch of the table remains and lying on it a flower that had before been unnoticed or, in any case, had taken up only a minute portion of the picture. Toward this flower, now the center of the action, grope the fingers of a hand, equally large, equally important, which was small and inconspicuous and played no part previously.

The sphere of operation of the film compared with that of the theater is thereby enormously enlarged. It must be added that, even if it were technically possible, emphasis upon the nonhuman element in the theater would be hardly appropriate. The theater depends on the spoken word; ordinary dramatic scenes, whose meaning lies in the dialogue, could never combine to give a homogeneous effect with scenes in which inarticulate things like animals or flowers carried on the action simply by their appearance or by movements accompanied or unaccompanied by sounds. Anything of this kind is only very exceptionally possible on the stage; and even in the kind of sound film that is based essentially on dialogue the introduction of such scenes at important points would produce a disturbing and incoherent effect.

Perhaps the point has never been made explicitly—and it seems significant that it occurs to very few theatergoers—how unnatural, how stylized, all stage art is because the actors never stop talking. Every action is overlaid and clothed with words. Even in the first outline, every scene is so planned that the plot shall be unfolded by unceasing conversation. Indeed every preponderance of mere action over the spoken word is regarded as a defect. The spoken word, the most important distinguishing trait of the drama, has developed into a medium of radical purity during the evolution of the art through thousands of years. That this method of presenting an event is not a matter of course will be clearly realized only after seeing from a good silent film how the action proceeds quite easily without any use of words at all.

Film can make inanimate objects attract attention to themselves. Let us suppose again that in a particular scene on the stage a flower is lying on a table. This flower could never, except with the help of the actors, attract the attention of the audience. The stage director or the playwright cannot rely on the possibility that the audience might in the course of the play notice the insignificant detail, because the audience's attention must always be directed to the precise point of the action.

The film artist has the best possible control of his audience's attention, for by placing the camera just where he wishes he brings onto the screen whatever is of greatest importance at the time and is able to give proper significance to objects without there being any need for the flower to call out, "Now look at me." The interest of the spectator is necessarily directed to it because at the time he is shown nothing else. Similarly other small events—a fly crawling, or the smoke of a cigarette—which would not be nearly emphatic enough on the stage to draw attention to themselves are given the requisite stress.

In a film, these little events, these roles played by accessories, are exactly of the same type as the "macroscopic" ones, those represented by the human actors. And hence arises a most satisfactory homogeneity.

The possibility of rapidly changing the distance from the object leads naturally to a relativization of the standards of size. Insofar as the spectator cannot use his past experience to judge what he sees—insofar as he does not know, for instance, that a fly is objectively small and a mountain large—he has nothing to go on in judging the objective size of what is shown. He has no means of knowing how far the camera stood from the object. A newsreel of an architectural exhibition showed several shots of houses that had been erected on the grounds, and, immediately afterward, shots of a little plaster model of the city of Rome. To the spectator both sets of buildings appeared of equal size, although in one they were of ordinary height and taken at the necessary distance and in the other the models were only a few inches high and photographed close to. Experience was here of no use to the spectator in judging the relative sizes.

This relativization results, on the one hand, in the possibility of making things of quite different sizes appear the same size, and thus of being brought into connection one with another. In a film on German university life the rounded belly of a corps student, who is snoring on a sofa, dissolves into a landscape shot—a similarly formed, gently rounded hill near Heidelberg. These two things which actually are of totally different sizes are simply and easily made to coalesce by the stomach's being photographed from close to and the hill from far away; and thereby the opportunity is given of making an amusing comparison between them.

On the other hand, particular effects may be induced by the spectators' being deceived as to the real size of what is shown. A critic once referred to a scene in the film version of Ibsen's *A Doll's House* as a standard example of the idiom of film art. A room is shown, and suddenly a huge hand is put into it, and thereby it is made clear that the room is actually quite small and only part of a doll's house. At first glance the room is assumed to be of normal size, for in the picture itself there is nothing to indicate that anything exceptional—a toy—

is involved. The sudden change brought about by perfectly natural means—the normal-sized human hand—brings home the symbolism of the happening to the spectator in the best way. What is only a conceptual identification of the human house and the toy house actually takes place here. Thus once again a "drawback" in film—the impossibility of giving any absolute standard of size—is turned to advantage and used for artistic effect.

THE COMPLETE FILM

The technical development of the motion picture will soon carry the mechanical imitation of nature to an extreme. The addition of sound was the first obvious step in this direction. The introduction of sound film must be considered as the imposition of a technical novelty that did not lie on the path the best film artists were pursuing. They were engaged in working out an explicit and pure style of silent film, using its restrictions to transform the peep show into an art. The introduction of sound film smashed many of the forms that the film artists were using in favor of the inartistic demand for the greatest possible "naturalness" (in the most superficial sense of the word). By sheer good luck, sound film is not only destructive but also offers artistic potentialities of its own. Owing to this accident alone the majority of art lovers still do not realize the pitfalls in the road pursued by the movie producers. They do not see that the film is on its way to the victory of wax museum ideals over creative art.

The development of the silent film was arrested possibly forever when it had hardly begun to produce good results; but it has left us with a few splendidly mature films. In the future, no doubt, "progress" will be faster. We shall have color films and stereoscopic films, and the artistic potentialities of the sound film will be crushed at an even earlier stage of their development.

What will the color film have to offer when it reaches technical perfection? We know what we shall lose artistically by abandoning the black-and-white film. Will color ever allow us to achieve a similar compositional precision, a similar independence of "reality"?

The masterpieces of painting prove that color provides wider possibilities than black-and-white and at the same time permits of a very exact and genuine style. But can painting and color photography be compared? Whereas the painter has a perfectly free hand with color and form in presenting nature, photography is obliged to record mechanically the light values of physical reality. In achromatic pho-

tography the reduction of everything to the gray scale resulted in an
art medium that was sufficiently independent and divergent from
nature. There is not much likelihood of any such transposition of reality into a qualitatively different range of colors in color film. To be
sure, one can eliminate individual colors—one may, for example, cut
out all blues, or, vice versa, one may cut out everything except the
blues. Probably it is possible also to change one or more color tones
qualitatively—for example, give all reds a cast of orange or make all
the yellows greenish—or let colors change places with one another—
turn all blues to red and all reds to blue—but all this would be, so to
speak, only transposition of reality, mechanical shifts, whose useful-
ness as a formative medium may be doubted. Hence there remains
only the possibility of controlling the color by clever choice of what
is to be photographed. All kinds of fine procedures are conceivable,
especially in the montage of colored pictures, but it must not be overlooked that in this way the subjective formative virtues of the camera,
which are so distinctive a characteristic of film, will be more and more
restricted, and the artistic part of the work will be more and more
focused upon what is set up and enacted *before* the camera. The
camera is thereby increasingly relegated to the position of a mere
mechanical recording machine.

Above all, it is hardly realistic to speculate on the artistic possibilities of the color film without keeping in mind that at the same time
we are likely to be presented with the three-dimensional film and the
wide screen. Efforts in these directions are in progress. The illusion
of reality will thereby have been increased to such a degree that the
spectator will not be able to appreciate certain artistic color effects
even if they should be feasible technically. It is quite conceivable that
by a careful choice and arrangement of objects it might be possible
to use the color on the projection surface artistically and harmoni-
ously. But if the film image becomes stereoscopic there is no longer
a plane surface within the confines of the screen, and therefore there
can be no composition of that surface; what remains will be effects
that are also possible on the stage. The increased size of the screen will
render any two-dimensional or three-dimensional composition less
compelling; and formative devices such as montage and changing camera angles will become unusable if the illusion of reality is so enormously strengthened. Obviously, montage will seem an intolerable
accumulation of heterogeneous settings if the illusion of reality is very
strong. Obviously also a change in the position of the camera will
now be felt as an actual displacement within the space of the picture.
The camera will have to become an immobile recording machine,

every cut in the film strip will be mutilation. Scenes will have to be taken in their entire length and with a stationary camera, and they will have to be shown as they are. The artistic potentialities of this form of film will be exactly those of the stage. Film will no longer be able in any sense to be considered as a separate art. It will be thrown back to before its first beginnings—for it was with a fixed camera and an uncut strip that film started. The only difference will be that instead of having all before it film will have nothing to look forward to.

This curious development signifies to some extent the climax of that striving after likeness to nature which has hitherto permeated the whole history of the visual arts. Among the strivings that make human beings create faithful images is the primitive desire to get material objects into one's power by creating them afresh. Imitation also permits people to cope with significant experiences; it provides release and makes for a kind of reciprocity between the self and the world. At the same time a reproduction that is true to nature provides the thrill that by the hand of man an image has been created which is astoundingly like some natural object. Nevertheless, various counter-tendencies—some of them purely perceptual—have prevented mechanically faithful imitation from being achieved hundreds of years ago. Apart from rare exceptions, only our modern age has succeeded in approaching this dangerous goal. In practice, there has always been the artistic urge not simply to copy but to originate, to interpret, to mold. We may, however, say that aesthetic theory has rarely sanctioned such activities. Even for artists like Leonardo da Vinci the demand for being as true to nature as possible was a matter of course when he talked theory, and Plato's attack on artists, in which he charged them with achieving nothing but reproductions of physical objects, is far from the general attitude.

To this very day some artists cherish this doctrine, and the general public does so to an even greater extent. In painting and sculpture it is only in recent decades that works have been appearing which show that their creators have broken with this principle intellectually and not merely practically. If a man considers that the artist should imitate nature, he may possibly paint like Van Gogh, but certainly not like Paul Klee. We know that the very powerful and widespread rejection of modern art is almost entirely supported by the argument that it is not true to nature. The development of film shows clearly how all-powerful this ideal still is.

Photography and its offspring, film, are art media so near to nature that the general public looks upon them as superior to such old-fashioned and imperfect imitative techniques as drawing and painting.

Since on economic grounds film is much more dependent on the general public than any other form of art, the "artistic" preferences of the public sweep everything before them. Some work of good quality can be smuggled in but it does not compensate for the more fundamental defeats of film art. The complete film is the fulfillment of the age-old striving for the complete illusion. The attempt to make the two-dimensional picture as nearly as possible like its solid model succeeds; original and copy become practically indistinguishable. Thereby all formative potentialities which were based on the differences between model and copy are eliminated and only what is inherent in the original in the way of significant form remains to art.

H. Baer in a remarkable little essay in the *Kunstblatt* has pointed out that color film represents the accomplishment of tendencies which have long been present in graphic art.

Graphic art [he says]—of which photography is one branch—has always striven after color. The oldest woodcuts, the blockbooks, were finished off by being handpainted. Later, a second, colored, plate was added to the black-and-white—as in Dürer's portrait of "Ulrich Varnbühler." A magnificent picture of a knight in armor in black, silver and gold exists by Burgmair. In the eighteenth century multicolored etchings were produced. In the nineteenth the lithographs of Daumier and Gavarni are colored in mass production. . . . Color invaded the graphic arts as an increased attraction for the eye. Uncivilized man is not as a rule satisfied with black-and-white. Children, peasants and primitive peoples demand the highest degree of bright coloring. It is the primitives of the great cities who congregate before the film screen. Therefore film calls in the aid of bright colors. It is a fresh stimulus.

In itself, the perfection of the "complete" film need not be a catastrophe—if silent film, sound film, and colored sound film were allowed to exist alongside it. There is no objection to the "complete" film as an alternative to the stage—it might help to take into remote places fine performances of good works, as also of operas, musical comedies, ballets, the dance. Moreover, by its very existence it would probably have an excellent influence on the other—the real—film forms, by forcing them to advance along their own lines. Silent film, for example, would no longer provide dialogue in its titles, because then the absence of the spoken word would be felt as artificial and disturbing. In sound film, too, any vague intermediate form between it and the stage would be avoided. Just as the stage will feel itself obliged by the very existence of film to emphasize its own characteristic—the predominance of dramatic speech—so the "complete" film could relegate the true film forms to their own sphere.

The fact is, however, that whereas aesthetically these categories of film could and should exist along with mechanically complete reproduction, they are inferior to it in the capacity to imitate nature. Therefore the "complete" film is certain to be considered an advance upon the preceding film forms and will supplant them all.

The

Cinematographic

Principle

and the

Ideogram

The following essay is from Film
Form (*Harcourt, Brace, New
York, 1949. Edited and translated
from the Russian by Jay Leyda*),
*one of the classic texts in film
literature. Although marred by
Eisenstein's inability to avoid politics and propaganda, this book, like
all of Eisenstein's writings, approaches the film with a dynamism
seldom found elsewhere. The concept of montage did not originate
with Eisenstein, but he theorized
and wrote about it extensively.*

by Sergei Eisenstein

IT IS A WEIRD and wonderful feat to have written a pamphlet on
something that in reality does not exist. There is, for example, no
such thing as a cinema without cinematography. And yet the author of the pamphlet preceding this essay* has contrived to write
a book about the *cinema* of a country that has no *cinematography*.
About the cinema of a country that has, in its culture, an infinite
number of cinematographic traits, strewn everywhere with the sole
exception of—its cinema.

This essay is on the cinematographic traits of Japanese culture

* Eisenstein's essay was originally published as an "afterword" to N. Kauf-
man's pamphlet, *Japanese Cinema* (Moscow, 1929).

that lie outside the Japanese cinema, and is itself as apart from the preceding pamphlet as these traits are apart from the Japanese cinema.

Cinema is so many corporations, such and such turnovers of capital, so and so many stars, such and such dramas.

Cinematography is, first and foremost, montage.

The Japanese cinema is excellently equipped with corporations, actors and stories. But the Japanese cinema is completely unaware of montage. Nevertheless the principle of montage can be identified as the basic element of Japanese representational culture.

Writing—for their writing is primarily representational.

The hieroglyph.

The naturalistic image of an object, as portrayed by the skillful Chinese hand of Ts'ang Chieh 2,650 years before our era, becomes slightly formalized and, with its 539 fellows, forms the first "contingent" of hieroglyphs. Scratched out with a stylus on a slip of bamboo, the portrait of an object maintained a resemblance to its original in every respect.

But then, by the end of the third century, the brush is invented. In the first century after, the "joyous event" (A.D.)—paper. And, lastly, in the year 220—India ink.

A complete upheaval. A revolution in draftsmanship. And, after having undergone in the course of history no fewer than fourteen different styles of handwriting, the hieroglyph crystallized in its present form. The means of production (brush and India ink) determined the form.

The fourteen reforms had their way. As a result:

In the fierily cavorting hieroglyph *ma* (a horse) it is already impossible to recognize the features of the dear little horse sagging pathetically in its hindquarters, in the writing style of Ts'ang Chieh, so well known from ancient Chinese bronzes.

But let it rest in the Lord, this dear little horse, together with the other 607 remaining *hsiang cheng* symbols—the earliest extant category of hieroglyphs.

The real interest begins with the second category of hieroglyphs —the *huei-i*, i.e., "copulative."

The point is that the copulation (perhaps we had better say the combination) of two hieroglyphs of the simplest series is to be regarded not as their sum, but as their product, i.e., as a value of another dimension, another degree; each, separately, corresponds to an *object*, to a fact, but their combination corresponds to a *concept*. From separate hieroglyphs has been fused—the ideogram. By the combination of two "depictables" is achieved the representation of something that is graphically undepictable.

For example, the picture for water and the picture of an eye signifies "to weep"; the picture of an ear near the drawing of a door "to listen";
a dog + a mouth = "to bark";
a mouth + a child = "to scream";
a mouth + a bird = "to sing";
a knife + a heart = "sorrow," and so on.[1]
But this is—montage!

Yes. It is exactly what we do in the cinema, combining shots that are *depictive*, single in meaning, neutral in content, into *intellectual* contexts and series.

This is a means and method inevitable in any cinematographic exposition. And, in a condensed and purified form, the starting point for the "intellectual cinema."

For a cinema seeking a maximum laconism for the visual representation of abstract concepts.

And we hail the method of the long-lamented Ts'ang Chieh as a first step along these paths.

We have mentioned laconism. Laconism furnishes us a transition to another point. Japan possesses the most laconic form of poetry: the *haikai* (appearing at the beginning of the thirteenth century and known today as "haiku" or "hokku") and the even earlier *tanka* (mythologically assumed to have been created along with heaven and earth).

Both are little more than hieroglyphs transposed into phrases. So

[1] Jean Pierre Abel Rémusat, *Recherches sur l'Origine et la Formation de l'Écriture Chinoise*. Paris.

much so that half their quality is appraised by their calligraphy. The method of their resolution is completely analogous to the structure of the ideogram.

As the ideogram provides a means for the laconic imprinting of an abstract concept, the same method, when transposed into literary exposition, gives rise to an identical laconism of pointed imagery.

Applied to the collision of an austere combination of symbols this method results in a dry definition of abstract concepts. The same method, expanded into the luxury of a group of already formed verbal combinations, swells into a splendor of *imagist* effect.

The concept is a bare formula; its adornment (an expansion by additional material) transforms the formula into an image—a finished form.

Exactly, though in reverse, as a primitive thought process, imagist thinking, displaced to a definite degree, becomes transformed to conceptual thinking.

But let us turn to examples.

The *haiku* is a concentrated impressionist sketch:

> A lonely crow
> On leafless bough,
> One autumn eve.
>
> BASHŌ

> What a resplendent moon!
> It casts the shadow of pine boughs
> Upon the mats.
>
> KIKAKU

> An evening breeze blows.
> The water ripples
> Against the blue heron's legs.
>
> BUSON

> It is early dawn.
> The castle is surrounded
> By the cries of wild ducks.
>
> KYOROKU[2]

The earlier *tanka* is slightly longer (by two lines):

> O mountain pheasant
> long are the feathers trail'st thou
> on the wooded hillside—

[2] Quoted in *Haiku Poems, Ancient and Modern*, translated and annotated by Miyamori Asatarō. Maruzen Company, Tokyo, 1940.

as long the nights seem to me
on lonely couch sleep seeking.

HITOMARO[?][3]

From our point of view, these are montage phrases. Short lists. The simple combination of two or three details of a material kind yields a perfectly finished representation of another kind—psychological.

And if the finely ground edges of the intellectual defined concepts formed by the combined ideograms are blurred in these poems, yet, in *emotional quality*, the concepts have blossomed forth immeasurably. We should observe that the emotion is directed toward the reader, for, as Yone Noguchi has said, "it is the readers who make the *haiku's* imperfection a perfection of art."[4]

It is uncertain in Japanese writing whether its predominating aspect is as a system of characters (denotative), or as an independent creation of graphics (depictive). In any case, born of the dual mating of the depictive by method, and the denotative by purpose, the ideogram continued both these lines (not consecutive historically but consecutive in principle in the minds of those developing the method).

Not only did the denotative line continue into literature, in the *tanka,* as we have shown, but exactly the same method (in its depictive aspect) operates also in the most perfect examples of Japanese pictorial art.

Sharaku—creator of the finest prints of the eighteenth century, and especially of an immortal gallery of actors' portraits. The Japanese Daumier. Despite this, almost unknown to us. The characteristic traits of his work have been analyzed only in our century. One of these critics, Julius Kurth, in discussing the question of the influence on Sharaku of sculpture, draws a parallel between his woodcut portrait of the actor Nakayama Tomisaburō and an antique mask of the semireligious Nō theater, the mask of a Rozo.

The faces of both the print and the mask wear an *identical expression. . . .* Features and masses are similarly arranged although the mask represents an old priest and the print a young woman. This relationship is striking, yet these two works are otherwise totally dissimilar; this in itself is a demonstration of Sharaku's originality. While the carved mask was constructed according to fairly accurate anatomical proportions, the proportions of the portrait

[3] Translation by Frederick Victor Dickins, in *Primitive and Mediaeval Japanese Texts.* Clarendon Press, Oxford, 1906.
[4] Yone Noguchi, *The Spirit of Japanese Poetry.* John Murray, London, 1914, p. 53.

print are simply impossible. The space between the eyes comprises a width that makes mock of all good sense. The nose is almost twice as long in relation to the eyes as any normal nose would dare to be, and the chin stands in no sort of relation to the mouth; the brows, the mouth, and every feature are hopelessly misrelated. *This observation may be made in all the large heads by Sharaku.* That the artist was unaware that all these proportions are false is, of course, out of the question. It was with a full awareness that he repudiated normalcy, and, while the drawing of the separate features depends on severely concentrated naturalism, their proportions have been subordinated to purely intellectual considerations. *He set up the essence of the psychic expression as the norm for the proportions of the single features.*[5]

Is not this process that of the ideogram, combining the independent "mouth" and the dissociated symbol of "child" to form the significance of "scream"?

Is this not exactly what we of the cinema do temporally, just as Sharaku did in simultaneity, when we cause a monstrous disproportion of the parts of a normally flowing event and suddenly dismember the event into "close-up of clutching hands," "medium shots of the struggle," and "extreme close-up of bulging eyes," in making a montage disintegration of the event in various planes? In making an eye twice as large as a man's full figure? By combining these monstrous incongruities we newly collect the disintegrated event into one whole, but in *our* aspect. According to the treatment of our relation to the event.

The disproportionate depiction of an event is organically natural to us from the beginning. Professor Luriya, of the Psychological

[5] Julius Kurth, *Sharaku*, 2nd edition, pp. 78–79. R. Piper, Munich, 1922. The Sharaku print referred to is that numbered 24 in the catalogue by Harold G. Henderson and Louis V. Ledoux, *The Surviving Works of Sharaki*. Published by E. Weyhe, in behalf of the Society for Japanese Studies, 1939.

Institute in Moscow, has shown me a drawing by a child of "lighting a stove." Everything is represented in passably accurate relationship and with great care. Firewood. Stove. Chimney. But what are those zigzags in that huge central rectangle? They turn out to be—matches. Taking into account the crucial importance of these matches for the depicted process, the child provides a proper scale for them.[6]

The representation of objects in the actual (absolute) proportions proper to them is, of course, merely a tribute to orthodox formal logic. A subordination to an inviolable order of things.

Both in painting and in sculpture there is a periodic and invariable return to periods of the establishment of absolutism. Displacing the expressiveness of archaic disproportion for regulated "stone tables" of officially decreed harmony.

Absolute realism is by no means the correct form of perception. It is simply the function of a certain form of social structure. Following a state monarchy, a state uniformity of thought is implanted. Ideological uniformity of a sort that can be developed pictorially in the ranks of colors and designs of the Guards regiments . . .

Thus we have seen how the principle of the hieroglyph—"denotation by depiction"—split in two: along the line of its purpose (the principle of "denotation"), into the principles of creating literary imagery; along the line of its method of realizing this purpose (the principle of "depiction"), into the striking methods of expressiveness used by Sharaku.[7]

And, just as the two outspreading wings of a hyperbola meet, as we say, at infinity (though no one has visited so distant a region!), so the principle of hieroglyphics, infinitely splitting into two parts

[6] It is possible to trace this particular tendency from its ancient, almost prehistorical source (". . . in all ideational art, objects are given size according to their importance, the king being twice as large as his subjects, or a tree half the size of a man when it merely informs us that the scene is out of doors. Something of this principle of size according to significance persisted in the Chinese tradition. The favorite disciple of Confucius looked like a little boy beside him and the most important figure in any group was usually the largest." —George Rowley, *Principles of Chinese Painting*. Princeton University Press, 1947, p. 56) through the highest development of Chinese art, parent of Japanese graphic arts: ". . . natural scale always had to bow to pictorial scale . . . size according to distance never followed the laws of geometric perspective but the needs of the design. Foreground features might be diminished to avoid obstruction and overemphasis, and far distant objects, which were too minute to count pictorially, might be enlarged to act as a counterpoint to the middle distance or foreground." (*Ibid.*, p. 66.)

[7] It has been left to James Joyce to develop in *literature* the depictive line of the Japanese hieroglyph. Every word of Kurth's analysis of Sharaku may be applied, neatly and easily, to Joyce.

(in accordance with the function of symbols), unexpectedly unites again from this dual estrangement, in yet a fourth sphere—in the theater.

Estranged for so long, they are once again—in the cradle period of the drama—present in a *parallel* form, in a curious dualism.

The *significance* (denotation) of the action is effected by the reciting of the *Jōruri* by a voice behind the stage—the *representation* (depiction) of the action is effected by silent marionettes on the stage. Along with a specific manner of movement this archaism migrated into the early Kabuki theater as well. To this day it is preserved, as a partial method, in the classical repertory (where certain parts of the action are narrated from behind the stage while the actor mimes).

But this is not the point. The most important fact is that into the technique of acting itself the ideographic (montage) method has been wedged in the most interesting ways.

However, before discussing this, let us be allowed the luxury of a digression—on the matter of the shot, to settle the debated question of its nature, once and for all.

A shot. A single piece of celluloid. A tiny rectangular frame in which there is, organized in some way, a piece of an event.

"Cemented together, these shots form montage. When this is done in an appropriate rhythm, *of course!*"

This, roughly, is what is taught by the old, old school of film making, that sang:

> "Screw by screw,
> Brick by brick . . ."

Kuleshov, for example, even writes with a brick:

If you have an idea-phrase, a particle of the story, a link in the whole dramatic chain, then that idea is to be expressed and accumulated from shot ciphers, just like bricks.[8]

"The shot is an element of montage. Montage is an assembly of these elements." This is a most pernicious makeshift analysis.

Here the understanding of the process as a whole (connection, shot montage) derives only from the external indications of its flow (a piece cemented to another piece). Thus it would be possible, for instance, to arrive at the well-known conclusion that streetcars exist in order to be laid across streets. An entirely logical deduction, if

[8] Lev Kuleshov, *Iskusstvo Kino*. Leningrad, 1929.

one limits oneself to the external indications of the functions they performed during the street fighting of February, 1917, here in Russia. But the materialist conception of history interprets it otherwise.

The worst of it is that an approach of this kind does actually lie, like an insurmountable streetcar, across the potentialities of formal development. Such an approach overrules dialectical development and dooms one to mere evolutionary "perfecting," insofar as it gives no bite into the dialectical substance of events.

In the long run, such evolutionizing leads either through refinement to decadence or, on the other hand, to a simple withering away due to stagnation of the blood.

Strange as it may seem, a melodious witness to both these distressing eventualities, simultaneously, is Kuleshov's latest film, *The Gay Canary* [1929].

The shot is by no means an *element* of montage.

The shot is a montage *cell.*

Just as cells in their division form a phenomenon of another order, the organism or embryo, so, on the other side of the dialectical leap from the shot, there is montage.

By what, then, is montage characterized and, consequently, its cell—the shot?

By collision. By the conflict of two pieces in opposition to each other. By conflict. By collision.

In front of me lies a crumpled yellowed sheet of paper. On it is a mysterious note:

"Linkage—P" and "Collision—E."

This is a substantial trace of a heated bout on the subject of montage between P (Pudovkin) and E (myself).

This has become a habit. At regular intervals he visits me late at night and behind closed doors we wrangle over matters of principle. A graduate of the Kuleshov school, he loudly defends an understanding of montage as a *linkage* of pieces. Into a chain. Again, "bricks." Bricks, arranged in series to *expound* an idea.

I confronted him with my viewpoint on montage as a *collision.* A view that from the collision of two given factors *arises* a concept.

From my point of view, linkage is merely a possible *special* case.

Recall what an infinite number of combinations is known in physics to be capable of arising from the impact (collision) of spheres. Depending on whether the spheres be resilient, nonresilient, or mingled. Among all these combinations there is one in which the impact is so weak that the collision is degraded to an even movement of both in the same direction.

This is the one combination which would correspond with Pud-ovkin's view.

Not long ago we had another talk. Today he agrees with my point of view. True, during the interval he took the opportunity to acquaint himself with the series of lectures I gave during that pe-riod at the State Cinema Institute. . . .

So, montage is conflict.

As the basis of every art is conflict (an "imagist" transformation of the dialectical principle). The shot appears as the *cell* of mon-tage. Therefore it also must be considered from the viewpoint of *conflict*.

Conflict within the shot is potential montage, in the development of its intensity shattering the quadrilateral cage of the shot and ex-ploding its conflict into montage impulses *between* the montage pieces. As, in a zigzag of mimicry, the *mise-en-scène* splashes out into a spatial zigzag with the *same* shattering. As the slogan, "All obstacles are vain before Russians," bursts out in the multitude of incident of *War and Peace*.

If montage is to be compared with something, then a phalanx of montage pieces, of shots, should be compared to the series of explo-sions of an internal-combustion engine, driving forward its automo-bile or tractor; for, similarly, the dynamics of montage serve as im-pulses driving forward the total film.

Conflict within the frame. This can be very varied in character; it even can be a conflict in—the story. As in that "prehistoric" period in films (although there are plenty of instances in the present as well), when entire scenes would be photographed in a single, un-cut shot. This, however, is outside the strict jurisdiction of the film form.

These are the "cinematographic" conflicts within the frame:
Conflict of graphic directions.

(*Lines—either static or dynamic*)

Conflict of scales.
Conflict of volumes.
Conflict of masses.

(*Volumes filled with various intensities of light*)

Conflict of depths.

And the following conflicts, requiring only one further impulse of intensification before flying into antagonistic pairs of pieces:
Close shots and long shots.

Pieces of graphically varied directions. Pieces resolved in volume, with pieces resolved in area.

Pieces of darkness and pieces of lightness.

And, lastly, there are such unexpected conflicts as:

Conflicts between an object and its dimension—and conflicts between an event and its duration.

These may sound strange, but both are familiar to us. The first is accomplished by an optically distorted lens, and the second by stop motion or slow motion.

The compression of all cinematographic factors and properties within a single dialectical formula of conflict is no empty rhetorical diversion.

We are now seeking a unified system for methods of cinematographic expressiveness that shall hold good for all its elements. The assembly of these into series of common indications will solve the task as a whole.

Experience in the separate elements of the cinema cannot be absolutely measured.

Whereas we know a good deal about montage, in the theory of the shot we are still floundering about amidst the most academic attitudes, some vague tentatives, and the sort of harsh radicalism that sets one's teeth on edge.

To regard the frame as a particular, as it were, molecular case of montage makes possible the direct application of montage practice to the theory of the shot.

And similarly with the theory of lighting. To sense this as a collision between a stream of light and an obstacle, like the impact of a stream from a fire hose striking a concrete object, or of the wind buffeting a human figure, must result in a usage of light entirely different in comprehension from that employed in playing with various combinations of "gauzes" and "spots."

Thus far we have one such significant principle of conflict: *the principle of optical counterpoint.*

And let us not now forget that soon we shall face another and less simple problem in counterpoint: *the conflict in the sound film of acoustics and optics.*

Let us return to one of the most fascinating of optical conflicts: the conflict between the frame of the shot and the object!

The camera position, as a materialization of the conflict between the organizing logic of the director and the inert logic of the object, in collision, reflects the dialectic of the camera angle.

In this matter we are still impressionistic and lacking in principle to a sickening degree. Nevertheless, a sharpness of principle can be had in the technique of this, too. The dry quadrilateral, plunging into the hazards of nature's diffuseness . . .

And once again we are in Japan! For the cinematographic method is used in teaching drawing in Japanese schools.

What is our method of teaching drawing? Take any piece of white paper with four corners to it. Then cram onto it, usually even without using the edges (mostly greasy from the long drudgery!), some bored caryatid, some conceited Corinthian capital, or a plaster Dante (not the magician performing at the Moscow Hermitage, but the other one—Alighieri, the comedy writer).

The Japanese approach this from a quite different direction: Here's the branch of cherry tree.[9] And the pupil cuts out from this whole, with a square, and a circle, and a rectangle—compositional units:

He frames a shot!

These two ways of teaching drawing can characterize the two basic tendencies struggling within the cinema of today. One—the expiring method of artificial spatial organization of an event in front of the lens. From the "direction" of a sequence, to the erection of a Tower of Babel in front of the lens. The other—a "picking out" by the camera: organization by means of the camera. Hewing out a piece of actuality with the ax of the lens.

[9] Illustration No. 12, "How to choose composition," in *Jinjo Shogaki Shintei Gaten Dai Roku Gaku Nen Dan Sei Yo* (Elementary Grade Drawing Manual for Sixth Grade Boys). Tokyo, Board of Education, 1910.

However, at the present moment, when the center of attention is finally beginning, in the intellectual cinema, to be transferred from the materials of cinema, as such, to "deductions and conclusions," to "slogans" based on the material, both schools of thought are losing distinction in their differences and can quietly blend into a synthesis.

Several pages back we lost, like an overshoe in a streetcar, the question of the theater. Let us turn back to the question of methods of montage in the Japanese theater, particularly in acting.

The first and most striking example, of course, is the purely cinematographic method of "acting without transitions." Along with mimic transitions carried to a limit of refinement, the Japanese actor uses an exactly contrary method as well. At a certain moment of his performance he halts; the black-shrouded *kurogo* obligingly conceals him from the spectators. And lo!—he is resurrected in a new make-up. And in a new wig. Now characterizing another stage (degree) of his emotional state.

Thus, for example, in the Kabuki play *Narukami*, the actor Sadanji must change from drunkenness to madness. This transition is solved by a mechanical cut. And a change in the arsenal of grease-paint colors on his face, emphasizing those streaks whose duty it is to fulfill the expression of a higher intensity than those used in his previous make-up.

This method is organic to the film. The forced introduction into the film, by European acting traditions, of pieces of "emotional transitions" is yet another influence forcing the cinema to mark time. Whereas the method of "cut" acting makes possible the construction of entirely new methods. Replacing one changing face with a whole scale of facial types of varying moods affords a far more acutely expressive result than does the changing surface, too receptive and devoid of organic resistance, of any single professional actor's face.

In our new film [*Old and New*] I have eliminated the intervals between the sharply contrasting polar stages of a face's expression. Thus is achieved a greater sharpness in the "play of doubts" around the new cream separator. Will the milk thicken or no? Trickery? Wealth? Here the psychological process of mingled faith and doubt is broken up into its two extreme states of joy (confidence) and gloom (disillusionment). Furthermore, this is sharply emphasized by light—illumination in no wise conforming to actual light conditions. This brings a distinct strengthening of the tension.

Another remarkable characteristic of the Kabuki theater is the principle of "disintegrated" acting. Shocho, who played the leading female roles in the Kabuki theater that visited Moscow, in depicting the dying daughter in *Yashaō* (*The Mask Maker*), performed his role in pieces of acting completely detached from each other: Acting with only the right arm. Acting with one leg. Acting with the neck and head only. (The whole process of the death agony was disintegrated into solo performances of each member playing its own role: the role of the leg, the role of the arms, the role of the head.) A breaking up into shots. With a gradual shortening of these separate, successive pieces of acting as the tragic end approached.

Freed from the yoke of primitive naturalism, the actor is enabled by this method to fully grip the spectator by "rhythms," making not only acceptable, but definitely attractive, a stage built on the most consecutive and detailed flesh and blood of naturalism.

Since we no longer distinguish in principle between questions of shot content and montage, we may here cite a third example:

The Japanese theater makes use of a slow tempo to a degree unknown to our stage. The famous scene of hara-kiri in *Chushingura* is based on an unprecedented slowing down of all movement—beyond any point we have ever seen. Whereas, in the previous example, we observed a disintegration of the transitions between movements, here we see disintegration of the process of movement, viz., slow motion. I have heard of only one example of a thorough application of this method, using the technical possibility of the film with a compositionally reasoned plan. It is usually employed with some purely pictorial aim, such as the "submarine kingdom" in *The Thief of Bagdad*, or to represent a dream, as in *Zvenigora*. Or, more often, it is used simply for formalist jackstraws and unmotivated camera mischief, as in Vertov's *Man with the Movie Camera*. The more commendable example appears to be in Jean Epstein's *La Chute de la Maison Usher*—at least according to the press reports. In this film, normally acted emotions filmed with a speeded-up camera are said to give unusual emotional pressure by their unrealistic slowness on the screen. If it be borne in mind that the effect of an actor's performance on the audience is based on its identification by each spectator, it will be easy to relate both examples (the Kabuki play and the Epstein film) to an identical causal explanation. The intensity of perception increases as the didactic process of identification proceeds more easily along a disintegrated action.

Even instruction in handling a rifle can be hammered into the tightest motor mentality among a group of raw recruits if the instructor uses a "breakdown" method.

The most interesting link of the Japanese theater is, of course, its link with the sound film, which can and must learn its fundamentals from the Japanese—the reduction of visual and aural sensations to a common physiological denominator.

So, it has been possible to establish (cursorily) the permeation of the most varied branches of Japanese culture by a pure cinematographic element—its basic nerve, montage.

And it is only the Japanese cinema that falls into the same error as the "leftward drifting" Kabuki. Instead of learning how to extract the principles and technique of their remarkable acting from the traditional feudal forms of their materials, the most progressive leaders of the Japanese theater throw their energies into an adaption of the spongy shapelessness of our own "inner" naturalism. The results are tearful and saddening. In its cinema Japan similarly pursues imitations of the most revolting examples of American and European entries in the international commercial film race.

To understand and apply her cultural peculiarities to the cinema, this is the task of Japan! Colleagues of Japan, are you really going to leave this for us to do?

[1929]

How

Films

Are Made

by René Clair

In a letter to the film critic of The New Statesman (*May 24, 1958*) *regarding the film* Touch of Evil, *Orson Welles made the following comment:* "*A typewriter needs only paper; a camera uses film, requires subsidiary equipment by the truckload and several hundreds of technicians. That is always the central fact about the film maker as opposed to any other artist: he can never afford to own his own tools. The minimum kit is incredibly expensive; and one's opportunities to work with it are rather less numerous than might be supposed. In my case I've been given the use of my tools exactly eight times in twenty years. . . .*" *René Clair's sobering exposition below* (*published by William Kimber, Ltd., London, 1953. Translated from the French by Vera Traill*), *taken from his book* Reflections on the Cinema, *spells out these difficulties. In no other art do the technicalities and complexities of production play such a crucial role. This is hardly news but it is a fact that altogether too many people are inclined to overlook.*

HOW A FILM IS CONCEIVED

To GIVE you some idea of the conditions in which a cinematographic work is conceived and executed, it can broadly speaking be compared to the building of a house. It very seldom happens that an architect builds a house or anything else for the sole satisfaction of his creative urge. Like a film maker, an architect must take his customers' tastes into account; he does not work alone, but with numerous collaborators, whose help is indispensable to him; and he is limited by the material means at his disposal. All this makes it impossible for an

339

architect, as it does for a film maker, to elude the rules of a profession which is related both to art and to industry; each side of this dual nature has its own characteristics, which cannot be reduced to a common denominator.

The choice of a subject. It would be difficult to say of each house in a given town why it was built in that particular manner and given that particular shape. It would be just as difficult to state the reason why a particular subject is chosen for film. The elaboration of a film should not be compared to that of a stage play. The idea for a film is sometimes born in an author's mind, but more often a film company has the intention of making a film and is thus moved to search among existing ideas for the one that suits it best. It is extremely seldom that a film craftsman, be he writer, director or producer, can follow the path of individual artistic creation open to a painter or a novelist.

Filmed theater. The advent of talking films has singularly complicated the choice of subjects. What a large part of the public, in the provinces especially, most enjoys seeing on the screen is a theater play which has previously gained a success on the stage of some big town. In this case, the cinema plays the same part as a publishing house which provides the means for disseminating a text which in manuscript form would be too rare and too costly to meet public demand. This formula naturally enjoys the support of most dramatists. Whatever we may think about the future of this kind of spectacle, it is clear that films can be divided into two main categories: those justly called "filmed theater," for which the cinema is solely a means of dissemination; and films endeavoring to utilize the particular resources of the screen, for which the cinema is a means of expression.

Adaptation of literary and dramatic works. The second category can be further subdivided into films whose themes were specially conceived for cinematic rendering, and films based on scenarios adapted from literary or dramatic works. Present-day cinema is addicted, either through taste or through habit, to such adaptations. And yet it has been proved by numerous examples that the best novels and the best plays seldom make the best films; and we do not have to possess any particular knowledge of the laws of the screen to realize that before the camera such subjects as *Andromaque* or *La Chartreuse de Parme* will lose their unique quality. Furthermore, the majority of works that made film history happen to have been based on stories whose titles had never been seen in print, be it on a theater program or on a book cover. However, observations like these make little impression on the rulers of the cinema, most of whom are businessmen. When choosing a story for a film, the businessman will naturally plump for the comedy or novel which has already known some success on the stage or in the bookshops, rather than take an original thing which provides no guarantee that it will be enjoyed by the public.

It does not follow, of course, that a novel or play cannot give birth to a genuine cinematic work. But in such a case the original story must be reshaped, either by the author himself, by specialized script-writers or else by the future director of the film. Whoever does it, this work of adaptation is subject to the same rule as literary translations from foreign languages: a faithful translation is often a betrayal of the original.

One knows that many famous plays and novels have proved a disappointment when adapted to the screen. Perhaps in principle any subject of a novel can be used as a film subject; but the style of a work of art cannot easily be transplanted. This difficulty is not peculiar to film making, but it is also to be met with in the theater. A play adapted from *Liaisons Dangereuses*, for instance, would very likely disappoint the readers of Laclos's novel.

Original scripts. Not all film subjects are taken from novels or plays. Some films are based on scenarios specially written for the cinema, although this does not mean that they necessarily possess cinematic qualities.

With very few exceptions, the best original scenarios have been written either by writers who knew the cinema particularly well, or by professional film workers. Although it may seem at first sight that anybody should be able to write a film scenario, experience shows that good scenarios are very rare. The manuscripts that pour in daily by the dozen to big film companies as well as those sent in to organized competitions have seldom been found satisfactory. These facts, observable in both Europe and America, indicate that a certain amount of knowledge of film technique is indispensable for the author of a film scenario.

THE SHOOTING SCRIPT

Whether it be an original script or an adaptation of a well-known literary subject, the scenario must be prepared for its cinematic realization. It is evolved in detail, scene by scene, with complete dialogue and acting directions. This final version of the scenario is known as the shooting script. This last can be more or less comprehensive, according to the director's methods, but very often it includes purely technical instructions on lighting, camera angles, interaction of visuals and sounds, etc. This elaboration of the shooting script, when done with care, constitutes the most important stage in the creation of a film. It corresponds to the work which Racine had done when, according to legend, he pronounced, "My tragedy is finished. All that is left for me to do is write it." At that stage, indeed, all that remained for the great tragedian to do was to compose the verses of a tragedy the plan of which was evolved. Similarly, when the shooting script has been completed, all that is left for the director to do is to realize in actual visuals and sounds what has already been written down; in other words, to bring the film to life and give it its style.

TECHNICAL PREPARATION

In its final form, the shooting script is subdivided by "numbers." These "numbers" correspond to every scene, or, to speak the language of the studios, to every shot which is to be made. The scenes are numbered not in the order in which they will appear to the public, but in which the sets in which they take place are to be erected and pulled down. Consequently, the first stage of the technical preparation consists in working out an exact timetable. This is done jointly by the producer, the director and the art director, who endeavor to foresee the work to be done on each successive day of shooting. When this timetable has been elaborated and the order of shooting has been finally fixed, the time has come to pass on to administrative aspects, that is to say, to fixing the period of employment of actors and technicians, ordering sets and costumes, drawing up the list of properties and establishing the final costing, which is not always an easy task.

It has frankly to be admitted that that preparatory work is not always carried out as carefully as it should be, either in France or in America, although it is commonly held that the film industry in Hollywood is better organized than anywhere else. The cinema is a new profession and film making is a gamble. This youthful, gambling spirit does not favor the observation of hard and fast rules, and hence film making cannot be classed as an industry in the most serious sense. If motorcar output, for instance, were not more strictly organized than film production, quite a number of cars would never start.

EQUIPMENT AND TECHNICIANS

The sets. The shooting of a film takes place either in a studio or "on location," or else in exterior sets.

The studio is a vast building (some studios measure over four hundred feet in length and two hundred feet in width) containing the electrical equipment for furnishing the necessary light and that for sound recording. Here the sets against which the action of a film is to take place are built.

The scenes shot "on location" are those that require a background which would be too difficult or too costly to reproduce within the studio (sea, countryside, typical aspects of a town, and the like). For all the ingenuity of studio electricians, some scenes shot "on location" undeniably benefit from lighting which it would have been very hard to reproduce artificially.

The technicians. The main artisans in the making of a film are the director, the art director, the cameraman and the sound engineer. Alongside these key men we must place the producer, whose exact role is hard to define; in many cases he is a mere administrator who supervises the execution of the work and keeps check of the expenses; but in exceptional instances he assumes, in addition, the main artistic responsibility and can be regarded as the real maker of the film.

The person known in English as the "director" (commonly called in French *metteur en scène,* a term less indicative of his real function than "director" or the German *regisseur*) in principle directs the realization of the film as a whole. But the director's task varies according to his personality, according to the film, and according to the methods employed. Some directors are genuine creators who impress the stamp of their personality onto the whole making of the film, from the shooting script to the final editing. Others are mere executives who receive from the producer a complete shooting script which they put into execution just as an architect might direct the construction of a building on the basis of somebody else's blueprint.

The "art director" (again improperly called in France *décorateur,* and more adequately in German *architect*) after reading the scenario prepares the models of the sets; then, after a discussion with the director, he supervises their building. He has a variety of skilled men under him: mechanics, carpenters, painters, upholsterers, locksmiths and the like. The producer is expected to supply him with the furniture and properties he may require, which are brought to him by "prop men." He keeps in touch with the chief cameraman, to ensure that the shape and color of his constructions suit the lighting to be provided.

The public is inclined to think of the "chief cameraman" as a kind of photographer who after focusing his lens begins to turn a handle round and round, with the gesture that symbolizes the cinema in the

public mind. This picture, however, dates back to the cinema's ancient history. In our time the chief cameraman is occupied almost
exclusively with camera angles, which he establishes in conformity
with the director's instructions, and with the regulation of the
lighting, which is attended to under his orders by the electricians.
Some chief cameramen never touch the camera, the latter being
handled by their assistants. But neither do these turn the legendary
handle, for this has long been replaced by silent motors.

The "sound engineer," who is responsible for the sound part of the
film, sits in a little room where all the sounds captured by his machines reach him through earphones. In the intervals between takes,
he comes to discuss with the director and the chief cameraman the
positioning of the microphone, which is not so simple an operation
as may seem at first sight. Indeed, the conditions of visual recording
and those of sound recording have not a single point in common, and
one of the director's tasks is reconciling the conflicting views of the
two technicians, each of whom insists on the rights of his respective
camera or microphone.

In addition to these principal collaborators whose professional
competence, talents and mutual understanding determine the technical success of a film, there are various other specialists attached to
the unit, such as the wardrobe staff, the studio manager, the still photographers, the make-up man, the continuity girl and others. All
these people, ranging from director to continuity girl, make up the
"technical" unit, as opposed to the "artistic" unit consisting of the
actors.

THE ACTORS

Most film-goers have but a very vague idea about the way a film
is made and know nothing about the director and the technicians who
made it. They are interested only in the actors. This interest, which
often takes a passionate and exaggerated form, manifests a tendency
too profoundly human to be resisted with any hope of success.

The American system of making films for the stars has found its
disciples in most film-producing countries. Spending considerable
sums of money on launching a new star can often be a good investment; a celebrated name can ensure even a mediocre film's takings.
But though this exploitation of star names may be commercially
profitable, it has its drawbacks where the spirit of the cinema and its
progress (largely dependent on unacknowledged work by directors
and technicians) are concerned.

It is only fair to point out that not all actors' reputations are usurped. There are great actors who fully deserve the success they enjoy. They are often the most modest, and the least attached to a glory whose vanity their knowledge of the realities of their profession helps them to perceive. But of most actors one can say that their value in a film corresponds precisely to that of their director. Mediocre actors have been known to give excellent performances under intelligent direction; it is much rarer to find an actor who remains at his best under a mediocre director.

The work of a film actor is entirely different from that of a stage actor. In the theater, the actor first rehearses his part for many days ahead and then sustains his character for several successive hours before the public. The film actor, however, is expected after a few minutes' rehearsal to give expression, in the silence of the studio, to an emotion which will there and then receive its final and probably irremediable form. In consequence of this, the film actor has to rely mainly on the director to estimate the quality of his acting.

THE TIME NEEDED TO MAKE A FILM

The shooting of every fragment of a scene is usually done in the following manner: The actor receives a few brief instructions from the director and goes through the movements he is asked to perform. During that time the chief cameraman has the camera placed in such a way as to follow the actor in his movements. While the lights are being regulated, the actor rehearses his movements and lines. When the director is satisfied with his performance and the sound engineer has succeeded in having at least one rehearsal made in complete silence, when the chief cameraman has finally regulated the last spotlight, then all is ready for the shooting. "Action!" Shooting begins. Usually the same fragment of a scene is recorded several times in succession, and it can happen that a fragment which took a whole day's work to shoot will occupy the screen for a few seconds. If the shooting of film lasts thirty days, and the projection an hour and a half, each day devoted to the shooting produces on the average three minutes of "useful" film.

The time it takes to make a film varies. In the case of first-feature films (that is, films shown in the second part of the cinema program) executed with some care, the average is about fifty working days, that is to say eight to nine weeks. With cheaper, mass-produced films, much less time is needed: twenty, fifteen or even ten days. Some films, notably a few of the silent period, have literally broken records of slowness; six months, and even a whole year, or two years have been spent on some of these costly productions, which often turned out to be "big" in no other than the budgetary sense.

EDITING

We have seen that in the shooting script each shot—that is, each fragment of a scene—bears a number, which serves as a kind of identity slip. This numbering must be made with scrupulous care. Indeed, if in a script containing five hundred numbers each of the five hundred shots is recorded three or four times, by the time the shooting is over fifteen hundred to two thousand little film strips, from which a selection will have to be made, will have reached the editing room.

The editing, done by one or several editors under the director's supervision, is a succession of operations during which the shots, recorded in their arbitrary order of shooting, will be assembled according to the script—that is, in the order in which the film will be shown to the public.

It is during this editing process that a film begins to take shape. Every fragment, or shot, will be gradually reduced (by cutting the actual strips) to the length that seems appropriate. Some shots will be considerably shortened or even cut out altogether, if the effect which the director aimed at has not been achieved, or if they seem to hold back the general tempo of the film. During the execution of this work, some visuals will be touched up in the laboratory (trick effects, such as "fades," "dissolves," "superimpositions," "wipes," etc., being introduced by means of a special machine) and some sounds will be added, or else combined with those already existing on the sound track ("dubbing" and "mixing").

When all these various jobs have been completed, the "rough cut"—that is, the first positive film—is ready. It consists of two separate strips, one of which carries the picture and the other the sound. These two strips are then projected simultaneously by a special apparatus, thus enabling one to judge the film as a whole, as it will appear before the public. This is rather like reading the proofs before the book is finally passed for printing.

After that the precious fragments of the negative films (visuals and sound) are taken from the vaults where they have been kept, and cut to the length of the corresponding fragments of the positive film which constitutes the "rough cut." This operation is called "editing the negative film." When it is done, the two negative films are sent to the printing laboratory, which will produce the final copies—that is, the positive copies on which the picture and the sound are merged on one film.

FILMS GROW OLD AND DIE

The number of positive copies varies according to the country and to the success of the film. In France we seldom make more than a hundred copies of the same negative. In America the figures are much higher. In theory, an almost unlimited number of copies can be printed from one negative, but in practice the negative, worn by handling and by its passage through the printing machines, soon loses its freshness.

At the present stage of film technique, it would be foolish to suppose that films can be preserved forever. A film grows old and dies. But even if it could remain physically intact, it would still lose its life in the spectators' eyes. Whoever has attended the performance of a film twenty or thirty years old will have been amazed by what he saw. People's appearance, in respect not only of their clothes but of their gestures and intonations, seems to change far more rapidly than we imagined before films first allowed us to observe. And the cinema itself, which pins down the fleeting aspect of people and things, in the end falls a victim to the time it challenged. The cinema remains, and will no doubt remain for a long time, a medium of expression of immense but ephemeral power, an art dedicated solely to the present.

Cocteau

on the Film

A Conversation

between

Jean Cocteau

and André Fraigneau

In the spring 1958 issue of Sight and Sound, *Alexandre Astruc, the young French film maker, was quoted—the lines are from his article* Le Camera-Stylo—*as follows: "The cinema . . . becomes bit by bit a language. By a language I mean the form in which and through which an artist can express his thoughts, however abstract they may be, or translate his obsessions, just as in an essay or a novel. That is why I call this new age of cinema that of the* Camera-Stylo." *When one considers that Jean Cocteau has been making films in this manner for some thirty years, it is strange to come upon this in 1958. In the following piece, which consists of excerpted fragments from* Cocteau on the Film, *Cocteau presents his conception of the film as a personal language. This book is a conversation with (and recorded by) André Fraigneau, published by Roy Publishers, New York, 1954. Translated from the French by Vera Traill.*

A.F.: I'd like this dialogue of ours to bear exclusively upon your activity in films, my dear Jean Cocteau. Would you be willing to approach our conversation from that angle?

J.C.: I can't do that, because for me the cinematograph is only one medium of expression among others. Speaking about it will inevitably lead me into other paths. I use the word *cinematograph* deliberately, in order to avoid any confusion between the medium it expresses and that which is commonly called the *cinema*, a somewhat dubious muse in that it is incapable of waiting, whilst all the other muses wait, and should be painted and sculpted in waiting poses.

Whenever people see a film for the first time, they complain

348

about some passages being too long or too slow. But quite apart from the fact that this is often due to the weakness of their own perception and to their missing the deep underlying design of the work, they forget that the classics, too, are full of passages that are long-winded and slow, but are accepted because they are classics. The classics must have faced the same reproaches in their lifetime. The tragedy of the cinematograph lies in its having to be successful immediately. It takes such a vast sum of money to make a film that it is necessary to get that money back as soon as possible by massive takings. That is a terrible, almost insurmountable handicap. I have just said that muses should be represented in attitudes of waiting. All arts can and must wait. They often have to wait for the death of their makers before they are able to live. Can, then, the cinematograph rank as a muse? Besides, muses are poor. Their money is invested. But the cinema muse is too rich, too easy to ruin at one go.

To this we must add that, for the public, films are just a pastime, a form of entertainment which they have been accustomed, alas, to view out of the corners of their eyes. Whereas for me the image-making machine has been a means of saying certain things in visual terms instead of saying them with ink on paper.

A.F.: Can you give me a more explicit definition of the *cinema* as a form of mass entertainment, and also tell me what you understand, in contrast, by the *cinematograph* as a medium of self-expression? I think that this would help readers to grasp the distinction you so persistently draw between the two terms.

J.C.: What is commonly called "cinema" has not been, up till now, a pretext for thought. People walk in, look (a little), listen (a little), walk out, and forget. Whereas the cinematograph, as I understand it, is a powerful weapon for the projection of thought, even into a crowd unwilling to accept it. *Orphée*, for instance, irritates, intrigues and shocks, but forces people to discussions with others and with their own selves. A book has to be read and reread before it comes to occupy its rightful place. And cinema managers have noticed that some spectators of *Orphée* returned to see it several times and brought other spectators with them. Besides, however inert and hostile an audience may be, it enables a few attentive individuals to see the film. Without such audiences, my message couldn't have reached the few unknown spectators for whom it was destined. You might say that if a film falls flat the message dies. Of course. And with *Orphée* I took enormous risks. But I was convinced that in the case of an unusual and difficult film, the curiosity that brings people to see it is stronger than the laziness that keeps them away. Every day I receive letters which show that I was right.

Their authors usually complain about the audience with which they
found themselves locked in for the duration of the performance.
But they forget that it's that very audience that enabled them to
see the film at all.

A.F.: I was struck by an expression you used earlier on: "the image-making machine." Do you mean that you use cinematic images
just as a writer uses literary images?

J.C.: No. The cinematograph requires a syntax. This syntax is obtained through the connection and the clash between images. No
wonder that the peculiarity of such a syntax (our style) expressed
in visual terms seems disconcerting to spectators accustomed to slap-
dash translations and to the articles in their morning paper. If the
wonderful language of Montaigne were transposed into images, it
would be as difficult for such spectators to watch as it is difficult for
them to read his writings.

My primary concern in a film is to prevent the images from flowing, to oppose them to each other, to anchor them and join them
without destroying their relief. But it is precisely that deplorable flow
that is called "cinema" by the critics, who mistake it for style. It is
commonly said that such and such a film is perhaps good, but that
it is "not cinema," or that a film lacks beauty but is "cinema," and so
on. This is forcing the cinematograph to be mere entertainment instead of a vehicle for thought. And this is what leads our judges to
condemn in two hours and fifty lines a film epitomizing twenty years
of work and experience.

A.F.: Now I understand how much it meant for you, at a given moment in your career, to discover the cinematograph as a vehicle for
thought—thought which you had previously expressed in so many
different ways. But did you find a greater freedom in that new
medium?

J.C.: No. Even if one is free to do as one pleases, there are, alas, too
many heavy burdens (capital, censorship, responsibility toward the
actors who agree to being paid later) to be what I would call completely free.

I am not thinking of actual concessions, but of a sense of responsibility which directs and restricts us without our even being fully
aware of it. I've been completely free only with *Le Sang d'un Poète*
because it was privately commissioned (by the Vicomte de
Noailles, just as Bunuel's *L'Age d'Or*), and because I didn't know
anything about film art. I invented it for myself as I went along, and
used it like a draughtsman dipping his finger for the first time in India ink and smudging a sheet of paper with it. Originally Charles
de Noailles commissioned me to make an animated cartoon, but I

soon realized that a cartoon would require a technique and a team nonexistent at that time in France. Therefore I suggested making a film as free as a cartoon, by choosing faces and locations that would correspond to the freedom of a designer who invents his own works. Moreover, I've often been helped by chance (or at least by what is commonly called chance but never is for one who lets himself be hypnotized by a task), including even the petty vexations of the studio, where everybody thought I was mad. Once, for example, as I was nearly at the end of *Le Sang d'un Poète*, the sweepers were told to clear up the studio just as we had started on our last shots. But as I was about to protest, my cameraman (Périnal) asked me to do nothing of the kind: he had just realized what beautiful images he would be able to take through the dust raised by the sweepers in the light of the arc lamps.

Another example: as I didn't know any film technicians, I sent out postcards to all the cameramen in Paris, giving them an appointment for the next morning. I decided to take the one who would come first. It happened to be Périnal, thanks to whom many images of *Le Sang d'un Poète* can vie with the loveliest shots of our time. Unfortunately, in those days a silver salt was used in film printing, which was done at a pace impossible today. This is why cinematic art is so fragile. A very old copy of *Le Sang d'un Poète* is as bright and shows as much contrast as any modern American film, whereas more recent copies look like old copies and weaken the whole effect of the film.

Although this too is arguable. To quote an instance: a friend of mine, whose intelligence I respect, detested *La Belle et la Bête*. One day I met him at the corner of the Champs Elysées and Rue la Boétie. He asked me where I was going and whether he could come with me. I said, "I'm going to work on the subtitling of *La Belle et la Bête*, and I'd hate to subject you to such an ordeal." He came along nevertheless, and I forgot him in a corner of the little cinema. I was working with my chief editor on a very old strip, almost unpresentable, gray and black and covered with stains and scratches. At the end of the projection I went back to my friend, and he announced that he found the film admirable. I concluded that he had seen it in a new perspective, rather as we do in film societies when we are shown old films in a disastrous condition.

A.F.: It seems to me that such strokes of chance, and all the miseries and splendors of film making, coupled with the difficulty of understanding a film, that is, to see and hear it with sufficient attention in the course of one fleeting projection, make it difficult, if not altogether impossible, for a message expressed in a film to have any *lasting* existence.

J.C.: Yes, indeed. The inevitable *invisibility* of any work of art which doesn't conform to public habits which make things visible— I mean, an invisibility arising from habits which were themselves acquired through contact with things that were not visible originally, but which have become visible through habit—this invisibility is an almost insuperable problem for those who treat the cinematograph as an art, as a vehicle of thought. It is almost impossible to solve it without resorting to some subterfuge which would make that thought visible in the immediate present, but would condemn it for the future. There is no future for such a film. Or, at best (provided the American laws become more sensible and one ceases destroying a story told in one manner for the sake of being able to retell it in another) the film will have a future of a sort with film clubs and a handful of amateurs. A film thus takes a reverse course compared to that followed by other works of art, which start on a small scale and reach a big one later, when they have proved their worth. The industrial machine forces films to begin on a large scale; after which they may live to reach a small one, if they survive the thousand perils threatening the existence of a negative: human carelessness, fire, and all the changes that technique is bound to bring into film production.

A film worthy of the name encounters the same obstacles as does a canvas by Vermeer, Van Gogh or Cézanne. But whilst these paintings land in the public museum only after a long time, a film must begin in it. Then it ascends a slope, gets classed, and from then on can only count on being seen by a few individuals, similar to the few who saw the paintings when they first appeared, before the eye and mind had grown accustomed to them. In short, a painting that isn't worth a penny to begin with will be worth millions later on. Whereas a film that was worth millions at the start will survive, if at all, in dire poverty.

A.F.: After these generalities on cinematography, will you allow me to ask you a more personal question? And will you promise to give me an exhaustive answer? Can you tell me the deep motives that brought you, first among the poets, to an art which most writers despise—even though we observe that they despise it less and less as time goes on?

J.C.: Before I reply to the main part of your question, I will say that these writers have a good excuse. Film making is a manual art, a craftsman's job. A work written by one man and then transposed onto the screen by another is no more than a translation, and can, indeed, be of very little interest for a genuine writer (or be of interest only to his pocket). Before film art can be worthy of a writer, the writer must become worthy of film art. I mean, he should not be content with leaving some left-handed work of his to be interpreted by other people, but should seize hold of it with both his hands and work hard at building an object in a style equivalent to his written style. A desk-and-pen man is naturally quite uninterested in films, and doesn't even value them as a means of propagating his ideas. And now let us go back to the personal problems you raised.

1. I am a draughtsman. It is quite natural for me to see and hear what I write, to endow it with a plastic form. When I am shooting a film, every scene I direct is for me a moving drawing, a painter's grouping of material. In Venice, you cannot look at a canvas by Tiepolo or Tintoretto without being struck by its "stage-setting" and by the deliberate singularity of planes, which goes so far as to allow a leg to protrude beyond the frame, in the bottom left-hand corner. (I'm not quite sure if it is in Tintoretto's Christ asleep in the boat, in the storm, but I think it is.) This method forces me to work in France where we still have disorder and even anarchy, to some extent. The severity of trade-union regulation in Hollywood and London makes it impossible to work without the intermediary of an army of specialists. But in France, film-making is a family affair, and no one rebels if his prerogatives are encroached upon—lighting, sets, costumes, make-up, music and so forth. All this rests in my hands, and I work in close collaboration with my assistants. Consequently, as my unit itself admits, the film becomes a thing of my very own to which they have contributed by their advice and skill.

2. Film-making isn't my profession. Nothing compels me to direct film after film, to chase after actors for a particular story or vice versa. That would have been a serious handicap. It is much easier to make a film from time to time, when you are seized by the imperative urge to make one, than to be ceaselessly driven to hunt for books and plays, and while you shoot one film to rack your brains over the problems of the next.

3. I sometimes wonder whether my perpetual malaise is not due to my incredible indifference toward the things of this world; whether my work is not a struggle to seize for myself the things that occupy other people; whether my kindness is not a ceaseless effort to overcome my lack of contact with my fellow-men. Unless I happen to become the vehicle of an unknown force, which I then clumsily help to take shape, I cannot read, or write, or even think. This vacuum is terrifying. I fill it up as best I can, as one sings in the dark. Besides, my mediumlike stupidity affects an

air of intelligence which makes my blunders pass for subtle cunning, and my sleepwalker's stumbling for the agility of an acrobat.

It isn't likely that this secret will ever come to light, and I shall probably continue to suffer after my death from a misunderstanding similar to that which makes my life so difficult.

When I have manual work to do, I like to think that I take part in earthly things, and I put all my strength into it like a drowning man clinging to a wreck. This is why I took up film-making, where every minute is occupied by work which shields me from the void where I get lost.

When I say I don't have ideas, I mean that I have embryos of ideas of which I'm not the master; and that I can start on a task only if instead of having an idea, an idea has me, and haunts, disturbs, torments me so unbearably that I am forced to get it out, to rid myself of it at any cost. Thus, work for me is a kind of torture. When this is finished, idleness becomes another kind of torture. And in the vacuum that comes back I feel that I shall never work again. . . .

A.F.: Now we come to *Orphée*, an extremely important film which winds up all your searchings, and sums up twenty years of your work in a medium which, because it is immediate, is dangerous. A film in which more forcibly than ever you have opposed poetry to the "poetic," and in which those of us who knew *Le Sang d'un Poète* have felt at home. Will you tell me in detail how you made that film? And whether the position you had gained through your other films (a position the continuity of which you have just proved to me) has made it easier for you to carry out a project that would have been beyond the reach of a newcomer?

J.C.: A book never ensures the success of another book. And a film, unless it is the copy of a previous one, encounters the same difficulties as those that hamper a newcomer. My first interview with the high-ranking officials of the Crédit National gave me good proof of that. As they began quibbling over my script, I cut them short and suggested that they might trust me, seeing that I had been very prompt in refunding all the credits they had granted me in the past. "But how can you say we don't trust you?" these gentlemen said. "Why, if an unknown young man submitted such a script to us we'd throw him out."

This terrible sentence seems to sum up the sole advantage of having a reputation such as mine. For the rest, I had to proceed exactly as though I were a newcomer: I founded a small company, scrounged around for every penny, and cut down on the costing; and in the end I managed to scrape through only thanks to my cast, who generously agreed to share the risks and wait for payment out of my problematic takings. There can be no doubt that if I had accepted the innumerable and absurd offers I had from various companies, I'd now be a rich man—rich "under the counter." But my conception of the cinematograph *versus* cinema condemns me to an unceasing struggle. On only one occasion, in my desire to cover the expenses in excess of costing which I had undertaken to pay off out of my own pocket, did I agree to cook up a story for some Mexican producers—with the result that they went off and shot quite another story (keeping my name on the credit titles), without Madame Maria Félix, who was playing a part in the film, or any other members of the unit knowing anything about it. This is an example of the kind of trap a film-maker constantly finds gaping at his feet. And this is why I refuse to call myself a film-maker; and also why the money-grubbers were flabbergasted by the success of *Orphée*.

A.F.: Why, after all your explorations in various directions, did you come back to the Orpheus myth, which had already inspired a play where you expressed yourself with complete freedom? Why did you deem it necessary to treat the same subject cinematically? And being one of those who saw *Orphée* in the Pitoeff production, I'd also like to know the reasons that determined the differences and the similarities between your play and the film.

J.C.: My mental work is that of a lame man, with one foot in life and the other in death. Therefore I am quite naturally drawn to a myth in which life and death meet face to face. Moreover . . . I realized that a film would serve much better to show the incidents on the frontier separating the two worlds. It was a manner of using tricks in the same way as a poet uses numbers, that is, never allowing them to fall into the visible, i.e. into the inelegant, and making them appear as a reality, or rather as a truth to the spectators. You'll understand that this compelled me to overcome the facility accorded by the cinematograph to fantasy and magic. I had to make magic *direct*, without ever using the laboratory and showing only what I saw myself and wanted others to see.

A.F.: What do you mean by *direct* magic?

J.C.: I mean a magic which, through an equilibrium between imagination and technique, through an extreme preliminary complexity ends by becoming as simple as would be, for a child who had seen sugar dissolve in water, the miracle that he himself does not dissolve in his bath. This equilibrium demands a close and unremitting understanding between the head cameraman and the director. Nicholas Hayer and myself, after our failure with conjurers and music-hall experts, sought only for means of showing on the screen what we had seen ourselves. This is the method of poets, who collect information but never use it. We had to give up our experiments with mirrors without silvering and with black velvet because they proved unusable in film lighting. I'll add, however, that such failures were useful in that they excited our imagination and set it going, compelling it to solve the problem of trick effects without resorting to any tricks. . . .

My film *Les Parents Terribles* is doing less well abroad than my other films. This is because the French language plays the leading part in it. The genius of the actors cannot overcome that difficulty. In *Orphée*, my ideas get through under the cover of the spectacle. This is what makes me hesitate about *Britannicus*. (*Hamlet* speaks a language of vast circulation.)

I will say it again: in order to reach a few we must be seen by all. Otherwise a book or a play would suffice.

The phenomenon we observe in all the arts, through which a brazen lie can convince people of a reality of a higher and deeper order, can be made to occur in a film only by an unusual use of people, gestures, words and places (a deliberate unusualness of costumes and settings would degenerate into a *masquerade*). It is only by a syntax of visual, common words placed in a certain order that the lie of art can be introduced into the cinematograph. I know only of *Caligari* where the lie was valid in spite of its operating in external forms.

Artistic creation is subject to the mechanism of all creation, which alters matter and appearance only by a different organization of the same atoms.

Some

Principles

of Documentary

_____

by Paul Rotha

For many years now Paul Rotha, the noted English documentary film maker, has been arguing for a method that would integrate film content with the social issues and political trends of the contemporary world. Both he and John Grierson, the father of British documentaries, have campaigned vigorously for what they believe to be the true aim of this medium: a propagandistic device for eliminating wars, poverty and oppression. Film art, Rotha feels, cannot avoid using politically pertinent data. The following selection, taken from Paul Rotha's book, Documentary Film *(third edition, revised and enlarged; written in collaboration with Sinclair Road and Richard Griffith. Faber and Faber, London, 1952), pretty much summarizes this point of view.*

EVERY TENDENCY in cinema reflects the social and political characteristics of its period, which in turn may, or may not, according to your reasoning, be a reflection of the obtaining economic conditions. The documentary method, as a distinct kind of film, as an interpretation of social feeling and philosophic thought quite different in purpose and form from the entertainment motives of the story film, has materialized largely as the result of sociological, political and educational requirements.

. . . We have tried to show that documentary is a genuine independent kind of cinema, as distinct from the story film or photoplay as is the biography from the novel. Further, we have tried to define the main characteristics that exist between the plain descriptive pictures of everyday life (travel pictures, nature films, educationals and newsreels) that fall short of documentary requirements and the creative dramatization of actuality and the expression of social analysis that are the first demand of the documentary method.

At any rate, it is clear, I think, that in purposeful documentary we enter a range of perception wider than has so far been attempted in descriptive films, for propaganda needs persuasive statements and implications that furrow deeply into the surface of modern experience. In the use of documentary for dialectical purpose, for example, we can conceive whole periods of time, symbolized by their existing heritages today, being arranged in dramatic shape to express a variety of outlooks. We can imagine how the fundamental sentiments of the human mind can be analyzed and dissected to suit a multitude of purposes. The immense range of discursive power made possible by film technique suggests the documentary method as an admirable instrument for clarifying and co-ordinating all aspects of modern thought, in the hope of achieving a fuller analysis that may in turn lead to more definite conclusions.[1] But how does this interpretation of the documentary method evolve from the traditions which we have just described? Before we can arrive at even first definitions, the existing tendencies require further analysis to discover if they are progressing on the most suitable lines.

Flaherty serves us well to demonstrate the elementary demands of documentary. He asks an observation of natural material on its actual location, from which the theme may arise. Further, he asks an interpretation of that material, to bring it alive as reality on the screen, which can be attained only by a complete understanding "from the inside" of such material and its relationships. For his own method, he prefers the inclusion of a slight narrative, not fictional incident or interpolated "cameos," but the daily routine of his native people. For his themes and locations he goes to those parts of the world where, supposedly, man has still to fight nature for his existence, although in most cases Flaherty reconstructs native life of a past or dying generation. The heroes of both *Nanook* and *Man of Aran*, for example, were waxwork figures acting the lives of their grandfathers. And it is precisely this choice which leads us to explore the validity of his approach in relation to documentary's social purpose.

In the modern world in which most of us live, it is doubtful if we are primarily interested in man's primitive relationship with

---

[1] Later practical examples of this theory have been the Canadian *World in Action* series, the U.S. Army's *Why We Fight* series, the argument films, *The World Is Rich* and *World of Plenty*, and Van Dongen's *News-Review No. 2*.

nature. Pushing back the sea to build a quay wall and damming a river to harness its energy admittedly present great achievements of scientific and engineering skill. But does not their importance, from a social aspect, lie less in the actual feat itself than in its resultant effect upon the geography of the landscape and ultimately the benefit to the economic life of the people concerned? The idyllic documentarist, it is true, is chiefly interested in man's conquering of natural objects to bend them to his ends. Admittedly, the sea was an obstacle to communication until man built ships to cross it. The air was useless to man's economic life, except as wind power, until he learned to fly through it. The minerals of the earth were valueless until man discovered how to mine. And, in the same way, production today is generally acknowledged to be more than sufficient to meet the needs of the community. But the success of science and machine-controlled industry has resulted in an unequal distribution of the amenities of existence under the relationships of the present economic system. Side by side with leisure and wellbeing there is also unemployment, poverty and wide social unrest. Our essential problem today is to equate the needs of the individual with production, to discuss the most satisfactory economic system and to present the social relationships of mankind in their most logical and modern ordering. Despite their braveries, man's fight against the fury of the sea, man's creation of unnatural pain to prove his manhood, man's battle against snow and ice and animals are of secondary interest in a world where so many urgent and larger problems demand our attention.

Granted that we may not expect the sentimentalist director to grapple with the materialist problems of our age, but at least we may expect from him an acknowledgment of their existence. Surely we have the right to believe that the documentary method, the most virile of all kinds of film, should not ignore the vital social issues of this year of grace, should not avoid the economic relationships which govern the present productive system and, consequently, determine the cultural, social and aesthetic attitudes of society?

Let Flaherty's fine feeling for photography stand, accept his unique sensibility to natural movements and his grand poetic vision of man against the sky, confess (in passing) that *Man of Aran* avoided all the important issues raised by sound, but let us realize, in the face of all the gilt of Venice, that the Flaherty method is an evasion of the issues that matter most in the modern world, is devoid of any attempt at serious social analysis. Give to Flaherty his credits; and they are many. Acknowledge our deep obligation to his pioneer spirit, his fierce battles to break down commercial stu-

pidity and the bravery of his struggle against the despicable methods
of exploitation from which he has suffered. But realize, at the same
time, and within the sphere of documentary, that his understanding
of actuality is a sentimental reaction toward the past, an escape into
a world that has little contemporary significance, a placing of sen-
timentalism above the more urgent claims of materialism.

No slums or factories, no employment exchanges or income tax
bureaus, no weekly rents or tithes exist in this fairy world of make-
believe created by the romantic tradition of documentary. Only
man against nature; cruel, bitter, savage and heroic but unrelated
to modern society. Industry and commerce are as remote as their
carved symbols which flank the Albert Memorial, or as the muscular stalwarts that lean nonchalantly on slender sledge hammers and
the bronzed workers who flourish torches of servility under the
nose of good Victoria. True, Flaherty observed in his own way the
craftsmanship of the potter and the glass blower when in the Midlands for *Industrial Britain,* but is it not significant that those very
trades are fading before the advance of mass production and machinery? And did not the filming of coal and steel and other heavy
industry in that film fall to other hands?

In every location which he has chosen there have existed social
problems that demanded expression. Exploitation of native labor,
the practices of the white man against the native, the landlords of
Aran, these have been the vital stories, but from them Flaherty has
turned away. Probably he realized that their exposure would have
clashed with the interests controlling the production and distribution of his films. It was not, we may grant, in his power to expose.
Instead he was content to present the "braveries of all time." Certainly he retreated into an acceptance of the irrelevance which is
the fate of all escapists. Idyllic documentary is documentary without significant purpose. It takes romanticism as its banner. It ignores
social analysis. It takes ideas instead of facts. It marks a reactionary
return to the worship of the heroic, to an admiration of the bar-
baric, to a setting up of the "Leader."

The symphonic approach of the Continental realists, on the other
hand, goes at first appearance to realism. But for the most part the
French and German directors see the documentary film as a work
of art in itself, as a symphony of tempos and movements, rather than
that the art should be an offshoot of the larger issue of a job well
done to meet a special purpose.

Thus the symphonic conception of *Berlin* provides a pleasant
enough pyrotechnical exercise, skimming over the many tantalizing
rhythms of modern life in street and factory and countryside, with-

out thought of the "how" and "wherefore" underlying the social scene. Yet, despite their exciting tempos, despite their bustle and thronging of modern city life, these big and little symphonies of big and little cities create nothing more valuable to civilization than a shower of rain. All the outward signs of a busy metropolis are there. People work and eat; a suicide and a wedding; but not one single implication underlies it all.

Again there is evasion, a deliberate self-satisfaction in the surface rhythms of a printing press or the processions of a milk-bottling machine, but nothing of inflated circulations or wages paid, nothing to suggest that the social and economic relations contained in the subject are the real material of documentary. The manufacture of steel is visually exciting. Ruttmann, Dr. Kaufmann and Basse have shown us that. But they did not think to show us that steel builds bridges, builds ships to cross the seas, radio masts to throw a girdle of communication round the earth, pylons to carry a new power up the length and breadth of the land, knives to eat with and needles to sew with. They did not tell us that steel is a state ceremony, that its foundrymen and smiths are in a sense national figures; nor that its labor might be underpaid, its risks horrifying and its markets cut across by private speculation.

Based on the same method of approach, but lacking the technical trickery that made *Berlin* of interest, Basse's film *Deutschland von Gestern und Heute* admirably epitomizes the realist tradition of the Continental school. Cross-sectioning in painful detail almost every aspect of German life, it is typical of the method in that it observes the pictorial surface of the scene but refuses to penetrate beneath the skin. It is said for Basse that he intended to show how the style of living in former times is still affecting modern life, that from the prehistoric forms of a primitive economic system the film leads historically over the Gothic style to Renaissance, from baroque to rococo, from the *Biedermeierzeit* to the complacency of present middle-class society, the provincial character of which makes possible the crescendo of a modern city's activity.[2] But I do not find Basse doing anything of the sort.

Instead, we have all the ingredients of the photographer's album, townspeople and countryfolk, pastimes and processions, customs and conventions, industry and agriculture, medieval city and modern metropolis. They are all neatly shuffled and labeled, arranged in order like a good picture book, with the camera roving here and there and round about. But as with Ruttmann, so with Basse. Nothing is

[2] *Vide* Arnheim, *Cinema Quarterly*, Vol. II, No. 3.

related socially. Nothing is said creatively. Nothing lives. The long-winded procession of images, some of them not too well photographed, meanders along without drive or purpose. Running to story-feature length, this film more than any other exposes the weakness of a purposeless theme. It is as if Basse just did not care how and why his images came to be. Unrelated geographically, they are put together in some form of contrast from which a mild implication might be drawn, but there is no essential aim behind it all. A few fleeting comments on the childishness of official parades, passing observations on the idiotic behaviorism of the *petite bourgeoisie*, but that is all. Had it been political, had it been sociological, had it been a compromise of respective description, it might have had point.

The visual arabesques of plunging pistons, the endless streams of trams and trains, the ballet movements of spinning bobbins, the belching issue of a steel furnace, the plow team and the harvest and the tractor, these as beautiful, exciting, poetic things in themselves are the main delights of the pseudo realist approach. More difficult, perhaps, than the noble savage hero, who in himself is a curious being, but even more escapist for its delight in surface values; more subtle because of its treating with familiar scenes but more dangerous because of its artistic avoidance of vital issues. Its virtue lies in the surface beauties of techniques and tempos; its value is craftsmanship with no end in view except its own virtuosity. It may have poetry, lyricism, beauty of movement, sensibility, but these are minor virtues. The point is well made in Grierson's criticism of Elton's *Voice of the World*, a documentary of radio-gramophone production.

Concentration on movement and rhythmic good looks obscures *importance* of the instrument. The building and *delivery* of the instrument, the key to the situation, not dramatized sufficiently. The result powerful but less than heroic. Elton possibly unappreciative of radio's social significance and therefore lacking in proper (aesthetic) affection for subject. This point important, as affecting almost all the tyros of documentary. Too damned arty and postwar to get their noses into public issues. Miss accordingly the larger dramatic themes possible to the medium.[3]

The Continental realists and their many imitators, then, are occupied principally by their interpretation of surface rhythms. They fail to appreciate the significance of their images or tempos. They

[3] *Cinema Quarterly*, Vol. I, No. 2.

give us a concerto of rotating wheels as a visual rhythm but do not realize that these stand as images of an epoch, symbols of an era of economic industrialism; and that only by relating these images to the human society which has given them existence can they become of real interest on the contemporary screen.

Analysis of all the tendencies of documentary, in fact, gives rise to the criticism that one of the real issues of modern society is being almost wholly avoided. In this age of social realism, surely one of the first aims of documentary should be to examine the problem of man's place in society? Surely it is pointless, if not impossible, to bring alive the realities of the modern world unless we do so in such a manner as to base our themes on the relationship of man to the world in which he lives? Machinery, agriculture, craftsmanship, culture and the rest cannot be divorced from their human fulfillments. Yet this is the very mistake into which some of our documentarists seem to have fallen. Apparently they fail to realize that the basis of the documentary method is a materialistic basis; that it is the material circumstances of civilization which create and condition the present cultural, sociological, political, religious and aesthetic ideas of society.

On almost every side, moreover, documentary has deliberately been allowed to avoid the existence of the human being as the main factor in civilization. Certainly people of many types have appeared in documentary but they have rarely been treated as anything but impersonal puppets. In following a path opposite to that of the story film, documentary has been permitted to prefer the mass to the individual, or, in some cases, simply an impersonal statement of facts. Not only have the documentarists failed to relate the mass to the individual, but, despite the fact that their material and subjects are naturalistic, they have also failed to relate their themes to current social consciousness.

It is interesting, at this point, to note that this problem of setting the human being against a naturalistic environment is the main subject of discussion in the present Soviet *kino*. Practically the whole of the preliminary closed conference preceding the Moscow Film Festival of 1935 was given over to criticism of the Soviet cinema's inability to recognize and incorporate the individual in its films. That is why *Chapayev*, a dull film technically, was accorded such praise. That is why we have Dinamov making the plea that "the theory of a film without a plot is a very dangerous theory," and Eisenstein stating that "a film without emotional feeling is scarcely worth consideration."

The fact is that since the Russians left their initial period of blood-and-thunder and strike, since the era of *Mother* and *Potemkin,* not one of them has succeeded in tackling the problems set by a new state of society, unless it will be Dovchenko in his new film *Air City.* It was one thing to evolve a set of rhythms which made the Odessa Steps massacre a scene of tremendous emotion, but quite another to relate the working of a milk separator to collective farming. So, in *The General Line,* we had a fine display of fireworks and slapstick by an expert showman; in *A Simple Case,* a set of artificial people with petty passions and a return to the Civil War for blood-and-thunder action, which all the splendid improvisations of a "Birth and Regeneration" sequence failed to justify. From his insistence that the real struggle lay at one's own back door, we might suspect that Pudovkin saw the fault in *Deserter,* but, as Grierson pointed out, he still evaded the issue by retreating to the street riots of Hamburg (so like the *St. Petersburg* location) and observed the working of his Russian factory with all the badness of a great artist.

Nor, when all was said and done, did the enthusiasms of a hundred thousand toilers in a Dziga Vertov cacophony do much to solve the task. Nearer the mark was *Counterplan,* in which the ideas were better than their fulfillment; but most progressive of all, to my mind, was *Men and Jobs,* which grappled with the problem of the untrained worker at the building of Dnieprostroy. Here, at least, was a bid to meet the issues of Russia going to school. The human being was, in a sense, related to the problems from which the theme arose. As persuasion for the shock-brigader to learn from American efficiency, it was probably effective. But observe that the philosophy was still unsound. Enthusiasm, no matter how inspired, can never conquer science. Together they may achieve idealist aims, but no engineer's science can be learned, as this film suggested. A crane is not worked by enthusiasm, although a film may have it so. A dam is not built by faith alone. A country cannot exist on a diet of ideology. And, in this measure also, *Men and Jobs* minimized its task.

Equally in their own sphere, the E.M.B. films of Britain avoided the major issues provoked by their material. That was inevitable under their powers of production. The real economic issues underlying the North Sea herring catch, the social problems inherent in any film dealing seriously with the industrial Midlands, lay outside the scope of a unit organized under a government department and having as its aim "the bringing alive of the Empire." The directors concerned knew this and wisely, I think, avoided any economic or important social analysis. Instead they contented themselves with attempting a simple statement of facts, dramatizing the action material of their themes, but leaving untouched the wider human fulfillments of the job.

It is strange that these many and varied efforts to realize and solve the problem of people in documentary are marked by an increasing, and perhaps dangerous, return to theatricalism. Having been freed from the banalities of the story film, having been developed along fresh and stimulating lines, documentary may now present the sad if faintly ironic spectacle of returning, in spirit if not in material, to the studio. With the Russians arguing for a discontinuance of "typage" and the resuscitation of the trained actor, with Ruttmann's linking of love with steel, and the G.P.O. unit romanticizing their savings banks and making a melodrama out of the designing of a stamp, it looks as if we shall yet see the all-star documentary, if indeed we have not already done so in *BBC: The Voice of Britain*.

But the fact remains that this, one of documentary's most important problems, must be faced. Clearly a full and real expression of the modern scene and modern experience cannot be achieved unless people are observed in accurate relation to their surroundings. To do this, there must be establishment and development of character. There must be the growth of ideas, not only in theme, but in the minds of characters. Your individuals must be of the audience. They must be familiar in type and character. They themselves must think and convey their thoughts to the audience, because only in this way will documentary succeed in its sociological or other propagandist purpose. Documentary must be the voice of the people speaking from the homes and factories and fields of the people.

And it is these very requirements which will continue to distinguish documentary from the story film. For in the latter, a character is seldom permitted to think other than trivial personal thoughts, or to have opinions in any way connected with the larger issues of existence. Just as in documentary the facts of the theme must be important facts, so also must be the characterization and outlook possessed by the individuals, for they are, in turn, conditioned by those same facts. In documentary this is possible, whereas in the story film, at any rate under present conditions of manufacture, facts and ideas as well as characterization are suppressed in the interests of the balance sheet, and technique alone is left to the director.

The foregoing severe criticism of purpose and method in documentary today is, of course, necessarily arbitrary. Documentary is a type of film possessing certain well-defined characteristics. Each of the films included in our estimate falls within its scope. But because they do not all carry the social analysis which, in some opinions, is documentary's most important task, this does not deny their often brilliant craftsmanship or our respect for their director's outlook. Rather does this signify that, quite reasonably, interpretations of the documentary method may differ; that there are different intentions underlying different observations; that whereas Flaherty, for example, can find his theme in the heroic braveries of all time expressed through some up-to-date "primitive" tribe, others find their material on the home front, in the back streets and factories and locations closer to those actualities among which so many of us live; that, whereas some prefer the attitude of romanticism, others of us set ourselves the task of building from a materialistic basis. It is purely a question of personal character and inclination, of how strongly you feel about satisfying private artistic fancies or communal aims. No director makes documentary simply for the wages he is paid. That we leave to the panjandrums of the story film. Your documentarist creates documentary and believes in the documentary method of cinema because he considers it the most powerful means of social expression available today.

Yet, despite my plea that the maker of documentary should be politically and socially conscious in his approach to everyday experience, he has no claim to the label of politician. His job is not upon a platform to harangue the mob but in a pulpit to persuade the mass to a wider consideration of human affairs. He is neither a fighter nor a barnstormer. Rather is he a prophet concerned with the broadest references of human associations. He is a propagandist making use of the most influential instrument of his time. He does not march with the crowd but goes just ahead, asking contemplation and discussion before action is taken on those problems with which he deals. In cinema, it is the documentary method which has proved the most suitable for these ends because it is a method of philosophic reasoning.[4]

The immediate task of the documentarist is, I believe, to find the means whereby he can employ a mastery of his art of public persuasion to put the people and their problems, their labor and their service, before themselves. His is a job of presenting one half of the populace to the other; of bringing a deeper and more intelligent social analysis to bear upon the whole cross section of modern society; exploring its weaknesses, reporting its events, dramatizing its experiences and suggesting a wider and more sympathetic understanding among the prevailing class of society. He does not, I think,

---

[4] Alas, how much of this has been forgotten or never learned by the postwar documentary film maker! (P.R.—1951.)

seek to draw conclusions but rather to make a statement of the case so that conclusions may be drawn. His world is in the streets, the homes, the factories and the workshops of the people, presenting this experience and that event to make his point. And if the documentary method today is being put to a double-headed use, if it is being employed to express a meaning within a meaning, then it is not the fault of the documentarist but of the time in which he lives.

. . . I have emphasized the documentary method rather than documentary as a particular kind of film. For this reason, although documentary has been characterized by its creative use of the materials and apparatus of cinema, although it has made special use of actualities rather than of artificialities, it is the method which prompts this practice that is important and not the type of film produced. The documentary method will not, I believe, remain fixed in a world defined, on the one side, by *Drifters* and, on the other, by *Nanook*. Already the limits have been expanded to embrace such a poem as *Coal Face* and such a piece of journalistic reporting as *Housing Problems*. Story, characterization and studio are likely to enter the documentary film but it will be the method and not the materials that will count. It will be the sociological, political or other purposes being served by the method which will continue to be of first importance.

In short, the documentary method is more complex than its traditions would have us believe. No longer is it the mere pictorial description of things and people and places of interest. Observation alone is not enough. Camera portrayal of movement, no matter how finely observed, is purely a matter of aesthetic good taste. The essential purposes of documentary lie in the ends applied to this observation. Conclusions must be indicated and the results of observation must be put across in a manner that demands high creative endeavor. Below the surface of the modern world lie the actuating economic issues of modern civilization. These are the real materials of purposeful documentary. In industry, commerce, civics and nature the mere superficial portrayal of actuality is insufficient. Such surface description implies no intellectual ability. Rather are the implications and fulfillments of his material the concern of the documentarist. It is the meaning *behind* the thing and the significance *underlying* the person that are the inspirations for his approach. To the documentary method, every manufacture, every organization, every function, every scheme of things represents at one point or another the fulfillment of a human interest.

In such circumstances, it seems improbable that your hero can still be the noble savage of Flaherty's choosing, or the centrifugal rhythms of a crankshaft which deceive the pseudorealist's mind. No matter whether they are politics, culture, economics or religion, we are concerned with the impersonal forces that dictate this modern world. The puny individual must be refocused into his normal relationship to the general mass, must take his place alongside in the community's solid struggle for existence and forsake personal achievement. Daily jobs, no matter how well described by rhetoric of camera and intimacy of microphone, are not documentary material in themselves. They must be related to the wider purposes of the community.

Above all, documentary must reflect the problems and realities of the present. It cannot regret the past; it is dangerous to prophesy the future. It can, and does, draw on the past in its use of existing heritages but it does so only to give point to a modern argument. In no sense is documentary a historical reconstruction, and attempts to make it so are destined to failure. Rather is it contemporary fact and event expressed in relation to human associations.

Frequently I hear it said that documentary aims at a true statement of theme and incident. This is a mistaken belief. No documentary can be completely truthful, for there can be no such thing as truth while the changing developments in society continue to contradict each other. Not only this, but technical reasons also preclude the expression of a completely accurate representation. It is often suggested that documentary has close similarity to the newsreel. By the trade they are naturally confused because they both, in their respective ways, deal with natural material.[5] But there the likeness ends. Their approach to and interpretation of that material are widely different. The essence of the documentary method lies in its dramatization of actual material. The very act of dramatizing causes a film statement to be false to actuality. We must remember that most documentary is truthful only in that it represents an attitude of mind. The aim of propaganda is persuasion, and persuasion implies a particular attitude of mind toward this, that or the other subject. To be truthful within the technical limits of the camera and microphone demands description, which is the aim of the instructional film, and not dramatization, which is the qualification of the documentary method. Thus even a plain statement of fact in documentary demands dramatic interpretation in order that it may be "brought alive" on the screen.

We may assume, then, that documentary determines the approach

---

[5] "The basis of all documentary, instructional and propaganda films is fundamentally the same as that of the newsreel. Truth."—*Kinematograph Weekly*, October 25, 1934.

to a subject but not necessarily the subject itself. Further, that this approach is defined by the aims behind production, by the director's intentions and by the forces making production a possibility. And because of the film camera's inherent capacity for reproducing a semblance of actuality and because the function of editing is believed to be the mainspring of film creation, it has so far been found that the best material for documentary purpose is naturally, and not artificially, contrived.

But it would be a grave mistake to assume that the documentary method differs from story film merely in its preference for natural material. That would imply that natural material alone gives the distinction, which is untrue. To state that only documentary makes use of analytical editing methods is equally mistaken. At least one leading exponent of the documentary tradition (Flaherty) was creating the living scene in film before the scientific experiments of the Russians became common knowledge, while the latter have applied their methods of technique to many purely fictional films. To postulate that documentary is realistic as opposed to the romanticism of the story film, with its theatrical associations, is again incorrect; for although documentary may be realistic in its concern with actuality, realism applies not only to the material but more especially to the method of approach to that material.

Such inspirations as I suggest are the essential aims of documentary demand a sense of social responsibility difficult to maintain in our world today. That I am fully prepared to admit. But, at the same time, your documentary director dares not be neutral, or else he becomes merely descriptive and factual.

The function that the film performs within the present social and political sphere must be kept constantly in mind. Relative freedom of expression for the views of the documentarist will obviously vary with the production forces he serves and the political system in power. In countries still maintaining a parliamentary system, discussion and projection of his beliefs within certain limits will be permitted only so long as they do not seriously oppose powerful vested interests, which most often happen to be the forces controlling production. Under an authoritarian system, freedom is permissible provided his opinions are in accord with those of the state for social and political advance, until presumably such a time shall arrive when the foundations of the state are strong enough to withstand criticism. Ultimately, of course, you will appreciate that you can neither make films on themes of your own choice nor apply treatments to accepted themes, unless they are in sympathy with the aims of the dominant system.

III

History

and

Personal

The intention here is simple and obvious: to present several episodes and personalities that figure prominently in the history of the film. It should be emphasized, however, that this section provides only a sampling. Many important figures such as Murnau, Epstein, Richter, Ophuls, Von Stroheim, and others are not represented here because of space limitations or inappropriate material.

First

Night

on Broadway

---

by Terry Ramsaye

The following is a chapter from Terry Ramsaye's two-volume work, A Million and One Nights (Simon and Schuster, New York, 1926). This book is the first important history of the film. It contains a wealth of information on both the early days of the film (after Lumière) and pertinent pre-film history. In a fascinating survey, Ramsaye traces the evolution of animated pictures from Aristotle to Edison, noting the work of such "precursors of the screen" as Leonardo da Vinci, Peter Mark Roget, William Friese-Greene and others.

CONTRACTS HAD BEEN signed for the launching of the Vitascope, Thomas A. Edison had agreed to lend his valued name, and his shops were building ten of the machines by the end of March 1896. But Edison had not seen it yet! He was that enthusiastic about the screen.

Raff & Gammon urged Gilmore to persuade Edison to attend a demonstration and he went to bed with a cold.

On April 1, Armat arrived from Washington to operate the machine and look over the Edison shop work.

On the evening of April 3 there was a demonstration of the Vitascope for Edison and the press at the Edison plant in West Orange. Edison saw the pictures with the reporters.

This line of publicity activity was not at all of the Edison pattern. It resulted from the aggressiveness of Norman C. Raff, anxious to merchandise the Vitascope as a novelty and more especially anxious to be sure that it was to be known as the latest of the marvels produced by the wizardly Edison. Thomas Armat and his brother, J. Hunter Armat, who was to remain at the West Orange plant in supervision of the making of Vitascopes, were discreetly in the background at the press showing.

Neither Edison nor Armat was especially fond of the arrangement, but it was accepted by them at the dictation of Raff as a matter of commercial expediency. It was ultimately to be proved of no especial value to any of them.

Just how completely the Vitascope was launched as an Edison enterprise may be gathered from the contemporary newspaper attentions. In its issue of April 4, 1896, the New York *Herald* proclaimed:

MR. EDISON'S LATEST

A Favored Few Treated to an Exhibition of the Inventor's Most
Recent Production.

CALLS IT THE VITASCOPE

Spectators Witness a Skirt Dance and
a Derby Race with Life
Size Figures.

THE KINETOSCOPE PERFECTED

What Will Be Possible When the Machine is Connected with an
Improved Phonograph?

A new invention by Thomas A. Edison was shown to a few favored persons last night. The new machine is really a grown up kinetoscope, and it is a success.

Mr. Edison calls his latest invention the Vitascope, which he says means a machine showing life, and that is exactly what the new apparatus does.

The vitascope, which has been in process of perfection at the Llewellyn laboratory for the last seven or eight months, under Mr. Edison's direction, is the ideal he had in mind, he says, when he began work on the kinetoscope machine, with which he has never been satisfied.

The vitascope is an improvement of the kinetoscope, by which moving life size figures of men, women and animals are thrown upon a screen by means of bright lights and powerful lenses. The trial of the new machine was made last night in a cold corner of the big foundry at the works, and Mr. Edison, with Richard N. Dyer, William J. Gilmour, manager of the phonograph works, Raff & Gammon, of New York, and a few invited guests huddled around a red hot stove and gazed at and admired the marvellous figures thrown upon the big white screen at one end of the room.

What the Visitors Saw

The first picture shown was a colored panorama of a serpentine dance by Anabelle, who went out to West Orange to pose one day last summer. The film roll on which the photographs were attached was arranged over a half dozen spools and pulleys, and the machine was set in motion.

Even the inventor himself was surprised at the result, although with his usual critical eye he discovered flaws in the film which he declared must be disposed of before the vitascope would come up to his ideal.

Anabelle danced for five minutes, and then a panorama of the latest English Derby was thrown upon the screen.

The feature of the new machine which astonished all who saw last night's views was the almost entire absence of vibration in the pictures as they appeared on the screen, and which had been the hardest obstacle to surmount in perfecting the apparatus.

The New York *Journal*'s account of the same date had a shade more color:

For the first time since Edison has been working on his new invention, the Vitascope, persons other than his trusted employees and assistants were allowed last night to see the workings of the wonderful machine. For two hours dancing girls and groups of figures, all of life size, seemed to exist as realities on the big white screen. . . .

No one was more pleased at the success of his work than the great inventor himself. Wrapped in a big overcoat which hung to his heels and rose to his hat brim, he walked about the cold room chuckling and joking with the men who had done so much to make his work what it is. . . .

. . . the inventor clapped his hands and turning to one of his assistants said:

"That is good enough to warrant our establishing a bald-head row, and we will do it, too."

The English Derby picture mentioned in the New York *Herald's* account of the press showing had been forwarded to Edison from Maguire & Baucus, the London agents of the Kinetoscope. The Derby picture had been photographed over there by Robert W. Paul as part of his independent supply of films for his own replica of the peep-show Kinetoscope.

Just how Edison really felt about this Armat machine is nicely indicated by his testimony in a later litigation. On the witness stand in 1898 Edison said:

Raff & Gammon got hold of this man named Armat and they wanted us to build the machine. The machine was brought over and we saw it was our machine except that it had a different movement for feeding the film along intermittently. Messrs. Raff & Gammon wanted us to build that machine and they wanted to use my name and as the movement seemed to be a good one and could be built very quickly and cheaply, I gave them permission to use the name for the reason that all there was in the machine that we did not have was simply his movement. And the machines were made and built by us and called the Edison Vitascope and the whole thing was mine except that one movement of Mr. Armat's.

We don't use that Armat movement any more but use our original Geneva stop movement.

In view of the fact that there is no important element of invention in a projection machine save the device that moves the film along intermittently, it would seem that Edison was a trifle conservative about giving credit to Armat.

However, this was testimony given in the heat of a lawsuit, not a statement made for publication. Today Edison is more inclined to rest his claim on the Kinetoscope.

In a letter to Armat in May 1922, discussing some misrepresentations of alleged screen history, Edison remarked incidentally:

You will probably notice that in interviews given by me I have stated that I had a projection machine, but that when you came on the scene I saw you had a very much better one than mine, and that I dropped my experiments and built yours, which was the first practical projection machine.

There is a certain finality in that letter of Edison's, written after the years have buried the biases of legal sparring for commercial advantages, that may well be the answer to many of the clamorous claims of priority for other inventors.

At the time when the Armat machine was new there was one tiny but amazing fact which doubtless chafed Edison. For years he had had standing in his laboratory a machine which lacked only about two minutes' work to make it a projection machine the equivalent of Armat's. The Edison camera, or Kinetograph, would have been a most excellent projection machine if only he had removed the shutter to allow the full flood of light to reach the screen. Edison's camera had an intermittent movement which held the film still nine times as long as it took to move it from frame to frame, but the camera shutter used only a fraction of this nine-to-one period. That shutter stood between Edison and the basic patent and principle of projection. Here is another of those obscure little technical facts which underlie the beginnings of the big and conspicuous affairs of the screen world. If Edison had been just a shade more interested in the screen he would long before have had that little shutter off and solved the problem first.

The technically minded reader may recall that Dickson tried that camera as a projector, . . . but Dickson did not then know that it would work better without the shutter. That made all the difference in the world.

Armat, the inventor of the Vitascope, was conspicuously absent from the press notices, as befitted the policy of the deal.

The story of the wonders of the Edison Vitascope went swiftly over the world and drew the usual obeisances and admirations on the editorial pages of the newspapers.

The Brooklyn *Eagle* offered promising comment:

Of course, now it is only an enlarged kinetoscope, the adaptation of a toy to the requirements of actual life, but that is just what was done with the telephone. Once that was a curious toy, now with it you can talk with a man in Chicago and recognize the tones of his voice. It will not be safe to decry the possibilities of the new living panorama. Edison is a mighty ingenious fellow—and electricity in its application to the arts is *in its infancy*.

For just thirty years since it has been the custom of editorial writers, critics, cultural uplifters and the like to refer to the motion pictures as being "in their infancy." It gives a glow of archaeological satisfaction to discover the origin of this hackneyed bit of cant in Brooklyn.

The press showing that cold night in West Orange was by way of tuning up the newspapers for the coming presentation at a theater, and to give the launching all of the wizardly stamp of Edison. It was sound merchandising.

The advertising of Koster & Bials' Music Hall, Thirty-fourth Street, Herald Square, for the week commencing Monday evening, April 20, 1896, announced the coming of "Thomas A. Edison's latest marvel, the Vitascope." The music hall was on the site now occupied by the Macy department store.

Thomas Armat came up from Washington to supervise the installation of the Vitascope on the balcony of the music hall.

The opening was delayed because of the time required for the installation of the machinery. The sensation was sprung on the night of April 23. Armat was in the projection booth at the machines while the crowd, thrilled with the dancing of Anabelle, life size on the screen, acclaimed Edison. Edison in a box at the show did not respond in person.

The pictures were thrown upon a twenty-foot screen, set in an overwhelming gilded frame. The program included pictures of a bit of the finale number of Hoyt's *The Milk White Flag*, a dash of prize fight, several dancing girls who displayed their versatility to the camera, and one of Robert W. Paul's pictures, the surf at Dover, in England. The Dover picture was accepted by the audience as something from down the New Jersey coast.

The Vitascope used at Koster & Bials' was equipped with a spool bank and endless loops of film, so that subjects might be repeated indefinitely without rewinding the pictures. The machine was capable of handling film on reels, but the idea of subjects that should occupy the length of a modern reel of a thousand feet was remote indeed from the picture makers of '96.

The audience was deeply puzzled at this magic of the screen. When the waves at Dover came rolling in to crash in jets of spume and spray there was a flurry of panic in the front seats.

In public attention on Broadway that week, honors were about equally divided between the new wonder of the screen and Albert Chevalier, the famous singer of coster songs, who was then appearing at Koster & Bials' in the glory of his first engagement, introducing to the eager American ear *My Old Dutch*, *The Nipper's Lullaby* and *Our Court Ball*.

Koster & Bials' audiences were as full of silk hats as an undertakers' convention. The amusement world was agog with speculation about the invention.

Charles Frohman, the rising star of theatrical magnates, was in that first night audience. He gave the New York *Times* an interview.

"That settles scenery [said Frohman]. Painted trees that do not move, waves that get up a few feet and stay there, everything in scenery we simulate on our stages will have to go. Now that art can make us believe that we see actual living nature the dead things of the stage must go.

"And think what can be done with this invention! For instance, Chevalier comes on the screen. The audience would get all the pantomime of his coster songs. The singing, words fitted to gestures and movements, could be done from the wings or behind the curtain. And so we could have on the stage at any time any artist, dead or alive, who ever faced Mr. Edison's invention.

"That in itself is great enough, but the possibilities of the Vitascope as the successor of painted scenery are illimitable."

Charles Frohman died before the screen had attained its greater triumphs of the modern period, but his prophecies have been translated into terms of practice. In a large sense the living shadows of the Vitascope have supplanted what he called the "dead things of the stage." Even the name that he left, Charles Frohman, Inc., today is the incidental property of Famous Players-Lasky, a motion picture corporation.

That showing of the Vitascope on the night of April 23, 1896, at Koster & Bials' Music Hall was the true introduction of the motion picture to Broadway. Herald Square, the scene of that première, was the heart of that gilded thoroughfare then. In thirty years the *Herald* has become a memory and, ten blocks up Broadway, Times Square rules as the capital of the amusement world, while on above in the northward path of Manhattan's march is the Capitol, the world's greatest theater, with a weekly turnover of more money than the first years of the whole motion picture industry saw.

To place this entry of the motion picture screen in a sense of time, note that the Greater New York consolidation bill, creating the city of today, had just been passed by the state legislature, and that this was the last year of the administration of Grover Cleveland, Democrat, statesman and fisherman of honored memory.

The same Monday newspapers which reviewed the offerings of the Vitascope at Koster & Bials' carried a story of a Sunday sermon by the Reverend D. Asa Blackburn, pastor of the Church of the Strangers, on the theme of "You cannot serve God and skylark on a bicycle." That was indeed a dim long ago. The bicycle as the out-

standing diversion of the public before the movie era was then the
orthodox subject of attack by the church. The fundamental sin of
the bicycle was in its involvement of the use of legs, the existence
of which was not admitted by any proper female person. Worse
yet, the bicycle led to bloomers, just as inevitably as, the Maine
Puritans say, "oysters lead to dancing." The Reverend Mr. Blackburn lost the great opportunity to have been the first to denounce
the movies, which daily reveal more and better legs than the entire
world's output of bicycles from the reign of Queen Victoria to date.

Méliès

by

Maurice Bardèche

and

Robert Brasillach

The following selection on Méliès is taken from The History of Motion Pictures *by Maurice Bardèche and Robert Brasillach (W. W. Norton, New York, 1938; translated from the French and edited by Iris Barry). Méliès was one of the most important figures in film history. A true visionary with an immense imagination, he was the first to free the camera from its bondage as mere instrument for banal reportage. He introduced the idea of painting-in-motion, a method that was further developed in the animated cartoons and abstract films of Walt Disney, Norman McLaren, Oscar Fischinger, UPA and others.*

T HERE IS NO knowing how long the film might have continued to be pure reportage and newsreel had it not been for the one man who brought to this new technical invention an immense number of really original ideas, and who finally made of the film something other than a mere offshoot of photography. Georges Méliès, born in 1861, was thirty-four years old when the Lumières produced their invention. To him, their first film show seemed a sort of miracle.

Long before it was over [he relates], I rushed up to Auguste Lumière and offered to buy his invention. I offered ten thousand, twenty thousand, fifty thousand francs. I would gladly have given him my fortune, my house, my family in exchange for it. Lumière would not listen to me. "Young man," said he, "you should be grateful, since although my invention is not for sale, it would undoubtedly ruin you. It can be exploited for a certain time as a scientific curiosity but, apart from that, it has no commercial future whatsoever."

Lumière was perfectly sincere in saying this. But Méliès would not listen to him. This young man had been a manufacturer, a mechanic, a cabinetmaker, a draftsman, a painter, a caricaturist on *La Griffe*, which he ran and illustrated almost entirely himself throughout the Boulangist period. For the last eight years he had been the manager and proprietor of the Théâtre Robert-Houdin at 16 Passage de l'Opéra, where he gave shows of magic and prestidigitation, produced puppet shows and devised various pieces of electrical apparatus by means of which to present tableaux and transformations like *The Marvelous Wreath*. Even at school at Louis-le-Grand he had constructed a Punch-and-Judy show in his desk.

He brought to the films wide experience and interests, and the resourcefulness of a jack-of-all-trades which enabled him to make anything he wanted at lightning speed, a robust and unspoiled talent much like that of the early painters, an imagination as rich and all-embracing as that of a child. He had a curious protean quality in a world which is both changeable and deceptive. "I was at one and the same time," he said one day in his delightfully simple way, "an intellectual worker and a manual worker. That explains why I loved the cinema so passionately."

This prestidigitator was just what the cinema needed. As he knew how to do everything, how to make anything, how to devise all sorts of tricks, the Lumière invention gave him a chance to unleash all his gifts. He began by showing Edison's films on the Boulevard des Italiens, then, realizing the possibilities of this new medium, soon became a producer and made a first *Trip to the Moon* at Montreuil. Films of marching regiments and of trains puffing into stations were not enough to satisfy him.

Almost immediately he attempted to apply to the new invention what he had learned in the Théâtre Robert-Houdin. *The Vanishing Lady* was his first tentative attempt in this direction. Success gave him confidence. He produced *The Bewitched Inn*, then in 1896 *The Devil's Castle*, a film nearly a reel long, and *The Laboratory of Mephistopheles*.

Chance played its usual jocular role in his development. One day when he was filming the traffic on the Place de l'Opéra, his camera jammed. It took him all of a minute to readjust it. He continued to crank and finished his picture, but when he came to develop it he perceived that while his camera had been out of gear the scene had undergone a change, and that a passing omnibus had suddenly been metamorphosed into a hearse—as unexpectedly as, twenty years later, another hearse also surprisingly appeared in *Entr'acte*. From this mishap, Méliès learned something extremely important —that in the realm of the cinema there is no such thing as fair play, that the hand of the director can control everything in a film and that, above all, the film's chief purpose is to entertain the public by tricks like this one which accident had just fortuitously discovered for him.

Méliès soon afterward produced his *One Man Band*, in which he, as the one and only actor, appeared in numerous roles simultaneously. Besides multiple exposure, he also introduced stop-motion photography, taken frame by frame, so that inanimate objects appear to move on the screen as, in 1925, we saw the furniture scuttling from the house in René Clair's *Italian Straw Hat*.

To these innovations another important one was shortly to be added. Early in 1897, the singer Paulus came to Méliès and asked him to make movies of him singing his songs.[1] At the last moment Paulus, made up as for the stage, refused to perform in the daylight. Faced with this problem, Méliès hurriedly painted some scenery, fixed up adequate illumination, and made the films indoors. The results were satisfactory, and thus the idea of a studio was born. . . .[2]

One of Méliès' earliest successes, late in 1898, was a series of films in which he reconstructed (in little incidents barely sixty feet long) the principal events in the Dreyfus case. Among them were "Dreyfus' Court-Martial—Arrest of Dreyfus," "Devil's Island—Within the Palisade," "Suicide of Colonel Henry," "Dreyfus Meets His Wife at Rennes" and "The Degradation of Dreyfus."

This admirable series of primitives, a sort of animated waxworks, somehow reminds one of the character in Pabst's *Dreigroschenoper* who sings of the various adventures of Mackie Messer to the music of a hand organ.[3]

[1] To be shown with phonograph accompaniment.
[2] The Edison "studio," the Black Maria, existed from 1893, but many Edison films, such as *The Execution of Mary Queen of Scots*, were made in the open air outside the Black Maria.
[3] Actually the Dreyfus film "reminds" one much more appropriately of the magic-lantern slides which were so popular before the invention of the motion picture; there is a definite relationship between them and primitive films of this sort.

A prototype of Mackie himself was about to appear in Zecca's *Story of a Crime*, issued by Pathé and one of that firm's biggest successes. It showed an apache with peaked cap and sinister forelock, engaged upon nefarious tasks in a dark street; then the night patrol and the discovery of the crime; magistrates in frock coats, and the medical officer with his precise gestures; witnesses giving evidence; the arrest in a wretched bar; and, finally, an early-morning scene at the guillotine. It was thought necessary to ban this final tableau. Censorship came into action almost before the film was out of its cradle.

A few months later, Pathé produced a series of *Capital Punishments in Various European Countries*—by the ax, by hanging, garroting, etc., each thirty feet long. Simultaneously, the magazine *Lectures pour Tous* ran some copiously illustrated articles on the same topic; public taste at the time ran very much in this direction. A similar source of inspiration gave us the film *Underworld of Paris* in 1906 and *The Exploits of Elaine* in 1915. For films of this type any current event might furnish a fresh subject.

An *Assassination of President McKinley* was re-enacted in one studio and followed by, suitably enough, *The Execution of His Murderer*, and by *The Death of Pope Leo XIII*, *The Assassination of the Serbian Royal Family* and *The Eruption of Mont-Pélé*. Foremost among reconstructed events, however, was the film of *Edward VII's Coronation* which Méliès made for the English firm, Warwick Trading Company. It was produced at Montreuil and provided the monarch himself with considerable amusement when he eventually saw it. . . .

The era of the short film persisted for a long time. We must remember that most of the first exhibitors were fairground people. In their eyes, a film had to provide a substitute for an acrobatic turn or a parade, and the films they liked best were comedies from sixty to one hundred and twenty feet long. The comedian Dranem in his first films appeared now as a baker's man, now as an old soldier, an elderly hag or a man smitten with the colic. The elderly dude, the policeman, the detective, the lady's maid, the pastry cook, the drunk and the porter were the principal characters in these comedies, which varied very little and were all based on the inexhaustible material drawn from circuses and pantomimes. Trick photography added ludicrous novelties—garments disappeared or flung themselves onto human torsos with unbelievable rapidity, beefsteaks vanished, pots of paint flew about, furniture executed a wild dance.

Then animated cartoons made their appearance. The first cartoon on film was made by Emile Cohl in 1908 with the appropriate title of *Phantasmagoria*. It was composed of two thousand drawings and was one hundred feet long. The essential technique of animated cartoons was exhibited in it, though the drawings themselves were crude. *Le Fétard* of 1908, for instance, is little more than schoolboy scribbling. Curiously enough, when the Russians began making animated cartoons in 1934[4] they used the same rather infantile fashion of drawing faces and bodies, just as if thirty years of technical improvement had not elapsed. Emile Cohl made many cartoons—such as *When Matches Struck*, *Merry Microbes* and his parody on *Chantecler*—but later on turned to the production of popular-scientific films.

FAIRY TALES AND TRANSFORMATIONS

The contribution of all these early producers cannot be overlooked. Despite the founding of American or Italian firms, the film throughout its first years was predominantly French—Gaumont, Pathé, Léar. Also, one must not overlook the part played by Mesguich[5]—one of Lumière's first projectionists and cameramen, who opened movie shows in the United States and all over the world. He traveled as far afield as Tibet and China, was the first man to photograph Lhasa and explored the country of the Tuaregs and the Far West. It was he who suggested having *A Trip to the Moon* accompanied by appropriate music. But the greatest creative worker was still Méliès.

His earliest fantastic films, such as *The Devil's Castle*, were much to the liking of the youthful audiences at the Théâtre Robert-Houdin. Partly out of a desire to please them, partly out of a personal predilection for the sumptuous settings, the diverse and fairylike flora of imaginary worlds, Méliès made films of adventures such as a child might dream. During the Exposition of 1900 he began work on his first superfilms, all nearly a whole reel long—*Cinderella, Red Riding Hood, Bluebeard*. The first one, *Cinderella*, set the type for them all. It was distributed by Pathé, and Méliès was vexed when Zecca cut it down from two thousand to nine hundred feet, thus sacrificing many of the trick scenes. After this, Méliès broke with Pathé. Among these lizards that turn into lackeys, rats that turn into coachmen without sacrificing their long whiskers, amid all this

---

[4] An error, perhaps a misprint for 1914. The first Russian animated cartoons were made by Starevich in 1913. After the Revolution, production was resumed in 1923.

[5] Mesguich has recounted his experiences in *Tours de Manivelle*, Grasset, Paris, 1933.

complicated and childish fairyland, Méliès had hit upon something. Out of his past experience, he discovered how to produce trick scenes and thus become quite independent of "reality." He was to turn all the fairy tales into films; and even they were not enough. The miracles of science, of speed, must be drawn upon, too. He concocted this new recipe for entertainment out of a droll and delightful combination in which monstrous machines from *La Science et la Vie* were allied to Jules Verne's plots. It was as though, in 1900, Méliès himself had been a twelve-year-old boy.

He turned out *A Trip to the Moon, An Adventurous Automobile Trip, Under the Sea, Rip Van Winkle, Robinson Crusoe, An Impossible Voyage, The Merry Frolics of Satan.* These films defied both technical limitations and current fashion. They were made for a public such as filled the Théâtre du Châtelet and were probably none the worse for that. With their good-humored air, their rough-and-ready cutting, their stilted acting, their settings which put one in mind of the opera at its worst, and their restricted movement, they display all the faults of the infant film. Yet from many points of view they are exceedingly rich and suggestive. A technical audacity which grew constantly bolder, an unflagging inventiveness and the virtuosity of an intellectual juggler earned for his work a special place and led him to open new paths for the motion picture. His prodigious fertility, his habit of disregarding obstacles and even of inviting them, and the ability of this Paganini of the film to juggle with *décor* were what particularly struck his contemporaries and gave him a front place in their ranks. But his films as a whole would seem to us little better than ingenious mechanical contrivances today were they not redeemed by more important elements. What we love in Méliès is a poetical quality, somewhat painstaking and clumsily archaic, but full of unexpected and sincere lovableness.

Castles copied from old missals, landscapes such as only fairyland knows, meticulous and primitive perspectives, a rather acid color, settings and characters straight out of Madame Tussaud's, all surge up in the thick of incredible adventures, reminding us sometimes of a valentine and sometimes of the little Tuscan villages in Lorenzetti's paintings—and all in bad taste so ingenuous that it is transformed in some strange way into the most elegant poetry. It is elements like these which combine to make his early masterpieces so precious.

This Jules Verne of the screen was not merely a gifted prestidigitator; he happened also to be the first poet of the cinema. There have not been many of them since. The nearest thing to these laboriously tinted films, with their deliberately unreal settings and infinite repertory of tricks, is the animated cartoons of today. The heir to Méliès is Walt Disney. But others, too, learned much from him. Otherwise, should we ever have had that ascension scene in *Liliom*, where Lang so charmingly created a paradise out of fairgrounds and merry-go-rounds? When we look at one of Méliès' exquisite scenes—some little seaport with its dainty fleet straight out of Gozzoli—we can readily forgive the heavy make-up and frenzied gesturing of the actors (who are the weakest part of his films). He has only to show us a gilded coach drawn by one old skeleton of a horse to put us in the frame of mind to set forth too, in fancy, with this quixotic steed, to realize that the Milky Way is a pretty girl in a 1900 costume, that the stars know how to play the lyre, or to accept the existence of a whole miraculous cosmogony such as we see at the end of *The Merry Frolics of Satan*. It seems quite natural that men should walk upside down on the ceiling, evil spirits spring out of clocks, Aurora and the Great Bear engage in a swimming contest, an umbrella turn into a giant mushroom, Saturn appear in the midst of his own rings and ten women come tumbling out of a parasol.

A BUSINESS ANECDOTE OF 1898

Méliès was going full blast. His firm, Star-Films, was pre-eminent in the French market and his product was widely circulated abroad. His competitors—Charles Pathé and Léon Gaumont in France, Urban and Warwick Trading Company in England, Ambrosio and Cines in Italy—followed his recipes and imitated his methods. In 1904, despite Edison's opposition, he opened a branch in the United States. In 1908, Méliès presided over the International Congress of Film Producers, at which all the most important film makers gathered. It was on this occasion that he succeeded, despite opposition, in getting a standard perforation of film stock adopted, a step which finally made possible a really international motion picture industry. President of the Chambre Syndicale du Cinéma which he had founded in 1897, he was the undisputed leader of the new industry. At the same time he was its most creative technician. To the innumerable trick effects he invented, which his fellow producers sought unavailingly to imitate, he had just added the "dissolve," which rendered unnecessary abrupt cuts between scenes. Here again a lucky accident helped him.

In his studio it had become customary gradually to diminish the aperture of the lens while shooting the last few feet of each scene, in order not to fog the film. When the work of editing followed, this portion was eliminated as being no part of the footage proper.

One day someone forgot to cut it, and when the film was projected, Méliès realized that a much smoother transition from one scene to the next could thus be achieved. He experimented with repeating the process inversely, commencing each new scene with the diaphragm almost closed, then opening the aperture gradually as the new scene started. By doing this at the beginning and end of each scene he effected a rough dissolve. Méliès also discovered the use of masking, of double exposure, and of slow-motion and rapid-motion photography.

His prosperity concealed one serious weakness, which was the financial organization of his firm, Star-Films. At the beginning of 1898, when Méliès' business was beginning to expand, an agent came to him to propose putting him in touch with important silent partners. Méliès agreed. A few days later, the agent called again with a Mr. W., who introduced himself as director of the Société d'Études Industrielles et Commerciales. Méliès explained how his business operated; they listened with interest. Next came an expert, then an engineer, then another expert. Each of them declared that the firm seemed extremely sound and that the Société d'Études would willingly undertake to find capital to invest in it. Only, there were certain steps to be taken first, they would probably have to sound out various parties and, in short, they asked Méliès to pay down twenty-five thousand francs. Méliès paid. Several months passed; Méliès waited. The Société d'Études gave no sign of life. Méliès became worried and finally reached the point where he should have started: he began investigations. They were sadly conclusive. The Société d'Études had engaged in various financial operations about which numerous firms in the entertainment business had little to report that was pleasant. Méliès wanted to bring suit. He was asked to lay out sixty thousand francs before he could appear against Mr. W. He felt disinclined to do so and left Mr. W. to pursue his course untroubled. This incident gave Méliès little liking for investments or for partners.

Some time later another man came to see Méliès. "I am M. Grivolas. I am in the electrical supply business and the films interest me."

"I see," said Méliès.

"Are you doing well?"

"Not badly," said he.

"And are you breaking into the foreign markets?"

"Here and there," said Méliès.

"M. Méliès," continued M. Grivolas, "it has occurred to me that the capital at my disposal [here Méliès pricked up his ears] might

be of considerable service to some sound firm in the motion picture
business able to offer me suitable inducements to invest in it."
Méliès had now reared up in alarming fashion, but the unsuspect-
ing M. Grivolas continued, "If you are willing to let my experts
come and see you and also to give me security, I am willing to invest the sum of—" M. Grivolas was unable to complete his sentence. Méliès had risen and in silent fury showed him the door.

M. Grivolas was much mystified but little disposed to argue. He
went to see M. Pathé instead and enabled him to form a limited
liability company with a capital of 2,600,000 francs. When Grivolas
meets Méliès he never fails to say, "If you had listened to me, today
you would own the firm of Méliès-Natan." When Méliès tells the
anecdote he sighs.

The situation generally was about to undergo a change. At first,
producers sold their films outright to the exhibitors, a system which
made it possible for independents like Méliès to compete with more
extensively financed producers. In 1904, however, three of Méliès'
assistants, Michaux, Astaix and Lallement, opened a film renting
agency. This enterprise, after initial difficulties, was so successful
that in 1907 Pathé decided to abandon the sale of films and to organize instead a chain of renting offices all over France. Méliès, feeling that he was ill-equipped for this method of operation, stuck to
outright sales. From that time on his position became that of a
lively and colorful pioneer, more interesting by reason of the variety and originality of his output than any of his competitors, but
destined to defeat at their hands in the field of commerce. Thence-
forward he specialized. He made a domain of the fantastic and
trick film, in which his superiority remained incontestable, but he
stood aside from the main avenues along which the motion picture
was now to progress. . . .

After 1900 the film was to enter upon a new phase, but in its
first years it most singularly recorded the death throes of an epoch.
More clearly even than in the advertisements of the magazines of
the period one may discern in the earliest films what the character
of the era was, the secret history of its fashions, its bad taste, its
aspirations and illusions. In the topical films and newsreels, in the
buffooneries of the vulgar little comedies and farces, one catches
the very flavor of the period when dining rooms, to be elegant, had to
be furnished with Tudor reproductions, when the *art-nouveau* entrances to the Paris subway stations were erected, when automobiles first chugged along the highways and melodramas were all the
rage. It is not a full photographic likeness of the time, but the cross
references are unmistakable and not very flattering. An involuntary

gesture can sometimes tell us more than a whole volume of memoirs, and the films with their abrupt and unstudied imagery really reveal the age. When the history of manners of 1897–1905 comes to be written the historians must not neglect to refer to these documents, for the authentic *look* of the epoch is there.

In all those first years, Méliès stood apart. Very much a man of his time, he was greatly impressed by "the marvels of science." As the Jules Verne of the cinema, he stems from the same impulses as produced the Eiffel Tower, the switchback railway and the novels of H. G. Wells. His predilection for make-believe was his salvation. He saw clearly that the cinema is not vowed to honesty and mere representation, that it knows no compulsion to logic or probability and that, above all else, it is a machine for creating illusions. Stamped all over his work is the great law of the cinema, "Thou shalt deceive," and thus he invented an art and forged far ahead of his rivals.

He was one of the first to love his work genuinely, to realize its potential richness and greatness.

The art of cinematography [he wrote] calls for so much experiment, necessitates so many different kinds of activity and requires so much sustained attention that I do not hesitate to say in all sincerity that it is the most alluring and the most interesting of all the arts, for it makes use of virtually all of them; drawing, painting, the drama, sculpture, architecture, mechanics and manual labor of every sort are all called into play in pursuing this extraordinary profession.

It was only much later that some extraordinary results of this attitude of his were to be seen, and they were to appear in another land. Using quite different methods from his, the animated cartoon was later to reveal what absolute freedom the moving image enjoys. The laws that govern the elements, the law of gravity, even life and death itself were to be suspended in favor of Mickey Mouse when trickery again became the inspiration of the cinema. But that was far ahead. When the champion in *Million Dollar Legs* flashed fifteen times around the stadium at the speed of a motorcycle, when the trees in the garden shed their bark to reveal cautious spies, when the dictator's palace proved to be a positive nest of trap doors and false panels, who could fail to recognize in this film a younger brother of *An Impossible Voyage* and *The Merry Frolics of Satan?*

Even if it had not been destined to constitute the first tentative step toward an original development of the film, the work of Méliès would still have been valuable. It can be studied today only in sadly few examples. In 1914 Star-Films was already insolvent when the government commandeered its offices and studios for military uses. There were several hundred kilograms of film there, the product of twenty years of work. In order to remove them, money was needed both for transportation and for new storage room. Méliès had lost most of his customers, his affairs were in bad shape, all entertainments had momentarily been closed, and so he accepted an offer from a junk merchant, who melted his four hundred films down into a substance used in the manufacture of footwear. M. Mauclères, founder of Studio 28, has since unearthed a few reels in an attic. They are the best-known ones—*A Trip to the Moon, The Merry Frolics of Satan, The Conquest of the Pole,* and one or two others. Caroly, a well-known prestidigitator, owns a few others, and that is all that remains in France of the work of this pioneer. There is some consolation, however, in the knowledge that Star-Films had a New York branch which prospered not at all: Vitagraph bought it out in 1913. An almost complete collection of Méliès' films is now owned by a Mr. S. He will neither sell them nor show them, presumably believing that some day they may have a value.

In 1928 M. Druhot, of the *Ciné-Journal,* discovered Méliès selling candy and toys in a booth at the Gare Montparnasse. He was given a banquet and much lauded; he was even given some sort of decoration. Today he lives at Orly.[6] The Chambre Syndicale, which he founded and of which for ten years he was president, offered him quarters in its Home for the Aged there. One would imagine that something more might have been managed, in recognition of the role he played and of his own eminence as well as that which he conferred on the French film internationally. He was the only one of the first producers who did not make a fortune.

[6] Georges Méliès died after a short illness in January 1938.

D. W. Griffith

---

by Lewis Jacobs

The following three chapters are from Lewis Jacobs' excellent book The Rise of the American Film (Harcourt, Brace, New York, 1939). Words of praise for D. W. Griffith's work are unnecessary here. His position as one of the giants of film history is firmly established. Although in his lifetime he produced several hundred films, most of them one- and two-reelers, his influence on film makers throughout the world is based on such films as The Birth of a Nation, Intolerance and Broken Blossoms. It was from his use of close-ups, intercuts, visual manipulation of images to effect ideas, that the Russians developed their theories of montage, which were in turn to become the very foundation of artistic film making.

I
NEW DISCOVERIES

THE THIRD MAJOR figure in the rise of the American film,* David Wark Griffith, did not want to make motion pictures. No contradiction proved more ironic, for, in the entire history of the American screen, no other director achieved greater success, none won more esteem. This "enigmatic and somewhat tragic" figure, as

* The other two major figures discussed by Mr. Jacobs in previous chapters of his book are Georges Méliès and Edwin S. Porter.—D. T.

Gilbert Seldes describes him, secretly cherished the ambition to become famous as an author and counted the moments until he should have sufficient money to quit the "flickers" and write. Ashamed of "selling his soul," he changed his name on entering the movies, only later to retrieve it and make it as familiar as the term "movie" itself.

Griffith further developed the art of Méliès and Porter, contributing devices of his own that made for greater unity, clarity, and effectiveness. Sensing from the beginning the need for a body of technique to catch and control the emotions of the spectator, he did more to realize a method and a viewpoint than any other man of his day. Although he was himself a former actor and playwright, he repudiated theatrical conventions and evolved a method of expression peculiar to the screen.

Griffith came to films at that propitious moment when they were in the plastic beginnings of artistic development. To them he brought new elements of form and a variety of resources, and he added at least two great productions to American motion picture achievement. The most revered and influential movie creator of his day, and perhaps of all motion picture history, he justified the new medium to the world. His productions became models for directors wherever films were made and to this day stand not only as important achievements in themselves but as the source of central motion picture developments.

In temperament Griffith was a conventional product of his origins and upbringing. Born into an impoverished family in Kentucky in 1880, nicknamed "Sugar," he was inculcated in his earliest years with Southern prejudices, Victorian sentiments, and a local social viewpoint which he never outgrew. His father, a former Confederate colonel known as "Thunder Jake" because of his roaring voice, filled him with tales of Johnny Reb, the old chivalrous South, and Confederate bravery, subjects romantic enough to fire a boy less imaginative and emotional than Griffith. This grand mural of a departed glory was later to appear time and again in Griffith's one-reel cameos of plantation life, Civil War battle episodes, and vignettes of Southern chivalry, and finally to culminate in that powerful film of Secessionist bigotry, *The Birth of a Nation*.

The sentimental bias implanted in Griffith by his father was reinforced by the boy's love of poetry in the Victorian manner. His adolescent dallying with the works of Browning, Kingsley, Tennyson, and Hood was later to be recalled and readapted for the screen in such films as *The Taming of the Shrew, Sands of Dee, Enoch Arden* and *Song of the Shirt*. Griffith's romantic values and poetic ideals persisted even after the rest of the world had abandoned

them. Many of his films were saturated with the saccharine sentiments and homilies characteristic of *Godey's Lady's Book*. Even
when on occasion he took up the cause of justice, tolerance, and
sympathy for the downtrodden, he could not refrain from becoming maudlin. Whether as fictioneer or pamphleteer, Griffith was a
man of sentimentality. That accounts in part for his phenomenal
prewar success and his swift postwar eclipse.

Griffith's romanticism determined not only his choice of subject
matter but his choice of players. His persistence in casting mere
slips of girls, fifteen or sixteen years old, blond and wide-eyed,
was due as much to Southern ideals of femininity and his immersion
in Victorian poetry as to the camera, always absolute in its demands
for pulchritude. All his heroines—Mary Pickford, Mae Marsh, Lillian Gish, Blanche Sweet—were, at least in Griffith's eye, the pale,
helpless, delicate, slim-bodied heroines of the nineteenth-century
English poets.

But Griffith had a strong creative urge that could divert attention
from his weaknesses. This quality of his character was in evidence
long before he came to movies. Sent to work at an early age, he
was dissatisfied with his short experience as a dry-goods clerk and
bookstore salesman; he aspired to become a writer. At seventeen he
got a job as newspaper reporter on the Louisville *Courier*. Soon he
became ambitious to write plays, and, following the advice of a
friend who told him that all great playwrights had been actors, he
left home to join a traveling stock company.

During the next few years, while acting, Griffith wrote continually, sending out poems, plays, and short stories to various editors
and occasionally making a sale. Once, when both acting and writing
failed to give him a living and he was stranded in California, he
became a hop picker. This experience he immediately turned into a
drama of an itinerant laborer, called *A Fool and a Girl*, which in
October 1907 played for two weeks in Washington and Baltimore.
Lukewarm though the newspaper criticism was, it throws light on
the outlook in the play later to appear in his films:

. . . if one wants to tell the old and beautiful story of redemption of
either man or woman through love, it is not necessary to portray the
gutters from which they are redeemed.[1]

The little money and slight public recognition that the play gave
him made Griffith more than ever determined to win fame as a
writer. Some of his poems and short stories were published in *Les-*

1 Quoted by Mrs. D. W. Griffith, *When the Movies Were Young*, p. 26.

lie's Weekly, Collier's Weekly, Good Housekeeping, Cosmopolitan.
He finished another play called *War*, based on firsthand information
from soldiers' diaries and letters which he diligently studied at the
Forty-second Street Library in New York City. The play proved
to be unsalable, but years later its data were put to use in his screen
drama *America*.

His creativeness is testified to by his wife, who recorded that he
tried to make every minute in his life count. When he was not
acting or writing he was inventing things. With his restless temperament and experimental turn of mind, he would astonish his wife
time and again with ideas for "nonpuncturable" tires, schemes to
harness the energy of the sea, methods of canning cooked foods—inventions that he thought might make him suddenly rich. This flair
for attempting the impossible, or the improbable, later led him to
discover new methods and devices in film making, to thrust aside the
objections made by technical men and to open up new resources of
the film medium.

Original and profound as a craftsman, Griffith however was never
to outgrow his Southern sentiments and Victorian idealism. When
his creative genius was most vigorous, it could lift him from sentimentality to dignity and art; when he surrendered to his emotional
impulsiveness, his films became orgies of feeling. This accounts for
the incongruity between the discipline of his structure and the lack
of restraint in his sentiment that mars even the best of his works.

Griffith's screen career falls into three periods: development, maturity, and decline. His years at Biograph Company, which he began
with *The Adventures of Dolly* (1908) and continued through some
hundreds of films to *Judith of Bethulia* (1914), can be characterized
as his apprenticeship period. He was then alert and active, displaying
a critical and fertile mind. He not only learned all there was to
know about the technique of motion pictures, but added to the
existing technique a host of new elements. His quick intuition
discovered the camera as a dramatic tool and developed its devices as
integral properties of film language: the full shot, the medium shot,
the close-up, the pan shot, and the moving camera. In addition his
employment of such narrative transitions as the cut, the spot iris,
the mask, and the fade contributed importantly to the art of continuity in films. But even more important than such integral devices
was his contribution to editing: an awareness of tempo and the
device of parallel and intercutting, which greatly expanded and
enriched the internal structure of movie art.

It was in 1907, when out of work in New York City, that Griffith first learned of the opportunities in the movies. An actor friend,

Max Davidson, advised him to apply to the American Mutoscope and Biograph Company for work to tide him over during the slack spring and summer months. Griffith applied for employment and found that he could make $5 a day for acting and $10 to $15 for story suggestions. Working hard, he acted and wrote a number of Mutoscope films. Among these were *Old Isaacs the Pawnbroker*, a bitter diatribe against the amalgamated association of charities then being muckraked; *The Music Master*, strongly reminiscent of Belasco; *At the Crossroads of Life*; *The Stage Rustler*; and *Ostler Joe*. At this time he appeared also in several Edison pictures. But like other movie craftsmen of that day Griffith was ashamed of his occupation and attempted to conceal it from his friends.

Poet, playwright, actor, inventor—a more fitting background for a motion picture director would be hard to define. Yet when an opportunity came to direct, Griffith debated with his wife: "In one way it's very nice . . . but you know we can't go on forever and not tell our friends and relatives how we are earning our living."[2]

He argued with his employers: "Now if I take to this picture directing and fall down, then, you see, I'll be out of an acting job."[3]

The vice-president of Biograph, Henry Marvin, reassured him. "If you fall down as a director, you can have your acting job back."

With this promise to hearten him, Griffith accepted the assignment, continuing with the name he had taken for stage purposes, Lawrence Griffith. He had told his wife that his real name was David Wark but that he would use it only when he became famous.

His plan was to make enough money in movies to enable him to quit them and return to his real interest: writing. But Griffith never was to leave the movies. From June 1908, when he undertook to direct his first picture for Biograph, he was to remain in the field for more than twenty years. Commenced apathetically, almost unwillingly, his directorial career was to bring to him personal fame and fortune, and to the movies fresh respect and importance. Medium and master had at last discovered each other, although neither suspected it.

Griffith took his first directorial job, *The Adventures of Dolly*, seriously. Before going to work on it he asked Marvin to run off a few films for him to study. What he saw was not very impressive, and he left the projection room confident that he could do better.

His talent for innovation was revealed at once. Stopping a stranger on Broadway because he recognized in him the type he wanted, Griffith selected his first leading man off the street. His

2 *When the Movies Were Young*, p. 43.
3 *Ibid.*, p. 47.

intuition was later vindicated; the stranger, Arthur Johnson, became one of America's first screen idols. For the leading female role Griffith chose his wife, Linda Arvidson, who had been playing background bits; and for the role of a villainous gypsy he persuaded a stage actor, Charles Inslee, to play in the "flickers." Having selected his cast with more care than was customary, he went to work.

The film that began Griffith's career as director was 713 feet long, a naïve tale picturing "kind providence thwarting the gypsies' attempt to kidnap a child for revenge" (all films of the day had to point a moral lesson). A synopsis of *The Adventures of Dolly* in the Biograph press sheet[4] reveals its quaint story as typical of contemporary productions:

On the lawn of their country residence sport mamma, papa, and baby Dolly. Near them flows a picturesque stream where mamma and Dolly watch the boys fishing. A band of gypsies . . . whose real motive is pillage, offers mamma some goods for sale. Her refusal rouses the ire of the gypsy and he attempts to steal her purse. Papa is attracted by her screams and comes on the scene with a heavy snake whip, lashing out at the gypsy unmercifully, driving him away with revengeful venom in his gypsy heart.

Later the gypsy gets his chance and kidnaps Dolly. Hiding her in a water cask, [the gypsies] put it on their wagon and speed away. As they pass over a stream, the cask falls off the wagon and into the water, where it is carried by a strong current downstream, over a waterfall, through seething rapids, finally to enter the quiet cove of the first scene. Fishing boys hearing strange sounds from the cask break it open and discover Dolly. Soon she is safe in the arms of her overjoyed papa and mamma.

In discussing *The Adventures of Dolly* years later, Billy Bitzer, the cameraman, said, "He showed it to me and I told him it was too long. Too long! In the light of a completed scenario today, I can readily say that Griffith was years ahead of us."[5]

Novice though Griffith was, *The Adventures of Dolly* compared favorably with the Biograph productions by more experienced directors. The company must have liked the picture, for they quickly had him sign a contract at $45 a week and a royalty of one mill for every foot of film sold.

Feeling his way in the new medium, Griffith turned out five pictures in the next four weeks, each within a reel: *The Red Man and*

4 July 1908.
5 New York *Journal*, January 29, 1937.

the Child, The Stage Rustler, The Bandit's Waterloo, The Greaser's Gauntlet, The Man and the Woman. All were in the conventional style and showed no deviation from the form initiated by Porter. Whatever distinction they may have had was due to greater care in the selection of the casts and in execution, for Griffith insisted on rehearsing scenes before shooting them, a procedure then uncommon and considered a waste of time. Dubbed the "once again" idea, it was later to be taken up by others.

The experience of directing these pictures and learning the rudimentary principles aroused Griffith to an awareness of the movies' limitations. He saw the need for a means whereby action could be developed and emphasized, characterizations built, atmosphere evoked, the whole story expressed with more fluidity and variety.

But it was one thing to be aware of a need and another to fill it. Resolved to experiment with his next assignment, Griffith chose Jack London's *Just Meat,* changing its title to *For Love of Gold.*

The climax of the story was the scene in which the two thieves begin to distrust each other. Its effectiveness depended upon the audience's awareness of what was going on in the minds of both thieves. The only known way to indicate a player's thoughts was by double-exposure "dream balloons." This convention had grown out of two misconceptions: first, that the camera must always be fixed at a viewpoint corresponding to that of a spectator in a theater (the position now known as the long shot); the other, that a scene had to be played in its entirety before another was begun (this was a direct carry-over from the stage).

Griffith decided now upon a revolutionary step. He moved the camera closer to the actor, in what is now known as the full shot (a larger view of the actor), so that the audience could observe the actor's pantomime more closely. No one before had thought of changing the position of the camera in the middle of a scene. Simple as this solution appears now, it was daring then.

The innovation was portentous, for it introduced the exploitation of camera mobility and the custom of breaking up a scene into separate shots. Such new methods would further the movie on its own course and free it from its crippling reliance on the stage. A closer view of the actor would make extravagant gestures, thought necessary on the stage, unnecessary—not to say unnatural and ludicrous—in the movie. Realizing this wonderful advantage of the full shot, Griffith saw that henceforth the movie must be weaned from the stage and given independence for self-development.

Excited at the effectiveness of his experiment and what it foreshadowed, Griffith employed the full shot throughout the many

films he made in the next three months. Of these the most outstanding were *The Heart of Oyama, The Barbarian, Ingomar, The
Vaquero's Vow, Romance of a Jewess, Money-Mad*. Gradually the
full shot became a regular device in the director's yet limited
repertory.

The next logical step was to bring the camera still closer to the
actor in what is now called the close-up. With this in mind, in
November 1908 Griffith had Frank Woods, soon to become known
as the film's major critic, make a screen adaptation of Tennyson's
Enoch Arden. Biograph opposed the story on the ground that it had
neither action nor a chase, the two conventional requisites for all
films. But their arguments were unavailing. Griffith was aiming for
something which to him was more important than gross action: in
the quiet ballad he saw the chance to use his new device, the close-
up. His hunch, bringing a new concept into the technique of
editing, made movie history.

Not since Porter's *The Great Train Robbery*, some five years
before, had a close-up been seen in American films. Used then only
as a stunt (the outlaw was shown firing at the audience), the close-
up became in *Enoch Arden* the natural dramatic complement of the
long shot and full shot. Going further than he had ventured before,
in a scene showing Annie Lee brooding and waiting for her husband's return Griffith daringly used a large close-up of her face.

Everyone in the Biograph studio was shocked. "Show only the
head of a person? What will people say? It's against all rules of
movie making!" With such naïveté was the close-up greeted.

But Griffith had no time for arguments. He had another surprise,
even more radical, to offer. Immediately following the close-up of
Annie, he inserted a picture of the object of her thoughts—her
husband, cast away on a desert isle. This cutting from one scene to
another, without finishing either, brought a torrent of criticism
down upon the experimenter.

"It's jerky and distracting! How can you tell a story jumping
about like that? People won't know what it's all about!"

Griffith was ready for all dissenters.

"Doesn't Dickens write that way?"

"Yes, but writing is different."

"Not much. These stories are in pictures, that's all."

But Biograph was greatly worried. It rechristened the film *After
Many Years*, sent it out, and watched its reception closely. To the
company's surprise it was immediately singled out as a masterpiece
and proved to be among the first American films honored by foreign
markets as worthy of importation.

Griffith's instinct had been right. In the close-up he had made use of one of the most valuable attributes of the moving picture camera, and in "cutting" from Annie Lee to her husband thousands of miles away he had broken away from the rigid one-shot-per-scene continuity and disclosed a more fundamental method of film construction. Not only was the scene made up of several shots, but one scene followed another without waiting for it to end. Not connected by time, separated in space, the shots were unified in effect by the theme. Thus Griffith proved not only that the basis of film expression is editing but that the unit of editing is the shot, not the scene.

Before the year was over Griffith had introduced other radical innovations. Ever since movies had been made in studios, the use of electric light had been considered a necessary evil. A scene was always lit from above, and it was considered bad taste and amateurish to leave any portions of a scene shadowed. There was no regard for any possible tonal or dramatic value that lighting might provide. To his two cameramen, Marvin and Bitzer, Griffith complained of the haphazard and disastrous results of lighting. The cameramen did not know what could be done, since the raw film was both "slow" and "color blind"; very strong light was needed to make any image on the film emulsion. The clumsiness of the lighting devices themselves—mercury vapor lamps—complicated the problem.

Griffith deliberately chose a story that involved a problem in lighting, *The Drunkard's Reformation*. In one scene the actors were to be illuminated by a fireside glow. The cameramen protested that the film would not take an image if they followed Griffith's directions—or that the peculiar lighting would cast ugly shadows on the players' faces. But Griffith disdained all their objections, and Marvin and Bitzer photographed the scene under his direction. Projected the next day in the studio, the scene was greeted with a murmur of admiration, and the cameramen were perhaps the most surprised and approving of all. From then on lighting was regarded more seriously as a means of enhancing the dramatic effect of a film story.

Aiming above the obvious and absurd "chase" melodramas of the day, fighting repeatedly for the privilege of making films that would force the stage, the critics, and the discriminating public to approve of the young art, Griffith realized that pictures could become significant only if their content was significant. He therefore led a raid on the classics for his material. Before his first year as a movie director was ended, he had not only adapted works by Jack London and Tennyson but had boldly brought to the screen Shakespeare, Hood, Tolstoy, Poe, O. Henry, Reade, Maupassant, Stevenson, Browning. Among the hundred or so pictures of this first year were *The Taming of the Shrew*, *The Song of the Shirt*, *Resurrection*, *Edgar Allan Poe*, *The Cricket on the Hearth*, *The Necklace*, *Suicide Club*, and *The Lover's Tale*.

Griffith soon saw that acting must be more natural, less a matter of "artistical attitudes." He canvassed theatrical agencies for fresh talent which could adjust itself to a more realistic style. Since it was not easy to persuade better-grade actors to appear before the camera, he paid as high as $10 a day for the services of such professionals as Frank Powell (later famed as the director and discoverer of Theda Bara), James Kirkwood, and Henry Walthall, a triumvirate which became, under Griffith, America's earliest anonymous screen idols. When $10 did not prove to be enough to attract Broadway talent, Griffith raised the offer to $20. Pitifully small though this salary appears today, it was then ridiculously high. By the end of the year, however, Griffith's pictures were being pointed out for their "more natural" performances as well as for their better stories and originality.

The climax of his early efforts was the film he directed just about a year after he came to Biograph: *The Lonely Villa*. In this he extended the editing method initiated in *After Many Years* and added to his technique one of its unique and most effective devices: intercutting. The story of *The Lonely Villa*, in a last-minute rescue, offered a more complex development of the chase pattern. To thwart a robbery and save his wife and children, a husband rushes home in a race against time. Griffith built suspense by prolonging the situation, intercutting from the helpless family and the burglars to the speeding husband in ever shortening intervals. The effect of such back-and-forth movement was to prolong the suspense and create a mounting tension in the audience, as they experienced by turns the fears of the family and the anxiety of the husband. Their relief at the rescue was therefore all the more pronounced.

So effective was this intercutting that it was immediately taken up by other directors, who honored its discoverer by calling it the "Griffith last-minute rescue." (Technically the device became designated as "the crosscut," "the cutback," "the switchback.") It solved a major problem of storytelling in films. Heretofore, to depict two actions taking place simultaneously at different places, directors had resorted to the double-exposure "dream balloons"; or they had given up the attempt to present any such simultaneous action at all. Griffith's *After Many Years* had been a step toward freedom from such a rigid method. Now, cutting back and forth before a scene was completed solved the space problem and, moreover, brought in the element of time to aid the director.

Until now the duration of a shot had been determined by the time the action would take in real life. *The Lonely Villa* proved that the duration of a shot need not be dependent upon its natural action but could be shortened or lengthened to heighten its dramatic effect. This manipulation of the time element not only increased the story's effectiveness but enabled the director to give his shots pace and rhythm.

Having within one year accomplished important innovations in technique, extended the scope of movie content, and improved motion picture acting, Griffith was regarded with mounting admiration in Biograph and in the industry generally. Everyone at Biograph now hastened to carry out his directions, wondering what great new thing he was now evolving, glad to have a hand in it. Rival directors would slip into theaters to watch his pictures and then hurry back to their studios to imitate them. Audiences and critics as well were singling out pictures with the "AB" trade-mark, the only distinguishing insignia of Griffith's films (as yet no individual credits were being given). In *The Moving Picture World* of July 3, 1909, the high regard for Griffith's pictures is expressed:

The other afternoon when I sat in my accustomed seat at the Bijou Dream on 14th Street and the title of the Biograph subject, *The Way of a Man*, appeared on the screen, there was a sudden hush. . . . Now this picture held the attention of the audience right up to the very last foot of film because the Biograph Company have got down to the root idea of a moving picture. . . . Their photographs are not mere snap shots or rapidly taken groups of small parties of puppets moving about on the stage. No. They are active photographs of thinking men and women. . . . Now all of this is indicative of progress in the making of moving pictures, in which the Biograph Company prominently shines. It is clear as day that all the other manufacturers will also have to advance. . . . The photographer does his work to perfection. He puts his camera near the subjects and the lens and you see what is passing in the minds of the actors and actresses. The total combination is that you get as perfect a picture play from the Biograph studio as it is possible in the present stage of moving-picture making to get.

Signing his second contract with Biograph in August 1909, Griffith little realized that all he had achieved so far was only a preparation for what he was yet to do. From the outset his second year with Biograph was triumphant.

For months he had been trying to convince his employers to let him make a film based on Browning's poem *Pippa Passes*. But it was not until a month after his new contract was signed—a busy month in the pastoral atmosphere of Cuddebackville, New York, where he made two mementos to the Revolutionary era, *Hessian Renegades* and *Leather Stocking*—that permission was granted him to film *Pippa Passes*.

Production began in mid-September 1909. Griffith at once turned to experiments with lighting. No doubt the success of his lighting effects in *The Drunkard's Reformation* had motivated his desire to do *Pippa Passes*, for the latter presented a complex lighting problem. Divided into four parts, Morning, Noon, Evening, Night, the film involved a more organic and dramatic use of lighting than Griffith had yet attempted. To his staff Griffith explained the problem and the kind of lighting effects he wanted. Cameramen Bitzer and Marvin were once again dubious, but Griffith—neither cameraman nor mechanic in his own right—laid out the procedure they were to follow for the first sequence, Morning. In her book *When the Movies Were Young*[6] Mrs. Griffith records her husband's plan:

He figured on cutting a little rectangular place in the back wall of Pippa's room, about three feet by one, and arranging a sliding board to fit the aperture much like the cover of a box sliding in and out of grooves. The board was to be gradually lowered and beams of light from a powerful Klieg shining through would thus appear as the first rays of the rising sun striking the wall of the room. Other lights stationed outside Pippa's window would give the effect of soft morning light. Then the lights full up, the mercury tubes a-sizzling, the room fully lighted, the back wall would have become a regular back wall again, with no little hole in it.

Marvin, remembering Griffith's past successes, was half inclined to give the new lighting scheme a try. Bitzer was wholly skeptical. Griffith, expecting more enthusiasm, exclaimed, "Well, come on— let's do it anyhow. I don't give a damn what anybody thinks about it."

The cameramen followed his orders grudgingly.

During the projection of the rushes there was great tension: "At first the comments came in hushed and awed tones, and then when the showing was over, the little experiment in light effects was greeted with uncontrolled enthusiasm."[7]

6 P. 128.
7 *When the Movies Were Young*, p. 129.

This was another victory for Griffith's imagination. When *Pippa Passes* reached the public in October 1909, the New York *Times* of October 10 commented enthusiastically, *"Pippa Passes* is being given in the nickelodeons and Browning is being presented to the average motion picture audiences, who have received it with applause and are asking for more."

This unsolicited praise had an immediate effect upon Griffith. His earnest struggles to master the medium were being recognized and approved by the world at large. No approbation could have been more heartening, nor could it have appeared at a better moment. It marked the turning point in Griffith's attitude toward the movies. Formerly oppressed by the thought that the motion picture had little future and that his attempts to better it would never bring him renown as an artist or writer, he now felt that his endeavors must have some significance after all.

Griffith's new hopes, however, were not quite free from doubts. When he went to a stage play, his new optimism and deepening conviction about the future of movies would be dissipated. He would go home in a temper, his high resolves about movies shattered. Even the sweet success of *Pippa Passes* did not rid him of nostalgic yearnings to be an author. He would reproach himself for giving up the only thing he really cared about, and became embittered at his own inability to leave the movies. Finally he would console himself with the money he was making and the secret thought that when he became a famous author nobody would know that David W. Griffith, the author, was once Lawrence Griffith of the nickelodeons.

Griffith was never to free himself from the labor of movie making. The more money he made, the more he seemed to need. Before the end of his second year he was earning $900 to $1,000 a month in royalties alone, but he kept putting off his impulse to quit the business. The more he worked, the more obstacles he saw to be overcome and the more willing he became to accept their challenge. Mechanical crudities, the lack of good stories, untrained and inexperienced actors—these, and the prevalent unconcern for quality and good taste, made his prospects dismal, but he kept on. Perhaps he was more suited to the new medium than he cared to admit even to himself.

About this time California had become the mecca of the independent movie makers. Griffith, seeing the pictures made there, was impressed with the landscapes and pictorial possibilities the state offered. Upon investigation he learned that not only mountains and beaches but historic missions, tropical vegetation, and deserts were easily accessible. His love for the picturesque, his eye for the sweep

of scenery and his enthusiasm for "artistic" backgrounds urged him
to leave New York and go West. Weather conditions, moreover,
always a serious problem in the East, seemed better in California;
they would help him to meet his expanded production schedule.

In the winter of 1910 Griffith took his company of Biograph
players to California, and on the outskirts of Los Angeles he improvised a studio. Wanting for his initial production a theme that
would impress the Biograph office back in New York, he wrote a
religious story about the old San Gabriel Mission. This film, *The
Thread of Destiny*, proved notable for three reasons. It featured
Mary Pickford; it employed a new lighting effect that was both
"dim" and "religious"; and, most important, its editing demonstrated
conclusively that the shot is the basis of scene construction.

Griffith desired to imbue the film with as much of the mission
atmosphere as possible. He photographed the mission in great detail, with its weather-beaten walls, decorative interiors, stairways,
choir loft, and cemetery—shots which were not called for in the
plot but which, when carefully edited, created an atmosphere and
background that greatly reinforced the narrative and action of the
story. No one, not even Griffith himself, had as yet taken shots of
the various details of a setting to build a scene. Any shot which
did not present a major phase of the scene's action had always been
regarded as impeding, even intruding upon, the flow of the story;
it was "a waste of footage" in the usual one-reel film. Griffith's
realization that the details of a background could not only enhance a
scene's mood and strengthen its action, but could also be basic in a
scene's construction, was a daring step forward in the refinement of
movie technique.

It was now clear to Griffith that the director must use the camera
not only to take the total content of a scene, but to select details
within the scene that bear relations to the content of the film as a
whole. This meant that a shot need not be regulated and restricted
by an imaginary proscenium; freed from this spatial bondage, the
camera could be stationed at any point, according to the director's
desire to select details and angles of the content that would lend
strength to a scene's structure and intensify its interest. This liberty
to direct attention to a vital element of a scene, to vary time-and-
space relationships for the sake of emphasis or contrast, gave the
director a powerful means of stimulating the spectator's responses.
Griffith suddenly understood how the art of the movie director
differs from that of the stage director: in movie making, guiding
the camera, even more than directing the actor, is the trick.

Acceptance of this new principle meant that hereafter the screen story would have to be conceived from a new point of view. Griffith had hit upon a truth with implications that all motion picture directors since then have been trying to command. It is that the primary tools of the screen medium are the camera and the film rather than the actor; that the subject matter must be conceived in terms of the camera's eye and film cutting; that the unit of the film art is the shot; that manipulation of the shots builds the scene; that the continuity of scenes builds the sequences; and that the progression of sequences composes the totality of the production. Upon the composition of this interplay of shots, scenes, and sequences depends the clarity and vigor of the story. Here, Griffith saw, is the epitome of motion picture method.

Working under commercial pressure, producing pictures at a steady pace in California throughout the winter of 1910, Griffith strove to apply what he had divined about camera composition, lighting, shot details, scene construction, transitions, and other phases of film technique. He constantly tried, moreover, to weld these elements into a personal style. The pictures he turned out during this period were *The Converts, The Way of the World,* and *The Two Brothers,* utilizing the missions and topography of California; semihistorical pieces such as *In Old California, Love among the Roses, The Romance of the Western Hills;* and *Ramona,* romanticizing dons, señoritas, and Indians.

Ramona provoked the most public excitement. For the privilege of adapting it Griffith had paid $100, an extraordinary sum for a story in those days. Biograph issued a specially illustrated folder which declared proudly that *Ramona* was the most expensive picture ever made. In this film appeared what Griffith subsequently was to call "the extreme long shots." These were shots of vast, distant panoramas and were intended to emphasize the spaciousness of the scene as a dramatic foil to the close shots.

Ramona was followed by a series of film sermons told in the idiom of the day: *Gold Is Not All, Over Silent Paths, The Gold Seekers, Unexpected Help, A Rich Revenge, As It Is in Life,* and *The Unchanging Sea.* The last is remembered as the "first masterpiece" of Griffith's West Coast series.

Returning to New York in the spring, Griffith set himself to work so industriously that Biograph's president, Arthur Marvin, sighed, "He'll die working." Besides editing his Western-made pictures, Griffith kept up with a production schedule more ambitious than ever. *In the Season of Buds, A Child of the Ghetto, What the Daisy Said, The House with the Closed Shutters, The Sorrows of the Unfaithful, The Call to Arms,* and *The Usurer* led a colorful array of dramas too numerous to list. The hard-working director's activity was constantly spurred by the increased attention of the trade papers to his pictures. The growing demand of exhibitors for Biograph products and the new phenomenon of fan letters singling out Griffith's pictures for praise indicated his increasing ability to outshine his contemporaries.

In the summer of this year Griffith signed his third contract with Biograph. This contract stipulated the relatively high salary of $75 per week and one eighth of a cent per foot royalty on all films sold. What made this agreement significant for Griffith was not so much the raise, however, as the fact that in it he abandoned his pseudonym "Lawrence" and for the first time used his real name, David. At last he was wholeheartedly accepting his career. From now on he was to work under his own colors. Happy over his decision, he set his face toward future accomplishments.

In 1911, again in California, Griffith produced *The Last Drop of Water, Crossing the American Prairies in the Early Fifties, The Lonedale Operator, The White Rose of the Wilds,* and *The Battle of Elderberry Gulch,* the last being released under the shortened title *The Battle.* All these films were distinguished from the general run of contemporary pictures by their content, careful attention to detail, and freshness of treatment. But in these pictures Griffith was seeking to master something new: movement of the action. Without knowing it, all he had discovered thus far had been an approach to it. Now he set about deliberately to create it by all the means he knew, and in *The Lonedale Operator* he was most successful. This was the usual last-minute-rescue type of story, stemming from *The Lonely Villa.* A girl held captive in a train depot telegraphs her father and sweetheart, railroad men, for help, and they commandeer a train and speed to her rescue. In filming the scenes Griffith seized every opportunity for emphasizing movement. Not only was there action within the shot, but the camera itself moved—not as in a pan shot, but by being placed on the moving train. The cutting back and forth from the speeding train to the captive gave momentum to the whole. The fluency of action which Griffith achieved by these devices brought a new kinetic quality to the screen.

Now Griffith began to chafe under the arbitrary limitation of a picture to one reel. One reel was hardly adequate to unfold a complete story; the limitation hindered development, curtailed incidents, and proved a general barrier to the choice of deeper themes. If the movie was ever to become a vital medium, reasoned Griffith, its length would have to be increased. But just as Porter in 1903 had had to convince his doubting employers that the public would sit through a picture a full reel in length, Griffith now had to struggle with Biograph's reluctance to lengthening films to two reels.

Finally disregarding protests, he made a two-reel picture, another version of the story which had already proved successful in one reel, *Enoch Arden*. Biograph refused to release the film as a whole; it was sold in two parts. But the movie audiences, unsatisfied after viewing only one reel, forced exhibitors to obtain both reels and show them one after the other. Biograph in turn had to comply with the requests of the exhibitors, and so the two-reel film was introduced.

The American two-reeler appeared none too soon, for almost immediately afterward two-reelers from European studios appeared. Their reception by audiences was anxiously watched by American producers. So enthusiastic was it that by 1912 two- and even three-reelers were acknowledged by the trade as inevitable.

Now allowed to expand his stories whenever he felt that they demanded more length, early in 1912 Griffith made two films which, for size and content, were his most ambitious efforts up to that time. Unlike any of his previous pictures, the first of these, *Man's Genesis*, was produced by a definite aesthetic urge, not a commercial one. The seriousness of its theme, a "psychological study founded upon the Darwinian Theory of the Evolution of Man," indicated Griffith's lack of concern for so-called entertainment values and his desire to do something "worth while." Needless to say, his employers were strongly opposed to the undertaking.

The philosophical and scientific aspects of the theme were dramatized in the conflict between the intelligence of "Weak-hands" and the body of "Brute-force." In the struggle brain finally conquers brawn. Though the film seems naïve to us today, it was then considered very advanced. The picture turned out to be one of the most discussed films of the year, provoking Vachel Lindsay to declare in his book *The Art of the Moving Picture:*[8]

It is a Griffith masterpiece, and every actor does sound work. The audience, mechanical Americans, fond of crawling on their stomachs to tinker their automobiles, are eager over the evolution of the first weapon from a stick to a hammer. They are as full of curiosity as they could well be over the history of Langley or the Wright Brothers.

Griffith's intuitive choice of such a serious subject was proved sound, for it inspired deeper respect for the screen among those who had been wont to scoff.

[8] P. 10.

Encouraged by this response, Griffith next ventured an ambitious historical re-creation of Custer's last stand, called *The Massacre*. Like *Man's Genesis*, this film was to be more than another program picture. Griffith went far beyond his budget in the production, paying no attention to the pained protests from Biograph's Eastern offices; he was determined to turn out a film greater than any he had yet done. With its casts, costumes, and sets on an unprecedentedly lavish scale, with its "hundreds of cavalrymen and twice as many Indians," the production forced Griffith to reach a new high in his series of technical triumphs. The film abounded in mass scenes, detailed shots of close fighting, vast panoramic pan shots, all skillfully blended and given a rapid continuity in a manner that presaged his later style in *The Birth of a Nation*. *The Massacre* was, in a sense, America's first spectacle film; for Griffith it was the beginning of a new and profounder turn of his talents.

But before the picture was released the American film world was disconcerted by a sudden and unexpected influx of European pictures of such dimensions that everything which had preceded them faded into insignificance. These foreign pictures, three, four, and even five reels in length, elaborately produced, with classics for subject matter, and starring such world-famed figures as Sarah Bernhardt, Helen Gardner, Asta Nielsen, Madame Réjane, stirred America deeply. *Queen Elizabeth, Camille, Cleopatra, Gypsy Blood, Madame Sans Gêne*, in their length and power of conception dwarfed contemporary American productions. The American companies, particularly those in the motion picture patents-trust group, regarded the invasion with mixed feelings of contempt and jealousy. Trade papers uneasily exhorted American producers to oust the foreigners. The aloof legitimate theater itself turned a fearful eye upon these new threats of celluloid. But the climax came with the startling announcement that a young arcade and nickelodeon upstart, Adolph Zukor, had signed a contract to feature "Famous Plays," all to run the foolhardy length of four reels. The industry was aghast.

In the midst of this excitement Griffith's *The Massacre* was released. Much to Griffith's chagrin, it was overlooked. Other events of momentous meaning had caught the attention of the movie world; in some quarters the anxiety over the rising popularity of long features, the foreign productions, and Zukor's Famous Players verged on hysteria. Everyone was wondering and fearing what would happen next. Griffith himself wanted to return to New York to view the foreign "miracles," but Biograph's winter production schedule kept him in California.

Smarting with the realization that foreign producers had thrust
him into the background, Griffith set to work angrily on the production of what he called his masterpiece, *Mother Love*. His impatient disregard of time and money threw Biograph into a panic,
but he insisted on his way: this new film was to be his answer to
the European invaders. His entire personnel sensed his anxiety;
they worked like demons, hoping to make the production come up
to Griffith's expectations. But their industry was in vain. Like *The
Massacre*, *Mother Love* was scarcely acknowledged in the sweeping
course of events. Even before the picture was completed, word
reached Griffith of a new sensation, the Italian picture *Quo Vadis*,
by far the most elaborate and best motion picture made to date.
The news was a shock to Griffith; twice now, with staggering sud-
denness and finality, he had been outclassed.

His ambition reinforced by intense envy, Griffith now resolutely
planned a reprisal that would force the world to acknowledge his
supremacy. His new production would be of such dimensions as
the world had never seen. To prevent rumors of his vast undertaking from spreading to the rest of the industry, he took his company to the town of Chatsworth, miles from the Los Angeles picture center. Not unnaturally, everyone working with Griffith was
highly curious. What was he up to? Never before had he taken
so many shots or been so exacting; never before had there been so
much activity and so little known of its nature. He was rehearsing
scenes over and over again, photographing and rephotographing
unceasingly. How many pictures was he making, anyhow? What
had inspired his new meticulous firmness? What was he driving at?
Why was he so secretive? But to all questions Griffith maintained
an unbroken reserve. Bitterness and envy rankled deep in him. His
only concern was to achieve a triumph so outstanding that every
movie ever seen before would, in comparison, seem like trash.

Finally in 1913 the secret production was completed: the first
American four-reel picture, *Judith of Bethulia*. And once again the
coincidence of events interfered with Griffith's hopes for an overwhelming success. *Judith of Bethulia* was not released until almost
a year after its completion, when, ironically enough, Griffith had
already forgotten it in an undertaking of far greater consequence.

As it turned out, *Judith of Bethulia* became Griffith's Biograph
swan song. When it did appear in 1914, it proved to be an extravagant treatment of the Bible story rewritten by Thomas Bailey
Aldrich, and without question the ablest example of movie construction to date. Though it appeared too late to overshadow *Quo
Vadis*, it was a far better film. Even if Griffith had done nothing

further than *Judith of Bethulia*, he would still be considered a sensitive and outstanding craftsman. A comparison of the usual puny American film of 1913 with the opulent and vigorous *Judith of Bethulia* proves Griffith's stature conclusively.

The unusual form of *Judith of Bethulia*, modeled on the four-part pattern of Griffith's earlier *Pippa Passes*, presaged the form of Griffith's future masterpiece, *Intolerance*. The four movements were in counterpoint not unlike a musical composition; they reacted to each other simultaneously, and the combination produced a cumulative, powerful effect. The individual episodes had a tight internal structure. The imagery was not only lavish in detail but fresh in camera treatment and enhanced by expert cutting.

The picture was produced in a deliberate effort to surpass the splendors of the Italian spectacle *Quo Vadis*, which, in fact, Griffith himself had not seen. *Judith of Bethulia* was crammed with colorful mass scenes and tremendous sets in a style that was later to be embraced by other American directors, notably Cecil B. De Mille. Such episodes as the storming of the walls of Bethulia, the chariot charges, and the destruction of the Assyrians' camp by fire "outspectacled" any movie yet produced in America.

Satisfied with his completed achievement, Griffith returned to New York to learn that Biograph, now in a new and modern studio in the Bronx, had contracted with the theatrical firm of Klaw and Erlanger to film their successful stage plays after the policy introduced by Zukor. During Griffith's absence a new tempo had been felt in the industry; the air was full of exciting predictions that the stage and the screen were henceforth to work together. European features had made America conscious of her own movie and stage talent and had started a craze for stage names and plays. All the Eastern companies were negotiating for stage alliances.

Griffith was now notified by Biograph that, because of his reckless extravagance with *Judith of Bethulia*, he would in the future supervise production instead of direct. Angered at his employers, bitter at being misunderstood, envious of the acclaim given the foreign pictures, Griffith decided to leave Biograph. He saw in a new company, Majestic-Reliance (Mutual), the opportunity to carry out a fresh and a more elaborate artistic offensive.

After getting his bearings and studying the foreign pictures for a time, he dramatically announced his break with Biograph. The announcement, listing all his technical discoveries, appeared as a full-page advertisement in *The New York Dramatic Mirror* for December 3, 1913. On October 29 the trade papers had already broken the news that Griffith was henceforth to be with Mutual Movies, and they had heralded a new era for the "Belasco of the Screen." The advertisement in *The New York Dramatic Mirror* confirmed what in October had been thought to be a mere rumor.

Asked at this time by Robert Grau, film and theater critic, whether he thought a knowledge of stagecraft was necessary to a command of motion picture direction, Griffith replied:

"No, I do not. . . . The stage is a development of centuries, based on certain fixed conditions and within prescribed limits. It is needless to point out what these are. The moving picture, although a growth of only a few years, is boundless in its scope and endless in its possibilities. . . . The conditions of the two arts being so different, it follows that the requirements are equally dissimilar. . . ."[9]

Griffith perceived what so many producers have since often forgotten: in the theater, the audience listens first and then watches; in the movie palace the audience watches first and then listens.

"The task I'm trying to achieve," said Griffith, "is above all to make you see."

Griffith's apprenticeship had ended. Only five years ago he had entered the industry, skeptical and even contemptuous of it; now he was America's ablest film craftsman. He stood sure of himself, eager for new achievements and a still higher reputation in the industry to which he had already made such remarkable contributions.

II

THE BIRTH OF A NATION
AND INTOLERANCE

The second period (1914–1917) of D. W. Griffith's career saw the production of his two greatest films, *The Birth of a Nation* and *Intolerance*. High points in the history of the American movie, these two pictures far surpassed other native films in structure, imaginative power, and depth of content, and they marked Griffith's peak as a creative artist. They foreshadowed the best that was to come in cinema technique, earned for the screen its right to the status of an art, and demonstrated with finality that the movie was one of the most potent social agencies in America.

Neither *The Birth of a Nation* nor *Intolerance* was an accident —a "lucky fluke" of directorial frenzy; both were the consummation of five years of intensive movie making. Griffith's Biograph apprenticeship is replete with presages of these two compositions. Ingenious organizational devices, startling compositional sketches, sentimental cameos, and high-powered episodes, which time and again had appeared in his hundreds of Biograph miniatures, reappeared in these two works with superlative effects. Without his experimental years at Biograph it is doubtful whether Griffith could have made at this time two such profound and triumphant films.

After leaving Biograph, Griffith produced for his new employers,

[9] *The Theatre of Science,* p. 86.

Mutual, four films in quick succession, none of which particularly interested him: *Home Sweet Home, The Escape, The Avenging Conscience (The Tell-Tale Heart)*, and *The Battle of the Sexes*. Griffith was getting $1,000 a week salary, and he did these minor pictures rapidly to accumulate money—this time not so that he could quit film making, but so that he could make bigger and better films than any he had yet done. The specter of the European film successes still tormented him. He had been constantly on the lookout for a subject that would lend itself to a spectacular use of his talents and would put him ahead of his foreign rivals. But he did not yet have more than a vague sense of what he wanted.

Discussing his needs with Frank Woods, the former film critic who had become a leading scenario writer through Griffith's encouragement, Griffith learned of Thomas Dixon's successful dramatization of his novel *The Clansman*. Woods rhapsodized over the novel's motion picture possibilities. He had already written a scenario of *The Clansman* for Kinemacolor Corporation, which had begun but was unable to finish the production. Griffith was naturally excited by the appeal of such a theme—the South and the Civil War—and the opportunity it offered for his particular talents. *The Clansman* seemed to fit his enlarged ambitions perfectly; so he bought the film rights.

In planning the story, Griffith added material from another Dixon book, *The Leopard's Spots*, and supplemented it with his own recollections of his father's reminiscences. The story he finally evolved was more extensive than any he had yet attempted. It covered the years immediately before the Civil War, the war itself, and part of the Reconstruction period. Griffith called it *The Clansman*.

Griffith now began production on a vast scale. Big though the undertaking was, it was still the creation of one mind. Like Georges Méliès before him, but with plans magnified a thousandfold, Griffith shouldered not only the responsibility of production but all the incidental business and financial obligations as well. Before he shot his first scene he put his company through six weeks of grueling rehearsals; then followed nine more weeks of painstaking shooting. An entire county is said to have been rented for the photographing of the rides and battle scenes. Unexpected difficulties developed when Griffith tried to get horses, which were urgently required in the war in Europe. Thousands of yards of cotton sheets had to be put on the "Clansmen," and this material too was a war scarcity. Whole communities were combed for white goods. But one of the heaviest burdens was the feeding, paying, and management of the hundreds of extras.

The making of the picture was marked by an unceasing struggle for money, an unbroken series of desperate financial difficulties and day-to-day borrowings. Everything Griffith possessed—his reputation, his personal fortune, whatever money he could raise from his friends—was poured into his gigantic enterprise. Besieged by mounting debts, hounded by creditors, discouraged by associates, he pushed the production to completion. According to his cameraman, Bitzer, he remained calm throughout, kept his troubles to himself, and moved steadily forward, filled with a creative urge that had to run its course regardless of time, personalities, debts, and other restraints or obstacles.

To the wonder of everyone, Griffith proceeded with his costly venture without a "shooting script." He had combined, condensed, and charted the material in his mind without the use of a written continuity. Even the details for the settings, costumes, properties, and specific scene actions were not written down. Carrying the general plan in his mind, he depended largely upon the intuition of the moment for specific action, and improvised freely as he went along. Lillian Gish, who played the heroine, revealed years later how Griffith quickly took advantage of every dramatic opportunity he saw and how he shaped his material as he went. Said Miss Gish:

At first I was not cast to play in *The Clansman*. My sister and I had been the last to join the company and we naturally supposed . . . that the main assignments would go to the older members. But one day while we were rehearsing the scene where the colored man picks up the Northern girl gorilla-fashion, my hair, which was very blond, fell far below my waist and Griffith, seeing the contrast in the two figures, assigned me to play Elsie Stoneman (who was to have been Mae Marsh).[1]

Such impulsive decisions were typical of Griffith. His method of work was in direct opposition to the careful planning of a director like Thomas Ince, who worked from minutely detailed shooting scripts. Griffith's reliance upon his instincts in shooting for continuity often explains the absurdities that sometimes crop up in his films. As Dwight Macdonald remarked, Griffith was

a practical genius who can make things work but who is not interested in "theory," i.e., the general laws that govern his achievements . . . his fitful talent throwing off the wretchedest as well as the most inspired productions. He grew up unaware of his own powers . . . guided only by his extraordinary flair for the cinema.[2]

[1] *Stage*, January 1937.
[2] *The Symposium*, April and July 1933.

Finally completed in February 1915, the production was the longest American film yet made, twelve reels—"a frightful waste and audacious monstrosity." The conservative coterie of film producers refused to handle its distribution, and Griffith was forced to form his own distribution outlets. In a letter supposed to have been written by William De Mille to Samuel Goldwyn on February 10, 1915, one can clearly sense the shortsightedness and narrow attitude of the industry generally:

I also heard rumors that the film cost nearly a hundred thousand dollars! This means, of course, that even though it is a hit, which it probably will be, it cannot possibly make any money. It would have to gross over a quarter of a million for Griffith to get his cost back and, as you know, that just isn't being done. Remember how sore Biograph was with Griffith when he made *Judith of Bethulia* and how much money that lost even though it was only a four-reeler? So I suppose you're right when you say there is no advantage in leading if the cost of leadership makes commercial success impossible. *The Clansman* certainly establishes Griffith as a leader and it does seem too bad that such a magnificent effort is doomed to financial failure.[3]

When we think of the great fortune the film reaped, such remarks seem ironic indeed.

The first American picture to get a two-dollar top admission, *The Birth of a Nation* enjoyed such enduring popularity that its total earnings make it one of the greatest money-makers in the history of the American screen.

The picture was first exhibited at Clune's Auditorium in Los Angeles on February 8, 1915, under the title of the book, *The Clansman*. On February 20 a print was run off in New York for the censors and a specially invited group. At this showing Thomas Dixon, the author of the original book, became so excited that during the applause he shouted to Griffith that the title *The Clansman* was too tame for so powerful a film, that it should be renamed *The Birth of a Nation*. This became the famous picture's title.

From the moment of its public opening on March 3, 1915, at the Liberty Theater in New York, *The Birth of a Nation* won phenomenal success. It was the first film to be honored by a showing at the White House. President Woodrow Wilson is said to have remarked, "It is like writing history with lightning." Critics, greeting the picture with boundless enthusiasm, called it "a new milestone in film artistry, astonishing even the most sanguine by its success, and

3 *Stage*, December 1937.

inspiring the most dramatic new departure in dissipating the supremacy of the theater."[4] *Variety* excitedly headlined its front page with "Griffith's $2 Feature Film Sensation of M. P. Trade," going on to say that "daily newspaper reviewers pronounced it the last word in picture making. . . . Mr. Griffith has set such a pace, it will be a long time before one will come along that can top him in point of production, action, photography, and direction," and concluding its lengthy panegyric with the pronouncement, "This picture is a great epoch in picture-making, great for the name and fame of D. W. Griffith and great for pictures."[5]

This great picture reviewed the Civil War, the despoiling of the South, and the revival of the South's honor through the efforts of the Ku Klux Klan. After a short introduction which showed the bringing of slaves to America and summarized the abolitionist movement, the story proper began with Phil and Tod Stoneman, of Pennsylvania, visiting their boarding-school chums, the Cameron boys, at Piedmont, South Carolina. Phil Stoneman falls in love with Margaret Cameron, while Ben Cameron becomes enamored of the daguerreotype of Phil's sister, Elsie Stoneman. Then the Civil War breaks out. Phil and Tod leave to fight for the Union, while Ben and his two brothers join the Confederate Army. During the ensuing war years the two younger Cameron boys and Tod are killed; Piedmont undergoes "ruin, devastation, rapine and pillage." Ben, the "Little Colonel," is wounded and becomes the prisoner of Captain Phil Stoneman. Nursed by Elsie Stoneman, Ben finally recovers. Elsie and his mother visit Lincoln, "the Great Heart," and win Ben's release.

The father of Elsie and Phil Stoneman is a leader in Congress; he agitates for the punishment of the South. Lincoln refuses to countenance revenge, but Stoneman persists with his plans and grooms the mulatto, Silas Lynch, to become a "leader of his people." After the surrender at Appomattox and the assassination of Abraham Lincoln, Stoneman swiftly gains power. With Elsie and Phil he goes to the South to carry out his "equality" program for the Negroes. He rents a house next door to the Camerons'. Elsie and Ben now become engaged, but Margaret cannot bring herself to accept Phil.

Meanwhile the Reconstruction period has started.

The reign of the carpet-baggers begins. The "Union League," so-called, wins the ensuing State election. Silas Lynch, the mulatto, is chosen Lieutenant-Governor. A legislature, with carpet-bag and Negro mem-

[4] *Variety*, March 12, 1915.
[5] *Ibid.*

bers in overwhelming majority, loots the state. Lawlessness runs riot. Whites are elbowed off the streets, overawed at the polls, and often despoiled of their possessions.[6]

The organization of the "invisible empire" of Clansmen is thus inspired and justified. Ben Cameron becomes their leader, and when Stoneman learns of it he forces Elsie to break her engagement to Ben.

Events rapidly arouse the ire of the Clan and fill Ben with a desire for vengeance. The Camerons' Negro servant, Gus, becomes a militiaman and joins Lynch's mob. When Gus makes advances to Flora, Ben's younger sister, she flees from him through the woods until, in despair, she hurls herself over a cliff. There Ben discovers her, dying.

Later Dr. Cameron is arrested for harboring the Clansman. Phil, desperate on seeing to what lengths the carpetbaggers are going, helps to rescue the doctor. With Mrs. Cameron, Margaret, and the faithful servants, Phil and the doctor find refuge in a log cabin. Here they attempt to fight off an attack by the Negro militia. Meanwhile Lynch, to whom Elsie Stoneman has come pleading that he save Phil and the Camerons, demands that she marry him, and he confronts her father with the proposal.

The climax comes when the Clansmen, headed by Ben, arrive in the nick of time to mow down the Negro militia, take the Lynch mansion, free Elsie and the Stonemans, kill Gus, and save the Camerons in the cabin just as they are about to be massacred. Thus the Ku Klux Klan heroically dispenses "justice." A double honeymoon, symbolic of the reunion of North and South, concludes the story. An epilogue rejoices that peace reigns once again:

> The establishment of the South in its rightful place is the birth of a new nation. . . . The new nation, the real United States, as the years glided by, turned away forever from the blood-lust of War and anticipated with hope the world-millennium in which a brotherhood of love should bind all the nations.

The film was a passionate and persuasive avowal of the inferiority of the Negro. In viewpoint it was, surely, narrow and prejudiced. Griffith's Southern upbringing made him completely sympathetic toward Dixon's exaggerated ideas, and the fire of his convictions gave the film rude strength. At one point in the picture a title

[6] From the special program notes given out at the initial Liberty Theater performance.

bluntly editorialized that the South must be made "safe" for the whites. The entire portrayal of the Reconstruction days showed the Negro, when freed from white domination, as arrogant, lustful, villainous. Negro Congressmen were pictured drinking heavily, coarsely reclining in Congress with bare feet upon their desks, lustfully ogling the white women in the balcony. Gus, the Negro servant, is depicted as a renegade when he joins the emancipated Negroes. His advances to Flora, and Lynch's proposal to Elsie Stoneman, are overdrawn to make the Negro appear obnoxious and audacious. The Negro servants who remain with the Camerons, on the other hand, are treated with patronizing regard for their faithfulness. The necessity of the separation of Negro from white, with the white as the ruler, is passionately maintained throughout the film.

The social implications of this celebrated picture aroused a storm of protest above the Mason and Dixon line. Negroes and whites united in attacking the picture because of its extreme bias. In Boston and other "abolitionist" cities race riots broke out. The Boston branch of the National Association for the Advancement of Colored People issued a pamphlet against the film. President Charles E. Eliot of Harvard charged the movie "with a tendency to perversion of white ideals,"[7] Oswald Garrison Villard condemned it as "a deliberate attempt to humiliate ten million American citizens,"[8] and Jane Addams was "painfully exercised over the exhibition."[9] Local politicians and officeholders jumped into the arena, choosing the side that offered the most votes.

In response to widespread attacks, Griffith himself became an outraged pamphleteer and published at his own expense *The Rise and Fall of Free Speech in America*. Its text contained extracts from editorials in various periodicals—*The Saturday Evening Post*, the Chicago *Tribune*, and the Boston *Transcript*, to mention three—upholding the right of *The Birth of a Nation* to freedom of the screen. He campaigned for "the freedom of the screen," issuing statements, making speeches, and writing letters to proclaim the "fundamental rights of expression" which he held to be self-evident. He must have realized, however, the wanton injury he had done to a race, for in a subsequent picture he attempted to atone for it by showing a white soldier kissing his wounded Negro comrade. Though heartfelt, such a sentimental concession could do little to compensate for the harm done by his prejudice in *The Birth of a Nation*.

[7] *A Million and One Nights*, Terry Ramsaye, p. 643.
[8] *Ibid.*
[9] *Ibid.*

The raging controversy awakened the nation to the social import
of moving pictures. But this realization was overshadowed by the
great acclaim for the picture's artistry, its rich imagery and powerful construction. So advanced was the film structurally that even today it stands as an accomplishment of great stature. All Griffith's
earlier experiments are here consolidated: the use of camera to build
scenes, the pacing of shots, the sensitive manipulation of camera
devices for transitions, simultaneous action, movement of all kinds—
all fused by brilliant cutting. The chief difference between this film
and Griffith's past efforts lies in the intensity and scale of the application of the cinematic elements. Griffith's conception had ripened;
an unerring command of the medium was now his.

The Birth of a Nation pulsates; it is life itself. From the very
beginning, shots are merged into a flux. Either the actions within
the shots have some kind of movement or the duration of shots is
so timed that the effect is one of continuous motion. This motion
creates a "beat" which accents the relationships of the separate elements of the film and produces a single powerful effect.

In the Petersburg sequences, the undercurrent of movement has
remarkable variety partly because of the nature of the raw material,
and it is marked by extensive and resourceful uses of cinematic principles. The passages that reach a climax in the battle itself, being
basically all action, are broken down by Griffith into juxtaposed
scenes of long, medium, close, and detail shots, varied in duration
and so contrasting in imagery that they re-create in the spectator the
excitement of the battle itself. In the hand-to-hand fighting, a group
of soldiers swarming across the left side of the screen are followed
by a group crossing at the right, so that the feeling of conflict is
intensified. Often the contrast of numbers is brought into play: shots
of individual soldiers are opposed to shots of many soldiers. There
is also opposition of space relationships, as in scenes in which an
extreme long shot is followed by an extreme close shot. Finally there
is the expressive opposition of a still shot of a dead body to the
moving shot of a soldier clambering up the ramparts to place a waving flag in position. Throughout this entire section of the film Griffith ingeniously employed these structural and dramatic oppositions,
giving the picture a dynamic quality that carried the spectator away
by its sheer sweep.

The Reconstruction sequences, starting with the struggle between
the defeated Southerners (the impoverishment of the Camerons is
significantly stressed) and the emancipated Negroes (made to appear vulgar, ostentatious, and arrogant), rises to a masterly climax in
the ride of the Clansmen. Here the tension is heightened by staccato

cutting. The dramatic power is enhanced by night photography, acute-angle shots, extreme long and close shots, sweeping pans, and moving-camera shots. The movement of the whole has a fast and uneven tempo emphasizing the excitement.

Typical of Griffith's vigorous style is the beginning of the "Grim Reaping" episode in the Reconstruction section. In the following excerpt from the script, made from the film by Theodore Huff of the Museum of Modern Art Film Library, can be seen Griffith's brilliant use of intercutting to relate simultaneous action and thus produce high tension:

Shot No.			Footage
1107	Full Shot	Lynch has Elsie Stoneman alone in his office. Lynch turns to her, raises his two hands.	2 feet
	Title	"See! My people fill the streets. With them I will build a black empire and you as a queen shall sit by my side."	10½ feet
1108	Full Shot	Lynch raises his arms in the air. Elsie sinks on chair. Lynch kneels, kisses the hem of her dress. She draws away in horror—rises—staggers to door, turning about. Lynch follows—sits at left. Elsie pounds on door.	21 feet
1109	Semi-Close-up	(Circle vignette) Lynch leaning back in chair—smiles—indicates his people outside.	7 feet
1110	(As 1108)	Elsie begs him—pleads with hands outstretched to let her go.	6½ feet
1111	(As 1109)	Lynch smiles at her.	2 feet, 13 frames
1112	(As 1110)	Elsie turns away—screams.	3 feet
1113	Long Shot	By the barn. Two Clansmen on horses come from right.	5½ feet
1114	Fade-in	Open country. Another Clansman dashes back.	7½ feet
	Title	"Summoning the Clans."	3 feet
1115	Semi-Close-up	Two Clansmen by the barn—one holding up the fiery cross—the other blowing a whistle.	3 feet
1116	(As 1113) Long Shot	By the barn. They ride forward.	6½ feet

Shot No.			Footage
1117	Fade-in (As 1114)	Open country. Clansman calling—comes forward.	7½ feet
1118	Iris-in (As 1116) Long Shot	By the barn. Five more Clansmen (having heard signal) come forward from barn.	8 feet
1119	¾ Shot	Lynch and Elsie. She rushes to window, left. Lynch after her—she pulls away—he shouts at her. Elsie sees it is no use—his people are outside.	9½ feet
1120	Medium Long Shot	Woods. Two Clansmen with a signal dash forward.	5 feet
1121	(As 1119)	Lynch and Elsie. Lynch pounds his chest with fist, boastingly.	3½ feet
1122	Fade-in Long Shot	Stream of water. Two Clansmen dash up stream. Fade-out.	9 feet
1123	(As 1121)	Lynch and Elsie. Lynch arrogantly points to window.	1 foot, 12 frames
1124	¾ Shot	Inner room. Man and woman listening, furtively.	1 foot, 12 frames
1125	(Back to 1123)	Lynch and Elsie. Lynch calls—Elsie is horrified.	1 foot, 1 frame
1126	(As 1124)	Inner room. Man at door hears Lynch's call.	2 feet, 13 frames
1127	Semi-Close-up	(Circle vignette) Door man—he enters Lynch's office.	1 foot, 12 frames
1128	¾ Shot	Office—different angle. Man comes to Lynch. Elsie rises.	3 feet
	Title	"Lynch, drunk with power, orders his henchman to hurry preparations for a forced marriage."	7½ feet
1129	(As 1128)	Office. Man goes. Lynch turns to Elsie —her hand over her mouth, shocked.	3 feet
1130	(As 1127)	(Circle vignette—door) Henchman rushes to carry out Lynch's order.	14 frames
1131	(As 1126)	Inner room. Henchman calls subordinate—sends him out, right.	10 feet
1132	(As 1125)	Elsie and Lynch. Elsie looks frantically about—rushes forward to door, left.	5½ feet

Shot No.			Footage	
1133	¾ Shot	(Circle vignette—door) Elsie speeds to it.	2 1	feet, frame
1134	(As 1132)	Elsie and Lynch. Lynch shouts to her to come back.	2	feet
1135	(As 1133)	(Circle vignette—door) Elsie tries to open door, can't, turns terrified.	1 11	foot, frames
1136	Fade-in Long Shot	Stream. A large group of Clansmen dash forward across shallow stream.	6	feet
1137	(As 1134)	Elsie and Lynch. Lynch calls Elsie back.	1 11	foot, frames
1138	(As 1135)	(Circle vignette—door) Elsie comes forward, terrified.	3½	feet
1139	(As 1137)	Elsie comes forward slowly.	4	feet
1140	Long Shot	Crossroads. Two Clansmen stop— give signal, dash on.	8	feet
1141	(As 1139)	Elsie and Lynch. Elsie pushes him away—rushes back to rear door—he after her—she escapes—comes forward around chairs—he chases her.	8	feet
1142	Fade-in Long Shot	Army of Clansmen lined up and form- ing—Ben in background.	7½	feet
1143	Semi- Close-up	(Circle vignette) Ben on horse—sur- veys army (mask off).	4	feet
1144	(As 1140)	Crossroads. Several more Clansmen come.	5½	feet
1145	Fade-in Long Shot	Field. Joining the army, Ben salutes.	6	feet
1146	Long Shot	Silhouette of hill. Horsemen (tiny specks) riding along ridge.	5	feet
1147	Medium Long Shot	Stream and cornfield. Two signal riders dash along.	3	feet
1148	Medium Shot	(Moving) Two signal riders (camera on car precedes them).	13	feet
1149	(As 1141)	Lynch and Elsie. Elsie rises from chair —she tries to get back.	5	feet
1150	Medium Shot	Street outside Lynch's office. Horse and wagons come, followed by Ne- groes, etc. Two men on horses enter, also.	10	feet

Shot No.			Footage	
1151	(As 1141)	Lynch and Elsie. Elsie falls back in faint—Lynch supports her.	3½	feet
1152	Medium Shot	Entrance to Lynch's office. Horse and carriage stop before it—crowd around cheering.	7	feet
1153	(As 1151)	Lynch, holding Elsie, hears—	2	feet
1154	¾ Shot	A carriage. Stoneman steps out.	4	feet
1155	Medium Shot	Stoneman goes on porch through cheering crowds.	3	feet
1156	(As 1153)	Lynch and Elsie. Lynch draws Elsie closer to him.	2 11	feet, frames
1157	¾ Shot	Hall. Stoneman comes—knocks.	1 15	foot, frames
1158	(As 1156)	Lynch hears—turns to Elsie.	2 3	feet, frames
1159	(As 1157)	Stoneman is impatient—asks guard the trouble—guard doesn't know.	6	feet
1160	(As 1158)	Lynch wonders what to do.	2 12	feet, frames
1161	(As 1159)	Hall. Stoneman impatient—paces— pounds cane—asks reason for delay.	12½	feet
1162	(As 1160)	Lynch and Elsie. Lynch carries Elsie forward.	6	feet
1163	¾ Shot	Inner dining room. Lynch brings her forward (unconscious, hair streaming)—sets her in chair, left. Orderlies instructed to guard her.	10	feet
1164	(As 1151)	Stoneman starts away.	2 10	feet, frames
1165	(As 1163)	Inner dining room. Lynch leaves— crosses room.	4	feet
1166	¾ Shot	Office. Lynch goes to outside door— unlocks it.	3½	feet
1167	(As 1161)	Hall. Stoneman hears—turns back—is admitted.	5½	feet
1168	(As 1166)	Office. Lynch and Stoneman come forward — Lynch apologizes — Stoneman gives him paper.	4	feet
1169	Long Shot	Clansmen forming in field. More going—Ben waves.	7½	feet

Shot No.			Footage
1170	(As 1168)	Office. Stoneman starts back. Lynch stops him.	5 feet
	Title	"I want to marry a white woman."	5 feet
1171	(As 1170)	Stoneman pats him on shoulder—"Sure, go right ahead"—shakes hands —smiles.	5 feet
	Title	"The Clans, being assembled in full strength, ride off on their appointed mission."	8 feet
1172	*Fade-in* *Long Shot*	Field. Several hundred Clansmen come forward (horses rearing) to Ben, who salutes them. He rides off—motions to others—they follow with banners and fiery crosses in clouds of dust.	28 feet
	Title	"And meanwhile other fates—"	4 feet

The conception in 1915 of such a remarkable cutting sequence, marked by significantly few titles, demonstrated an unusual mastery of the movie medium. As can be seen from the footage of the shots, they are trimmed down so that only one essential fact is given each time. The effect builds up shot by shot, and the suspense increases, in a manner which the great Russian directors were later to develop with amazing skill. There is, furthermore, an extraordinary audacity displayed in the cutting from one scene to another without allowing either to terminate and from one episode to another so that the threads of meaning are cunningly interwoven. The tension that develops in the spectator is not relieved until Griffith resolves both episodes. This "constant shifting of scenes" is the essence of filmic technique. Henry MacMahon was one of the first to realize Griffith's accomplishment and succinctly pointed out in the New York *Times*, June 6, 1915:

Every little series of pictures, continuing from four to fifteen seconds, symbolizes a sentiment, a passion, or an emotion. Each successive series, similar yet different, carries the emotion to the next higher power, till at last, when both of the parallel emotions have attained the nth power, so to speak, they meet in the final swift shock of victory and defeat.

Many other episodes could be cited to prove the excellence of the film's structure. Of the rioting of the Negroes in the streets, for

example, Vachel Lindsay in 1915 said, "Splendidly handled, tossing
wildly and rhythmically like the sea."[10] A typically striking use of
the "switchback" occurs in the episode of Phil's proposal to Margaret. We see a medium shot of Margaret considering the offer; then
the film flashes back to scenes of her brothers being killed by North-
erners. The following close shot of Margaret refusing her suitor is
thus made forceful to the spectator without use of words, titles, or
pantomime. Again, the three-cornered chase involving Flora, Gus,
and Ben in the woods is filled with fearful suspense through cumulative editing: the contrast of extreme long and close shots and
Flora's zigzagging course convey to the audience the desperation of
Flora in her wild, headlong run.

These impressive devices are supplemented by another celebrated
one: the iris, strikingly used in the sequence of Sherman's march
to the sea and the burning of Atlanta. In the upper left-hand corner
of a black screen, a small iris discloses the pitiful detail of a mother
and three children huddled together. Gradually the iris opens to
reveal more of the scene, and when it is fully opened we see the
reason for the misery of these figures: in the valley below an army
of Northern invaders is marching through the town the woman has
just fled. The scene is startling in its implications; the dramatic effect
is far more gripping than it would have been if, through mere cutting, the shot of the army had been placed to follow the shot of the
mother and children. The iris functioned not only as a dramatic
means of presenting an action and its cause, but as a transitional
device to frame the sequence. A daring and masterly use of the
camera for a psychological effect, it shows Griffith's precise sensitivity to the dramatic possibilities of the medium.

Besides having such prime technical devices, *The Birth of a
Nation* was one of the first films to make much use of symbolism.
Suitable objects and animals were introduced to heighten a mood,
sharpen an inference, or delineate a character. In an ecstasy of emotion, Elsie (Lillian Gish) embraces a mahogany bedpost. (Years
later Greta Garbo as Queen Christina, after being closeted with her
lover for three days, plays the scene similarly.) Lynch, the villainous mulatto, is shown mistreating an animal. The "Little Colonel" is
shown fondling small birds (a symbol taken over notably by Von
Stroheim in *Greed,* and since used so often that today it is a cliché).

The Birth of a Nation also introduced the practice of accompanying movies with a specially arranged orchestral score. Although this
was not actually the first time music had been so used—as early as

[10] *The Art of the Moving Picture,* p. 49.

1908 several imported French pictures had carried musical score sheets—Griffith had exploited the possibilities of music far beyond the ordinary practice of the day.

The cultural world rapturously hailed *The Birth of a Nation*, and Griffith was enthroned as the film's first master. The acclaim was sweet to his ears, more than compensating for the public's temporary neglect of him during the preceding year, when the sensational European films had held America's admiration. He now stood at the peak of his career, the summit of his six years of struggle to make the movie an eloquent, vital, and respectable medium for art.

The Birth of a Nation was produced less than a decade and a half after motion pictures had learned to narrate. But its technique was incomparably superior to that of its primitive progenitors. If *The Great Train Robbery* was the giant of American pictures in 1903, *The Birth of a Nation* made it seem a pygmy in 1915.

The Birth of a Nation propelled the film into a new artistic level. A high point in the American movie tradition, it brought to maturity the editing principle begun with Méliès and furthered by Porter. So rich and profound in organization was this picture that for years thereafter it directly and indirectly influenced film makers everywhere, and much of the subsequent filmic progress owes its inspiration to this master achievement.

The commotion produced by *The Birth of a Nation* awakened Griffith to the effectiveness of pictures that dealt with social controversies, and it influenced him to increase the dimensions of his next film. Before the excitement attending *The Birth of a Nation* had completely subsided, he was at work on *The Mother and the Law*. The story for this picture was based upon the Stielow case, then making headlines in newspapers, and upon a Federal industrial commission's report of the killing of nineteen employees by a chemical manufacturer's "Goths" (as Griffith termed the militia) during a strike for higher wages. Griffith enlarged the original idea and expanded his theme so that it became more than a simple exposé; it was an elaborate condemnation of hypocrisy and cruelty resulting from prejudice—a theme that was ironic in view of his own bigotry in *The Birth of a Nation*. To suit the magnitude of his new undertaking, the title was finally changed to *Intolerance—A Drama of Comparisons*. Said Griffith, "If I approach a success in what I am trying to do in my coming picture, I expect a persecution even greater than that which met *The Birth of a Nation*."[11]

Presumably in answer to the attacks upon *The Birth of a Nation*,

[11] *Photoplay*, December 1916.

his pamphlet *The Rise and Fall of Free Speech in America* had been published to prepare the public for the theme of this picture. The pages of this booklet were shrewdly sprinkled with such phrases as "Intolerance is the root of all censorship," "Intolerance martyred Joan of Arc," "Intolerance smashed the first printing press," "Intolerance invented Salem witchcraft." The recurrent emphasis on intolerance appears too deliberate to have been anything but a calculated advance blast for the forthcoming picture.

In making *Intolerance* Griffith was faced with financial problems even greater than those encountered in the making of *The Birth of a Nation*. Although he had command of plenty of money after the triumph of that film, his expenditures on this new enterprise reached a fantastic high. The payroll alone amounted to as much as $12,000 a day. Settings for Babylonian walls three hundred feet high and for elaborate streets in Paris, Judea, and New York (miniatures and processing were still unknown), not to mention the expense of costumes, cost thousands more. The grandiose banquet scene for Belshazzar's feast is said to have cost $250,000. The photography for the picture consumed 300,000 feet of negative—a stupendous quantity even for today's epic productions. When Griffith's backers became alarmed and refused to put up any more money, Griffith bought them out, going heavily into debt to do so. When the costs were finally totaled, the figure was reported to be $1,900,000. *Intolerance* was by far the costliest production up to that time and for many years after.

The complete picture was thirteen reels long and contained three other stories in addition to the original one of *The Mother and the Law:* the fall of Babylon, the Christ legend of Judea, and the massacre of the Huguenots on St. Bartholomew's Day. The whole was, as Griffith himself stated, "a protest against despotism and injustice in every form."[12] To tie the four stories together Griffith used a symbol, the recurring image of a mother rocking a cradle, suggested by Walt Whitman's lines, ". . . endlessly rocks the cradle, Uniter of Here and Hereafter."

The scope of the theme required a most exacting and uncommon craftsmanship. A unique structural form, stemming from Porter's *The Kleptomaniac* and from Griffith's own *Judith of Bethulia*, but magnified a hundredfold, was planned. Declared Griffith:

[the] stories will begin like four currents looked at from a hilltop. At first the four currents will flow apart, slowly and quietly. But as they

[12] In the program given out at the revival showing, November 10, 1933, at the 55th St. Playhouse, New York.

flow, they grow nearer and nearer together, and faster and faster, until in the end, in the last act, they mingle in one mighty river of expressed emotion.[13]

The picture opens with a statement of the theme, then the presentation of the symbol of the Mother, "Today as yesterday, endlessly rocking, ever bringing the same human passions, the same joys and sorrows."[14] Then a book—referred to when each of the other stories is introduced—opens and "our first story . . . out of the cradle of the present" begins by sarcastically depicting reformers and the evils of prohibition. Then the story switches to Babylon and its scheming priests. Next is the sequence in Palestine, in which the motivation of the Crucifixion begins. Finally the spectator is taken to Paris to witness the plotting of the St. Bartholomew's Day massacre. These parts, separated in time and space, are linked through parallel and contrast editing; structural cohesion gives them a united effect. Their interplay brings out the emotional values in each and, as they progress toward a common climax, they force the audience to appreciate Griffith's message: "Each story shows how hatred and intolerance, through the ages, have battled against love and charity."[15]

The modern story was the most carefully thought out and dramatically motivated sequence of the four. It has the most "bite" and despite minor absurdities is as telling today in its ironic denunciation of reformers and profiteers as it was then. A group of "Uplifters" obtain the financial support of Jenkins, an industrial magnate, through his sister, an embittered old maid. In order to gain more money to donate to this "false charity," he cuts the wages of his mill workers and a strike follows. The militia is called out and the strikers are ruthlessly mowed down. When strikebreakers are employed, many of the destitute townspeople are forced to leave. Among these are the Dear One and her father, the Boy, whose father was killed in the strike, and the Friendless One. All four arrive at the neighboring big city.

Here, unable to get work, the Friendless One is enticed by a "Musketeer of the Slums"; the Boy robs a drunkard and becomes a member of the Musketeer's gang; Dear One's father dies. The Boy and Dear One marry but the Musketeer "frames" the young husband, who has decided to "go straight," and he is arrested and sent to prison. During his absence, Dear One has a baby but it is taken from her by the "Uplifters." On the pretext that he will get back

13 Robert Edgar Long's *David Wark Griffith*.
14 A main title in the film.
15 From the main title prefacing the film.

the child, the Musketeer forces his way into Dear One's room, not knowing that the Friendless One, now his mistress, is jealously spying. Just as he attacks Dear One, the Boy, who has been freed from jail, arrives. During the ensuing struggle the jealous girl perches herself on a ledge outside the window, and when the Boy is about to be overcome she shoots the Musketeer, throws the gun into the room and escapes. In the confusion the Boy picks up the gun, and he is found with it in his hands when the police arrive. Arrested for murder, he is tried and sentenced to be hanged. Dear One seeks a pardon from the Governor but is unsuccessful. At the final moment, however, the murderess confesses. There is a last-minute chase, first to get the pardon from the Governor before he leaves on a trip, then to reach the prison in time to stop the execution. The pardon is presented as the noose is to be cut. The Boy is saved, the family reunited.

The second story depicted the fall of Babylon through the treachery of the High Priest of Bel. The tale of the mountain girl's love for Belshazzar and her futile attempts to save Babylon from Cyrus and the Persians made this the next most dramatically defined sequence. In opulence it has rarely been equaled, the scenes of the Feast of Belshazzar and the attack and counterattack on Babylon, particularly, reaching heights of unprecedented grandeur.

The third and fourth sequences, or "rings," as they were then sometimes called—Christ in ancient Jerusalem and the massacre of the Huguenots in France on St. Bartholomew's Day—were the least developed in plot.

The four stories culminate in a plea for tolerance: symbolic double exposures of angels, prison walls dissolving into open fields, children playing and kissing each other, and as a finale, after a vast multiple exposure, a close shot of the recurrent symbolic image, the Mother rocking the Cradle of Humanity.

Profound though its theme is, the commanding feature of *Intolerance* is its internal organization. Years ahead of its time (it was to become a major influence on the Soviet school of directors), *Intolerance* surpassed even *The Birth of a Nation*. The comparatively simple editing pattern of the latter film, based on one single event and story related in time and space, was in *Intolerance* expanded into a complex form with four movements, all progressing simultaneously. The film cuts freely from period to period as the theme of intolerance in each is developed. Episode is paralleled with episode. With bold, staccato cutting, Griffith interweaves the motifs of Christ struggling toward Calvary, the Babylonian mountain girl speeding to warn Belshazzar that his priests have betrayed him, the massacre on St. Bartholomew's Day by the French mercenaries, and Dear One rushing frantically to save her husband at the gallows.

These passages are vividly motivated by every means Griffith had at his disposal. A shot is cut before the completion of its action; the moving camera parallels and reinforces a movement; iris and masks are used to emphasize a significant detail or eloquently effect a transition; large detail close-ups and extreme long shots produce effects of intensity and vastness. All these camera devices are brought into play to create a rich and varied film which flows in unbroken and mounting suspense until the end. Here, as in *The Birth of a Nation*, an underlying movement creates a rhythmic beat, which increases in frequency as the four climaxes approach. There is not a moment, not a shot, that is not controlled, timed, and selected for what it means and adds to the whole.

In the climactic sequences, particularly, is Griffith's artistry supreme. Here all the opulent details of the lavish scenes are subjected to an unceasing movement, action follows action, and none is ever allowed to terminate as the rhythm sweeps along. Christ is seen toiling up Mount Calvary; the Babylonian mountain girl is racing to warn her king of the onrushing enemy; the Huguenot is fighting his way through the streets to rescue his sweetheart from the mercenaries; the wife is speeding in an automobile to the prison with a pardon for her husband, who is about to be hanged.

Images whirl across the screen, startling the spectator with their pace and holding him spellbound by their profusion, rhythm, suspense. They are a visual symphony, swelling steadily until the final moment when all the movements are brought together in a grand finale. As Iris Barry wrote of these passages, "History itself seems to pour like a cataract across the screen."[16]

Individual episodes within each movement also have striking beauty of structure. At one point in the modern story, for example, the reformers, whom Griffith satirically called Vestal Virgins of Reform, are shown going to workers' homes, led by a rich industrialist's wife who gives the workers charity and moral guidance, keeping them from drinking, gambling, and prostitution. Following this are scenes showing factory workers being shot down by militia called out by the industrialist.

This is one of the many striking episodes; recorded shot by shot from the film by Theodore Huff, it is given below in its complete form. It is a vivid instance of Griffith's cutting. By an overlapping of movement from one shot onto the next, a double edge is given

[16] Museum of Modern Art Film Library Program Notes (III).

to the images and strong tension is created. Each shot, moreover, is cut to the minimum; it gives only the essential point. Facts build upon one another in the audience's mind until, in the very last shot, all the facts are resolved and summarized through the introduction of another type of shot, longer than any of its predecessors and significantly different in character. Not only the cutting and treatment of the sequences, but the deliberate documentary quality of the shots themselves, are remarkable. In this episode the origins of the remarkable Soviet technique are clearly evident.

Shot No.	Title		Footage
	Title	"Resuming our story of today—Dividends of the Jenkins mills failing to meet the increasing demands of Miss Jenkins' charities, she complains to her brother, which helps decide him to action."	17 feet
198	*Long Shot*	Large, bare office. Jenkins and assistant at desk. Sister hurries in from left—sits at desk—hands paper to brother.	6 feet
199	*¾ Shot*	Assistant getting number—hands telephone to Jenkins.	3 feet
200	*¾ Shot*	Factory manager answering phone.	2 feet,
201	(As 199)		4 frames
		Jenkins phoning to manager.	5 feet
	Title	"Order a ten per cent cut in all wages."	2 feet
			9 frames
202	(As 200)	Manager hangs up telephone—surprised—nervously wipes forehead and mouth. Iris out.	5 feet
203	*Long Shot*	Iris-in of men at gate of factory.	3 feet
204	*Medium Shot*	Iris-in of gate—men posting sign ordering the wage cut.	3 feet
205	*Long Shot* (As 203)	Gate of factory—crowds agitating. "A great strike follows."	2½ feet
	Title		2 feet,
			3 frames
206	*Long Shot*	Another part of the factory. Mob of workers agitating. The Boy in foreground. Man addresses crowd.	4 feet

Shot No.			Footage	
	Title	"They squeeze the money out of us and use it to advertise themselves by reforming us."	9	feet
207	¾ Shot	The Boy, angry—others, also. Argues.	3½	feet
208	(As 206)	The mob.	3½	feet
209	Long Shot	A mound. Workers' families grouped on hill watching the strike.	6½	feet
210	Long Shot	A row of small houses—families standing by gates and on sidewalk, listening.	3	feet
	Title	"Hungry ones that wait to take their places."	3	feet
211	Medium Shot	Group of men at gate, waiting.	5	feet
212	Long Shot	Road by factory. Militia come forward.	3	feet
213	Long Shot	Strikers fleeing.	5½	feet
214		The militia come forward—set up a line across the road.	6	feet
215	Medium Shot	The Girl's yard. She comes forward, stoops to pick up kindling wood.	4	feet
216	Long Shot	Militia barricade in street.	3	feet
217	Medium Shot	Cannon—men lying down with rifles.	2 5	feet, frames
218	Semi-Close-up	Rows of men and rifles—rifles are cocked.	4	feet
219	Medium Long Shot	Strikers shaking fists.	3	feet
220	Extreme Long Shot	From above—the lines of soldiers at the factory.	1 12	foot, frames
221	Long Shot	People on the hill—they shake their fists.	5	feet
222	Medium Long Shot	Cannon—they start firing.	5	feet
223	Long Shot	Strikers—they run back, down the hill.	2 11	feet, frames
224	Long Shot	Families on the hill—some run.	3	feet
225	Long Shot	Row of houses—people excited.	2	feet
226	¾ Shot	The Girl—frightened (hand to mouth)—drops wood—runs back toward house but comes forward again.	9	feet

Shot No.			Footage	
227	Medium Long Shot	Cannon firing.	2 11	feet, frames
228	Medium Long Shot	Strikers—man in foreground bares chest, daring soldiers to shoot him.	1 12	foot, frames
229	Long Shot	Inside factory fence: 4 strikers beyond—factory guards in foreground.	1 12	foot, frames
230	Medium Shot	Manager and assistant agitated—manager runs forward.	2½	feet
231	Medium Shot	Factory door—manager runs in.	2 2	feet, frames
232	¾ Shot	Office—manager runs forward to telephone. Calls Jenkins.	1 12	foot, frames
233	Medium Shot	Bars of fence—strikers behind, shaking fists and sticks.	1 10	foot, frames
234	Long Shot	Jenkins' office—he answers phone.	2 3	feet, frames
235	(As 232)	Manager at telephone, excited.	1 13	foot, frames
236	Medium Shot	Jenkins at telephone, answering calmly.	1	foot
237	Another Angle	Jenkins.	14	frames
238	(As 235)	Manager hangs up receiver—hesitates.	1 15	foot, frames
239	¾ Shot	Jenkins sitting at desk—staring ahead —indomitable.	2 6	feet, frames
240	(As 238)	Manager rushes back to door in rear.	1 12	foot, frames
241	(As 231)	—runs out door.	1 13	foot, frames
242	Long Shot	Factory guards—manager comes with order—group starts back toward fence.	4	feet
243	Medium Shot	Strikers by fence—shake fists—a few have revolvers.	1 12	foot, frames
244	(As 242)	Factory guards firing.	13	frames
245	Long Shot	People on hill.	5	feet
246	(As 244)	Guards firing.	9	frames
247	(As 243)	Strikers shake fists and fire.	1½	feet
248	Medium Long Shot	Guards firing.	1 14	foot, frames

Shot No.			Footage
249	¾ Shot	The Boy helping wounded father— others fleeing in background.	4 feet
250	(As 233)	Men sticking fists through pales of fence.	1 foot, 9 frames
251	(As 249)	Others fleeing and falling. Smoke.	3½ feet
252	Long Shot	Group on hill—people run frantically.	4 feet
253	(As 225)	Rows of houses—people excited.	2½ feet
254	(As 226)	The Girl—frightened—puts hand over her mouth fearfully.	3 feet
255	Extreme Long Shot	Camera pans slowly from strikers shooting to the factory crowd firing. On the fence in background the sign, in large letters, "The same today as yesterday."	13 feet

As in its cutting, so in its details *Intolerance* had impressive originality. Huge close-ups of faces, hands, objects, are used imaginatively and eloquently to comment upon, interpret, and deepen the import of the scene, so that dependence upon pantomime is minimized. A celebrated instance is the huge close-up of the clasped hands of Mae Marsh, suggesting her anguish during the trial of her husband. Camera angles are used to intensify the psychological impact: the extreme long shot of the industrialist alone in his office (lord of his domain) characterized him better than any action, incident, or subtitle. The handling of crowds as organized units in movement, as in the firing of the militia or in the notable Babylonian sequences, heightened the dramatic intensity of such scenes. The deliberate use of artificial sky above the onrushing Persian chariots gave the panorama great depth and massiveness, heightening the sense of impending doom as no natural sky could have done, and incidentally introducing to film technique the "process shot."

The singling out of significant action on one part of the screen by lights, irises, or masks—examples of which appeared in almost every sequence—indicated Griffith's sensitive regard for the apt image. With admirable ease, he cuts daringly into the square shape of the screen and blocks out whole sections, sometimes leaving them blocked out for the duration of the scene, sometimes opening the frame to its size. But whether he uses it closed in or opened out, he rarely uses the same shape twice in succession, but contrasts them so that the eye of the spectator is kept moving. For example, if the

screen opens in a semicircle from the lower right-hand corner to
the upper left, as in the opening mass scene of Babylon, the next
time, the screen opens in a semicircle from the upper left-hand corner, then opens out and down diagonally to the lower right.

This dramatic "framing" of the image throughout the film is done
with a variety and skill that have rarely been equaled. The screen is
sliced down the center, revealing only the middle (the great wall
of Babylon), then opens out. The screen is cut across diagonally,
sometimes from upper left to lower right, sometimes from upper
right to lower left. Details are thus brought to our attention and
yet kept part of the larger scene itself in a more precise way than
the use of close-up insertions could afford. This movement and variety of screen shapes keep the image ever fresh and vital and
heighten the momentum of the whole.

If the "framing" of the screen is remarkable, no less so is the fluid
and active participation of the camera. Its physical capacities for
movement and dramatic angle—generally conceded to be the original contributions of the postwar German craftsmen—must have
strained to the taxing point whatever was known then of camera
grace and flexibility. Yet there is never a sense of striving for sheer
mechanical wonder, but always a subordination of such capabilities
to the subject and the point to be made. The unceasing use of the
camera to drain everything that is significant out of the scene accounts in no small measure for the overwhelming sense of lavishness
and opulence that is so impressive to all. For example, we are shown
the court of France, 1572, first from an extreme long shot. The camera is stationary for a few moments as we take in the elaborate
scene; then the camera begins slowly to "truck" into the court, moving in on King Charles receiving on his throne; then the camera
"pans" to the right around the crowded room to pause on the Prince-
Heir, who, incidentally, is portrayed as a decadent fop with a realism worthy of Von Stroheim. Later in the film, in the marriage market of ancient Jerusalem, the camera "pans" to the right, showing
the painted women framed in a diagonal strip across the screen from
lower left to upper right. Again, in the Temple of Sacred Fire in
Babylon, the camera plays caressingly over the white nudeness of
erotic and sensual women clothed in flimsy chiffons, beflowered and
bejeweled, by "panning" from right to left, then from left to right;
then the screen frame closes in, then moves out, and in again with
marvelous facility.

More spectacular than any of these devices, however, was the
remarkable "trucking" camera shot which traveled, without a pause
or a cut, hundreds of feet from an extreme distant view of the entire

grandeur of ancient Babylon to a huge close-up of the scene itself. This shot, embracing immense sets, thousands of people and animals, was unprecedented and is still an amazing piece of camera bravura.

The film also utilized dramatically tinted film stock. Then a comparatively common device, it was seldom used on as large a scale or with as great variety. Night exteriors are tinted blue; sunny exteriors or lighted rooms are in various tones of yellow; blackness drapes the figures in the Temple of Sacred Fire; the Babylon battle at night is highlighted by red flares. Throughout the tints attempt to approximate reality; they show Griffith's awareness of the emotional values to be gained from the use of color.

With all its profound excellence, *Intolerance* nevertheless had many unfortunate weaknesses that marred its complete realization. The most obvious were Griffith's inherent sentimentality and his tendency to overdramatize. These weaknesses had appeared in *The Birth of a Nation* but, in view of that picture's subject and story, were less glaring. In *Intolerance* the maudlin names "little Dear One," "Brown Eyes," "Princess Beloved," all hangovers from the movies' past, are laughable. The extravagant posturing and the black-and-white characterizations are also hangovers from the prewar period. The massacre of the Huguenots and the Babylonian episode are full of bloodshed and violence, which reach a ludicrous high when the soldier of Belshazzar cuts off the head of his enemy so that the audience can see it topple off (a scene that had appeared in *Judith of Bethulia* and the older *Mary, Queen of Scots*, and was apparently acceptable in its day). Griffith's overindulgence in pious, highly moral, and frequently saccharine explanatory titles is another defect.

The greatest fault of *Intolerance* was what Julian Johnson, reviewing the film for *Photoplay*,[17] was the first to comment upon: "The fatal error of *Intolerance* was that in the great Babylonian scenes you didn't care which side won. It was just a great show." The overemphasis upon the spectacle outweighed the message. The formal concept ran away with the thematic; the execution was brilliant, but the point was forgotten. This discrepancy between the admirable structure and the uncertainty of the message is the reason why many people regard *The Birth of a Nation* as the greater of the two films. In that film one is forced, by the way the case is presented, to side with the South; in *Intolerance* the spectator is emotionally aroused but not as a partisan.

[17] December 1916.

First shown publicly September 5, 1916, the film evoked mixed criticism. Many of the critics of the day were bewildered by the cutting style, could not follow the story from period to period, and were confused by the "interminable battle scenes" and the recurring "mother rocking her baby." They found the idea obtuse and the effects exhausting. Like other publications *Variety*,[18] giving it far less attention than that accorded *The Birth of a Nation*, called it "a departure from all previous forms of legitimate or film construction . . . so diffuse in the sequence of its incidents that the development is at times difficult to follow." Heywood Broun declared that the bathing-beauty spectacle *Daughter of the Gods*, starring Annette Kellerman, "has the enormous advantage over *Intolerance* that it tells a story."[19] Years later Pudovkin, in his book *Film Technique*,[20] praised Griffith's structural innovations in *Intolerance* but thought the film "so ponderous that the tiredness it created largely effaced its effect."

At the time of the picture's release something like a war spirit was growing in the nation, and people could not reconcile the pacific intentions of *Intolerance*—intentions which they understood mainly through its titles—with the current militarism. As the country moved closer to active participation in the war, opposition to the film grew more vigorous. Censured and then barred in many cities, the picture suffered a sad and ignoble fate. Although it stands as a milestone in the progress of the American film, for Griffith it proved to be a financial disaster of crippling proportions. Through its failure he lost his independence and, no doubt, much of his great zeal.

Modern criticism of *Intolerance* has been increasingly favorable. The film has been called "a timeless masterpiece"[21] (Richard Watts, Jr.); "the end and justification of that whole school of American cinematography"[22] (Iris Barry); "an opulence of production that has never been equaled"[23] (Frank S. Nugent). It has thus reclaimed its rightful position as a peak in American movie making, the consummation of everything that preceded it and the beginning of profound new developments in the motion picture art. Its influence has traveled around the world, touching directors in Germany, France, and Soviet Russia in particular. A testament to Griffith's maturity, it marked the end of his second and most brilliant period and the

[18] September 8, 1916.
[19] The New York *Tribune*, October 20, 1916.
[20] P. 8.
[21] Quoted in the program given out at the revival showing, November 1933, at the 55th St. Playhouse.
[22] Museum of Modern Art Film Library Program Notes (III).
[23] The New York *Times*, March 8, 1936.

turning point in his career. Although continuing actively in movie making in the next years, and maintaining his high reputation, he was never again to equal *Intolerance*, or its predecessor, *The Birth of a Nation.*

III

THE DECLINE OF D. W. GRIFFITH

The third period of D. W. Griffith's career is bounded by the financial fiasco of his masterpiece, *Intolerance*, in 1916 and his hurriedly recalled swan song, *The Struggle*, in 1931. Fifteen years separated these two films—one the finest expression of craftsmanship on the American screen in its time, the other a sorrowful example of ineptness. Between these dissimilar efforts Griffith's career as a director steadily fell back to make way for Griffith's career as a businessman; both careers came at last to an obscure end. Pre-eminent in the American movie world in 1918, achieving international acclaim in 1919, by 1931 Griffith was out of movies altogether. Newcomers who knew better how to keep up with the swiftly changing times had supplanted him.

The reasons for Griffith's decline were twofold. First, he lost interest in films as such, and with each new picture he became further out of touch with the altered postwar audience. Second, an increasing regard for wealth and success compromised his integrity. That spirit of inquiry and humility which had once been his outstanding trait was replaced by a spirit of self-aggrandizement and ostentation. He began to concentrate upon exploiting his personality and reputation; it made no difference what he did, so long as the name "Griffith" appeared in print. He prophesied the future of pictures; he planned seventy-two-reel movies, and a chain of Griffith theaters from coast to coast that would show only his pictures; he spoke before chambers of commerce about the blessings of the movie trade; he criticized the government income tax rate; he railed against censorship; he took public credit for every artistic advance made in movies. And all the time his films were becoming worse.

Revolutionary changes in moral attitudes during these years were irreconcilable with Griffith's nineteenth-century orthodoxy. He clung to a moral code which was disdained and mocked as "old-fashioned." Even when he choose up-to-date themes, his outmoded and deep-seated prejudices were obvious; all his films appeared stilted, forced, ludicrously colored by prewar ideals. Griffith's great weakness was his inability to move with the times.

Even after the financial debacle of his *Intolerance*, Griffith was regarded as the "dean of American screen art"; no other director was so renowned or esteemed. When the Federal Government mobilized the motion picture industry on America's entrance into the World War, Griffith was one of the first to be recruited. Feted and acclaimed, he was sent to England to produce two propaganda pictures, one to arouse anti-German sentiment and the other to show "the regeneration of British society through its war activities." These pictures were made with the earnest co-operation of the officials of the Allied governments. England put all her stage, screen, and society notables at Griffith's service, and the French and Belgian governments conducted him on a tour of their battle fronts. No financial or artistic restraints were placed upon him. Thus, allowed unlimited resources and assured of the widest distribution governments could provide, Griffith made *Hearts of the World* and *The Great Love*.

Hearts of the World depicted the German occupation of a French village. Germans were shown, in the fashion of the day, as "Huns" —as plunderers, debauchers, and horsewhippers of beautiful French girls. Such titles as "Month after month piled up its legend of Hunnish crime on the book of God" may have been, as one critic of the day put it, a "powerful stimulus to patriotic emotions,"[1] but they certainly served the film in no other way. This is the film in which Griffith, to compensate for his anti-Negro prejudices in *The Birth of a Nation*, deliberately inserted a scene showing a white soldier kissing a dying Negro soldier who is crying for his mother. Though perhaps an honest gesture, this was out of place and certainly could not make up for his bigoted portrayal of the Negro race in the older film. Altogether maudlin and biased, *Hearts of the World* had the faults of Griffith's sentimental style at its worst.

Much was expected of Griffith's English war film, *The Great Love* (circulated exclusively in England). This too proved to be a mediocre effort. Numerous shots of royal personages and scenes of important places so overburdened the film that it evolved as nothing more than a glorified newsreel of Who's Who and What's What in wartime England. After the remarkable structure and fine humanity displayed in *Intolerance*, *The Great Love* no less than *Hearts of the World* seemed like a picture made by another man—by anybody but Griffith. Both of these war pictures, written by Griffith him-

[1] *Variety*, August 11, 1919.

self under pseudonyms, were devoid of that formal distinction which had made his previous efforts so startling; both were rabidly militaristic and revealed little comprehension of the great issues at stake. In a statement to reporters on his return to America, Griffith revealed his superficial understanding of the war by remarking that his sets for *Intolerance* had been more impressive than anything he saw in war-torn France and Belgium. "Viewed as drama," he said, "the war is in some ways disappointing."[2]

The armistice found Griffith, like most movie makers, unprepared for peace. While waiting to see what type of story the public wanted now—war pictures became a drug on the market—Griffith recut *Intolerance* into two pictures, *The Fall of Babylon* and *The Mother and the Law*, and in addition quickly made a number of typical prewar idylls: *True-Hearted Susie*, *The Romance of Happy Valley*, *The Greatest Thing in Life*, and *The Girl Who Stayed at Home*.

To the Babylonian picture were added many love scenes which had been omitted from the *Intolerance* version. They caused one critic to comment, "The picture is given a velvety touch which was originally lacking, as it is it appeals not only to the eye but to the emotions."[3]

The Mother and the Law was released as an "indictment of the conditions that permit the oppression of the poor through the medium of 'Uplifters' who work for self-aggrandizement; also a plea for tolerance in law."

The other films, the titles of which were symptomatic of a past day, were released in 1919 to a cynical and sophisticated audience who had just come through a war. The films were greeted with snickers and laughter. This was the first clear indication that Griffith's unchanged moral outlook had become dated.

Griffith was now floundering in the commercial revolution the industry was undergoing. New companies were springing into existence; mergers were changing the status of older firms; great new studios were being built; huge and elaborate movie theaters were appearing on the nation's main streets; thousands of additional people of varied talents were being drawn into the feverish activity that characterized the movies' postwar boom days. Before Griffith found a secure berth, he made two pictures for two different companies: *Scarlet Days* (1919), a Western melodrama of Joaquin Murieta, and *The Greatest Question* (1919), dealing with spiritualism. Neither was released at first because they were of such poor quality.

[2] *Photoplay*, 1918.
[3] *Motion Picture News*, August 2, 1919.

When finally exhibited, they were widely criticized as mediocre efforts, unworthy of a great director.

In the fall of 1919, Griffith and three other leading Hollywood figures—Charles Chaplin, Mary Pickford, and Douglas Fairbanks—formed a producing-distributing company, the United Artists Corporation. The prestige of the names of this "Big Four" assured financial support and made the firm a potential force in the new order of things. Griffith, like each of the others, was to direct and supervise his own productions, relying upon the pool for distribution and exhibition. While this seemed a perfect arrangement for a craftsman like Griffith, in reality it soon proved to be a great hindrance. For when Griffith became a member of United Artists, he became a part of that circle of producers whose only criterion for movie art was the box office. Hereafter all his efforts were directed toward getting the dollar; he made pictures on a strictly business basis, relying upon his prestige and associations to sell them. His new ambitions were power, fame, and money.

This change in Griffith, dictated by the pressure of the times and the vast capital investments in the business, paralleled the change in national attitudes. Movies having become big-scale operations, necessitating large returns, there was no longer room in the industry for independence or daring. Deviations from a closely knit manufacturing system involved great risks. In short, Griffith could no longer take chances.

The first picture made for United Artists was his last outstanding cinematic achievement, *Broken Blossoms* (1919). This picture, his most successful and most acclaimed effort since *The Birth of a Nation* and *Intolerance*, supported his sagging reputation. A distinguished if not a great work, the film contained a number of features that were deliberately chosen for their publicity value and revealed Griffith's growing esteem of showmanship: the racial issue (a Chinese man in love with a white girl); the unusual locale (the Limehouse district of London); "impressionistic photography" (gauzes and soft-focus effects, then new enough to be startling); and the novelty of tinted sequences and beams of pastel-colored lights, thrown from a projector while the picture was in progress to endow the sequences with additional emotional overtones. All these elements were reasons for the stir and admiration that greeted the film on its release.

Broken Blossoms, based on Thomas Burke's *Limehouse Nights* and in particular on "The Chink and the Child," is a poignant, romantic tragedy of the love and care of a "Chinaman" for a mistreated girl. Its mood is set by a pseudopoetic preface which ends, "It is a tale of tears." This note is sustained throughout the leisurely but dramatic unfolding of the story. Despite its lapses into sentimentality, the whole has a reality and plausibility that represented Griffith at his best, from the opening scenes in the streets of the Orient with the carousing American sailors and the religious solemnity of the Chinese, to the fog-drenched docks of Limehouse and the lurid interior of the smoking den.

Impressive as the atmosphere is, it is equaled by the characterizations. Richard Barthelmess as the Chinaman appears as sensitive and fragile as the story wants us to believe. Slender and pale, with his tilted head, his withdrawn, curved body, and his dreamy countenance emphasized in large close-ups time and again, he is a vivid character in contrast to the large, restless, energetic Brute (Donald Crisp).

There are many splendid moments in the film that suggest Griffith's faculties in their prime. There is, for example, the beating of the waif by the Brute—subtly edited so that one does not see the suffering girl during her torture; or the intensely dramatic closet scene in which the terrified Lillian Gish, knowing that there is no escape for her, spins despairingly around and around in the small space as the Brute pounds on the door; or the suspense up to the climax, when the spy tells the Brute the girl has gone to live with the Chinaman.

The fine execution and cutting of these scenes were supported by a sustained use of the camera to evoke moods, feelings, pictorial qualities. The "soft focus" suited the tenderness of the tale. Altogether *Broken Blossoms* was a brilliant culmination for the "sweet-and-innocent" era in American movies, already dying and being succeeded by the sophisticated, daring "triangle" era.

Griffith's own press books[4] are full of the glowing praise critics heaped upon *Broken Blossoms*. The New York *Evening Telegram* declared, "It is as if Dickens had spoken by means of the camera." According to the Chicago *News*, the film was "an eloquent and decisive flight beyond the speaking stage," while the *Literary Digest* concluded that "on that night [of the opening] the screen jumped five years . . . with the showing of *Broken Blossoms* a new art arrived, an art as important as music or poetry." Said the New York *Morning Telegraph*, more effusively, "Such art, so real one can think only of the classics, and of the masterly paintings remembered through the ages; so exquisite, so fragile, so beautifully and fragrantly poetic is *Broken Blossoms*."

The conservative New York *Times*[5] was no less enthusiastic: "All his mastery of picture making, the technique that is pre-eminently

4 Griffith Scrapbooks at the Museum of Modern Art Film Library.
5 October 19, 1919.

his by invention and control, the skill and subtlety with which he can unfold a story, has gone into the making of *Broken Blossoms*. It is a masterpiece."

Not even *The Birth of a Nation* had aroused such widespread adulation. Once called "the Belasco of the screen," Griffith was now acknowledged as "the Shakespeare of the movies."

With his head in the clouds, Griffith sent out a series of lofty pronouncements. His next picture was to be the world's largest film, consisting of seventy-two reels; he was going to build his own theater, the "Griffith"; he was going to build a chain of theaters all over the country to show only his films. Imperious, affiliated with money interests, powerful, he began to lecture, prophesy, advise, find fault with the industry and the nation at large. He assailed the income tax:

The income tax . . . is one of the most unjust systems of taxation known to modern civilization. . . . The income tax does not weigh upon the rich in any way as heavily as upon the workers and creators. . . . With the crash of nations falling before the menace of Bolshevism around the world, we believe it is very good time to pause and take thought about the matter. Bolshevism in the old days had small chance of gaining a foothold in America because the American worker . . . knew that the rich of America had begun just as he had . . . but we believe that the income tax makes it impossible to feel the same in this regard and gives a potent reason for discontent.[6]

About this same time he released *The Greatest Question* (1920), which he had made before *Broken Blossoms* and which he now hoped would benefit by that picture's success. In connection with the new film a singular event occurred which placed Griffith's name on the front pages of newspapers throughout the country. At the moment when the picture which "tried to answer the question whether communication with the dead was a fact or fancy" appeared, word was received that Griffith and his party, on board the yacht *Rosanda* en route to the Bahamas to film some scenes for his next production, had disappeared. The news was headlined on the front pages of all the New York papers on December 13, 1919. That afternoon thousands of people stormed the Strand Theater, where *The Greatest Question* was playing, and even overflowed into the Rialto and the Capitol, besieging the managements of those neighboring theaters for details of Griffith's whereabouts.

During the next few days the press continued to feature the story, made the more exciting now by the intervention of the United States

[6] Los Angeles *Times* Magazine Section, October 26, 1919.

government, which had dispatched Navy planes, a submarine chaser, and Coast Guard cutters to search for Griffith along the Florida coast. Finally, a week later, word was flashed that Griffith and his entire crew had been found safely cruising off the coast. The nation heaved a sigh of relief, and Griffith presently came home, a national celebrity.

Soon, however, the air was filled with angry insinuations that a hoax had been perpetrated. This was vehemently denied by the Griffith office. But an editorial in the Baltimore *Sun*, October 18, diplomatically summed up the matter, commenting that "the most expert press agent of all stagedom could not have invented a more thrilling and effective publicity stunt had he worked a year on it, than this wholly unpremeditated one."

There was no disputing Griffith's showmanship thereafter. The new role of producer-director pleased him immensely. Everything he touched for the next five years received widespread publicity. His activities were always colorful copy. The old ambition to become a famous writer had long since disappeared; he was more famous than the best of writers.

If fame was welcome to Griffith, the business of making pictures was rapidly becoming a burden. After twelve years in the industry, during which he had made several hundred films, he found the effort no longer exciting. Though the rewards had greatly increased, picture making had become more and more a hard discipline, even though Griffith now had a staff of directors under him to carry out his plans. Gradually he lost his passion for movies and concentrated more intently on his career as a business magnate.

The pictures Griffith produced during the next few years were costly but were formula pictures with out-of-date themes; they were sold on his past reputation and showed a steady decline in his directorial faculties. *The Idol Dancer* (1920), which he went to the Bahamas to make, and *The Love Flower* (1920) were both criticized as "unworthy of the master." *Way Down East* (1920), which got great publicity because of the $175,000 paid for the story, turned out to be a stilted treatment of an outdated social problem with little meaning during these rebellious years. *Dream Street* (1921) was a weak attempt to repeat the success of *Broken Blossoms*. Declared the Baltimore *Sun*,[7]

One doesn't expect these things from the most loudly lauded director-producer of the day, nor does one take kindly to such a plentiful evi-

[7] May 24, 1921.

dence of crude, amateurish acting, such wholesale symbolism, such mawkish sickening sentimentality. Where is the D. W. Griffith of yesteryear?

Griffith's next film, *Orphans of the Storm* (1922), was the work
of a man who was no longer influencing the movies but being influenced by them. A drama of the French Revolution, it clearly bore
the marks of the German historical dramas then the rage.

Griffith was rapidly becoming a "back number." Pictures had taken
over the attributes and point of view of a jazz-conscious world. It
was De Mille and Lubitsch, with their sophisticated films about
marital infidelity, bathtubs, and forbidden paradises, who were now
the leaders. Even other men who had trained under Griffith were
beginning to supersede him in popularity. The time was not far off
when De Mille's forecast, recalled to Harry Carr years later,[8] was
to become fact: "Some day Griffith would take a hard bump—due to
his refusal to take ideas from the trend of the day."

At a time when the country was fast breaking its prohibition laws,
winking and drinking recklessly, rejoicing in the daily stock market
rise, throwing traditional morals to the winds, Griffith made a number of futile attempts to regain his foothold in the industry. *One
Exciting Night* (1923) was a melodramatic mystery, "jumbled and
pointless."[9] He sent out notices that he was having great difficulty in
finding the right sort of material. Tamar Lane, West Coast film critic,
attacked him as being unable "to get away from the situation of the
attacking, raping, or wronging of the defenseless girl,"[10] in almost
every one of his screen stories of the past few years.

The White Rose (1923) was so hopelessly prewar in outlook that
F. J. Smith, in *Photoplay*,[11] remarked, "Somehow he seems to us to
be a great man living within a circle of isolation, surrounded by
minor advisers, genius out of touch with the world, as it were."

This lack of touch with the times was notable also in his next
film, *Isn't Life Wonderful* (1924-1925). Simple to the point of bareness, it appeared drab and out of place beside the films of glamour
and elegance then in vogue. Although it was moving and honest in
its theme—the tragedy in Germany during the war—and was adroitly
constructed, it was received unsympathetically. People of the twenties were concerned chiefly with physical sensations and had little
time for honest appraisals of social conditions; Griffith was blindly
bucking the tide. His succeeding film, *America* (1924), scarcely im-

---

[8] *Cinema Digest*, May 1932.
[9] *Photoplay*, January 1923.
[10] *What's Wrong with the Movies*, p. 63.
[11] August 1923.

proved his position; absorbing bits of realism culled from his research, years before, in soldiers' diaries, it was undoubtedly inspired by the phenomenal success of *The Covered Wagon*.

The end was not far off. By 1925 Griffith was no longer his own producer. At Paramount he became merely one of a large staff of directors. Here he was subjected to the commercial pressure he had always abhorred: he had to make pictures on schedule, to stay within the budget, to turn out "program" features.

A minor director now, he made a series of romantic films which attempted to capture the time spirit. *Sally of the Sawdust* (1925), a circus tale, was slow in a fast age, prewar in temper. *That Royle Girl* (1926), despite "clever touches," remained a Victorian melodrama. *Sorrows of Satan* (1926–1927), an obvious imitation of the day's outstanding sensation from Germany, *Variety*, emerged as a hackneyed morality tale. The industry whispered that Griffith was "through."

For two and a half years thereafter, Griffith made no films. What he was doing, what he was thinking, no one knew. All sorts of rumors circulated, but he did nothing. Then in 1928 he suddenly returned to United Artists—in which he still held stock—and once more resumed motion picture directing. Expectations of a brilliant comeback were put to an end after his production of *Drums of Love* (1928), based on the Paolo and Francesca legend; *The Battle of the Sexes* (1928–1929), a rehash of his 1913 film; and *The Lady of the Pavements* (1929), a romantic melodrama to which sound was added.

Into his first all-talking film Griffith poured a great deal of effort. Choosing a story and a background he knew well, he filmed *Abraham Lincoln* (1930). As one of the earliest of the all-talking films, it was typically static and had no feeling for the movie medium. There were so many moments of absurd sentimentality—the death of Ann Rutledge and the pardon of the boy soldier, to mention two glaring instances—that the whole carried little weight.

Griffith has made only one film since then: *The Struggle* (1931). Independently financed, a halfhearted effort, it was recalled from exhibition after a few showings—a sad finishing touch to Griffith's career. Sound had confirmed Hollywood's conviction that Griffith was an "old-timer."

So fast has the motion picture world moved in thirty years that today Griffith is in the peculiar circumstance of being regarded as an "old master," although he is still alive. Notwithstanding all his great contributions and his early talent, he has unquestionably declined since the war. As soon as he was no longer moving forward, he disintegrated as an artist. The profound film form of which he achieved mastery could not sustain or compensate for the superficiality of content and the commercial motives revealed in his postwar work. His romantic leanings, inbred prejudices, and moral inflexibility, while serving him well in their day and age, at last became millstones around his neck. Of this misfortune he apparently was unaware, since he became absorbed in high finance and the personal glories of success. The name of Griffith, nevertheless, has come to signify American motion picture art; his contributions to it enriched its traditions and gave it vital momentum.*

* D. W. Griffith died in Hollywood in July 1948.—D.T.

Caligari

by Siegfried Kracauer

This is a chapter from Siegfried Kracauer's stimulating book on the German film from 1918 to 1933, From Caligari to Hitler (Princeton University Press, Princeton, New Jersey, 1947). His central thesis—that it was unrest and the search for authority that led to the rise of Hitler—is exhaustively documented. The essay below is an account of the genesis of the famous German expressionist film, The Cabinet of Dr. Caligari.

THE CZECH HANS JANOWITZ, one of the two authors of the film *Das Cabinet des Dr. Caligari* (*The Cabinet of Dr. Caligari*), was brought up in Prague—that city where reality fuses with dreams, and dreams turn into visions of horror.[1] One evening in October 1913 this young poet was strolling through a fair at Hamburg, trying to find a girl whose beauty and manner had attracted him. The tents of the fair covered the Reeperbahn, known to any sailor as one of the

[1] The following episode, along with other data appearing in my pages on *Caligari*, is drawn from an interesting manuscript Mr. Hans Janowitz has written about the genesis of this film. I feel greatly indebted to him for having put his material at my disposal. I am thus in a position to base my interpretation of *Caligari* on the true inside story, up to now unknown.

449

world's chief pleasure spots. Nearby, on the Holstenwall, Lederer's gigantic Bismarck monument stood sentinel over the ships in the harbor. In search of the girl, Janowitz followed the fragile trail of a laugh which he thought hers into a dim park bordering the Holstenwall. The laugh, which apparently served to lure a young man, vanished somewhere in the shrubbery. When, a short time later, the young man departed, another shadow, hidden until then in the bushes, suddenly emerged and moved along—as if on the scent of that laugh. Passing this uncanny shadow, Janowitz caught a glimpse of him: he looked like an average bourgeois. Darkness reabsorbed the man and made further pursuit impossible. The following day big headlines in the local press announced: "Horrible sex crime on the Holstenwall! Young Gertrude . . . murdered." An obscure feeling that Gertrude might have been the girl of the fair impelled Janowitz to attend the victim's funeral. During the ceremony he suddenly had the sensation of discovering the murderer, who had not yet been captured. The man he suspected seemed to recognize him, too. It was the bourgeois—the shadow in the bushes.

Carl Mayer, co-author with Janowitz of *Caligari*, was born in the Austrian provincial capital of Graz, where his father, a wealthy businessman, would have prospered had he not been obsessed by the idea of becoming a "scientific" gambler. In the prime of life he sold his property, went, armed with an infallible "system," to Monte Carlo, and reappeared a few months later in Graz, broke. Under the stress of this catastrophe, the monomaniac father turned the sixteen-year-old Carl and his three younger brothers out into the street and finally committed suicide. A mere boy, Carl Mayer was responsible for the three children. While he toured through Austria, peddling barometers, singing in choirs and playing extras in peasant theaters, he became increasingly interested in the stage. There was no branch of theatrical production which he did not explore during those years of nomadic life—years full of experiences that were to be of immense use in his future career as a film poet. At the beginning of the war, the adolescent made his living by sketching Hindenburg portraits on post cards in Munich cafés. Later in the war, Janowitz reports, he had to undergo repeated examinations of his mental condition. Mayer seems to have been very embittered against the high-ranking military psychiatrist in charge of his case.

The war was over. Janowitz, who from its outbreak had been an officer in an infantry regiment, returned as a convinced pacifist, animated by hatred of an authority which had sent millions of men to death. He felt that absolute authority was bad in itself. He settled in Berlin, met Carl Mayer there, and soon found out that this eccentric young man, who had never before written a line, shared his revolutionary moods and views. Why not express them on the screen? Intoxicated with Wegener's films, Janowitz believed that this new medium might lend itself to powerful poetic revelations. As youth will, the two friends embarked on endless discussions that hovered around Janowitz' Holstenwall adventure as well as Mayer's mental duel with the psychiatrist. These stories seemed to evoke and supplement each other. After such discussions the pair would stroll through the night, irresistibly attracted by a dazzling and clamorous fair on Kantstrasse. It was a bright jungle, more hell than paradise, but a paradise to those who had exchanged the horror of war for the terror of want. One evening, Mayer dragged his companion to a side show by which he had been impressed. Under the title "Man and Machine" it presented a strong man who achieved miracles of strength in an apparent stupor. He acted as if he were hypnotized. The strangest thing was that he accompanied his feats with utterances which affected the spellbound spectators as pregnant forebodings.

Any creative process approaches a moment when only one additional experience is needed to integrate all elements into a whole. The mysterious figure of the strong man supplied such an experience. On the night of this show the friends first visualized the original story of *Caligari*. They wrote the manuscript in the following six weeks. Defining the part each took in the work, Janowitz calls himself "the father who planted the seed" and Mayer "the mother who conceived and ripened it." At the end, one small problem arose: the authors were at a loss as to what to christen their main character, a psychiatrist shaped after Mayer's archenemy during the war. A rare volume, *Unknown Letters of Stendhal*, offered the solution. While Janowitz was skimming through this find of his, he happened to notice that Stendhal, just come from the battlefield, met at La Scala in Milan an officer named Caligari. The name clicked with both authors.

Their story is located in a fictitious North German town near the Dutch border, significantly called Holstenwall. One day a fair moves into the town, with merry-go-rounds and side shows—among the latter that of Dr. Caligari, a weird, bespectacled man advertising the somnambulist Cesare. To procure a license, Caligari goes to the town hall, where he is treated haughtily by an arrogant official. The following morning this official is found murdered in his room, which does not prevent the townspeople from enjoying the fair's pleasures. Along with numerous onlookers, Francis and Alan—two students in love with Jane, a medical man's daughter—enter the tent of Dr. Caligari and watch Cesare slowly stepping out of an upright, coffinlike box. Caligari tells the thrilled audience that the somnambulist will answer questions about the future. Alan, in an excited state, asks how long he has to live. Cesare opens his mouth; he seems to be dominated by a terrific, hypnotic power emanating from his master. "Until dawn," he answers. At dawn Francis learns that his friend has been stabbed in exactly the same manner as the official. The student, suspicious of Caligari, persuades Jane's father to assist him in an investigation. With a search warrant the two force their way into the showman's wagon and demand that he end the trance of his medium. However, at this very moment they are called away to the police station to attend the examination of a criminal who has been caught in the act of killing a woman, and who now frantically denies that he is the pursued serial murderer.

Francis continues spying on Caligari and, after nightfall, secretly peers through a window of the wagon. But while he imagines he sees Cesare lying in his box, Cesare in reality breaks into Jane's bedroom, lifts a dagger to pierce the sleeping girl, gazes at her, puts the dagger away and flees, with the screaming Jane in his arms, over roofs and roads. Chased by her father, he drops the girl, who is then escorted home, whereas the lonely kidnaper dies of exhaustion. As Jane, in flagrant contradiction of what Francis believes to be the truth, insists on having recognized Cesare, Francis approaches Caligari a second time to solve the torturing riddle. The two policemen in his company seize the coffinlike box, and Francis draws out of it —a dummy representing the somnambulist. Profiting by the investigators' carelessness, Caligari himself manages to escape. He seeks shelter in a lunatic asylum. The student follows him, calls on the director of the asylum to inquire about the fugitive, and recoils horror-struck: the director and Caligari are one and the same person.

The following night—the director has fallen asleep—Francis and three members of the medical staff whom he has initiated into the case search the director's office and discover material fully establishing the guilt of this authority in psychiatric matters. Among a pile of books they find an old volume about a showman named Caligari who, in the eighteenth century, traveled through North Italy, hypnotized his medium Cesare into murdering sundry people, and, during Cesare's absence, substituted a wax figure to deceive the police. The main exhibit is the director's clinical records; they evidence that he desired to verify the account of Caligari's hypnotic faculties, that his desire grew into an obsession, and that, when a somnambulist was entrusted to his care, he could not resist the temptation of repeating with him those terrible games. He had adopted the identity of Caligari. To make him admit his crimes, Francis confronts the director with the corpse of his tool, the somnambulist. No sooner does the monster realize Cesare is dead than he begins to rave. Trained attendants put him into a strait jacket.

This horror tale in the spirit of E. T. A. Hoffmann was an outspoken revolutionary story. In it, as Janowitz indicates, he and Carl Mayer half intentionally stigmatized the omnipotence of a state authority manifesting itself in universal conscription and declarations of war. The German war government seemed to the authors the prototype of such voracious authority. Subjects of the Austro-Hungarian monarchy, they were in a better position than most citizens of the Reich to penetrate the fatal tendencies inherent in the German system. The character of Caligari embodies these tendencies; he stands for an unlimited authority that idolizes power as such and, to satisfy its lust for domination, ruthlessly violates all human rights and values. Functioning as a mere instrument, Cesare is not so much a guilty murderer as Caligari's innocent victim. This is how the authors themselves understood him. According to the pacifist-minded Janowitz, they had created Cesare with the dim design of portraying the common man who, under the pressure of compulsory military service, is drilled to kill and to be killed. The revolutionary meaning of the story reveals itself unmistakably at the end, with the disclosure of the psychiatrist as Caligari: reason overpowers unreasonable power, insane authority is symbolically abolished. Similar ideas were also being expressed on the contemporary stage, but the authors of *Caligari* transferred them to the screen without including any of those eulogies of the authority-freed "New Man" in which many expressionist plays indulged.

A miracle occurred: Erich Pommer, chief executive of Decla-Bioscop, accepted this unusual, if not subversive, script. Was it a miracle? Since in those early postwar days the conviction prevailed that foreign markets could be conquered only by artistic achievements, the German film industry was of course anxious to experiment in the field of aesthetically qualified entertainment.[2] Art assured export, and export meant salvation. An ardent partisan of this doctrine, Pommer had moreover an incomparable flair for cinematic values and popular demands. Regardless of whether he grasped the significance of the strange story Mayer and Janowitz submitted to him, he certainly sensed its timely atmosphere and interesting scenic potentialities. He was a born promoter who handled screen and business affairs with equal facility and, above all, excelled in stimu-

[2] Vincent, *Histoire de l'Art Cinématographique*, p. 140.

lating the creative energies of directors and players. In 1923, Ufa was to make him chief of its entire production.[3] His behind-the-scenes activities were to leave their imprint on the pre-Hitler screen.

Pommer assigned Fritz Lang to direct *Caligari*, but in the middle of the preliminary discussions Lang was ordered to finish his serial *The Spiders;* the distributors of this film urged its completion.[4] Lang's successor was Dr. Robert Wiene. Since his father, a once famous Dresden actor, had become slightly insane toward the end of his life, Wiene was not entirely unprepared to tackle the case of Dr. Caligari. He suggested, in complete harmony with what Lang had planned, an essential change of the original story—a change against which the two authors violently protested. But no one heeded them.[5]

The original story was an account of real horrors; Wiene's version transforms that account into a chimera concocted and narrated by the mentally deranged Francis. To effect this transformation the body of the original story is put into a framing story which introduces Francis as a madman. The film *Caligari* opens with the first of the two episodes composing the frame. Francis is shown sitting on a bench in the park of the lunatic asylum, listening to the confused babble of a fellow sufferer. Moving slowly, like an apparition, a female inmate of the asylum passes by: it is Jane. Francis says to his companion, "What I have experienced with her is still stranger than what you have encountered. I will tell it to you."[6] Fade-out. Then a view of Holstenwall fades in, and the original story unfolds, ending, as has been seen, with the identification of Caligari. After a new fade-out the second and final episode of the framing story begins. Francis, having finished the narration, follows his companion back to the asylum, where he mingles with a crowd of sad figures—among them Cesare, who absent-mindedly caresses a little flower. The director of the asylum, a mild and understanding-looking person, joins the crowd. Lost in the maze of his hallucinations, Francis takes the director for the nightmarish character he himself has created and accuses this imaginary fiend of being a dangerous madman. He screams, he fights the attendants in a frenzy. The scene

3 *Jahrbuch der Filmindustrie*, 1922–23, pp. 35, 46. For an appraisal of Pommer, see Lejeune, *Cinema*, pp. 125–31.

4 Information offered by Mr. Lang.

5 Extracted from Mr. Janowitz' manuscript. See also Vincent, *Histoire de l'Art Cinématographique*, pp. 140, 143–44.

6 Film license, issued by Board of Censors, Berlin, 1921 and 1925 (Museum of Modern Art Library, clipping files); *Film Society Programme*, March 14, 1926.

is switched over to a sickroom, with the director putting on horn-rimmed spectacles which immediately change his appearance: it seems to be Caligari who examines the exhausted Francis. After this he removes his spectacles and, all mildness, tells his assistants that Francis believes him to be Caligari. Now that he understands the case of his patient, the director concludes, he will be able to heal him. With this cheerful message the audience is dismissed.

Janowitz and Mayer knew why they raged against the framing story: it perverted, if not reversed, their intrinsic intentions. While the original story exposed the madness inherent in authority, Wiene's *Caligari* glorified authority and convicted its antagonist of madness. A revolutionary film was thus turned into a conformist one—following the much-used pattern of declaring some normal but troublesome individual insane and sending him to a lunatic asylum. This change undoubtedly resulted not so much from Wiene's personal predilections as from his instinctive submission to the necessities of the screen; films, at least commercial films, are forced to answer to mass desires. In its changed form *Caligari* was no longer a product expressing, at best, sentiments characteristic of the intelligentsia, but a film supposed equally to be in harmony with what the less educated felt and liked.

If it holds true that during the postwar years most Germans eagerly tended to withdraw from a harsh outer world into the intangible realm of the soul, Wiene's version was certainly more consistent with their attitude than the original story; for, by putting the original into a box, this version faithfully mirrored the general retreat into a shell. In *Caligari* (and several other films of the time) the device of a framing story was not only an aesthetic form, but also had symbolic content. Significantly, Wiene avoided mutilating the original story itself. Even though *Caligari* had become a conformist film, it preserved and emphasized this revolutionary story —as a madman's fantasy. Caligari's defeat now belonged among psychological experiences. In this way Wiene's film does suggest that during their retreat into themselves the Germans were stirred to reconsider their traditional belief in authority. Down to the bulk of Social Democratic workers they refrained from revolutionary action; yet at the same time a psychological revolution seems to have prepared itself in the depths of the collective soul. The film reflects this double aspect of German life by coupling a reality in which Caligari's authority triumphs with a hallucination in which the same authority is overthrown. There could be no better configuration of symbols for that uprising against the authoritarian dispositions which apparently occurred under the cover of a behavior-rejecting uprising.

Janowitz suggested that the settings for *Caligari* be designed by the painter and illustrator Alfred Kubin, who, a forerunner of the surrealists, made eerie phantoms invade harmless sceneries and visions of torture emerge from the subconcious. Wiene took to the idea of painted canvases, but preferred to Kubin three expressionist artists: Hermann Warm, Walter Röhrig and Walter Reimann. They were affiliated with the Berlin Sturm group, which, through Herwarth Walden's magazine *Sturm*, promoted expressionism in every field of art.[7]

Although expressionist painting and literature had evolved years before the war, they acquired a public only after 1918. In this respect the case of Germany somewhat resembled that of Soviet Russia, where, during the short period of war communism, diverse currents of abstract art enjoyed a veritable heyday.[8] To a revolutionized people expressionism seemed to combine the denial of bourgeois traditions with faith in man's power freely to shape society and nature. On account of such virtues it may have cast a spell over many Germans upset by the breakdown of their universe.[9]

"Films must be drawings brought to life"; this was Hermann Warm's formula at the time that he and his two fellow designers were constructing the *Caligari* world.[10] In accordance with his

[7] Mr. Janowitz' manuscript; Vincent, *Histoire de l'Art Cinématographique*, p. 144; Rotha, *Film Till Now*, p. 43.

[8] Kurtz, *Expressionismus*, p. 61.

[9] In Berlin, immediately after the war, Karl Heinz Martin staged two little dramas by Ernst Toller and Walter Hasenclever within expressionist settings. Cf. Kurtz, *ibid.*, p. 43; Vincent, *Histoire de l'Art Cinématographique*, pp. 142-43; Schapiro, "Nature of Abstract Art," *Marxist Quarterly*, Jan.-March 1937, p. 97.

[10] Quotation from Kurtz, *Expressionismus*, p. 66. Warm's views, which implied a verdict on films as photographed reality, harmonized with those of Viking Eggeling, an abstract Swedish painter living in Germany. Having eliminated all objects from his canvases, Eggeling deemed it logical to involve the surviving geometrical compositions in rhythmic movements. He and his painter friend Hans Richter submitted this idea to Ufa, and Ufa, guided as ever by the maxim that art is good business or, at least, good propaganda, enabled the two artists to go ahead with their experiments. The first abstract films appeared in 1921. While Eggeling—he died in 1925—orchestrated spiral lines and comblike figures in a short he called *Diagonal Symphony*, Richter composed his *Rhythm 21* of squares in black, gray and white. One year later, Walter Ruttmann, also a painter, joined in the trend with *Opus I*, which was a dynamic display of spots vaguely recalling X-ray photographs. As the titles reveal, the authors themselves considered their products a sort of optical music. It was a music that, whatever else it tried to impart, marked an utter withdrawal from the outer world. This esoteric avant-garde movement soon

beliefs, the canvases and draperies of *Caligari* abounded in complexes of jagged, sharp-pointed forms strongly reminiscent of Gothic patterns. Products of a style which by then had become almost a mannerism, these complexes suggested houses, walls, landscapes. Except for a few slips or concessions—some backgrounds opposed the pictorial convention in too direct a manner, while others all but preserved them—the settings amounted to a perfect transformation of material objects into emotional ornaments. With its oblique chimneys on pell-mell roofs, its windows in the form of arrows or kites and its treelike arabesques that were threats rather than trees, Holstenwall resembled those visions of unheard-of cities which the painter Lionel Feininger evoked through his edgy, crystalline compositions.[11] In addition, the ornamental system in *Caligari* expanded through space, annulling its conventional aspect by means of painted shadows in disharmony with the lighting effects, and zigzag delineations designed to efface all rules of perspective. Space now dwindled to a flat plane, now augmented its dimensions to become what one writer called a "stereoscopic universe."[12]

Lettering was introduced as an essential element of the settings—appropriately enough, considering the close relationship between lettering and drawing. In one scene the mad psychiatrist's desire to

---

spread over other countries. From about 1924, such advanced French artists as Fernand Léger and René Clair made films which, less abstract than the German ones, showed an affinity for the formal beauty of machine parts, and molded all kinds of objects and motions into surrealistic dreams.—I feel indebted to Mr. Hans Richter for having permitted me to use his unpublished manuscript, "Avantgarde, History and Dates of the Only Independent Artistic Film Movement, 1921–1931." See also *Film Society Programme*, Oct. 16, 1927; Kurtz, *Expressionismus*, pp. 86, 94; Vincent, *Histoire de l'Art Cinématographique*, pp. 159–61; Man Ray, "Answer to a Questionnaire," *Film Art*, No. 7, 1936, p. 9; *Kraszna-Krausz, "Exhibition in Stuttgart, June 1929, and Its Effects," Close Up*, Dec. 1929, pp. 461–62.

11 Mr. Feininger wrote to me about his relation to *Caligari* on Sept. 13, 1944: "Thank you for your . . . letter of Sept. 8. But if there has been anything I never had a part in nor the slightest knowledge of at the time, it is the film *Caligari*. I have never even seen the film. . . . I never met nor knew the artists you name [Warm, Röhrig and Reimann] who devised the settings. Some time about 1911 I made, for my own edification, a series of drawings which I entitled: 'Die Stade am Ende der Welt.' Some of these drawings were printed, some were exhibited. Later, after the birth of *Caligari*, I was frequently asked whether I had had a hand in its devising. This is all I can tell you. . . ."

12 Cited by Carter, *The New Spirit*, p. 250, from H. G. Scheffauer, *The New Spirit in the German Arts*.—For the *Caligari décor*, see also Kurtz, *Expressionismus*, p. 66; Rotha, *Film Till Now*, p. 46; Jahier, "42 Ans de Cinéma," *Le Rôle Intellectuel du Cinéma*, pp. 60–61; "The Cabinet of Dr. Caligari," *Exceptional Photoplays*, March 1921, p. 4; Amiguet, *Cinéma! Cinéma!*, p. 50. For the beginnings of Werner Krauss and Conrad Veidt, see Kalbus, *Deutsche Filmkunst*, I, 28, 30, and Veidt, "Mein Leben," *Ufa-Magazin*, Jan. 14–20, 1927.

imitate Caligari materializes in jittery characters composing the words "I must become Caligari"—words that loom before his eyes on the road, in the clouds, in the treetops. The incorporation of human beings and their movements into the texture of these surroundings was tremendously difficult. Of all the players only the two protagonists seemed actually to be created by a draftsman's imagination. Werner Krauss as Caligari had the appearance of a phantom magician himself weaving the lines and shades through which he paced, and when Conrad Veidt's Cesare prowled along a wall, it was as if the wall had exuded him. The figure of an old dwarf and the crowd's antiquated costumes helped to remove the throng on the fair's tent street from reality and make it share the bizarre life of abstract forms.

If Decla had chosen to leave the original story of Mayer and Janowitz as it was, these "drawings brought to life" would have told it perfectly. As expressionist abstractions they were animated by the same revolutionary spirit that impelled the two script-writers to accuse authority—the kind of authority revered in Germany—of inhuman excesses. However, Wiene's version disavowed this revolutionary meaning of expressionist staging, or, at least, put it, like the original story itself, in brackets. In the film *Caligari* expressionism seems to be nothing more than the adequate translation of a madman's fantasy into pictorial terms. This was how many contemporary German reviewers understood, and relished, the settings and gestures. One of the critics stated with self-assured ignorance, "The idea of rendering the notions of sick brains . . . through expressionist pictures is not only well conceived but also well realized. Here this style has a right to exist, proves an outcome of solid logic."[13]

In their triumph the Philistines overlooked one significant fact: Even though *Caligari* stigmatized the oblique chimneys as crazy, it never restored the perpendicular ones as the normal. Expressionist ornaments also overrun the film's concluding episode, in which, from the Philistines' viewpoint, perpendiculars should have been expected to characterize the revival of conventional reality. In consequence, the *Caligari* style was as far from depicting madness as it was from transmitting revolutionary messages. What function did it really assume?

During the postwar years expressionism was frequently considered a shaping of primitive sensations and experiences. Gerhart Hauptmann's brother Carl—a distinguished writer and poet with

13 Review in *8 Uhr Abendblatt*, cited in *Caligari-Heft*, p. 8.

expressionist inclinations—adopted this definition and then asked how the spontaneous manifestations of a profoundly agitated soul might best be formulated. While modern language, he contended, is too perverted to serve this purpose, the film—or the bioscop, as he termed it—offers a unique opportunity to externalize the fermentation of inner life. Of course, he said, the bioscop must feature only those gestures of things and of human beings which are truly soulful.[14]

Carl Hauptmann's views elucidate the expressionist style of *Caligari*. It had the function of characterizing the phenomena on the screen as phenomena of the soul—a function which overshadowed its revolutionary meaning. By making the film an outward projection of psychological events, expressionist staging symbolized— much more strikingly than did the device of a framing story—that general retreat into a shell which occurred in postwar Germany. It is not accidental that, as long as this collective process was effective, odd gestures and settings in an expressionist or similar style marked many a conspicuous film. *Variety*, of 1925, showed the final traces of them. Owing to their stereotyped character, these settings and gestures were like some familiar street sign—"Men at Work," for instance. Only here the lettering was different. The sign read, "Soul at Work."

After a thorough propaganda campaign culminating in the puzzling poster, "You must become Caligari," Decla released the film in February 1920 in the Berlin Marmorhaus.[15] Among the press reviews—they were unanimous in praising *Caligari* as the first work of art on the screen—that of *Vorwärts*, the leading Social Democratic Party organ, distinguished itself by utter absurdity. It commented upon the film's final scene, in which the director of the asylum promises to heal Francis, with the words: "This film is also morally invulnerable inasmuch as it evokes sympathy for the mentally diseased, and comprehension for the self-sacrificing activity of the psychiatrists and attendants."[16] Instead of recognizing that Francis' attack against an odious authority harmonized with the party's own antiauthoritarian doctrine, *Vorwärts* preferred to pass off authority itself as a paragon of progressive virtues. It was always the same psychological mechanism: the rationalized middle-class propensities of the Social Democrats interfering with their rational

[14] Carl Hauptmann, "Film und Theater," *Der Film von Morgen*, p. 20. See also Alten, "Die Kunst in Deutschland," *Ganymed*, 1920, p. 146; Kurtz, *Expressionismus*, p. 14.

[15] *Jahrbuch der Filmindustrie*, 1922–23, p. 31.

[16] Quoted from *Caligari-Heft*, p. 23.

socialist designs. While the Germans were too close to *Caligari* to appraise its symptomatic value, the French realized that this film was more than just an exceptional film. They coined the term *"Caligarisme"* and applied it to a postwar world seemingly all upside down; which, at any rate, proves that they sensed the film's bearing on the structure of society. The New York première of *Caligari*, in April 1921, firmly established its world fame. But apart from giving rise to stray imitations and serving as a yardstick for artistic endeavors, this "most widely discussed film of the time" never seriously influenced the course of the American or French cinema.[17] It stood out lonely, like a monolith.

Caligari shows the "Soul at Work." On what adventures does the revolutionized soul embark? The narrative and pictorial elements of the film gravitate toward two opposite poles. One can be labeled "Authority," or, more explicitly, "Tyranny." The theme of tyranny, with which the authors were obsessed, pervades the screen from beginning to end. Swivel chairs of enormous height symbolize the superiority of the city officials turning on them, and, similarly, the gigantic back of the chair in Alan's attic testifies to the invisible presence of powers that have their grip on him. Staircases reinforce the effect of the furniture: numerous steps ascend to police headquarters, and in the lunatic asylum itself no less than three parallel flights of stairs are called upon to mark Dr. Caligari's position at the top of the hierarchy. That the film succeeds in picturing him as a tyrant figure of the stamp of Homunculus and Lubitsch's Henry VIII is substantiated by a most illuminating statement in Joseph Freeman's novel, *Never Call Retreat*. Its hero, a Viennese professor of history, tells of his life in a German concentration camp where, after being tortured, he is thrown into a cell:

Lying alone in that cell, I thought of Dr. Caligari; then, without transition, of the Emperor Valentinian, master of the Roman world, who took great delight in imposing the death sentence for slight or imaginary offenses. This Caesar's favorite expressions were: "Strike off his head!" —"Burn him alive!"—"Let him be beaten with clubs till he expires!" I thought what a genuine twentieth-century ruler the emperor was, and promptly fell asleep.[18]

This dreamlike reasoning penetrates Dr. Caligari to the core by conceiving him as a counterpart of Valentinian and a premonition of

[17] Quotation from Jacobs, *American Film*, p. 303; see also pp. 304-5.
[18] Freeman, *Never Call Retreat*, p. 528.

Hitler. Caligari is a very specific premonition in the sense that he uses hypnotic power to force his will upon his tool—a technique foreshadowing, in content and purpose, that manipulation of the soul which Hitler was the first to practice on a gigantic scale. Even though, at the time of *Caligari*, the motif of the masterful hypnotizer was not unknown on the screen—it played a prominent role in the American film *Trilby*, shown in Berlin during the war—nothing in their environment invited the two authors to feature it.[19] They must have been driven by one of those dark impulses which, stemming from the slowly moving foundations of a people's life, sometimes engender true visions.

One should expect the pole opposing that of tyranny to be the pole of freedom; for it was doubtless their love of freedom which made Janowitz and Mayer disclose the nature of tyranny. Now this counterpole is the rallying point of elements pertaining to the fair— the fair with its rows of tents, its confused crowds besieging them, and its diversity of thrilling amusements. Here Francis and Alan join the swarm of onlookers; here, on the scene of his triumphs, Dr. Caligari is finally trapped. In their attempts to define the character of a fair, literary sources repeatedly evoke the memory of Babel and Babylon alike. A seventeenth-century pamphlet describes the noise typical of a fair as "such a distracted noise that you would think Babel not comparable to it," and, almost two hundred years later, a young English poet feels enthusiastic about "that Babylon of booths—the Fair."[20] The manner in which such Biblical images insert themselves unmistakably characterizes the fair as an enclave of anarchy in the sphere of entertainment. This accounts for its eternal attractiveness. People of all classes and ages enjoy losing themselves in a wilderness of glaring colors and shrill sounds, which is populated with monsters and abounding in bodily sensations— from violent shocks to tastes of incredible sweetness. For adults it is a regression into childhood days, in which games and serious affairs are identical, real and imagined things mingle, and anarchical desires aimlessly test infinite possibilities. By means of this regression the adult escapes a civilization which tends to overgrow and starve out the chaos of instincts—escapes it to restore that chaos upon which civilization nevertheless rests. The fair is not freedom, but anarchy entailing chaos.

Significantly, most fair scenes in *Caligari* open with a small iris-in exhibiting an organ-grinder whose arm constantly rotates, and, behind him, the top of a merry-go-round which never ceases its cir-

[19] Kalbus, *Deutsche Filmkunst*, I, 95.
[20] McKechnie, *Popular Entertainments*, pp. 33, 47.

cular movement.[21] The circle here becomes a symbol of chaos. While freedom resembles a river, chaos resembles a whirlpool. Forgetful of self, one may plunge into chaos; one cannot move on in it. That the two authors selected a fair with its liberties as contrast to the oppressions of Caligari betrays the flaw in their revolutionary aspirations. Much as they longed for freedom, they were apparently incapable of imagining its contours. There is something Bohemian in their conception; it seems the product of naïve idealism rather than true insight. But it might be said that the fair faithfully reflected the chaotic condition of postwar Germany.

Whether intentionally or not, *Caligari* exposes the soul wavering between tyranny and chaos, and facing a desperate situation; any escape from tyranny seems to throw it into a state of utter confusion. Quite logically, the film spreads an all-pervading atmosphere of horror. Like the Nazi world, that of *Caligari* overflows with sinister portents, acts of terror and outbursts of panic. The equation of horror and hopelessness comes to a climax in the final episode, which pretends to re-establish normal life. Except for the ambiguous figure of the director and the shadowy members of his staff, normality realizes itself through the crowd of insane moving in their bizarre surroundings. The normal as a madhouse: frustration could not be pictured more finally. And in this film, as well as in *Homunculus,* is unleashed a strong sadism and an appetite for destruction. The reappearance of these traits on the screen once more testifies to their prominence in the German collective soul.

Technical peculiarities betray peculiarities of meaning. In *Caligari* methods begin to assert themselves which belong among the special properties of German film technique. *Caligari* initiates a long procession of 100 per cent studio-made films. Whereas, for instance, the Swedes at that time went to great pains to capture the actual appearance of a snowstorm or a wood, the German directors, at least until 1924, were so infatuated with indoor effects that they built up whole landscapes within the studio walls. They preferred the command of an artificial universe to dependence upon a haphazard outer world. Their withdrawal into the studio was part of the general retreat into a shell. Once the Germans had determined to seek shelter within the soul, they could not well allow the screen to explore that very reality which they abandoned. This explains

21 Rotha, *Film Till Now,* p. 285. For the role of fairs in films, see E. W. and M. M. Robson, *The Film Answers Back,* pp. 196–97.—An iris-in is a technical term for opening up the scene from a small circle of light in a dark screen until the whole frame is revealed.

the conspicuous role of architecture after *Caligari*—a role that has struck many an observer. "It is of the utmost importance," Paul Rotha remarks in a survey of the postwar period, "to grasp the significant part played by the architect in the development of the German cinema."[22] How could it be otherwise? The architect's façades and rooms were not merely backgrounds, but hieroglyphs. They expressed the structure of the soul in terms of space.

Caligari also mobilizes light. It is a lighting device which enables the spectators to watch the murder of Alan without seeing it; what they see, on the wall of the student's attic, is the shadow of Cesare stabbing that of Alan. Such devices developed into a specialty of the German studios. Jean Cassou credits the Germans with having invented a "laboratory-made fairy illumination,"[23] and Harry Alan Potamkin considers the handling of the light in the German film its "major contribution to the cinema."[24] This emphasis upon light can be traced to an experiment Max Reinhardt made on the stage shortly before *Caligari*. In his *mise-en-scène* of Sorge's prewar drama *The Beggar (Der Bettler)*—one of the earliest and most vigorous manifestations of expressionism—he substituted for normal settings imaginary ones created by means of lighting effects.[25] Reinhardt doubtless introduced these effects to be true to the drama's style. The analogy to the films of the postwar period is obvious: it was their expressionist nature which impelled many a German director of photography to breed shadows as rampant as weeds and associate ethereal phantoms with strangely lit arabesques or faces. These efforts were designed to bathe all scenery in an unearthly illumination marking it as scenery of the soul. "Light has breathed soul into the expressionist films," Rudolph Kurtz states in his book on the expressionist cinema.[26] Exactly the reverse holds true: in those films the soul was the virtual source of the light. The task of switching on this inner illumination was somewhat facilitated by powerful romantic traditions.

The attempt made in *Caligari* to co-ordinate settings, players, lighting and action is symptomatic of the sense of structural organization which, from this film on, manifests itself on the German screen. Rotha coins the term "studio constructivism" to charac-

[22] Rotha, *Film Till Now*, p. 180. *Cf.* Potamkin, "Kino and Lichtspiel," *Close Up*, Nov. 1929, p. 387.
[23] Cited in Leprohon, "Le Cinéma Allemand," *Le Rouge et le Noir*, July 1928, p. 135.
[24] Potamkin, "The Rise and Fall of the German Film," *Cinema*, April 1930, p. 24.
[25] Kurtz, *Expressionismus*, p. 59.
[26] *Ibid.*, p. 60.

terize "that curious air of completeness, of finality, that surrounds each product of the German studios."[27] But organizational completeness can be achieved only if the material to be organized does not object to it. (The ability of the Germans to organize themselves owes much to their longing for submission.) Since reality is essentially incalculable and therefore demands to be observed rather than commanded, realism on the screen and total organization exclude each other. Through their "studio constructivism" no less than their lighting the German films revealed that they dealt with unreal events displayed in a sphere basically controllable.[28]

In the course of a visit to Paris about six years after the première of *Caligari,* Janowitz called on Count Étienne de Beaumont in his old city residence, where he lived among Louis Seize furniture and Picassos. The Count voiced his admiration of *Caligari,* terming it "as fascinating and abstruse as the German soul." He continued, "Now the time has come for the German soul to speak, monsieur. The French soul spoke more than a century ago, in the Revolution, and you have been mute. . . . Now we are waiting for what you have to impart to us, to the world."[29]

The Count did not have long to wait.

[27] Rotha, *Film Till Now,* pp. 107–8. *Cf.* Potamkin, "Kino and Lichtspiel," *Close Up,* Nov. 1929, p. 388, and "The Rise and Fall of the German Film," *Cinema,* April 1930, p. 24.

[28] Film connoisseurs have repeatedly criticized *Caligari* for being a stage imitation. This aspect of the film partly results from its genuinely theatrical action. It is action of a well-constructed dramatic conflict in stationary surroundings—action which does not depend upon screen representation for significance. Like *Caligari,* all "indoor" films of the postwar period showed affinity for the stage in that they favored inner-life dramas at the expense of conflicts involving outer reality. However, this did not necessarily prevent them from growing into true films. When, in the wake of *Caligari,* film technique steadily progressed, the psychological screen dramas increasingly exhibited an imagery that elaborated the significance of their action. *Caligari*'s theatrical affinity was also due to technical backwardness. An immovable camera focused upon the painted *décor;* no cutting device added a meaning of its own to that of the pictures. One should, of course, not forget the reciprocal influence *Caligari* and kindred films exerted, for their part, on the German stage. Stimulated by the use they made of the iris-in, stage lighting took to singling out a lone player, or some important sector of the scene. *Cf.* Barry, *Program Notes,* Series III, Program 1; Gregor, *Zeitalter des Films,* pp. 134, 144–45; Rotha, *Film Till Now,* p. 275; Vincent, *Histoire de l'Art Cinématographique,* p. 139.

[29] From Janowitz' manuscript.

Charlie Chaplin:

Portrait

of the Moralist

---

by Robert Payne

The genius of Charlie Chaplin has resulted in a vast literature on the subject. Hundreds of articles and scores of books and monographs have been written on his achievements. He is one of the very few movie figures to transcend his métier and become a global personality. The following selection is taken from The Great God Pan *(Hermitage House, New York, 1952), a book on Chaplin by Robert Payne. There are several other books on Chaplin worth reading—notably those by Louis Delluc, R. J. Minney, Theodore Huff and Parker Tyler.*

W E LIVE IN RIDICULOUS and desperate times; we are catching up with the Keystone comedies. We know that world only too well. The incompetent flat-footed cops, the mad bank presidents, the thugs in the alleyway, the piecrusts which are disguised sticks of dynamite, the perpetual vision of peace in a world where every stone marks a hidden detonator and every road leads nowhere, all these we know because they are part of the world we now travel in. We travel blind, sustained by the hope that the blindness may miraculously fall from our eyes, and we do our best to remain deadpan in spite of the possibility that our cities and all the people in them and all the works of art may be instantaneously transformed in a rainbow-colored cloud. There was something prophetic in Mack Sennett's world, that world which Charlie explored with the utmost abandon. There was a time not long ago when we laughed at the television face in the factory, at the mechanical feeders and the cogwheels that forgot which way they were going. We do not laugh so much now. Today the thugs are waiting down the alleyway, and the cops overwhelm us always, and sooner than we think we may be living in flophouses or wandering down uninviting empty roads. The world is bleak and cold, with the wind coming through the worn rafters. In this dilemma, where do we stand?

We may, of course, take our consolations where we can. We pay our income tax regularly and read the books on child psychology; it is up to God and society to protect us. It is pleasant to repose in the justice of our cause, but it is no longer sufficient. We live in desperate times. We have no real assurance of victory. We blunder, and do not know where we are going. The roads ahead are blacker than they have ever been. In this extremity the only certain weapon is defiance, the purely human and instinctive courage to go on, whatever the cost, however many bodies we stumble on. Like the hanged highwayman who kicks off his shoes in a final gesture of invincibility, we may find that the only final consolation lies in our determination to go on dancing to the end.

Charlie, who represents to such an extraordinary degree the whole human race caught in its habitual rattrap, does kick off his shoes, and we are abundantly convinced of the validity of his gesture of invincibility. But the matter is not so simple. The joyful contempt he flings at the face of his enemies has many origins. It is partly pure braggadocio. There is warmth in it, and extreme cold. There is a sense of human dignity and a splendid nonchalance. He will whistle to himself and take pleasure in the sudden panic-stricken look on the face of his conquerors when they see he is unconquerable. All his life Charlie has lived on the edge of things, as today we live on the edge of things, but he has behaved with decorum—the decorum is only too plainly underscored—and when the last moment arrives he has no regrets, because he has a clear conscience. (He has stolen occasionally, but to steal food when one is hungry is, as St. Ambrose observed long ago, one of those sins which are immediately pardoned in heaven). Indeed, far more than Sir Galahad, he represents the heroic figure of the man who remains pure and undefiled, and he is all the more credible because he is reduced to a human scale. And since human heroism consists in the refusal, even the absolute rejection, of all those things which tend to degrade the human splendor, Charlie emerges as the knight-errant of the back streets, the knight of faith, the devout tightrope walker who, simply by maintaining his balance on the tightrope, holds the circus tent and everyone in it from falling into a bottomless abyss, and he can only do this out of his sense of impudent defiance—that complex defiance which, as we have seen, derives from so many different sources. He is a master of defiance, but some times when the highwayman kicks off his shoes he will imitate defiance by accident—there must be many times when what seemed to be defiance was no more than the nervous spasms of the trembling bones.

Kierkegaard has spoken at great length of the knight of the faith, the simple person who arrived at faith without difficulty, without ever having to cross the abysses, the man with no chink in his armor, the most enviable of the saints. It occurred to Kierkegaard that the knights of faith were subtly disguised. The great prelates who attained to holiness by the use of hair shirts and midnight flagellations, the philosophers who pushed thought to the very end of thought, the nuns who sacrificed themselves—yes, they possessed an admirable holiness, and it would be folly to dispute their love of God. But did God love them? It seemed to Kierkegaard that God loved most of all the tobacconist at the corner, the man who puffed at his pipe and had a little joke for his customers and took his family along the shore every Sunday afternoon. In such a man it might be possible to find a faith so final that it put the faith of the nuns and the theologians to shame. Something of the same thought must have passed through the mind of Flaubert when, seeing some peasants in the evening gathered at table, he said, *"Ils sont dans le vrai."* The man who had spent his life in a titanic struggle with art, producing it little by little, chipping it from his breastbone, came to see at the end of his days that art flowered naturally round the peasants' table, so naturally that they were hardly aware of its presence and took its existence for granted.

In all this Charlie has his place, and there is nothing at all fanciful in seeing him as one of those rare archetypal figures like Don Juan, Pierrot and Faust, who arise unexpectedly and flower and take on the colors of their time, and inevitably there will be more Charlies later. Faust, passing through the hands of Marlowe, Goethe and a hundred others, demonstrated the human spirit's hunger for experience and power at periods when that hunger was keenest. Don Juan emerged from the hands of Father Gabriel Tellez, the dramatist Tirso de Molina, already a rounded figure, though he was to acquire a forest of cock's feathers in the year to come, and he was born anew, with a fierce aplomb and a studied indifference to harm, in the hands of the obscure Da Ponte. As for Pierrot, he had lived through a hundred lives before he was blessed with maturity from the hands of Deburau; and like Don Juan, who descended from the figure of Larva in the Jesuit tragedies and even beyond, he had a respectable ancestry. Don Juan demonstrated the human spirit's appetite for the conquest of women, but of Pierrot a more subtle claim must be made: He represented an awareness of pity, the knowledge that failure is important and often desired, and that out of failure arise the most triumphant conquests. Pierrot partakes of the glory of Don Juan, for all men in a sense fail to accomplish the one thing they most desire, which is to possess a woman, and Don Juan fails more tragically than most.

The dancing figure of Charlie represents a human and more practical quest. He has no desire for conquests. His desire is for freedom in a trammeled world. He is the virgin spirit of liberty who refuses to be oppressed, refuses to talk in mock profundities, refuses to concern himself with the origin of the universe or with anything except the practical things of the moment, *l'homme moyen sensuel* raised to the pitch of perfection, desiring above all that the world should provide him with sleep, rest, food and amusement, bewildered by machines, and still more bewildered by himself, by the fact that a man is a man. He is the least dangerous of the great archetypes, the most human, the most incorrigibly concerned with things as they are. His characteristics are a terrible enthusiasm and an odd mania for laughing at the world's incongruities, and in his own capricious way he is determined, like Cinderella, that the last should be first, but he goes further, for with the crook of his bamboo cane or a jab in the eye he ensures that the guilty are condemned. And since he is nothing more than the great god Pan reduced to human size and wearing a human dress, there is no reason why we should be surprised to find him among the archetypes, and of all the archetypes he is the one whose emergence is fraught with most consequence, for he is the only one who is not evil.

Faust's sin, like the sin of Don Juan, was one of blazing spiritual pride. They knew no limits to their power. They were determined upon rebellion and presumption, on the breaching of divine law; and in the popular imagination they were always conceived in the glare of infernal fires. They were dark spirits, with the look of demonic majesty on their faces, cruel, merciless and terribly real, so that people recognized themselves in the flame-lit characters. They were cruel not in order to be kind or because they saw virtue in cruelty for cruelty's sake, but because they regarded other people as in their way; they must destroy others to achieve their victory, and every virgin and every honorable man was their legitimate prey. But Charlie is no hunter, desires no prey, is in quest of no El Dorados, and he remains a great personage because he transcends life and the limitations of ordinary life by his infinite resource in dealing with life as it is lived. In this sense he is a far more heroic figure than Faust, who merely transacts a legal document with Mephistopheles, or Don Juan, who goes out of his way to erect barriers between himself and the women he inconveniently desires; for he lives in the real world, his enemies real enemies, his blunders real blunders from which he can extricate himself only by real and human acts. He is no Don Quixote wandering in a land of dreams. He desires the princess, and he knows that she is already married to her prince, and therefore he must go on his way. No windmills fall before him. He has a gypsy's love for simple things, the open road, flowers, the flesh of women, a good meal, and all the excitements of incongruity and irony. It is odd that it has been rarely recorded of him that he is essentially a moral figure, and that he came to birth in an age when morality was in decline and he could have come to birth only in such an age. What is even more astonishing is that the author of this prodigious archetype has been so bitterly attacked.

The failure of the public to recognize the validity and delicacy of *Monsieur Verdoux* springs from many causes; not the least of them was the blunting of our sensibilities by the war. Charlie was playing dangerously in the shadow of total annihilation, that shadow which we fear above all things; even in that shadow he dared to laugh, and not only because he was himself wearing the faintly sinister disguise of someone who pretends to be the agent of annihilation. Refusing to face such a shadow, we become a little like the resourceful Countess Aurélie who, living in her underground cellar, habitually read *Le Gaulois* of March 22, 1903, because this was the best issue the editors ever published, though she added that it was always a shock to see in the columns reserved for the lists of the dead the name of a close acquaintance who seemed to die every morning. When *Monsieur Verdoux* appeared we were still living in the past. "Who wants to have imaginary people staring at us, especially strangers?" says one of the other characters in Giraudoux's wonderful play, and something very similar must have been said by the people who saw *Monsieur Verdoux* and went away disgusted. If they had looked a little closer they would have noticed that the imaginary person was no stranger, but someone who lived far too close to their hearts for comfort.

It had been like that from the very beginning: Charlie had leaped out of space to find his home in the human heart. The man who acted the part, and who was terror-stricken by the creation of his imagination, was a prodigious actor who acted with his whole body, limbs and torso, but it was Charlie rather than Chaplin who gave back to the soul its earthly covering of body. In time Chaplin will be forgotten, but Charlie will remain. He will have a place in the cosmography of the imagination which every generation maps afresh, but in every thousand years only a few new legends are permitted to enter. He will live in the world inhabited by Alexander the Great, Napoleon and the Borgias, with Robin Hood, King Arthur and the Wandering Jew as his companions; Punch, Pierrot and Harlequin will be his accomplices in mischief, and somewhere to the north of his favor there will be Faustus and Don Juan, wearing their legendary masks, striking their legendary attitudes, and like them he will disappear out of history into masquerade. Don Quixote lives there, and so does Ulysses. In this world, where Nausicaa is forever playing ball by the seashore and Falstaff is forever quaffing his flagons of rude ale, Charlie's place is assured. It is even possible that his place is at the very center of the fabulous island, since of all the heroes he is most like ourselves once we have removed our false beards, ear trumpets and magnifying spectacles and show ourselves more naked than we care to be. The formula for Charlie was potent. The elements have been so mixed in him that the recreative activities of latter-day actors will hardly be able to change him. For all the foreseeable future he will walk down the brightly lit roads of the mind, swinging his cane and dexterously picking up cigarette butts, flaunting his absurdly human dignity in the face of the world's importunity, a pirate nailing his flag to the mast, but instead of crossed bones and a skull the flag shows a pair of battered boots and a polished derby, those signs of our human dignity and waywardness.

Charlie was not, of course, the only clown to show an appreciation of human dignity and thereby launch himself into eternity. In our own age at least one other has appeared. Raimu, with his equatorial waistline, his buttony mustache and his foolscap of knitted wool, had some of Falstaff's fervor and Falstaff's inability to recognize the harshness of the world, even though he complained about it. He takes his pleasure where he can. He, too, covers the soul with flesh, and he knows Charlie's trick of claiming a place in both worlds, the world of bouillabaisse and Provençal women and the timeless world of contemplation. In *The Baker's Wife* Raimu is the proud possessor of a young and pneumatic wife. He is the friend of everyone in the village, and he even has a good word to say for an exasperating and long-necked priest, who is a model of the young curé who is determined to change the ways of the village. He is a baker and therefore possesses a sacramental function in the village, but the baker's wife is a jade who runs away with a handsome farm hand. The villagers attempt to comfort Raimu, and while comforting him they get drunk, and when in their drunkenness they bring him a pair of antlers, he refuses to accept their mockery. He refuses indeed to understand them. Why have they come? What are these antlers in comparison with what he has lost; and so he falls to bed, dreaming of his wife, patting and smoothing down the bedclothes where he expects her to be, and then jumping up in the middle of the night to hurl imprecations on a world so unjust that it removes from him his chief source of felicity. Even when he attempts to commit suicide, he is responsible only to himself, for no one else must suffer. The antlers, the drunken friends have nothing to do with his death. The act of suicide is no more than a bewildered recognition of the tumult in his own soul, a gesture of despair wrung from his heart rather than from their deeds. But in the middle of this nightmare he remembers the bread, and with a steadfast air of dignity he wanders from the bedroom to the bakery. There, at a slower pace and without the staccato rhythm which Charlie has made peculiarly his own, we are aware that we are in the presence of the same theme which runs providentially through *The Bank*, *The Kid*, *City Lights*, and half the intervening films. It is odd that in none of Chaplin's films except *A Woman of Paris* is there an unfaithful wife, for in the history of Charlie infidelity clearly has a place. An unfaithful wife is promised in *Limelight*, and this is perhaps as it should be, for only at the very end can Charlie be expected to reveal all his secrets.

Raimu and Chaplin share the eminence. Fernandel with his charming leer and his horse face belongs to carnival; it is a face copied from the painted ten-foot dolls. The Marx brothers possessed an anarchic fire until the seeds of Brooklyn respectability addled them. W. C. Fields was wholly given over to anarchic fire, but the fire alone is hardly sufficient. Donald Duck, the one great creation of the Disney studios, died of the weariness of repeating a single barking cackle, but he was majestic while he lasted, and in Elysium he follows on Charlie's heels. Close to the eminence are Ben Turpin, Slim Summerville, Harry Langdon and Buster Keaton, and Roscoe Arbuckle is not far behind. The great deadpan faces of the Keystone and Roach comedies were wonderful evocations of American legend, the stone faces springing out of the folklore of the tramps, the bums and the I. W. W. They came from the same cradle which produced the man so lean that he cast no shadow; six rattlesnakes struck at him once, and every one missed him. Charlie was not dead-pan, though he would sometimes with great effort suggest that he could be. As for Chaplin, who can clown as well as Charlie, he is, as Mack Sennett has said repeatedly, "simply the greatest actor who has ever lived," but this is probably the least important fact about him.

As he grows older, reflecting on the impermanence of fame and the permanence of legends, Chaplin has not lost his love of clown-ing. The great clown tends to be lost in the greater Charlie. It is probably a pity. There are times when Chaplin at his eternal game of mimicry could hoot Charlie off the stage; and there is as much magic about the man as in the character he invented. Charlie was an accident—we remember Mack Swain's mustache and Roscoe Ar-buckle's trousers. What if they had not been there? There are a hundred comic characters which Chaplin could have played, if he had ever allowed himself to dwell for more than a few moments on the imps which crowd in his brain. I have seen him do things which I thought only Indian fakirs could do. His deep-blue smoky eyes can change color. In a moment his splendidly arched brow can be-come low and mean. His face and neck can swell out until he resembles to perfection the latest news photograph of Winston Churchill, or he can suck in his cheeks until he resembles some poor devil in a prison camp, and by some unwarranted process of magic he can speak the very words they would utter. He still enters a room so superbly quiet that you hardly notice he is there, and there is nothing about him in the least like Charlie. As in his youth he re-sembled Keats, so in age he bears (in the rare moments when his face is in repose) an astonishing resemblance to the elder Yeats, with a great mane of white hair, the face bronzed, the lips pursed, the hands at rest; and just as he enters quietly, so he can disappear as quietly—gone like a flash, leaving the air quivering behind him.

I have seen him many times, and it was always the same—the odd quietness, and the curious passion for disappearing, so that he gives at times the appearance of a man who desires to watch, and only to watch. He is not tall, but he gives the impression of tallness. He still talks with the faintest of Cockney accents, but the mellowness of southern American accents—where did he learn them?—is also there, a professor's voice, or a scholar's, the voice of a man who is accustomed to live alone, and is surprised to hear himself speaking. You are not conscious of his clothes; you are conscious only of that head, glowing in the sun, a head which grows stronger and more leonine as the years pass, so that you wonder how it was ever pos-sible that a man who looks like a president of a vast company or a poet should be remembered as the little chalk-white tramp with the long boots and the waving cane, running madly in the face of authority, as a moth runs at a candle flame.

But when the mood takes him another Chaplin appears who is infinitely remote from the presiding genius of United Artists. Chaplin the clown has all of Beckmann's powers. He comes into the room unobserved and unannounced, very casually, with that curious power of self-effacement, and then suddenly, no one knows how it begins, he is the center of the stage. He begins to gesture. He tells a story. It may be a story about a fishing trip to Santa Barbara or Catalina Island, but the story becomes something else—it becomes pure comedy. With gestures Chaplin outlines the fish, the line, the ship, the watching sea gulls, the way the line is thrown, the way the fish with greedy eyes runs scampering after the bait. You are no longer conscious of the presence of Chaplin, but of the roar of the sea, the desperate struggles of the fish, the creaking of the ship's timbers. The fight goes on. The fish butts the boat, the fisherman falls overboard, and now the fish has become as large as Leviathan. The tremendous battle is waged in the room, and you are convulsed and helpless with laughter, and at the moment when you can bear the sight of the comic battle no longer, he introduces another fish which comes to the rescue of the first, and then the ship springs a leak, and then crowds of small fishing boats come out of nowhere, and somewhere in the sea he is struggling in mortal combat with Leviathan, and there is no end to it, for always at the moment when you think the story is coming to its conclusion Chaplin has introduced from nowhere some miraculous element, some new and outrageous adventure which must be followed to its conclusion, but there is no conclusion, and it is only when you are sick with laughing and crying that he will pause long enough to let you breathe again. Give him a lace handkerchief; he will become an old dowager, a señorita, a Russian noblewoman congratulating Chaliapin on his voice, the lace handkerchief becoming a fichu, a mantilla, the little square of silk in which the Russian noblewoman drowns her sobs. In the end, of course, with something of Charlie's nonchalance, he may wipe his nose very brusquely with the handkerchief, and so put an end to the performance, but when he was taking the part of the old dowager, she was there, and like Beckmann she brought with her the air she lived in, the whole furniture of her mind, her hobbling walk, the delicate way in which her fingertips touched the furniture in her room. With relish he will play the part of one of those girls who haunt Japanese bathhouses, or a city stockbroker, or any politician. They are all observed minutely, with love and irony. He could, if he wanted to, mimic the New York telephone book or the Selective Service Act, and at once they would become both ideally true and hilariously funny.

There are blind beggars who wander over North China with bells fixed to their knees and clapboards attached to their legs and a great collection of musical instruments slung over their chests or tied to their ankles; one blind beggar alone tells a story to the sound of a full orchestra. When Chaplin tells a story, you are conscious of the presence of a full orchestra. Somehow, by some miracle, he conveys the story in all its depths. There will be ten or twelve characters in the story. By a gesture, by a tone of voice, by some trick of shading, you come to know each of them as you know your friends. Then, when the story is over, it is quite likely that he will disappear from the room, vanishing as mysteriously as he entered it; it is only long afterward that you remember he was wearing an outrageous red velvet coat and a pair of gray slacks.

There are mysteries in Chaplin which no one will ever dare to plumb. The perfection of the technique is bewildering; he is over sixty, but the casual sureness of gesture and mime remains, increasing in brilliance with every day that passes; and like the elder Yeats he seems to acquire power with age. There are moments when he wearies of Charlie. He will say, "I am so sick of him. I'd like to wring his neck. I'll never make another film with him." The next moment he is drawing out of the air the most impossible situations, the most ridiculous distortions, and through all these mazes he pictures Charlie at his wrecker's game, humbling the proud, falling in love with all the pretty women, almost delighting to be repulsed, at odds with the malevolence and idiocies of the world. Whole volumes concerning the life of Charlie have been left on the cutting-room floor; more volumes have been told by Chaplin with that quietly disingenuous air of someone revealing the sacred mysteries. I asked him once where Charlie was going during the fade-out, when he wanders down an empty lane, shrugging his shoulders and kicking at a stone. He said darkly, "He is going nowhere. He is only the blind mole digging into his hole." The blaze of neon lights from a deserted sandwich joint on Wilshire Boulevard fell on his face. For a moment he looked like Mephistopheles.

It was one answer; there were a thousand others. Like Proteus, Chaplin can assume a thousand shapes, hint at a thousand ironies, balance his thousand legs upon a thousand tightropes. Chaplin at his clowning has a wider range than Charlie, but in some subtle fashion Charlie always included those possibilities which the clown has explored, and we know that when he is amusing himself quietly in some evil-smelling doss-house, where all the misery of the world is accumulating, Charlie will invent for himself those creatures who are continually being invented by Chaplin with prodigious abandon. Chaplin and Charlie have one thing in common: they are concerned with ultimates. The dowager is the ultimate of dowagers. The fish caught off Catalina Island is the ultimate of fishes. The Japanese bath girl is the ultimate of Japanese bath girls. And the mole digging into his hole is the ultimate of moles.

Because he deals with ultimates, Chaplin is inevitably the child of paradox. He will say, for example, "Why shouldn't I mock poverty? The poor deserve to be mocked. What fools they are!" He will say this savagely, the face becoming a mask of horror-stricken accusation. "Why don't they rebel against poverty? Why do they accept it? It is the ultimate stupidity to accept poverty when there are all the riches of the world—every man should have them." The next moment, confronted with human misery, knowing that it is there, knowing that there is almost nothing he can do about it, he will say, "The whole world is full of poor devils caught in the trap. How will they ever get out? I've tried to help them to forget the trap in my films, but the trap is still there." He once told the Russian producer Eisenstein, "You remember the scene in *Easy Street* where I scatter food from a box to poor children as if they were chickens? You see, I did this because I despise them. I don't like children." Those were the words which Eisenstein remembered, and it is likely enough that Chaplin said them, but it would be absurd to accuse Chaplin of a savage intolerance on the basis of a remembered phrase. He has shown too many times a tenderness for children so real, so overwhelming that it is like a wound. It is possible to go insane by loving too much, by being tender too much. The tortured sensitivity of the artist is the price he pays for the abundance of his love, and when he scattered food to the poor children he was remembering, and subtly transforming, the way in which food had been served to him at an orphanage in London.

The presence of a comic genius in our civilization presents almost as many problems as the presence of Charlie. What role is to be played by the comic genius? The Roman emperors took care that the great mimes should be close to the throne. Every manner of honor was showered upon them. They were known to be dangerous. They were like walking explosives. They had the power to turn the people against the Emperor, and they were known to be afraid of nothing. Two clowns were executed by the Emperor Tiberius for mimicking him and so bringing his rule into jeopardy. The court jesters of the Middle Ages were sometimes roped to the throne by little golden chairs, perhaps for fear they might escape and jest before the people. Dimly, it was recognized that they possessed powers denied to the Emperor. They were closer to the sources of life. They spoke, when they spoke at all—for mostly they claimed a prodigious indifference and were silent for long periods—only at moments of illumination, and so they were cousins to the Sybils, who lived mysteriously in caves and uttered prophecies over braziers. The Emperor was thought to have absolute power over the empire, but he knew that with one word, with one laugh pitched to the exact pitch, the clown could destroy the kingdom, as a singer will destroy a wineglass. It has never happened, of course, but it is conceivable that it might happen; in the totalitarian states comedians may never approach a live microphone. The dangers and triumphs of comedy are very real, and they are especially real in totalitarian times. The opposite of the dictator is the clown. Between them there can be no peace; hence Chaplin's dilemma when he attempted to play both roles. Because he is the opposite of the dictator the clown is dedicated to playing a heroic role, perhaps the most heroic of all, for since his moral function is to remind us of our common humanity and take delight in it, he is the enemy of bureaucracy equally, of all the pigeonholes into which governments, acknowledging their incompetence to deal with human beings, attempt to squeeze us. Secretly the clown rules. More than the poet he is the unacknowledged legislator of our lives, and we may thank God that this is so. Out of the nettle danger he plucks a sense of our real humanity each for the other. There was a time when this was called morality.

The achievement of Chaplin was a singularly moral achievement. He has invented an archetype whose purpose was a moral one, and he gave the game away when he came to utter the anguished and impassioned cry which concludes *The Great Dictator:*

> The good earth is rich and can provide for everyone.
> The way of life can be free and beautiful,
> But we have lost the way.
> Greed has poisoned men's souls,
> Has barricaded the world with hate,
> Has goosestepped us into misery and bloodshed.
> We have developed speed,
> But we have shut ourselves in.
> Machinery that gives abundance has left us in want.
> Our knowledge has made us cynical.
> Our cleverness, hard and unkind.
> We think too much and feel too little.

More than machinery we need humanity.
To those who can hear me, I say—Do not despair!
The misery that has come upon us is but the passing of greed,
The bitterness of men who fear the way of human progress.
The hate of men will pass, and dictators die,
And the power they took from the people will return to the people.
And so long as men die, liberty will never perish.

So long as men die . . . We might have known from the beginning that a clown's confession of faith would implicate mortality.

We are hungrier for morality than we know, so hungry that we leave the flesh outside and go spinning after peace of mind. It is not peace of mind so much as peace of body which will put an end to our miseries; and we have not begun to learn to comfort others bodily. The clown does it by making us laugh, by pulling the curtain aside and showing us the world as it really is, the joyful abandon underneath the frigid mask; and Charlie, hungry to the point of undiscriminating excess, feverishly in love with love, points the way to the substance of the moral life. He knows that men create themselves by their acts, not by their conventions; therefore he acts with the freshness of a child and asks why one should act in any other way. He makes his conventions as he goes along, and always with daring, and always with courage. He cares not a fig for the dictators and bullies; he will throw them down as calmly as he will kick a lump of mud in the road. If we are frightened and would like to sleep because we are afraid, he will tell stories to keep us awake. He knows, as the elders of the Church once knew and then forgot, that divine grace is not conferred on all the schoolmen or even on all the prophets; the charwoman may be the possessor of a saint's nimbus; grace is not conferred only on certain individuals but on all alike. The moral of his story is that there is no moral except the dignity of man under heaven. As for Chaplin's own achievement, as distinguished from Charlie's (which belongs to another order), he knows mortality too well to care very much for recognition—to seek recognition as a person is foolishly to deny one's own doubleness. The world is as it is; men turn into clay; the canisters of film will also perish. But at least for a brief while he has held up a candle which dazzles with a joyful light. In the end his achievement is a part of the divine love in mankind which will one day succeed in abolishing the idea of particular persons altogether, those individual ghosts who haunt us all, packaged and labeled with our names, as though names were more than scratches haphazardly put together. Scotus Erigena believed that in the end we become mere points of light swimming in the divine consciousness, an unhappy fate, for the sunlit waves can do this sort of thing better. St. Paul and earlier schoolmen believed in a nobler destiny: that on the Day of Judgment we shall arise in flesh and in joy. A pity we should have to wait so long.

Now that we live in the long shadow of the rainbow-colored clouds, it is good to remember Charlie, who arises in flesh and in joy and impudence and sheer delight of the world around him, fiercely jubilant, as men often are when under fire, and with no cares to speak of, no guilt to wash clean. Like St. Francis he tips his hat at the birds and trees, and will sing a song with the farm girls. Smitten by the moon, he comes with the gifts of Pan, and in these treacherous days one can do worse than fall into step and beat a drum beside him.

Renaissance
of the
French Film

Feyder, Renoir,
Duvivier, Carné
1934-1940
by Georges Sadoul

This is a chapter from Georges Sadoul's French Film *(Flammarion, Paris, 1949), a book that relates the history of the French film from its beginnings to 1950. As suggested by the films mentioned in it, some of the greatest works came out of France during the 1930s.*

This piece has been translated by Adrienne Foulke.

JACQUES FEYDER left the United States for good at the end of 1933. Five years earlier, he had set out for Hollywood, full of hope and dreaming of the immense technical and financial possibilities he would find there. He found them, indeed, and, by way of a handsome bonus, he was given the great Greta Garbo for his first film. But the Midas-like "golden touch" sterilized his whole personality; the enormous film factory Von Stroheim had nicknamed "the sausage machine" inhibited his real gifts. While in Hollywood Feyder did serve up some tasty, well-seasoned dishes for international consumption, but they lacked body and vitamins (*Olympia, Le Spectre Vert,* etc.). As far as his art was concerned, those five years were a total

479

loss. Back in France, after much talk and several false starts, he was given *Le Grand Jeu* to direct. With his wife, Françoise Rosay, his assistant, Marcel Carné, and a whole company of actors and technicians he set out for North Africa, where he had filmed his first great success, *L'Atlantide*.

Charles Spaak had written the script for the new film. With the advent of the talkies and a growing awareness of the need for more careful development of subjects, the French screen writer was becoming increasingly important. Except for Delluc, the French had ignored the importance of a good script and it is a moot point whether the Impressionist school may not have failed to influence the international film world partly because there was no talented writer at hand, no French Carl Mayer, for example.[1]

Charles Spaak, although he had no very marked individuality, was a prolific, skillful and cultivated script writer; if he produced much work that was routine, he also wrote scripts for some masterpieces of Feyder, Renoir and Duvivier. His chief rival was Jacques Prévert, a poet of the Surrealist school, who was a stronger writer of dialogue than of plot. Prévert's style and outlook on life were to influence profoundly Marcel Carné, on all of whose films but one he collaborated.

Spaak and Feyder, who worked together on the scenario for *Le Grand Jeu*, as on all Feyder's European films, succeeded in transforming a conventional story about the French Foreign Legion into a powerful film. They gave it a psychological background, picking up the Pirandellian theme dear to the author of *L'Image:* Does one ever know with whom one is in love? To highlight the hero's uncertainty, Marie Bell played both women involved, but a second voice was dubbed in for her in the prostitute's role.

The value and influence of *Le Grand Jeu* are not to be measured by these artistic devices of dual casting and voice dubbing any more than the merit of *Crainquebille* is to be found in trick photography. The film's importance is in its portrayal of the Legion and its colonial atmosphere. Pierre Richard Wilm's and Marie Bell's roles are less significant than Françoise Rosay's and Charles Vanel's interpretation of two aging cabaret performers set up in a ménage on the edge of the desert. Nostalgia and the sense of human failure permeate the film's best scenes, set in a stuffy back room where Françoise Rosay tells fortunes for homesick legionnaires. Now that he was

[1] Carl Mayer will be remembered as the writer for *Caligari, Sylvester, Scherben, Der Letzste Mann, Berlin Symphonie eine Grosse Stadt*, and numerous other great successes of the German films from 1920 to 1930.

back in France again, Feyder was returning to the naturalism of Zola and De Maupassant.

Pension Mimosas surpassed *Le Grand Jeu*. Françoise Rosay played a modern Phèdre, in love with her adopted son; to snatch him away from a young rival, she leads the boy to suicide. Charles Spaak's story line is closer to melodrama than to tragedy. But the real subject of the film is gambling: gambling in Monte Carlo, in Paris society and among the toughs of the suburbs. Backgrounds are of such documentary exactness that they assume primary dramatic importance. The rundown family boarding house, from which the film takes its title, is actually a character in the drama, as are the roulette room and the low night club by the Seine where Françoise Rosay finds her adopted son in the company of crooks. The film became the source of one of the tendencies in French film-making to which Marcel Carné later adhered.

Feyder's *Le Grand Jeu* and Duvivier's *La Bandera*, for both of which Spaak wrote the scripts, were the joint roots from which other new trends were to develop.

Julien Duvivier was no newcomer to films. He had begun working immediately after the war and directed twenty-odd silent films, each as undistinguished as the next. They were chiefly adaptations of Henri Bordeaux novels, melodramas, adventure and religious propaganda films. With the talking film, Duvivier found in dialogue a means of expression which he had lacked, and this workmanlike director, who certainly knew his trade, suddenly and surprisingly began to emerge from mediocrity. Following *David Golder*, in which Harry Bauer played a modern, watered-down version of Balzac's *Père Goriot*, *Poil de Carotte* was widely admired for its beautiful photography, for the skillful direction of young Robert Lynen, and a tender understanding of childhood. This last is to be found also in Jean Benoit-Lévy's very nearly contemporary *La Maternelle*, which may even be considered superior to *Poil de Carotte*. In the best French tradition, it offered a credible portrait of the outskirts of Paris, whereas Duvivier's film had weakened the vigorous, trenchant work of Jules Renard by its sentimentality and concessions to popular taste.

For the *La Bandera* script, Charles Spaak borrowed the background of *Le Grand Jeu* with one minor change. He replaced the French Foreign Legion with the Spanish Foreign Legion, then commanded by General Franco, to whom the film was dedicated. The love interest was unimportant. Jean Gabin, an actor who was just beginning to attract attention after a series of routine films, played a criminal who tries to forget his past in the army. The high spots of the film are the death of legionnaires beseiged in a fort (an episode reminiscent of the recently successful *La Patrouille Perdue*) and a free-for-all in which Duvivier, who obviously had the American gangster film in mind, exploited several technical devices such as oblique camera shots which he was to use again and with greater effect in *Carnet de Bal.*

La Bandera was a great box-office success. No such reception was given in that same year—1935—to *Toni*, by Jean Renoir. This modest film, which is too little known, marked a turning point in the work of the producer and was the forerunner of the work being done to-day by Rossellini and De Sica.

Renoir, who shot *Toni* in the south for Marcel Pagnol, found his subject in a news item and re-created the story simply by having his actors play the witnesses of the crime. The crime, therefore, is nothing more than an incident in the film. The real subject is the study of a definite social phenomenon—*i.e.*, the situation of Italian and Spanish emigrant workers in the agricultural regions of southern France. Dialogue and interpretation were trimmed to an extreme naturalism, and the photographic style, twelve years before Rosselini, was documentary. The work, even if it did not venture far beyond the descriptive, was strong and telling; it opened the way to a genuine realism, and it had social purpose, siding firmly with the emigrants, against whom (in the film) a xenophobic, almost racist campaign had been unleashed.

1934 was not only the year of *L'Atalante, Le Grand Jeu, Le Dernier Milliardaire, Angèle* and the contract for *Toni*. It was also the year which witnessed the economic crisis that precipitated grave troubles in French political life and saw a mob storm from the Place de la Concorde to besiege the Palais Bourbon. Mass counter-demonstrations responded to this violence, the police fired on the crowds, and the dead were counted by the dozens. On the wave of this major crisis France entered the prewar period. The subsequent outbreak of hostilities in Ethiopia, then in Spain, sharply pointed up the turn history was taking.

Popular pressure groups were quick to organize. Demonstrations became commonplace. Millions of men joined together to halt a movement such as the one which had just brought Hitler to power. The Popular Front was formed in a spirit of enthusiasm that quickly influenced the films, as *Le Crime de Monsieur Lange* by Prévert and Renoir and *La Belle Équipe* by Spaak and Duvivier both testify.

It has always been hard to appreciate Prévert's dialogue because seriously defective recording made *Le Crime de Monsieur Lange* almost incomprehensible. The film had been made on a shoestring by an independent amateur producer. Experience was to prove with time that the reign of such money-minded independents created fewer problems for directors than had the monopoly formerly imposed by the big companies. Directors and their associates who agreed to work for these mushrooming—often unscrupulous—production companies ran the risk of not being paid or of seeing their funds dry up before their films were completed. Renoir, for example, could not finish his *Nuit de Carrefour*. When it was released, the film made very little sense because half of the scenes he had planned had never been shot. But coupled with these risks was a relative freedom in the choice of subject. A strong director could persuade an amateur producer to give him a free hand, whereas the selection committees of the big companies mercilessly rejected ideas that strayed too far from the beaten path. The golden age of the French cinema was born out of the poverty which was in turn engendered by this relatively free competition.

Le Crime de Monsieur Lange is the story of a small printing shop in the outskirts of Paris. The owner of the firm—a shrewd businessman not too unlike the new breed of film producer—absconds with the company funds. The employees form a co-operative and bring out the novels of an obscure writer, Monsieur Lange (extremely well played by the star of *Le Million*, René Lefèbre). Under the workers' management, the business prospers. The unscrupulous employer hears of this and tries to take back control of the concern. An outraged Monsieur Lange accidentally kills him.

In relation to other films of its period, *Le Crime de Monsieur Lange* stands out as a signpost. Yet neither in intention nor in fact was it a propaganda film. Almost without conscious effort Prévert and Renoir had touched a responsive chord in their French public. They had learned how, in a style different from that of René Clair, to portray the man in the street—the butcher and baker, printer and porter—with the exactness of Émile Zola or Auguste Renoir, the father of Jean.

Shortly after he had finished *Le Crime de Monsieur Lange*, Jean Renoir read Spaak's script for *La Belle Équipe*. He was immediately enthusiastic and wanted to direct it, but Duvivier, who had acquired the rights, refused to release them and finally directed the film himself.

The opening situation is the same as in *Le Million*. A group of down-and-out men wins a big lottery prize. The penny-pinching types of René Clair, appropriate for the old prosperity days, are here replaced by a group of strikers who live in a wretched hotel. They are shown tramping the streets in a vain search for work, standing by posters that are an affront to their poverty, and then back in their furnished room where at nine sharp the proprietor cuts off the electricity. There, in the darkness, as their rage is about to explode, they suddenly get word of their great luck.

The prize they have won is not enough for them all to live on. The story goes beyond the point where the René Clair film ended and emphasizes the need for people to work together. The friends —*la belle équipe*—join in an effort to build their collective security on the periphery of society by buying a dilapidated music hall which they try to get running again.

In certain respects the film surpassed *Le Crime de Monsieur Lange* by demonstrating that a little group of men of good will can, through some vague co-operative scheme, find a kind of cure for the ills of society. Also, *La Belle Équipe* criticized without pessimism the notion, dear to the French, that a little white house with green shutters is a guarantee of happiness. . . . The film nonetheless ended on a weakly ambiguous note.

Toni, Le Crime de Monsieur Lange, and *La Belle Équipe* introduced into French films a new character, rarely present in the films of other countries—the working man. In the Spaak–Duvivier film the new character was perfectly created by Jean Gabin. He originated the young man in the cloth cap, attractive, brave, gentle, hot-tempered, slightly brutal—a figure which mirrored a very important French type of the period—and quickly won international fame.

As for Jean Renoir, when he was unable to secure rights to *La Belle Équipe*, he turned to an adaptation of the famous novel by Maxim Gorky, *The Lower Depths*, in which he starred Jouvet and Jean Gabin. It was a work of mixed and uneven quality. But his next film, *La Grande Illusion*, was a distinguished success on every level and secured his reputation as a great realist. The subject, less restricted than in *Toni*, was a powerful treatment of the burning issue of war.

Little by little the conviction was spreading in Europe that a new world war was imminent. Faced by what seemed its near certainty, men were asking themselves how they should meet the coming situation but found no satisfactory answer.

Renoir thought he might have found a solution and in *La Grande Illusion*, which he wrote with Charles Spaak, he gave it dramatic expression. He made use of his own experiences as a young officer who had spent long years in German prisoner-of-war-camps. The film strove to show that social conditioning can be more important than wars in determining human relations. In the palace-prison the well-born German and French officers (Erich von Stroheim and

Pierre Fresnay) fraternize, finding a basis of sympathy in memories of friendships, polo games—in short, memories of their common world. A fraternization no less real but based on quite different elements flourished among the soldiers of working-class origins. *La Grande Illusion* was affirming that war does not abolish social distinctions or affinities and that these transcend national boundaries even though they do not eliminate nationalist feelings. Thus, when the French prisoners learn of the victory at Verdun, they organize an evening of amateur theatricals as an excuse to sing *"La Marseillaise"* and bait the Germans. And when the Junker officer shoots his French "friend," he also with genuine regret places a treasured sprig of geranium on the man's coffin.

In one sense, *La Grande Illusion* was a final, sincere but hopeless appeal to Germany to recapture the spirit of fraternization which marked the end of the World War I, and to prevent the masters she either had accepted or was enduring from unleashing a new world conflict. Dr. Goebbels did not mistake the sense of the message. He banned the film in the Third Reich and put maximum pressure on Mussolini to prevent its being awarded a prize at the Venice Film Festival.

Just before writing *La Grande Illusion*, Charles Spaak had prepared the script for Feyder's *La Kermesse Héroique*. This film was also concerned with the problem of war, but it offered a different solution.

Actually, the authors of *La Kermesse* did not fully realize that they were dealing with a matter of conscience crucial to the Europe of 1935-40. After finishing the rather somber *Pension Mimosas,* Jacques Feyder was eager to do a light film which would allow him to popularize and publicize throughout the world the great painters of his native Flanders. A short story by Spaak provided the substance of the idea; the dramatist Bernard Zimmer prepared the adaptation; Jean Murat, Françoise Rosay, Louis Jouvet and Alerme played the leads in this costume farce. Lazare Merson (who died shortly thereafter) created the sumptuous backgrounds of a seventeenth-century Flemish village, and scenes were set up in such a way that they resembled magnificent paintings. Feyder's sense of movement and rhythm gave fresh life to the film. It is a major work, so exceptionally beautiful that it could be compared to a cavalcade or ballet, had its historical subject not acquired powerful timeliness because of the world political situation of the '30s.

In the seventeenth-century the troops of the Spanish Governor of Flanders, the fierce Duke of Alba, are nearing a small village; memories of recent massacres plunge the citizens into a panic. The men lose their heads completely, but the women decide to offer the enemy army a sumptuous welcome and so hopefully avert disaster. After a night of truly heroic feasting, the handsome soldiers move on, and the Flemish women tenderly watch the departure of alien men who had brought a taste of adventure into the monotony of their daily lives.

La Grande Illusion had raised the problem of fraternization. La Kermesse Héroique dealt—as early as 1935—with the problem of collaboration. It relegated the possibility of a nation's being occupied to a dreamily remote world, it ridiculed the possibility of resisting an invader, and it in effect glamorized an idyll in which the defeated protect their security by sharing bed and board with their conquerors. . . .

If, after 1940, hindsight allows us to find this moral in La Kermesse Héroique, it certainly was no part of its authors' intentions in 1935. The film did provoke incidents, but paradoxically they came from Flemish nationalists who a few years later became the worst collaborators of the German occupation troops that persecuted Feyder and his colleagues. The fact remains that Dr. Goebbels permitted the film (financed by the Tobis, which he controlled) to be presented in Berlin as the film event of the season, whereas La Grande Illusion was banned there.

Renoir's next film, La Marseillaise, again had war as its theme. One of its best scenes shows French emigrés at Coblentz plotting with Germany to hurl the armies of the Duke of Brunswick against Paris. These well-born eighteenth-century traitors were prototypes of the twentieth-century "collaborators," putting class interest before the safety of their country and scornfully dubbing "patriotism" the business of the "rabble."

To a certain extent such behavior reflected the France of 1937 and seemed to foreshadow the coming war. And the use of "La Marseillaise" is significant. Popular history has the French troops sweeping to victory at Valmy, singing their then new national anthem. (Goethe even described Valmy as opening a new era in human history.) But in his film Renoir made only a passing allusion to the battle, and showed the French soldiers lost in a fog, which is historically correct; as he utilized the fog, it became almost a symbol. The work was often, even abusively, attacked; it was uneven, but it had many fine sequences.

La Marseillaise opened in Paris six months before Munich. . . . But even earlier the rumblings of cannon from beyond the Pyrenees had made many people—including the film makers—feel that they were being swept forward by an irresistible fatality which no human or social force could resist. The resulting theme of escapism, already found in Pagnol's *Marius*, was eventually followed by the theme of isolation.

Pépé le Moko bears the imprint of its director, Julien Duvivier, and of its script writer, the gossip columnist Henri Jeanson. But it is not simply a clever French version of *Scarface* or *Underworld*. While it transplants the gangsters of Chicago to the colorful and picturesque background of the Algerian Casbah, it also deals with the theme of escape.

Pépé, played by Jean Gabin, certainly dreamed of escape. But his revolt led the Parisian to the jungle of the Casbah, where the police themselves do not dare appear and prefer to work through stool pigeons. Pépé is more securely confined in the exotic world of his "escape" than in any prison. He becomes homesick. He dreams of flight with a woman he loves on a ship (the symbolic ship which, in the Pagnol film, bore Marius away). But the film's end brings Pépé face to face with a fatal iron gate that bars his way to the departing ship, and he is shot down by the police. (Later Carol Reed will remember this device in *Odd Man Out*.)

Similar in theme, *Carnet de Bal* made its point less explicitly. It was a clever commercial confection, a series of sketches that brought together the ranking French actors of the period (Fernandel, Raimu, Harry Bauer, Louis Jouvet, Pierre Blanchar, Françoise Rosay, etc.). Twenty years after her first ball, a woman comes across her old dance program. Now a widow, she tries to rekindle the charm which had delighted her young admirers of long ago. One by one she discovers that each man has become a failure. And this is the film's meaning: man is destined to failure; the hopes of youth are illusory, effort is futile; only folly, degradation and old age are real. It is significant that the finest sequences—starring Louis Jouvet and Pierre Blanchar—were those in which the decadence and ruin of their heroes was the most nearly complete.

Duvivier's last prewar film was *La Fin du Jour*. Scripted by Charles Spaak, this dealt with some tragic old actors who, broken down by physical infirmity and approaching death, still struggle to make a comeback.

Charles Spaak had traveled a long way from *La Grande Illusion*, and Julien Duvivier no less far from his run-of-the-mill *Golem*, which he had filmed in Prague, on the theme of revolt and the law of the slave.

The role of destiny was also a guiding theme for the work of Marcel Carné and Jacques Prévert. The first production of this team of poet and ex-journalist was *Jenny*. With the guarantee that

Françoise Rosay would play the title role, Jacques Feyder persuaded a small producer to finance this project of his assistant on *Le Grand Jeu* and *Pension Mimosas*. *Jenny* offered the great actress the role of an ailing mother such as she had played in *Mimosas*.

The plot was rather awkwardly melodramatic. The beautiful closing shots, however, in which Françoise Rosay stands on a suburban railroad bridge, silhouetted against the sky, shows that Marcel Carné was another lyric poet of the films. While following in the footsteps of Jasset, Feuillade, René Clair and Jean Renoir, he had demonstrated the originality of his own gift, especially in treating a subject such as the Paris suburbs.

For their next film they decided to enlarge upon Jacques Prévert's first success, *L'Affaire Est dans le Sac*. Their attempt in *Drôle de Drame* to combine burlesque with a touch of Mack Sennett and *l'Opéra de Quat'sous* was an interesting effort, but the results were uneven and static. The characters were abstractions, creatures of imagination, developed against schematic backgrounds. Nor did they succeed in handling the elements of fantasy and caricature in showing either London or England in general. Carné, like Feyder, needed to know his background thoroughly in order to function well.

On the heels of this partial failure, *Quai des Brumes* was a complete triumph and ranks as one of the most significant films of the prewar period. Title and plot came from the novel of Pierre Mac-Orlan; the book's action took place in the famous Montmartre café, Le Lapin Agile, which in 1914 and before was the meeting place of Picasso, Francis Carco, Apollinaire and Max Jacob. Prévert took the liberty of updating the action and of installing his Bohemians, artists and toughs in a cabaret built by the sea near the great port of Le Havre. A deserter (Jean Gabin) turns up, looking for a ship in which to escape the police; in a fit of anger he has committed a murder. While still searching, he falls in love with Michèle Morgan and her memory-haunting beauty. Before he can carry her off to happiness in some new and faraway land, he must overcome their enemies—her despicable guardian (Michel Simon) and his hoodlum friends. He kills the uncle, but is killed in turn by one of the gang (Pierre Brasseur). Once again death and the door of fate prevent an escape to happiness.

During their formative years Prévert and Carné had enormously admired Murnau and Von Sternberg. For a time the gangster (of *Underworld*, for example) seemed to them the true hero of modern times and his sawed-off machine gun, defying the world, the one weapon against social injustice. By 1930 they had changed their point of view. The superman was found to have too much in common with Hitler's SS men. The gangster in *Quai des Brumes*, for example, was no longer a hero; he was quite simply a coward.

The rebellious Gabin was not a professional criminal; he was the accidental criminal, driven to murder by some rather ill-defined social injustice. For him murder was not a solution but a form of misfortune. All he asked of life was to be able to live in peace, far from the world, with the woman he loved. But as bad fairies used to hover over the cradles of innocent children, forces of good and evil fight over the bed of these lovers. The good forces, represented by a tramp, a painter and an innkeeper, are arrayed against the bad, a shopkeeper—a "fence"—and the ruffians. Evil wins out over good; happiness has no place in this world; it is human destiny that good people and lovers always be defeated. The struggle is not futile, however; although defeat lies at the end of the road, the kind or good deed must always be performed and herein lies the meaning of life.

To a certain extent *Le Quai des Brumes* may be said to have followed from and developed aspects of Von Sternberg's *The Docks of New York*. Its successor, *Hôtel du Nord*, was a fairly free adaptation of a book by Eugène Dabit, a masterpiece of the social novel. It was reminiscent in at least one of its episodes of Rouben Mamoulian's *City Streets*, in which the lovers have no alternative but suicide. This film lacks the flowing unity of *Quai des Brumes*, perhaps because Jacques Prévert had no part in it. And while the poetic charm of a famous Parisian neighborhood, the Canal St. Martin, was captured with rare intensity, the film remains a minor one in Carné's production.

On the other hand, *Le Jour se Lève*, filmed on the eve of World War II, was a masterpiece. As in Von Sternberg's *Underworld*, the hero is tracked down and cornered by the police and kills himself in the end. Gabin in *Pépé le Moko* was safe so long as he did not leave the Casbah where he had friends and lovers. Gabin in *Le Jour se Lève* is hopelessly alone, imprisoned in a tiny room, and his hours are numbered. From the depths of his despair, he strains with all his strength for total annihilation.

This situation challenged Carné and Prévert to do their utmost to find an adequate artistic solution. Their hero was a foundry worker, in love with a flower-shop clerk. He stumbles onto the path that is to lead him to crime and to death by falling in with two depraved people, the broken-down dog-trainer (Jules Berry) and his mistress (Arletty). Carné created these two characters through background, action and costume rather than dialogue. The dog-trainer is the sum of all corruption and vice; he *is* evil incarnate. The flower-shop girl (Jacqueline Laurent) is the eternal feminine—ambiguous, ingenuous, perverse. The worker in his cap and sweater talks like a pseudo-intellectual of the Left Bank, carefully choosing the metaphors he uses to describe the tragedy of the human dilemma and the inescapability of destiny.

Le Jour se Lève, offspring of crisis, turmoil and much soul-searching, was a perfect example of artistic achievement. Jean Gabin reached the peak of his art in a role made to order for him. Arletty, bitter, provocative, cynical, yet with a good heart, is the partner of a despicable, weak and ignoble Jules Berry, who listens at keyholes, seduces young girls, tortures dumb animals and lies with every breath he draws. He personifies all that is both evil and inevitable; the fusion of these two in a single character gives it extraordinary strength.

On the eve of the war, then, a spirit of somber gloom and fatalism pervaded the French film world. Carné was possessed by a quasi-metaphysical confusion, whereas the bitterness of his master Feyder—the fruit of hard personal experience—was tempered by profound albeit disillusioned sympathy for human frailty. Duvivier, on the other hand, found man fundamentally evil and despicable.

After finishing *La Kermesse Héroique*, Feyder accepted Alexander Korda's proposal to direct *Knight without Armor* in London, with Marlene Dietrich and Robert Donat. It turned out to be as great a mistake as his Hollywood venture. Then, in Munich, he filmed *Les Gens du Voyage* in a French and German version. While this was more interesting, especially the excellent scenes of a traveling circus, the childish, melodramatic plot quite defeated Feyder's characteristic strengths—his skillful direction of actors, his sense of atmosphere, the clarity of his story line and his plastic yet precise photography. It is a pity that, during this golden age of the French cinema, its greatest pioneer should have lived primarily abroad and chosen to work with facile, colorful subjects rather than with solid, well-defined material. His last great French film, *La Loi du Nord* (shown in a mutilated version during the German occupation) suffered for being shot against a synthetic American background haphazardly put together in French studios; a few exteriors were filmed, however, in the then completely unknown Norwegian port of Narvik. The film's ending was tragic: the love of three men for the same woman led them all to their deaths. . . .

Jean Renoir's optimism, triumphant in *Le Crime de Monsieur Lange*, also turned to bitterness. *La Bête Humaine* was taken from one of Zola's gloomiest, most pedestrian novels. Despite the director's sincere effort to remain faithful to his model, the film transformed the book. In Zola the mechanic Lantier was the victim of the physiological doom which hung over the Rougen Macopiart family (a pseudo-scientific formulation of the vengeful gods' pursuit of the Atridae in classical Greek poems). Like Carné, Renoir has Lantier driven to a life of crime almost accidentally, because "life is such a dirty business." In another period—for example, when he was directing *Thérèse Raquin*—Renoir would probably have given a very different motivation and had the frustrated sensuality of the heroine be the force which made her hate men so much that she was driven to crime. However, while passional conflict had a place in this film, the essential theme was man in relation to his work. *La Bête Humaine*'s chief merit is the documentary accuracy with which the two journeys from Paris to Le Havre are filmed and the graphic record of the daily life of an express-train engineer.

Since *La Chienne* Renoir had been fascinated by untried camera possibilities. Now he turned away from conventional methods of photography. He used varying depths of focus to unite his characters with their surroundings, careful to keep the backgrounds in as sharp focus as the foregrounds. The technique was harshly criticized at the time, yet three years later Gregg Toland was to introduce it to the United States. Renoir never applied these ideas blindly or mechanically, but adapted them as required. Stjostom in *Les Proscrits* had already faded the background out of focus when he wanted to spotlight action. In the murder scene of *La Bête Humaine*, which is very close to a similar scene in *La Chienne*, the man and woman stand out alone against an almost neutral background. Yet in both films, a song with resonant counterpoint diminishes our sense of their isolation and serves to bind them to the rest of the world.

La Règle du Jeu, Renoir's last French film, was one of his finest. Leaving his characteristic dramatic sequences, social settings and props behind him, the director staged a comedy in the luxurious surroundings of a rich man's property. This was an already familiar world, and even before 1900 the novelist Paul Bourget had baptized it "Cosmopolis." The film is polarized around a great reception which ends in tragedy. A similar sequence occurred in *Les Bas-Fonds*, *La Grande Illusion* and *La Bête Humaine*. . . .

Renoir wrote scenario and dialogue, acted one of the major roles and improvised a whole section of the film which—in a great departure from the usual procedure—he directed scene by scene in the exact order each would be seen on the screen. When he directed *La Règle du Jeu*, Renoir was at the peak of his fame, he was master of his art and of his materials, and yet the film was a total failure. It was withdrawn a few days after its opening and never reached a wide public. A few weeks later war broke out, the film was banned by the censor, and since then it has not been shown in France or abroad.

La Règle du Jeu was nonetheless the only French work which expressed in film terms the spirit of confusion that prevailed after Munich and into the first months of the Second World War. In certain respects, Jean Renoir did achieve the ambition recorded in the epitaph to his work: that, on the eve of a conflict which everyone acknowledged was imminent, he should give France a work of magnitude equal to *Le Mariage de Figaro*, which Beaumarchais presented on the eve of the Revolution.

Renoir, however, had seriously misjudged popular taste, which demanded entertainment to relieve the tensions of the day. Nor did he himself avoid a conflict of expressions in the film. At the end, when a series of slapstick blunders causes the tragic death of the most sympathetic of heroes, the film's moods are so dissonant that what was intended to be gripping was actually laughable. Renoir might have overcome this—and several other discrepancies—had he not been so taken up by his new enthusiasm for amateur acting that he allowed his actors to work on their own initiative, with the result that some characters lost even a semblance of reality.

As in the earlier *Le Million*, *La Règle du Jeu* was centered around a chase. Brandishing a revolver, the jealous gamekeeper rushes through the great rooms of the château in hot pursuit of the local poacher who has been trying to ensnare his wife, the parlor maid. Elsewhere in the castle, on a stage set up for amateur theatricals, the guests, dressed as Bavarian peasants, are rehearsing the martial *"En revenant de la revue,"* which from the time of Méliès has been the rallying song of the partisans of the reactionary General Boulanger. The master of the chateau, a collector of antique mechanical toys, is proudly exhibiting his mechanized portable organ. To the tune of its childish melody, the servants' chase picks up speed, while the family and their guests fall into a fight over the mistress of the château, like so many brawling porters amid the books, bibelots and stuffed birds. The hurly-burly scene gives way to the ghosts and skeletons who perform a macabre dance on the stage. This brilliant sequence, following a chase of genuine and chilling ferocity, is a film metaphor which translates with uncommon imaginative power the troubled atmosphere of 1939. As Renoir was directing these very scenes, the European radio was reporting the entry of Adolph Hitler into Prague. And Sologne, that lovely corner of France with its châteaux and hunting terrain, forests and swamplands, whose natural beauty Renoir captured so remarkably, was one year later to become the battlefield for the last stand of the French Army in 1940. *La Règle du Jeu*, both in style and in theme, was *the* film of the moment. Renoir had profoundly believed in this film. When it proved a failure, he was in such confusion and despair that he left France and went to Rome to direct *La Tosca*. René Clair, who had come to Paris to direct *Air Pur* (in which the protagonists are children), saw his work decisively interrupted by the war. Mobilization and growing unease completely disorganized the Paris studios. For years French production had averaged 125 films a year; in 1939 it fell to seventy-five.

If, by virtue of their great talents, Renoir, Feyder, Marcel Carné and René Clair had dominated the French cinema from 1930 to 1940, film output was not limited to their work alone. Directors from the silent days were also active, but they produced hardly anything during this period which is worth remembering.

Abel Gance after finishing *Napoléon*, undertook his gigantic, bombastic *Fin du Monde;* distributed as a talkie, it was a total failure. He was then obliged to direct or produce a series of second-rate films (*Le Roman d'un Jeune Pauvre, Lucrèce Borgia, Jérôme Perrau, Le Maître de Forges*, etc.). Occasionally he remade his earlier master-pieces (*Mater Dolorosa, J'accuse*). Perhaps his best film was *Un Grand Amour de Beethoven*, in which he experimented with inter-esting sound effects, but the film was ruined by Harry Bauer's over-acting. His moving *Paradis Perdu* had considerable charm.

Marcel L'Herbier produced numerous films (*Le Mystère de la Chambre Jaune, Le Bonheur, Le Scandale, Les Hommes Nouveaux, La Porte du Ciel, Veille d'Armes, La Citadelle du Silence, Forfaiture, Nuits de Feu*, etc.) and he made a speciality of historical films (*La Tragédie Impèriale, Adrienne LeCouvreur, Entente Cordiale*, etc.).

Baroncelli continued his policy of filming adaptations of plays and popular novels (*L'Ami Fritz, L'Arlésienne, Le Père Goriot*) and colonial subjects (*S.O.S. Sahara, L'Homme du Niger*). His patriotic melodramas (*Nitchevo, Feu*) always fell short of the mark.

Léon Poirier followed much the same road (*Soeurs d'Armes, Brazza, L'Appel du Silence*), although occasionally he showed that he had not forgotten his earlier experiments with the documentary technique.

Raymond Bernard's best film was his adaptation of *Les Misérables*, presented in several episodes, but *Anne-Marie, Le Coupable, Le Cavalcade d'Amour* and even *Les Otages* are best forgotten. *Les*

Otages had a fine subject which was ruined by poor taste and a poor script.

The record of those who joined the industry after 1930 and seemed then to be the hope of the French cinema was no better. Marc Allegret was the most brilliant of the lot. He tried to repeat his success of *Lac aux Dames* with *Les Beaux Jours* and again with *Sous les Yeux d'Occident*. But it seemed as if he lacked the vigor needed to make this the great film it could have been (it marked the film debut of Jean-Louis Barrault). *Gribouille* had a good scenario from Marcel Achard and was excellently acted by Raimu. *Orage*, adapted from Bernstein, starred Charles Boyer and revealed the very appealing talents of Michèle Morgan. (She and Jean Gabin were perhaps the most typical and familiar faces of the prewar French films.) *Entrée des Artistes* was intelligent but lacked impact; its interesting documentary study of the Paris Conservatoire was spoiled by Henri Jeanson's melodramatic script.

After his routine *Mutinés de l'Elseneur*, Pierre Chenal turned to melodrama and lapsed into total failure of taste with *L'Alibi* and *La Maison du Maltais*. He succeeded somewhat better with *L'Affaire Lafarge*, based on a well-known trial, and *Le Dernier Tournant*, adapted from James Cain's *The Postman Always Rings Twice*.

Jean Benoît-Lévy had had a genuine success with his charming and perceptive *La Maternelle*, *Itto*, *Hélène* (adapted from the Vicki Baum book) and *Altitude 3,200* were failures, but his *Mort du Cygne*, although rather melodramatic, was a moving film and offered a fine documentary study of the dance world.

Dimitri Kirsanoff's *Rapt*, while interesting, was nonetheless a failure. Kirsanoff then seemed to settle for subjects with sure box-office appeal, but he still managed to inject some of his experimental ideas into them (*Franco de Port, La Plus Belle Fille du Monde, L'Avion de Minuit*). *Quartier sans Soleil* portrayed life in the slums; it was a sympathetic but awkward and melodramatic effort.

After directing *Ciboulette*, an operetta on which the then novice Jacques Prévert collaborated, Claude Autant-Lara went on to make quite ordinary films for Maurice Lehmann such as *Le Ruisseau* and *Fric-Frac*. Lehmann adapted *Fric-Frac* from Édouard Bourdet's hit, and Michel Simon and Arletty were the stars.

The contribution of foreign directors working in France was of minor importance. The Russian Léonide Moguy made his debut with a stirring vaudeville film, *Le Mioche*, and seemed to have achieved definite power with *Prison sans Barreaux*, in which two new actresses, Corinne Luchaire and Ginette Leclerc, made their debuts. But he had greater facility than strength, as succeeding films showed

(*Conflit, Je t'Attendrai, L'Empreinte de Dieu*), all of which were as meticulous as they were uninspired.

After *Don Quichotte*, that beautiful yet quite unmoving photo album, and after his Hollywood fiasco, G. W. Pabst produced only decadent efforts such as *Le Drame de Shangai, De Haut en Bas, Jeunes Filles en Détresse* and *Mademoiselle Docteur*, where little of the old *Opera de Quat'-sous* is to be found aside from his taste for setting his stories in disreputable surroundings.

Anatole Litvak remade *L'Équipage*, a silent film of Maurice Tourneur, and then proceeded to the considerable commercial success of *Mayerling*, which took director and stars (Charles Boyer and Danielle Darrieux) to Hollywood. This clever success brought nothing of artistic value to the French cinema; nor did Kurt Bernhardt's stirring *Le Vagabond Bienaimé*, or Max Ophuls' sensitive—and boring—*Werther*, Robert Siodmak's *Mister Flow*, a remarkable pastiche of the famous *Trouble in Paradise* by Lubitsch, or the pathetic *Ultimatum*, the last film of Robert Wiene, director of *Caligari*, who died shortly after; Fedor Ozep's pompous *Dame de Pique*, the less than mediocre *Bataille* of Farkas, or *Le Mensonge de Nina Petrovna* of Tourjanksy.

French critics were puzzled by the success Sacha Guitry's films enjoyed abroad. When he made his debut in the early 1900s, Guitry's contributions as author-actor had some originality. But in the period between the two wars, his fashionable comedies became quite stereotyped. He filmed several (*Le Mot de Cambrone, Désiré, Quadrille*) and in the process of always playing to the camera with the most astonishing self-complacency, he discovered that by exploiting every trick in the trade, including the most varied make-ups, he could present evening-long monologues. This otherwise unfortunate predilection did allow him to produce his most clever success, *Le Roman d'un Tricheur*, which in technique was almost like a silent film but with running commentary. It was nothing but a trick, but this time it worked. On the other hand, *Les Perles de la Couronne* and *Remontons les Champs-Elysées*, the latter a series of ostentatious sketches of fashionable society, did not rise above the level of an inferior *Folies Bergères*.

The world of Sacha Guitry does not extend beyond the fashionable boulevards of city life. The world of Pagnol, a colleague of his from the theater, draws its originality and vigor from the soil and atmosphere of Provence. The director-author had had an almost perfect success with *Angèle*. He hoped to score as well with *Régain*. Adapted from a Giono novel, the film portrays an abandoned village of Haute Provence, and its "back-to-the-land" theme is offered as a universal cure for war, unemployment, social corruption, mechanization and all other ills from which society suffers. This primitive and rather overblown ideology, plus one or two mistakes, spoiled a film which, had it really studied the causes for the decline of the Provençal village, could have been both poetic and illuminating.

Pagnol was more at ease in *La Femme du Boulanger*, which was again a Giono subject. Unmarred by philosophical pretensions, it was a simple tale, a straight farce in the style of a lesser Molière. The baker's wife in a small village runs off with a handsome shepherd. In despair, her husband refuses to bake his bread. When all appeals to him fail, the entire village sets out to look for the missing wife. She is found, returned, and life also returns to normal. The truly great gifts of Raimu, the sensuality of Ginette Leclerc, and above all the slightly facile but accurate skill with which local characters are drawn—the priest, the schoolmaster, mayor, squire, the village *boule* players—all these contribute to making *La Femme du Boulanger* second only to *Angèle* in Pagnol's work. Despite theatrical touches, the film unquestionably belongs among the best work of the French film of its day. It is easy to understand the great success it enjoyed abroad, in London and even more in New York. This amusing and in some respects powerful work should not, however, be allowed to overshadow numerous other films produced in France during the same period which were both more original and more powerful. . . .

If the hopes engendered by the introduction of the talkies had not been generally realized (not even by Georges Lacombe, whose *Les Musiciens du Ciel* had considerable merit), several important film personalities appeared in the immediate prewar period.

Foremost among them was Jean Grémillon. The unmerited failure of *La Petite Lise* closed the doors of French studios to him. He worked for a while in Spain (*La Dolorosa*) and then went to Berlin to make French films. The first were quite inferior, but *Gueule d'Amour*, for which Charles Spaak wrote a fine scenario based on a novel by André Beucler, showed virile qualities that *L'Étrange Monsieur Victor*, which provided Raimu with one of his best roles, fully confirmed. Grémillon next undertook *Remorques*, with Jean Gabin and Michèle Morgan. It has some very beautiful scenes, among them the melancholy wedding in a summer garden by the seashore which is interrupted by the grim news of a ship in distress; everyone deserts the wedding to rush to the rescue. Even if the subject was rather forced, Jacques Prévert's treatment and dialogue make it convincing and throughout Grémillon showed his gift for characterization.

Jacques Prévert was also one of the group responsible for the moving and successful *Les Disparus de Saint Agyl*. It is based on a detective story by Pierre Véry, the action taking place, just before 1914, in a boy's school. The director, Christian Jaque, had produced numerous mediocre commercial films, but, like Duvivier before him, he had genuine talent and capacity for growth. The adaptation by Jacques Prévert (which he did not sign) was a beautifully sensitive treatment of childhood, such as Christian Jaque was not completely equal to when shortly afterward he directed *L'Enfer des Anges*. These successes, however, established Jaque and he never lapsed into any more mass-produced melodramas. Another prewar film that cannot be overlooked is Jef Musso's *Le Puritain*, an expressionist version of a novel by Liam O'Flaherty, with Jean-Louis Barrault and Viviane Romance in the leading roles.

Just before war was declared, the novelist André Malraux gave a one-night performance in Paris of *Espoir*, which he had directed in Spain during the last months of the Civil War. The film was an adaptation of several episodes from his book of the same title. It clearly showed the influence of the silent Soviet films and the gangster classics. Circumstances delayed his finishing the work, and the declaration of war postponed its release until 1945. Because it remained unknown for so long, *Espoir*, contrary to some opinion, could scarcely have influenced the neo-realism of the Italians, although they have much in common. Certain crowd scenes where the author is fired by Spanish revolutionary enthusiasm, are extremely successful. Sequences in which his characters soliloquize on the "human dilemma" sound false—perhaps because the actors are so poor. The French, fresh from the war from liberation, sensed the artificiality of *Espoir*. The film was relatively unsuccessful and remained an isolated effort to film literature, without great influence on other French film makers.

In 1939, despite *La Règle du Jeu* and *Le Jour se Lève*, the new French film group was giving signs of evident weariness. Whether it would be able to achieve its own rebirth was the moot question confronting it when the long-feared, long-awaited war broke out.

The

Golden

Age

———

by Henry Miller

There is hardly an aspect of modern life about which Henry Miller has not written. He has covered such things as bread in America, the Brooklyn Bridge, mysticism, starving in Paris, hitch-hiking throughout America, painting, literature, to mention a few. It was inevitable that Mr. Miller would have his say on the film, and as usual he makes his share of interesting and entertaining observations. In the following piece, taken from a collection of essays called The Cosmological Eye *(New Directions, 1939), he uses the Luis Bunuel-Salvador Dali film* L'Age d'Or *as a springboard for his comments on film art and the film public in general.*

AT PRESENT THE CINEMA is the great popular art form, which is to say it is not an art at all. Ever since its birth we have been hearing that at last an art has been born which will reach the masses and perhaps liberate them. People profess to see in the cinema possibilities which are denied the other arts. So much the worse for the cinema!

There is not one art called the Cinema but there is, as in every art, a form of production for the many and another for the few. Since the death of avant-garde films—*Le Sang d'un Poète*, by Cocteau, was I believe the last—there remains only the mass production of Hollywood.

The few films which might justify the category of "art" that have appeared since the birth of the cinema (a matter of forty years or so) died almost at their inception. This is one of the lamentable and amazing facts in connection with the development of a new art form. Despite all effort the cinema seems incapable of establishing itself as art. Perhaps it is due to the fact that the cinema more than any other art form has become a controlled industry, a dictatorship in which the artist is dominated and silenced.

Immediately an astonishing fact asserts itself, namely, that the greatest films were produced at little expense! It does not require millions to produce an artistic film; in fact, it is almost axiomatic that the more money a film costs the worse it is apt to be. Why then does the real cinema not come into being? Why does the cinema remain in the hands of the mob or its dictators? Is it purely an economic question?

The other arts, it should be remembered, are fostered in us. Nay, they are forced upon us almost from birth. Our taste is conditioned by centuries of inoculation. Nowadays one is almost ashamed to admit that he does not like this or that book, this or that painting, this or that piece of music. One may be bored to tears, but one dare not admit it. We have been educated to pretend to like and admire the great works of art with which, alas, we have no longer any connection.

The cinema is born and it is an art, another art—but it is born too late. The cinema is born out of a great feeling of lassitude. Indeed lassitude is too mild a word. The cinema is born just as we are dying. The cinema, like some ugly duckling, imagines that it is related in some way to the theater, that it was born perhaps to replace the theater, which is already dead. Born into a world devoid of enthusiasm, devoid of taste, the cinema functions like a eunuch: it waves a peacock-feathered fan before our drowsy eyes. The cinema believes that what we want of it is to be put to sleep. It does not know *that we are dying*. Therefore, let us not blame the cinema. Let us ask ourselves why it is that this truly marvelous art form should be allowed to perish before our very eyes. Let us ask why it is that when it makes the most heroic efforts to appeal to us its gestures are unheeded.

I am talking about the cinema as an *actuality*, a something which exists, which has validity, just as music or painting or literature. I am strenuously opposed to those who look upon the cinema as a medium to exploit the other arts or even to synthetize them. The cinema is not another form of this or that, nor is it a synthetic product of all the other this-and-thats. The cinema is the cinema and nothing but. And it is quite enough. In fact, it is magnificent.

Like any other art the cinema has in it all the possibilities for creating antagonisms, for stirring up revolt. The cinema can do for man what the other arts have done, possibly even more, but the first condition, the prerequisite in fact, is—*take it out of the hands of the mob!* I understand full well that it is not the mob which creates the films we see—not technically, at any rate. But in a deeper sense it *is* the mob which *actually* creates the films. For the first time in the history of art the mob has dictated what the artist should do. For the first time in the history of man an art is born which caters exclusively to the masses. Perhaps it is some dim comprehension of this unique and deplorable fact which accounts for the tenacity with which "the dear public" clings to its art. The silent screen! Shadow images! Absence of color! Spectral, phantasmal beginnings. The dumb masses visualizing themselves in those stinking coffins which served as the first movie houses. An abysmal curiosity to see themselves reflected in the magic mirror of the machine age. Out of what tremendous fear and longing was this "popular" art born?

I can well imagine the cinema never having been born. I can imagine a race of men for whom the cinema would have been thoroughly unnecessary. But I cannot imagine the robots of this age being without a cinema, *some kind of cinema.* Our starved instincts have been clamoring for centuries for more and more substitutes. And as substitute for living the cinema is ideal. Does one ever remark the look of these cinema hounds as they leave the theater? That dreamy air of vacuity, that washed-out look of the pervert who masturbates in the dark! One can hardly distinguish them from the drug addicts: they walk out of the cinema like somnambulists.

This of course is what they want, our worn-out, harassed beasts of toil. Not more terror and strife, not more mystery, not more wonder and hallucination, but peace, surcease from care, the unreality of the dream. But *pleasant* dreams! *Soothing* dreams! And here it is difficult not to restrain a word of consolation for the poor devils who are put to it to quench this unslakable thirst of the mob. It is the fashion among the intelligentsia to ridicule and condemn the efforts, the truly herculean efforts, of the film directors, the Hollywood dopesters particularly. Little do they realize the invention it requires to create each day a drug that will counteract the insomnia of the mob. There is no use condemning the directors, nor is there any use deploring the public's lack of taste. These are stubborn facts, and irremediable. The panderer and the pandered must be eliminated—*both at once!* There is no other solution.

How speak about an art which no one recognizes as *art?* I know that a great deal has already been written about the "art of the cinema." One can read about it most every day in the newspapers and the magazines. But it is not the *art* of the cinema which you will find discussed therein—it is rather the dire, botched embryo as it now stands revealed before our eyes, the stillbirth which was mangled in the womb by the obstetricians of art.

For forty years now the cinema has been struggling to get properly born. Imagine the chances of a creature that has wasted forty years of its life in being born! Can it hope to be anything but a monster, an idiot?

I will admit nevertheless that I expect of this monster-idiot the most tremendous things! I expect of this monster that it will devour its own mother and father, that it will run amuck and destroy the world, that it will drive man to frenzy and desperation. I cannot see it otherwise. There is a law of compensation and this law decrees that even the monster must justify himself.

Five or six years ago I had the rare good fortune to see *L'Age d'Or,* the film made by Luis Bunuel and Salvador Dali, which created a riot at Studio 28. For the first time in my life I had the impression that I was watching a film which was pure cinema and nothing but cinema. Since then I am convinced that *L'Age d'Or* is unique and unparalleled. Before going on I should like to remark that I have been going to the cinema regularly for almost forty years; in that time I have seen several thousand films. It should be understood, therefore, that in glorifying the Bunuel-Dali film I am not unmindful of having seen such remarkable films as:

The Last Laugh (Emil Jannings)
Berlin
Le Chapeau de Paille d'Italie (René Clair)
Le Chemin de la Vie
La Souriante Madame Beudet (Germaine Dulac)
Mann Braucht Kein Geld
La Mélodie du Monde (Walter Ruttmann)
Le Ballet Mécanique
Of What Are the Young Films Dreaming? (Comte de Beaumont)
Rocambolesque
Three Comrades and One Invention
Ivan the Terrible (Emil Jannings)
The Cabinet of Dr. Caligari
The Crowd (King Vidor)
La Maternelle

Othello (Krause and Jannings)
Extase (Machaty)
Grass
Eskimo
Le Maudit
Lilliane (Barbara Stanwyck)
A Nous la Liberté (René Clair)
La Tendre Ennemie (Max Ophuls)
The Trackwalker
Potemkin
Les Marins de Cronstadt
Greed (Eric von Stroheim)
Thunder over Mexico (Eisenstein)
The Beggar's Opera
Mädchen in Uniform (Dorothea Wieck)
Midsummer Night's Dream (Reinhardt)
Crime and Punishment (Pierre Blanchard)
The Student of Prague (Conrad Veidt)
Poil de Carotte
Banquier Pichler
The Informer (Victor McLaglen)
The Blue Angel (Marlene Dietrich)
L'Homme à la Barbiche
L'Affaire Est dans le Sac (Prévert)
Moana (Flaherty)
Mayerling (Charles Boyer and Danielle Darrieux)
Kriss
Variety (Krause and Jannings)
Chang
Sunrise (Murnau)
nor
three Japanese films (ancient, medieval and modern Japan) the titles of which I have forgotten;
nor
a documentary on India
nor
a documentary on Tasmania
nor
a documentary on the death rites in Mexico, by Eisenstein
nor
a psychoanalytic dream picture, in the days of the silent film, with Werner Krause

nor
certain films of Lon Chaney, particularly one based on a novel of
Selma Lagerlöf in which he played with Norma Shearer
nor
The Great Ziegfeld, nor *Mr. Deeds Goes to Town*
nor
The Lost Horizon (Frank Capra), the first *significant* film out of
Hollywood
nor
the very first movie I ever saw, which was a newsreel showing
the Brooklyn Bridge and a Chinese with a pigtail walking over the
bridge in the rain! I was only seven or eight years of age when I
saw this film in the basement of the old South Third Street Presby-
terian Church in Brooklyn. Subsequently I saw hundreds of pictures
in which it always seemed to be raining and in which there were
always nightmarish pursuits in which houses collapsed and people
disappeared through trap doors and pies were thrown and human life
was cheap and human dignity was nil. And after thousands of slapstick, pie-throwing Mack Sennett films, after Charlie Chaplin had
exhausted his bag of tricks, after Fatty Arbuckle, Harold Lloyd,
Harry Langdon, Buster Keaton, each with his own special brand of
monkeyshines, came the chef-d'oeuvre of all the slapstick, pie-throwing festivals, a film the title of which I forget, but it was among the
very first films starring Laurel and Hardy. This, in my opinion, is the
greatest comic film ever made—because it brought the pie throwing
to apotheosis. There was nothing but pie throwing in it, nothing but
pies, thousands and thousands of pies and everybody throwing them
right and left. It was the ultimate in burlesque, and it is already
forgotten.

In every art the ultimate is achieved only when the artist passes
beyond the bounds of the art he employs. This is as true of Lewis
Carroll's work as of Dante's *Divine Comedy,* as true of Lao-tse as of
Buddha or Christ. The world must be turned upside down, ran-
sacked, confounded in order that the miracle may be proclaimed. In
L'Age d'Or we stand again at a miraculous frontier which opens up
before us a dazzling new world which no one has explored. *"Mon
idée générale,"* wrote Salvador Dali, *"en écrivant avec Bunuel le
scénario de* L'Age d'Or, *a été de présenter la ligne droite et pure de
conduite d'un être qui poursuit l'amour à travers les ignorables
idéaux humanitaires, patriotiques et autres misérables mécanismes de
la réalité."* I am not unaware of the part which Dali played in the
creation of this great film, and yet I cannot refrain from thinking

of it as the peculiar product of his collaborator, the man who directed the film: Luis Bunuel. Dali's name is now familiar to the world, even to Americans and Englishmen, as the most successful of all the surrealists today. He is enjoying a temporal vogue, largely because he is not understood, largely because his work is sensational. Bunuel, on the other hand, appears to have dropped out of sight. Rumor has it that he is in Spain, that he is quietly amassing a collection of documentary films on the revolution. What these will be, if Bunuel retains any of his old vigor, promises to be nothing short of staggering. For Bunuel, like the miners of the Asturias, is a man who flings dynamite. Bunuel is obsessed by the cruelty, ignorance and superstition which prevail among men. He realizes that there is no hope for man anywhere on this earth unless a clean slate be made of it. He appears on the scene at the moment when civilization is at its nadir.

There can be no doubt about it: the plight of civilized man is a foul plight. He is singing his swan song without the joy of having been a swan. He has been sold out by his intellect, manacled, strangled and mangled by his own symbology. He is mired in his art, suffocated by his religions, paralyzed by his knowledge. That which he glorifies is not life, since he has lost the rhythm of life, but death. What he worships is decay and putrefaction. He is diseased and the whole organism of society is infected.

They have called Bunuel everything—traitor, anarchist, pervert, defamer, iconoclast. But lunatic they dare not call him. True, it is lunacy he portrays in his film, but it is not of his making. This stinking chaos which for a brief hour or so is amalgamated under his magic wand, this is the lunacy of man's achievements after ten thousand years of civilization. Bunuel, to show his reverence and gratitude, puts a cow in the bed and drives a garbage truck through the salon. The film is composed of a succession of images without sequence, the significance of which must be sought below the threshold of consciousness. Those who were deceived because they could not find order or meaning in it will find order and meaning nowhere except perhaps in the world of the bees or the ants.

I am reminded at this point of the charming little documentary which preceded the Bunuel film the night it was shown at Studio 28. A charming little study of the abattoir it was, altogether fitting *and* significant for the weak-stomached sisters of culture who had come to hiss the big film. Here everything was familiar and comprehensible, though perhaps in bad taste. But there was order and meaning in it, as there is order and meaning in a cannibalistic rite.

And finally there was even a touch of aestheticism, for when the slaughter was finished and the decapitated bodies had gone their separate ways each little pig's head was carefully blown up by compressed air until it looked so monstrously lifelike and savory and succulent that the saliva flowed willy-nilly. (Not forgetting the shamrocks that were plugged up the assholes of each and every pig!) As I say, this was a perfectly comprehensible piece of butchery, and indeed, so well was it performed that from some of the more elegant spectators in the audience it brought forth a burst of applause.

It is five years or so ago since I saw the Bunuel film and therefore I cannot be absolutely sure, but I am almost certain that there were in this film no scenes of organized butchery between man and man, no wars, no revolutions, no inquisitions, no lynchings, no third-degree scenes. There was, to be sure, a blind man who was mistreated, there was a dog which was kicked in the stomach, there was a boy who was wantonly shot by his father, there was an old dowager who was slapped in the face at a garden party and there were scorpions who fought to the death among the rocks near the sea. Isolated little cruelties which, because they were not woven into a comprehensible little pattern, seemed to shock the spectators even more than the sight of wholesale trench slaughter. There was something which shocked their delicate sensibilities even more and that was the effect of Wagner's *Tristan and Isolde* upon one of the protagonists. Was it possible that the divine music of Wagner could so arouse the sensual appetites of a man and a woman as to make them roll in the graveled path and bite and chew one another until the blood came? Was it possible that this music could so take possession of the young woman as to make her suck the toe of a statued foot with perverted lasciviousness? Does music bring on orgasms, does it entrain perverse acts, does it drive people truly mad? Does this great legendary theme which Wagner immortalized have to do with such a plain vulgar physiological fact as sexual love? The film seems to suggest that it does. It seems to suggest more, for through the ramifications of this Golden Age Bunuel, like an entomologist, has studied what we call love in order to expose beneath the ideology, the mythology, the platitudes and phraseologies the complete and bloody machinery of sex. He has distinguished for us the blind metabolisms, the secret poisons, the mechanistic reflexes, the distillations of the glands, the entire plexus of forces which unite love and death in life.

Is it necessary to add that there are scenes in this film which have never been dreamed of before? The scene in the water closet, for example. I quote from the program notes:

Il est inutile d'ajouter qu'un des points culminants de la pureté de ce film nous semble cristallisé dans la vision de l'héroïne dans les cabinets, où la puissance de l'esprit arrive à sublimer une situation généralement baroque en un élément poétique de la plus pure noblesse et solitude.

A situation usually baroque! Perhaps it is the baroque element in human life, or rather in the life of civilized man, which gives to Bunuel's works the aspect of cruelty and sadism. Isolated cruelty and sadism, for it is the great virtue of Bunuel that he refuses to be enmeshed in the glittering web of logic and idealism which seeks to mask from us the real nature of man. Perhaps, like Lawrence, Bunuel is only an inverted idealist. Perhaps it is his great tenderness, the great purity and poetry of his vision which forces him to reveal the abominable, the malicious, the ugly and the hypocritical falsities of man. Like his precursors he seems animated by a tremendous hatred for the lie. Being normal, instinctive, healthy, gay, unpretentious he finds himself alone in the crazy drift of social forces. Being thoroughly normal and honest he finds himself regarded as bizarre. Like Lawrence again his work divides the world into two opposite camps—those who are for him and those who are against him. There is no straddling the issue. Either you are crazy, like the rest of civilized humanity, or you are sane and healthy like Bunuel. And if you are sane and healthy you are an anarchist and you throw bombs. The great honor which was conferred upon Luis Bunuel at the showing of his film was that the citizens of France recognized him as a true anarchist. The theater was taken by assault and the street was cleared by the police. The film has never been shown again, to my knowledge, except at private performances, and then but rarely. It was brought to America, shown to a special audience, and created no impression whatever, except perplexity. Meanwhile Salvador Dali, Bunuel's collaborator, has been to America several times and created a furor there. Dali, whose work is unhealthy, though highly spectacular, highly provocative, is acclaimed as a genius. Dali makes the American public conscious of surrealism and creates a fad. Dali returns with his pockets full of dough. Dali is accepted—as another world freak. Freak for freak: there is a divine justice at work. The world which is crazy recognizes its master's voice. The yolk of the egg has split: Dali takes America, Bunuel takes the leavings.

I want to repeat: *L'Age d'Or* is the only film I know of which reveals the possibilities of the cinema! It makes its appeal neither to the intellect nor to the heart; it strikes at the solar plexus. It is like kicking a mad dog in the guts. And though it was a valiant kick in the guts and well aimed it was not enough! There will have to be other films, films even more violent than Luis Bunuel's. For the world is in a coma and the cinema is still waving a peacock-feathered plume before our eyes.

Wondering sometimes where he may be and what he may be doing, wondering what he *could* do if he were permitted, I get to thinking now and then of all that is left out of the films. Has anybody ever shown us the birth of a child, or even the birth of an animal? Insects yes, because the sexual element is weak, because there are no taboos. But even in the world of the insects have they shown us the praying mantis, the love feast which is the acme of sexual voracity? Have they shown us how our heroes won the war —and died for us? Have they shown us the gaping wounds, have they shown us the faces that have been shot away? Are they showing us now what happens in Spain every day when the bombs rain down on Madrid? Almost every week there is another newsreel theater opened up, but there is no news. Once a year we have a repertoire of the outstanding events of the world given us by the news getters. It is nothing but a series of catastrophes: railroad wrecks, explosions, floods, earthquakes, automobile accidents, airplane disasters, collisions of trains and ships, epidemics, lynchings, gangster killings, riots, strikes, incipient revolutions, *putsches*, assassinations. The world seems like a madhouse, and the world is a madhouse, but nobody dares dwell on it. When an appalling piece of insanity, already properly castrated, is about to be presented, a warning is issued to the spectators not to indulge in demonstrations. Rest impartial!—that is the edict. Don't budge from your sleep! We command you in the name of lunacy—*keep cool!* And for the most part the injunctions are heeded. They are heeded willy-nilly, for by the time the spectacle is concluded everybody has been bathed in the innocuous drama of a sentimental couple, plain honest folks like ourselves, who are doing exactly what we are doing, with the sole difference that they are being well paid for it. This nullity and vacuity is dished up to us as the main event of the evening. The hors d'oeuvre is the newsreel, which is spiced with death and ignorance and superstition. Between these two phases of life there is absolutely no relation unless it be the link made by the animated cartoon. For the animated cartoon is the censor which permits us to dream the most horrible nightmares, to rape and kill and bugger and plunder, without waking up. Daily life is as we see it in the big film: The newsreel is the eye of God; the animated cartoon is the soul tossing in its anguish. But none of these three is the reality which is common to all of us who think and feel. Somehow they have worked a camouflage on us, and though it is our own camouflage we accept the illusion for reality. And the reason for it is that life as we know it to be has become absolutely unbearable. We flee from it in terror and disgust. The men who come after us will read the truth beneath the camouflage. May they pity us as we who are alive and real pity those about us.

Some people think of the Golden Age as a dream of the past; others think of it as the millennium to come. But the Golden Age is the immanent reality to which all of us, by our daily living, are either contributing or failing to contribute. The world is what we make it each day, or what we fail to make it. If it is lunacy that we have on our hands today, then it is we who are the lunatics. If you accept the fact that it is a crazy world you may perhaps succeed in adapting yourself to it. But those who have a sense of creation are not keen about adapting themselves. We affect one another, whether we wish to or not. Even negatively we affect one another. In writing about Bunuel instead of writing about something else I am aware that I am going to create a certain effect—for most people an unpleasant one, I suspect. But I can no more refrain from writing this way about Bunuel than I can from washing my face tomorrow morning. My past experience of life leads up to this moment and rules it despotically. In asserting the value of Bunuel I am asserting my own values, my own faith in life. In singling out this one man I do what I am constantly doing in every realm of life—selecting and evaluating. Tomorrow is no hazardous affair, a day like any other day; tomorrow is the result of many yesterdays and comes with a potent, cumulative effect. I am tomorrow what I chose to be yesterday and the day before. It is not possible that tomorrow I may negate and nullify everything that led me to this present moment.

In the same way I wish to point out that the film *L'Age d'Or* is no accident, nor is its dismissal from the screen an accident. The world has condemned Luis Bunuel and judged him as unfit. Not the whole world, because, as I said before, the film is scarcely known outside of France—outside of Paris, in fact. Judging from the trend of affairs since this momentous event took place I cannot say that I am optimistic about the revival of this film today. Perhaps the next Bunuel film will be even more of a bombshell than was *L'Age d'Or*. I fervently hope so. But meanwhile—and here I must add that this is the first opportunity, apart from a little review which I wrote for *The New Review*, I have had to write about Bunuel publicly—meanwhile, I say, this belated tribute to Bunuel may serve to arouse the curiosity of those who have never heard the name before. Bunuel's name is not unknown to Hollywood, that I know. Indeed, like many another man of genius whom the Americans have got wind of, Luis Bunuel was invited to come to Hollywood and give of his talent. In short, he was invited to do nothing and draw his breath. So much for Hollywood.

No, it is not from that quarter that the wind will blow. But things are curiously arranged in this world. Men who have been dishonored and driven from their country sometimes return to be crowned as king. Some return as a scourge. Some leave only their name behind them, or the remembrance of their deeds, but in the name of this one and that whole epochs have been revitalized and recreated. I for one believe that, despite everything I have said against the cinema as we now know it, something wondrous and vital may yet come of it. Whether this happens or not depends entirely on us, on you who read this now. What I say is only a drop in the bucket, but it may have its consequences. The important thing is that the bucket should not have a hole in it. Well, I believe that such a bucket can be found. I believe that it is just as possible to rally men around a vital reality as it is around the false and the illusory. Luis Bunuel's effect upon me was not lost. And perhaps my words will not be lost either.

The

Great

Goldwyn

by Alva Johnston

The following is a chapter from The Great Goldwyn (*Random House, New York, 1937*). *Samuel Goldwyn stands out as one of the few really independent producers in Hollywood. There is no detail too trivial for his attention; he supervises wardrobe, lighting, grips —everything and everyone. His films are among the biggest box-office successes of all time.*

Sᴀᴍ Gᴏʟᴅᴡʏɴ has always had a passion for quality. When he was a nineteen-year-old glove salesman, he tried to organize a company to manufacture gloves of unparalleled quality. The plan collapsed because the financial backer withdrew on learning that Sam was a minor and could not be bound by a contract.

"Quality" pictures were Sam's aim when he entered the films in 1913, and he was a leading factor in the change from the Wild West thrillers and the white-slave shockers to the modern feature picture. In 1919, Sam wanted to elevate the pictures again. For several years he had had the idea that the writer should be the key man in the pictures; that the scenario or script should be something better than a rough draft for a director to follow or throw away, as he saw fit. Sam had an inspiration; he would corner the world supply of literary artists; all great writers would be Goldwyn writers.

In his enthusiasm, Sam thought that he might be able to advertise the names of the writers in big lights and the names of the stars in small lights. If the movie public accepted this, it would solve Sam's problem. When he broke away from Zukor and Lasky in 1916 and founded his own company, Goldwyn's great difficulty was that of finding stars. His competitors had most of the popular favorites under contract. If Sam could make the public more excited over Gertrude Atherton than over Mary Pickford or wilder over Gouverneur Morris than over Douglas Fairbanks, the Goldwyn company would lead the field.

Sam organized The Eminent Authors, Inc. His first consignment of genius to arrive in Hollywood included Rex Beach, Rupert Hughes, Mary Roberts Rinehart, Gertrude Atherton, Basil King, Gouverneur Morris and Leroy Scott. Sam's new move frightened his competitors. They doubted if men of letters would become great box-office stars, but they wanted to be protected. Sam had cleaned up the home market so thoroughly that his rivals had to import Elinor Glyn, Sir Gilbert Parker, Somerset Maugham, Arnold Bennett and others. Ordinary writers were weeded out of the studios to make room for famous authors. One of the ousted scenarists was Darryl F. Zanuck, now chief of Twentieth Century-Fox, who was reduced to working in a shipyard.

For a time the heaviest duty of Sam's eminent authors was that of being photographed in the act of gazing admiringly at Sam. When they started to write for the pictures, the results were not uniform.

Sam read the first work of Leroy Scott and said: "Mr. Scott, you are undoubtedly the greatest writer in the world, but maybe this is not good for the movies."

When he read the first scenario by Basil King, Sam said, "Mr. King, you are undoubtedly the greatest writer in the world, but maybe this is not good for the movies."

Every Goldwyn author was told that he was undoubtedly the greatest writer in the world, and so on. The venture was not wholly a failure, however. Sam got his money's worth in publicity, and Rupert Hughes wrote the script of *The Old Nest*, which drew more than a million dollars at the box office.

Sam wanted to make a Goldwyn writer of George Bernard Shaw. They discussed it over tea one day in London. Shaw thought Sam was too aesthetic to be a practical man. A version of the conversation was cabled over to Howard Dietz, Goldwyn's publicity chief;

he compressed Shaw's words into: "The trouble, Mr. Goldwyn, is that you are only interested in art and I am only interested in money." This was cabled back to London and released there. It added considerably to Shaw's reputation as a wit.

The most eminent of Goldwyn's Eminent Authors was Maurice Maeterlinck. The great Belgian poet had come to the United States shortly after the war for a lecture tour. His first appearance was at Carnegie Hall. Maeterlinck spoke no English. He wrote the lecture in French and had it translated literally into English. Then he had each English syllable retranslated into a French syllable. Each English sound was to be rendered by an approximate French sound. The result was a lecture in mispronounced anagrams. Delivered to a Franco-American audience, it was equally unintelligible to the French and to the Americans. It was a new literary form; it was not even nonsense, so it topped Gertrude Stein.

The lecture caused the cancellation of the rest of the lecture tour. Maeterlinck was free, and Sam went after him. Since his words had to be translated, Sam was shorn of half of his sales craft; his gestures and grimaces failed to synchronize with his selling points. Thus handicapped, Sam made slow progress. He thought the poet's weakness was vanity, and he tried to play on this infirmity by explaining what it meant to Maeterlinck to get to be a Goldwyn writer; how proud the folks back home would be. Sam made a success story of it—a rookie becoming a big-league star overnight. Maeterlinck looked blank. Sam tried again to fire the man's ambition. "You'll get equal treatment with Rex Beach," he said. Maeterlinck still had an expression of bewilderment which Sam took for an expression of incredulity. Sam ordered all the contracts with eminent authors to be brought in.

"You're getting as much money as any of them," said Sam. To verify this, he handed the Basil King contract to Maeterlinck.

"You know Basil King?" said Sam.

This was translated to Maeterlinck, who said, "*Non*."

Other contracts were handed to the Belgian, and other questions translated by the interpreter.

"You know Rupert Hughes?"

"*Non*."

"Mary Roberts Rinehart?"

"*Non*."

"Rex Beach?"

"*Non*."

Sam went down the list, getting a "*Non*" at each name.

He turned to his press agent and whispered, "What's the matter with this guy? Is he dumb?"

Maeterlinck understood five figures, however, and he joined the Goldwyn literary colony. The private car which had been used by Woodrow Wilson when he stumped the country for the League of Nations was obtained by Howard Dietz, the publicity chief, for Maeterlinck's trip from New York to Hollywood. A publicity man was placed on the car to issue, at every stop, statements by Maeterlinck glorifying America and Goldwyn.

America was eager to hear from the poet. The *Blue Bird* craze started by Maeterlinck's play was fresh in the public mind. The publicity scheme was a disappointment, however, to Dietz and Goldwyn. One member of the party in the private car was Maeterlinck's lecture manager. Maeterlinck would soon pick up enough English to make a million-dollar lecture tour of America, according to the manager's reasoning, and he had a contract for a percentage of the receipts. He reasoned further that, if Maeterlinck gave away a lot of words now, he would not be able to sell them later. To the lecture manager, every Maeterlinck statement to the press today meant a hundred empty seats sometime in the future. The entire journey was a battle between the publicity man and the lecture manager, the poet siding with the lecture manager, who wore a frock coat and called him "Master." For hundreds of miles at a stretch, the Maeterlinck special got less publicity than a cattle train.

Goldwyn's representative at Dallas was a go-getting Texan named Lew Remy. He arranged a banquet there for Maeterlinck. The mayor of Dallas, the governor of Texas and all the leading citizens of the Southwest came. The banquet was a disappointment. The great Belgian did not arrive. The lecture manager had rerouted the private car and made it miss Dallas entirely. Lew Remy learned the new route that the Maeterlinck party was taking and wired to a Texas friend at another town to meet the train and page the lecture manager. "Then punch him in the nose," concluded Remy's message. The lecture manager was duly paged.

"Are you Mr. ——?" asked Remy's friend.

"I am," said the manager.

Instantly he was stretched out flat on the platform.

Arriving finally at Hollywood, Maeterlinck demanded a house on a hilltop, so that he could see the sun better. That was provided. There are witnesses in Hollywood who will sign affidavits that Maeterlinck's first effort was a film adaptation of his *Life of the Bee*, and that, on reading it, Goldwyn ran out screaming, "My God, the

hero is a bee!" Goldwyn's own recollection is that Maeterlinck's
first scenario was about a little boy and a mattress and a lot of blue
feathers.

In order to saturate the poet in Hollywood psychology, he was
then taken, day after day, to projection rooms to see action pictures.
His next scenario started with the lid slowly rising from a sewer in
a street of Paris; up from the sewer came the face of a gory and
bedraggled female Apache with a dagger gripped between her teeth.
Maeterlinck's Hollywood writings were not made into pictures. It
is said that, when Maeterlinck left Hollywood, Goldwyn saw him
to the station, patted him on the shoulder and said, "Don't worry,
Maurice. You'll make good yet."

Maeterlinck was at Cannes a year ago when Goldwyn was there
with Lord Beaverbrook. Sam was asked if he wanted to meet Maeterlinck. "No," he said, "I saw enough of that man years ago."

In spite of his experiences with Maeterlinck and certain other
members of Eminent Authors Pictures, Inc., Goldwyn always stuck
to his theory that the writers were the most important people in the
pictures. Goldwyn is king, but writers are those nearest the throne.
Sam will go anywhere, do anything, to sign a man he thinks is a
great writer. To some extent he has suffered because of his worship
of letters. For nearly a quarter of a century he has surrounded himself with crack novelists and playwrights. They studied Goldwyn
as a strange zoological specimen. They treasured his curious sayings
and constantly added to the Goldwyn legend. Some intimates of
Sam assert that he does not make any more breaks in English than
any other man who was not reared by a governess, but that Sam's
breaks are always caught and preserved. Except for years of close
association with writers, Goldwyn would not be known today as a
surrealist word painter and master of the misspoken word. On the
other hand, Sam has benefited by his association with writers. He
can be articulate when he abandons his mind to it; much of the time,
however, he is struggling with ideas and lets expression take care of
itself. Sam may be lucky that his English education consisted only
of one year at night school; his power seems to consist in a simplicity and elemental directness of mind which does not always
flourish under higher education. There was not even a dictionary at
the night school that Sam attended. He was astonished at the enormous size of a volume which was brought forth at a Hollywood
party to be consulted at the game of Guggenheim.

"What a big book!" said Sam. "Who wrote it?"

"Webster," was the reply.

"It must have taken him a long time."

"About a century."

"My, my!" said Sam. "Fifty years!"

Sam laid no claim to being an artist when he organized the Lasky company in 1913. He was the salesman and businessman of the company. When he organized his own company in 1916, he was everything. He found that he had to do his own editing and cutting in order to keep studio politics and studio amours out of the pictures. Some of the directors were more intent on their own romances than on those of the pictures; close-ups and other scenes were sometimes slipped in for reasons not connected with the plot. Salesmanship was Goldwyn's specialty, and he found that he ought to know all about his pictures in order to sell them.

For example, after the war Sam saw a chance to invade England, so he looked for pictures that he could sell to the British public. Among others he made *Lord and Lady Algy* and *The Gay Lord Quex*. He went abroad to sell them. One of his cables home was, "I went to see Lord and Lady Algy three nights ago and I am still sick." Sam insisted on better pictures, so that he could sell them better. He absorbed picture knowledge rapidly and developed into one of the shrewdest judges of story values.

Sam's competitors were slow in admitting his talent as a producer, but they venerated him as a salesman, showman and publicity man. He has always been considered unequaled at stirring up excitement about his forthcoming pictures. Theater owners bleated about Sam's prices, but they nearly all paid them. One of Sam's rare defeats in a duel between buyer and seller was inflicted on him by the late Abraham Finkelstein, of Minneapolis. Salesmen reported that Finkelstein was obdurate; he positively refused to buy a Goldwyn picture at the price asked. Sam gave the agent an inspirational talk by telephone; the agent tackled Finkelstein again, but failed again. "I'll go there myself and show you how to sell pictures," said Sam.

He was off for Minneapolis. Finkelstein, a tall, elderly, stoop-shouldered man, listened to Sam with grave courtesy until Sam named the price; then he pressed a buzzer. Two men in the uniforms of lunatic asylum attendants came in and led Sam out. Sam came back later and announced that he would build a theater in Minneapolis and run Finkelstein out of business. Finkelstein reached for his hat and coat. "Come with me," he said, "and I'll show you the best sites." He drove Sam around town, pointing out the good locations for movie palaces, but Sam didn't build.

Sam's love of publicity for the name of Goldwyn has been attributed to egotism. This theory is not utterly fantastic. Sam does not try to conceal the fact that he has an ego. In a word battle with

Herman Shumlin, the Broadway producer, Sam could think of nothing more withering to say than "You're a bigger egotist than I am." Publicity for the name of Goldwyn, however, is important in salesmanship. The public may not be stampeded into picture houses by the mere name of Goldwyn, but the name does mean something to proprietors and managers of motion picture houses. If Sam made inferior pictures, his personal publicity would be injurious to him. His name would be associated in the minds of exhibitors with vacant seats and red ink. While Sam steadily produces superior pictures, his personal publicity is an important department of salesmanship. Sam has had many of the best press agents in the country, but they have never got enough publicity to satisfy him for long. Pete Smith, now the famous Voice of the Films, was a Goldwyn press agent. He did satisfy Sam once for two or three days by a publicity coup.

Pete Smith proposed the idea that Sam should get himself talked about by announcing that there were only thirteen real actors in Hollywood and naming them. Sam was afraid at first; he thought it would create thirteen ingrates and a thousand enemies. Finally Sam had a stroke of genius himself; he said, "I'll name twelve and say the thirteenth is a mystery, and every actor and actress in Hollywood will think he's the mystery." It made a sensation, and Sam followed it up next day with a column discussing possible entries for the thirteenth place.

Sam was abroad part of the time while Pete Smith was his press agent. He returned to Hollywood full of enthusiasm. Laying some large photographs of himself before the press agent, Sam said, "What do you think of those?"

"All right," said Smith.

"Only all right?" inquired Sam.

"They do justice to you," said Smith. "They look as if they would reproduce all right."

"Pete, I'm disappointed in you," said Goldwyn. "Don't you see they're eleven by fourteen inches? They're too big for the newspapers to put in one column. Don't you grasp the idea? From now on they'll have to print my picture in two columns."

The publicity man broke his employer's heart by explaining that newspapers could take a photograph as big as a billboard and reduce it to a one-column cut. Pete Smith, like some other hard-boiled publicity men who worked for Goldwyn, did not take him too seriously, and put up with his tantrums as long as he paid well.

Sam had a love of being met by impressive turnouts on his arrival from New York or Europe. Smith managed to get a couple of bonafide news photographers down to the train and then padded out the camera battalion by calling on personal friends to show up at the station with cameras.

Sam, always a tremendous walker, used to make Smith walk with him in the mornings from the Goldwyn home to the Goldwyn studio, a distance of four or five miles. One morning Sam saw a rival's advertising banner stretched across Beverly Boulevard.

"That's good advertising," said Sam. "That's what I want for our première. Only instead of one banner, I want hundreds—one on every corner, all the way to the theater."

Smith saw that the banner stretched across the street between two pieces of property owned by the rival company. He could see that Goldwyn's idea of hundreds of banners would mean hundreds of negotiations with property owners. Furthermore, there was a city ordinance against such banners. He knew, however, that opposition would only make Sam rabid in favor of the idea. His only escape from an impossible task was to make a bad argument in favor of it.

He estimated that the banners would cost about fifteen dollars apiece, and he said, "That's a great scheme. Those banners will only cost a hundred and fifty or a hundred and seventy-five dollars apiece. We can put up two hundred of them for about thirty thousand dollars, or more if you like."

It ended with Goldwyn rebuking Smith for having such an expensive and mediocre idea.

The Goldwyn publicity department is a sort of public-health department at times. The streak of the absolute monarch in Sam inspires him with real anxiety for the health of all the potentates of the earth. He is said to identify himself with them so closely that when one is sick Sam goes on a diet; when one dies Sam feels that his own time has come.

He is like a certain princess of Tarente, who put on mourning whenever a member of any royal house died in any part of Europe. On one occasion she did appear in brilliant colors; Madame de Sévigné said, "Madame, I rejoice in the health of Europe." Similarly, if Sam is gay it means there are not likely to be any big obituaries in the paper tomorrow. He does at times worry about other than the top personalities. One Saturday afternoon he met a studio executive who seemed seriously stricken. "You look all run down," said Sam. "Go home. Don't come back till Monday morning." Sam was discovered one day in distress. He had before him a letter telling him not to send any more money to an aged woman living in New York, because she had died; she had been Sam's first landlady when he arrived in New York as a boy, and had fed and lodged him when he was broke. Another streak of humanity asserted itself in Goldwyn once when he recognized an extra on one of his sets. "Come away quick," he said to his studio manager. The extra had once been a Goldwyn star; she had quarreled with him, had become a free lance and had bad luck. "I didn't want her to see me," said Goldwyn. "It would embarrass her." His chief anxiety, however, is for great people.

He called up his press agent one morning and asked, "How is the President?"

"Fine," said the press agent. "I was with him last night and he was fine."

"What do you mean, you were with him last night?"

"Mr. Schenck and I were together last night," said the press agent, referring to Joseph Schenck, president of United Artists.

"No, no," said Goldwyn. "I mean Roosevelt. The paper says he has a cold. Find out how he is and let me know at once."

The press agent telephoned to a friend at United Press and found out the President was all right. He then telephoned to Goldwyn and said, "I had the UP carry a special wire to the White House saying Mr. Goldwyn was anxious to know how the President was this morning, and the President thanks Mr. Goldwyn for his kindness and says that he is feeling much better."

"That's the kind of service I like," said Goldwyn. He was satisfied with the press agent for hours.

As Pete Smith used to pad the welcoming camera batteries with dummies, another press agent used to upholster the Goldwyn interviews with fraudulent interrogators. Two or three local reporters would be present. In addition, the publicity man would call in eight or ten reliable pals who would be presented to Goldwyn as "Mr. Wolgast of the Chicago *Tribune*, Mr. Berlenbach of the New York *Times*, Mr. Greb of the London *Daily News*," and so on. Devices of this kind, however, were used only when it was considered important to put on a special show. The Goldwyn publicity man's brain is usually working with great rapidity in the interest of getting big displays in newspapers and magazines. Goldwyn men have to have their hearts in the cause.

There has always been an argument among Goldwyn scholars as to whether his rages are genuine or part of a routine. Sam is an old head salesman both in gloves and in pictures. A head salesman's business is to scourge the soul of the junior salesman in order to fill him with enterprise. You blast his morale, accuse him of wrongfully

cumbering the earth and cheating potter's field, and then send him
forth to overwhelm the customers with his victorious personality.
However, Goldwyn does not discriminate in favor of his own subordinates in his rages and furies; he has had shouting affrays with
nearly all the big figures in the industry, and when he lets go there
is not a word in or out of the language that he hesitates to use. The
theory that his tornadoes are artificial is based on the fact that he
can turn off the ferocity and turn on the charm in an instant. He
has no hangover from one mood to another. An outburst that might
leave another man sick for days is completely out of Sam's system
the moment the uproar is over. He is too busy to waste time in the
transition from one emotional state to another. A split second separates Ivan the Terrible from Mr. Pickwick.

One day Sam blazed away at his current press chief, Jock Lawrence, most of the afternoon. After going to bed that night, Sam
summoned the press agent and started blazing away again. Samuel
Goldwyn, Jr., then a boy of seven or eight, entered the room to say
good night to his father. Sam's fist stopped in mid-air; he beamed;
he chatted gaily about school problems; at last he tenderly advised
his son to run along and get plenty of sleep.

As the boy was leaving the room, Sam made a genial gesture in
the direction of Jock Lawrence, and cooed, "Kiss Uncle Jock good
night."

The boy obeyed and left.

"And furthermore . . ." resumed Sam, furiously addressing the
publicity man, starting to rail at him again from the precise point
at which he had been interrupted by the entrance of Sam Junior.

Sam thinks so fast that the latter end of his argument sometimes
refutes the beginning.

"I have never had a lawsuit in my career," he said. "That shows
you that I'm easy to get along with. I'm the most reasonable man
out here. I've never had a lawsuit worth mentioning. Three or four,
maybe. Right now I'm being sued by Paramount for five million
dollars. It's one of the most important lawsuits in the country."

He started a speech to salesmen once by telling them to be reasonable with theater owners, some of whom had complained of being
gouged. He asked the salesmen to be very moderate in their demands.
But in his peroration the old sales instinct seized him, and he exhorted them to go after the last cent. The final line of his speech is
generally quoted. "This business is dog eat dog, and nobody is going
to eat me."

He complained by telephone because another studio had borrowed a Goldwyn writer for a few hours without his permission. Sam was told that every effort had been made to get in touch with him, and that it was finally assumed that he would have been agreeable.

Sam kept repeating, "If you only had the decency to ask me."

"What would you have said, Mr. Goldwyn?"

"I would have said no," replied Sam.

Sam fears contentment. He has seen contentment ruin many of the great figures in the industry. He is afraid of making the people around him contented; that is one cause of his being more liberal with blame than with praise. A press agent once wanted to resign; one reason was that Goldwyn had never said a good word about his work. "If I don't say it's bad, it's good," said Sam. He hates yes men; he loves no men, but he is fond of having no men answer him in the affirmative. This becomes complicated. Sam once became greatly smitten with a Hollywood executive noted for his rugged way of saying no. Sam hired him at an enormous salary; the man turned out to be a yes man; he could say no to others, but not to the furious Goldwyn. The contract expired; the employee was held over on a weekly salary to finish a job; no longer in awe of Sam, he was able to say, "It stinks. . . . It's awful. . . . It's gruesome," and so on. Sam, impressed, put him under contract again; the man again started saying, "It's fine. . . . It's great. . . . It's wonderful," and was useless again.

Sam is at his best when talking to one person. He is a tête-à-tête evangelist. His man-to-man conferences become rousing revivals or camp meetings and usually end with the party of the second part on the mourner's bench, putting his signature on a contract. The day before his death last January, Richard Boleslazski, the director, said that one of his most memorable experiences was a talk with Goldwyn.

"My book, *The Way of a Lancer*, had just come out," he said. "Sam called me over in great haste and wanted to buy it then and there. I told him there were two other interested parties and that I couldn't sell it without their permission. He handed me two telephones and said, 'Get them.' I got one in New York and one in Ohio. Sam battled with them over the price, but a good stiff one was finally agreed on. 'We'll sign right now,' said Sam, putting five hundred dollars option money in my hand. I said I thought I ought to see my lawyer. He put his arm around me and said, 'I'll be your lawyer.' I tried to argue, but he hypnotized me. There was no standing up against his impetuosity. He drew up the contract and I signed it. Later he changed his mind and didn't want to make *The Way of a Lancer*. I thought the contract called for the amount agreed on, but it only called for the five hundred dollars option money. I never felt that Sam intended to take advantage, but I thought I would have been better advised to see a lawyer. That was my only personal contact with him, but I am one of his greatest admirers. He has a real and spontaneous love of beauty. He hates the phony and will do anything to get the real thing."

The

Movie

Colony

————————

by Leo C. Rosten

In this chapter from his book Hollywood *(Harcourt, Brace, New York, 1941), Leo Rosten, a social scientist, makes a clinical examination of the mores of various strata of the film colony. Using questionnaires, team research, graphs and charts, Rosten comes up with much revealing data on Hollywood, some of which explodes a number of popular myths about the people who operate and run the dream factories. Although the book was written in 1939-40, his picture of life in Hollywood remains substantially unchanged.*

THE DAZZLING SPOTLIGHT which Hollywood turns upon its Personalities throws into shadow the thousands who work in the movie studios—technicians and craftsmen, musicians and sound engineers, painters, carpenters, laboratory workers. These, plus the thousands of extras whose faces are used in an agglomerate mass, are the anonymous people who swarm over the sound stages, the lots, and the offices wherever pictures are fabricated. They are movie workers, as distinguished from what we shall call movie makers.

The movie workers lead ordinary lives; they live in middle-class homes or apartments; their incomes are sometimes higher and often

lower than those of their relatives in Cleveland or St. Paul.[1] They
go to church, play golf, crowd the beaches. They are no more or
no less attractive, secure, or neurotic than America at large. They
are never seen at the fashionable night clubs or restaurants. They
never set foot in the majestic homes. They may affect the manners
and the superlatives of Hollywood's elite, but they are not a part of
the Hollywood which is the symbol of affluence and allure. They
may boast of their proximity to the gods, bask in reflected glory, or
cherish their identification with the fabled world of the screen. But
they enjoy no social status within the movie colony, and they have
no individual identity to the world beyond. They are in Hollywood,
but they are not of Hollywood.

Hollywood is composed of three concentric circles. The largest
circle embraces all of the thirty thousand movie workers and movie
makers; the middle circle encompasses the movie makers alone
("the movie colony"), the producers, actors, directors, and writers
who participate in Hollywood's social and professional life; and the
smallest circle, the one at the center of power and prestige, encloses
the movie elite, some two hundred and fifty persons who, to set an
arbitrary but useful index, earn $75,000 or more a year. . . .

It is often said that Hollywood has no sense of reality and spins
its fables in some Nirvana out of space and time. One of the less
original aphorisms with which we are all familiar is "Hollywood
is only a state of mind." Hollywood is in the southwestern nook of
the United States, only a hundred-odd miles from Mexico. But it is
2,741 miles from Washington, 2,901 miles from New York, 2,219
miles from Chicago, 1,925 miles from St. Louis, 1,938 miles from
New Orleans.

These are not simply figures; they are signs of psychological as
well as geographical distance. The climate of Hollywood is like that
of Capri or the Riviera, not the East or the South or the Middle
West; and the mental climate complements the weather. Upheavals

[1] Annual earnings (1938) of the following groups averaged:

2,906	carpenters	$1,066	533	sound men (all classes)	$2,919
1,695	electrical operators	1,575	299	wardrobe people	1,255
1,312	"grips"	1,738	278	still photographers	2,347
957	painters	1,426	136	hairdressers and	
948	prop makers	1,215		make-up appliers	3,477

And so on. Furthermore, in 1940 only 3.1 per cent of the extras *who were employed* averaged $150 or more a month; only 9 extras earned $2,500–$3,000; only 45 earned $2,000–$2,500; 579 received $1,000–$2,000; the rest earned less than $1,000 each.

in Washington, droughts in Kansas, convulsions in Wall Street seem muffled and remote in a town where the sun is felicitous and the houses are brightly colored, a town where the daily energy is exhausted in slashing at the Gordian knot of a fictitious Story. The Los Angeles papers offer scanty international news compared with the newspapers of the East, and New York newspapers and national political journals arrive in Hollywood four to five days late. Even the radio is less immediate in its impact; some national programs do not come through at all; others are rebroadcast from disks at inconvenient hours. The salubrious climate and the pervading sense of isolation led one melancholy screenwriter to say, "Hollywood is a warm Siberia."

There are other reasons for the antipodean character of the movie colony. Hollywood is a one-industry town. Its people sleep, eat, talk, and think movies. They are engaged in the creation of symbols rather than of material goods. Movie making is one prolonged, involuted fantasy. It is often said that the movies are an escape for the masses; it is rarely suggested that they are also an escape for the movie makers. When a movie producer or actor, director or writer goes to sleep he leaves the world of fantasy and enters the world of reality.

It is stories, roles, dramatic artifices which tyrannize Hollywood's attention, not goods or crops or machines. And this preoccupation with the fanciful must tend to blur perceptions of the real. To personalities lost in fantasy, reality passes through a distorted receiver; either it ceases to seem as threatening as it ought to, as in the case of children, or it becomes absurdly ominous, as in the case of psychotics. In either case, the real world—of men and things and events—loses its proper proportion and becomes exaggerated at an extreme. The singular anxiety of some of the movie makers, and the singular indifferentism of others, are end points on Hollywood's psychological horizon. If Hollywood is a community of people who work and live in fantasy, then it is to be expected that their life should take on the attributes of the fantastic. The greater wonder, one visitor exclaimed to this writer, is that Hollywood is sane.

The movie colony's intense engrossment in its work gives Hollywood a feverish, self-fascinated quality and lends a despotic priority to its own values. This can be illustrated by a few classic examples. When Tom Mooney was released from San Quentin—an event which was front-page news on the seven continents—a columnist in the *Hollywood Reporter* solemnly announced: "The labor activities of Tom Mooney have very likely cost him a picture contract."

When Mussolini's legions marched into Ethiopia and the world waited for the League of Nations to act, a producer was asked by a breathless friend, "Have you heard any late news?" To which that child of Hollywood replied hotly, "Italy just banned *Marie Antoinette!*" And in the week in which Mussolini raped Albania, Louella Parsons, correspondent for all the Hearst papers and dean of Hollywood's gossip writers, began one of her extraordinary columns: "The deadly dullness of the past week was lifted today when Darryl Zanuck announced he had bought all rights to *The Blue Bird* for Shirley Temple."[2]

Let us examine this escapist haven more closely.

Hollywood is young. The movie colony itself is barely thirty years old, and its people are young. Not as young as the public seems to think, or as the publicity would have it, but compared with other industries or professional groups Hollywood would probably show a marked youthfulness. An analysis of 707 cases[3] showed that 46.2 per cent of the movie colony are under 40 years of age; over a third are between 30 and 40. If we break the data into groups, we find:

Producers: Over a fourth are under 40; over half (52.6 per cent) are under 45; three fourths are under 50. The median average age is 43.

Directors: Over a third are under 40; over two thirds are under 45; less than a tenth are 50 or over. The median age is 42.

Actors: Almost a third are under 35; 37.6 per cent of the actresses are under 30 and over a fifth are under 25. The median age for actresses is 34, for actors (including veteran "character" players) 46, for both, 42.

Writers: 31.7 per cent are under 35, well over half (57.6 per cent) are under 40; 70.9 per cent are under 45, and 84.2 per cent are under 50. The median age is 37.

Assistant Directors: Over a third are under 35; almost two thirds are under 40. The median age is 37.

[2] Miss Parsons, called by one commentator "the most consistently inaccurate reporter who ever lived to draw $600 a week," announced on various occasions that RKO was in the process of negotiating with W. H. Hudson to do a screen version of *Green Mansions;* that Paramount intended to remake *Peter Ibbetson,* "by Henrik Ibsen"; and that D'Annunzio's inamorata was a famous Italian actress named Il Duse. She (Miss Parsons) once burst into verse in her column with this line: "Oh, to be in England now that it's May," and lightly corrected the *faux pas* the next day by writing: "Oh, to be in England now that May is here."

[3] Comprising 271 actors and actresses, 92 producers, 20 executives, 66 directors, 120 writers, 79 assistant directors, 41 first film editors, 18 directors of photography.

First Film Editors (cutters): Over 85 per cent are under 45. The median age is 37.

There is more striking evidence of the role of youth in Hollywood. The history of the movie colony and the motion picture industry is crammed with the saga of "boy geniuses." Movie production at the studios, involving the millions of dollars that were cited earlier, is often placed in the hands of very young men. In few other industries are comparable power and freedom delivered into such callow (and gifted) hands. The late Irving Thalberg, for instance, was in his twenties when he began to soar through the movie firmament, and he was breaking precedents and box office records before he was 30. At 22, Darryl F. Zanuck was writing scenarios for Rin Tin Tin; but at 26 he became the head producer at the big Warner Brothers plant, at 30 he was one of the most influential figures in Hollywood and tore up his $5,000-a-week contract, and within a year he was put into the top production chair at Twentieth Century-Fox as vice-president. David O. Selznick was vice-president in charge of production at RKO when he was 29; he was a vice-president and producer at M-G-M when he was 31. Hal B. Wallis stepped into the chief executive-producer post at Warner Brothers when he was 32. Matthew Fox became assistant to the president of Universal when he was 29. Pandro Berman took over the reins at RKO when he was less than 32. And a 26-year-old like Garson Kanin directed top-flight pictures, the budgets for which were around $750,000. Youth is at a premium in Hollywood, and those who are not so young spend a conspicuous amount of effort in offering visible indications of their rejuvenescence.

The emphatic youthfulness of many of Hollywood's central personalities brings up a point which is not generally given the attention it deserves: The movie people—famous, pampered, rich—are very young to be so famous, so pampered, and so rich. Probably never in history has so immature a group been accorded such luster, such sanctions, and such incomes. "Youth on the prow, and Pleasure at the helm . . ."

Hollywood's wealth is first-generation wealth, possessed by people who have not inherited it, spent by people who have not been accustomed to handling it, earned as a reward for talent (or luck) rather than heritage. It is not surprising that the movie colony has not achieved stability or integration; it is too young, too new, and too uncertain. The people of the movie colony are characterized by showmanship, not breeding; glibness, not wisdom; audacity, not poise. Of Hollywood it might be written, as was written of the

America of the 1880s, that here is "a society that for the first time found its opportunities equal to its desires, a youthful society that accounted the world its oyster and wanted no restrictions laid on its will."[4]

In a professional community which is itself young, and whose population is weighted toward youth in its composition, one would expect optimism to flourish; and when the dominant industry in that community demands buoyant, creative types, then we would expect optimism to be at a maximum. Hollywood is optimistic. Hollywood demands optimism. Hollywood's restaurants, parties, and offices are characterized by much levity and verbal horseplay. Despite the perennial crises in the motion picture industry (labor strife, wholesale layoffs, shrinking box office receipts) Hollywood possesses a sense of insulation from the electrical displays of our economy.

To Hollywood, economic reversals seem to be but passing fevers. The long trend of the movie business has been one of phenomenal prosperity and expansion, with greater and greater profits to the industry and higher and higher rewards to most of its personnel.[5] The Hollywoodian therefore suspects that when a producer complains that business is not good he means that it isn't as superlatively good as he had hoped it would be, or that it isn't as good as it was last year (when it was unusually good), or that although it is fine at the moment it *may* get worse. And secretly, the producer generally does not believe his own lamentations either; his mind is focused on a smash hit just around the corner.

"You've got to be an optimist to be in pictures," a New York film executive told this writer. "It is wild, unbeatable optimism that built the industry. The way Hollywood makes pictures and the fortunes they cost would terrify ordinary businessmen—but Hollywood makes profits. Enthusiasm pays huge dividends in the motion picture industry."

Wherever optimism is too conspicuous and too determined, the observer has reason to doubt its appearance. Along with the insistent optimism, there is in Hollywood a vague, restless fear that "it can't go on," that the mighty structure is impermanent, that its foundations are unsound. From many choirs in the movie colony this uneasy refrain ascends: "It can't last. Pictures cost too much; producers get

[4] Vernon Louis Parrington, *Main Currents in American Thought*, Vol. III: 1860–1920, *The Beginnings of Critical Realism in America* (Harcourt, Brace, 1930), p. 10.
[5] A studio such as M-G-M has made net earnings of well over seven million dollars a year in each and every year from 1935 to the present date (1941). In one year, 1937, the net earnings were $14,334,000.

too much; actors ask too much; writers earn too much; directors make too much. It *can't* go on this way."

[Hollywood] is a serene principality on its surface, but one need not scratch deep to discover that it is afraid of its shadow, still more afraid of the shadow it casts upon the world's screens. Fear is behind its production code, a fear of giving offense which might, in turn produce an offensive onslaught on the box office. Fear is behind its players, writers, and directors—a fear that one bad picture will wipe out the memory of all their good ones. Fear is what makes [Hollywood] the unreal world that it is, fear far more than glamour, far more than wealth and beauty and the Southern California sunshine.[6]

Optimism and insecurity run through the movie colony side by side. This is no paradox, for optimism is often a narcotic to deaden anxiety, and in Hollywood anxiety serves as a restraint on excessive elation and as a kind of penance for extravagances of income, spending, conduct, or business operations. There seems to be an unconscious *need* for anxiety in the movie colony, and anxiety is provoked, nursed, and kept alive (note the popularity of gambling, for example) in a manner which suggests self-punishment for obscure and disturbing guilts.

Hollywood tries to resolve its anxieties by keeping other people anxious about the same things. It is for this reason that conclaves in the movie colony—whether at the Brown Derby or a Guild meeting—tend to keep attention focused on a threatening future. "Something's going to crack up at M-G-M. . . . Such-and-such a studio is headed right for bankruptcy. . . . It can't last. . . ." These points help to explain the constant "suffering" of Hollywood, the morbidity and self-deprecation which the movie people cultivate— and, if you please, enjoy. Optimism is the desideratum of Hollywood, but Cassandra is its prophet.

Hollywood's chronic dissatisfaction has impressed many visitors. The comedians want to play parts with social significance; the tragedians yearn for a chance at farce; the directors complain about their scripts; the writers fondle dreams of the Great American Novel. One columnist, impressed by Hollywood's variations on the lachrymose theme, exclaimed:

I doubt if any town in history ever had as many carpers, cry babies, belly-achers, and habitual self-pitiers as does this "gay and glittering"

6 Frank S. Nugent, in Douglas Churchill and Frank S. Nugent, "Graustark," *We Saw It Happen*, edited by Hanson W. Baldwin and Shepard Stone (Simon and Schuster, 1939), p. 127.

city of Hollywood. To tour a studio, one must wade through a sea of tears. My desk is piled high with letters, my telephone is kept buzzing with calls and my reception room is crowded with visitors—all with complaints.[7]

There are many reasons for the perennial complaints, as we shall see. One of the most important is that dissatisfaction is inevitable in a place where there are *no fixed goals*. It is natural for the actress who earns $20,000 a year to envy the actress making $50,000, who envies the actress getting $100,000. In a community where one can make $350,000 a year, $75,000 is not especially impressive—either to the group or to the self. Where there is no reasonable point at which to fix "success," where salaries are as well known and as widely discussed as they are in Hollywood, where the scale of rewards against which people measure their success and their prestige is so long and so extensible—there the ego suffers many rebuffs. In the movie colony there are few places for the ego to rest in peace, except at the very top—and the top in Hollywood is very high. "In this town," one unhardened soul said, "I'm snubbed socially because I only get a thousand a week. That hurts."

The personalities who make pictures are impulsive, volatile, and creative. They always will be; movies can't be made by punch-press operators. And the fact that the movies, as a business, are exposed to a daily ballot of dimes and quarters means that the expectations of months can be smashed or galvanized by the box office returns of a day. The vicissitudes of movie studios can be illustrated by a few striking examples:

The net earnings of Paramount skyrocketed 820 per cent in one year (1935–36).

The net earnings of RKO plummeted 110 per cent in one year (1938–39).

The *deficit* of Warner Brothers was $7,918,605 in 1931 and $14,095,054 in 1932; in 1935 the *net earnings* were $674,150; in 1936 they were $3,177,313 (a jump of 371 per cent); in 1937 they had jumped to $5,876,183, and in 1939 they had dropped to $1,741,000.

The record of many movie individuals reflects the record of the motion picture companies. In Hollywood, men who have earned several thousand dollars a week can go unemployed for years. The writers of several pictures which won Academy Awards were not

7 Jimmie Fidler in the Los Angeles *Times*, December 3, 1940.

able to get jobs a week later. Actors who enjoy majestic salaries may become "box office poison" before they quite understand what has happened. Mae West earned $326,500 in one year, but found it difficult to get a contract the next. The late John Gilbert's career collapsed overnight when sound pictures came in; so did Ramon Novarro's. Luise Rainer won two Academy Awards and the fame which attends them, then dropped out of movies because her drawing power had vanished. The rolls of the Motion Picture Relief Fund and of the Los Angeles bankruptcy courts are studded with once dazzling names.

There are few places in our economy where fluctuations in earnings and security can be as violent and unpredictable as they are in Hollywood. We have heard of the startling rapidity of movie success. (One actor, for example, received a weekly salary of $100 and earned a total of $3,100 in 1928; the next year his salary jumped to $1,000 a week; and in 1939 he got $3,000 a week and earned $180,000 for the year.) But there are ample cases to illustrate the rapidity of the collapse of movie careers. Note the earnings of the following movie directors, for example:[8]

	1936	1937	1938
A.	$30,000	$75,000	none
B.	80,000	40,000	$7,000
C.	15,000	4,500	1,500
D.	63,000	42,000	none

The volatility of fortune in Hollywood subjects its personalities to a severe and persistent strain. "You're only as good as your last picture" is a byword in the movie colony, and an hour after a picture is previewed the solemn consensus that "Griffith is slipping" or "Rogers is through" races through the town. This is scarcely a climate conducive to psychological serenity or efficient digestion. The movies require creative—hence temperamental—personalities; the objective conditions of the business are hazardous; and the combination of an erratic milieu and quivering personalities intensifies the insecurity of both.

The pace is too swift, things change too fast, success and failure are too close together. You can't expect people to gait their lives to the pace of the world outside. Normally a man builds all his life; he may succeed, enjoy a few easy years, and then he is ready to retire. Here success may

[8] The cases are taken from replies to questionnaires.

come overnight and vanish overnight. How can you have that happen and expect to find people living as they do elsewhere?[9]

The movie colony gets a curious satisfaction out of drumming these facts home—to itself. The stories which begin, "You see that man over there—the one in the shiny serge suit? Well, two years ago . . ." serve to remind the movie makers of the precarious foundation of their careers. The movie makers frighten themselves into caution. They also feel less frightened when they see someone more frightened. They also keep anxiety alive by their identification with the sad fate of others.

The reckless and flamboyant acts for which the movie makers are renowned betray their abysmal insecurity. Bravado typifies Hollywood, bravado in its publicity, its manners, its romances. And bravado is a revealing trait, for it is an attempt—like whistling in the dark— to cover up uncertainty. If Hollywood is afraid "it can't last," then the defiant conduct and compulsive spending of the movie makers represent an effort to act as if it *will* last. The psychic game of "as if" is played by those who are haunted by a suspicion that their extraordinary fortune is unreal or undeserved, subject, in any event, to the caprices of luck; they act *as if* it will last. This kind of behavior is partly designed to negate doubt; it is also a form of magical thinking, an effort to make reality conform to wish. The bravado which is rooted in deep-seated fears drives the movie people to commit acts which, to the outsider, seem to defy the fates, and these are another manifestation of the effort to impress, to spur, to challenge the self: "Now that I've bought this big house (or built this big swimming pool), I'll *have* to do better work, I'll *have* to succeed, I'll *have* to get a higher salary and a long-term contract. . . ."

Hollywood is famed for its "individuality" and "temperament," and these, too, spring from the bravado which shields the ego. There is a juvenile tone in the extremes to which the movie colony resorts in order to flaunt its individuality. One actor for years won attention by wearing a sweat shirt to formal parties. Another actor followed the quaint whim of driving to the studio in a cavalcade of seven Cadillacs, each chauffeured and with a secretary, a maid, a hairdresser, and a trainer ensconced in station. The director who dresses like a cross between an African explorer and a polo player is familiar to the public. These puerilities are symptomatic of several things: the desire to attract attention and gain exhibitionistic gratification; the urge to "show them"; and the need to release the rebelliousness

[9] Frank S. Nugent, in Churchill and Nugent, *op. cit.*, pp. 133–34.

in which so many of Hollywood's personalities are steeped. The
psychological protests of the movie colony are often expressed in
the violation of unimportant customs—especially in garb and deportment. The movie makers are given to acts of pointless defiance—
but the meaning is not to be found on the surface of their acts. Like
children who assume that age brings peace and maturity, the movie
makers are disturbed when they discover that getting older does
not mean getting more adult.

The movie makers are engaged in an endless search for deference
—from the world, their colleagues, themselves. They seem to be lost
in a long, unhappy effort to win respect from symbolic juries. The
hunger for praise is marked in Hollywood, and the hunger for
orientation amidst the confusion of the world. In an epoch charged
with catastrophic crises and violent social change, the people who
play the game of movie making are periodically overcome by the
urge to "do something important." For Hollywood is plagued by
a vague contempt for itself, a revulsion against the make-believe of
its life and work. The movie makers always devalue what they have
achieved and continue to set greater and greater goals for their
talents. This perennial dissatisfaction, this relentless comparison of
what they are or what they are doing with utterly utopian desires
heightens the discontent in which they are lost. People of this type
are driven to surround themselves with a human and indulgent environment, because they demand constant response—to maintain their
inner security and their professional output.

This helps to explain the profusion of yes men in the movie
colony. To say that yes men are unnecessary in Hollywood is like
saying that gondoliers are unnecessary in Venice. The yes men are
quite necessary to those executives and producers who cannot
function without consistent admiration. The yes man buttresses the
ego and the confidence of his superiors; he shields them from doubt
and indecision. The yes man is not really superfluous; he is simply
overpaid. There is a functional niche in Hollywood for those who
carry the banner of confidence and forever cry, "Swell! That's
great! It'll roll them in the aisles!" They may be wrong and generally are; but they counterbalance the congenital uncertainty with
which Hollywood's creators are cursed. They pour ebullience into
those who cannot create without it.

Hollywood needs face-to-face stimulation. The movie colony is
highly gregarious. The craving for company at almost every hour
of day or night exposes the great loneliness which lives under Hollywood's façade of gaiety. The movie makers make a career out of
their neuroses and their anxiety. They are overcome by depression

when they are alone; hence they do not like to be alone. Anxiety, like misery, loves company.

Hollywood is exhibitionistic. Its mansions, its clothes, and its conduct are devices for conspicuous display. Now, exhibitionism is to be expected among actors, who earn their living in an occupation which maximizes vanity and is devoted to the exploitation of the self; and in a community dominated by actors—"every producer, director, or writer has a bit of the ham in him"—unconventionality becomes as common as ulcers. The picture people have created a milieu in which uniqueness thrives; they infect one another with their narcissism and with their exhibitionism. (Someone has said that the movie colony is governed by the rule of "an I for an I.") In Hollywood, which is populated by temperamental and egocentric personalities, the inhabitants exacerbate each other's abnormalities. In Rome, the Romans make Romans more Roman.

There is an amusing aspect to the devious ways in which exhibitionism rears its head in the movie colony. Movie stars cannot shop or walk down the street without precipitating a parade. They love this, on the whole, but they experience occasional irritation with their fishbowl fate and yearn for anonymity—partial anonymity, at least. One solution of the dilemma was found in the widespread use of sunglasses—but sunglasses with large white rims. These novel blinders concealed indentity but attracted attention. They identified the wearer as a movie star, but forbade recognition of which movie star it was. They were a triumph of conspicuous anonymity. White-rimmed sunglasses won special popularity in Hollywood because they served two powerful and contradictory forces with exquisite efficacy: they announced "Celebrity!" and simultaneously signaled "in search of privacy." When waitresses and extras took up the fad, Hollywood became a baffling sea of Celebrities Hiding Identity.

The movie colony is full of those who, lacking character, become characters. The California climate encourages exhibitionism, and a community full of actors is certain to be full of exhibitionists. In subtropical Hollywood, exhibitionism has free rein. The dress seen on Hollywood Boulevard, the Peacock Alley of the movie extras, is wondrous to behold. Fur coats are worn over lounging pajamas, slacks, or, so far as this author can judge, shorts. The girls, a species renowned for pretty faces and an astonishing resemblance to one another, affect colors in their coiffure which quite defy description. The movie men are alarmingly comfortable in slacks, scarves, and sandals, and they specialize in jackets with shoulders which are a tribute to their tailors rather than their physiques.

Exhibitionism is by no means unique to Hollywood, though it is rampant and inescapable there. William James put it down as a postulate of human nature that "we have an innate propensity to get ourselves noticed, and noticed favorably, by our kind. No more fiendish punishment could be devised . . . than that one should be turned loose in society and remain absolutely unnoticed . . ."[10] (Modern psychiatrists hold that there is a period of "infantile exhibitionism" through which all of us—hermits as well as stripteasers—pass.) In Hollywood, exhibitionism is simply more dramatic, conspicuous, and widespread than it is in, say, Fort Dodge.[11]

The Hollywood of today is popularly supposed to be a community of unconventionality, of individualism and of general personal freedom; just a gay, carefree lot of youngsters having a perpetual good time. But a glance beneath the surface of the gaiety soon convinces a careful observer that in Hollywood, as in other places, conformity rules with an iron hand. If you would be considered a part of it you must follow its customs; if the fashion is unconventional clothing you, too, must wear it or be thought of as a reactionary. . . . You must drive a costly car and live expensively or be condemned as unimportant or, worse yet, as reflecting upon the studio which pays you so generously. Above all, you must go to Sunday cocktail parties, particularly those given by prominent executives, where nothing is talked but shop and nothing is played but cards.[12]

Hollywood fosters and encourages exhibitionism—eccentric deportment makes excellent publicity. Publicity is, of course, good business in the world of entertainment, but the fanatical craving for publicity, to which so many of Hollywood's people are enslaved, suggests a *need* for self-dramatization. Not all the applause or attention of the outside world can sate the publicity hunger of those possessed by implacable drives for self-dramatization. One producer

---

[10] William James, *Psychology* (Holt, 1899), Chap. 12.

[11] When a banker buys a car, it is long, impressive, and black; when an actor buys a car, it is low, sleek, and colorific. The difference is symbolic; but the differences in tradition were not always so. The history of the *haut monde* of the nineties is full of tales of glittering phaetons and brightly caparisoned lackeys. One celebrated dowager wrote: "The most childish and insane ways of showing off met with the approval of Society. . . . I recall seeing one matron driving down Bellevue Avenue in her Victoria. She had a monkey on each shoulder and a plump well-washed pig on the seat beside her."—Mrs. John King Van Rensselaer (in collaboration with Frederic Van de Water), *The Social Ladder* (Holt, 1924), pp. 238-39.

[12] William C. De Mille, *Hollywood Saga* (Dutton, 1939), p. 298.

admitted that he takes advertising in a certain trade paper in order
to guarantee flattering comment. "Of course I pay for the praise—
but a fellow likes to read nice things about himself in the papers."

The student of design is struck by the blurring of sex lines in the
film colony's dress. Women's clothes are masculinized; men's clothes
are feminized. The vogue for color in men's clothes (green trousers,
orange sneakers, pastel neckerchiefs) and for masculinity in women's
attire (slacks, tweeds, socks, shorts) lends an epicene quality to the
garb of Hollywood. This applies to manners and language as well
as dress. Hollywood uses "dear" and "darling" with a sanguine disregard of sex. The theatrical tradition has long encouraged the
wholesale use of an affectionate lingo—but "dear," "sweetheart," "darling," and "honey" are bandied about in Hollywood with a frequency which confirms the suspicion that jealousies are often
cloaked in the phrases of flattery.

Hollywood talks and thinks in superlatives. Movie people do not
"like" things; they are "mad about" them. They do not dislike
things; they loathe or detest them. All phenomena, from filigree
brooches to tidal earthquakes, can be marvelous, terrific, colossal, or
stupendous—or, in reverse English, cute, cunning, or chic. In its
language, as in its behavior, Hollywood reveals a strenuous effort to
deny doubt, by self-induced elation. The excessive use of adjectives
such as "terrific" or "sensational" sets a Gresham's Law to work as
inexorably in vocabulary as it does in money—superlatives drive
sobriety out of circulation. The revealing story is told of two movie
producers meeting on the street. "How's your picture doing?" asked
the first. "Excellent." "Only excellent? That's too bad!"[13]

Hollywood sleeps, eats, thinks, and talks movies. The remarkable
point is that the chief concern in Hollywood is not movies, but
making movies. Shop talk is paramount in the movie colony—and
it is an intriguing topic, packed with amusing dilemmas and astonishing personalities. But almost no attention is paid to the film as an
entity, a force, a factor in society. One explanation for this lies in
the uneasiness which besets Hollywood wherever theories are in-

[13] Hollywood has a vocabulary of its own, and the argot is rich and expressive. *Flesh peddlers* and *ten-percenters* are agents; *juicers* are electricians and
grips are property men. *Switcheroo* denotes a change (switch) in plot structure; *double take* refers to the facial expressions which accompany delayed
comprehension (a pleased smile, a pause, a sudden look of consternation). The
vernacular of the trade journals is equally rich in abbreviation and ingenuity.
B.O. means box office; *biz* means business, and *pix* is shorthand for pictures.
Meggers (from "megaphone") are directors. *Stinkeroo* refers to a flop and
smasheroo to a hit. The classic headline, "*Stix Nix Hix Pix*," from *Variety*
some years ago, announced, in its own way, that rural audiences were disinclined to patronize pictures of the unsophisticated genre.

volved. The movie makers work with hunches, not logic; they trade in impressions rather than analyses. It is natural that they court the intuitive and shun the systematic, for they are expert in the one and untutored in the other.

But there is another reason why the movie people like to talk of movie making and do not like to talk about movies. "Hollywood," one story editor remarked, "is sitting on a powder keg of talents and possibilities and the unrealized scope of the screen." The concentration on talk about making movies is, in part, a defense mechanism, an escape from a recognition of the enormous potentialities of the screen and therefore of the enormous *responsibilities* of the movie makers. Hollywood is a little afraid to face those responsibilities. So energy is used up in an endless elaboration of stories and problems which deal with the technique of picture making, the curious impasses, the hilarious cul-de-sacs, the colorful clashes of temperaments. Hollywood is nervous about the power of the screen, because the movie makers are not sure how to use it.

Where talk in Hollywood leaves the primary zone of shop talk, it is concerned with gossip and anecdotage. Conversation and gossip are synonymous in the movie colony. The salaries and feuds, plans and romances of all the generals and most of the lieutenants in the production army are manna to a town overrun with magpies and agog with news of contracts and kisses, options, droptions, careers, and debacles. A thousand tongues are loyal to the cause of rumor, and, for all the skepticism about the gossip columns, they are followed with more avidity and credence than anyone likes to admit.

The talk about pictures is endless, and picture talk is endlessly absorbing. After-dinner conversation and studio talk are very similar: story problems, production problems, new pictures, old pictures, what Goldwyn said and what Curtiz didn't, who is working where, the purge at Paramount, the shakeup at RKO, and—above all—who is doing what with, for, or to whom. No phrase is so common in Hollywood as the titillating "I heard . . ." Gossip, in Hollywood as in Waco, is a disguised and sanctioned form of slander. Derogatory anecdotes, Hollywood's largest noncommercial export, compensate their purveyors for inferior status and power. Derisive stories and insinuating revelations are safety valves for envy and frustration. The movie people talk to each other about each other, and they infect each other with the sweet virus of rumor.

Most people in Hollywood tell a story well, and few other communities are as rich in story material. But the concentration on anecdotes serves to distract attention from more relevant—hence disturbing—social or interpersonal problems. A Hollywood party quickly resolves itself into a tournament of anecdotes, and the earnest competition in storytelling is heightened by those who *must* perform for deference, who depend upon plaudits for their sense of security, who interpret the social success of others as a rebuff to themselves.

Hollywood has the greatest collection of mimics on earth, and the actors have by no means a monopoly on the talent—as any conference with a producer, director, or writer will prove. Now, skill in mimicry is a revealing characteristic. Children practice mimicry as a means of playing "grown up"; they also use it as a device to master fears by imitating threatening objects. Adults who devote excessive energy to imitating seem to be driven by the urge to test themselves in other roles, other identities which may be more pleasing to the self than the protean personality which mimics usually possess. Mimicry, in children, ends when a definite identity is chosen for the self. Adults who prolong, cherish, and refine their talent for playing someone else are, we might say, still exploring the world to discover other characters they might like to be.

Our society stresses specialization and frowns upon those who continue to postpone the acceptance of a functional identity for themselves. A striking thing about Hollywood is that it is full of so many characters in search of a character; they remain a combination of many. It is this which makes them seem insincere; it is this, in part, which makes them colorful, unpredictable, and "irrational." For here are adults who sustain their juvenility (and their creative fantasy), who lend their profession that infantilism which is so typical of the screen and the stage. Here are creators in search of a stable personality. Here are the rich in fantasy.

When Orson Welles (of whom someone said, "There, but for the grace of God, goes God") was first shown through a studio he exclaimed, "This is the biggest electric train any boy ever had!" The remark is acute and revealing. Movie making is a game; the movie makers play it with great zest and, as in all games, the players surrender to periodic impatience with the game's illusory significance. An interesting refrain runs through Hollywood: "This is a crazy business. It ruins your digestion. It undermines your self-respect. It drives you nuts. But I wouldn't be doing anything else for the world!" This hymn of woe, which might be dubbed the Hollywood Lament, always ends with an emphatic "I wouldn't be doing anything else for the world!"

The movie makers love their work. The actors complain about their stories and their directors; the directors complain about the producers and the scripts; the producers complain about their directors and their writers; the writers complain about the producers, the directors, the actors, and the industry. But they all love making movies. There is no tedium in making pictures, except for the repetitive "shooting" on sound stages. There is no serenity, either. Hollywood takes immense nervous energy out of those caught in the controlled delirium of movie making. Weeks of tension follow weeks of semi-indolence; there is no encompassing routine into which life can fall, no certain progression in which personalities can find long-range equilibrium.

The movie people cannot stay away from Hollywood without falling into boredom and uneasiness. Time and again a producer or a director will announce that he is going away for a six-month vacation—and is back in Hollywood within six weeks. The movie makers do not seem to be able to endure extended residence in the world outside the movie colony. This can be understood; what other environments are as indulgent as Hollywood's, or as variegated, or as distracting? What other places offer such exhilarating conflicts, such opportunities for self-dramatization? Where else are there so many aggressive people who by their hostility excuse counter-hostility? Where else can narcissism be so richly fed? "I always bragged of the fact that no second of those contained in the twenty-four hours ever passed but that the name of William Fox was on the screen, being exhibited in some theater in some part of the world."[14] A movie director confessed, "When the credits dissolve on that screen and the music comes up and it says 'Directed by'—I get a lump in my throat."

The movie makers enjoy making movies and, for the most part, they like the jobs they hold. Sample comments from several hundred answers to questionnaires illustrate the point:

> I feel happier at directing than anything else.
> No two days are alike.
> I actually enjoy the work.
> Greatest medium of self-expression.
> Thrilling, exciting.
> Most creative of all branches.
> I love the work.

[14] Upton Sinclair, *Upton Sinclair Presents William Fox* (Upton Sinclair, 1933), p. 5.

This presents a point of the utmost importance. Most Americans live in two separate universes, the world of work and the world of play. Our schools, our churches stress the idea that play *follows* work, that work is something unpleasant which sanctions play. But in Hollywood the work is a form of play, and the people love their work, and they are paid handsomely for having fun. The movie makers are paid to dream their dreams and exploit their reveries. They are paid for doing things which other people would like to do without being paid. Is it any wonder that the movie makers are plagued by ambiguous guilts? In a society where work means sacrifice or the performance of distasteful routines, those who are rewarded for having fun may be expected to be ridden by remorse. And where the rewards are as high as they are in Hollywood, and, in addition, are coupled with adulation from the populace, the guilts would be all the greater. Is it for this reason that so many people in the movie colony jump at the chance to impress the listener with how hard they work? They seem to be defending themselves. They seem to be trying to convince themselves. They seem to think that no one believes that they do work hard; and they themselves, when they look at their bankbooks and their homes, their press clippings and their social calendars, can't believe that they worked *that* hard.

Love of work is especially noteworthy in a society in which work has become increasingly dull, routinized, and mechanistic. The best comment on the morale of the movie factories is that they have the atmosphere of a high-school dramatic club. The joy of craftsmanship, which characterized prefactory work and was swept away by the Industrial Revolution, still thrives in Hollywood's plants.[15] The movie maker gets personal attention and individual approbation; in few other fields are men so encouraged to "express yourself," in few other fields does the ego receive such sustained and deferential rewards. Psychological income is high in Hollywood.

No one retires voluntarily in Hollywood. There is no precedent or expectancy that the attainment of a given age or a certain estate will be followed by professional retirement and a life of leisure. This is partly because of the absence of fixed goals, partly because movie making is forever fascinating, partly because the kind of people who make movies can never rest in the effort to prove their

[15] Even the carpenters, property men, and messenger boys get a certain amount of awe from their wives and friends because of their proximity to the wonders and demigods of the sound stage. Such envy is not accorded to most laborers in our society. Two union leaders told this writer that studio painters and electricians feel quite superior to painters and electricians in the Los Angeles locals.

skill and potency to the world, and partly because the expiation of
guilts is a lifelong proposition. Those who retire from Hollywood
are forced to retire and those who have been forced out plan desperately to get back. In the movie colony, the champ never retires
undefeated; if he did, everyone would say knowingly, "No wonder
. . . he was going blind!"

The ex-romantic star tries character parts; the ex-glamour girl
accepts matron roles; the producer organizes a small company; the
director takes less attractive jobs. The simplest explanation is that
the comparative inaction and anonymity of the world outside are
intolerable after the exhilarating work and life of Hollywood. True
enough—but there are more penetrating reasons. The movie makers
depend upon praise for their inner security; they are driven by an
urgency to keep on working; their need for testimonials to their
talent is bottomless; their need for support to their ego is infinite;
their need to remain preoccupied with problems outside themselves
is ubiquitous. Hollywood is almost Japanese in the value it places
upon "face," and saving face is a double-sided matter—the preser-
vation of prestige in the eyes of the community, and the retention
of a sense of value by the self.

So it is that the aging Adolph Zukor, once the most powerful man in
films and more recently relegated to positions of high-sounding
vacuity, continues to fight for activity and power in the Paramount
plant. Harold Lloyd, who could retire for life, produces pictures
now that he has passed the apex of his popularity as a comedian.
Gloria Swanson and Richard Barthelmess, after years of retirement
and travel, have embarked on comeback careers. Mary Pickford
continues to plan productions which she will finance, and yearns
for a chance to act. Winfield Sheehan, once head of the Fox studio,
drifts in and out of studios in secondary production capacities.
Dozens of men and women in the movie colony who have ample
money and fat scrapbooks cannot face the prospect of life outside
the gratifying realm of movie making.

. . . no one ever retires on his laurels. . . . The minute that a man is
no longer an active participant he loses all standing in the community
and may even be taunted with the fact that he was once a big man. . . .

The only recognized, valid motivation . . . is the desire to succeed
and to continue to succeed. A successful man must always continue the
game, which is played for no fixed prize. Retirement is without honor,
and means that such an individual is henceforth to be ignored as a non-

entity. The whole of the social life is integrated into this one pattern; no field of social life is exempted from it.

This quotation, so pertinent to Hollywood, was written by Dr. Margaret Mead—about the Manus tribe in the Admiralty Islands.[16]

Hollywood is cosmopolitan. A random inspection of movie biographies disclosed actors from Tasmania, Brooklyn, Stockholm; directors from Pasadena, Tiflis, Sicily; writers from Budapest to Wapakoneta, Ohio; cameramen from China to New York; producers from Minsk to Wahoo, Nebraska. The largest collection of Indians outside of a government reservation is said to reside in Hollywood. On the social margins of the movie colony there are such fugitive groups as the Indian Actors Association, the Latin Writers Association, the Malayan-Filipino Club, the Chinese Screen Actors Association, the Hawaiian Actors Association and others.

The endless search for new faces and rare skills has brought people to Hollywood from the unnumbered places of the world. There are almost as many accents in Hollywood as in Shanghai, and the assemblage of skills surpasses the collection of nationalities. Within the circumference of the movie colony one has no difficulty in finding deep-sea divers, snake charmers, hog callers, dust manufacturers, walrus trainers, glass blowers, Cossacks, yogis, Foreign Legionnaires, and so on and on.

The potency of "Hollywood" as a symbol of quick opportunities and lavish rewards, like the symbol of "America" a generation earlier, has become a giant magnet to the world. The stream of actors, technical advisers, movie hopefuls, and tourists, the swarm of new faces and new careers, the sporadic changes in personnel, give Hollywood (as Washington) the character of a hotel lobby. In the movie colony, everyone seems to be from somewhere else.

In the days of silent pictures, a foreign accent may have presented a problem on Broadway, but not in Hollywood. The dislocations of postwar Europe impelled many entertainers and movie technicians to migrate to Hollywood, and the catastrophic impact of Hitler over Europe drove hundreds of artists off the Continent, to strike out for new careers in South and North America.

How large a proportion of the movie makers are foreign-born? An analysis of 555 cases (producers, actors, directors, writers)

[16] Margaret Mead, "The Manus of the Admiralty Islands," in *Competition and Cooperation Among Primitive Peoples,* edited by Margaret Mead. (McGraw-Hill, 1937), pp. 217, 218, 238.

showed that 78.2 per cent were born in the United States and 21.8 per cent outside the United States.[17] (80.2 per cent were born in the United States and Canada.) About a fifth of the four major skill groups in Hollywood, therefore, were born outside the United States. Foreign birth does not, of course, imply alien status. Many of the movie makers who were born abroad, like many other Americans, came to the United States at a tender age and were raised and educated here. By countries, the origins of the movie makers are:

		Per Cent
United States		78.20
Great Britain and Dominions		12.25
Great Britain	7.03	
Canada	1.98	
Ireland	1.98	
Union of South Africa	.54	
Australia	.36	
India	.18	
British West Indies	.18	
Russia		2.53
Germany		1.98
Hungary		1.26
Austria		1.08
France		.72

Under one-half of one per cent each: Sweden, Poland, Japan, Italy, China, Mexico, Norway.

The distribution of foreign-born among the four major groups offers a little surprise:

	Per Cent
Directors	28.7
Actors and actresses	25.3
Producers	17.4
Writers	13.9

[17] Comprising 221 actors and actresses, 132 producers and executives, 108 writers, 94 directors. The percentage of foreign-born whites 21 years old and over in the United States is 11.6. The 21.8 per cent foreign-born of Hollywood's movie makers is a smaller proportion than the foreign-born whites in the following cities: Boston (29.4), Cambridge, Mass. (28.4), Waterbury, Conn. (27.8), Providence, R. I. (25.5), Detroit (25.5), San Francisco (24.2), Rockford, Ill. (21.2), and so on (1930 census figures). But the concentration within one area, one profession, one general social group, and one field of identification gives the movie colony a more cosmopolitan flavor than is found in the cities mentioned.

The high proportion of movie directors of foreign birth is explicable by the fact that European directors were more expert and inventive than other film groups on the Continent; they found a readier market in Hollywood for their experience and skills. Besides, the director, unlike the actor or the writer, needs little command of English; he works . . . with visual rather than verbal techniques.

It was Dorothy Parker who said, "Authors and actors and artists and such, never know nothing and never know much." The educational background of Hollywood presents another surprise to those who hold the impression of widespread illiteracy in the movie colony. An analysis of 706 cases,[18] ranging from executives and actors to film editors and cinematographers, showed:

57.1 per cent went to college.

38.5 per cent went to high school but not to college.

9.2 per cent undertook postgraduate work beyond the four-year college level.

4.4 per cent did not go to high school.

Hollywood is characterized by sudden wealth and sudden success; it is typified by brash personalities and assertive behavior; it seems dedicated to ostentation and self-indulgence.

With all the opulence and splendor of this city, there is very little good breeding to be found. I have not seen one real gentleman, one well-bred man, since I came to town. At their entertainments there is no conversation that is agreeable; there is no modesty, no attention to one another. They talk very loud, very fast, and all together.[19]

This statement, oddly enough, was not made of Hollywood. It was made by John Adams, second President of the United States, and he was referring to the society of eighteenth-century New York. It is a particularly fitting quotation here, since it epitomizes the reaction of the Brahmin to persons who lack lineage and decorum. Hollywood—new, thriving, socially ambitious—lacks both. The disdain with which Hollywood is customarily regarded is, in its essence, similar to the scorn which Cabot Lodge cast upon the vulgarity and intellectual poverty of the elite of the nineties. It is similar to the icy contempt which the patricians of Southampton held

[18] Comprising 251 actors and actresses, 121 producers and executives, 133 writers, 66 directors, 17 directors of photography, 79 assistant directors, 39 first film editors.

[19] Quoted in Miriam Beard, *A History of the Business Man* (Macmillan, 1938), p. 505.

toward Newport (!) because that celebrated spa worshiped "cash rather than culture, arrogance rather than aristocracy."[20] The condescension with which the movie colony is generally discussed is, it would seem, a contemporary version of an ancient snobbery. Hollywood lacks urbanity. Its people are characterized by notoriety, not pedigree; its position rests on money, not birth; its fame depends on publicity, not ancestry. To paraphrase the words of a *grande dame* who despised the merchant princes of her day, society represents a wealthy aristocracy, but Hollywood represents an aristocracy of wealth.

For Hollywood is *nouveau riche*. Its magnificos are young, untrained in the art of the good life, untempered by old codes of behavior. In the movie colony there is being formed an amusement aristocracy, to use Miriam Beard's phrase, and Hollywood is assuming the social function of European royalty—"that of luxuriously diverting itself in public and diverting others. . . . In such an elite, gradually enlarged and diversified . . . the people sees itself mirrored and seeks its models."[21]

[20] Van Rensselaer, *op. cit.*, p. 236.
[21] Miriam Beard, *op. cit.*, p. 759.

Everything

Has Just

Gone Zoom

by Lillian Ross

The following chapter from Lillian Ross's Picture *(Rinehart and Company, New York, 1952. The contents of the book originally appeared as a series of articles in* The New Yorker) *details—to an eyelash—the making of the John Huston production of* The Red Badge of Courage. *Miss Ross uses a direct, spare, reportorial style. She does not comment on her material. The result is a witty, satirical portrait of Hollywood life. At the same time she presents a great deal of inside information on modern big-scale picture making.*

THE WEEK BEFORE rehearsals started on *The Red Badge of Courage*, Gottfried Reinhardt and John Huston found it a little hard to believe that they actually had a starting date (August 25, 1950) and a work schedule (nine rehearsal days and thirty-four shooting days). As the rehearsals approached, Reinhardt kept repeating to Huston that they would make "a *great* picture"; the picture would be profitable to Loew's, Inc., and at the same time it would duplicate the quality of the Stephen Crane novel and be *great* artistically. Huston, in turn, kept repeating that the picture had "a wonderful cast, with wonderful faces." Whenever Huston or Reinhardt received an inter-office communication from one of the thirty-two departments involved in the production of their picture, he was able to reassure

himself of the reality of the project by noting that on the memo the
"Subject" was described, convincingly, as "Production No. 1512"
and that copies were going to all the key executives, including
Nicholas Schenck himself, in New York. If a memo went to
Schenck, it was real. A couple of times, when Huston was looking
over a memo, he said to Reinhardt, "You know, we're really going
to *make* the picture."

On the eve of the first rehearsals, I dropped in on Reinhardt and
Huston at Reinhardt's house, where they were working on the
script. Reinhardt lived in Bel Air, on a winding, narrow road high
in the hills overlooking Beverly Hills. The house was in a hollow,
and it resembled the English mansion in the movie version of *Wuth-
ering Heights*—gabled, dark, and forbidding. I found the two men
in a study that had deep leather armchairs, two love seats, and a
green-tiled fireplace, in which stood a couple of tropical plants. Beyond a wide archway was a gloomy, cavernous room where the outline of a grand piano was visible. Reinhardt, holding a copy of the
script, was pacing back and forth in front of an armchair in which
Huston, comfortably dressed in a pink-checked cotton shirt, gray
flannel slacks, and loafers, lay sprawled, his long legs stretched out
and a copy of the script on his lap. Reinhardt's collar was unbuttoned and his necktie hung loosely around his shoulders. A long
strand of hair had fallen over his right eye, and the stub of a cigar
was in his mouth. He explained to me that they were devising dialogue for a scene in which the Youth and his comrades, marching
to their first battle, are taunted by battle-scarred veterans.

"You got anything?" Reinhardt asked Huston, stepping over his
legs. Albert Band, Huston's assistant, entered the room and started
pacing behind Reinhardt. Huston was rhythmically banging his
chin against his chest. Then, after drawing little sketches of Reinhardt in the margin of his script, he scribbled some words. "Write
this down, Albert," he said. " 'Hang your clothes on a hickory limb,
and don't go near the battle!' "

"Good," Band said, writing it down. "Very good."

"Now!" Reinhardt said, standing still for a moment. "We need
words for Scene 110. Or you can ad-lib it on the set."

Huston turned the pages of the script, a mimeographed booklet
stamped on the cover with the words "Production No. 1512," to
the scene:

MEDIUM SHOT—BACK OF THE LINE OF FIRING MEN
A private is fleeing, screaming, from his place in the line. He is met
and stopped by the captain of the reserves who grabs him by the collar.

The private is blubbering and staring with sheeplike eyes at the captain, who is pounding him.

Huston said, "I think this would be good if it's not said. Just have this little bit of action."

"You have to say *something*," Reinhardt said.

"We'll do it on the set," said Huston. "I want to see how it looks first."

Reinhardt rotated the cigar stub in his mouth. "Albert, go tell the cook we'll eat in half an hour," he said, and Band left the room.

Huston shifted to a love seat and lay back, his hands clasped behind his head. He seemed lost in some remote thought. Suddenly he jerked his head in a conspiratorial way at Reinhardt and, taking a piece of paper from his pocket, said he wanted to read something aloud. On April 23, 1863, he said, his great-grandfather, Colonel William P. Richardson, received a silver-sheathed sword from the noncommissioned officers and privates of the Twenty-fifth Regiment, Ohio Volunteer Infantry, and he was going to put the sword in the movie; it would be worn by the actor playing the part of the Youth's general. "We ought to put this kind of talk in the picture, too," he said. "Listen. This is from the speech my great-grandfather's superior officer made when he presented it to him: 'Wealth, influence, or favoritism might procure such a gift as this, but the esteem and confidence of brave men cannot be bought.' Jesus, Gottfried, people don't talk like that any more!"

Reinhardt nodded, then glanced impatiently at his script.

"My mother had that speech copied," Huston said. "He was her grandfather. I've got a Brady of him."

"Your mother would have been pleased to know that you're making *The Red Badge of Courage*," Reinhardt said. He looked rather taken with his own adroitness in bringing his director back to the task of the hour.

"Nothing I ever did pleased my mother," Huston said.

Band came back, and Reinhardt said that they would have to work on the script every night after rehearsals. Huston told him they were farther ahead than he seemed to think.

"We accomplished a lot today," Band said.

"We really must finish," Reinhardt said, with restrained desperation.

"Don't worry about it, *amigo*," said Huston.

"Remember that night in this room when we both said we wanted to make the picture?" Reinhardt said. "I said to you, 'What about making *The Red Badge of Courage?*' And you said, 'That's my

dream.' And we shook hands." Reinhardt looked very serious.
"L. B.[1] begged me not to do this picture," he said. "He was like a
father to me."

Mrs. Reinhardt came in, wearing black jersey ballet tights and
shirt, and ballet slippers. She had a black apron tied over the tights,
and the apron strings floated behind her like a tail. She was accompanied by Mocha, her black French poodle. Band started to sit down
in an armchair, but Mocha beat him to it.

"Today, Mocha ate four bananas," Mrs. Reinhardt said.

Reinhardt did not look at her. He said to Huston, "L. B. called
me into his office and talked for hours about the kind of pictures
that make money. He said he was telling me for my own good. I
thought he would weep."

"L. B. is *weeping?*" Mrs. Reinhardt said.

"He didn't want us to make the picture, honey," Huston said.

Mrs. Reinhardt said, "Gottfried, should I let Mocha eat strawber-
ries?"

Reinhardt said, "L. B. told Dore if *he* thought we should make
the picture, to go ahead and make it."

"Hang yourselves, boys, in other words," Huston said cheerfully.

Reinhardt looked at him shyly and laughed. "Now L. B. puts
Dore on the spot with this picture," he said. "He has his arm around
Dore. And he says he loves Dore." He laughed, and then he looked
serious. "Frankly, I'm worried," he said. "The book is about the
thoughts of the Youth. Will we show what really goes on inside
the boy?"

"Audie Murphy will show it, Gottfried," Huston said.

"You wanted Audie," said Reinhardt.

"Yes," Huston said in a patient tone.

"Montgomery Clift—" Reinhardt began.

"Don't worry, Gottfried," Huston said.

"This must be a *great* picture," Reinhardt said.

"Don't worry, Gottfried," Huston said.

Around the same time, Huston's agent, Paul Kohner, submitted
the script to a local psychologist for reassurance that the theme of
The Red Badge of Courage—that of a boy who runs away from his
first battle and then, when he returns to his comrades, performs
heroic acts in his next battle—was valid. The psychologist turned in
a typewritten report stating that the script told the story of a soldier who surmounts his fear complex and becomes a hero, in ac-

[1] L. B. Mayer.

cordance with the established theory that a courageous action can be a direct reaction to cowardice. "Of course, it is presupposed dramaturgically that the psychosis of fear is taken as a fact," he wrote. "And so automatically the question arises as to whether such a conception can be generalized. . . . Since the motives of his heroism are of purely psychopathic origin it should be stated that the filmic description of the psychological evolution fails to convince at the important moments. This is a cardinal fault in regard to the conception of the matter." He then suggested several additional scenes that would explain the Youth's change from cowardice to heroism in battle. "These differentiated psychological *Zwischentöne* have to be plastically formed," he wrote, and added that if his suggestions were followed, "the picture could be the outstanding one of the year."

Huston and Reinhardt read the analysis, exchanged bleak looks, and had it filed.

The morning of the day rehearsals were to start, on Huston's ranch, Huston, a red-and-green-checked cap on his head, a brown cigarette in his mouth, and his arms folded on the top bar of a white rail fence separating a small ranch house from his stables, watched his adopted son, Pablo, saddle a big black horse. It was the horse from whose back Huston intended to direct the picture. The horse moved impatiently under the saddle.

"All right, baby," Huston said soothingly.

"Take it easy, baby," said Pablo. "Dad, you want me to walk him a little bit?"

"Just hold him there, Pablo," said Huston, and exhaled a stream of cigarette smoke with an expression of happy fulfillment. He mounted the horse, and with a quick, dramatic gesture he pulled his cap down farther over his forehead, and then, taking the reins in both hands, he sat facing the dry, rutty dirt road leading away from the stables. The big horse stood motionless. Huston sat in silence, staring grimly ahead for a moment. "Well now, Pablo," he said, with intense emphasis on each syllable. "Keep an eye on everything back here, *amigo*." Then he started the horse down the road (MEDIUM SHOT) at an easy, rocking walk, stirring up a cloud of dust in his wake.

Huston stopped his horse beside a large oak tree next to a dry, barren, yellow field. Studio limousines and a large studio bus were parked in the field. A pyramid of rifles was stacked near the bus. Under the oak tree sat Harold Rosson, the cameraman, with Reggie Callow, assistant director; Lee Katz, unit manager; Andrew

Marton, the "leapfrog" director; Colonel Paul Davison, the technical adviser; and Albert Band.

Callow stepped forward and gave a brisk salute. "The troops are in good shape, Mr. Huston, sir," he said. "Been drilling them for an hour."

"Very good, *amigo*," Huston said.

"Rough day," Katz said. "Hot, hot."

A dozen of the studio's stock actors, in blue uniforms and kepis, lounged about on the grass. Not far from them was another group, consisting of a script clerk, a still photographer, a few assistant and second assistant directors, a few assistant and second assistant cameramen, grips (the movie equivalent of stagehands), and property men. The leading members of the cast, all in blue uniforms, sat in a circle on the ground playing poker: Audie Murphy, the Youth; Bill Mauldin, the Loud Soldier; John Dierkes, the Tall Soldier; Royal Dano, the Tattered Man; and Douglas Dick, the Lieutenant.

"All right, lads," Huston said. He dismounted, tied his horse's reins to a branch of the tree, and spent the next hour conferring with Rosson on camera problems. The stock players lolled about, blank-faced and resigned. They were being paid a hundred and seventy-five dollars a week, and audiences wouldn't notice them enough to remember their faces. Some were on the way up; that is, they were being given work more and more regularly. Others were on the way down. All of them had the manner of men who expected no major surprises. The leading actors made a great show of casualness and boredom, and then became genuinely bored, genuinely casual, and gave up the poker game. Bill Mauldin, his kepi pushed back and a cigarette holder stuck jauntily in his mouth, held the others' attention for a while with a series of jokes.

"Hell, this is ditchdiggin' work," Mauldin remarked at one point. "I'm just here raisin' scratch, so's I can go back home and work on my play." He started to roll a cigarette.

Dano took a pack from his pocket and held it out.

"Hell," Mauldin said, "I was rollin' my own when you was in three-cornered pants."

"Gosh, Bill," Dierkes drawled. "You talk just like the Loud Soldier."

"Hell," Mauldin said, looking proud and pleased, and ducked his head.

Dano remarked amiably that working in pictures was fine with him. He seemed at ease and as well suited to the role of the Tattered Man as Mauldin was to the Loud Soldier. He was unshaven and gaunt—so skinny that his bones protruded. He has large dark eyes, long lashes, and black hair, which was hanging raggedly over his ears. His uniform was torn and his shirttail was outside his trousers. He looked as though he had always worn tatters. He yawned, stretched out on the ground with his head on a rock, and went to sleep.

Dierkes turned to Murphy, who, with a troubled expression, was staring at the top of a tree, and asked him how he felt.

Murphy said that his malaria was acting up again, that he had had an attack of nausea while driving out to the ranch, and that he was going to lie down in Huston's ranch house.

As Murphy walked slowly away, Dierkes shook his head and said to Mauldin that he was amazed whenever he realized that Murphy was the most-decorated soldier of the last war. "When the war ended, he wasn't even old enough to vote," he added. In a tone of deep respect, Dierkes, who has an enormous interest in other people, said that Murphy was one of nine children of a Texas share-cropper who abandoned his family when Murphy was fourteen. The mother died two years later. Murphy was working in a radio repair shop when the war came. He tried to enlist in the Marines and then in the paratroops but was turned down because he was underweight. He finally got into the infantry. Among his decorations were the Medal of Honor, the Distinguished Service Cross, the Silver Star, the Legion of Merit, the Bronze Star, the Croix de Guerre, and the Purple Heart. "Now look at the little sport," Dierkes said.

"Hell, amigo, he's in a war picture, ain't he?" Mauldin said.

"All right, lads!" Huston called. They woke Dano up, and the first rehearsal began.

The rehearsals concentrated less on the acting than on prepa-rations for getting the actors photographed. Huston studied his actors from various points through a finder and conferred with Rosson about the placing of the camera, composing the basic plan of each scene with the meticulous care of a painter at work on a picture. A scene in which the Loud Soldier was to run up to a group of comrades and shout that the Army was moving into battle would have to look as if it were near a river where, in the previous scene, the Loud Soldier had heard the news. The latter scene would be filmed at the Sacramento River location, near Chico, California, several hundred miles north of the ranch. At the end of the nine-day rehearsal period, the company would go up to Chico for several days of additional rehearsal and shooting.

After a couple of hours, the cast and crew had lunch, provided by an M-G-M catering truck, in the field. Lee Katz told Huston that in the course of making the picture ten thousand five hundred box lunches would be served, at a cost to Metro of $15,750—one of the smaller items in the picture's budget. During lunch, a prop man brought Huston a box containing old-fashioned watches of several styles and asked him to choose one for a scene in which the Loud Soldier, fearing that he will be killed in battle, gives his watch to the Youth. Another prop man carried over three small, squealing pigs and asked Huston to choose the one that would be stolen from a farm girl in a scene featuring a soldier pillaging a farmyard. Huston chose a watch and cast a pig, and then called for a rehearsal of a scene between Murphy and Mauldin just before their first battle.

Murphy sat under an oak tree, and Mauldin sat several yards behind the tree. Huston and Rosson squatted in front of them. Callow, his script open to the scene, stood behind Huston. The script clerk, whose name was Jack Aldworth, conferred with Callow about time schedules. Colonel Davison sat at the roadside with Marton, who began to tell how he had narrowly escaped death at the hands of African natives while making *King Solomon's Mines*. The stock players lolled nearby.

"All right, Billy, come on down," Huston said to Mauldin, putting the finder to his eyes. Through it he watched Mauldin come down and lean over Murphy's shoulder, saying, "Why, hello, Henry. Is it you? What yeh doin' here?"

"Oh, thinkin'," said Murphy.

Huston did not seem to be paying any attention to the performances of the actors. Occasionally, he interrupted to ask them to look in this direction or that, and he discussed with Rosson where the camera should be placed and how much of the tree should be in the picture.

After the rehearsal of the scene was over, Huston made his first comment on the acting. He drew Murphy aside and told him that there was a humorous aspect to the Youth's fear. "Fear in a man is something tragic or reprehensible, you know, Audie?" he said. "But fear in a youth—it's *ludicrous*."

Murphy nodded solemnly.

"All right, *amigo*," Huston said, clapping him on the shoulder. "You just work it out for yourself."

"Here comes the producer, boys!" someone shouted. "Act busy!"

Reinhardt plodded slowly across the sun-baked, yellow field. A

fresh cigar was in his mouth, and a blue beret was on his head. He
shook Huston's hand and asked him how things were going.

"Wonderful, Gottfried," said Huston. "Just wonderful."

As the rehearsals progressed, Huston seemed to show a greater
interest in the acting of some scenes, and he was particularly interested in one in which Murphy discovered his comrade the Tall
Soldier, Dierkes, in the line of wounded men straggling away from
the battle the Youth had run away from. Dano, the Tattered Man,
trudged along a dirt road, one arm dangling at his side. Murphy
came from behind a clump of bushes and fell in with him. The
Tattered Man looked fervently at him. "Th' boys ain't had no fair
chanct up t' now, but this time they showed what they was," Dano
said. "I knowed it'd turn out this way. Yeh can't lick them boys.
No, sir! They're fighters, they be. Where yeh hit, ol' boy?" Dierkes
came shuffling past them. Murphy started after him, calling his
name, and put a hand on his arm.

At this point, Huston fell into step with Murphy and Dierkes,
his face signaling grotesque and terrible emotions, which were not
apparent in the faces of the actors. Band brought up the rear,
following the lines in the script.

"I was allus a good friend t' yeh, wa'n't I, Henry?" Dierkes said,
in a kind of delirium. "I've allus been a pretty good feller, ain't I?
An' it ain't much t' ask, is it? Jest t' pull me along outer th' road?
I'd do it fer you, wouldn't I, Henry?"

Murphy tried to get Dierkes to lean on him for support.

"No, no, no, leave me be," Dierkes said, pulling away.

Huston elbowed Dierkes aside and put Murphy's hand on his
own arm. "When you say 'No, no, no, leave me be,' start to go
down and make him let go of you," he told Dierkes. He stumbled
and fell forward, loosening Murphy's grip. "All right, try it again—
by yourselves this time."

Huston lit a brown cigarette as the actors moved back up the
path to do the scene again. Inhaling deeply, as though in anger, he
said that Dano was wonderful. "That boy is an *actor*," he said.
"He's a great actor. I don't have to tell him a goddam thing. The
only other actor I've known who had that was Dad. But Dierkes
will be wonderful in the picture. That face! Even when an actor is
limited in his acting experience, you can cover for him. You can
get him to do things that don't require acting." He threw his cigarette down and ground it out. "You make him let go of you as you
start to go *down*," he said to Dierkes in a soft voice.

Dierkes looked puzzled. "Don't I pull my arm away from him?"

"Do whatever you want to do with your goddam arm," said the director. "The point is you *make* him let go of you by falling." Dierkes looked more puzzled. "I see, John," he said.

"Once more," Huston said crisply.

There were only a few days left of the allotted rehearsal time. The company had become tense. With a certain air of impatience with the problem, Huston had tried to communicate to the others his ideas and feelings for composing the various shots, and he had talked about the way things might eventually look on the screen. The others had tried to demonstrate that they understood just what he was driving at. But the strain was beginning to tell. One joke that made the rounds of the cast and crew was "This is getting to be a long war." The most popular one was "Did you hear about the coward who quit M-G-M to join the Army?"

Reinhardt was becoming dissatisfied with the script. He acted like a man under pressure. He lost weight and smoked more cigars every day. Huston showed no sign of being under any pressure. He was able to turn from one thing to another with ease, good humor, and concentration. In a single hour one day, he did the following: When Dusty, the official cowboy on Huston's ranch, wanted to know when he would be given a part in the picture, Huston entered into a long, involved discussion with him about why it was necessary for a man to choose between a career in pictures and life on the range, and how much better the latter was in the long run. From Dusty, he turned to Audie Murphy and asked him to look through the finder at the hilltop where the Tall Soldier would die. "He goes to die in the open, Audie," Huston said. "Do you feel the sense of expanse up there?" He went into a long, involved explanation of why a man chooses to die in the open. From Murphy, Huston turned to Rosson, to work out the details of placing the camera on a dolly, or wheeled platform, and of building dolly tracks for scenes in which the camera would have to roll along with moving actors. From Rosson, Huston turned to a telephone to take a call from Sam Spiegel, his partner in Horizon Pictures; he told Spiegel he might be free to work on Horizon's next picture, *The African Queen*, in four months. From the telephone, he turned to Hans Peters, the art director, to inquire whether a night scene filmed on a set at the studio would look as real as one filmed outdoors. From Peters, Huston turned to a newspaper photographer who wanted him to pose with Mrs. Huston, who was watching rehearsals, for what he called a happy-go-lucky family shot, and he agreed to pose later that day. From the photographer, Huston turned to a tree branch lying in the road and demonstrated with it how a jockey twirls a whip. From the tree branch, Huston turned to his wife, who told him that he was expected to appear in an hour, in black tie, at a dinner party at the home of L. B. Mayer.

The operating budget for Production No. 1512 was by now complete. It showed that the total cost was supposed to come to $1,434,789, including:

Direction	$156,010
Story and Continuity	41,992
Cast	82,250
Departmental Overhead	238,000
Rent and Purchase Props	80,800
Extras	145,058
Cameramen	25,500
Sound	35,177
Cutters and Projectionists	15,650
Producer's Unit Charge	102,120
Production Staff	30,915
Stills and Stillmen	6,995
Picture Film and Dev.	17,524
Sound Film and Dev.	8,855
Music	12,620
Wardrobe	43,000
Makeup and Hairdressers	13,915
Auto and Truck Hire	49,125
Meals and Lodging	35,385
Travel and Transportation	6,360
Location Fees and Expenses	18,255
Misc.	23,850

In a breakdown of these figures, the estimate showed that Audie Murphy was scheduled for forty-seven working days at a salary of $2,500 a week; his cost to the production would be $25,000. Bill Mauldin, working the same number of days at $2,000 a week, would cost $15,667. John Dierkes would work thirty days at $600 a week and would cost $3,000; Douglas Dick, forty-six days at $800 a week, would cost $6,133; Royal Dano, twenty-four days at $750 a week, would cost $3,000. The Story and Continuity cost included $10,000 paid to the estate and the publisher of Stephen Crane for the rights to film the novel, and $28,000 paid to the writer of the screenplay—Huston. The Directorial charges included Huston's $4,000-a-week salary, totaling $137,334.

The Rent and Purchase Props included $33,370 for the use of horses and the services of their trainers. The figures for the battle scenes indicated that they would be violent as well as expensive. Eighty thousand rounds of ammunition, at $110 per thousand, would come to $8,800; three caissons had to be reconditioned at $25 each; two hundred and fifty 45-70 rifles with bayonets and slings would come to $200. There would be ten Confederate flags ($65) and two Union flags ($13). Six dummy horse carcasses were to be bought at $275 each. Among the battle regalia that was being rented were two Union battle drums, at $5 each per week; two short bugles, at $3.50 each per week; twenty pairs of carbine boots, at $1.50 a pair per week; thirty nose bags, at one dollar each per week; a hundred infantry packs and blanket rolls suitable for foreground use, at $1.50 each per week; and twenty-five cavalry sabers, at $5 each per week. The Production Staff charge of $30,915 included the cost of Lee Katz ($8,718), of two assistant directors ($5,366, half of which represented Reggie Callow's cost to the picture), of two second assistant directors ($2,609), and of Jack Aldworth, the script clerk ($1,430). The estimate explained that Aldworth would be paid $160 a week while on location, and $140 a week at the studio. Of the money to be paid to the cameramen, Rosson, at a weekly salary of $750, would receive $11,250.

The Sound charges were broken down in this fashion: Twenty-nine days of recording at the studio would cost $7,337; two days of playback, $506; the use of the public-address system for fifty-eight days, $4,002; and 30,000 feet of rerecording, or dubbing, at sixteen cents a foot, $4,800. The estimate for Picture Film and Dev. showed the expenses involved in buying and processing both negatives and positives, and that the job would take more than forty times as much film as was expected to appear in the final product. The 180,000 feet of black-and-white negative, at 4.1 cents a foot, would cost $7,380; the processing of 165,000 feet of black-and-white negative, at 2.5 cents a foot, would cost $4,125; 155,000 feet of black-and-white positive, at 1.283 cents a foot, would cost $1,989; and the processing of it, at 2.6 cents a foot, would cost $4,030.

The breakdown of the Wardrobe charges of $43,000 revealed that uniforms for officers would cost more than those for soldiers in both the Union and Confederate armies. In addition to old uniforms on hand in the wardrobe department, there would be a hundred and twenty-five new ones for Union soldiers at $50 each, ($6,250), twenty-five new Union officers' outfits at $75 each

($1,875), and ten Confederate officers' uniforms at the same price
($750). The cost of Music, including a thirty-five-piece orchestra,
was figured on a basis of $600 an hour. Box lunches, as Lee Katz had
pointed out, would cost $15,750.

The cost of extras and bit players was broken down scene by
scene:

EXT. Fording River (Chico)
    Sc. 65-66—soldiers slide down bank, cross stream, and climb
    hill—$2,850
EXT. Farm (Ranch)
    Sc. 43-47—soldiers side with farm girl as she berates fat
    soldier for attempting to snatch pig

fat soldier	$150
girl	$150
ad-libs (4) @ $55	$220
extras—total	$2,431

One of the least expensive shots would show the body of a dead
soldier in the woods. (The Youth would come upon the body
after he had run away from the battle.) The only cost for this,
other than the overhead and Murphy's salary, would be the wages
of the extra who would play dead—$25. Extras who spoke lines
would be paid an additional $23 for each day they spoke. The
battle scenes would be the most expensive. The Confederate charge
that causes many Union soldiers, including the Youth, to flee would
cost $16,469.

Reinhardt, Huston, and the cast and crew of The Red Badge
of Courage were accompanied to Chico, for the first shooting on
the film, by Mrs. Huston, Pablo, and Mrs. Reinhardt. The Hustons,
the Reinhardts, and the leading members of the cast were quartered
in the Oaks Hotel there. (The other members of the company were
scattered about the town.) The Oaks is a small, neat, rectangular
building in the center of a small, neat, rectangular town.

Late in the morning of the first day, Mrs. Reinhardt sat gloomily
in a high-backed chair in the lobby. She was wearing a high-necked
dress of mossy-green sheer silk with a golden butterfly at the throat,
and high-heeled black pumps. She looked chic and elegant. The
other lobby-sitters were for the most part gentlemen dozing under
ten-gallon hats. A newspaper lay in Mrs. Reinhardt's lap; a black
banner head stretched from one side to the other: "AMERICANS
SMASH RED ROADBLOCK." Huston and Reinhardt were on the Sacra-

mento River, eight miles away, with some stunt men who were
trying to find a safe and cinematically attractive site for the scene
in which the Youth's regiment would cross a river. The actors were
rehearsing in a park four miles away. It was a twenty-four-hundred-
acre park, and Mrs. Reinhardt told me she did not have the faintest
notion where to find anybody in it, even if she were dressed for
the excursion.

"It's wilderness and you need trousers," she said to me. "Gottfried
loathes me in trousers. The temperature outside is *one hundred and
five degrees.* Have you read the news?" She opened the newspaper
and pointed to a headline read-in, "MOVING PICTURE CREWS ARRIVE
IN CHICO FOR FILMING OF CIVIL WAR DRAMA SHOTS."

"We are famous," Mrs. Reinhardt said dryly. She closed the
newspaper and sighed in utter despair. "Why am I here?" she asked.

Huston was in an expansive mood. He was sitting behind the
desk in a room in the Oaks Hotel, his chair tipped back and his
heels resting on the desk, and looking over some local citizens who,
in response to advertisements, were applying for bit parts in the
picture. He loved to use the faces of nonprofessional actors in his
pictures, he told me, and besides it cost less to hire bit part players
and extras—a couple of hundred men would be engaged at $10 a
day each to appear as members of the Youth's regiment in the
Union Army—locally than it would to transport them from Hollywood. The first applicant to come in was an eager, hard-breathing
young man named Dixon Porter. He had a round, innocent face
and an incongruously heavy black beard. Huston gave him a gra-
cious nod. "Nice beard you've got there, Dixon," he said. He picked
up a long pad of yellow paper and started making sketches of Dixon
and various types of beards.

Reggie Callow, who was attending the audition, along with
Colonel Davison and the other assistant director, Joel Freeman, said
beards were almost as important as talent for these bit parts.

"M-G-M offers a five-dollar bonus to every man with a good
beard!" Callow said, in a raucous voice. "Go ahead, Dixon. Read."

Dixon Porter read, " 'Ain't they a sight to behold, in their brand-
new uniforms! Hang yer clothes on a hickory limb and don't go
near the battle!' "

"Thank you, Dixon," Huston said. "Very good, Dixon. Thank
you very much."

"We'll let you know, Dixon," Callow said mechanically, ushering
the applicant out.

"That boy is good," Huston said. "Not tough but good. We'll

find *some* use for him. Now let's get some real grizzled sons of bitches." He went back to his sketching.

The next applicant was a thin young man with a long, dolorous face, horn-rimmed glasses, and a soft beard. He said he belonged to a local little-theater group. After he had read and departed, Huston told Callow they needed tougher-looking men, tough as hell.

"Every time you get little-theater, you get these delicate fellas," Callow said.

The third applicant, who was accompanied by his three-year-old daughter, explained earnestly that he hadn't been able to get a baby-sitter. Huston tore off the page he had been sketching on, crumpled it up, and threw it on the floor. The earnest father and the three-year-old went out again.

"Joel!" Huston said sternly to the other assistant director, a serious young man with a crew haircut. "Joel, you go out tonight to the poolrooms! To the gas stations! Find the tough guys and bring them back. We need guys who look tough."

"You mean guys who look—" Freeman began.

"Tough!" said Huston.

Reinhardt had finally pinned Huston down to the job of revising the script with him. They worked in Huston's hotel room, with Albert Band, making some changes requested by Joseph I. Breen, the Motion Picture Production Code Administrator. Huston lay on the bed, his back resting against the headboard, and sketched thoughtfully on a yellow pad as Band read off the lines that were considered objectionable.

" 'Gawd, he's runnin',' " Band read.

" 'Look, he's runnin',' " Huston said in a bored voice.

" 'It'll be hell to pay,' " Band read.

" 'It'll be the devil to pay,' " said Huston.

"You can't say that," Reinhardt said.

Huston said, "The hell you can't."

"Joe Breen—" Reinhardt began.

"All right," Huston interrupted. " 'It'll be the *dickens* to pay.' "

" 'Damn tobacco,' " Band continued.

"Take 'damn' out," said Huston.

"That takes care of your censor problem for now," said Band.

Reinhardt directed him to make copies of the changes and send them to Metro's Script Department. Then he looked uncertainly at Huston. "You don't like to write?" he asked.

"When I put pencil to paper, I find myself sketching," Huston said. "I can't write alone—I get too lonely. I have to dictate."

Reinhardt asked him to try to write some dialogue for the Youth's officers just before the regiment went into action, to give the audience an idea of the position of the Youth's regiment in relation to the battle. Reluctantly, Huston set to work. Reinhardt went to his own room for a cigar. When he returned, Huston said, "Here's a speech. The Colonel rides up behind the lines and says to the Captain, 'Captain, the Rebs are on that hill over there. We're goin' to try an' push them off. Maybe we will, maybe we won't. Anyway, take positions on that road down there and hold it whatever happens!' Captain says, 'We'll stand, Colonel, sir!'"

"Good!" Reinhardt said explosively.

"It's got to be kept simple," Huston said, looking pleased.

"Good!" Band said explosively.

The telephone rang. Band answered it and told Huston it was Sam Spiegel, calling from Hollywood. Huston said to say he wasn't in. Reinhardt bit off the end of his cigar and smiled happily.

Late in the afternoon of the day before the shooting of the picture was to start, Huston asked Harold Rosson if he wanted to go fishing. Rosson said no, adding that he had been bitten by a wasp, burned by the sun, and exhausted by tramping through underbrush in search of locations, and besides he had a bad dust cold; he was going to bed. Undaunted, Huston said that he was going fishing. Pablo escorted Mrs. Reinhardt on a shopping trip, from which she returned with an outfit, recommended by Pablo, to wear on location—a pair of Army suntans, a green T shirt, and a green porkpie hat. At the Oaks, Andrew Marton passed around a copy of the *Hollywood Reporter* in which the column "Trade Views," written by W. R. Wilkerson, the paper's owner, was devoted entirely to the leapfrog method being used in making *The Red Badge of Courage*. (This was a reference to Marton's job of getting scenes lined up for Huston so that they could be shot without delay.) The column said, "Reinhardt and Huston are trying to make the picture with as little cost as possible. Such activity is to be congratulated and given every encouragement."

At two o'clock in the morning of the day the shooting was to start, Reinhardt sat down and wrote a letter to Huston:

Dear John:

Well—today is the day! After all the cliffs and shallows we have had to circumnavigate, it seems almost miraculous that this day should have come at all and so soon. How well I remember that night in my house, when at two o'clock we suddenly, enthusiastically, almost recklessly decided on The Red Badge of Courage! *Well, the first phase is completed. We didn't "run." However, taking a leaf from our book, that isn't enough. We now must prove that we are real heroes. Or better, you must prove it. For I, the more or less unarmed lieutenant, can merely egg you on. It is you who will have to engage the enemy from today on, and I know that you will give a wonderful account of yourself. To that end you have my very best wishes, my unshakable confidence, and, if you want, my help.*

I needn't tell you that the course ahead will be far from an easy one. The deep waters we have reached offer far greater dangers than the petty little political cliffs and financial shallows we were able to avoid. And they require much more than your amazing talents (which are a pleasure to watch) or whatever circumspection I was able to lend our venture. They require your constant, untiring watchfulness.

Let me—on this day—point out the main problems as they come to mind one by one:

(1) Audie Murphy. He needs your constant *attention, all your ingenuity (photographically and directorially), all the inspiration you can give him. He shouldn't be left alone for a single second. Nothing should be taken for granted. At the risk of making myself a tremendous bore,* CONCENTRATE ON AUDIE MURPHY! *I watched him. I believe he will be good. How good (and the whole picture depends on the degree) depends entirely on the support you give him.*

(2) Variety. Change of pace. At the speed you are going to do this in all respects terribly difficult picture and the crazy continuity you will shoot it in, there is the danger of losing the rhythm of the continuity; the tempo might become too even, the moods too similar. In view of the general sameness of the background and the subtlety and introspectiveness of the development, I beg you to examine and re-examine every scene in the light of what precedes and follows the action. This may sound like childish advice. But I know how easy it is to get bogged down in the physical difficulties alone.

(3) Humor. Wherever you see the opportunity, bring it out; wherever you can, inject it!

(4) Geography. I know you are aware of that. But I repeat: it is imperative that we always know where we are. Especially the transitions from one locale to another must be smooth and clear.

(5) Script. Every hour you can spare (and I know this is going to be tough from now on) you ought to spend on the script until, from beginning to end, it is in a shape to your own satisfaction. Needless to say, I am at your disposal all the time. You have no idea—or maybe you

have—how the days and hours you spent on the script (away from the set) in the last few weeks improved it.

That is all. Regarding the last point, I must add that you made me very unhappy last night. You know I was waiting for you. But it wasn't so much your failure to tell me that you went fishing which disturbed me (although it wouldn't have hurt if you had done it), but I know we would have accomplished a lot, maybe finished the script, if you had kept our appointment. Now that the shooting starts it will be twice as difficult. After all, that is the main reason why I came. If we can't get together, I might as well pack up and go home. I hope you won't mind my frankness in telling you this. You asked me once to be your "boss." I can't do that. I can only be your accomplice and friend. And in those capacities, I am anxious and ready to lend you whatever assistance I can.

And now, good luck! I have a feeling something quite extraordinary is likely to come out of all this. But whatever will be the outcome, I can tell you one thing already: it has been a great experience to be associated with you. And somehow I am quite calm: we will steer our ship safely and proudly into port.

> *Always,*
> *Gottfried*

Reinhardt's letter was not the only one Huston received in the morning. At breakfast with Murphy and Mauldin, he read a letter from Dore Schary that said, "Today's your day, and with it goes all my best to you. I'm sure, John, we'll get a damned good movie out of *Red Badge*—one that we'll all be proud of. Good luck and good shooting. Sincerely, DORE." Joe Cohn, the head of Metro's Production Office (logistics, budgets, etc.), wired Huston, "YOU ARE DOING A WAR PICTURE. SHOOT—SHOOT—SHOOT."

The atmosphere at the breakfast table was one of readiness. Murphy and Mauldin, the two leading men, had on their blue uniforms and kepis. They listened abstractedly as Huston, putting his correspondence aside and playing nervously with a couple of quarters, told them about Nate Leipsig, who he said was the greatest coin manipulator in history. Then Huston, who was wearing regulation Army suntans, stood up, put a Mexican straw hat on, took a gulp of coffee, and said he would see the boys outside. A few minutes later, Huston and Reinhardt, who wore blue cotton slacks and a matching knit shirt and was carrying a pith helmet, came out. Both men were looking grim. "I want to ride out with *you*, Gottfried," Huston was saying. Reinhardt nodded benignly and clapped the helmet on his head.

The first scene to be shot, No. 72, read:

MEDIUM SHOT—NEW ANGLE

The regiment encounters the body of a dead soldier and the ranks open covertly to avoid the corpse.

It was being set up on a dirt road running through the thickly wooded park. A couple of hundred Chicoans, many of them sporting five-dollar-bonus beards and all of them dressed in Union blues and carrying rifles or swords, were lined up on the road in a column of fours. Near the head of the column stood Dixon Porter, wearing the sword and red sash of a lieutenant; he was one of the extras. A long dolly track, with wooden rails, had been laid beside the road. The camera, fixed on a tripod, stood on a rubber-wheeled dolly at one end of the track. The trees lining the road arched high over the heads of the warlike array. Everybody in Huston's crew seemed, with a harassed awareness of the dollar value of every minute, to be rushing everyone else. Rosson, standing on the dolly and peering through the camera at the line of soldiers, gave hurried signals to assistants helping him get the camera in position. Huston and Reinhardt made a hasty inspection of the Chicoan army. Marton dashed at Mauldin, collared him, and thrust him into the Union ranks behind Murphy and Dierkes. The time was 8:38 A.M.

In the road, ahead of the troops, lay a soldier, face down, his uniform disheveled, a rifle under his limp arm, his legs sprawled. Callow was arranging and rearranging the legs. A still photographer aimed a Speed Graphic at the dead man; his flash bulb popped, and he quickly turned his camera on the waiting troops. Band arrived and began to tag after Huston, who walked over to the camera.

"Good morning, boys," Huston said to Rosson and his assistants. "Good luck, gentlemen!"

Jack Aldworth was writing in a hard-covered notebook. The first page was headed "LOG—PROD. NO. 1512—HUSTON." Under the heading, he had already written:

7:45–8:00—*Travel to Location*
8:00–8:20—*Spot Equip. and Unload Trucks*
8:20–8:32—*Line up Dolly Shot with Soldiers*

He now wrote:

8:32–8:40—*Set up camera with it on dolly—meanwhile reh. and drill soldiers.*

Aldworth would submit his daily log to Reinhardt and to Callow, who would submit it to Lee Katz, who would submit copies of it to Joe Cohn, Dore Schary, and L. B. Mayer, in Culver City, and to Nicholas Schenck, in New York. (Along with the daily log would go a daily report on the time the crew left for location, the time shooting started and finished, the number of scenes filmed, and the number of extras used.) Reinhardt was standing beside the camera, reading a letter that had just been handed to him by a messenger:

Dear Gottfried:

Well, we're off! And we're off to a good start. I'm certain it will be good, Gottfried, damned good. We'll make it so. Good luck and my best.

Sincerely,
Dore

The rehearsal began. Callow yelled, "Here we go, boys! Get in line!" The troops started marching toward the man lying in the road. Callow told them to pause and look down at the body as they passed it. Huston peered into the camera and watched the procession, then called to the troops that this was the first dead man they had ever seen, and told them to keep this in mind when they looked down at the body. The time was 8:56.

For all the tension, hurry, and confusion, it was very quiet. At Callow's command, the Union soldiers, having passed the body, moved back to their starting point. They were silent, and their silence was respectful. A smoke machine mounted on a truck, which had been hidden in the woods off the road, started up with a clatter, and smoke drifted slowly among the trees in the almost windless heat of the morning.

Huston moved about quickly and smoothly. He strode over to the dead man in the road and called for a bucket of water. A prop man scurried off and was back with it in a few seconds. Huston quickly mussed the man's hair and sprinkled dirt over his hair, face, and knapsack. Reinhardt looked down with a cynical smile as Huston mixed a handful of earth with water and daubed mud over the man's face and hands. Huston stood up. Aldworth was holding out a clean white handkerchief. Huston wiped his hands on it and called for blood. A make-up man sprinted over with a tube of "panchromatic blood"—mineral oil with vegetable coloring. Huston, thumbs hooked in the back of his belt, directed the bloodying process. Callow rushed up and said, "Mr. Huston, have the troops lost their knapsacks by this time or haven't they?" Huston, thoughtfully star-ing at the dead man, said they still had knapsacks. He sprinkled another handful of dirt over the man. Marton hurried up and asked whether the troops still had their knapsacks on, and Huston gave him the same answer he had given Callow. It was 9:10.

Colonel Davison came up to tell Huston that the drummer boys in the column looked too naked with only their drums. Huston directed a prop man to put packs on the boys. Aldworth was writing:

8:40–9:12—*Cont. line up Dolly Shot*

A make-up man fussed with Mauldin's wig under his kepi until it covered the better part of his neck. Huston saw the wig and said it was all wrong. The wig was removed, and a smaller one was sub-stituted. Smoke now lay over everybody and everything. The smoke machine sounded like a couple of steam shovels. "Kill that motor!" Callow bawled.

A man carrying a loud-speaker box on his shoulder and a micro-phone in his hand walked over to Huston. "All right," Huston said in a dramatically calm voice into the mike. "All right, boys." Every-body looked at him. "The idea is these troops are coming into a battle area," he said. "This is the first time you have heard gunfire. I'm going to fire a revolver. This will be the first shot you have ever heard. Each soldier as he passes the dead man will slow down. This is the first dead man you have ever seen. All right." The time was 9:26.

There was a brief silence—a lull before a battle. Huston told a smoke man not to make smoke, because this would be a rehearsal. Callow reminded the troops that they were not to step over the dead man but pass around him. Huston went over to the camera and called for action. Callow told the men to get going. They began to shuffle toward the dead man. The camera trained on them rolled on ahead, pulled along the dolly track by grips. Huston walked back-ward behind the dolly, looking intently at the faces of the troops. He gave the Chicoans a menacing look and slowly raised the re-volver over his head. He fired the revolver, still watching grimly, then fired again. The troops shuffled uneasily around the body of the dead man. Callow called "About face!" and the men returned to their starting position. Huston went over to the dead man and sprinkled more dirt on him. Reinhardt laughed. "How he loves to do that!" he said.

The time was 9:35. Jack Aldworth was writing:

9:12 = 9:35–*Reh*

Katz said to Reinhardt, "Joe Cohn asked me last night when you were coming back."

"I wish I knew," Reinhardt said.

"Consider the whole thing unasked," said Katz. At the end of each day, he told Reinhardt, the film that had been shot would be flown back to Culver City for developing.

Reinhardt said he wanted to see each day's film—called rushes, or dailies—the following day. He didn't want to wait two or three days. "I don't care how they feel about spending the money," he added.

"May I quote you?" Katz asked, smiling.

"It's important," said Reinhardt.

"Let me just find my studio notes," Katz said, digging in his pockets.

"If we can get them two *hours* sooner, I want them," said Reinhardt.

Katz took out his notes and studied them. "It would mean a difference of ten or twelve dollars a night," he said. "I'll talk to Joe Cohn about it."

"All this for two lines in the script," Albert Band said. "Would television go to all this trouble for two lines in a script?"

Callow announced that everyone was to be very quiet, because they were going to start shooting. A prop man was chalking on a small slate:

Huston   Scene 72
Prod 1512   Set 01
EXT ROAD AND DEAD SOLDIER

The smoke machine started again. Aldworth wrote:

9:35–9:40–*Put in smoke effect in BG* [background]

Pistol in hand, Huston knelt directly in front of the camera.

"Quiet and roll it!" Callow shouted.

The camera buzzed. The prop man held his slate in front of the camera for a moment.

"*Action!*" Huston said. The soldiers moved forward. The camera moved ahead of them.

Reinhardt looked at Huston with a long sigh. "Now there is no turning back," he said. "We are committed."

On their fourth encounter with the body since the shooting had begun, the troops apparently gave the performance Huston wanted. "Cut! That's it," he said. "Print it!"

Aldworth wrote down:

9:40–10:00—*Shoot four take* (*Takes* 1-2-3–NG [*no good*] *action*)

The dead man got up and wiped a muddy palm over his muddy face. He asked Band whether he would be paid extra for lying in the road a couple of hours.

"Over Joe Cohn's dead body," Band said.

At 2:30 P.M., the temperature in the woods was a hundred and eight. Eight Chicoans had collapsed while Huston was rehearsing a scene that required some troops to run off the road and into the forest and start digging ditches, as the Lieutenant of the Youth's platoon, played by Douglas Dick, walked toward the camera, smoothing his mustache, youthfully arrogant as he looked forward to his first taste of battle. At 2:32, Huston ordered his crew to print the shot of the troops.

At 4:02, Huston began working on a close-up of Dick smoothing his mustache. Huston lifted his own shoulder slightly to signify youthful arrogance and encouraged Dick to imitate him. At 4:28, after seven takes, Huston said, "That's it."

At 4:45, Huston started working on close-ups of the soldiers digging in.

"Do we expect an attack?" Dixon Porter asked him.

"You don't know what the hell to expect. That's why you're digging," said Huston.

Katz came over and said he didn't want to rush anybody, but the film had to be flown out of Chico at 6:30. Huston nodded curtly.

Huston directed the camera to be set up behind an elderly Chicoan who was digging in. The man had a long, deeply lined face. Kneeling alongside the camera, behind the man, Huston ordered him to relax and said he would tell him exactly what to do. "Action!" he called. "All right, sir. Move a little forward, sir. Now turn around and look behind you, slowly. That's right. Now dig. With your scabbard. Hard at it. Now with your plate! Hard. Harder. Very good. Cut!" He thanked the man and looked very happy. It was a face he liked.

Huston was rehearsing a group of soldiers in a digging scene when Rosson told him that they were fighting a losing battle with the sun. In the scene, Arthur Hunnicutt, an actor with a careworn face, was leaning on his rifle, watching half a dozen comrades dig a hole. "I don't hold with layin' down and shootin' from behint a little hill," he was saying. "I wouldn't feel a bit proud doin' it. I aim t' do my fightin' standin' up." One of the soldiers digging said, "If yeh want t' get shot that's yer own business." Hunnicutt said, "Well, I ain't goin' t' lay down *before* I'm shot—and that's all there is to it!"

"Light's going!" Rosson cried. "Let's take it."

Jack Aldworth wrote:

6:10–6:17—*Moving camera and actor to get sunlight*

At 6:20, Huston took his last shot of the day. Then he walked over to a rotting log and sat down. He put his elbows on his knees and cupped his face in his hands.

Jack Aldworth noted in his report—a copy of which would be in Nicholas Schenck's New York office the next day—that eleven scenes had been shot for *The Red Badge of Courage*, out of a total of three hundred and forty-seven.

On the second day of shooting, John Dierkes, the Tall Soldier, arrived at the day's location ahead of the other actors. A dusty dirt road wound through patches of wood and brush to the location, which was a broad, level, barren field beside the Sacramento River. Near the riverbank, grips were working on a twenty-five-foot-high tower of steel scaffolding, from which the camera would shoot scenes of the Union soldiers drilling on the field. A dolly track ninety feet long ran across the field at right angles to the river. On the track was the camera, which was to photograph a scene of soldiers drilling before a row of Army tents. Dierkes walked to the far end of the dolly track and sat down on one of the rails. He rubbed the back of one hand over an orange stubble of beard, and with the other he unbuttoned the stiff, high collar of his tunic. He took his kepi off and put it on the ground. With a crumpled bandanna, he wiped the perspiration from his neck. The sun was already hot in the clear sky, and the morning air was humid and buzzing with swarms of giant flies. Two trucks were lumbering past, manned by eight grips, who all had wrestlers' muscles. Dierkes stood up and saluted them. The grips did not return the salute. They seemed detached and superior, impervious to heat, humidity, flies, and isolation, fixed as though forever in one another's company, and completely absorbed in their truckloads of tools, ladders, ropes, reflectors, two-by-fours, and tripods. The trucks stopped. The head grip shouted that some small trees were needed. The grips took saws and axes and headed for a patch of woods. A sound truck was being maneuvered into position near the camera. As it came to a halt, a young man jumped out and set up a microphone boom by the camera. In a little while a property truck came up. The barrel-chested man in charge of it was stripped to the waist, revealing tattoos on his arms, chest, and back. Cheerfully, he let the truck's tailboard bang down; inside were stacks of rifles, swords, kepis, and extra uniforms. A few minutes later, buses arrived with the blue-coated army of Chicoans, and they lined up to get their rifles from the prop man. Then the studio limousines brought the other leading players and Huston.

Huston made a brisk tour of inspection past the row of tents, their pyramids of rifles stacked in front of them. Behind Huston came Reinhardt, his pith helmet pulled down over his forehead, and behind him, under another pith helmet, came Band. Huston conferred briefly with Reinhardt, then walked toward Audie Murphy. Dierkes slapped his kepi back on and went over to one of the studio's limousines and put his head in at the window. The driver was dozing over a newspaper.

"They workin' ya hard, Ferd?" Dierkes asked the driver.

Ferd looked up. "Am I burned up!" he said. "I was all set to get a couple of guys tomorrow and drive to Reno and hit them everlovin' crap tables. Then I hear they got news for me. We work. On *Sunday*."

"Gosh, Ferd," said Dierkes.

"Sunday is supposed to be a day of rest," said Ferd.

"I guess they don't want the picture to get behind schedule," said Dierkes.

"Behind schedule is all I hear," Ferd said, and returned to his paper.

Over the loud-speaker, Callow was bellowing for the actors to form ranks preparatory to drilling. Dierkes, on his way to pick up a rifle, walked past the camera dolly. Huston was standing on it, talking to the cameraman. Dierkes stopped, took off his kepi, and mopped his face again. Huston kept on talking to the cameraman. Dierkes got his rifle and took the long way around to the drill field, past the dolly again. He waited a moment, then said good morning to Huston and the cameraman. Huston returned the greeting exuberantly but mechanically. Then, as though something had just occurred to him, he stepped down from the dolly and motioned Dierkes to come closer with one of his conspiratorial gestures. The two men squatted on the ground. "I just want to tell you how glad I am to have you in the picture," Huston said, with slow, dramatic emphasis. "I just know you'll be good, John."

The orange stubble of beard appeared to redden as Dierkes said, "Thanks." Then he added, "I sure wish the picture was shot."

"It'll be over before you know it," said Huston. "It always is. Too soon."

"A picture, if it is a hit, is the director's hit," Reinhardt said over dinner that night. "If it is a flop, it is the producer's flop." He was confident that *The Red Badge of Courage* would not be a flop, that it would, in fact, be both a work of art and a commercial success. The film shot the first day had been developed, and M-G-M's head cutter, Margaret Booth, whose official title is Executive Film Editor, had telephoned to tell him she had seen the first rushes.

"Margaret says everything looks fine," Reinhardt reported to Huston. "The march into the forest she loves. She says the trees look terrific, and Audie, too. The dead-man shot is very interesting, she says."

"That's something, if this dame says it's good," said Huston. "People put more stock in what she says than anybody else. She's tough as hell."

"And she told Dore," Reinhardt said.

On the third day of shooting the picture, the nervous excitement that had permeated the company at the start abruptly disappeared. Even the army of Chicoans seemed suddenly to lose all their eager anticipation. "Pretty cheap outfit, M-G-M," said one during a break in marching around on the hot drill field. "Ten dollars a day, and it turns out to be *work*."

Dixon Porter said to a friend, "I suppose out of all this chaos comes order eventually."

His friend said, "All this hurry up and wait. It's just like the Army."

Reinhardt had brought along a 16-millimeter motion-picture camera, and he was shooting his private movie of the making of the movie. "Mine will be in Technicolor," he told me. His wife arrived on the set wearing her newly purchased trousers and porkpie hat. Reinhardt groaned when he saw her outfit. "Gottfried!" she announced. "I will keep you supplied with bottles of soda pop."

Mrs. Reinhardt put a brown cigarette in the corner of her mouth. "Silvia!" Reinhardt cried in horror.

"We are in a constant state of osmosis," Mrs. Reinhardt said, paying no attention to Reinhardt's agitation. "Osmosis has been going on for a very long time. A liquid of a lesser density flowing toward a liquid of a greater density through a thin membrane." She uttered a shrill, hopeless laugh and gave a hitch to her Army suntans.

Reinhardt wiped his face with a large silk handkerchief. It was immediately soaked with perspiration. He looked morosely at the wet silk as Katz came over to him, smiling gaily. "This is a scorcher, in case you haven't noticed," Katz said. "Anything I can do you for?"

Reinhardt asked him whether the studio had given permission for the army to ford the Sacramento River.

"Insurance men are studying the river for safety," Katz said. "They're going into it themselves."

"I will go in with them," Reinhardt said.

"Good, good," said Katz.

Huston came along and asked about the river crossing.

"Maybe if I were made head of the studio, I would go to you and say, 'No river crossing!' " Reinhardt said.

"Watch out, or that may happen," said Huston. He gave his choked kind of laugh.

"Then let's do the river crossing quickly," said Reinhardt.

A few minutes before midnight that night, I accompanied Huston and Reinhardt to the Vecino Theater, on Main Street, in Chico. The marquee was flashing the current attraction in electric lights—Jack Carson in *The Good Humor Man*. Waiting under the marquee were Rosson, Marton, Callow, and Band. After the regular program was over, we were going to see the first rushes of *The Red Badge of Courage*. The rushes were being returned in forty-eight, rather than twenty-four hours.

"This is it, pals," Rosson said in a low voice as we joined them.

For a few moments, nobody said anything. The men looked at one another nervously. They seemed held together by the same tense expectancy that had marked the first day of shooting. "Let's go, guys," Huston said finally.

We followed Huston into a roaring darkness; on the screen several men and a girl were hitting each other over the head with sticks. We found seats in the rear. On the screen, a donkey kicked a man, and the crashes on the sound track mixed with the crashing laughter of the audience. Then Jack Carson was holding a girl in his arms, there was a final blast of music, and the house lights went on. "Christ!" Huston said. He stared blankly at the audience making its way out of the theater.

"Sit yourself still," Katz said, and sat down behind him.

"Cigarette, Albert," Huston said. Band quickly gave him one and lighted it.

"You gentlemen ready?" a man called from the projection booth.

"Go ahead," Huston said, in a voice that sounded very loud in the now empty theater. He slumped in his seat, putting his long legs over the back of the seat in front of him. Reinhardt knocked the ash off his cigar and sighed deeply. The house lights went off.

On the screen, the Chicoan army shuffled along the road; the faces reflected the feeling of tense expectancy that had marked the entire first day's shooting, and somehow the effect on the screen was just right dramatically. After the raucousness of Jack Carson, the shuffling of soldiers' feet sounded weirdly subdued. There was a cut to a close-up of the dead man in the road and then to one of Audie Murphy, starting at the sound of Huston's revolver. The scene of the column scattering into the woods was followed by two close-ups of Douglas Dick smoothing his mustache. In the first one, Dick held his shoulders rigid, and the fingers he passed over his mustache seemed unsure of where they were going, of where the mustache was. In the second scene, he lifted one shoulder arrogantly, in an approximation of the way Huston had shown him how to play it. Huston exhaled some smoke and changed his position so that his knees pressed against the seat in front of him. "We use the second one, Albert," he said. "Make a note."

When the house lights came on, Huston and Reinhardt walked out of the theater rapidly.

"Well, now, the stuff looks very good, *very* good, Gottfried," Huston said.

Reinhardt agreed that most of the scenes looked good, but he did not like the shot of the regiment coming upon the dead soldier. There wasn't shock in the scene, he said. It didn't serve its purpose—to show the Youth's first frightening impression of war.

Huston said that the shot would be just fine—all it needed was a darker print. "The body is too light, that's all," he said impatiently.

Reinhardt still looked troubled. "There is no *surprise*," he said.

"It'll be fine, Gottfried," Huston said.

Dixon Porter had been promoted from extra to bit player. He was now one of the ragged veteran soldiers taunting the Youth and the other recruits. Huston sprayed Porter's face with water, then threw dirt in his face, and finally told him to roll around in a puddle of mud, all of which was intended to make him look tough. Another veteran was the man who had played dead. He was a painter and steeplejack named Jack O'Farren, and while he was waiting for the shot to be taken, he handed out business cards reading "The Sky's the Limit with Jack O'Farren" to all the recruits. Two of the other veterans, a real-estate salesman named Smith and a Chico State College art student named Feingold, rolled in patches of river moss, on their own initiative, after Huston had ordered them to roll in mud. They looked wonderful, he told them. He seemed exhilarated. He led the veterans in loud, boisterous laughter for their scene, slapping his knee and guffawing, and told the veterans they were great, just great; after the shot was taken, he led the spectators in applause for the performance.

With a good deal of zest, Huston then prepared to film the scene in which the Youth comes upon the body of a dead officer propped up against a tree at the edge of the woods. The effect, according to the script, was to be that of a cathedral interior, with the rays of the sun breaking through a thick haze of battle smoke. Huston showed the extra playing the dead man how he should stare open-eyed in death at the tops of the tall trees, and then he showed Murphy how he should approach the sight and move back in slow, hypnotized fascination. Then Huston switched back to the role of the dead officer. He seemed to more than identify himself with the characters; the identification extended to the scene as a whole, including the tree. He sat against the tree, his hand clutching his sword, and again the look of death came into his eyes. Quickly he rose and strode back to the Youth's position, and again he demonstrated his idea of how one reacted when one came upon the horror of death. Reinhardt stood by watching. Huston did not talk to him.

That afternoon, Reinhardt appeared depressed. Because he was impatient to have a look at the latest rushes, he went to see them in the afternoon, while Huston was still shooting. I accompanied him to the theater. Katz was standing outside. He told us to go on in and sit down, and said he would bring Reinhardt a soft drink.

"He'll bring the wrong thing, you'll see," Reinhardt said to me. "He'll bring me root beer and I hate root beer."

Katz returned with a bottle of root beer, and the house lights dimmed. There were scenes of the soldiers drilling, of Dierkes marching with Murphy and Mauldin, and of Murphy running through the woods, and, at the end, another take of the dead-man shot that had disappointed Reinhardt. "Much better," Reinhardt said to me. "I had them print this other take." He seemed to be working himself toward a more cheerful evaluation of the picture. The drill field, he said, looked just like a Brady photograph. Great atmosphere, he told Katz, but they should have used more men in the scene.

"It looks like a lot of people," Katz said. "It looks almost
crowded."

Reinhardt did not argue the point. Dierkes looked wonderful, he
said. Huston had certainly known what he was doing when he
picked him. And in the second print the dead soldier *looked* like a
dead soldier and produced a more startling, shocking effect. Murphy
would be very good. "John can charm anybody into anything," he
added.

When we returned to the set, Reinhardt told Huston that the
rushes were wonderful. Huston seemed pleased. They walked to a
shady spot and sat down.

"Tell me all about it, Gottfried," Huston said.

"The dead soldier is all right now," Reinhardt told him. "If I had
seen that take, I wouldn't have kicked at all."

"It's all right now, then, Gottfried?" Huston asked, grinning at
him for the first time since they had seen the first rushes together.

Reinhardt laughed a relieved laugh and said yes. "And it is really
Virginia, because there is a cloud," he said.

Mrs. Huston and Mrs. Reinhardt had gone back home. "I leave in
a great rush, in confusion, in a sudden gust of ambivalence toward
Chico, actors, directors, producers, and the Civil War," Mrs. Reinhardt wrote in a terse note of farewell to me. "I am returning to
Mocha, who understands me."

The Legal Department of M-G-M had finally given permission
for two hundred and fifty uniformed, armed Chicoans to walk across
the Sacramento River while two cameras turned. It was to be one of
the most important scenes in the picture, Reinhardt told me, and
it had been saved for the last day in Chico. At four that morning,
Huston went fishing with Murphy. Four hours later, I drove out to
the site of the river crossing with Reinhardt and Band. A hired
motor launch took us across the river, and we landed near the spot
where the camera had been set up, on a platform. Huston was not
around. Rosson, wearing only a pair of swimming trunks, was hovering over his camera, surrounded by his assistants, and Callow was
supervising the setting up of a fairly elaborate public-address system,
over which he and Huston would call out orders to the men crossing the river. Reinhardt was getting his own movie camera ready for
the big scene. "I wish Dore could see this," he said.

On the other side of the river, the soldiers were lining up.

"Everybody ready for D Day?" one of the cameramen shouted.

Rosson said they had to wait for Huston. He stepped down from
the camera platform and hunted around in the tall grass along the

riverbank, and there he came upon Huston, sound asleep. Rosson woke Huston, who followed him back to the camera, shaking his head sleepily. The director climbed on the platform and sat there, complaining that he and Murphy had not caught a single fish. He looked around glumly at the frenzied preparations for the crossing.

"Let's go, pals!" Rosson called.

"I'm scared to death," Reinhardt said, putting his 16-millimeter camera to his eye.

Huston, over the public-address system, ordered the crossing to begin. The Chicoan army crossed the river and emerged soaked but triumphant. Huston stepped to the public-address system and told the men that they had been just great. "When you see this picture, you're going to see one of the most impressive scenes ever filmed," he said. "Now we need some volunteers for another shot. It means going back into the river part of the way."

"I'll go," Dixon Porter said, right up front, as usual.

"Good boy, Dixon," said Huston.

Porter brightened. "Had to chop water all the way across the first time," he said.

"You looked wonderful, just wonderful," said Huston.

Albert Band turned up in a blue uniform, grabbed a rifle, and went into the river with the volunteers, as he had once warned Huston and Reinhardt he would. "It felt wonderful," he said when he came out.

During the day, a new joke made the rounds. Everybody told everybody else that the river crossing scene would have to be reshot because one wig had been wrong. Reinhardt put in a call to Dore Schary as soon as he had returned to his hotel. The next time Reinhardt saw Huston, he said he had given Schary a full report on the river crossing.

"Dore said to me, 'O.K., baby,' " Reinhardt told Huston.

Jack Aldworth had made his final log note for the work in Chico ("Wrap up—return to hotel—crews start loading equipment for return to studio"), and the company was getting ready to go back to Los Angeles. Huston, Reinhardt, and Band were going to drive back in Reinhardt's convertible, and they offered me a lift.

Band seemed to have been highly stimulated by his recent military experience. "One-hup-reep-foh-lelf-righ-lelf! One-hup-reep—" he chanted, marching in soldierly circles around Reinhardt.

"Albert!" Reinhardt said.

Band stopped and saluted.

"Get my camera, Albert," said Reinhardt.

Band saluted again and went off, chanting his drill field refrain. Huston showed up shortly afterward, and read a newspaper while Band stowed the luggage. Reinhardt put his movie camera to his eye and focused on Huston reading the headline "U. S. TROOPS ATTACK REDS."

"Put the camera in the back seat, Albert," said Reinhardt. He sighed and said he was fed up with taking his own movies. "I've spent a fortune on this picture already," he added.

Band climbed into the rear seat, and the rest of us sat up front.

"Well!" Huston said as we started off. "How much ahead of schedule are we, Gottfried?"

"A day and a half," said Reinhardt. "Reggie says if we had done that shot of the river crossing in the tank at the studio, it would have cost twelve thousand dollars more than this did. Albert, the box of cigars. Under my coat next to you."

"We can have the river crossing on the screen for a minute," Huston said.

"That long?" asked Reinhardt, who was driving.

"It's worth it," Huston said. He slumped down in his seat, arranging his long legs in a comfortable position. Reinhardt stepped on the gas. "Don't rush," Huston said, looking out at passing fields of haystacks. "We're in no hurry, Gottfried. I like to see this kind of country. I just love to see this."

Nobody spoke for a while, and then Huston said, "I'm so happy about what we did in Chico."

"It was not so bad, was it?" Reinhardt said.

"One-hup-reep-foh—" Band said from the rear.

Huston sat up and said slowly, "I made a mistake."

Reinhardt started.

"On the veterans' close-ups," said Huston. "I forgot to dolly. The long shot was a dolly shot. I forgot that on the close-ups."

Reinhardt closed his lips around the cigar. Maybe they could do some retakes when they returned to the ranch, Huston said. He closed his eyes and went to sleep. Reinhardt stepped on the gas.

One of the first things Reinhardt did when he got back to his office at Metro-Goldwyn-Mayer was to write a letter to Dore Schary:

Dear Dore:

Upon returning from the wilds of Chico, I find that in the heat of fighting the Civil War (and I mean "heat"!) I missed your birthday so

please let me send you my very best wishes belatedly today. Your
presents are the rushes and the time in which they were shot.

With kindest personal regards,
Yours,
Gottfried

P.S. *And I mean "fighting." I even forded single-footed the Sacra-*
mento River in order to convince the insurance man that it could be done
without too big a risk. After all, what nobler gesture can a studio make
than risk the lives of its producers?

The scenes that were shot at Chico had been pieced together in
approximately the order they would follow in the finished picture,
and Reinhardt had seen them in this form. Now Huston was looking
at the film in a projection room at the studio, and Reinhardt was
waiting for him in his own office. Schary had seen the film, too, he
said, but Mayer would not see any part of the movie until it was
previewed. "Mayer really *hates* the picture," he said. "He will keep
on hating it as long as he thinks we do not have a story. He would
like to see us rewrite the script and give Stephen Crane's story a
new *twist*." He laughed sadly. "It reminds me of the time Sam Hof-
fenstein was given a Tarzan picture to rewrite. He was told to give
it a new twist. He rewrote it—he put it all into Yiddish." He gave a
shy smile. "I love that story. It's a great story."

Huston burst into the office, followed by Albert Band.

"The stuff looks awfully good, Gottfried," Huston said. "It'll cut
like a cinch. I have very few criticisms."

"What criticisms do you have?" Reinhardt asked.

"Well, practically nothing, *amigo*," said Huston. He sat down and,
tilting back, put his feet on Reinhardt's desk.

Reinhardt leaned back and put his feet up on the desk, too. "This
is an American custom I have embraced wholeheartedly," he said.
"What criticisms?"

"I'll say right now Audie is superb," said Huston. "He's just
marvelous. Sensitive. Alive. This boy is something."

Reinhardt said, "Will you do me a favor, John?"

"What?" Huston asked.

"Get Audie to smile in the picture," Reinhardt said. "Just once."

"All right, Gottfried," Huston said graciously.

A few days later, it was Huston, rather than Reinhardt, who
seemed to have become dissatisfied. He was worried about the script
for his picture. Specifically, he told Reinhardt that day, he was worried about the way the picture seemed to be turning into an account

of the struggle between the North and the South in the Civil War. "All we want to show is that what the Youth is doing has nothing to do with the big battle," he said. "The battle has gone on for three days and it's going to go on for another three days. The Youth gets on the roulette wheel and stays for a little while and then he's thrown off, and that's all we have to be concerned with. We have to get something for the end that will show that." All they had at the end now, Huston said, was a scene in which the Youth's regiment took a stone wall held by the Confederates, and that was the last action scene in the picture. It bothered him, he said, that there was no big scene at the finish. He felt that something was missing.

Reinhardt said it was better not to strive for climaxes. "Sometimes the quiet ending is the more impressive," he said. "I always think of the strong effect of the quietness of *Till Eulenspiegel*. The average motion picture guy would say that it is anticlimax. I do not think so." Reinhardt seemed to be getting immense enjoyment out of this kind of discussion.

Huston, ignoring the reference to *Till Eulenspiegel*, merely repeated that they would have to get something new for the ending. "I'd just like the situation to be clarified," he said. "The Youth and his comrades have been fighting all that day and the day before. Now we open the last battle by following the general on his white horse riding along the lines. We go to the Youth and his regiment. They're part of this big thing. They capture a fragment of the wall. We begin with a big thing and end with a little thing. If the battle depended on this wall, then we would know what the situation is. But we don't know quite what happened."

Reinhardt said, "They take the wall. You think, This is the big thing. They take prisoners. Suddenly they get a command to fall in and march away, and they watch as another regiment is committed."

"I'd like to know from the standpoint of the battle itself what's happening," Huston said. "And I don't know. I don't even know." He laughed, and said he would think of something. "Another thing, Gottfried," he said, at the end of the discussion, "I don't like the dead soldier Audie finds in the woods. It looks too stagy."

Reinhardt protested that he liked the scene.
Huston said that he would do it over.

In his living room every night after dinner, Dore Schary ran the rushes of all the pictures in production at M-G-M, and one night he invited me to come over and see the rushes of *The Red Badge of Courage*. Schary lives in Brentwood, a fashionable residential district, where he has a cream-colored English stucco house. The doormat at the front door bears the words "Schary Manor"—the name of his parents' Newark home, from which they ran a catering business. In the summer of 1950, Schary was forty-five—one year older than Huston, seven years older than Reinhardt, and twenty years younger than Mayer. He was born in Newark, the youngest of five children. He attended public grade school, quitting at the age of thirteen after an argument with a teacher about a problem in algebra. Six years later, having meanwhile worked off and on in the family business, been a necktie salesman, and tried other jobs, he returned to school and, by attending day and night, went through high school in a year. In 1928, he joined the Stuart Walker Stock Company in Cincinnati as an actor, and remained there for one season. He subsequently spent a summer as assistant recreation director at the Flagler Hotel in the Catskills (the director was Moss Hart), and from that he went on to play small parts in the Broadway production of *Four Walls* and *The Last Mile*. Schary wrote a play that was not produced but was read by Walter Wanger, who signed him to a hundred-dollar-a-week contract as a writer at Columbia Studio in 1932. He took the job, but at the end of twelve weeks Wanger didn't pick up his option. Schary stayed on in Hollywood, and several months later he helped write the script of M-G-M's *Big City*, starring Spencer Tracy. Then, also for M-G-M, he collaborated on the writing of *Boys Town*, for which he won an Academy Award. He next collaborated on *Young Tom Edison* and *Edison, the Man*, and was given a job at M-G-M supervising a studio production unit, which made *Joe Smith, American*, *Journey for Margaret*, and *Lassie Come Home*. After this, Schary joined David O. Selznick's independent producing company, where he produced *The Farmer's Daughter* and *The Bachelor and the Bobby-Soxer*. The success of these films led to Schary's appointment as head of production at RKO, and for that company he made *Crossfire* and *Mr. Blandings Builds His Dream House*. He returned to M-G-M in the summer of 1948, at the invitation of L. B. Mayer. Before long, in addition to serving as superintendent of production for the whole studio, he himself produced *Battleground*, starring Van Johnson, and *The Next Voice You Hear*. . . .

Schary met me at the door of his house with an easygoing, home-spun grin and told me that he was just about to view the last of the day's rushes. He was wearing gray flannel slacks and a blue blazer with white buttons. He took me into a large sitting room. At one end of the room was his wife, who paints under the name Miriam Svet, his three children (Jill, fifteen; Joy, thirteen; and Jeb, eleven) and M-G-M's chief cutter, Margaret Booth, a thin woman with a thin, bony face. Schary led me to a chair near them and snapped his fingers. A wide panel in the wall at the opposite end of the room slid up, exposing a white screen, and the room was darkened. A projectionist in a booth behind us showed us *The Red Badge of Courage* scenes. These were followed by Technicolor scenes of Clark Gable and an Indian girl making love on a mountaintop. Schary told Miss Booth how he wanted the scenes trimmed, and the lights came on. The children thanked their father for being allowed to see the movies. He kissed them and sent them off to bed, adding that if they were good they could see the rushes the next night, too. Miss Booth said she had a date to go to a movie, and left. Mrs. Schary excused herself, saying that she had to work on a painting.

Schary sat down. The rushes of *The Red Badge of Courage* had been magnificent so far, he told me. "John and Gottfried have proved their point that they could make this picture," he said. "The original estimate on this picture was close to two million, and our estimators said it would take forty-eight days. John and Gottfried said they could do it in thirty and hold the cost down to a million five. Nobody believed it. But *I* believed it. I believe that no picture is like any other picture. So I believed the boys could do what they wanted to do. I believe that one of the most debilitating things is to have too large a frame of reference."

Before production started, Schary said, Huston and Reinhardt had seemed almost overwhelmed with doubt, and he had had to steady them. They had come to see him at home, when he was ill. "They were so concerned I went over the whole thing with them. I said, 'I have no way of comforting you guys by telling you that this is going to be a great picture. I only know that John is a brilliant director. The script is wonderful. This can be an inspiring picture. I don't think anybody will be able to say it's a bad picture. Let's follow our first hunches and first instincts, and let's make the picture! Let's make it as efficiently and as economically and with as much enthusiasm as we can. Let's stop thinking about it as an *if* picture. It's to be made. That's all.' From that time on, everything has just gone zoom."

Schary gave me a candid look. "I love John," he said. "That guy will live forever. He's a hearty, tough soul. When he wants something from you, he sits down next to you and his voice gets a little husky, and pretty soon you're a dead pigeon. He wanted Audie for the Youth and he got him." He shrugged benevolently. "A creative man, when he wants to win a point, he uses effective and dramatic arguments." Schary shrugged again. "I love to do this imitation of

John when he says hello to you," he said. He did the imitation—getting up and giving a quarter twist to his body and saying "hel-lo" —and then sat down and chuckled at his performance. "I had visualized the Youth as a taller, blonder, freckle-faced kind of kid, sort of a younger Van Johnson," he continued. "I said, 'John, you're a big ham. If you were twenty years younger, you'd love to play this part yourself.' He said I was right. That's the kind of guy I had in mind—a guy with an odd, interesting kisser, with hair that falls down in front. But in the final test, I was sold on Audie. John never lost his hunch, and now he's got something there. Great guy, John. He's always flying back and forth. He goes here, there, everywhere, in a plane. A schlemiel like myself gets on a plane and it crashes. I love John."

Schary grinned broadly. "Show business!" he said. "I'm crazy about show business. I'm crazy about making pictures. All kinds of pictures. But my favorites are the simple, down-to-earth pictures, the ones about everyday life. *The Next Voice You Hear* . . . was that kind of picture. I'm crazy about that picture. I *love* it." Schary went on to say that he enjoyed seeing the rushes every night. "I like to reaffirm myself," he said. "The biggest job is the transfer of an image to the screen. For *The Red Badge of Courage* I had an image in mind of dark-blue uniforms against light, dusty roads. This was an image that John moved successfully into the realm of production." Schary gave a professorial nod. "The boys are making an impressive picture. The only controversy about *The Red Badge of Courage* is whether it will be a success or a failure. It's as simple as that."

Enter,

the Movies

by Ben Hecht

In this excerpt from Ben Hecht's autobiography, A Child of the Century *(Simon and Schuster, 1954), he tells of his experiences in Hollywood, where he wrote over sixty movies and made fantastic sums of money. Irrepressible, galvanic, Hecht belongs to that small band of screenwriters who wrote the scenarios of some of the most successful movies in a matter of a few days.*

For MANY YEARS I looked on movie writing as an amiable chore. It was a source of easy money and pleasant friendships. There was small responsibility. Your name as writer was buried in a flock of "credits." Your literary pride was never involved. What critics said about the movie you had written never bothered you. They were usually criticizing something you couldn't remember. Once when I was a guest on a radio quiz show called "Information Please," the plot of a movie I had written a year before and that was playing on Broadway then was recited to me in full. I was unable to identify it.

For many years Hollywood held this double lure for me, tremendous sums of money for work that required no more effort than a game of pinochle. Of the sixty movies I wrote, more than half were written in two weeks or less. I received for each script, whether written in two or (never more than) eight weeks, from fifty thousand to a hundred and twenty-five thousand dollars. I worked also by the week. My salary ran from five thousand dollars a week up. Metro-Goldwyn-Mayer in 1949 paid me ten thousand a week. David Selznick once paid me thirty-five hundred a day.

Walking at dawn in the deserted Hollywood streets in 1951 with David, I listened to my favorite movie boss topple the town he had helped to build. The movies, said David, were over and done with. Hollywood was already a ghost town making foolish efforts to seem alive.

"Hollywood's like Egypt," said David. "Full of crumbled pyramids. It'll never come back. It'll just keep on crumbling until finally the wind blows the last studio prop across the sands."

And now that the tumult was gone, what had the movies been? A flood of claptrap, he insisted, that had helped bitch up the world and that had consumed the fine talents of thousands of men like ourselves.

"A few good movies," said David. "Thirty years—and one good movie in three years is the record. Ten out of ten thousand. There might have been good movies if there had been no movie industry. Hollywood might have become the center of a new human expression if it hadn't been grabbed by a little group of bookkeepers and turned into a junk industry."

"I'm writing a book about myself," I said, "and I keep wondering what I should write about the movies, which are, in a way, part of me."

"Write the truth," said David. "Before you start bragging about your fancy Hollywood exploits, put down the truth. Nobody has ever done that!"

I doubt if the truth about Hollywood is as novel as my friend, in his new disillusion, believed. It is novel enough, however, and I shall try to put down as much of it as I know.

WHAT THE MOVIES ARE

The movies are one of the bad habits that corrupted our century. Of their many sins, I offer as the worst their effect on the intellectual side of the nation. It is chiefly from that viewpoint I write of them— as an eruption of trash that has lamed the American mind and retarded Americans from becoming a cultured people.

The American of 1953 is a cliché-strangled citizen whose like was

never before in the Republic. Compared to the pre-movieized
American of 1910–1920, he is an enfeebled intellect. I concede the
movies alone did not undo the American mind. A number of forces
worked away at that project. But always, well up in front and never
faltering at their frowsy task, were the movies.

In pre-movie days, the business of peddling lies about life was
spotty and unorganized. It was carried on by the cheaper magazines, dime novels, the hinterland preachers and whooping politicians.
These combined to unload a rash of infantile parables on the land.
A goodly part of the population was infected, but there remained
large healthy areas in the Republic's thought. There remained, in
fact, an intellectual class of sorts—a tribe of citizens who never read
dime novels, cheap magazines or submitted themselves to political
and religious howlers.

It was this tribe that the movies scalped. Cultered people who
would have blushed with shame to be found with a dime novel in
their hands took to flocking shamelessly to watch the picturization
of such tripe on the screen.

For forty years the movies have drummed away on the American
character. They have fed it naïveté and buncombe in doses never
before administered to any people. They have slapped into the
American mind more human misinformation in one evening than
the Dark Ages could muster in a decade. One basic plot only has
appeared daily in their fifteen thousand theaters—the triumph of
virtue and the overthrow of wickedness.

Two generations of Americans have been informed nightly that
a woman who betrayed her husband (or a husband his wife) could
never find happiness; that sex was no fun without a mother-in-law
and a rubber plant around; that women who fornicated just for
pleasure ended up as harlots or washerwomen; that any man who
was sexually active in his youth later lost the one girl he truly loved;
that a man who indulged in sharp practices to get ahead in the world
ended in poverty and with even his own children turning on him;
that any man who broke the laws, man's or God's, must always die,
or go to jail, or become a monk, or restore the money he stole before
wandering off into the desert; that anyone who didn't believe in
God (and said so out loud) was set right by seeing either an angel
or witnessing some feat of levitation by one of the characters; that
an honest heart must always recover from a train wreck or a score
of bullets and win the girl it loved; that the most potent and brilliant
of villains are powerless before little children, parish priests or young
virgins with large boobies; that injustice could cause a heap of trouble but it must always slink out of town in Reel Nine; that there are

no problems of labor, politics, domestic life or sexual abnormality but can be solved happily by a simple Christian phrase or a fine American motto.

Not only was the plot the same, but the characters in it never varied. These characters must always be good or bad (and never human) in order not to confuse the plot of Virtue Triumphing. This denouement could be best achieved by stereotypes a fraction removed from those in the comic strips.

The effect on the American mind of this forty-year barrage of Mother Goose platitudes and primitive valentines is proved by the fact that the movies became for a generation the favorite entertainment of all American classes.

There are millions of Americans who belong by nature in movie theaters as they belong at political rallies or in fortuneteller parlors and on the shoot-the-chutes. To these millions the movies are a sort of boon—a gaudier version of religion. All the parables of right living are paraded before them tricked out in gang feuds, earthquakes and a thousand and one near rapes. The move from cheap books to cheap movie seats has not affected them for the worse.

But beside these grass-root fans of platitude sit the once intellectual members of the community. They are the citizens whose good taste and criticism of claptrap were once a large part of our nation's superiority. There is little more in them today than the giggle of the movie fan. Watching the movies, they forget that they have taste, that their intelligence is being violated, that they are being booted back into the nursery. They forget even that they are bored.

In the movie theaters, all fifteen thousand of them, the U.S.A. presents a single backward front.

There is a revolution brewing and movie audiences are beginning to thin out. I shall take up this revolt later and mention here only that it is not an intellectual uprising. It is a revolt downward.

THE CAPTIVE MUSE

The persistent banality of the movies is due to the "vision" of their manufacturers. I do not mean by manufacturers, writers or directors. These harassed toilers are no more than the lowest of *Unteroffizieren* in movieland. The orders come from the tents of a dozen invisible generals. The "vision" is theirs. They keep a visionary eye glued to the fact that the lower in class an entertainment product is, the more people will buy it.

Since their start, the movies have been, practically, in the hands of the same dozen. A few have died, to be replaced by men of identical indifference to every phase of entertainment save one—its profits.

These dozen Tops of the industry have nothing to do with the making of movies. They have to do only with the *sort* of movies that are to be made—commercial ones. There is no murmur of revolt. Only hosannas rise from the movie slave pens.

In no industry into which I have peered have I seen the wanton boss flattery that is normal in movieland. Proud and wealthy men of intelligence are not ashamed to prostrate themselves publicly before the hollow-headed big boss—the Owner. They will gasp with wonder over his dullest droppings and see in his fumbling efforts to understand what is going on the constant mark of genius. No workman I have ever seen is as afraid of a boss, no servant as aquiver before a master as are the movie factotums who come near the golden throne of the movie company Owner.

The fear that inspires this kowtowing is as deep as religious fear. It rises from the same source—guilt. Nearly all who work in the making and even selling of movies are guilty of distorting, constantly, their minds and in one way or another of violating their tastes and their instincts.

The only movie figure exempt from such guilt is the company Owner. He is usually a man who has no taste to be violated or intelligence to be distorted. He admires with his whole soul the drivel his underlings produce in his factory.

This boss fear-adulation is the chief color of movieland. My contacts with the studio Owners and their viziers who ran the studios for them informed me early in my movie service that most of them were nitwits on a par with the lower run of politicians I had known as a reporter. Yet they all moved in an aura of greatness, and the reports of their genius would have embarrassed Michelangelo.

In addition to the guilt of violating their culture, which brought these courtiers to heel, there was a money guilt. The greater were the sums these underlings received, the more fearful of the boss they grew. When you overpay small people you frighten them. They know that their merits or activities entitle them to no such sums as they are receiving. As a result their boss soars out of economic into magic significance. He becomes a source of blessings rather than wages. Criticism is sacrilege, doubt is heresy.

In the court of the movie Owner, none criticized, none doubted. And none dared speak of art. In the Owner's mind art was a synonym for bankruptcy. An artist was a saboteur to be uprooted as quickly from the company's payroll as a Communist with a pamphlet.

Whenever the movie company Owner found himself with three or more employees at his feet he made a pronouncement. "I'm a Showman," he said, "and as long as I remain a Showman all you geniuses who work in my studio don't have to worry. You will have jobs—and big wages."

The movie company Owner was and is no more Showman than he is a pilgrim bound for Mecca. His single objective as Owner is to see that his movies make profits. He asks nothing else of them. He has no more instinct to gamble with the contents of his product than have the makers of Flit. What the public wants, he proclaims, is "solid entertainment, and for God's sake, Ben, don't stick those ideas of yours into this film. You want to help make a successful film, don't you? A picture people will be glad to see? All right then —don't insult the things they believe in. Make 'em realize how wonderful life is, and what a fine fella this hero of yours is, so that everybody will be glad to have him elected senator."

The movie Owners are the only troupe in the history of entertainment that has never been seduced by the adventure of the entertainment world—by the dream of diverting people with something a "little better," or a "little different." Their fixation on peddling trash has many causes. For one thing, they are further removed from the creation of their product than any showmen have ever been before. Showmen in the theater read manuscripts, interview actors, select out of their tastes the product on which they put their names. The gypsy aroma of entertainment goes to their heads, however hard they are. And however greedy they are, the tinkle of show bells becomes as winsome to them as the tinkle of money. The movie showmen, however, read no scripts, consort with no actors. They have no ideas to offer. They stick no finger in the pie. Thus they have no spiritual or mental stake in their product. No show bells tinkle in their counting rooms.

Their product, also, is a more expensive one than any heretofore peddled by showmen. Millions of dollars and not mere thousands are involved. Men who manipulate the spending of millions must put aside enthusiasm for anything but money. The artists they employ may bask in press notices. The Owners can afford to bask only in box office returns.

The fame of the movie company Owners is small in the public eye. It is even small in movieland, where the movies are made. In my years in and out of the Hollywood studios I have not managed to learn all the names of my true bosses—the "men of vision" who dictated my work. I have encountered some of them: L. B. Mayer,

Howard Hughes, the Schencks, the Cohens, the Warners, the Bala-
bans. There are others as unknown to me as to any outsider.

The major triumph of the movie company Owners lies in this
fact—The barrage of movie trash has conditioned the public to the
acceptance of trash only. A "different" movie is usually scorned by
Americans. They will sneer and catcall during its showing and leave
the theater with cries of having been cheated.

Yet the movie Owner's victory is not a solid one, and here I come
to the little revolution that stirs among the sixty million movie fans.
The movie industry is beginning to wobble. The sound track is beginning to echo cavernously in its theaters. Although the American
will still run from a "different" movie as from a smallpox sign, he
has shown a mounting aversion to the hog feed he has hitherto gob-
bled. The studios continue to manufacture this mush with undimin-
ished cunning and largess. No sum is too vast for the making of a
Great Epic of Roman History, or of the Indian Wars or of the Song
Publishing Business. Nevertheless the movie fan has begun to stay
away from the movie palaces that cater fiercely to his love of trash.

Surveying their sagging box office charts, the movie Owners point
wildly to television as the villain responsible. I have a notion that
my old bosses are wrong.

Put a squirrel on a treadmill and he will run gayly and happily
for hours on end. But there comes an hour when the squirrel's soul
feels the falseness and insufficiency of the treadmill as a road for
travel. The squirrel begins, then, to twitch, to roll its eyes, to chatter
frenziedly. And if not removed from the treadmill the bewildered
little animal will fall dead.

The American moviegoer, experiencing these squirrel-like
twitches, is removing himself from the movie trash treadmill. Confronted by the double problem of being unable to enjoy any longer
the dime novel movie, and of disliking angrily still any departure
from it, the American has retreated into his parlor to stare at another
national eruption of trash on his television set. And acquire another
set of twitches.

MONEY IS THE ROOT

As a writer in Hollywood, I spent more time arguing than writing
—until the last four years, when the British boycott left me without
much bargaining power. My chief memory of movieland is one of
asking in the producer's office why I must change the script, eviscer-
ate it, cripple and hamstring it? Why must I strip the hero of his
few semi-intelligent remarks and why must I tack on a corny ending

that makes the stomach shudder? Half of all the movie writers argue
in this fashion. The other half writhe in silence, and the psychoan-
alyst's couch or the liquor bottle claim them both.

Before it might seem that I am writing about a tribe of Shelleys
in chains, I should make it clear that the movie writers "ruined" by
the movies are for the most part a run of greedy hacks and incompetent thickheads. Out of the thousand writers huffing and puffing
through movieland there are scarcely fifty men and women of wit
or talent. The rest of the fraternity is deadwood. Yet, in a curious
way, there is not much difference between the product of a good
writer and that of a bad one. They both have to toe the same mark.

Nor are the bad writers better off spiritually. Their way is just
as thorny. Minus talent or competence, the need for self-expression
churns foolishly in them and their hearts throw themselves in a wild
pitch for fame. And no less than the literary elite of Hollywood
they feel the sting of its knout. However cynical, overpaid or inept
you are, it is impossible to create entertainment without feeling the
urges that haunt creative work. The artist's ego, even the ego of the
Hollywood hack, must always jerk around a bit under restraint.

The studio bosses are not too inconvenienced by this bit of
struggle. Experience has proved that the Hollywood artist in revolt
is usually to be brought to heel by a raise in salary. My own discontent with what I was asked to do in Hollywood was so loud that I
finally received a hundred and twenty-five thousand dollars for four
weeks of script writing.

APULEIUS' GOLDEN STOOGE

I have taken part in at least a thousand story conferences. I was
present always as the writer. Others present were the "producer,"
the director and sometimes the head of the studio and a small tense
group of his admirers.

The producer's place in movie making is a matter that, in Hollywood, has not yet been cleared up. I shall try to bring some clarity
to it.

The big factory where movies are made is run by a superproducer
called Head of the Studio who sits in the Front Office and is as difficult of access as the Grand Lama. He is the boss, appointed by the
studio Owner himself. Thus, despite the veneration in which he is
held by the thousand studio underlings, he is actually the greatest
of the movieland stooges. He must bend his entire spirit to the philosophy of the movie Owner—"make money." He must translate this
greedy cry of the Owner into a program for his studio. He must

examine every idea, plot or venture submitted to him from the single point of view of whether it is trite enough to appeal to the masses.

If he fails in this task, he is summoned from his always teetering studio throne to the movie Owner's New York Office, in which nothing ever teeters. Here he receives a drubbing which the lowest of his slaves would not tolerate. He is shown pages of box office returns. He is shoved into the presence of homicidal theater Owners snarling of empty seats. Proof is hurled at his head that he has betrayed his great trust, that he is ruining the movie industry, and that he is either an idiot or a scoundrel.

Shaken and traumatized, he returns to his throne in the studio. Here he must wiggle himself into the Purple again and be ready to flash his eyes and terrorize his underlings with his Olympian whims.

His immediate underlings are the producers. He has hired them to do the actual movie making for him. After all, no one man can weigh, discuss and manipulate fifty movie plots at one time. He has to have lieutenants, men who will keep their heads in the noisy presence of writers and directors and not be carried away by art in any of its subversive guises.

ILLUSTRATIONS BY DORÉ (GUSTAVE)

There are different kinds of producers in the studios, ranging from out-and-out illiterates to philosophers and aesthetes. But all of them have the same function. Their task is to guard against the unusual. They are the trusted loyalists of cliché. Writers and directors can be carried away by a "strange" characterization or a new point of view; a producer, never. The producer is the shadow cast by the studio's Owner. It falls across the entire studio product.

I discovered early in my movie work that a movie is never any better than the stupidest man connected with it. There are times when this distinction may be given to the writer or director. Most often it belongs to the producer.

The job of turning good writers into movie hacks is the producer's chief task. These sinister fellows were always my bosses. Though I was paid often five and ten times more money than they for my working time, they were my judges. It was their minds I had to please.

I can recall a few bright ones among them, and fifty nitwits. The pain of having to collaborate with such dullards and to submit myself to their approvals was always acute. Years of experience failed to help. I never became reconciled to taking literary orders from them. I often prepared myself for a producer conference by swallowing two sleeping pills in advance.

I have always considered that half of the large sum paid me for writing a movie script was in payment for listening to the producer and obeying him. I am not being facetious. The movies pay as much for obedience as for creative work. An able writer is paid a larger sum than a man of small talent. But he is paid this added money *not* to use his superior talents.

I often won my battle with producers. I was able to convince them that their suggestions were too stale or too infantile. But I won such battles only as long as I remained on the grounds. The minute I left the studio my victory vanished. Every sour syllable of producer invention went back into the script and every limping foot of it appeared on the screen.

Months later, watching "my" movie in a theater, I realized that not much damage actually had been done. A movie is basically so trite and glib that the addition of a half dozen miserable inanities does not cripple it. It blares along barking out its inevitable clichés, and only its writer can know that it is a shade worse than it had to be.

DIAVOLO, AGAIN—

Such is half of my story of Hollywood. The other half is the fun I had during the heyday of the movies—1925 to 1945. There was never a more marzipan kingdom than this land of celluloid.

There was only one factory rule. Make a movie that went over big at the preview, and the town was yours. You could be as daft as you wanted, as drunk and irreverent as Panurge, and still the bosses bowed as you passed. The bosses were all earthy fellows with the smell of junk yards, tire exchanges and other murky business pasts clinging to their sport ensembles. Though we wore their yoke, we were nevertheless literary royalty, men of grammar.

In the time when I first arrived in it, the movie world was still young. Djinn and ogres, odalisques, Sindbads and earth shakers were still around in wholesale lots, especially the ogres. And whatever the weather elsewhere in the world, it rained only gold in Hollywood.

Mankiewicz' telegram had told the truth. Hollywood, 1925, was another boom town, and my nerves were alive to its hawker's cry an hour after I had left the train. It reminded me happily of that other Eldorado—Miami. Miami had run up the price of its real estate. Hollywood was doing the same thing for talent, any kind of talent, from geese-trainers to writers and actors.

Hungry actors leaped from hall bedrooms to terraced mansions. Writers and newspapermen who had hoboed their way West began hiring butlers and laying down wine cellars. Talent, talent, who had talent for anything—for beating a drum, diving off a roof, writing a joke, walking on his hands? Who could think up a story, any kind of story? Who knew how to write it down? And who had Ego? That was the leading hot cake—Ego or a pair of jiggling boobies under morning-glory eyes. Prosperity chased them all. New stars were being hatched daily, and new world-famous directors and producers were popping daily out of shoe boxes.

I went to work for Paramount Pictures, Inc., over which the Messrs. Zukor, Lasky and Schulberg presided. They occupied the three Vatican suites on the main floor of a long plaster building that looked like a Bavarian bathhouse. It still stands, empty of almost everything but ghosts.

Most of the important people got drunk after one o'clock, sobered up around three-thirty and got drunk again at nine. Fist fights began around eleven. Seduction had no stated hours. The skimpy offices shook with passion. The mingled sound of plotting and sexual moans came through the transoms. It was a town of braggadocio and youth. Leading ladies still suffered from baby fat (rather than budding wattles as today) and the film heroes had trouble growing mustaches.

Nor was the industry yet captive. There were as many wild-catters around as bankers. And the movies, God bless 'em, were silent. The talkies had not yet come to make headaches for the half-illiterate viziers of the Front Office. In fact, to the best of my recollection, there were no headaches. There were no unions, no censor boards, no empty theater seats. It was Round Three and everybody looked like a champion.

Movies were seldom written. They were yelled into existence in conferences that kept going in saloons, brothels and all-night poker games. Movie sets roared with arguments and organ music. Sometimes little string orchestras played to help stir up the emotions of the great performers—"*Träumerei*" for Clara Bow and the "Meditation" from *Thaïs* for Adolphe Menjou, the screen's most sophisticated lover.

I was given an office at Paramount. A bit of cardboard with my name inked on it was tacked on the door. A soiree started at once in my office and lasted for several days. Men of letters, bearing gin bottles, arrived. Bob Benchley, hallooing with laughter as if he had come on the land of Punch and Judy, was there; and the owlish-eyed satirist Donald Ogden Stewart, beaming as at a convention of March Hares. One night at a flossy party Don appeared on the dance floor in a long overcoat. "That's silly and showing off, to dance in an overcoat," said the great lady of the films in his arms. "Please take it off." Don did. He had nothing on underneath. F. Scott Fitzgerald was there, already pensive and inquiring if there were any sense to life, and muttering, at thirty, about the cruelty of growing aged.

Listening to Mankiewicz, Edwin Justus Mayer, Scott Fitzgerald, Ted Shayne and other littérateurs roosting in my office, I learned that the Studio Bosses (circa 1925) still held writers in great contempt and considered them a waste of money. I learned, also, that Manky had got me my job by a desperate coup. The studio chieftain, the mighty B. P. Schulberg, smarting from experience with literary imports, had vowed never to hitch another onto the payroll. Manky had invaded the Front Office, his own two-year contract in his hand. He had announced that if his friend Hecht failed to write a successful movie they could tear up his contract and fire us both.

I was pleased to hear this tale of loyalty and assured Manky the New York *Times* would be happy to take him back on its staff if things went awry.

On my fourth day, I was summoned and given an assignment. Producer Bernard Fineman, under Schulberg, presented me with the first "idea" for a movie to smite my ears.

An important industrialist, said he, was shaving one morning. His razor slipped and he cut his chin. He thereupon sent out his butler to buy an alum stick to stop the flow of blood. The butler was slowed up by a traffic jam and the great industrialist, fuming in his onyx bathroom, had to wait fifteen minutes for the alum stick. The movie I was to make up was to show all the things that were affected in the world by this fifteen-minute delay. I recall of the details only that something went wrong with the pearl fisheries. The whole thing ended up with the great industrialist's mistress deserting him, his vast enterprises crashing, and his wife returning to his side to help him build a new life.

I relate this plot because my distaste for it started me as a successful scenario writer. I had seen no more than a dozen movies but I had heard in my four days in Hollywood all that was to be known about the flickers.

"I want to point out to you," said Manky, "that in a novel a hero can lay ten girls and marry a virgin for a finish. In a movie this is not allowed. The hero, as well as the heroine, has to be a virgin. The villain can lay anybody he wants, have as much fun as he wants cheating and stealing, getting rich and whipping the servants. But you have to shoot him in the end. When he falls with a bullet in his forehead, it is advisable that he clutch at the Gobelin tapestry on the library wall and bring it down over his head like a symbolic shroud. Also, covered by such a tapestry, the actor does not have to hold his breath while he is being photographed as a dead man."

An idea came to me. The thing to do was to skip the heroes and heroines, to write a movie containing only villains and bawds. I would not have to tell any lies then.

Thus, instead of a movie about an industrialist cutting his chin, I made up a movie about a Chicago gunman and his moll called Feathers McCoy. As a newspaperman I had learned that nice people —the audience—love criminals, doted on reading about their love problems as well as their sadism. My movie, grounded on this simple truth, was produced with the title of *Underworld*. It was the first gangster movie to bedazzle the movie fans and there were no lies in it—except for a half-dozen sentimental touches introduced by its director, Joe von Sternberg. I still shudder remembering one of them. My head villain, Bull Weed, after robbing a bank, emerged with a suitcase full of money and paused in the crowded street to notice a blind beggar and give him a coin—before making his getaway.

It was not Von Sternberg who helped me put the script together but another director, Arthur Rossen. Art Rossen was the first of these bonny directorial gentlemen with whom I was for many years to spend happy days locked away in fancy hotel rooms sawing away at plots. Art was one of the best of them, but, with a few nightmarish exceptions, they were all good. They were the new sort of storyteller produced by the movies, and, to this day, they remain the only authentic talent that has come out of Hollywood.

The Paramount viziers, all four of them, including the ex-prize fighter Mr. Zukor, listened to my reading of *Underworld*. It was eighteen pages long and it was full of moody Sandburgian sentences. The viziers were greatly stirred. I was given a ten-thousand-dollar check as a bonus for the week's work, a check which my sponsor Mankiewicz snatched out of my hand as I was bowing my thanks.

"You'll have it back in a week," Manky said. "I just want it for a few days to get me out of a little hole."

My return to New York was held up for several weeks while Manky struggled to raise another ten thousand to pay me back. He gambled valiantly, tossing a coin in the air with Eddie Cantor and calling heads or tails for a thousand dollars. He lost constantly. He tried to get himself secretly insured behind his good wife Sarah's back, planning to hock the policy and thus meet his obligation. This plan collapsed when the insurance company doctor refused to accept him as a risk.

I finally solved the situation by taking Manky into the Front Office and informing the studio bosses of our joint dilemma. I asked that my talented friend be given a five-hundred-a-week raise. The studio could then deduct this raise from his salary and give it to me. Thus in twenty weeks I would be repaid.

I left the Vatican suite with another full bonus check in my hand; and Manky, with his new raise, became the highest paid writer for Paramount Pictures, Inc.

THE CLOWNS: PINK PERIOD

Making movies is a game played by a few thousand toy-minded folk. It is obsessive, exhausting and jolly, as a good game should be. Played intently, it divorces you from life, as a good game will do. For many years I was one of the intent, though part-time, players. I paid some twenty visits to Hollywood and remained there each time only long enough to earn enough money to live on for the rest of the year. This required from two weeks to three or four months of work. With my bank balance restored, I would seize my hat and fly. Nearing penury again, I would turn again to Hollywood. There went with me, usually, Rose, a relative or two, two or three servants, many trunks and suitcases, all my oil paintings and whatever animals we possessed.

I remember, along with my indignation, the sunny streets of Hollywood, full of amiable and antic destinations. I remember studios humming with intrigue and happy-go-lucky excitements. I remember fine homes with handsome butlers and masterpieces on the walls; vivid people, long and noisy luncheons, nights of gaiety and gambling, hotel suites and rented palaces overrun with friends, partners, secretaries and happy servants. I remember thousands of important phone calls, yelling matches in the lairs of the caliphs, baseball, badminton and card games; beach and ocean on diamond-sparkling days, rainstorms out of Joseph Conrad and a picnic of money-making. More than all these pleasant things, I remember the camaraderie of collaboration.

Although I wrote most of my sixty movies alone, all my movie writing was a collaboration of one sort or another. The most satisfactory of these were my actual literary collaborations with Mac-

Arthur, Lederer or Fowler. The Hollywood party grew happier at such times.

But even without collaborators, the loneliness of literary creation was seldom part of movie work. You wrote with the phone ringing like a firehouse bell, with the boss charging in and out of your atelier, with the director grimacing and grunting in an adjoining armchair. Conferences interrupted you, agents with dream jobs flirted with you, and friends with unsolved plots came in hourly. Disasters circled your pencil. The star for whom you were writing fell ill or refused to play in the movie for reasons that stood your hair on end. ("I won't do this movie," said Ingrid Bergman of *Spellbound*, "because I don't believe the love story. The heroine is an intellectual woman, and an intellectual woman simply can't fall in love so deeply." She played the part very convincingly.) The studio for which you were working suddenly changed hands and was being reorganized. This meant usually no more than the firing of ten or twenty stenographers, but the excitement was unnerving. Or the studio head decided it would be better to change the locale of your movie from Brooklyn to Peking. You listened to these alarms, debated them like a juggler spinning hoops on his ankles, and kept on writing.

Of the bosses with whom I collaborated, Selznick and Zanuck and Goldwyn were the brightest. David, in the days he loved movie making, was a brilliant plotter. He could think of twenty different permutations of any given scene without stopping to catch his breath. Darryl was also quick and sharp and plotted at the top of his voice, like a man hollering for help. Goldwyn as a collaborator was inarticulate but stimulating. He filled the room with wonderful panic and beat at your mind like a man in front of a slot machine, shaking it for a jackpot.

Of the directors with whom I collaborated, most were sane and able fellows. I remember them happily—the young, piano-playing Leo McCarey, with a comedy fuse sputtering in his soul; the ex-clog dancer Ernst Lubitsch, who loved rhythm and precision in his scripts; the drawling fashion plate Howard Hawks, apurr with melodrama; the moody and elegant Harry D'Arrast; the gentlemanly Alfred Hitchcock, who gave off plot turns like a Roman candle; the witty and Boccaccian Otto Preminger; the antic Jack Conway; the hysterical Gregory Ratoff; the chuckling, wild-hearted Willie Wellman; the soft-spoken, world-hopping Henry Hathaway; the aloof and poetical Victor Fleming. These and many others were all men of talent with salty personalities. Working with them was like playing a game—"Gimmick, Gimmick, Who's Got the Gimmick?"

There were directors, however, who added some depressing rules to the game and made collaboration a messy affair. These were the humorless ones to whose heads fame had gone like sewer gas. They resented a scenario writer as if he were an enemy hired by the Front Office to rob them of their greatness. They scowled at dialogue, shuddered at jokes, and wrestled with a script until they had shaken out of it all its verbal glitter and bright plotting. Thus they were able to bring to the screen evidence only of their own "genius." This consisted of making great psychological or dramatic points by using props, scenic effects or eye-rolling close-ups instead of speech. Knowing these pretenders well and the foolish egomania that animated their work, I managed to avoid most of them. A few, however, fell like rain into my life and darkened some of my days.

This sickly "greatness" is, however, rare in Hollywood. I remember little of it. At dinner parties where all the guests were famous movie stars and directors, none acted famous or even felt famous. Their world-known faces were full of shyness or sociability. The enormous publicity that flared around stars and directors seldom touched their inner personalities, which were as modest and eager as those of factory workers on a picnic. The only strut I remember was the strut of power. A few of the studio caliphs were inclined to make lordly entrances and to relish a bit of homage.

My favorite collaborator in Hollywood was neither writer, director nor boss, but the cameraman Lee Garmes. It was with Lee as a partner that I made all my own pictures, starting with *Crime without Passion* and *The Scoundrel, Specter of the Rose* and *Actors and Sin*. Lee introduced me to the real magic of the movie world —its technical talents. He was not only one of the finest camera artists in Hollywood but more learned about movie making than anyone I met in movieland. The camera was a brush with which he painted, but in his painting was the knowledge of the hundred hazards of a movie set. Nothing I ever encountered in the movies was as uniquely talented as the eyes of Lee Garmes. I prided myself on being an acute observer, but beside Lee I was almost a blind man. Driving his car at fifty miles an hour he would inquire if I had noticed the girl in the back seat of a car that had passed us, speeding in the opposite direction. What about her, I would ask. Lee would beam, "We ought to put that in a picture sometime. She was using daisies for cuff links, real daisies."

Standing on a set, Lee saw a hundred more things than I did. He saw shadows around mouths and eyes invisible to me, highlights on desk tops, inkstands and trouser legs. He spotted wrong reflections and mysterious obstructions—shoulders that blocked faces in the background, hands that masked distant and vital objects. These were all hazards that no look of mine could detect. He corrected them with a constant murmur of instructions. While ridding the set of its wrong nuances of light and shade, Lee also watched the grouping of figures and carried the cutting of the picture in his head. He knew the moods of space, the value of planes, the dynamics of symmetry as well as any painting master. And all this wisdom went into his pointing of the camera.

Working with Lee, I became aware of the other fine talents that are part of movie making. The gaffer, or head electrician, taking his orders from Garmes was a fellow as fond of his work and as full of technical skill. Carpenters, prop men, painters, special-effects men all moved about with quick and economic gestures. They were as removed from laborers as the master craftsmen working beside Cellini in his silver smithy. As director of the movie being shot, I was the final word on all matters. But I would sit by silent and full of admiration as Lee and his overalled magicians prepared the set for my "direction." My job seemed to me little more than putting a frame on a finished canvas.

A FEW TEN-PER-CENTERS

I had another sort of company in my Hollywood work. This was an overenergized and exasperating fellow known as my agent. During my years in Hollywood I employed dozens of them. There was little variation among them. When my fortunes were high, they swarmed around me like Oriental courtiers. When my fortunes were low, they clapped on their turbans and bolted. But high or low, they continued to detach ten per cent from my earnings and harass me with charges of infidelity and duplicity. It was the theory of each of my agents that he alone was entitled to nab ten per cent of my studio checks. I saw no sense in the entire agency business. But I took no stand against them. Most of them were good companions, and their preposterous existence was, somehow, a natural part of the movie scene.

The first and most important of my agents was Leland Hayward. Leland had launched himself as a ten-per-center by sneaking a manuscript from my desk in Beekman Place and selling it to Metro behind my back. The manuscript was a short story I had discarded as unfit for publication. (It was produced as *The Green Ghost*, with Lionel Barrymore directing it.)

Leland's immediate demand for a cut of fifteen hundred dollars startled me. It was the first time such inroad into my earnings had been attempted. I hurried indignantly to the Metro office in New York and insisted on an extra fifteen hundred dollars for my story, and sent this added boodle to Leland. Thereafter I became reconciled to paying over great sums to men who seemingly did nothing but notify me they had secured a task for me which either I did not want or had already finished.

Leland had become an agent out of a boyish veneration for writers. This mood deserted him early in his agent's career. He became disdainful of writers and easily irritated by them. He said they had disillusioned him—"So help me God, they're more hammy and hysterical than even actors, and more ungrateful." But the truth was that Leland had become disillusioned with writers because of their eagerness to throw away their high talent and turn into movie hacks. Although he made his fortune out of this flaw in the literary soul, Leland was complex enough to sneer at it. He was always more perked up over my refusing to do a movie chore than over my having done it. A good part of my reputation as a troublesome fellow in Hollywood was based on Leland's happy pronouncements to the studio caliphs—"You can't get Hecht. He read the story and thinks it stinks. I tried to argue with him, but all he said was you haven't got enough money to get him to do such kind of crap."

Leland shuffled between New York and Hollywood like a man in a fever, sometimes flying his own plane and getting lost for days. He was continually vanishing, becoming involved in mysterious enterprises, flying into hysterics and losing total track of who his clients were and what they were doing. Yet in the midst of more confusion than all his secretaries could untangle, Leland managed to unload millions of dollars' worth of talent a year on the studios. Unload was Leland's own concept of his activities. He came away from a studio deal grinning like a con man who had disposed of a hole in the lake.

Among Leland's partners was an even eerier businessman than himself. This was Myron Selznick. They were partners only briefly, for not even a movie agency could house two such exotics long.

Myron's attitude toward writers was different from Leland's. Not that he loved writers, but to Myron the writer was an important weapon in his war on the movies. Myron considered the movie owners as his enemies. They had brought low his father, Lewis Selznick, who had been among the first of the great movie showmen, and Myron had sworn in his soul to avenge him.

His work of vengeance changed the Hollywood climate. It doubled and quadrupled the salaries of writers, actors and directors—myself among them. Myron making a deal with a studio head was a scene out of Robin Hood. He was not only dedicated to the task of bankrupting the studio, but ready to back up his sales talk with fisticuffs, if the discussion went not to his liking. Brooding in his tent after a sortie on a major studio, Myron would chortle, "I'll break them all. I'll send all those thieves and fourflushers crawling to the poorhouse. Before I'm done the artists in this town will have all the money." Myron rose to great riches in Hollywood before his untimely death. But even the respect of the bosses failed to win him over against the artists or dim his personal courage in their behalf.

A VISIT FROM SCARFACE

My first dealing with Myron involved going to work for Howard Hughes. I told Myron I didn't trust Mr. Hughes as an employer. I would work for him only if he paid me a thousand dollars every day at six o'clock. In that way I stood to waste only a day's labor if Mr. Hughes turned out to be insolvent.

Myron was pleased by my attitude and put the deal over with dispatch. The work I did for Hughes was a movie called *Scarface*. News that it was a biographical study of Al Capone brought two Capone henchmen to Hollywood to make certain that nothing derogatory about the great gangster reached the screen. The two henchmen called on me at my hotel. It was after midnight. They entered the room as ominously as any pair of movie gangsters, their faces set in scowls and guns bulging their coats. They had a copy of my *Scarface* script in their hands. Their dialogue belonged in it.

"You the guy who wrote this?"

I said I was.

"We read it."

I inquired how they had liked it.

"We wanna ask you some questions."

I invited them to go ahead.

"Is this stuff about Al Capone?"

"God, no," I said. "I don't even know Al."

"Never met him, huh?"

I pointed out I had left Chicago just as Al was coming into prominence.

"I knew Jim Colisimo pretty well," I said.

"That so?"

"I also knew Mossy Enright and Pete Gentleman."

"That so? Did you know Deanie?"

"Deanie O'Banion? Sure. I used to ride around with him in his flivver. I also knew Barney.

"Which Barney?"

"Barney Grogan—Eighteenth Ward," I said.

A pause.

"O.K., then. We'll tell Al this stuff you wrote is about them other guys."

They started out and halted in the doorway, worried again.

"If this stuff ain't about Al Capone, why are you callin' it *Scarface?* Everybody'll think it's him."

"That's the reason," I said. "Al is one of the most famous and fascinating men of our time. If we call the movie *Scarface*, everybody will want to see it, figuring it's about Al. That's part of the racket we call showmanship."

My visitors pondered this, and one of them finally said, "I'll tell Al." A pause. "Who's this fella Howard Hughes?"

"He's got nothing to do with anything," I said, speaking truthfully at last. "He's the sucker with the money."

"O. K. The hell with him."

My visitors left.

SOME GILDED ASSIGNMENTS

Writing under handicaps of one sort or another—deadlines to be met, censors to be outwitted, stars to be unruffled—was normal procedure. Writing to please a producer who a few years ago had been a garage owner or a necktie salesman was another of the handicaps. But given a producer literate as Anatole France, there was still the ugly handicap of having to write something that would miraculously please forty million people and gross four million dollars. The handicaps, including this last Liverpool Jump, only added bounce to the job. They made it always a half-desperate performance. If there was little excitement in the script, there was more than enough in its preparation to keep me stimulated.

Goldwyn, Selznick and Eddie Mannix of Metro were my favorite handicap makers. I wrote million-dollar movies for Mannix in a week each. They had to be rushed to the camera to catch release dates set long in advance. For Goldwyn I rewrote an entire script in two days. It was called *Hurricane. Nothing Sacred*, done for Selznick in two weeks, had to be written on trains between New York and Hollywood.

One of my favorite memories of quickie movie writing is the doing of half the *Gone with the Wind* movie. Selznick and Vic

Fleming appeared at my bedside one Sunday morning at dawn. I
was employed by Metro at the time, but David had arranged to
borrow me for a week.

After three weeks' shooting of *Gone with the Wind,* David had
decided his script was no good and that he needed a new story and
a new director. The shooting had been stopped and the million-dollar
cast was now sitting by collecting its wages in idleness.

The three of us arrived at the Selznick studio a little after sunrise. We had settled on my wages on the way over. I was to receive
fifteen thousand dollars for the week's work, and no matter what
happened I was not to work longer than a week. I knew in advance
that two weeks of such toil as lay ahead might be fatal.

Four Selznick secretaries who had not yet been to sleep that night
staggered in with typewriters, paper and a gross of pencils. Twenty-
four-hour work shifts were quite common under David's baton.
David himself sometimes failed to go to bed for several nights in a
row. He preferred to wait till he collapsed on his office couch.
Medication was often necessary to revive him.

David was outraged to learn I had not read *Gone with the Wind,*
but decided there was no time for me to read the long novel. The
Selznick overhead on the idle *Wind* stages was around fifty thousand
dollars a day. David announced that he knew the book by heart and
that he would brief me on it. For the next hour I listened to David
recite its story. I had seldom heard a more involved plot. My verdict
was that nobody could make a remotely sensible movie out of it.
Fleming, who was reputed to be part Indian, sat brooding at his own
council fires. I asked him if he had been able to follow the story
David had told. He said no. I suggested then that we make up a
new story, to which David replied with violence that every literate
human in the United States except me had read Miss Mitchell's book,
and we would have to stick to it. I argued that surely in two years
of preparation someone must have wangled a workable plot out of
Miss Mitchell's Ouïdalike flight into the Civil War. David suddenly
remembered the first "treatment," discarded three years before. It
had been written by Sidney Howard, since dead. After an hour of
searching, a lone copy of Howard's work was run down in an old
safe. David read it aloud. We listened to a precise and telling narrative of *Gone with the Wind.*

We toasted the dead craftsman and fell to work. Being privy to
the book, Selznick and Fleming discussed each of Howard's scenes
and informed me of the habits and general psychology of the characters. They also acted out the scenes, David specializing in the
parts of Scarlett and her drunken father and Vic playing Rhett

Butler and a curious fellow I could never understand called Ashley. He was always forgiving his beloved Scarlett for betraying him with another of his rivals. David insisted that he was a typical Southern gentleman and refused flatly to drop him out of the movie.

After each scene had been discussed and performed, I sat down at the typewriter and wrote it out. Selznick and Fleming, eager to continue with their acting, kept hurrying me. We worked in this fashion for seven days, putting in eighteen to twenty hours a day. Selznick refused to let us eat lunch, arguing that food would slow us up. He provided bananas and salted peanuts. On the fourth day a blood vessel in Fleming's right eye broke, giving him more of an Indian look than ever. On the fifth day Selznick toppled into a torpor while chewing on a banana. The wear and tear on me was less, for I had been able to lie on the couch and half doze while the two darted about acting. Thus on the seventh day I had completed, unscathed, the first nine reels of the Civil War epic.

Many of the handicaps attending script writing I invented without anyone's aid. I often undertook to do two or more movies at the same time. Once I did four simultaneously, writing two of them with Lederer, one with Quentin Reynolds and one by myself. The house in Oceanside where this mass composition went on swarmed with secretaries, and producers motored down from Beverly Hills to spy on me. Lederer and I had small time for our favorite diversions, which were Klabiash, badminton, horseshoes on the beach and cooking up Napoleonic schemes for getting rich without effort.

MY POVERTY ROW

When I came to Hollywood alone I usually stayed in a Beverly Hills hotel. One of my favorite memories of my hotel existence in Hollywood is of the "breakfasts" over which I presided in the Beverly-Wilshire Hotel.

My activities and social duties had made it impossible for me to see the innumerable people "of no standing" whom I still knew. Unemployed and often hungering writers and actors kept my telephones ringing constantly. I decided to consort with them at breakfast, from seven to ten. Accordingly, each morning my suite filled up with raucous and embittered fellows—newspapermen who had turned up only cinders in Eldorado, actors whose bad luck was as fantastic and inexplicable as the good luck of the movie favorites. They drank up bottles of champagne each morning, emptied tins of caviar and filled the air with calumny of Hollywood's Fortunatuses. I was pleased to offer them behind-the-scenes tales proving their contentions that the town was run by cretins and monsters. There was little more I could do for them. Despite their wit and even talent, unsuccess was in their eyes. The need to be underdogs and rail against existence was as strong in them as their lust for fame and money. You could not only see it in their faces but hear it in the gloat with which they detailed their misfortunes.

There is little that can be done in Hollywood to alter the status of its indignant misfits. Jobs obtained for them, lyrical introductions written out for them, are valueless. They fall out of jobs overnight and the high prose commending them brings only a frown to the boss's face. He knows their real objective, which is to add another sonofabitch to their roster of employers who misused and misunderstood them. Occasionally one of these has-beens or never-weres erupts into fame. But much more frequent in Hollywood than the emergence of Cinderella is her sudden vanishing. At our party, even in those glowing days, the clock was always striking twelve for someone at the height of greatness; and there was never a prince to fetch her back to the happy scene.

SEX IN HOLLYWOOD

The sexual activities of Hollywood have a vast number of kibitzers, most of them waving pennants. There are some necks straining here and there for a peek that disapproves. But this is an old moral trick that even the clergy has begun to see through. Denouncing sin is one of the few ways open for virtuous people to enjoy it. A sermon against the evils of promiscuous sex indulgence can send a congregation home to masturbate as quickly as a reading from Fanny Hill.

Not many years ago the sex life of Hollywood would have stirred thunder from the pulpits of the land and set the vigilantes riding. In fact, it did. But something has changed—sex, of course. The Devil is out of it. It has almost the status of a game. And as in all games, the public looks toward champions.

Thus Hollywood is to sex what the major leagues are to baseball. The glamorous Hollywood figures perform in a sort of World Series sex match. The public rises to its feet with a happy roar when another one of its marriages is wrecked by a great base-running siren. A celebrated cocksman batting four hundred against the curves and inshoots spreads joy in the bleachers.

Hollywood's love-making is as spotlighted as its movie making for its insiders as well as outsiders. Much of the conversation in movieland is concerned with the venal doings of the ladies and gentlemen of the screen. A great star returning from her honeymoon to start her divorce proceedings told of her first night with her new, third, husband. He had asked her for an unnatural caress. "And I said to him," the beautiful young bride related, " 'Nix, I don't have to do that any more. I'm a star now!' "

A male star hosting a party at Chasen's Restaurant asked for advice. He was starting a picture in the morning. He had reason to believe that his director was his wife's lover. What was the best way to handle the situation? His own paramour, beside him, spoke up. "Have her come on location with you. In that way it will seem that she's devoted to you, and all the columnists will write about your happy home life. And she'll be able to be with the director. And so everybody will be happy." The star took the suggestion and his movie was shot in Arizona with happiness enow for all.

In movieland fidelity is as passé as sideburns. Boccaccio would have delighted in its parties. Crébillon would have found among them a perfect cast of lewd and witty duchesses and nimble chevaliers.

The chief advance (or backslide) the movie people have made is freeing sexual activity from social censure. A woman who is known to change her lovers five times a year is as acceptable socially as any virgin—a meaningless statement, that, that marks my age. Virgins have never been acceptable in Hollywood. In all the time I spent there I never heard virginity discussed any more than the canals of Mars.

Even married women who are known to be betraying their husbands with chauffeurs, actors or salesmen are under no cloud. Friends may caution such a wife about running into a blackmailer, but no door closes against her, and there is amusement rather than sting in the gossip she stirs. Men who have been the targets of rape and bastardy charges and who make seduction a profession remain honorable figures in Hollywood society.

I have sat at a dinner party of twelve, knowing that my host, in the last two years, had seduced all six of his feminine guests. There was no hint of tension at the table. No memory of love or sin put a stutter in the talk. Similarly, I have sat in a room where one of the lady stars present had bedded with five of the men chatting around her. She could not have been more at ease had they been five beaux who had taken her canoeing and no more.

News that a group of stars and caliphs have been engaging in orgies is received casually by the movie dinner parties. Information from a qualified source that a certain great star is perverse in her love-making and will engage in amour only in a bathtub full of warm milk, or that a local Casanova has taken to substituting electrical appliances for phallic attentions makes the smallest of ripples. You will see the lacteal siren and the sexual Edison at dinner the next evening and there will be no nudging or winking. People's sex habits are as known in Hollywood as their political opinions, and much less criticized. In fact, they are hardly noticed. In a world of tigers it is difficult for a stripe to stand out.

The absence of moral censure makes gossip depend on its wit or freshness. My friend, on the verge of getting married, told this anecdote about himself: "What can I do? She's cold, and difficult to get along with. Her last husband refuses even to come to the United States as long as she's here. And she's going to drive me crazy with her idea that she's an actress. But on the other hand I am only potent with her. Since falling in love with her, I have tried five other girls. Nothing! With my fiancée, I am like a lion. Of course I had to tell her this. My mistake. As soon as she found it out she insisted on marriage."

Men embarking on love affairs seek counsel with their predecessors on the quickest way to gain entry into the bedroom of the mutual friend. "Don't boast to her of how successful you are," said one Don Juan to the other. "She hates Hollywood success. She says it's a sign of stupidity. Attack Hollywood, the studio, the movies. Tell her they're eating up your soul. She's very artistic."

A friend said to me, "You know, she was my mistress for four years. We were as close as any husband and wife. She cooked me dinner sometimes, rubbed my back. Suddenly she announced, 'I don't love this man I met, but he's a railroad vice-president and rich. And he's asked me to marry him. I told him I would see you first. He's waiting in New York right now for me.'

"I said to her, 'Darling, you're wonderful. I can't ask you to marry me. I wouldn't be sincere. So—go to him. And be happy.'

"Well, we got undressed, went to bed for an hour. She was so wonderful, I cried. Both of us cried. At three-thirty she jumped out of bed. 'Darling, I must hurry. I'll miss the train to New York. It leaves at five. Don't get up. You don't have to take me to the station. I'd rather remember you lying in bed like that—smoking a cigarette.' I asked her if she had her ticket and drawing room. Yes, she had them. The railroad vice-president had taken care of that. She walked out. And I lay there on my bed. At first I was just numb. Then I began to suffer. At four o'clock I was like a man being choked to death. I wanted to get down on the floor and cry. I did. I wanted her back. I kept looking at the clock. I could call her at the station. It's easy to have somebody paged. At four-thirty I grabbed the phone. I thought I would die, I was suffering so. And I

called. I had her paged. I couldn't live without her. The thought of
her going to bed with this railroad vice-president was like a knife
in my heart. The voice on the phone said to me, 'Sorry, sir. The
train has already left for New York.' I told him he was stupid and
crazy. It was only twenty minutes to five. He tells me it is five
minutes after five. My clock is twenty-five minutes slow. I hang
up. My God, that was the greatest moment of my life. Such a relief
came over me, I wanted to yell. I felt suddenly twenty years old,
new, fresh, saved!"

Unmarried women discuss their lovers openly, concentrating
usually on their sexual failings. "Good God, a man with his reputation. You'd think he'd know something! All I can tell you is we
got to the bedroom at exactly two-thirty. We went straight there
from Romanoff's. At exactly two-forty-five we were dressed again
and leaving. How do you like that for a big lover! No more actors
for me."

"Well, lay off producers. They're worse. I said to Joe last night
at Chasen's 'For God's sake, everybody thinks we're mad lovers and
we haven't been to bed for three weeks!' He answered me, 'Don't
be selfish, darling. We're having a shakeup at the studio.' "

At a dinner table once in a movie caliph's home, I showed surprise
at the recently publicized infidelity of a movie star whom I and the
public had considered always a chaste wife. All fifteen of the diners
turned on me with derision. They supplied me with a list of ten men
with whom my heroine had copulated in the past two years. My
delusion about the lady seemed a larger flaw in their eyes than her
ten defections. When I riposted with this, one of the other famous
ladies present said, "What's so wrong about a woman having ten
lovers, if they don't interfere with her career or make her unhappy?"

Concealment is not only passé in Hollywood but the publicizing
of sin is actually the rule, as much for the girls as the men. Actresses
and near-actresses hire press agents to notify the newspaper columnist of their new love affairs. Or else they call up the newspaper
themselves—"Oh, darling, it's the greatest love of my life! He's so
wonderful! Oh, no, that affair is over. I haven't seen Mr. J. for God
knows how long. But this time it's real, darling! I'm swooning so I
don't know if I'll be able to act in my next picture. No, not *Hold
Me Forever*. That's been postponed. I'm playing the feminine lead
in *Lady of the Swamps*. Thank you, darling. I wanted you to be the
first to know how happy I am."

Items that a starlet (which in Hollywood is the name for any
woman under thirty not actively employed in a brothel) has hit the
hay with a new glamour boy are an important aid to her career.

The movie caliphs are averse to hiring unknowns. In the caliph's eyes any reputation is better than none. A girl who has figured in a dozen "romances" with men of any sort of prominence (even prominent drunkards will do) has proven she is a good prospect for further exploitation. The phrase is: She's star material.

As I hinted a few pages back, it was otherwise once. In the twenties, women's clubs boycotted actresses who changed husbands. Civic organizations picketed theaters in which some recently exposed fornicator was cooing on the silver screen.

Movie stars whose sexual activities slopped over into print were actually dropped by the studios. In fact, the moguls were so intent on keeping their stars sexually pure in the public eye that they did their best to suppress the news that an actress was honorably married. How expect the public to buy a heroine fighting to preserve her virginity when it knew she was being bounced every night in a marital bed?

It was the theory of the studio caliphs in that time that the public demanded purity above all other things in an actress, and that its absence was punished with artistic as well as box office failure. There was no middle ground between virgin and vampire.

The switch to selling strumpets instead of pure girls to the public was a gradual one. No one press agent or studio philosopher merited an Oscar for the deed. As with other Hollywood trends, it was actually what the public wanted. It wanted no ladies with their legs nobly crossed. It wanted bacchantes and satyrs chasing them, or vice versa.

The moguls have as yet been unable to cater to this great box office yen for immorality. The churches and the civic leagues still stand guard against the art of underpants. The movie censorship code still demands that no woman shall sleep with a man unless married to him, and that if she seems to be sleeping with any man to whom she is not married, she shall be either sent to jail or killed at the end of the film—as a lesson.

The movie makers have not been too stymied by this part of their self-imposed curbs. They have learned how to hint at fornication in a hundred masterful ways and so much so that I, for one, watching a movie, am ready to believe that all its males and females fall to futtering one another as soon as the scene "dissolves."

A rash of Bible pictures has recently solved the fornication problem for the major studios. Although the historian Cecil B. De Mille pointed the way decades ago, the movie makers hung back, dubiously. But, no longer. Immorality, perversion, infidelity, cannibalism, etc., are unassailable by church and civic league if you dress them up in the togas and talliths of the Good Book.

DON JUAN IN HOLLYWOOD

Don Jaunism is part of society everywhere. In Hollywood it is the standard. Love and marriage are secondary matters there to sexual exercise. And oddly, it is my impression that there is less successful sex in Hollywood than in Wichita, Kansas. I have no five hundred fieldworkers to bring me morning reports on the situation, as the good Professor Kinsey had, but I have my own accumulation of data. It convinces me that Hollywood, uninhibited center of venery, is more headquarters for impotence than for stallion play.

I have known a number of Don Juans who were good studs and who cavorted between the sheets without a psychiatrist to guide them. But most of the busy love-makers I knew were looking for masculinity rather than practicing it. They were fellows of dubious lust.

And their conquests were most often ladies of similar lack. Their female sexuality was nearly all in their clothes, their mannerisms and their reputations. The glamour girls of Hollywood number many an honest set of glands among them, and there are even some nymphomaniacs of note to be met. But, as with the male Don Juans, the ladies hopping from lover to lover brought more ambition to bed than passion.

On this subject my friend Fanny Brice used to say, "Men always fall for frigid women because they put on the best show."

I can add little to Fanny's observation—except that Don Juan is apt to prefer the hullaballoo of spurious passion to the simpler noises of honest sex. His own love racket is also more windy than seminal.

With all the infidelity going on in movietown and with its large sexual turnover, you would expect much smolder and violence. There is some alcoholic torch carrying to observe and an occasional explosion to read in the papers. But pain and explosion are rare in the love annals of Hollywood. Marriages break up with a minimum of emotional pother. What bitterness appears has usually to do with property division. Great romances which have kept the public shaking with vicarious passion collapse suddenly, and usually their only epitaph is a new Great Romance, announced in the press on Monday.

This is one of the reasons for the human feebleness of the movies. They are made by these same folk. Most movies deal with matters foreign to their makers—the agonies of love, the miseries of infidelity and the wonders of a safe and loyal marriage that lasts till "death do us part."

The movie makers are able to put more reality into a picture about the terrors of life at the ocean bottom than into a tale of two Milwaukeeans in love. They know more about the former matters.

I remember a phone call to Nyack from the M-G-M Studio in Hollywood. Bernie Hyman, then the studio head, wished my help on a plot problem that had arisen in a two-million-dollar movie being prepared for shooting.

"I won't tell you the plot," he said. "I'll just give you what we're up against. The hero and heroine fall madly in love with each other—as soon as they meet. What we need is some gimmick that keeps them from going to bed right away. Not a physical gimmick like arrest or getting run over and having to go to the hospital. But a purely psychological one. Now what reasons do you know that would keep a healthy pair of lovers from hitting the hay in Reel Two?"

I answered that frequently a girl has moral concepts that keep her virtuous until after a trip to the altar. And that there are men also who prefer to wait for coitus until after they have married the girl they adore.

"Wonderful!" said the Metro head of production. "We'll try it."

FAREWELL, SOLDIER

I knew few actors and actresses well in Hollywood. Adventures and work shared with actors are not enough to make friendships. Actors are modest and warmhearted but they remain stubbornly in their own world. One of the few exceptions was Jack Gilbert. He became a friend, suddenly. We met at a dinner party and Jack came home with me and talked all night.

In the time of Hollywood's most glittering days, he glittered the most. He received ten thousand dollars a week and could keep most of it. He lived in a castle on top of a hill. Thousands of letters poured in daily telling him how wonderful he was. The caliphs for whom he worked bowed before him as before a reigning prince. They built him a "dressing room" such as no actor ever had. It was a small Italian palace. There were no enemies in his life. He was as unsnobbish as a happy child. He went wherever he was invited. He needed no greatness around him to make him feel distinguished. He drank with carpenters, danced with waitresses and made love to whores and movie queens alike. He swaggered and posed but it was never to impress anyone. He was being Jack Gilbert, prince, butterfly, Japanese lantern and the spirit of romance.

One night Jack sat in a movie theater and heard the audience laugh at him in a picture. It was his first talkie. His squeaky boy's voice accompanying his derring-do gestures turned him into a clown.

After the preview the Metro caliphs decided not to use him again. His contract for ten thousand a week still had many years to run. He would draw his salary and remain idle.

Jack called in three vocal coaches. He worked two hours a day with each of them. He started breaking into the front offices crying out, "Listen to me now. I can talk." And he recited passages from Shakespeare and the poets. The caliphs remembered the laughter in the theater and waved him away.

One day he entered Walter Wanger's office, fell on his knees and pleaded for the male lead in *Queen Christina*. Garbo, one of his former leading ladies, was being starred in it.

"Listen to me talk," said Jack. "It's a real voice, a man's voice." Tears fell from his eyes.

Wanger gave him the lead. Gilbert played it well, but the movie failed to bring him back to fame. The Gilbert voice no longer made audiences laugh. It left them, however, unimpressed. Jack played in no more pictures. He became a ten-thousand-dollar-a-week beachcomber. He strutted around the movie lot and gave drinking parties in his Italian-palace dressing room. There was no gloom visible in him. He played Jack Gilbert to a small audience of masseurs, fencing and boxing instructors, vocal coaches, barkers, whores, hangers-on and a few friends.

One rainy afternoon I called on him in his dressing room. He was lying down on one of his five-thousand-dollar beds reading one of my books. He asked me to autograph it. I wrote in it, "To Jack Gilbert—Dumas loaned him a mustache." I regretted the sentence as soon as I put it down. Jack grinned as he looked at it. "So true," he said. "Can you have dinner with me tonight?"

The rain became a tropic storm. Four of us drove out to Gilbert's house on Malibu Beach. MacArthur was one of the guests. Another was one of Jack's staunchest friends, Dick Hyland, the athlete and sports writer.

We drank and told stories after dinner. The wind howled in the night and the dark sea came crashing almost up to the windows. Gilbert was silent. He sat drinking and smiling at us. At eleven o'clock he sprang to his feet.

"I've got a date," he said. "I'm swimming out and returning a mustache to Dumas. Good-by—everybody—sweethearts and sonsa-bitches, all."

He waved a bottle of liquor at us and was gone. We saw him for a moment racing in the storm toward the roaring ocean. No one moved.

"For God's sake!" young Hyland said. "He's gone to drown himself!"

Hyland watched the storm for a few minutes and then left to find Jack. He returned in an hour, drenched and wearied. We were still drinking and talking.

"I couldn't find him," Hyland said. "He's gone."

I looked at MacArthur and asked, "What do you think, Charlie?"

"I don't know," said my friend, "but if a man wants to kill himself that's his privilege. Everybody destroys himself sooner or later."

MacArthur stood up unsteadily. He had remembered a phrase out of the Bible, which was always half open in his head.

"A man fell in Israel," he quoted, and resumed his drinking.

The noises of the storm filled the room. The door opened sud-denly. Rain and wind rushed in. A dripping Jack Gilbert stood weaving in the doorway. He grinned and tried to speak. Instead he vomited and fell on the floor.

"Always the silent star," said MacArthur.

I thought of the Hans Christian Andersen tale of the Steadfast Tin Soldier. He had been swept away to sea in a paper boat, and in his ears as he was drowning had sounded the voice of one he loved.

Farewell, soldier, true and brave,
Nothing now thy life can save.

A few months later Gilbert went to a gay Hollywood party. While he was dancing with a movie queen, his toupee fell off. Amid shouts of laughter he retrieved it from under the dancer's feet. He was found dead the next morning in bed—in his castle on the hill.

Notes on the Contributors

ÉLIE FAURE (1873–1937) was a French art critic and historian. He wrote many books on art history and painting, including the celebrated five-volume work, *History of Art*. He was also a surgeon.

ERWIN PANOFSKY, the distinguished art historian, has been associated with the Institute for Advanced Study at Princeton, New Jersey, since 1935. He is the author of *Gothic Architecture and Scholasticism, Studies in Iconology, The Life and Art of Albrecht Dürer, Pandora's Box* (with Dora Panofsky), and many monographs on medieval, Renaissance and baroque art.

ALLARDYCE NICOLL, teacher and writer, has written widely on the history of English drama. He succeeded George Pierce Baker as director of Yale University's celebrated Drama Workshop. Since 1951 Mr. Nicoll has been director of the Shakespeare Institute at Stratford-on-Avon.

SUSANNE LANGER, philosopher and writer on aesthetics, has taught philosophy at Radcliffe College, Columbia University and elsewhere. She is the author of *Philosophy in a New Key*.

PARKER TYLER has been writing on film aesthetics for many years. He has published three books on the film. His articles on painting, literature, the movies and the dance have appeared in *View, Art Digest, Kenyon Review* and *Film Culture*. He has also published three volumes of poetry.

ARNOLD HAUSER, art historian, has been lecturing on the history of art at the University of Leeds, England, since 1951. He has written several articles on the film which have appeared in *Sight and Sound, Life and Letters* and *Partisan Review*.

SEYMOUR STERN has been engaged in film criticism, teaching and film making for over twenty-five years. He has written several articles and monographs on D. W. Griffith. Since 1955 he has been teaching film history at U.C.L.A.

MARGARET KENNEDY has written plays, novels and screenplays. Her first book was a textbook on modern European history. She is best known for her novel *The Constant Nymph*, which was made into a film.

JOHN GRIERSON has been making documentaries and writing about films for about thirty-five years. He has been a dynamic force behind the documentary film in England, Canada and elsewhere. Among his many positions, he was Director of Mass Communications at UNESCO from 1945 to 1948. Many prominent film makers, including Paul Rotha, Basil Wright and Norman McLaren, have studied under him.

JAMES AGEE, who died in 1955, was a film critic, poet, novelist and screenwriter. He wrote the scenarios of *The African Queen* (with John Huston) and *The Bride Comes to Yellow Sky*, and the narration of the documentary film *The Quiet One*. His last film work was a scenario, written with Howard Taubman of the New York *Times*, on Tanglewood in the Berkshires.

ROBERT WARSHOW was managing editor of *Commentary* for several years. He wrote many essays on the film and on other aspects of American culture which appeared in *Commentary, Partisan Review* and *The American Mercury.*

MANNY FARBER, painter and art critic, has written about films for *The Nation* since the early 1940s. Along with Harry Alan Potamkin, Otis Ferguson, Gilbert Seldes and James Agee, he has done some of the finest movie reviewing in America.

PAULINE KAEL, who lives in Berkeley, California, is a young writer who has written several articles on the movies for *Sight and Sound* and *Partisan Review.*

GILBERT SELDES coined the phrase "the seven lively arts." He has been involved in all aspects of these arts for many years as critic, creator and production executive.

GEORGE BLUESTONE has written short stories and articles on the film and on literature for *The Atlantic Monthly, The Quarterly of Film, Radio and Television, Sewanee Review* and *Film Culture.*

MARTHA WOLFENSTEIN has taught philosophy and psychology at Hunter College, C.C.N.Y. and New York University. She has written on various aspects of art and literature.

NATHAN LEITES, currently on the staff of the Rand Corporation, has taught at the University of Chicago. He has also been connected with the Office of War Information and UNESCO.

V. I. PUDOVKIN (1893–1953) studied chemistry and physics in college. He went into films after seeing D. W. Griffith's *Intolerance.* He subsequently made several films, of which *Mother* and *The End of St. Petersburg* rank among the film classics.

BÉLA BALÁZS (1884–1951), a Hungarian, wrote on film aesthetics and made films in German. He was the first film critic to run a column in a daily paper. He is the author of two important books on film aesthetics and theory, *Der Sichtbare Mensch (The Visible Man)*, 1923, and *Der Geist des Films (The Spirit of Films)*, 1930. He also wrote children's books and was Béla Bartók's librettist.

RUDOLPH ARNHEIM has written widely on the film, the dance, sculpture and painting for many publications in Germany, Italy and the United States. His most recent book was *Art and Visual Perception: A Psychology of the Creative Eye*, a remarkable work on the aesthetics of the visual arts. He teaches at Sarah Lawrence College.

SERGEI M. EISENSTEIN was one of the great figures of the film. Teacher, writer, film maker, he created several screen classics, including *October, Potemkin* and *Alexander Nevsky*. He died in 1948.

RENÉ CLAIR is one of the most important film makers of the past thirty years. Among others, he made such superior films as *The Italian Straw Hat* (1927), *Sous les Toits de Paris* (1929–30), and *A Nous la Liberté* (1931).

JEAN COCTEAU has written art, poetry and drama criticism, philosophical works, plays, novels, poetry and travel sketches. He has also produced such outstanding films as *Blood of A Poet, The Strange Ones, Orpheus, Beauty and the Beast*, and *The Eternal Return*.

PAUL ROTHA has been making documentary films and writing on documentary methods for many years. He is the author of a history of the film, *The Film till Now* (1930, 1949) and many articles which have appeared in *Cinema Quarterly, Sight and Sound*, and other film magazines. The films which best reflect his point of view on documentary techniques are *World of Plenty* (1943), *Land of Promise* (1945), and *The World Is Rich* (1948).

TERRY RAMSAYE worked for The Chicago *Tribune* before writing *A Million and One Nights*. He has also served as an editorial consultant for several large picture companies. Since 1943 he has been editor of the *Motion Picture Herald*.

MAURICE BARDÈCHE, in addition to writing on the film, has published books on such assorted subjects as the Nuremberg war trials, the French resistance, European politics, Balzac and Stendhal.

ROBERT BRASILLACH (1909–1945), coauthor with Maurice Bardèche of *The History of Motion Pictures*, wrote a book on World War II and the German occupation of France entitled *Journal d'un Homme Occupé*, published in Paris in 1955.

LEWIS JACOBS has been associated with film criticism and film making for close to thirty years. He has written for almost all of the significant film journals in America. He has worked in Hollywood on several films. At present he is making films in New York City.

SIEGFRIED KRACAUER has been engaged in writing on the film for close to thirty years. He was the film critic of the *Frankfurter Zeitung* from 1920 to 1933. Since coming to the United States in the thirties, he has been doing research on mass communications, propaganda, sociology and the aesthetics of the film.

ROBERT PAYNE has written in the neighborhood of fifty volumes of criticism, travel sketches, novels, biographies and essays; he has also edited anthologies. He has taught English in China and the United States.

GEORGES SADOUL is an internationally known film historian who has published many articles in his field. He is the author of *Histoire Générale du Cinéma*, the largest general history of the film yet undertaken. Most of this multivolume work has already been published (Paris, 1946 to present).

HENRY MILLER requires no introduction. He is world-famous for his books *Tropic of Cancer* and *Tropic of Capricorn*. He lived in Paris from 1930 to 1939 and then returned to his native America. He is now living in Big Sur, California, high up in the hills, writing and painting.

ALVA JOHNSTON, who died in 1950, was one of America's outstanding reporters. For many years he was a regular contributor to *The New Yorker*, the New York *Times* and *The Saturday Evening Post*. He wrote several books, including *The Legendary Mizeners*.

LEO C. ROSTEN is a social scientist, screenwriter, novelist and journalist. Under the name of Leonard Q. Ross, he wrote *The Education of H*Y*M*A*N K*A*P*L*A*N*. At present he is an editorial adviser to *Look* magazine.

LILLIAN ROSS worked for many years as a reporter for *The New Yorker*. She is well remembered for her witty profile of Ernest Hemingway which appeared in that magazine.

Ben Hecht is a famous screenwriter, well known for his work on *Underworld, Scarface, Gone with the Wind, Specter of the Rose, A Farewell to Arms* (Selznick version in 1958), and many others. He has also written plays, novels, essays and poetry.

Bibliography

The standard bibliography on the film is *The Film Index: A Bibliography*, edited by Harold Leonard, New York, 1941. There is also a large and diversified bibliography in *The Rise of the American Film* by Lewis Jacobs, covering books, special articles, documents, catalogues, pamphlets and periodicals from 1896 to 1939. For foreign material, particularly books and articles in German, the bibliography in Siegfried Kracauer's book *From Caligari to Hitler* is worth looking into.

The following bibliography is limited to those articles and books which supplement the contents of this anthology. It would be worth while, for example, to read Dwight Macdonald's article on Hollywood directors (listed below) in conjunction with Grierson's selection in this book, or Arnold Hauser's article in *Sight and Sound* with Paul Rotha's piece on the documentary, and so on. All the books and articles mentioned in the foregoing text are excluded from the list.

Agee, James, *Agee on Film.* New York, 1958.

Aristarco, Guido, *L'arte del film; antologia storico-critica.* Milan, 1950.

Arnheim, Rudolph, *Art and Visual Perception.* Berkeley and Los Angeles, 1954, pp. 304–34.

Arnheim, Rudolph, "Epic and Dramatic Film." *Film Culture,* Vol. 3, No. 1 (11), 1957.

Arnheim, Rudolph, "Who Is the Author of a Film?" *Film Culture,* January 1958.

Balázs, Béla, *Der Sichtbare Mensch: Eine Film-Dramaturgie.* Halle, Germany, 1924, 2nd edition.

Balázs, Béla, *Der Geist des Films.* Halle, Germany, 1930.

Benoît-Lévy, Jean, *The Art of the Motion Picture.* New York, 1946. Translated from the French by Theodore R. Jaeckel.

Betts, Ernest, *Heraclitus, or the Future of Films.* New York, 1928.

Bloem, Walter S., *Soul of the Moving Pictures.* New York, 1924. Translated from the German by Allen W. Porterfield.

Bluestone, George, "In Defense of 3-D." *Sewanee Review,* Autumn 1956.

Brustein, Robert, "America's New Culture Hero." *Commentary,* February 1958.

Chiaromonte, Nicola, "Italian Movies." *Partisan Review,* June 1949.

Cohen-Séat, Gilbert, *Essai sur les Principes d'une Philosophie du Cinéma* (Paris, 1946), Vol. 1.

De Laurot, Edouard L., "Audio-Visualism versus Education." *Film Culture,* Winter 1955.

Dreyer, Carl, "Thoughts on My Craft." *Sight and Sound,* Winter 1955–56.

Eisenstein, Sergei, *The Film Sense,* edited and translated from the Russian by Jay Leyda. Meridian Books, New York, 1957. This paperback edition also includes the entire text of *Film Form.*

Elliott, Eric, *Anatomy of Motion Picture Art.* Territet, Switzerland, 1928.

Epstein, Jean, *Le Cinéma du Diable.* Paris, 1947.

Epstein, Jean, *Esprit de Cinéma.* Geneva and Paris, 1955.

Feild, Robert, *The Art of Walt Disney*. New York, 1942.

Grierson, John, "Flaherty as Innovator." *Sight and Sound*, October–December 1951.

Hampton, Benjamin, *A History of the Movies*. New York, 1931.

Hauser, Arnold, "The High Road or the Low Road." *Sight and Sound*, Winter 1938–39.

Hauser, Arnold, "Can Movies Be 'Profound'?" *Partisan Review*, January 1948.

Hodgins, Eric, "Amid the Ruins of an Empire a New Hollywood Arises." *Life*, Vol. 42, No. 23 (June 10, 1957), pp. 146–66.

Hutchins, Patricia, "James Joyce and the Cinema." *Sight and Sound*, October–December 1951.

Kracauer, Siegfried, "The Found Story and the Episode." *Film Culture*, Vol. 2, No. 1 (7), 1956.

Kyrou, Ado, *Le Surréalisme au Cinéma*. Paris, 1953.

Lambert, Gavin, "Fritz Lang's America." This article appeared in two parts in *Sight and Sound*, Summer and Autumn 1955.

Lawson, John Howard, *Theory and Technique of Playwriting and Screenwriting* (New York, 1949), pp. 309–450.

Lindsay, Vachel, *The Art of the Moving Picture*. New York, 1915.

Macdonald, Dwight, "Notes on Hollywood Directors." *Symposium*, April–July 1933.

Macdonald, Dwight, "A Theory of 'Popular Culture.'" *Politics*, February 1944.

Manvell, Roger (editor), *Experiment in the Film*. London, 1949.

Marcouelles, Louis, "French Cinema . . . the Old and the New." *Sight and Sound*, Spring 1958.

Marías, Julián, *La Imagen de la Vida Humana*, pp. 49–73. Buenos Aires, 1955.

Mayer, J. P., *Sociology of the Film*. London, 1946.

Moholy-Nagy, L., *Vision in Motion* (Chicago, 1947), pp. 270–91.

Moussinac, Léon, *Panoramique de Cinéma*. Paris, 1929.

Reisz, Karel, *The Technique of Film Editing*. London and New York, 1953.

Richter, Hans, "The Film as an Original Art Form." *Film Culture*, January 1955.

Riesman, David, *The Oral Tradition, the Written Word and the Screen Image*. A public address published by the Antioch Press, Yellow Springs, Ohio, 1956.

Rotha, Paul, *The Film Till Now*. With an additional section by Richard Griffith. New York, 1949.

Seton, Marie, *Eisenstein: A Biography*. New York, 1952.

Shelton, Robert, "Movie Men of Few Words." The New York *Times*, Section 2, June 15, 1958, p. 8.

Spottiswoode, Raymond, *Film and Its Technique*. Berkeley and Los Angeles, 1951.

Spottiswoode, Raymond and Nigel, *The Theory of Stereoscopic Transmission and Its Application to the Motion Picture*. Berkeley and Los Angeles, 1953. This is an extremely technical book intended for professionals.

Stauffacher, Frank (editor), *Art in Cinema*. A symposium on the avant-garde film. Published by the Art in Cinema Society, San Francisco Museum of Art, 1947.

Stern, Seymour, *Monograph on D. W. Griffith. Cinemages*, New York, Special Issue No. 1, 1955.

Taylor, Robert Lewis, *W. C. Fields: His Follies and Fortunes*. New York, 1949.

Tyler, Parker, "The Film Sense and the Painting Sense." *Perspectives* USA 11, Spring 1955.

Tyler, Parker, *Magic and Myth of the Movies*. New York, 1947.

Warshow, Robert, "The Gangster as Tragic Hero." *Partisan Review*, February 1948.

Welles, Orson, "The Third Audience." *Sight and Sound*, January–March, 1954.

Young, Vernon, "The Not-so-innocent Eye." *Arts*, December 1955.

A NOTE ON FILM MAGAZINES

An exhaustive list of film journals of recent years can be found in a bibliographical issue of *Cinemages* (April 15, 1957). The result of two years of research, it lists the names and addresses of 1,151 film periodicals in all parts of the world. Incidentally, *Cinemages* itself is excellent. It is published by the Group for Film Study, 3951 Gouverneur Avenue, New York 63, N.Y., under the editorship of Mr. Gideon Bachmann. It differs from the other film magazines in that it stresses records, filmographies, and film scholarship; it also runs regular articles. Established in 1955, it brought out at first six issues per year, plus special supplements now and then; since 1957 the magazine has appeared irregularly. For those film enthusiasts who seek a historical insight into the art of the film, every issue is worth reading. There is a wealth of valuable information—some of it new—on the work of such film masters as Eric von Stroheim, D. W. Griffith, G. W. Pabst, Luis Bunuel, Jean Epstein and many others.

The following is a select list of film magazines and other magazines of a critical nature that run articles on the film:

1. FILM MAGAZINES

Cahiers du Cinéma, Paris.

Cinema Quarterly, Edinburgh, 1932–35.

Close Up, Territet, Switzerland, and London, 1927–33. This was one of the earliest magazines devoted exclusively to the film as an art form. It published articles by Gertrude Stein, Osbert Sitwell, Havelock Ellis, André Gide, Dorothy Richardson, Bryher, Jean Prévost, René Crével, Herman G. Weinberg, Ernest Betts, Kenneth MacPherson, Harry Alan Potamkin and others.

Film Art, London, 1934–37.

Film Culture, New York. Edited by Jonas Mekas. This is the leading magazine on the film in America today.

Film Quarterly, Berkeley, California. Edited by Ernest Callenbach. Established in the fall of 1958, this is an outgrowth of *The Quarterly of Film, Radio, and Television* (Berkeley, 1951–58).

Films, New York, 1939–40.

Museum of Modern Art Library (New York) clipping files.

Sight and Sound, London. This is the leading international film magazine.

2. NONFILM MAGAZINES

American Mercury, 1950–52.

Arts, 1955.

Commentary

Hound and Horn—one of the outstanding literary magazines of the 1920s and early 1930s. See the series of five articles by Harry Alan Potamkin on René Clair, G. W. Pabst, Pudovkin, Eisenstein, and a film academy plan. Ran contiguously from the issue of October–December 1932 to that of October–December 1933.

Hudson Review

Kenyon Review

Partisan Review

Perspectives USA

Politics, 1944–49. A first-rate polemical magazine which ran many interesting reviews and articles on the movies.

Sewanee Review

View, 1940–47. This stimulating magazine, edited by Charles Henri Ford, ran many articles and reviews on the film.

Finally, the following magazines have regular film departments: *The Nation, The New Republic, The New Yorker, Commonweal, Time, Newsweek, The New Leader, The Saturday Review.*

Index

B

C

E

H

I

N

S

T

U

W

V

Y

Z

About the Editor

DANIEL TALBOT, *a New Yorker, has worked for eight years in book publishing and for three as Eastern Story Editor of Warner Brothers Pictures, Inc. He has recently returned from Spain, where he spent a year writing and working on a film. He plans to produce films in the near future.*